Police Administration

FIFTH EDITION

Police Administration

James J. Fyfe
Temple University

Jack R. Greene
Temple University

William F. Walsh
University of Louisville

O. W. Wilson
Late Dean Emeritus, School of Criminology
University of California, Berkeley, and
Superintendent of Police (Retired), Chicago, Illinois

Roy Clinton McLaren
Late Chief of Police
Arlington, Virginia and Miramar, Florida
and former Director, Field Operations Division,
International Association of Chiefs of Police
Gaithersburg, Maryland

Boston, Massachusetts   Burr Ridge, Illinois   Dubuque, Iowa
Madison, Wisconsin New York, New York San Francisco, California St. Louis, Missouri

McGraw-Hill

A Division of The McGraw-Hill Companies

POLICE ADMINISTRATION

This book is printed on acid-free paper.

5 6 7 8 9 0 DOC DOC 0

ISBN 0–07–022566–4
Library of Congress Catalog Card Number: 96–75689

This book was set in Palatino by Ruttle, Shaw & Wetherill, Inc.
The editor was Marge Byers.
The production supervisor was Paula Keller.
The cover was designed by Amy Barovick.
Cover inset photo by New York City Police Department Photographic Unit, Deputy Commissioner of Public Information.
Background photo by The Image Bank, A. M. Rosario.
The photo editor was Anne Manning.
Project supervision was done by The Total Book.
R. R. Donnelley & Sons, Company was printer and binder.

8. Financial Management and Budgeting   250

9. Personnel Management I: Hiring and Entry-Level Training   270

10.   Personnel Management II: Human Resource Management   318

About the Authors

JAMES J. FYFE is Professor of Criminal Justice and Senior Public Policy Research Fellow at Temple University, Philadelphia. He holds a baccalaureate from John Jay College of Criminal Justice, City University of New York, and earned master's and Ph.D. degrees in criminal justice at the State University of New York at Albany.

Fyfe served sixteen years with the New York City Police Department and is a former senior fellow of the Police Foundation. He is a commissioner of the Commission on Accreditation for Law Enforcement Agencies, recently chaired the American Society of Criminology's Task Force on Police, and was the editor of *Justice Quarterly,* the official journal of the Academy of Criminal Justice Sciences. He has published six books and more than 75 articles and book chapters, including *Above the Law: Police and the Excessive Use of Force* (with Jerome H. Skolnick, 1993).

Fyfe has won several professional awards for his research on police use of force, and has consulted with many police and law enforcement agencies in the United States and abroad. He has testified as an expert on police practices in federal and state courts and in the United States Senate and House of Representatives. His research was cited by the U.S. Supreme Court in *Tennessee v. Garner,* on which he consulted and for which he drafted the Police Foundation's *amici curiae* brief.

JACK R. GREENE, Professor of Criminal Justice at Temple University, has written extensively on matters of police management and organization, as well as the evaluation of police services. He is intimately involved in organizational change and the implementation of community policing in several major city police departments, including Philadelphia and Los Angeles. He regularly serves as a consultant/advisor to the National Institute of Justice, several police agencies, and policy research organizations. His research and writing blend the intellectual and practical sides of police management and administration with the day-to-day world of the police.

Dr. Greene received his Ph.D. from Michigan State University, where he specialized in criminal justice and criminology, organizational sociology, and public policy analysis. Among his numerous publications and reports, are three books which he has edited, the most recent of which, *Community Policing: Rhetoric and Reality* (1988), was the first to critically assess a national movement to shift policing toward community and problem-focused issues. He is also the editor of *Managing Police Organizations: Issues and Analysis* (1982).

Professor Greene is the Director of Temple University's Center for Public Policy, a multidisciplinary, applied policy-research organization which provides timely and policy-focused analysis across a wide range of governmental and civic issues, including those of crime and justice. He is currently directing programming and research on the implementation of community policing in public housing settings, the assessment of organizational change needs within the Philadelphia Police Department, the climate and culture of safety within Philadelphia middle schools, the use and effectiveness of "safe corridors" in travel to and from school, and the social and physical rebuilding of a large section of North Philadelphia.

WILLIAM F. WALSH is the Director of the Southern Police Institute and Associate Professor in the Department of Justice Administration at the University of Louisville. The Southern Police Institute is an advanced education and training center dedicated to enhancing the professional development of law enforcement practitioners, with emphasis on training current and future police executives. Walsh's students hold police command positions throughout the United States, Europe, and the Pacific Rim nations.

A former member of the New York City Police Department with 21 years' service, Walsh holds undergraduate and master's degrees from John Jay College of Criminal Justice and a Ph.D. in sociology from Fordham University. Before joining the University of Louisville faculty, Walsh was a professor in the Administration of Justice department at The Pennsylvania State University, where he received the National Continuing Education Association Faculty Service Award in 1988.

Walsh's research on public and private police has been published in *Issues in Community Policing* (Peter Kratcoski and Duane Dukes, eds., 1995), the *American Journal of Police, Justice Quarterly, Journal of Police Science and Administration, Journal of Criminal Justice, The Justice Professional, Security Journal,* and *Police Chief.* With Edwin J. Donovan of The Pennsylvania State University, Walsh co-authored *The Supervision of Police: A Performance Based Approach.* He has served as a consultant to police departments throughout the United States and Europe, most recently in the emerging democracies of Hungary and Romania.

Contents

PART 2
Leadership and Administration   83

4. The Police Chief Executive As Leader   85

PART 3
Operations   535

16. Uniformed Services: Patrol, Traffic, and Special Operations   537

17. Crime Prevention and Criminal Investigation   587

Preface

When O. W. Wilson published the first edition of this book in 1950, he defined the state of the art of police administration. The ideal in 1950, generally, was a highly bureaucratized reaction to the unprofessional and politicized style of policing that existed in many American cities, towns, counties, and states. Wilson, who had entered policing during the great corruption of the Prohibition Era, believed with some of the brightest of his contemporaries that police independence from political influences—which, at the time, were almost all bad—was an ideal earnestly to be desired and sought.

The 26 years between the first and fourth editions of *Police Administration* altered American society dramatically. Between 1950 and 1976, the police found themselves in the middle of the civil rights movement, urban disorder, rapidly rising crime rates, political violence, antiwar demonstrations, a variety of liberation movements, an activist Supreme Court that overhauled American criminal procedure, and a growing and militant labor movement in their own ranks. Because these pressures and forces made the police such interesting research subjects, these years also saw the beginning of scholarly study and systematic research into matters of the police and police policy. For the first time, policing was no longer the virtually exclusive subject of practitioner-authors like Wilson and his mentor August Vollmer. Instead, police policy and practice became informed by the perspectives and methods of political scientists, management specialists, sociologists, operations researchers, and others from outside the police field. The work of these social scientists was one of several factors that caused the police to rethink the ways in which they had done many things. In the years that followed, policing—like society—changed dramatically. Still, four editions of *Police Administration* continued to define the state of the art.

Wilson's mastery of his subject matter and his ability to keep *Police Admin-*

O. W. Wilson at a Chicago Police Department staff meeting. Listening attentively to Wilson is his young aide and protégé, Herman Goldstein, who subsequently wrote the landmark *Policing a Free Society* and created the idea of problem-oriented policing. *Courtesy of Wichita, Kansas Police Department.*

istration apace of the times had many sources. Perhaps most important, he was joined in the third and fourth editions by coauthor Roy C. McLaren, who had been his student at the University of California—Berkeley. In addition, Wilson certainly kept his hand in the real world of policing: He served as Chicago Police Superintendent for seven years. There, in attempting to reform a troubled department while working under Mayor Richard Daley, Wilson showed great courage and political acumen. Before taking his job, he extracted from Daley a promise that he would be allowed to run the department free of partisan influences and deal making. Daley, the leader of perhaps the greatest American political machine, gave his word—but most knowledgeable observers viewed this as a streetwise pol's manipulation of a naïve out-of-towner. Daley, many felt, had hoodwinked Wilson into taking the superintendent's job in order to legitimize the deal making they were sure would continue while Wilson, the ascetic professor from Berkeley, had his nose buried in his books. The observers underestimated Wilson, and perhaps Daley: The promise was kept, and Wilson and his staff had a free hand in running the department.

Still, shortly after Wilson's retirement from Chicago, there occurred an event that showed both how fast things were changing at that time and how difficult it is for even the most able police administrator and staff to quickly effect reform in police agencies. The Democratic National Convention was held in Chicago in 1968, at a time when the United States was deeply divided over both the Vietnam War and the national direction generally. Demonstrators and provocateurs poured into town to goad the Establishment and, of course, the police. The result has generally been termed a "police riot." Angry and apparently beyond discipline, police clubbed demonstrators, bystanders, and journalists indiscriminately. Tear gas poured from the streets onto the convention floor. Clearly, as far as the police had come during Wilson's tenure in Chicago, there was much room for improvement there, and in policing generally.

Since that riot and the last two editions of *Police Administration,* the changes have continued. We have learned much about what the police can, and cannot, do. Police administration has become better informed through improved training and education, career development, and the application to policing of management styles and philosophies that have proved successful in other fields of endeavor. Indeed, one major lesson is that police organizations are not as unique as they had formerly been believed to be, and that what works in other settings may also work in policing. At the street level, we have seen a progression of alternative organizational arrangements, running from variants of team policing to the community and problem-oriented policing models that currently are being adopted throughout the country.

Although problem solving has always been a part of good police work, problem-oriented policing did not exist as a distinct concept when the fourth edition of this book was published in 1976. Nor was it prevalent in 1989, when Roy McLaren died. Still, we are certain that both Wilson and McLaren would have approved of the movement toward community and problem-oriented policing. Fyfe came to know McLaren while both worked in quarters shared by the Police Foundation and the Police Executive Research Forum (PERF); Fyfe was a senior fellow of the Foundation, and McLaren oversaw PERF's end of the creation of the Commission on Accreditation for Law Enforcement Agencies and its standards. There, interspersing his latest jokes, McLaren regularly expounded on the need to eliminate artificial walls between police and community and to get police to see beyond pure law enforcement and to look for additional ways of solving community problems and improving neighborhoods. That Wilson would approve of community and problem-oriented policing is beyond question: The person generally recognized as the father of these new policing styles is Professor Herman Goldstein of the University of Wisconsin, whose monumental influence on policing began with service as Wilson's aide in Chicago. Thus, in continuing the Wilson/McLaren tradition, it was easy for us to decide that goal-oriented styles of policing and management—COP, POP, MBO, etc.—should be featured prominently in this edition. This material may be different from what Wilson and McLaren wrote, but policing also is a lot different now from what it was then. Were Wilson and McLaren still with us, we are confident that both would have insisted on including this material and, probably, on writing it themselves.

Other materials in this edition also are new and, in some cases, actually in conflict with information included in past editions. These conflicts, however, do not indicate that Fyfe, Greene, and Walsh are in disagreement with the Wilson/McLaren tradition. The Wilson/McLaren tradition is to present readers with the state of the art of police administration, rather than to perpetuate information that may be time-locked in earlier years. The fact is that the state of the art has changed since 1976: It is our honor to continue in the tradition of O. W. Wilson and Roy C. McLaren by attempting to present the state of the art as it exists at this writing.

Acknowledgments

Writing a text on police administration requires a delicate balance between the theoretical and conceptual world of those who study police organizations and their environments and the practical and more immediate needs of police administrators. Such writing also requires a sensitivity to and understanding of the complexity of policing and of police management. Several people have tried to influence the development of this perspective in all three of us: we hope their efforts show in this volume.

Our views and analyses of policing and its role in a democratic society have been influenced heavily by many writers, including Egon Bittner, Raymond Fosdick, Herman Goldstein, William Ker Muir, August Vollmer, James Q. Wilson, and, obviously, O. W. Wilson and Roy C. McLaren. For the opportunity to express our analyses and views in this volume and for urging and helping us to bring it to fruition, we owe other debts. At McGraw-Hill, we are grateful to Annette Bodzin, Marge Byers, Bridget Isacsen, Anne Manning, Laura Warner, and —especially—to Phil Butcher. We thank also the reviewers who pored through this manuscript and who made many useful suggestions: Sam Chapman, University of Nevada–Reno; Victor Strecher, Sam Houston State University; Paul Coupland, Western Iowa Technical Community College; Walter Roger, Nassau Community College; Lynn Button, California State University–Fresno; David Carter, Michigan State University; Peter Phillips, Utica College of Syracuse University; Vincent Del Castillo, John Jay College of Criminal Justice; George L. Kelling, Kennedy School of Government, Harvard University; Peter Horne, Mercer County Community College; William P. McCamey, Western Illinois University; Vergil L. Williams, University of Alabama; James Sewell, Florida Department of Law Enforcement.

In addition, each of us is particularly grateful to individuals who have affected us along our paths to this page. As a police officer, Fyfe worked with and for so many fine people that listing them all here would require a separate volume. They ranged in rank from police administrative aides to police commissioners, and they know who they are. As an undergraduate at John Jay College, Fyfe was influenced heavily by John Cronin, Lloyd Sealy, and Jack Sulger, all of whom have gone on to more peaceful surroundings. At SUNY-Albany, Hans Toch, Richard A. Myren, Fred Cohen, Donald J. Newman, and Michael Hindelang showed Fyfe what it meant to think critically about the police, and crime, and justice.

Thomas Brady, Brian Forst, George Kelling, Daniel Rosenblatt, Lawrence Sherman, and Cynthia Sulton of the Police Foundation, as well as the late Gary P. Hayes of the Police Executive Research Forum, helped Fyfe to meld police scholarship into police practice. There were differences among those who worked at the Foundation and down the hall at PERF but, under the guiding hand of Patrick V. Murphy, the Foundation and PERF had an enormous effect on policing—and on Fyfe. Jerome H. Skolnick and Rita J. Simon, Fyfe's last two coauthors, provided examples of collegiality and expertise that helped immensely in writing this book. Fyfe's education continues, primarily under the tutelage of his colleagues at Temple; at the Commission on Accreditation for Law Enforcement Agencies; and at home, in the person of his wife, Professor Candace S. McCoy of the School of Criminal Justice at Rutgers University.

On the academic side, Jack Greene is indebted to Professors Robert Sheehan of Northeastern University and Victor Strecher and Louis Radelet of Michigan State University, who provided him the opportunity to better understand the "theory" of policing, police and community relations, and police administration. Professor Sheehan, a "philosopher, friend, and guide," also stressed the importance of the human side of the policing enterprise—the men and women who join police agencies to help others. For Greene, such intellectual lessons made this book worth writing.

Former Police Commissioner Kevin Tucker of the Philadelphia Police Department and Chief Willie L. Williams of the Los Angeles Police Department gave Greene an opportunity to see and feel police administration as it is played out in an often turbulent and uncertain world. Such professional mentorship is a continuing and invaluable source of real world grounding, adding a view from the *eagle's nest* to one from the *ivory tower.* Deputy Commissioner William T. Bergman, former Deputy Commissioner Thomas Seamon, and Chief Inspector Edward McLaughlin of the Philadelphia Police Department and Commander Garrett W. Zimmon of the Los Angeles Police Department have also influenced this work by bringing to their jobs a clarity of thought, intellect, and vision that befits the new generation of police managers.

Greene's wife and children and mother and father are continuing sources of support, love, and tolerance. They have taught him how important it is to be directed by others—the hallmark of effective leadership and administration.

For 21 years, William Walsh labored with the men and women of the New York City Police Department, each of whom has had an influence on the contents of this book. Walsh is particularly indebted to Edwin J. Donovan, his long-time colleague and friend at both the New York City Police Department and at Pennsylvania State University. By example and encouragement, Ed has shown that transitions from the streets to the classroom and back can be made with integrity and excellence. At John Jay College, Arthur Niederhoffer and Alexander Smith were both intellectual and moral role models for Walsh, and left marks that have proven indelible. Michael J. Farrell of the Vera Institute of Justice harnessed Walsh's street knowledge and academic training into his first significant research and writing projects; Mike's marks are also to be found in this book. At the University of Louisville, Walsh is especially grateful to Deborah G. Wilson, Assistant Provost and former Department Chair, who encouraged him throughout the preparation of this book. Walsh's greatest debts, however, are to his family—Anne, William, Sean, and Peter.

James J. Fyfe
Jack R. Greene
William F. Walsh

PART ONE

The Police Role

RESPONSIBILITIES, PROBLEMS, AND RELATIONSHIPS

1

Police:
The Historical Perspective

KEY WORDS AND PHRASES

Police power
European police systems
Tything
London Metropolitan Police
Sir Robert Peel
Charles Rowan
Richard Mayne
Peel's Principles
Police and politics
Stephen James O'Meara
August Vollmer
Orlando W. Wilson

Omnipresence
Wickersham Commission
Crime clearance rates
Bureaucratic model
Societal forces
Kerner Commission
Due process revolution
Limited police authority
Strategic tests
Community policing
Problem-oriented policing

All organizations, especially municipal police departments, are shaped by their historical, community, and political environments. Our nation has evolved from an isolated collection of agriculturally based communities to a complex technological and information age society. The majority of its population now live in megametropolitan areas consisting of numerous independent suburban communities bordering on larger central cities. This transformation has caused vast economic and social changes in our society.

Policing, like our society, has also undergone a transformation. It has evolved from the responsibility of the colonial sheriff and citizen nightwatch into a high-profile, professionally organized, 24-hour, 365-day, occupational specialty. Today, police administrators are accountable for an array of responsibilities that include public safety, law enforcement, human resource manage-

3

ment, and information and fiscal management. Police officers have become the most visible representatives of government on our streets and the most commonly encountered authority figures in our communities (Palmer, 1988).

Police administration is currently experiencing an intense period of examination, reflection, and experimentation. There exists a debate regarding strategies of police governance and service delivery. Some administrators favor the professional bureaucratic model with its emphasis on efficiency and crime control. Others believe that community and/or problem-oriented policing is a more appropriate way of addressing the needs of our communities. The paradigmatic debate over police macrostrategies is a direct outgrowth of the historical development of professional policing.

This chapter will examine a selection of historical events that highlight the origins of the police function and the development of American policing.* Its purpose is to contribute to our understanding of how contemporary police administration and the current debate evolved.

POLICING: ORIGINS OF THE CONCEPT

The origins of the term "police" are found in the Greek word *politeia*, which referred to the organization and government of the city. When it is used in the modern phrase *"police power"*—the power of the state to regulate or govern—the original meaning of the word becomes more apparent (McDowell, 1993). The French, who established a police force as early as the fourteenth century, used the word as a subject noun—for example, *la police de Paris*—and as a transitive verb, *policer*, which referred to the act of bringing order, to civilize or organize (Palmer, 1988:69). In English, the use of the word "police" to define an organized group established for the purpose of maintaining order began in the eighteenth century.

The need to maintain order and control conflict, policing, has always existed in some form or another whenever people have lived in groups. Tribal groups practiced a form of self-policing through the collective efforts of their adult members. Standards of conduct were enforced by tribal heads, elders, and religious leaders. When permanent settlements began to evolve, the methods of providing order and safety became more complex. There is evidence of formalized policing in ancient China, Egypt, the Greek city-states, and Rome (Fuld, 1971; Kelly, 1973). In medieval free cities in Europe civic authorities assumed responsibility for safety and security; however, there was no organized police force. It was the emergence of national states after the Middle Ages that created the need for a more organized form of policing.

The national states of continental Europe that emerged after the Middle Ages developed policing systems whose purpose was to serve the interests of the political authority that created them. These departments consisted of armed officers organized in military fashion. They were responsible for controlling political opposition as well as citizen behavior. Reaction to the perva-

---

*A more comprehensive account of police history can be obtained from Critchley, 1972; Richardson, 1974; Walker, 1977; Monkkonen, 1981; and Palmer, 1988.

sive and intrusive nature of continental policing systems influenced the Anglo-American belief that excessive centralization of police power should be avoided and that the police should be held accountable for the methods they used to perform their duties.

OUR ENGLISH HERITAGE

Although the United States of America became a nation by revolting against England, our legal system has been strongly influenced by English traditions. These traditions are reflected in the fact that American police officers possess limited authority defined in law instead of the broader powers enjoyed by their counterparts in other nations. Secondly, in the United States, police departments are controlled by local governmental authorities instead of the central government. Lastly, this form of control contributes to a highly decentralized and fragmented system that has produced in excess of 17,000 separate state and local police agencies (Walker, 1992:4).

Today, supporters of community policing claim that it is different from other forms of policing because it derives its priorities in part from community input and need (Kelling, 1988; Trojanowicz and Carter, 1988). They maintain that community self-defense against crime and disorder is primarily a matter of private social control supported by the police (Kelling and Stewart, 1989:8). The concept of community self-policing has its origins in the laws and customs of the tribal groups that invaded and subsequently settled in the British Isles. One such group, the Saxons, developed an obligatory self-policing system during the reign of King Alfred (871–900).

All males in the community between the ages of 12 and 60 were organized into groups called *tythings*. If a crime was committed by a member of the tything, the other members were obligated to apprehend the offender and hold the individual for trial. Overall command of this collective security system was given to the shire reeve, later to be contracted to sheriff, who held office through a king's appointment (Critchley, 1972).

After the Normans invaded and conquered England in 1066, the Anglo-Saxon collective community control system was modified and expanded. Under the Normans, however, it became necessary to impose harsh fines on all members of the tything if the tything failed to perform its obligatory duties (Klockars, 1985:23). Sanctions became necessary to ensure that individuals did not place their self-interest before their community duties and because the Norman authority was resented by the Saxons. Today, as in the past, it remains a difficult task to obtain voluntary citizen cooperation and support for community self-policing, especially in our more crime-ridden and disorderly communities (Skogan, 1990).

At the end of the thirteenth century the efficiency of the English community self-policing system based on citizen voluntary obligation was in decline. At about this time formal law enforcement agencies began to emerge. The constable, formerly a servant of the manor lord, became a governmental officer. The term *comes stabuli* (count of the stable) initially referred to an individual who was the principal representative of the lord of the manor. However, this position evolved into an officer of the crown having the responsibility for keeping the "King's Peace," the first police officer (Critchley, 1973:5; Uchida, 1993). Constables served under the sheriff or mayor and were required to report on community crime prevention, defense, and crime control to the traveling justices (McDougall, 1988). At first, able-bodied men served in this position, but because of its increasing burdens and unpleasant duties, affluent men began to pay deputies (often of low mental ability or destitute) to take their place.

The Statute of Winchester, passed in 1285, codified and formalized a system of watch and ward to assist the constable in maintaining order in towns. The watch was to contain at least 16 men, who would station themselves at the gate of their walled community. They had the power to arrest individuals during hours of darkness and bring them to the constable. In addition, the administration of justice was centralized under the control of the office of justice of the peace, in 1361. This system of policing remained in place until it also became insufficient toward the end of the seventeenth century.

The quality of the office of constable and the justice of the peace began to decline during the sixteenth century (Critchley, 1972). Dishonest law enforcers emerged as products of a system that exacted a fee for every act performed. Corruption was so epidemic that immunity from prosecution could be bought with ease (South, 1987). Lastly, the massive growth of urban centers and the expansion of the English population from 6 to 12 million contributed to an increase in crime.

Industrialization, migration, and urbanization during the mid-eighteenth century were the forces that turned English cities into squalid, overcrowded, disorderly, and criminal places. At the same time, the corrupt justice system serving its own ends was unable to restore order and safety. The resulting societal breakdown in law and order created the need for reform that eventually would lead to the development of an organized public civil policing system unlike any that had evolved in Europe (Kelling and Stewart, 1991).

Anglo-American police historians have traditionally traced the origins of organized policing to a series of police reforms that began in London, in response to the conditions of eighteenth-century life. One such reform was the "Bow Street Runners," who were founded in 1750, a salaried constabulary that grew into an organization of 18 patrols, 13 to patrol the highways around London and the streets within the parish of Bow Street (Stead, 1985; McDougall, 1988). The Runners were the creation of the brothers John and Henry Fielding. Both brothers served as magistrates at Bow Street Court in London—John from 1748 to his death in 1754 and Henry from 1754 to 1780. But this force never exceeded 160 men (Reppetto, 1978:15), and there was little popular or governmental support for the creation of a salaried, organized police force throughout England at this time.

ORGANIZED PUBLIC POLICING

In 1829, the English Parliament after many years of debate passed the Metropolitan Police Act. This act created the London Metropolitan Police, an organized, paid police force, initially consisting of 3,000 officers, assigned in shifts to provide a 24-hour foot patrol for the metropolis of London. This department would eventually become the model for future American municipal police forces, even though paid organized police departments existed in many other European cities. Sir Robert Peel is credited with the act's passage as well as with the organizational formation and administrative direction of the new police force. The importance of his contribution is that he created a new mission and strategy in policing while employing a traditional administrative model of command and control.

The essential difference between the London force and the other police departments of its day is that it was purposely created from the beginning to be a homogeneous and democratic body, in tune with and drawing its authority from the people (Critchley, 1972:52). Its primary mission, the prevention of crime and the maintenance of order, was to be achieved through preventive patrol. Officers were required to maintain a continual visible presence in the community by patrolling a fixed geographic area called a *beat* (Walker, 1992:5). They were commanded to treat citizens with respect. This approach was taken because the ordinary people of England, especially the lower middle class and the working class, strongly objected to this force they called "Peel's Bloody Gang" (Palmer, 1988:303–308). They feared the creation of a repressive police system similar to those existing in Europe. Therefore, it became essential that the mission, administration, and operational strategy of the department be designed in a manner that would obtain the support and respect of the very individuals who were subjected to its control—a unique concept for this period in history and a critical one for today.

Peel organized the "New Police" in military fashion, with ranks and a hierarchical authoritarian system of administration similar to that used by European police departments. Ranking officers were promoted, on the basis of merit, from within the organization. The basic police officer, the uniformed constable, was a legal officer with limited authority who was unarmed except for a small hardwood truncheon that was kept concealed on his person.

Executive leadership and strong administration were the critical elements in the success of the London police in achieving acceptance. Miller (1975) credits this to Peel's appointment of Army Colonel Charles Rowan and barrister Richard Mayne as the first "Commissioners of Police." They succeeded in instilling the notion of impersonality into the structure and practice of the force while maintaining tight discipline. In the first eight years of their administration's existence, every position on the entire force was refilled three times over by firings or forced resignations (Klockars, 1985:42). While a majority of these dismissals were for drunkenness on duty, firing also resulted from inappropriate behavior toward citizens, unlawful use of force, lateness, and disorderly uniforms. The centrally administered, disciplined, military-style Metropolitan Police eventually won the respect and support of the community it policed. Similar police departments, controlled by local authorities, replaced older established departments and watch systems throughout England by the middle of the nineteenth century (Reppetto, 1978).

Moore and Stephens (1991) observe that for a particular strategy to be successful, the following three tests must be met:

BOX 1-1. Peel's Principles of Law Enforcement

1. The basic mission for which the police exist is to prevent crime and disorder as an alternative to their repression by military force and severity of legal punishment.
2. The ability of the police to perform their task is dependent on public approval of their existence, actions, behavior, and on the ability of the police to secure and maintain public respect.
3. The police must secure and maintain the respect and approval of the public as well as the cooperation of the public in the task of observance of laws.
4. To recognize always that the extent to which the cooperation of the public can be secured diminishes, proportionately, the necessity for the use of physical force and compulsion for achieving police objectives.
5. To seek and to preserve public favor, not by catering to public opinion, but by constantly demonstrating absolutely impartial service to law, in complete independence of policy, and without regard to the justice or injustice of the substance of individual laws; by ready offering of individual service and friendship to all members of the public without regard to their wealth or social standing; by ready offering of sacrifice in protecting and preserving life.
6. To use physical force only when the exercise of persuasion, advice and warning is found to be insufficient to obtain public cooperation to an extent necessary to secure observance of law or to restore order; and to use only the minimum degree of physical force which is necessary on any particular occasion for achieving a police objective.
7. To maintain at all times a relationship with the public that gives reality to the historic tradition that the police are the public and that the public are the police; the police being only members of the public who are paid to give full-time attention to duties which are incumbent on every citizen, in the interests of community welfare and existence.
8. To recognize always the need for strict adherence to police executive functions, and to refrain from even seeming to usurp the powers of the judiciary or avenging individuals or the state, and of authoritatively judging guilt and punishing the guilty.
9. To recognize always that the test of police efficiency is the absence of crime and disorder, and not the visible evidence of police action in dealing with them.

Source: Lee (1901).

First, the articulated goals and objectives must describe a purpose that is plausibly valuable to society. *Second*, the purpose must be operationally feasible and should take advantage of the distinctive competencies and capabilities of the organization. *Third*, the purpose must be able to continue to attract support from those in political and legal positions who authorize the continuation of the enterprise.

The London Metropolitan Police provides a historical example of this observation. Its administrative guidance was based on a value system embodied in a mission statement known today as Peel's Principles of Law Enforcement. This mission statement embodied the values of the British legal system and people. The leadership of the "New Police" created the nineteenth-century London "bobby," a respected civil servant, and an organization that became a respected national institution.

A thoughtful reading of Peel's nine principles (see Box 1-1) suggests that policing should be a preventive, lawfully carried out endeavor based on public need, respect, and cooperation. The power of police officers should be limited to that authorized by law, and the application of officer-administered "street justice" is not to be tolerated. These principles are as much the relevant "reason for being" of policing now as they were in 1829 (Braiden, 1986:5).

The political and social characteristics of England also contributed to the evolution of this police system. By the beginning of the nineteenth century, England had become the world's greatest empire. This empire was ruled by a strong central government, with an established aristocracy, a middle class, an independent judiciary, and a strong civil service. While class divisions existed along with social unrest, the country contained a homogeneous population and an established body of law. As the creation of the Home Secretary and Parliament, the London police drew their authority from and gave their allegiance to the representatives of the national government, not local politicians. Thus, they obtained their capacity to control from the profoundly social authority and power of the institution of which they were part (Klockars, 1985:49). In America, a different set of political and social factors assisted in creating a policing system that failed to achieve this status.

POLICING IN AMERICA: THE EARLY YEARS

America established a process of law enforcement and administration of justice that was based on English traditions modified to conform to the American political, social, and cultural environment. This system in colonial times employed the sheriff, constable, and civilian watch (Walker, 1992). In the rural areas, especially in the south, the county sheriff evolved as the dominant official, while in the pre-Revolutionary urban centers like Boston and New York, the constable and watch system was employed. At first, these positions were unpaid, but by the mid-seventeenth century they received compensation for their services. The policing duties of these early urban constables were similar to those of the county sheriff. The watch patrolled at night, reported fires, raised the hue and cry, maintained street lamps, and arrested or detained suspicious persons (Uchida, 1989).

The quality of law enforcement in seventeenth- and eighteenth-century America was inadequate for the needs of the colonies. Sheriffs and constables were reactive law enforcers who depended on the men of the community to assist them with apprehensions. The agents of the law before and after the Revolution were accountable to local governmental authority. The justice system was plagued by inefficiency, corruption, and political interference, which quickly emerged as American traditions (Walker, 1992). On the frontier, beyond the Appalachian Mountains, vigilantism arose in response to the absence of law enforcement. Settlers took the law in their own hands; rounded up suspicious or disorderly persons; captured law violators; and administered swift punishment, including death, to their prisoners (Brown, 1969).

Our Founding Fathers' fear of strong centralized authority led them to create a federal government with limited powers. State and local municipal governments were delegated the responsibility for policing. As a result, American law enforcement during the first years of the new nation remained essentially what it was before the Revolution. However, at the end of the eighteenth century and throughout the nineteenth century the forces of urban growth, industrialization, large-scale immigration, religious strife, urban riots, and ethnic and racial violence created a need for change. From 1840 to the 1880s new immigrants, mostly German and Irish, clashed with the native-born American power structure for political and economic survival. American cities became battlegrounds between those who possessed wealth and power and those who wanted it. Cities became divided into subcommunities, separated from one another by barriers of class and culture, their streets pathways of danger (Richardson, 1970).

The archaic watch and constable law enforcement system that required citizen support lost its foundation and became inadequate as a social control mechanism, as it had in England (Lane, 1967; Richardson, 1970). Initially, the American response to the problems of the cities was to add personnel to the nightwatch and/or to create a day patrol. However, the success and acceptance, in England, of Peel's London Metropolitan Police resulted in demands for the adaptation of a similar police system in urban America. Although Charleston, South Carolina; Richmond, Virginia; and Savannah, Georgia, had established organized foot and mounted slave patrols in the eighteenth century and Texas its Rangers in 1835, there was some resistance to an organized police force as being inappropriate for a democratic society. New York, in 1845, became the first American city to establish a police force loosely patterned on the London model. Chicago followed in 1851; Boston and Philadelphia in 1854. Most major American cities created similar policing systems by the middle of the nineteenth century.

The creation of municipal police departments in America did not produce effective crime control, well-policed cities, or an efficient, professional public service. The problems associated with the development of policing throughout the nineteenth century resulted from the political, social, and economic forces of that period. In the United States, instead of a strong central authority to establish the police mandate as was the case in London, there existed an ideological commitment to "popular democracy" with an emphasis on local community control. Local political authorities themselves were evolving during this period, and as a result politics dominated American policing as well as other developing governmental services (Strecher, 1992).

European immigrants organized political machines that fought native-born Americans for control of city governments. Police departments were used as a source of political patronage that provided jobs for people the machines needed for their vote. As a result, governmental control of some police departments fluctuated between native-born state legislatures and city governments in the control of immigrant-dominated political groups.

This created decentralized, partisan, politically dominated police departments whose officers selectively used force and intimidation to control the lower or disreputable classes in American cities (McDougall, 1988:48). Palmer (1988:20) claims that nowhere was the relationship between police and politics tighter than in America during this period. Police chiefs and officers were appointed and removed by political mandate. Police officers who owed their positions to local political leaders employed whatever means possible to make sure their candidates stayed in office (Kelling and Moore, 1988).

The nineteenth-century police officer's mandate to maintain order flowed from the local political power structure, but his ability to gain citizen compli-

Nineteenth-century policing was tumultuous. In 1857, New York reformers tried to end corruption in the existing Metropolitan Police Department by disbanding it and creating a new Municipal Police Department. When the new Municipals attempted to evict the Metropolitans from City Hall, a riot followed. The Metropolitans beat off the outnumbered Municipals and, for several months, New York City was policed by two separate departments. A court decision then upheld the reform, and the Metropolitans passed into history.
From The Gangs of New York *by Herbert Asbury, Garden City Publishing Co., 1928.*

ance often depended on his physical power. Out of necessity, he developed a style of policing that employed a degree of discretion and personalized use of force far greater than that of his London counterpart. This style of policing helped create the myth of the tough street cop who maintained a clean beat and could right all wrongs—an image still idolized in the myths of police lore and Hollywood portrayals. However, as the only municipal service in many cities, the nineteenth-century police officers engaged in more than crime control activities. They performed social welfare and safety-related services as well as the enforcement of law and the application of street justice (Lane, 1967; Richardson, 1970). Unfortunately, corruption, inefficiency, political interference, and discriminatory law enforcement characterized policing during this period.

The Beginning of Reform

A movement to reform municipal government with a focus on policing began in the latter half of the nineteenth century. The reformers from the middle and upper classes believed that the way to bring an end to machine politics, corruption, and inefficiency was to stop the use of police departments as a source of patronage, political graft, and power. They sought to free police chiefs from politics by giving them tenure in office, as well as the power and the authority of European police commissioners. They wanted rank-and-file officers to be appointed and promoted on the basis of civil service examinations, not membership in a political party. What they envisioned was an impersonally administered, tightly disciplined, rational legal bureaucratic organization similar to that which developed in London under Commissioners Rowan and Mayne. The nineteenth-century municipal reformers failed in their primary objective of freeing the police from municipal politics, but they were successful in having many police departments adopt the civil service examination process.

The one American police department that came close to exemplifying the reformers' ideal was the Boston Police Department under Stephen James O'Meara, 1906 to 1918. Raymond Fosdick in *European Police Systems* (1915:121–122) identified it as the best police department in the United States. O'Meara's ability as a leader and the manner in which he used the power of his office contributed to his success. The following factors helped establish his power over the department and its operations:

1. O'Meara was appointed police commissioner for a five-year term.
2. He had the authority to hire, fire, and promote virtually at will.
3. The officers were selected from the working class of Boston, avoiding connotations of an army of occupation.
4. The department maintained a relatively high ratio of police to population, which permitted full utilization of the beat system.
5. Management and supervision ensured that a high standard of integrity and legality was maintained.

O'Meara's administration is an example of a strong administrator using the powers of his office to create change and successfully control the organization. Rowan and Mayne used a similar approach with the London Metropolitan Police. This strategy has been repeated in numerous departments throughout the modern era. Unfortunately, history has proved that the impact of these change agents usually lasts only during their tenure in office. The Boston Police Department was not without its weaknesses (Harrison, 1934), and the Boston Police Strike of 1919 destroyed the achievements of O'Meara's administration (Reppetto, 1978:97–105).

The Emergence of the Bureaucratic-Efficiency Model

The first attempt to reform policing had been stimulated from the outside by civilians interested in obtaining political control. In the early twentieth century a new reform emerged, led by police administrators motivated by the desire to make policing a respected profession (Johnson, 1981). These individuals sought to create a neutral, apolitical, efficient police through managerial control over police operations and officer discretion (Goldstein, 1990). They rejected politics as the basis of police legitimacy and instead sought to establish a new mandate for policing in law, scientific methods of investigation, and their vision of police professionalism (Johnson, 1981). They sought to replace the politically directed public service activities of police departments with a police

August Vollmer explains fingerprint science to a
class at the University of California at Berkeley.
Vollmer, who was O. W. Wilson's mentor, was
the most influential police reformer of the early
twentieth century.
AP/Wide World.

function consisting of crime control and criminal apprehension (Kelling and
Moore, 1988; Monkkonen, 1981; Roberg and Kuykendall, 1993). Their conception of policing, grounded in the principles of scientific management and military command, evolved into the dominant police administrative philosophy of
this century (Moore and Stephens, 1991:1; Wilson, 1989).

August Vollmer, one of the first great reformers to come from within policing, is considered the founder of this movement. He served as chief of police in
Berkeley, California, from 1905 to 1932, with a one-year leave to serve as the
police chief of Los Angeles. Vollmer advocated the application of concepts
drawn from the developing fields of management, sociology, social work, and
psychology, as well as the use of modern technology in policing. He was the
first police administrator to suggest that police officers should have a college
education, and his department attracted many university students into its
ranks. Vollmer helped to establish the first university-level police training program in the United States in 1916 at the University of California at Berkeley.
The principal administrative architect of this reform's organizational strategy,
Orlando W. Wilson, was one of Vollmer's college-educated officers and his
protege (Kelling and Moore, 1988).

O. W. Wilson's distinguished career included service as chief of police in
Fullerton, California, during 1925 and in Wichita, Kansas, from 1928 to 1939;
professor and dean at the University of California's School of Criminology at

Berkeley from 1939 to 1960; and superintendent of the Chicago Police Department from 1960 to 1967. Wilson was a proponent of strong managerial control through a centralized command structure, rigid hierarchical organizational structures, and operational efficiency. He supported motorized patrol units over foot patrols, the use of radio dispatch communication systems, and crime control through preventive patrol. He theorized that motorized, radio-directed preventive patrolling provided the police with a method of quick response to crime and created a sense of omnipresence (the police were everywhere) that struck fear in criminals. Wilson influenced countless numbers of police administrators through his authorship of *Police Records* (1942), *Police Planning* (1957), and several editions of this volume beginning in 1950. More than 100 of his former students achieved important positions in policing, where they implemented his ideas (Johnson, 1981).

The reformers' redefinition of the police function received support from the first national commission to study law enforcement in the United States. In 1929, the National Commission on Law Observance and Enforcement (known as the Wickersham Commission) published Report 14, *The Police,* which focused on police administration. Its principal author, August Vollmer, restated the ideals of the professional reform movement and supported the belief that the true role of the police was crime fighting through the enforcement of the law (Wilson, 1968).

Another significant police reformer of this era was J. Edgar Hoover, director of the Federal Bureau of Investigation from 1924 to 1972. During the depression years, the publicity associated with the exploits of famous criminals created a crime wave fear throughout the nation (Walker, 1992). Federal laws in 1934 provided the FBI with the jurisdiction to investigate kidnapping, bank robbery, and espionage. Hoover established the bureau's reputation for competence, integrity, and crime fighting during the investigation of these high-profile crimes. As a result, the FBI became the premier law enforcement organization in the United States. Hoover, as leader of this organization, offered the technological and training services of his agency to local police departments, many of which were unable to provide these services.

In 1930, the FBI was given control of the Uniform Crime Reports, a national system of crime statistics developed in 1922 by August Vollmer with the support of the International Association of Chiefs of Police. In effect, this made the FBI the unofficial monitor of police efficiency and the voice of American policing (Alpert and Dunham, 1992; Walker, 1992). All local police agencies send their statistical reports to the bureau in Washington, D.C., and each year, the FBI announces the annual crime rate and individual police department crime clearance rates. Crime clearance rates evolved into the principal measures of success for police administrators. In 1935, the bureau established the National Academy for the training of police managers, many of whom were considered to be the future leaders of their departments. The benefits of the National Academy reached beyond its training program: it created the first opportunity for police managers from different departments to work together in a controlled learning environment. This permitted the exchange of knowledge and the networking of ideas between these law enforcement leaders. The FBI's National Academy; its crime lab, opened in 1932; and the Uniform Crime Reports all assisted in supporting crime fighting as the primary police mission (Walker, 1992).

In the years between 1930 and 1970, a rational-legal bureaucratic form of police professionalism slowly came to dominate policing, and a new administrative leadership grounded in its "Principles" emerged. These individuals were management-oriented pragmatic leaders who transformed many politically dominated watchman-style departments into legalistically styled organizations with an emphasis on crime control (Guyot, 1991). They sought to control their organizations and improve the quality of police personnel, training, and integrity. The basic "Principles" of this model of policing are as follows:

1. The primary function of policing is crime control.
2. Police departments should be independent of politics.
3. Effectiveness and efficiency result from a highly centralized command structure and standardized operating procedures.
4. The police organization should be hierarchical and subdivided according to a division of labor and task specialization.
5. Officers should be selected on the basis of established recruitment standards.
6. Officers should be well trained and disciplined.
7. Preventive random motorized patrol deters crime.
8. Policing should use modern technology.
9. Police officers should enforce laws impartially.
10. Crimes are solved by scientific investigative methods (Goldstein, 1990).

The major exemplar of this model of policing was William H. Parker, chief of the Los Angeles Police Department from 1950 to 1966. A contemporary of O. W. Wilson, he transformed a corrupt police department into the nation's leading model of police bureaucratic professionalism (Walker, 1992). His use of strong discipline and swift handling of internal problems gained him public respect and freedom from political interference. Parker simplified the department's command structure, enhanced its use of technology, stressed the use of planning, and instituted rigorous personnel selection procedures and training. The LAPD under Parker projected a public image of its officers as tough, competent, polite, impartial, and effective. This ideal image received national exposure through Jack Webb's portrayal of Los Angeles detective Sgt. Joe Friday, who always wanted "just the facts" in the TV program *Dragnet*. Unfortunately, Parker's power enhanced his authoritarian management style, and he had little tolerance for criticism of his department (Johnson, 1981). During Parker's administration and that of subsequent heads of the Los Angeles Police Department, this style of policing was maintained until the Rodney King beating incident led to an external review and a person from outside the department being named chief in 1992.

The advocates of the bureaucratic-efficiency model of police professionalism sought to create an independent, centrally controlled organization, primarily concerned with crime control while at the same time remaining isolated from the corrupting influences of the community in which it existed. They succeeded in making crime control and crime solving the dominant goals in policing, and in making preventive patrol by automobile and rapid response to calls for service its major tactics (Kelling and Moore, 1988; Moore and Trojanowicz, 1988). In their desire for reform, the movement's leaders and their supporters created a distinct profession and a field of study, police administration. They

enhanced the educational and training levels of police personnel and introduced modern technology into policing. However, critics of this reform movement claim that it also created professionally remote, internally oriented, legalistic, formalized, and rigid police departments concerned more with
organizational survival and efficiency rather than effectiveness and the needs
of the communities they served (Braiden, 1986; Goldstein, 1990; Kelling and
Moore, 1988; Moore, 1992). These departments, in their zeal to separate themselves from corrupting community influences, created barriers between themselves and the citizens they served, especially in urban minority communities
(Williams and Murphy, 1990). In doing this, they violated Peel's warning for
his police to act in a manner that will gain the support of those whom they
controlled. The separation between police departments and the people they
served and the style of policing employed by many street patrol officers eventually became the flash points that ignited a storm of controversy beginning in
the 1960s that is still affecting policing today.

THE STORM OF CHANGE

During the 1960s and 1970s American society experienced a period of intense
social unrest and change that involved the civil rights and anti–Vietnam war
movements, increases in crime, and fear and riots in our cities. At the same
time, the exclusionary rule and more stringent standards of procedural conduct were applied to the police by the courts. The control of police administrators was challenged by employee unions, research raised doubts about the validity of police operational methods, and the police relationship to the
communities they served became subject to debate. Policing entered a period
of crises and self-examination that Skolnick and Bayley (1986:10) identified as
the beginning of the social reconstruction of American policing.

The American public, as a result of the efforts of the police themselves, had
come to expect that the police could and would control crime. However, crime
began to increase at an alarming rate in the 1960s despite increases in police
personnel, the reorganization and reform of some departments, the use of
rapid motorized response to calls for service, and modern telecommunication
dispatch systems. This increase in the crime rate was particularly dramatic for
those crimes people feared the most, violent personal crimes. The robbery rate,
for example, almost tripled between 1960 and 1970 (Uchida, 1989). Citizen fear
became widespread, even among those who lived in low-crime areas. The public began to question the ability of the police to prevent and control crime.

At the same time, the civil rights and anti-Vietnam war movements directly challenged the legitimacy of the police. Police tactics used to control protestors were questioned by many citizens who observed them on national television for the first time. Minority citizens, especially African Americans,
protested police mistreatment, inadequate police services, and discriminatory
hiring practices. Beginning in 1963 America experienced over 300 incidents of
urban disorder. Major riots erupted in the minority communities of New York
City, 1964; Los Angeles, 1965; Detroit, 1967; and Miami and Newark, 1968.
President Lyndon Johnson, alarmed by the magnitude of the urban unrest, es-

tablished the National Advisory Commission on Civil Disorders (known as The Kerner Commission, 1967–1968) to identify the causes of these disturbances. The commission concluded that institutional racism was the underlying cause of the civil disorders. However, it also found that many of the riots had been directly triggered by a police action toward minority citizens. The commission noted that use of aggressive patrol tactics, brutality, and the unwarranted use of deadly force against minorities were sources of hostility. Interestingly, many of the serious disorders took place in cities where the police had a reputation for being professionally led, organized, and trained (National Advisory Commission on Civil Disorders, 1968:301). The commission's findings made it clear that police-public relations, especially with inner-city minority residents, needed improvement. National attention became focused on police–minority group relations and officer misconduct.

Another major factor associated with the civil rights and anti–Vietnam war movements was that they expanded civil protest beyond the inner city to middle-class colleges, main-street America, and television. They brought large numbers of middle-class and minority protestors into open conflict with the police. When the police employed tactics that included the use of force and mass arrests against protestors, they were portrayed as agents of repression who maintained order at the expense of justice. As a result, the rational-legal bureaucratic model of policing began to be questioned by a broader spectrum of the American people.

The Due Process Revolution

At the same time the police were having trouble controlling crime and were gaining a negative reputation because of their handling of social protest, the U.S. Supreme Court decided a series of landmark cases that extended the Fourteenth Amendment to the states and set restrictions on police behavior. This series of cases (see Box 1-2 for a summary of these cases) created a due process revolution in American jurisprudence because they applied the Bill of Rights to the states' criminal proceedings and elevated individual rights over those of the states (Walker, 1992). These cases had a sweeping impact on the day-to-day criminal investigation activities of all police officers, whether they worked in a small town or a large city department. They required that police interaction with suspects conform to constitutional standards, while at the same time they increased public awareness of what was appropriate police procedure.

These decisions generated a storm of controversy within and outside of policing. Critics claimed that the Court was soft on crime, handcuffing police at a time when the crime rate was rising. Many thought that the Supreme Court had become too liberal and that it now favored the rights of criminals over those of law-abiding citizens. Looking back over the years, however, these cases have had a more positive effect on the police profession than any of their critics could have imagined. Police departments, responding to the procedural standards imposed by the Court, raised recruitment standards, improved in-service legal training of their officers, and established procedures to govern officer behavior. The result is that these cases have proved to be a major force in upgrading the professional status and expertise of all police officers.

Research and the Police

The turbulence of this decade also began an in-depth debate and examination regarding the nature of policing and the justice system. Two national studies, conducted by the President's Commission on Law Enforcement and the Administration of Justice (1967) and the National Advisory Commission on Criminal Justice Standards and Goals (1973), were the products of this review. The reports issued by these commissions focused on improving the organization, personnel, education, training, and administration of police departments. However, these studies also raised important questions about the function of police and their accountability and relationship to the communities they served (Goldstein, 1990:10). These issues generated an interest in scholars which eventually led to a revolution in police research. Fueled by funding that became available when Congress passed the Safe Streets Act in 1968 and from private sector sources such as the Ford, Guggenheim, and Charles Stewart Mott Foundations, scholarly examination of policing by researchers from outside the police profession dramatically increased during the 1960s and 1970s.

Studies by William Westley (1951; published, 1970), Wayne La Fave (1965), Jerome H. Skolnick (1966), Arthur Niederhoffer (1966), Egon Bittner (1970), James Q. Wilson (1968), and Albert J. Reiss, Jr. (1971) provided critical descriptions and analyses of actual police work that bridged the gap between the ideal image and reality of policing. We came to understand that police officers employ a great deal of discretion in their work, that the majority of their patrol

RANDOM PATROL

The Kansas City (Missouri) Preventive Patrol Experiment demonstrated that changes in the amount of random, motorized patrol neither significantly reduced crime nor affected citizen fear of crime (Kelling et al., 1974).

SPEED OF RESPONSE

A Kansas City (Missouri) Police Department study found that rapid response to calls has no effect on the arrest of criminals or on the satisfaction of involved citizens. Speed of response means very little because citizens usually delay calling the police. Therefore, the employment of technological innovations and human resources to reduce police response time will have a limited impact on crime outcomes. These findings were confirmed in studies conducted in Jacksonville, Florida; San Diego, California; Peoria, Illinois; and Rochester, New York (Spelman and Brown, 1981).

CRITICALITY OF CALLS

The National Institute of Justice sponsored Police Executive Research Forum studies of differential response strategies by police departments in Wilmington, Delaware, and Birmingham, Alabama. It was found that citizen satisfaction with rapid response was associated with the victims' expectations about response time rather than the actual time. PERF field-tested and evaluated a Differential Police Response Model that classified calls according to their criticality, dispatching an immediate response to the most critical and stacking and delaying reports on those of a noncritical nature. This system saved police resources without a negative impact on citizen satisfaction.

CRIMINAL INVESTIGATION

In 1975, The Rand Corporation conducted a nationwide study of criminal investigation entitled *The Criminal Investigation Process*. This study found that the information needed to solve a case usually resulted from the preliminary investigation conducted by the patrol officer who initially handled the case. Further, it found that detectives usually worked from known suspects to corroborating evidence (Greenwood, Petersilia, and Chaiken, 1977).

---

time is not spent engaged in crime control, and that most police work is initiated by citizens rather than police officers. This initial body of research led to an understanding that the problems associated with the practice of policing directly resulted from the complexity of the police function in our society (Goldstein, 1990:8).

In the 1970s, the validity of the assumptions that supported the operational orthodoxy of policing—preventive patrol, response time, and criminal investigation—were examined. These assumptions rested on the belief that random patrolling by motorized police units prevented crime and made citizens feel safe, that rapid response to calls for service enhanced the chance of making an arrest and resulted in citizen satisfaction, and that serious criminal cases could be solved through postevent investigation by specially trained detectives. The studies conducted during this period concluded that in general, traditional police strategies were not very effective crime control tactics. (See Box 1-3 for a summary of these studies and their findings.)

These findings increased the debate and controversy surrounding the practice of policing. They contributed to a period of unprecedented exploration, experimentation, and openness to research in policing that has involved both police administrators and line officers in project development. Research has influenced major changes in the policy and practice of patrol operations, criminal investigations, and specialized offense and offender operations (Petersilia, 1989). It has also raised serious questions about what must be done to provide safe and secure communities.

A NEW REFORM ERA: COMMUNITY POLICING

Social unrest, the due process revolution, research, and experimentation helped to create a doubt in the effectiveness of traditional police operational methods. Some police executives faced with limited personnel and resources while required to respond to an ever increasing number of calls for service began, in the 1980s, to direct their departments away from the reactive operational strategies of the bureaucratic crime control model toward a philosophy and practice that supports proactive crime prevention, problem solving, and community engagement. They engaged in efforts to obtain community cooperation and support in controlling crime and disorder. These efforts have created a new reform that is loosely called community policing.

Community Relations Programs

This new direction differed from the police-community relations programs that originated in the 1940s. These programs developed as a result of the teachings of Joseph D. Lohman and Gordon Allport with organizational support from the National Conference of Christians and Jews and the National Institute of Police and Community Relations founded at Michigan State University in 1955 (Radelet, 1980). Their objective was to improve police–minority group relations through communication and education programs. Many police departments attempted to achieve this goal by forming special Community Relations Units, often staffed by minority officers. However, these units never achieved the support of the rank-and-file officers, who viewed them as not being engaged in legitimate police work. The worst of them were half-hearted, understaffed, and underfunded attempts by police departments to overcome community dissatisfaction through public relations without making any substantive change (Trojanowicz and Bucqueroux, 1990:61–67). The riots of the 1960s and the report of the National Advisory Commission on Civil Disorders (1968) underscored the fact that despite these efforts, civil disorder still occurred.

Team Policing

Team policing in the late 1960s and 1970s represented the first tentative step toward a community-oriented approach to policing which involved decentralization of police services. Team policing assigned a group of police officers (ranging from 14 to 56 officers), usually under the direction of a sergeant or a lieutenant, the responsibility of providing police services in a specific geographic area on a 24-hour basis. In theory the team was expected to break down the barriers between the police and the neighborhood it served, provide improved services, and increase the job satisfaction of the patrol officers. A number of urban police departments implemented some form of team policing. However, team policing still employed traditional police crime control tactics.

The Police Foundation systematically examined team policing in Dayton, Detroit, New York City, Los Angeles, Holyoke, Syracuse, and Richmond, California (Sherman, Milton, and Kelly, 1973). This analysis and one conducted by the National Sheriffs Association and the Law Enforcement Assistance Administration (LEAA) in 19 cities produced inconclusive findings regarding the effectiveness of this strategy (Gay, Day, and Woodward, 1977). As a result, the hypothesis that team policing is a more effective and efficient way of providing patrol services remained an unresolved issue (Larson and Cahn, 1981). In fairness, however, ambiguity about the effectiveness of team policing was at least partially attributable to the open resistance of traditional managers, who refused to share power and responsibilities with the teams and their commanders. Teams were also resented by line officers, who believed that these units drained personnel resources from where they were needed in the incident-driven patrol units. Also, many team members and supervisors were inadequately trained to perform their new service roles in the community (Sherman, Milton, and Kelly, 1973).

Community- and Problem-Oriented Policing

Starting in the 1980s, experimentation with different organizational and service delivery approaches commenced. These experiments were supported by the National Institute of Justice, the Police Foundation, the Police Executive Research Forum, and the Charles Stewart Mott Foundation. Police departments in Newark, New Jersey; Boston, Massachusetts; Houston, Texas; Flint, Michigan; New York City; and Santa Ana, California, reinstituted the traditional strategy of foot patrol, but with a greater emphasis on community problem solving. Evaluation of these efforts found that foot patrol contributed to the quality of community life, reduced fear, increased citizen satisfaction with police, improved police attitudes toward citizens, and increased officer morale and job satisfaction (Trojanowicz and Bucqueroux, 1990).

At the same time, Herman Goldstein (1979, 1990) noted that systematic analysis was seldom applied to underlying substantive community problems that create the major proportion of a police department's service demand. He suggested that management take a problem-oriented approach to police work. Problem-oriented policing holds that the basic unit of policing should be changed from the isolated, self-contained "service call" to the "problem." A problem consists of a group of incidents or calls that are related because they contain similarities such as behavior, location, persons involved, or victim characteristics. Goldstein (1990:33) advises that a more in-depth interest in these community problems should be taken by analyzing the conditions and factors that cause them. Underlying this suggestion is the belief that these problems cannot be addressed in isolation. The successful control of a problem can only be achieved if those members of the department and the community who have a vested interest in the problem are included in its analysis and solution.

Spelman and Eck (1987:2) analyzed a problem-oriented policing project conducted by the Police Executive Research Forum with the support of the National Institute of Justice in Newport News, Virginia. They state that:

Problem-oriented policing is the outgrowth of 20 years of research into police operations that converged on three main themes: *increased effectiveness* by attacking underlying problems that give rise to incidents that consume patrol and detective time; *reliance on the expertise and creativity of line officers* to study problems carefully and develop innovative solutions; and *closer involvement with the public* to make sure that the police are addressing the needs of citizens.

Problem-oriented policing was tested in Madison, Wisconsin, and Baltimore County, Maryland, as well as in Newport News. Cities that have experimented with various forms of community policing that have a problem-oriented component include Flint, Michigan; New York City; Los Angeles and Oxnard, California; Savannah, Georgia; Tulsa, Oklahoma; Houston, Texas; Evanston, Illinois; and Edmonton, the capital of Alberta, Canada (Goldstein, 1990). Holden (1994:25) notes that problem-oriented policing may involve the whole department or a specific unit. Therefore, the department need not change its traditional operational methods.

Critics of these methods of policing point out that law enforcement and crime detection have become ends in themselves instead of the means to a more complete end, community safety and security (Braiden, 1986). Community policing is a response to this type of criticism. It involves the decentralization of patrol services for the purpose of community engagement, crime prevention, and problem solving. Community-oriented patrol officers have the dual objective of not only becoming acquainted with people on their beats and their problems but also taking an active role in trying to solve these problems (Farrell, 1988).

The community policing movement reflected a critical and creative phase in the development of policing that involved researchers, academics, and police executives thinking and working closely together. Mastrofski (1988:67) points out that this reform has stimulated more debate and innovation among police and researchers than the police profession has seen since the days of August Vollmer. Community policing does not constitute a single coherent program like the reform movement that began in the 1930s. Instead, police departments are experimenting with a variety of new programs, all resting on the rational, not always clearly articulated premise that police must involve the community in a practical way in the police mission and engage in operational problem solving. Community policing has evolved into an ideology, an organizing framework for many activities, and a set of individual programs (Greene and Mastrofski, 1988).

The future of this latest reform movement is uncertain, and its actual effect on policing will not be known for some time. The acceptance of community involvement by law enforcement officials constitutes a fundamental shift from a legalistic, professional insularity to an orientation that sees the community and its police as both having a responsibility for crime prevention and control. It requires that a service orientation become the dominant style of policing. This orientation emphasizes accountability of the police to the community and the personalization of police service through decentralization. The ultimate goals of community policing are the maintenance of civil authority and the preservation of the community (Kelling and Stewart, 1989). However, the successful

implementation of this reform will require major changes in the training of police officers, supervisors, and managers, as well as in the staffing, organization,
and administration of police departments, all of which will take a significant
amount of time and resources to carry out. To what extent this will occur is unknown. Community policing, like the earlier reform of this century, will require many years of experimentation and analysis before its actual impact on
the police profession can be assessed with any validity. It remains to be proved
whether these efforts can control the crime and disorder that are currently
plaguing our cities.

SUMMARY

The two major factors that have consistently determined the mandate and
methods of policing throughout its development are government—the political institution from which the police draw their authority—and community—
the society in which the police function. In homogeneous, nonmobile, agriculturally based societies, security and safety needs were handled by community
self-policing, neighbor protecting and watching neighbor. The emergence of
more complex societies, urban centers, and national states created the need for
a more organized form of policing.

In Europe, when social and political control became particularly difficult,
complex policing organizations were created. These departments were organized like military units. They were armed and given the authority to control
and suppress political opposition as well as enforce the law. The communities
they policed were often hostile toward them. The first urban police forces in
the United States also drew their mandate from and gave their service to the
political organizations that created them. Like their European counterparts,
they were responsible for a number of municipal services, as well as for the
suppression of opposing political views.

A significant change in policing's political mandate occurred with the
founding of the London Metropolitan Police in 1829. The concepts of limited
police authority and community accountability were operationalized in this
police department through the administrative leadership of its first Commissioners of Police, Rowan and Mayne. Their adherence to Peel's Principles provided this organization with a mission and a core set of values that helped
them turn a hated experiment into a respected national institution. Peel's
legacy, the creation of an unarmed municipal policing system based on community accountability and strict adherence to the law, represents one of the
great administrative accomplishments in the history of policing.

In America, a reform movement that began earlier in this century led the
police in a different direction. This movement contributed to the development
of a powerful police managerial orthodoxy rooted in the traditions of the military and scientific management (Moore and Stephens, 1991). It was an internal
administrative reform that attempted to supplant the dominance of machine
politics with a mandate derived from the law and crime control. In its most advanced stage, this movement created a highly centralized, bureaucratically
controlled, reactive police organization concerned primarily with internal ac-

countability. However, social forces within the society—i.e., unrest, research, the due process revolution, and increasing crime and disorder—challenged the basic assumptions of this movement and helped make police accountability and effectiveness a major political issue.

Community policing is now calling for a fundamental rethinking of the police role and a redesign of police services to respond to changing social conditions. A basic goal of this reform is the development of a more accountable and responsive police service not unlike the Peelian reform of the last century. However, in the last several years, cuts in federal assistance, the faltering economy, and the political difficulty of raising taxes have led more states and cities to cut back on services and diminish police resources. Social unrest, drug trafficking, and rising levels of personal crime and violence are straining the scarce resources of municipal police departments. Police administrators are currently under intense pressure from their governmental authorities and communities to demonstrate the accountability of their personnel and the efficiency and effectiveness of their management practices. The rest of this book will address these issues with the purpose of contributing to the enhancement of the police administrative function.

QUESTIONS FOR DISCUSSION

1. Discuss the meanings attached to the term "police" in history.
2. Explain the Saxon system of "collective security."
3. How did the "New Police," created in 1829, differ from all previous police forces in Europe and Ireland?
4. Are Peel's *Nine Principles of Law Enforcement* as relevant today as they were in 1829?
5. Define the "Professional Model" of policing. How does it differ from the "Community Problem Solving Model" of policing? What factors have accounted for the trend from one to the other over the last generation?

SOURCES

ALPERT, GEOFFREY P., and ROGER G. DUNHAM (eds.). *Policing Urban America,* 2d ed. (Prospect Heights, Ill.: Waveland, (1992).

BAYLEY, DAVID H. "Police and Political Development in Europe," pp. 328–379 in Charles Tilly (ed.), *The Formation of National States in Western Europe* (Princeton, N.J.: Princeton University Press, 1975).

BIECK, WILLIAM H., WILLIAM SPELMAN, and THOMAS J. SWEENEY. "The Patrol Function," pp. 59–95 in William A. Geller (ed.), *Local Government Police Management*, 3d ed. (Washington, D.C.: International City Management Association, 1991).

BITTNER, EGON. *The Functions of the Police in Modern Society: A Review of Background Factors, Current Practices, and Possible Role Models* (Chevy Chase, Md.: National Institute of Mental Health, 1970).

BRAIDEN, CHRIS. "Bank Robbers and Stolen Bikes: Thoughts of a Street Cop," *Canadian Police College Journal,* 10:1–30 (1986).

BROWN, RICHARD M. "The American Vigilante Tradition," pp. 121–129 in Hugh Davis Graham and Ted Gurr (eds.), *Violence in America: Historical and Comparative Perspec-*

tive, report to the National Commission on the Cause and Prevention of Violence (Washington, D.C.: U.S. Government Printing Office, 1969).

CORDNER, GARY W. "Fear of Crime and the Police: An Evaluation of a Fear Reduction Strategy," *Journal of Police Science and Administration,* 14,3:223–233 (September 1986).

CRITCHLEY, T. A. *A History of Police in England and Wales,* 2d ed. (Montclair, N.J.: Patterson Smith, 1972 reprint of original 1967 manuscript).

Escobedo v. Illinois, 378 U.S. 478 (1964).

FARRELL, MICHAEL J. "The Development of the Community Patrol Officer Program: Community-Oriented Policing in the New York City Police Department," pp. 73–88 in Jack R. Greene and Stephen D. Mastrofski (eds.), *Community Policing: Rhetoric or Reality?* (New York: Praeger, 1988).

FOSDICK, RAYMOND B. *European Police Systems* (Montclair, N.J.: Patterson Smith, 1969 reprint of 1915 original).

FULD, LEONARD F. *Police Administration: A Critical Study of Police Organizations in the United States and Abroad* (Montclair, N.J.: Patterson Smith, 1971 reprint of 1909 original).

GAY, WILLIAM G., H. TALMADGE DAY, and JANE P. WOODWARD. *Neighborhood Team Policing in the United States* (Washington, D.C.: U.S. Government Printing Office, 1977).

GELLER, WILLIAM A. (ed.). *Local Government Police Management,* 3d ed. (Washington, D.C.: International City Management Association, 1991).

GOLDSTEIN, HERMAN. "Improving Police: A Problem Oriented Approach," *Crime and Delinquency,* 25:236–258 (April 1979).

———. *Problem-Oriented Policing* (New York: McGraw-Hill, 1990).

GREENE, JACK R., and STEPHEN D. MASTROFSKI (eds.). *Community Policing: Rhetoric or Reality?* (New York: Praeger, 1988).

GREENWOOD, PETER, JOAN PETERSILIA, and JAN CHAIKEN. *The Criminal Investigation Process* (Lexington, Mass.: Heath, 1977).

GUYOT, DOROTHY. *Policing as Though People Matter* (Philadelphia: Temple University Press, 1991).

HARRISON, LEONARD V. *Police Administration in Boston* (Cambridge, Mass.: Harvard University Press, 1934).

HOLDEN, RICHARD N. *Modern Police Management,* 2d ed. (Englewood Cliffs, N.J.: Prentice-Hall, 1994).

JOHNSON, DAVID H. *American Law Enforcement: A History* (St. Louis: Forum Press, 1981).

Kansas City Police Department. *Response Time Analysis,* 3 vols. (Kansas City, Mo.: Board of Commissioners, 1977–1979).

KELLING, GEORGE L. "Police and Communities: The Quiet Revolution," *Perspective on Policing,* no. 1 (Washington, D.C.: National Institute of Justice and Harvard University, 1988).

———. "Foreword," pp. v–vii in Robert Trojanowicz and Bonnie Bucqueroux (eds.), *Community Policing: A Contemporary Perspective* (Cincinnati, Ohio: Anderson, 1990).

——— and MARK H. MOORE. "The Evolving Strategy of Policing," *Perspectives on Policing,* no. 4 (Washington, D.C.: National Institute of Justice and Harvard University, 1988).

———, TONY PATE, T. DUANE DIECKMAN, and CHARLES E. BROWN. *The Kansas City Preventive Patrol Experiment: A Technical Report* (Washington, D.C.: Police Foundation, 1974).

——— and JAMES K. STEWART. "Neighborhoods and Peace: The Maintenance of Civil Authority," *Perspectives on Policing,* no. 10 (Washington, D.C.: National Institute of Justice, 1989).

——— and ———. "The Evolution of Contemporary Policing," pp. 3–21 in William Geller (ed.), *Local Government Police Management,* 3d ed. (Washington, D.C.: International City Management Association, 1991).

KELLY, MARTIN A. "The First Urban Policeman," *Journal of Police Science and Administration*, 1:56–60 (January 1973).

KLOCKARS, CARL B. *The Idea of Police* (Beverly Hills, Calif.: Sage, 1985).

LA FAVE, WAYNE. *Arrest: the Decision to Take a Suspect into Custody* (Boston: Little, Brown, 1965).

LARSON, RICHARD C., and MICHAEL F. CAHN. *Synthesizing and Extending the Results of Police Research Studies: Final Project Report* (Cambridge, Mass.: Public Systems Evaluations, Inc., 1981).

LANE, ROGER. *Policing the City—Boston, 1822–1885* (Cambridge, Mass.: Harvard University, 1967).

LEE, W. L. MELVILLE, *A History of Police in England* (London: Methuen, 1901).

Mapp v. Ohio, 367 U.S. 643 (1961).

MASTROFSKI, STEPHEN D. "Community Policing as Reform: A Cautionary Tale," pp. 47–68 in Jack R. Greene and Stephen D. Mastrofski (eds.), *Community Policing: Rhetoric or Reality?* (New York: Praeger, 1988).

McDOUGALL, ALLAN K. *Policing: The Evolution of a Mandate* (Ottawa: The Canadian Police College, 1988).

McDOWELL, CHARLES P. *Criminal Justice in the Community,* 2d ed. (Cincinnati, Ohio: Anderson, 1993).

MILLER, WILBUR R. "Police Authority in London and New York City, 1830–1870," *Journal of Social History,* 81–101 (Winter 1975).

Miranda v. Arizona, 384 U.S. 436 (1966).

MONKKONEN, ERIK H. *Police in Urban America, 1860–1920.* (Cambridge, Eng.: Cambridge University Press, 1981).

MOORE, MARK H. "Problem Solving and Community Policing," pp. 99–158 in Michael Tonry and Norval Morris (eds.), *Modern Policing* (Chicago: University of Chicago Press, 1992).

—— and DARRELL W. STEPHENS. *Beyond Command and Control: The Strategic Management of Police Departments* (Washington, D.C.: Police Executive Forum, 1991).

—— and ROBERT C. TROJANOWICZ. "Corporate Strategies for Policing," *Perspectives on Policing,* no. 6 (Washington, D.C.: National Institute of Justice and Harvard University, 1988).

National Advisory Commission on Civil Disorders. *Report of the National Advisory Commission on Civil Disorders* (Washington, D.C.: U.S. Government Printing Office, 1968).

NIEDERHOFFER, ARTHUR. *Behind the Shield* (Garden City, N.Y.: Doubleday, 1967).

PALMER, STANLEY H. *Police and Protest in England and Ireland, 1780–1850* (New York: Cambridge University Press, 1988).

PETERSILIA, JOAN. "The Influence of Research on Policing," pp. 230–247 in Roger Dunham and Geoffrey Alpert (eds.), *Critical Issues in Policing: Contemporary Readings* (Prospect Heights, Ill.: Waveland, 1989).

Police Foundation. *The Newark Foot Patrol Experiment* (Washington, D.C.: Police Foundation, 1981).

RADELET, LOUIS A. *The Police and the Community* (New York: Macmillan, 1980).

REISS, ALBERT J., JR. *The Police and the Public* (New Haven, Conn.: Yale University Press, 1971).

REPPETTO, THOMAS A. *The Blue Parade* (New York: Free Press, 1978).

RICHARDSON, JAMES F. *The New York Police: Colonial Times to 1901* (New York: Oxford University Press, 1970).

——. *Urban Police in the United States* (Port Washington, N.Y.: National University Publications, 1974).

ROBERG, ROY R., and JACK KUYKENDALL. *Police & Society* (Belmont, Calif.: Wadsworth, 1993).

RUBINSTEIN, JONATHAN. *City Police* (New York: Ballantine, 1974).

SHERMAN, LAWRENCE W., CATHERINE H. MILTON, and THOMAS V. KELLY. *Team Policing: Seven Case Studies* (Washington, D.C.: Police Foundation, 1973).

SKOGAN, WESLEY G. *Disorder and Decline: Crime and the Spiral of Decay in American Neighborhoods* (New York: Free Press, 1990).

SKOLNICK, JEROME H. *Justice without Trial* (New York: Wiley, 1966).

———— and DAVID H. BAYLEY. *The New Blue Line: Police Innovation in Six American Cities* (New York: Free Press, 1986).

SOUTH, NIEGEL. "Law, Profit, and Private Persons: Private and Public Policing in English History," pp. 72–109 in Clifford D. Shearing and Philip C. Stenning (eds.), *Private Policing* (Newbury Park, Calif.: Sage, 1987).

SPELMAN, WILLIAM, and DALE K. BROWN. *Calling the Police: Citizen Reporting of Serious Crime* (Washington, D.C.: Police Executive Research Forum, 1981).

———— and JOHN E. ECK. "Problem-Oriented Policing," *Research in Brief* (Washington, D.C.: National Institute of Justice, 1987).

STEAD, PHILIP J. *The Police of Britain* (London: Macmillan, 1985).

STRECHER, VICTOR G. "Current Perspectives on Policing," pp. 324–355 in Larry T. Hoover (ed.), *Police Management: Issues and Perspectives* (Washington, D.C.: Police Executive Research Forum, 1992).

————. "History and Future of Policing: Readings and Misreadings of a Pivotal Present," *Police Forum*, 1:1–9 (1991).

TAFT, PHILLIP B., JR. *Fighting Fear: The Baltimore County COPE Project* (Washington, D.C.: Police Executive Research Forum, 1986).

TONRY, MICHAEL, and NORVAL MORRIS (eds.). *Modern Policing* (Chicago: University of Chicago Press, 1992).

TROJANOWICZ, ROBERT, and BONNIE BUCQUEROUX. *Community Policing: A Contemporary Perspective* (Cincinnati, Ohio: Anderson, 1990).

———— and DAVID CARTER. "The Philosophy and Role of Community Policing," *Community Policing Series No. 13* (East Lansing, Mich.: National Neighborhood Foot Patrol Center, School of Criminal Justice, Michigan State University, 1988).

UCHIDA, CRAIG D. "The Development of the American Police: An Historical Overview," pp. 16–32 in Roger G. Dunham and Geoffrey P. Alpert (eds.), *Critical Issues in Policing: Contemporary Readings,* 2d ed. (Prospect Heights, Ill.: Waveland, 1993).

WALKER, SAMUEL. *A Critical History of Police Reform* (Lexington, Mass.: Lexington Books, 1977).

————. *The Police in America: An Introduction,* 2d ed. (New York: McGraw-Hill, 1992).

WASSERMAN, ROBERT, and MARK H. MOORE. "Values in Policing," *Perspectives on Policing,* no. 8 (Washington, D.C.: National Institute of Justice, U.S. Department of Justice and Harvard University, 1988).

WESTLEY, WILLIAM A. *Violence and the Police* (Cambridge, Mass.: M.I.T. Press, 1970).

WILLIAMS, HUBERT, and PATRICK V. MURPHY. "The Evolving Strategy of Police: A Minority View," *Perspectives on Policing,* no. 13 (Washington, D.C.: National Institute of Justice and Harvard University, 1990).

WILSON, JAMES Q. *Varieties of Police Behavior: The Management of Eight Communities* (Cambridge, Mass.: Harvard University Press, 1968).

————. *Bureaucracy: What Government Agencies Do and Why They Do It* (New York: Basic Books, 1989).

2

The Police Role in Society

KEY WORDS AND PHRASES

Occupational mandate
Law enforcement
Conditions and cases
Criminal justice system
Mapp v. Ohio
Miranda v. Arizona
Permanent underclass
Problem-oriented policing
Herman Goldstein
Discretion

Coercion
Protecting lives, rights, and property
Preserving order
Evaluation
Quantification
Qualitative measures
Accountability
Monell v. New York City Department of
  Social Services

Thus far, we have seen that the development of police in the Western world generally has paralleled broader social history. For the most part, the history of Western civilization has been positive. We have suffered setbacks and disasters, but the quality of life has improved significantly over the last few centuries in terms of increased life expectancy, broadened distribution of wealth, improved social welfare, vastly increased productivity, and technological advancement. The hazards and problems of primitive life—disease, tribal combat, exposure to extremes of climate, scarcity of food, and the need to expend enormous amounts of energy just to contend with these difficulties from day to day—are no longer a part of most people's lives.

Still, the progress of humanity has created or been accompanied by new problems and potential disasters. Since the last edition of this book was written, the risk of nuclear holocaust appears to have diminished with the end of nearly a half-century of cold war. Yet, turmoil continues in the Middle East and in many developing parts of the world. For the nations of eastern Europe and their closest neighbors, the near future promises years of social and political upheaval. Choices, freedoms, and rights that were only vague dreams in that part of the world when Wilson and McLaren wrote the last edition of this book, have suddenly become real and will greatly complicate the tasks of governing and policing. We also are concerned with other problems that either did not exist or had not yet been discovered in the 1970s. AIDS, depletion of Earth's ozone layer and predictions of a disastrous greenhouse effect, and fears that unstable Third World dictators may become capable of waging nuclear or chemical warfare all have recently landed on our list of looming crises. In short, as society moves forward and becomes more complex, new problems arise.

NEW OCCUPATIONS AS RESPONSES TO PROBLEMS

Chapter 1 suggests that one response to emerging problems is the creation of new occupations or professions to deal with them. In just such a manner, the police have developed as the growth of society has weakened the ability of such informal means of social control as families and communities to maintain peace and harmony. The police rarely are needed when everybody knows or is related to everybody else; when everybody shares the same political, social, and moral views; and when there exists a common definition of right and wrong. When and where this happy state of affairs has changed, the police came into being. Where it did not change—as in primitive tribal societies and in some of our own small homogeneous communities—the community has taken care of its own problems, and there has been no need for a formal police occupation.[1]

Most occupations enjoy very clear *mandates,* or roles, that have been developed through a process of negotiation and education involving the general public and its leaders and opinion makers, as well as the members of the occupation. Sociologist Peter K. Manning was among the first to point out (Manning, 1977) that this has not been true of the police. The role of the police is ill-defined, and rather than having enjoyed—*or having seized*—the opportunity to help structure their own responsibilities, the police historically have been told what to do by people without experience or training in police work.[2] The absence of a clear mandate that has been developed with substantial input from members of the police occupation has had major consequences for the police, their performance, and the manner in which they are perceived by the public and public officials.

In most cases, occupational (or organizational) mandates can be concisely and acceptably described in a few words. The mandate of medicine is to prevent disease, to treat diseases it could not or did not have the opportunity to prevent, and to search for cures to diseases for which there exist no successful treatments. The mandate of the fire service is similar: to prevent fires and to extinguish as quickly as possible those that its efforts did not prevent. However complex and mysterious its work, the mandate of the Central Intelligence Agency can also be put into a few words: to protect the interests of the United

States by developing and analyzing information about potential threats against it and by working to minimize such threats.

Clear occupational mandates offer many advantages. The process of creating a mandate gives all participants the opportunity to decide and articulate just what they expect of an occupation and its members. This, in turn, helps to decide where to draw the lines between the work and responsibilities of related occupations such as medicine and dentistry, social work and psychiatry, and carpentry and bricklaying. A clear mandate also makes it easy to establish performance standards for the occupation. This helps in evaluating personnel and organizations and in establishing requirements for entry to the occupation and for remaining and advancing in it. It simply is not possible to establish defensible hiring standards for jobs that have not been clearly defined.

In other words, it helps everybody concerned with an occupation—its members and its clients—if there is a clear understanding of the occupation's responsibilities.

DEFINING A POLICE MANDATE

As the first lines of virtually every police department's manual state, there is general agreement that the primary responsibilities of the police are as follows:

1. To protect life, property, and constitutional guarantees
2. To preserve order

These responsibilities serve as the basic standards for establishing police policy and for evaluating police conduct. Certainly, no police administrator should direct his or her personnel to engage in conduct that endangers life, property, or constitutional guarantees or that serves to create disorder. Nor, obviously, should any administrator tolerate such conduct.

Problems in Setting Police Priorities

Beyond this bottom line, however, these two brief prescriptions give little precise guidance as to how these noble goals are to be achieved or how priorities should be arranged among them. Is it more important to protect constitutional guarantees or to preserve order? For example, the police could probably prevent some disorders and ensuing disruption to many lives by clamping down on the attempts of controversial small groups to exercise their First Amendment right to gather and speak in public. When faced with applications for parade permits from the Ku Klux Klan or other organizations that periodically seek to air despicable views, most police chiefs are sorely tempted to send them on their way with rude suggestions that they go elsewhere to promote hate. For good reasons that have nothing to do with the merits of individual groups' beliefs, however, the police generally cannot take this easy way out of the quandary between the Constitution and the need for order. Instead, the police usually swallow their distaste, permit the parades, and take extraordinary and expensive steps to preserve order. In doing so, they invariably are second-guessed ("Why should my tax dollars go to pay overtime to police in order to protect people who spout un-American messages of hate?"), especially when disorder occurs despite police precautions ("'We Told You So,' Says City Council, Demanding Chief's Ouster for Permitting Parade That Resulted in Downtown Mini-Riot").

Failure to Distinguish the Police from Other Occupations

In addition to its lack of clarity, this statement of primary police responsibilities suffers another liability: it does not define a mandate unique to the police. Bits and pieces of these two responsibilities also are the duties of other occupations. Firefighters and rescue personnel also protect life and property; the courts also have a major responsibility to protect constitutional guarantees; and, usually on an international level, the military preserves order. In short, these two goals are not much help in drawing clear lines that distinguish the work of the police from that of other occupations. One consequence of this absence of uniqueness is that the duties of the police in relation to those of other organizations vary throughout the United States. In some jurisdictions, police also provide firefighting, rescue, and ambulance service; in others, they provide rescue and emergency services only in cases that do not involve flames or smoke, which are the responsibility of fire departments; in still others, separate fire, rescue, and ambulance services exist, and police are responsible only for rendering temporary aid pending the arrival of specialists at the scenes of fires or other emergencies.

A second consequence of this lack of uniqueness is that police have been assigned many responsibilities simply because nobody else has been readily available 7 days a week, 24 hours a day, to handle them. Would the local merchants like someone to stoke their fires early in the morning so that their shops will be toasty when the first customers arrive? Firefighters also are on duty at these hours, but their mandate requires that they extinguish rather than start fires, and this type of duty might make them unavailable to do so. Let's assign this job to the beat officers on the graveyard shift and tell them that it's a way of protecting property, many city fathers decided early in the century. Do we need someone to get cats out of trees? to open doors for people who have locked themselves out of their homes or cars? to intervene in family arguments that break out in the middle of the night, when social workers and marriage counselors are home in bed? The police are around, so let's tell them to do it. How should we distribute food and coal to home relief clients? It's hard for poor folks to travel downtown, and it looks bad to have so many scruffy people around city hall, so let's do this at easily accessible neighborhood police stations: somebody is always on duty in them.

The range of such assignments during the history of U.S. policing has been extremely wide, and sometimes it has borne only the slightest relation to the responsibilities of protecting life, property, and rights and preserving order. But since the lines defining *police work* are so blurry, officers have had to become jacks-of-all-trades as new tasks are routinely added to their duties. The advent of community and problem-oriented policing models is not likely to change this.

LAW ENFORCEMENT: A CLEAR DIRECTIVE OR A VAGUE SUGGESTION?

One popular way to define a unique mandate for the police is to think of them in terms of *law enforcement.* At first glance, this sounds relatively straightforward and logical. But when examined more carefully, the law enforcement tasks of the police become only a hazy set of responsibilities.

We frequently use the terms "police" and "law enforcement" interchangeably (as in police career, law enforcement career; police officer, law enforcement officer), but these simply are not the same. As Chapter 1 has indicated, the roots of the word "police" have to do with government generally rather than with law enforcement. Further, as we shall see, most police work involves activities other than law enforcement. Note, for example, that the two primary police responsibilities defined above—protecting life, property, and constitutional guarantees and preserving order—make no mention of law enforcement.

In addition, while we expect the fire service to respond to all fires all the time, nobody *really* expects the police to enforce all the laws all the time. If the police truly were expected to enforce all the laws all the time, we would make sure that they had the personnel and equipment to arrest every jaywalker, to ticket every car parked more than 12 inches from a curb, and, in the great number of states in which fornication remains a crime, to investigate and arrest everybody who has sex outside of marriage. Even if the police had the resources to vigorously enforce all laws, we would expect them not to do so. Instead of full enforcement, we expect the police to tolerate some offenses and to use "common sense" and "mature judgment" in exercising their enforcement powers: What motorist would not complain about being ticketed for traveling 3 or 4 miles an hour over the speed limit on an empty highway? Who, listening to such a complaint, would not conclude either that the police officer had been overzealous or that the motorist was not telling the whole truth about what led to a ticket in such circumstances?

The point is that while law enforcement generally is considered a core police responsibility, including it in a concise description of the police occupational mandate would ignore the reality that we expect the police not to enforce some laws in some situations. Indeed, if the police did not refrain from arresting or ticketing when there occurred some *minor* or *understandable* violations of law, life would quickly become tiresome—but we don't agree on which violations of law may be written off as minor or understandable. Most of us would probably agree on the point at which firefighters should be summoned because a barbecue has turned into a dangerous fire, for example. We are sharply divided, however, about the point at which people's conduct becomes offensive or dangerous enough to warrant police attention, even when such conduct—like illegal gambling, fornication, or even drug use—is specifically prohibited by law. Many of us view these as terrible vices that should be the subject of vigorous law enforcement; many others think that some or all of

Civil rights and antiwar demonstrations in the 1960s caused major reassessment of whether police at demonstrations should vigorously enforce all laws or should place primary emphasis on maintaining order while protecting citizens' right to protest. In this 1969 photo, a group of Washington, D.C., officers chats with a young peace demonstrator.
Charles Gatewood/Image Works.

these activities are harmless *victimless crimes*—private matters that should be ignored so that police can concentrate on enforcing laws against crimes with identifiable victims. The result is that while we would be angry if doctors chose to ignore some diseases and some sick people, we expect the police to ignore violations of some of the laws they presumably are sworn to enforce.

In addition, the police ignore some law violations because, instead of helping to keep order, enforcing the law might actually contribute to disorder. Controversial public issues once again provide a useful illustration. Emotional participants at public demonstrations over contentious matters—war and foreign policy, abortion, civil rights—sometimes engage in disorderly conduct, trespass, or other public order offenses because they get caught up in the temper of the moment. Others do so intentionally, specifically to call attention to their cause by provoking the police to forcibly arrest them. At more casual and only slightly less volatile events such as rock concerts, police attempts to arrest spectators for offenses such as marijuana smoking sometimes have led to near riots. One doesn't have to hold a strong view on whether the police should vigorously enforce the law in such circumstances to realize that doing so sometimes creates more immediate problems than it solves.

The reality of police discretion in whether to enforce the law suggests the proper place of law enforcement in any consideration of the police role. Law enforcement does not belong in the list of police responsibilities that includes protection of life, property, and rights and preservation of order. These all are valid ends in themselves, but law enforcement is not. Instead, law enforcement is most appropriately regarded as one of many *tools* the police use to achieve their ends of protecting life, rights, and property and preserving order. Sometimes, in meeting their responsibility to protect life and property, the police use law enforcement as a tool. On other occasions—as when they warn motorists rather than issue tickets—they use other means of achieving the same end. The same principle holds where other police responsibilities are concerned. At some demonstrations, protection of rights and preservation of order may be accomplished merely by warning demonstrators to cease unlawful conduct. At other demonstrations, only arrests will get the job done.

In addition, experience has shown that arrest is not always an effective means of preserving order. In many cities, police administrators frequently hear residents and merchants complain that groups of "undesirables" (street prostitutes, drug abusers, panhandlers, rowdy teenagers, street drunks, and the like) have been drawn to certain streets and neighborhoods. When officers respond to these complaints by making arrests, however, they often get the sense that the courts are too lenient with the individuals whose offenses may have extremely negative effects on an entire community's quality of life. The frustration of the police is understandable, but so are the slaps on the wrist typically delivered to such offenders by the courts.

In such situations, the problem the police confront is a general *condition:* many people committing offenses against public order which, individually, are very minor but which, when committed by enough people in a small area, may make life miserable for everybody else. The courts and the law, however, are not geared to deal with conditions. Instead, the courts apply laws that are oriented to *cases* and *individuals.* The courts may apply laws against disorderly conduct and loitering in all the cases brought to them by the police, but the minor penalties they mete out are not much of a deterrent, especially when street conditions typically involve so many offenders that the police are capable of hauling before the courts only a small percentage of the total. Further, even if penalties were increased, judges would be hard-pressed to justify applying them when most jails already are overcrowded with individually more serious offenders like robbers and burglars. This leaves the police stuck between community demands that the police clean up a condition and the realities of a court system that is more capable of dealing with individual big cases—and more interested in doing so than in cracking down on apparently minor offenders.

POLICE: A CRIMINAL JUSTICE AGENCY?

Over the last quarter-century, recognition of quandaries like the need to reconcile the police focus on street conditions with the courts' focus on individual cases has led to great expansion of *criminal justice* as a formal academic field of study. Most of the college and university programs in which this book is used were created during this period. Other programs that can trace their histories back further in time changed their titles from "police science," "police studies," or "law enforcement" to "criminal justice" during these years.

The growth of criminal justice programs on college and university campuses reflects a concern with growing rates of crime. In addition, there grew a realization in the 1960s that the best way to study the police or other criminal justice agencies (e.g., courts and corrections) is in the context of the whole system rather than in isolation from each other. This realization was based on the reasoning that the criminal justice system—*or nonsystem*—could be improved only if its constituent parts stopped thinking of themselves as islands unto themselves. Instead, commentators such as President Johnson's blue-ribbon Commission on Law Enforcement and Administration of Justice urged that police, courts, and corrections be convinced to view themselves as part of a continuing process that begins with police investigation and that ends when convicts complete their sentences (President's Commission, 1967).

Recognition of the need for formal study of criminal justice has led to major improvements in the performance of American police, courts, and corrections. But it also has prompted many of even the most knowledgeable people—including the police themselves—to think of the police strictly in terms of crime, law enforcement, and criminal justice. As suggested above, for example, it seems especially inappropriate to describe patrol personnel as law enforcement officers. Law enforcement may be one of the most important duties performed by patrol officers, but it is only one of many things they do.

Importantly, recognition of criminal justice as a legitimate field of academic study also has caused many people to think of "the criminal justice system" as some sort of expensive and all-powerful monolith that should be able to solve the crime problem with little assistance from anybody else. We have learned by experience that this is not so. For many of the same reasons that law enforcement is an inadequate descriptor of the police or their mandate, defining either the police or their mandate in criminal justice terms leaves out much of their work. The most relevant research suggests that the percentage of police patrol work involving crime and law enforcement may have increased in recent years, but it is less than one might expect. James Q. Wilson (1968) reported that only 10 percent of calls to the Syracuse (N.Y.) Police Department during a week in 1966 afforded an opportunity for law enforcement. Albert J. Reiss, Jr., (1971) found that Chicago police classified as "criminal" only 17 percent of the calls they received. Richard J. Lundman (1980) studied the work of five varying police departments and found that only 30 percent of their patrol officers' time involved law enforcement. More recently, Stephen Mastrofski (1983) reported that 29 percent of the incidents handled by patrol officers in 24 police departments involved crime.

True criminal justice agencies—courts and corrections—interact exclusively with people who have been accused of crime, were victimized by crime, or have witnessed crime. Except for those in specialized assignments, however, police officers' workdays include contacts with a wide range of people who have nothing to do with crime. Among these are motorists in need of directions, traffic violators, lost children, the sick and injured, homeowners or merchants concerned about noisy groups of kids, family members who have engaged in loud arguments, and all others who call the police for help or are subjects of such calls. When police come into contact with such people and their problems, their work has little to do with crime or law enforcement. Instead, as Egon Bittner indicated in a pointedly worded and oft-quoted description, most police patrol work consists of putting an end to "something-that-ought-not-to-be-happening-and-about-which-somebody-had-better-do-some-thing-*now*" (Bittner, 1974:30). Even when this *something* involves conflicts, minor disorder, or other types of behavior that may involve real or potential law violations, Bittner suggests, the mere presence of the police usually is enough to resolve it without police use of any law enforcement powers. This form of police work has led Ericson (1982) to conclude that what police really do is to *reproduce* order after it has been disturbed.

The traditional view of the police as a criminal justice—or law enforcement—agency, therefore, is a narrow one that overlooks the fact that most police work does not involve crime or enforcement of the criminal laws. Certainly, no other agency fights crime in precisely the manner of the police, but crime, law enforcement, and criminal justice are only one part of the police role.

Confusion about the mandate of the police and the goals and means of policing is more than merely academic. It is evidence that a most fundamental question concerning the police—*What do we expect from them, and how do we expect them to do it?*—has not been thought out nearly as well as have the roles of other occupations.[3] When we think of the police as law enforcement officers, we define them in terms of one of the tools they use rather than in terms of what they are responsible for accomplishing with the tools available to them. Other occupations typically draw a clearer distinction between what they expect to accomplish and the tools of their trade. If doctors defined their profession's core responsibility as "doing surgery" or "prescribing drugs," we would think their view shortsighted and narrow, and we would point out that we expected them to try their best to cure disease, no matter what it took. The police, however, are often referred to as law enforcement officers, even though (as the street-condition example suggests) this means of accomplishing the police goal doesn't always achieve the desired end. When we describe the police as a part of the criminal justice system, we are only partly correct, because much police work has nothing to do with crime or criminal justice and involves no interaction with courts or corrections. Conversely, virtually every bit of the business of the criminal courts or correctional agencies begins with something a police officer does.

MORE DETAILED STATEMENTS OF POLICE RESPONSIBILITIES

The result of all this is that beyond the very brief—*and very incomplete*—statement that we expect the police to protect life, property, and rights and to preserve order, we have developed no universally accepted mandate for the police. Instead, and often without meaningful input from police themselves, the police have been assigned a dizzying array of duties largely because they enjoy

great authority to use force and because they are available 24 hours a day, 7
days a week. When he tried to identify the police mandate, Manning (1977:8)
concluded that "the police have staked out a vast and unmanageable social domain." Even though the American Bar Association (ABA) used less colorful
language in attempting to define police responsibilities, its list (1973:4–5) illustrates why Manning reached this conclusion. Consider the conflicts and ambiguous messages in the following:

> In assessing appropriate objectives and priorities for police service, local com-
> munities should initially recognize that most police agencies are currently
> given responsibility, by design or default:
>
> i. to identify criminal offenders and criminal activity and, where appro-
>   priate, to apprehend offenders and participate in subsequent court
>   proceedings;
> ii. to reduce the opportunities for the commission of some crimes
>   through preventive patrol and other measures;
> iii. to aid individuals who are in danger of physical harm;
> iv. to protect constitutional guarantees;
> v. to facilitate the movement of people and vehicles;
> vi. to assist those who cannot care for themselves;
> vii. to resolve conflict;
> viii. to identify problems that are potentially serious law enforcement or
>   governmental problems;
> ix. to create and maintain a feeling of security in the community;
> x. to promote and preserve civil order; and
> xi. to provide other services on an emergency basis.

After a few years of further consideration, Herman Goldstein, who drafted
this list for the ABA, amended it in his classic book *Policing a Free Society*
(1977). The list of police obligations that resulted from these changes is shown
in Box 2-1.

BOX 2-1. The Objectives of State and Local Police in the United States

1. To prevent and control conduct widely recognized as threatening to life and property (serious crime).
2. To aid individuals who are in danger of physical harm, such as the victim of a criminal attack.
3. To protect constitutional guarantees, such as the right of free speech and assembly.
4. To facilitate the movement of people and vehicles.
5. To assist those who cannot care for themselves: the intoxicated, the addicted, the mentally ill, the physically disabled, the old, and the young.
6. To resolve conflict, whether it be between individuals, groups of individuals, or individuals and their government.
7. To identify problems that have the potential for becoming more serious problems for the individual citizen, for the police, or for government.
8. To create and maintain a feeling of security in the community.

Source: Goldstein, 1977:35.

In explaining his more recent thinking, Goldstein said:

> This list differs from that approved by the ABA committee in several respects. I have deleted the references to apprehending offenders, participating in court proceedings, and working to reduce crime through preventive patrol, on the assumption that these are more accurately characterized as methods employed by the police than ultimate objectives to which they are committed. I have dropped the objective of promoting and preserving civil order because this is covered adequately under resolving conflict. Some might want to add to this list the regulation and control of private morals, not because it should be a police responsibility but because the police are currently expected to devote substantial resources to this end. (Goldstein, 1977:44, fn. 25)

Thus, even after all his experience in police administration and scholarship, Goldstein had to admit that the list of police responsibilities he had helped develop for the ABA was fuzzy. He also viewed it as unrealistic. In 1977, he wrote:

> Many of the problems coming to the attention of the police become their responsibility because no other means has been found to solve them. They are the residual problems of society. It follows that expecting the police to solve or eliminate them is expecting too much. It is more realistic to aim at reducing their volume, preventing repetition, alleviating suffering, and minimizing the other adverse effects they produce. (Goldstein, 1977:243)

Goldstein's thinking on this subject should be kept in mind by all students and practitioners of policing. To state the major point of agreement between him and Manning (as well as most other police scholars), *there is no such thing as a police problem; there are only social problems we ask the police to confront. Since most of these problems are caused by factors that the police did not create and cannot change, the police cannot be expected to solve most of them.* Frequently, however, we ask the police to correct specific and temporary *conditions* caused by broader social problems. The police often are able to do so with dispatch, but the problems underlying these conditions—all the factors that lead to a family argument so noisy that it leads neighbors to call the police, for example—usually are beyond the capacity of the police.

THE PROBLEM OF CRIME

Crime and violence probably are the best illustration of the intransigence of the problems many of us expect the police to solve. The police crime-fighting role has been subjected to great scrutiny since researchers first discovered that it constituted a surprisingly small percentage of officers' time and effort. When the study of criminal justice began in earnest, most of the public (and some police officials) apparently assumed that most crime could be eradicated by improving the administration and operations of police, courts, and corrections. Since then, we have suffered nearly three decades of continuing and great increases in crime and violence. This trend has not occurred because the police have become less proficient at fighting the war on crime. Every knowledgeable observer would agree that police—as well as the courts and corrections systems—today are much more technically sophisticated and better trained, educated, and equipped than they were before crime started to increase during the early 1960s.

Nor is this increase in crime attributable to the various U.S. Supreme Court decisions some regard as "handcuffs" on police crime-fighting ability. The 1961 decision in *Mapp v. Ohio*[4] ruled that unconstitutionally seized evidence could not be used in state criminal cases and is frequently cited as an unrealistic obstacle to police and prosecutors. Yet no study has found that exclusion of improper evidence results in the dismissal of more than 1.5 percent of criminal cases, the great majority of which are *possessory* offenses (possession of weapons or drugs) rather than crimes of violence such as murder, rape, or robbery.[5] Indeed, one of the most interesting effects of the *Mapp* decision is that it may have encouraged the police to increase training related to search and seizure (see Davies, 1983), which certainly was not a bad outcome.

Critics of *Miranda v. Arizona*,[6] the decision requiring officers to issue the famous Miranda warnings to silence and counsel before questioning suspects, frequently do not realize that violations of this rule do not automatically result in dismissed criminal charges. Instead, violations result only in exclusions of resulting unconstitutional confessions and evidence obtained through them, and they do not affect the admissibility of independent physical and eyewitness evidence. As a result, the number of prosecution cases lost because of *Miranda* violations is far smaller even than the number dismissed because of *Mapp*. Even Ernesto Miranda ultimately was convicted in the famous case that bears his name: in his case, as in most others affected by it, the only thing dismissed was his confession, and he was convicted on the basis of all the other evidence against him. Indeed, there is no evidence that any Supreme Court decision has had any effect whatever on rates of crime or on public safety or police effectiveness.

We also often hear that *turnstile justice* accounts for rising crime. What's to keep us from committing crime, this argument goes, as long as our courts specialize in plea bargaining and in issuing penalties that are laughably minor? Certainly, there are miscarriages of justice, and some serious offenders do receive overly lenient treatment. Generally, however, our trial courts have become far tougher on crime in recent years. During the 1980s, the average length of sentences handed down by the courts steadily increased, with the result that prison and jail populations approximately doubled: more than 1 million Americans currently are incarcerated (U.S. Department of Justice, 1991). Further, crime rates among the states seem to vary without any relationship to sentencing severity (U.S. Department of Justice, 1984).

Thus, it does not appear that the general upward trend in American crime and violence can be attributed to any failure or weakness of the police or the rest of the criminal justice system. The police, judicial, and correctional systems all are working hard—*and tough*—but in many places they are overwhelmed by the volume of crime and violence they face and are frustrated by their inability to reverse it. This is so because, in our search for a simple solution to the problem of crime, we have tried to unload this *social* problem on the police and the rest of the criminal justice system. This has been a mistake.

Common sense and experience dictate that putting an end to a problem requires that we identify and eliminate its cause. The best doctors and nurses, for example, will not solve the problem of AIDS by treating people who are already afflicted with it. Instead, they must teach us how to try to prevent AIDS from spreading, and, in the long run, medicine must identify and eliminate its causes.

The same logic applies to crime and violence. However well-intended, hardworking, and competent, no police officer or criminal justice official can hope to solve the crime problem merely by hunting down and confining people who have already committed a crime. Instead, in the long run, the causes of crime must be identified, and, insofar as possible, they must be eliminated. In trying to do so, two realities must be acknowledged. First, while the police have a great—*and often unrecognized*—responsibility to work and speak out against the causes of crime, this is not a job that can be handled exclusively by the police or, indeed, even by the whole formal system of criminal justice. Second, neither the causes of crime nor crime itself will ever be totally eradicated. As the great sociologist Emile Durkheim observed many years ago, some members of even the most orderly societies behave in ways that draw condemnation:

> Imagine a society of saints, a perfect cloister of exemplary individuals. Crimes, properly so called, will there be unknown; but faults which appear venial to the layman will create there the same scandal that the ordinary offense does in ordinary consciousness. If, then, this society has the power to judge and punish, it will define these acts as criminal and will treat them as such. (Durkheim, 1977:659)

Criminologists and others have put forth a vast array of theories about the causes of crime. Because criminologists' explanations usually are so heavily influenced by their varied training and interests as sociologists, psychologists, and geneticists, their theories and proposed solutions also vary widely. Further, because the term "crime" is itself used to describe an enormous range of conduct committed by different types of people for completely different reasons, we will never find one authoritative theory or explanation for all crime. The acts of Wall Street swindlers, serial murderers, drug users, spouse abusers, and political criminals are all *crimes*, but the backgrounds and motivations of the people who commit them are simply too different to be explained by a single theory that has any implications for eliminating all this wrongful behavior.

Still, we do not ask the police to deal with *all* crime. With rare exception, prevention and detection of financial and political crimes generally are the responsibilities of specialized regulatory and investigative agencies such as the Securities and Exchange Commission, the Federal Bureau of Investigation, or the Secret Service. Most of the police work in this country is done at the local and state levels, and we typically ask these officials to combat what criminologists call *peasant* crime: predatory crimes against people, property, and public order. This crime is highly visible and causes great fear in the average citizen. Unlike political crime, corruption by public officials, and other white-collar crime, peasant crime typically does not involve offenders whose crimes are abuses of their occupation or positions. Together with drug and vice crimes, the offenses included in the FBI's Crime Index—murder and manslaughter, assault, rape, robbery, larceny, vehicle theft, burglary, and arson—constitute most of the crime-related workload of local and state police.

Even when the police share of the crime problem is narrowed down this far, however, police efforts to prevent and detect crime are hindered by major obstacles. Many of the most serious crimes take place indoors and cannot be deterred by any amount of police presence on the street. Drug trafficking, fencing of stolen property, labor racketeering, and the other activities of organized crime are difficult to detect because, voluntarily or through intimidation, the only people who know about these offenses take part in a rigidly enforced code of silence. Other high-profit "professional" crimes are committed by people who have so carefully planned their acts that they simply do not anticipate that they will be detected. Crimes of passion—spouse killings and drunken assaults—are committed by people who are so far out of control that, for the moment at least, they do not care whether their acts are detected. Some of the most ghastly crimes are the handiwork of seriously disturbed people who appear to have no understanding of or respect for the dignity or value of human life. Peasant crime probably is most frequent in what some observers have called a *permanent underclass.* Among the criminal members of this underclass, arrest and incarceration are rites of passage rather than causes for fear. Arrest involves no losses among people who have nothing to lose; imprisonment imposes little deprivation on people whose lives on the outside already are impoverished. Instead, arrest and survival in prison increase one's status by demonstrating toughness and total commitment to a criminal lifestyle.

Thus, a broad array of social, economic, genetic, and psychological factors is associated with the crime the police traditionally have been asked to prevent and detect. Criminologists differ about the relative weight and influences of these factors, but it is clear to all that the most violent and crime-ridden neighborhoods in this country are those of the underclass. These areas are afflicted by poverty, weak or nonexistent family structures, the absence of strong positive role models for young people, inadequate schools and support for education, ignorance, social isolation, inequity, lack of opportunity, and hopelessness. Certainly, not everybody exposed to such conditions succumbs to criminality, but as is true of kids who swim in polluted waters, a large percentage become infected.

Dealing meaningfully with the crime that occurs in these neighborhoods, and that sometimes reaches out beyond their boundaries, requires that these causes of crime be addressed. The administration of criminal justice may be made more effective and more efficient and speedier by good legislation, sound court decisions, and progressive management—or it simply may be made more harsh—but these efforts alone are unlikely to make substantial dents in the crime problem because they do not address the problems that are at its heart. Instead, all that these steps accomplish is to collect the unpaid debts to society that are owed by isolated offenders. However necessary, putting deserving individuals behind bars in this way will not solve the crime problem anytime soon. Unless this is clearly understood, public expectations of the police are bound to be unrealistic, and the police themselves will continue to be frustrated by their failure to live up to these unrealistic expectations.

This consideration of the crime problem has great implications for any attempt to define the role of the police. Certainly, the police should be expected to work hard to prevent and detect crime on a day-to-day basis, but over the

As the expression on the face of this eleven-year-old stabbing victim suggests, many urban kids grow up in environments that harden them early.
Jill Freedman.

long term the most important tasks in the police crime-fighting role may be educational and inspirational. The police—who, with the courts and correctional systems, have been given most of the responsibility for the crime problem—must continually and vigorously point out to policy makers and the public that significant long-term reductions in crime can only be achieved by changing the social conditions that breed most crime. The police also must continually inspire others to take action on this information.

PROBLEM-ORIENTED POLICING

Herman Goldstein's concept of problem-oriented policing incorporates the idea that police attempts to ease the problems of crime and disorder should include educational and inspirational efforts. Most generally, Goldstein argues that while many of the most complex problems confronted by police—crime, as an example—are beyond easy resolution, police can be expected to ease them. In addition, individual police officers can increase their ability to correct many of the temporary unacceptable *conditions* created by these problems. Police accomplish this by viewing themselves not exclusively as law enforcement officers but as *diagnosticians,* charged with identifying problems and mobilizing whatever resources are necessary to combat them (see Eck and Spelman, 1987; Goldstein, 1990). Several principles underlie this recent and promising trend:

1. Traditional police responses to community problems have proved ineffectual.
2. These responses have generally been reactive, and police rarely have made serious attempts to anticipate and head off community problems or to develop strategies to deal with long-term problems.
3. In attempting to deal with community problems, the police generally have looked only to themselves and have rarely enlisted the aid of other community institutions and resources.
4. The police response to the problems they confront has been characterized by an overreliance on law enforcement.
5. Traditional measures of police performance have overemphasized numbers (of arrests, tickets, response time in minutes, etc.) without regard to whether these quantitative measures reflect the quality of police service.
6. Since police and community situations and problems vary so greatly, no hard-and-fast set of rules can be devised to guide performance in all situations.
7. The fiction that police officers do not exercise discretion should be finally abandoned because even in the most rigidly law enforcement–oriented police departments, officers exercise great discretion.
8. Like other professionals' discretion, police discretion should be acknowledged and structured in ways that more directly address the problems they are expected to confront.
9. Since police hold such broad authority, they must be held closely accountable for exercising it in ways that best serve to address community problems.

Fundamental to all this is the development of a broad perspective that avoids the automatic presumption that law enforcement is the most appropriate tool for most problematic police situations. Certainly, where serious violations have occurred, laws must be enforced, but law itself frequently is no solution to many minor annoying conditions.

Police Work as Coercion

Problem-oriented policing defines in general ways the methods employed by police to address long-term problems and correct temporary conditions, but it does not define with specificity the strategies and tactics typically employed in *good* policing. To fill in this blank, the work of political scientist William Ker Muir (1977) is extremely useful.

Muir carefully studied 28 police patrol officers and concluded that the essence of their work was *coercion.* Like politicians, Muir argued, police are in the business of convincing people to do things they would not otherwise be inclined to do. And like politicians who head countries, police face a major challenge in trying to avoid the use of force in their attempts to get others to behave in certain ways. In legislatures, suggested Muir, politicians use a carrot-and-stick approach to convince both their colleagues and their constituents to vote in certain ways. So, too, he indicated, good police officers spend much of their time in skillful and smooth manipulation of other people's behavior. The mere sight of a police car on the highway is a form of manipulation that slows would-be speeders. A blank stare from an officer in a pausing patrol car often can convince noisy corner groups of teenagers to take their parties elsewhere. Police phone calls to people who park in others' driveways usually get immediate results. A police officer's arched eyebrow or skeptical expression convinces traffic violators that continuing pleas are falling on deaf ears and, yes, that the officer really does want the license and registration. In some cases, like hostage negotiations or investigators' attempts to turn criminals against their colleagues, this coercion is very subtle and consists of leading subjects to recognize the decisions that they must make to serve their own interests. In other cases, as when officers make arrests or use deadly force, police coercion is far more overt and puts a quick and involuntary end to wrongful behavior. Sometimes, police coercion involves actual law enforcement. On most occasions, however, police change behavior merely by manipulating their subjects' knowledge that officers can always resort to law enforcement if inappropriate behavior is not changed immediately. Stated most simply, therefore, Muir's view is that good police officers are masters of legal coercion: the art and science of marshaling the authority of their office and their own personal powers to get other people to behave in ways the police define as appropriate.

The Noncoercive Work of the Police

Certainly, not all the work that has been assigned to the police involves coercion. Most such noncoercive work, however, could easily be performed by others (e.g., social workers, rescue and medical squads, locksmiths, humane societies) and has become the duty of the police only because of their around-the-clock availability. But the *core* of police work—*protecting life, rights, and property and preserving order*—is coercive. Accomplishing this work requires that the police be given broad authority to use force when more gentle forms of coercion (persuasion, warning, etc.) are insufficient. The police have been given such authority. In Bittner's words (1970:122), the police are "an institution with the monopoly to employ non-negotiably coercive force in situations where its use is unavoidably necessary."

A DEFINITION OF POLICE WORK

This lengthy discussion leads us to our definition of police work. We begin with a version of the statement of primary police responsibilities presented at the beginning of the chapter, altered to reflect our view that protection of constitutional guarantees holds a higher priority than protection of property. To it, we add a summary of what U.S. police actually do and how they do it. The result is the following:

1. The primary responsibilities of police in the United States are to protect life, constitutional guarantees, and property and to preserve order, in that priority.

2. In attempting to meet these responsibilities, the police maintain a 24-hour-a-day capacity to address problems and conditions that require the use of legally authorized force or coercion and/or that are not the clearly delineated responsibility of other official agencies.

This definition of police work leads directly to two questions:

1. How does one determine whether police have acted appropriately to meet their responsibilities?

2. What measures should be in place to hold police accountable for doing so?

Evaluating Police Performance

Determining whether police have used their broad authority in ways most likely to protect life, rights, and property and to preserve order is not an easy task. Indeed, one likely reason that *law enforcement* has been so readily accepted as a definition of the police mandate is that it has been so easy to measure and, presumably, to evaluate. Where law enforcement has been defined as the core of the police task, evaluation measures typically have consisted only of *numbers:* of arrests, of crimes cleared by arrests, of summonses.

This *quantification* of police performance also has been extended beyond law enforcement measures. As a result, most police annual reports prominently feature pages of tables that count calls for service and that present elaborate analyses of response time. However interesting these numbers may be, they tell us little about the quality of police work or, as in our driveway example, of whether enforcement—*or quick response time*—helped to correct the con-

---

BOX 2-2. Police Code of Ethics

In 1957, the International Association of Chiefs of Police adopted the following statement of police responsibilities and conduct as its official Code of Ethics:

As a law enforcement officer, my fundamental duty is to serve mankind; to safeguard lives and property; to protect the innocent against deception, the weak against oppression or intimidation, and the peaceful against violence or disorder; and to respect the Constitutional rights of all men to liberty, equality and justice.

I will keep my private life unsullied as an example to all; maintain courageous calm in the face of danger, scorn, or ridicule; develop self-restraint; and be constantly mindful of the welfare of others. Honest in thought and deed in both my personal and official life, I will be exemplary in obeying the laws of the land and the regulations of my department. Whatever I see or hear of a confidential nature or that is confided to me in my official capacity will be kept ever secret unless revelation is necessary in the performance of my duty.

I will never act officiously or permit personal feelings, prejudices, animosities, or friendships to influence my decisions. With no compromise for crime and with relentless prosecution of criminals, I will enforce the law courteously and appropriately without fear or favor, malice or ill will, never employing unnecessary force or violence and never accepting gratuities.

I recognize the badge of my office as a symbol of public faith, and I accept it as a public trust to be held so long as I am true to the ethics of police service. I will constantly strive to achieve these objectives and ideals, dedicating myself before God to my chosen profession . . . enforcement.

dition to which the police had been called. Operations researchers and professional program monitors consider an evaluation measure *valid* only when it accurately reflects the extent to which a goal has been accomplished. By that simple standard, most quantitative measures of police performance are invalid because they do not measure how well police meet their responsibilities of protecting life, rights, and property and preserving order. Instead, these quantitative measures typically tell only how *often* or how *quickly* police did certain things.

A fuller understanding of whether police have done everything possible to protect life, rights, and property and preserve order—either generally or in specific circumstances—requires the use of *qualitative* measures. Merely counting the number of tickets issued tells us nothing about whether police have cleared up a double-parking condition in a business area or done everything possible to clear it up. Instead, we should observe the area in question after the police have taken action—whether it be issuing tickets; merely warning merchants, residents, and customers; or some combination of the two—and determine whether the condition has been alleviated. We should also watch to see whether there occur renewed complaints about the same condition. In doing so—as in evaluating any other police endeavor—we should keep in mind that, because of factors beyond police control, even the best police efforts may sometimes be inadequate to eliminate a problem.

Similarly, response time indicates little about whether police have satisfactorily dealt with a complaint of a noisy party. Instead, we should ask the complainant whether the noise was quelled and whether he or she was satisfied with whatever action the responding officers took. Just as the medical profession does not measure surgeons' job performance by counting the number of sutures they sew or determining how quickly operations are completed, the police should rely only secondarily on quantitative measures of job performance. In medicine and policing, the best measure of job success is whether the people involved did everything reasonably possible to address the problem or correct the condition they confronted.

In both medicine and policing, this measure—*Under the circumstances, did the professional(s) do everything reasonably possible to address the problem or correct the condition?*—is an even more valid assessment of job performance than is the question of whether desired results were attained. Consequently, this measure of *process* should be considered independent of, and more important than, the results in any specific incident. The old saw that "the operation was a success, but the patient died" is far more than a dark joke. In every field of endeavor, there are hopeless cases that even the most exemplary and extraordinary professional efforts cannot solve. Some cancers are so far along that cures are impossible; some suspects are so irrational that force simply must be employed to take them into custody; some crimes involve so little evidence that no amount of investigation will solve them. In such cases, it makes little sense to evaluate professional performance in terms of results. Ironically, in fact, exclusively *result-based* evaluation measures often penalize the best performers in any profession or occupation. The best doctors usually are the ones asked to treat patients with the lowest survival chances. The best patrol officers frequently are assigned to the toughest neighborhoods, where both crime rates and the probability of having to use force are great. The best homicide investigators usually are assigned to investigate the well-planned murders of organized crime, while their less able colleagues boost their clearance rates with assignments to clear-cut cases of domestic homicide.

Equally important, overreliance on result-based performance measures tends to reinforce unreasonable and inappropriate behavior. On many if not most occasions, even the most egregious conduct in any profession, or in any other aspect of life, results in apparently happy endings. Drunks involved in terrible collisions frequently tell officers that their driving ability could not have been affected by their high blood alcohol counts because they have years of accident-free experience driving home from local pubs. A few police officers who act in the most reckless and provocative ways come to believe that their behavior is appropriate because its worst-possible consequences have not yet been realized. Some investigators come to believe that violating the rules of obtaining and handling evidence is acceptable because the people they arrest simply plead guilty without challenging the manner in which the cases against them were built or mishandled.

Clearly, we wish police to behave in manners likely to achieve successful results because we have a great interest in successful police outcomes. But we should not be so blinded by our interest in results that we forget that good outcomes sometimes occur despite inappropriate behavior and that unhappy endings sometimes are unavoidable despite good intentions and efforts. When police performance is measured in a one-dimensional, result-based manner, exemplary conduct is penalized and inappropriate behavior is rewarded and perpetuated. *The acid test of police behavior is whether, on the basis of information available at the time, the police act in a manner that is congruent with their primary responsibilities to protect life, rights, and property and to preserve order, in that priority.*

Police Accountability

Scandals involving politicians' political meddling in police matters have led to a sentiment that *professional* policing requires that police and their departments be insulated from all politics. Instead, this logic holds, police should be strong and independent of politics and politicians. Further, according to such advocates of professional policing, this state can only be accomplished if police chief executives, like their officers in most places, hold lifetime tenure in their jobs. Advocates of professional policing also believe that, by virtue of their training and experience, police should be exclusively responsible for holding officers accountable for their actions (see, e.g., Fogelson, 1977; Johnson, 1981).

Certainly, history is full of examples of improper ties between police and politicians. Further, nobody can offer defensible reasons for denying police chief executives the right to serve as the primary authority figures over their officers or to manage police operations on a day-to-day basis. Still, the view of police as an independent monolith is shortsighted and ignores several realities. The first is that for better or for worse American police typically are arranged in a hierarchical, military organizational model. In our conception, the top of the military organizational model is not a professional soldier or sailor. Instead, the commander in chief of the military of the United States and every country that has modeled its government on our own is a democratically elected civilian politician. The reason for this is simple. The military is an enormously powerful force with the capability of changing all our lives. In a democracy, therefore, military policy cannot be set by a few unelected professional soldiers. Instead, military policy must be the responsibility of a civilian commander in chief who holds authority through the will of the people and who is advised by military professionals who serve at his or her pleasure.

This analogy applies with even more force to the police. Police have both enormous authority and great discretion to decide how to use it. When the police are led in ways that do not reflect the legitimate interests of their communities as demonstrated in the democratic electoral process, their authority can easily be used for oppressive purposes or for reasons that serve some narrow definition of the public good. Where the police or other officials with law enforcement powers have been granted independence from elected authorities, the ultimate results invariably have included widespread sentiment that their authority has been used in unreasonable and/or discriminatory ways.[7]

Further, the notion of politically autonomous police apparently flies in the face of the American tradition of *home rule*. In order to ensure that local citizens had real influence on their own fates, the Founding Fathers granted to state and local governments as many functions as possible. As we have seen, there were virtually no police at that time, but except for national defense, virtually all government functions were decentralized in the apparent desire to see that these operated as responsively as possible to local conditions. Given that history, it makes no sense to remove elected officials, and thus citizens, from participation in the processes of formulating police policy and holding police accountable for their actions.

This is not to suggest that police should return to the tight partisan control that frustrated and angered the great police reformers earlier in this century. Instead, as Goldstein (1977:141) has pointed out, we must recognize that there is a difference "between the political decision-making process in its broadest sense and narrow partisan politics." In fact, the police are a government agency, and government is political. It is proper and appropriate, therefore, that police policy formulation and accountability also be treated as political matters; it would not be proper to treat them as narrow partisan issues. It is proper that police chiefs' broad philosophies, styles, and policies reflect the priorities of elected chief executives, since these elected representatives presumably represent the will of the people. It also is proper that police chiefs be required to demonstrate to mayors and to the electorate that they hold officers accountable for abiding by these philosophies, policies, and styles. It would not be proper for police to be accountable for formulating or applying policies that benefit partisan or other narrow interests.

Thus, accountability for police policy and for specific actions should not end in the police chief's office. Indeed, regardless of the specific arrangements or understandings between any individual police agency and the rest of the executive branch of government, the time when it was possible for police accountability simply to end in either the chief's office or the mayor's office has passed. This is so because of the recent growth in the courts' role of assuring that police actions and policies accord with fundamental constitutional principles and common understandings of reasonableness.

Although hard figures are difficult to obtain, civil litigation alleging wrongful police behavior apparently has increased considerably in recent years.[8] One of the major vehicles for this increase was *Monell v. New York City Department of Social Services,*[9] a 1978 Supreme Court decision that greatly increased local government liability for employees' violations of federal civil rights laws. Most generally, *Monell* holds that plaintiffs who can prove that the civil rights violations they suffered at the hands of government employees were the result of serious shortcomings in agency custom and practice—such as deficient supervision or training—may recover damages from government treasuries as well as from the employees involved. The effect of this decision, in other words, was to open government's *deep pockets* to plaintiffs and to hold police agencies accountable in the courts for formulating and enforcing reasonable standards of police behavior.

Monell, therefore, brings this discussion full circle to the appropriate means of evaluating police conduct. When juries in civil suits examine police actions, the standard they employ is precisely that described on p. 47:

> On the basis of information available at the time, did the police act in a manner that is congruent with their primary responsibilities to protect life, rights, and property and to preserve order, in that priority?

When the answer to this question is negative, juries ask a second, similar question:

> Was the unreasonable police action a predictable result of supervisory and training practices so deficient that they were not congruent with the primary police responsibilities to protect life, rights, and property and to preserve order, in that priority?

Monell provides a powerful incentive for police to assure that their officers' actions and the policies and practices that guide officers can pass these tests of reasonableness. Indeed, when future historians study the significance of Supreme Court decisions affecting American police practice, they are likely to find that *Monell* has been much more important than *Mapp, Miranda,* or any other ruling involving criminal procedure. This is so because *Monell* and the cases that have followed it impose a standard for assessing police behavior and policy that is so logical—Have we done everything reasonable to protect life, rights, and property and to preserve order?—that it should have long ago been adopted as the universal test of police conduct.

SUMMARY

These first two chapters have traced the history of police and have attempted to derive a statement of the police role that serves as a basis for much of the rest of this book. We have not been hesitant to criticize other definitions, and we anticipate—*and hope*—that others will criticize ours. Advances in the science of policing require continual reevaluation and definition of the police role and of the ways in which we attempt to determine how successfully it is being performed. The degree to which policing is done successfully, we are convinced, cannot be determined with quantitative measures alone. Instead, anyone who seeks to measure the quality of police work should look more carefully at *how* it is done than at whether it results in some number that can be entered in a favorable column on a graph. Quite often, the outcome of police work is the result of matters beyond police control, but the degree of reasonableness and thoroughness with which police work is done is never beyond police control.

QUESTIONS FOR DISCUSSION

1. It has often been suggested that all police tasks other than law enforcement could be better handled by other official agencies. Is this a practical idea? What advantages, disadvantages, and problems would be involved?
2. What are the consequences of defining police primarily, or exclusively, in terms of *law enforcement* and *criminal justice*? How do such definitions affect the views and expectations of (*a*) the public, (*b*) political and elected leaders, (*c*) the media, and (*d*) police officers themselves?
3. How much are rates of crime and violence influenced by police effectiveness?
4. Devise measures of police performance in dealing with the following frequently encountered problems and conditions: (*a*) traffic congestion caused by double parking, (*b*) domestic violence, (*c*) drunk driving, and (*d*) street prostitution and drug sales.
5. The next chapter discusses the accountability of police chief executives. Before reading it, consider and discuss the advantages and disadvantages of each of the following arrangements:
   a. Civil service tenure, with removal only "for cause"
   b. Serving at the pleasure of the mayor or some other government chief executive
   c. Direct election of police chiefs, as in the manner of choosing county sheriffs
   d. Fixed, renewable, contractual terms that overlap mayors' terms of office

NOTES

1. Whether police work is an occupation or a profession is a debate considered later in this book. For now, all fields of endeavor will be defined as occupations.
2. Even today, most writing by police scholars and practitioners (including this book) is "how-to" material, designed to provide information about how responsibilities assigned to the police by legislators and others outside the occupation should be performed. Except for occasional debates about "victimless crimes" (e.g., Should drugs be decriminalized? Should police enforce laws against gambling or prostitution?) and the merits of assigning traffic enforcement to some nonpolice agency, police scholars and, *especially*, practitioners have written very little about the fundamental question of what the police should be doing.
3. This discussion owes much to Herman Goldstein's landmark article "Improving Policing: A Problem-Oriented Approach" (Goldstein, 1979).
4. 367 U.S. 643, 84 S.Ct. 1684, 6 L.Ed. 2d 1081 (1961).
5. Perhaps the most comprehensive summary of research on the effects of the exclusionary rule is Davies (1983).

6. 384 U.S. 436, 86 S.Ct. 1602, 16 L.Ed. 2d 694 (1966).
7. Extensive discussions of the effects on the Federal Bureau of Investigation and the Los Angeles Police Department of freedom from accountability to elected officials are found in Powers (1986) and Christopher et al. (1991).
8. Americans for Effective Law Enforcement, a nonprofit group that conducts training and research related to police liability, estimates that suits against police in federal and state courts increased from 1,723 in 1967 to 10,233 in 1976 to approximately 25,000 in 1983 (Schmidt, 1986:228–229).
9. 436 U.S. 658 (1978).

SOURCES

American Bar Association Project on Standards for Criminal Justice. *Standards Relating to the Urban Police Function* (New York: American Bar Association, 1973).

BITTNER, EGON, "Florence Nightingale in Pursuit of Willie Sutton: A Theory of the Police," in Herbert Jacob (ed.), *The Potential for Reform of Criminal Justice* (Beverly Hills, Calif.: Sage, 1974).

————. *The Functions of the Police in Modern Society* (Rockville, Md.: National Institute of Mental Health, 1970).

CHRISTOPHER, WARREN, et al. *Report of the Independent Commission on the Los Angeles Police Department* (July 1991).

DAVIES, THOMAS. "A Hard Look at What We Know (and Still Need to Learn) about the 'Costs' of the Exclusionary Rule: The NIJ Study and Other Studies of 'Lost' Arrests," *American Bar Foundation Research Journal,* 611–690 (1983).

DURKHEIM, EMILE. "Crime as a Normal Phenomenon," pp. 657–661 in Sir Leon Radzinowicz and Marvin E. Wolfgang (eds.), *Crime and Justice,* vol. I: *The Criminal in Society,* 2d ed. (New York: Basic Books, 1977); reprinted from Emile Durkheim, *Rules of Sociological Method,* 8th ed., Sarah A. Solvay and John H. Mueller (trans.), George E. G. Catlin (ed.) (Glencoe, Ill.: Free Press, 1950).

ECK, JOHN E., and WILLIAM SPELMAN. *Problem Solving: Problem-Oriented Policing in Newport News* (Washington, D.C.: Police Executive Research Forum, 1987).

ERICSON, RICHARD V. *Reproducing Order: A Study of Police Patrol Work* (Toronto: University of Toronto Press, 1982).

FOGELSON, ROBERT M. *Big-City Police* (Cambridge, Mass.: Harvard University Press, 1977).

GOLDSTEIN, HERMAN. *Problem-Oriented Policing* (New York: McGraw-Hill, 1990).

————. "Improving Policing: A Problem Oriented Approach," *Crime and Delinquency,* 25:236 (April 1979).

————. *Policing a Free Society* (Cambridge, Mass.: Ballinger, 1977).

JOHNSON, DAVID H. *American Law Enforcement: A History* (St. Louis: Forum Press, 1981).

LUNDMAN, RICHARD J. "Police Patrol Work: A Comparative Perspective," pp. 52–65 in Richard J. Lundman (ed.), *Police Behavior: A Sociological Perspective* (New York: Oxford University Press, 1980).

MANNING, PETER. *Police Work: The Social Organization of Policing* (Cambridge, Mass.: M.I.T. Press, 1977).

Mapp v. Ohio, 367 U.S. 643, 81 S.Ct. 1684, 6 L.Ed. 2d 1081 (1961).

MASTROFSKI, STEPHEN D. "The Police and Non-Crime Services," in Gordon P. Whittaker and Charles David Phillips (eds.), *Measuring Performance of Criminal Justice Agencies* (Beverly Hills, Calif.: Sage, 1983).

Miranda v. Arizona, 384 U.S. 436, 86 S.Ct. 1602, 16 L.Ed. 2d 694 (1966).

Monell v. New York City Department of Social Services, 436 U.S. 658 (1978).

MUIR, WILLIAM K. *Police: Streetcorner Politicians* (Chicago: University of Chicago Press, 1977).

POWERS, RICHARD G. *Secrecy and Power: The Life of J. Edgar Hoover* (New York: Free Press, 1986).

President's Commission on Law Enforcement and Administration of Justice. *The Challenge of Crime in a Free Society* (Washington, D.C.: U.S. Government Printing Office, 1967).

REISS, ALBERT J., JR. *The Police and the Public* (New Haven: Yale University Press, 1971).

SCHMIDT, WAYNE W. "Section 1983 and the Changing Face of Police Management," pp. 226–236 in William A. Geller (ed.), *Police Leadership in America: Crisis and Opportunity* (New York: Praeger, 1986).

United States Department of Justice, Bureau of Justice Statistics. *Justice Expenditure and Employment Extracts: 1980 and 1981 Data from the Annual General Finance and Employment Surveys* (Washington, D.C.: U.S. Government Printing Office, 1984).

———. *National Update* (Washington, D.C.: U.S. Government Printing Office, July 1991).

VOLLMER, AUGUST. *The Police and Modern Society* (Montclair, N.J.: Patterson Smith, 1972 reprint of original 1936 manuscript).

WILSON, JAMES Q. *Varieties of Police Behavior* (Cambridge, Mass.: Harvard University Press, 1968).

3

The Police and Politics

KEY WORDS AND PHRASES

Politicization

Home rule

Decentralization

Community control

City manager

Strong mayor

Police commission

Director of public safety

Partisan politics

Political influences

Ombudsmen

Personnel deployment

Labor negotiations

Power structure

Openness

Policing is a function of the executive branch of government. Like other executive agencies—most significantly, the military services that provided the organizational model on which police are structured—police departments in the United States are held accountable to the public through the electoral process. Just as the military reports ultimately to an elected commander in chief—the president of the United States—police professionals typically report to elected mayors, supervisors, or governors. This process of law enforcement accountability to the electorate is even more direct in sheriffs' departments, where chief law enforcement executives are themselves elected officials.

This line of authority seems rather straightforward and appears to put the police squarely into the political process. This is as it should be, because police are involved in some of the most sensitive public decision making. Police at every level exercise broad discretion, and their deliberations—both those of chiefs in paneled offices and those of officers in dark alleys—should be informed by and responsive to the philosophies and policies of their elected commanders in chief. As President Truman's dismissal of General MacArthur illustrates, this principle is not unique to the police, nor did it originate in the police service. Like the U.S. military, the U.S. police ultimately answer to elected officials.

Except for spectacular events like a feisty president's dismissal of the nation's most revered soldier, however, political officials' oversight of the military causes little debate. Despite frequent disagreement about whether the military should be deployed in specific circumstances, there is little dissent from the principle that elected officials, rather than career soldiers, should decide this issue, as well as the question of how, once committed to doing so, we wage war. When American soldiers took part in Operation Desert Storm, we all watched as the military experts advised President Bush about options, strategies, and tactics. But as we watched and waited, we knew that the politicians—rather than the generals—would decide what to do and how to do it.

SOURCES OF CONFUSION ABOUT POLICE AUTHORITY

We are less certain of who does or should make decisions where police are concerned. In the United States, police frequently are locked into uneasy relationships with politicians who don't quite know how to deal with the powder kegs that are their police departments. If these officials stand too close, they may be tarred with scandal; if they stay at a distance, they may allow their police to become entities unto themselves, complete with agendas that may place their own narrow interests above those of the public. At the same time, some of the police chiefs who complain most loudly about the "politicization" of law enforcement have used their own autonomy to become major actors on their local political scenes (see, e.g., Skolnick and Fyfe, 1993).

Police Decentralization

One of the major sources of the confusion and irregular relations between police and politicians is the American tradition of *home rule,* which, among other things, has made the U.S. "system" of policing the most decentralized in the world. Here, as in most other countries, some police and law enforcement agencies are organized at the national level. The great majority of American police departments, however, are creatures of local government. These agencies enforce ordinances enacted by the cities, towns, and counties of which they are a part, as well as the laws of the 55 separate state and territorial jurisdictions in which they are found. Federal law enforcement agencies have limited police powers and are carefully regulated by laws that place most policing authority as close as possible to the local level. But while its own enforcement role is limited, the federal government does play some role in assisting and overseeing state and local policing. The Federal Bureau of Investigation, for example, has long made training and scientific and technical assistance available to state and local police. Through the National Institute of Justice and the Bureau of Justice Assistance, the Justice Department has funded police research, experimentation, training, and the development of model police projects. Although the extent of their efforts varies with the philosophies of presidential administrations, the Justice Department's Civil Rights Division and Community Relations Service have also been valuable as a check that police operate within constitutional limits and as a resource for mediating police-community tensions.

Policing and law enforcement authority is also divided horizontally across the executive, legislative, and judicial branches of federal, state, and local governments. When the public thinks of federal law enforcement, for example, executive agencies such as the FBI, the Drug Enforcement Administration, and the Secret Service generally come most quickly to mind. In addition, however, there exist some limited-jurisdiction police agencies within both the federal judiciary and the legislature. The judiciary supervises the U.S. Supreme Court Police, while the Congress oversees the U.S. Capitol Police. Although the U.S. Marshal Service is organized within the Justice Department, much of its work is supervised by the federal courts. At the state level, police and highway patrols are part of the executive branch of their governments, but probation officers—who exercise enforcement powers—report to judges.

State involvement in local police matters, obviously, includes the legislation that authorizes jurisdictions to create police departments, as well as the laws that define criminal behavior and how to deal with it. Increasingly, state governments also have taken it on themselves to set minimum standards for local police policy, training, and performance. Although some object to this apparent violation of the home rule principle, the standards generally are so minimal that they cannot seriously be considered interventions in the administrative discretion of any but the most derelict agencies. The state-imposed minimum police recruit training requirement in Missouri, for example, is 120 hours (Flanagan and Jamieson, 1988), hardly a number that would require expansion of training by any reasonably informed police or law enforcement agency. More recently, Florida and Texas have initiated programs that allow state agencies to decertify local police officers from further eligibility for police work on findings of serious misconduct.

When there are so many jurisdictions with authority to oversee policing, it is understandable that lines of authority sometimes are blurred. Where a single police agency operates under the authority of a strong national chief executive, only one relationship between police and politicians must be designed and implemented. If, as is usually the case, the national leader in such a place holds the country together through both formal power and personal strength—and, perhaps, ruthlessness—there will be little doubt about who is in charge and who will design and implement the system. In a country with as many police jurisdictions as in the United States, however, police-government relations must necessarily vary all over the lot.

Community Control. During the 1960s and 1970s, this variation increased in some places with the advent of *community control*. Where police were concerned, community control meant the transfer of decision-making authority over police policy from the local government at large to smaller neighborhood units within the area encompassed by that government (see, e.g., Altshuler, 1970:64–65).

Efforts at community control were bred by the alienation and abuse of minorities, the lack of some neighborhoods' influence in setting enforcement priorities, imbalance in police resource allocation, and the inability to secure a rightful share of police resources. Advocates of community control argued that many of the problems affecting urban residents could be alleviated if the means of control were put directly into the hands of neighborhood representatives rather than into the hands of representatives who are elected by the citizens at large. Certainly, it was acknowledged by community control advocates, such arrangements might not be as efficient as centralized control by established government, but these advocates were more interested in the legitimacy of government than in its efficiency (Altschuler, 1970).

Community control never got very far. Even in Berkeley, California, which was at the time a hotbed for the movement, the issue was soundly defeated in a public referendum. Inefficiency was certainly an issue[1] in the decline of community control, but it had other shortcomings as well. First, it is very difficult to precisely describe or draw lines around "communities." Most of the places in which community control is most badly needed are not homogeneous and, indeed, are not "communities" at all. Instead, James Q. Wilson has suggested, inner cities typically are home to poor and middle-class blacks, young white singles, and elderly white couples who lack either the interest or the ability to form true communities (Wilson, 1983:33). Thus, as O. W. Wilson and McLaren pointed out in the last edition of this volume, there could be no assurance that leaders who emerged from neighborhood organizations had that much more legitimacy with all the citizenry in the neighborhood than a city council member elected from the same political ward, or even a council member or executive who was elected at large. Instead, community control mechanisms were fated to encourage conflicts with existing legislative bodies. How, for example, would community control boards interact with city councils over matters of budget? However much individual council members might agree with the concept of community control for *their neighborhoods*, it is simply not in the nature of politicians to give up control of the purse strings to inexperienced newcomers, most of whom represent other neighborhoods.

Second, community control advocates sometimes seemed to believe that responsiveness to community desires was an adequate gauge of police performance. In doing so, however, they may have overlooked the fact that police response to the wishes of many American communities would result in systematic violation of the rights of the people community control sought to empower. If police responsiveness were an adequate measure of the quality of policing, then officers who can be seen brutalizing civil rights demonstrators in the grainy films with which we are now all familiar—ironically, only a few years before the blossoming of the community control movement—surely would have passed muster. In short, community control may have accorded a higher priority to the standards of community squeaky wheels, no matter how far out of line, than to the standards of due process and professionalism to which police aspire.

Third, in some ways, community control was a regression to the old ways of local ward bosses' control of the police. As we had found out during the nineteenth century, such an arrangement frequently involved corruption, profiteering, and politics in all the wrong senses, while it excluded the public interest.

Problem- and Community-Oriented Policing. Nevertheless, community control advocates focused needed attention on the need for decentralization

Community policing has changed the way police policy and decisions are made. Here, a community group at a public meeting examines and discusses the Poughkeepsie, New York, Police Department's proposal for deploying officers.
McLaughlin/Image Works.

of influence on police policy and operations. This activism and a long line of research—and, some skeptics would add, a desire to be aboard the latest fad's bandwagon—led police administrators to see how tightly linked they and their operations were to local political, social, and economic environments, and how much these varied within jurisdictions. Out of this realization has come the drive toward problem-oriented policing and community-oriented policing.

This new philosophy of policing does not change the lines of accountability or our traditional notions of due process. It does add greatly to the number of sources of input to police decisions about how to tackle problems. Consequently, as Robert Trojanowicz and Bonnie Bucqueroux note, it demands "profound changes in the way traditional police departments view their role" (1990:6).

Statutory Provisions and Inadequacies

Variations in statutory provisions for control of the police are extensive and often blur the line from police to government chief executives. In some cases, police management responsibility is simultaneously vested in a city council and/or police commission, a mayor, a city manager or administrator, a director of public safety, and a chief of police. The cause of all this confusion usually is a legislative body. Rural-dominated state legislatures, distrusting those in urban centers to run their own affairs, sometimes have unrealistically limited cities' policing authority by creating single departments to police both inner cities and surrounding suburban areas. In such circumstances, affluent, better organized, and more sophisticated outlying areas typically have bent police policies to their ends. In other cases, nineteenth-century state legislatures took policing authority out of the hands of city fathers; police in New York City, Detroit, Cleveland, New Orleans, Cincinnati, Boston, and Omaha were placed under the supervision of state officials (Fogelson, 1977:14–15).

Similarly, legislation that blurs authority and makes every police decision an exercise in committee politics has been enacted by city councils that have been both inexperienced and overly anxious to ensure that their branch of government has some authority over police matters. Frequently, the resulting city charters or governing ordinances are overly specific about details relating to police management and, at the same time, ambiguous as to who actually exercises control. On occasion, consultants of the International Association of Chiefs of Police have encountered police ordinances that set out in detail the organizational structure of the department, including the numbers of personnel to be assigned to each rank and such matters as salaries and working conditions, as well as rules and regulations for the conduct of departmental business.

A detailed ordinance is unnecessary and undesirable. The best ordinances are brief and general, as illustrated in Box 3–1, showing the model ordinance developed by the International Association of Chiefs of Police.

When the department is encumbered by a detailed ordinance that infringes on the authority of the chief of police to carry out day-to-day operations, the chief should take the initiative in seeking to have a simpler form adopted. One like the model ordinance in Box 3-1 is usually acceptable to city managers and mayors, since it gives them more control than would be the case if the police ordinance were highly detailed. The manager or mayor may thus be receptive to bringing the ordinance problem to the attention of the city council. In some cases, a poor police charter provision can be changed only by public referendum, which may require the support of a citizens' group or charter commission before the change can be realized. The merits of this change dictate that chiefs should not hesitate to recommend it out of fear that people will assume that their only motive for doing so is a desire to be independent of the legislative body. Realistically, however, chiefs should be alert to this sentiment and might consider enlisting the aid of influential citizens and persons in the government who can carry the flag without drawing as much controversy.

A proper ordinance or charter should set out the chain of command for control of the department and for reporting purposes. Even when the ordinance or charter fails to specify the proper chain of command, the chief should attempt to secure agreement by the manager or mayor and the council through a written memorandum or a directive that serves the same purpose.

BOX 3-1. International Association of Chiefs of Police Model Police Ordinance

POLICE DEPARTMENT

There is hereby created a Police Department for the City of which shall consist of a Chief of Police and as many employees as the City Council may designate from time to time.

Appointment and Removal of the Chief of Police

The Chief of Police shall be appointed by the (Mayor) (City Manager) with the approval of a majority of the City Council, from a list of eligible candidates supplied by the Civil Service Commission (or central personnel agency). The Chief of Police shall serve at the pleasure of the (Mayor) (City Manager) and may be removed by the (Mayor) (City Manager) at any time thereafter with the consent of a majority of the City Council.

Supervision and Control of the Chief of Police

The (Mayor) (City Manager) shall be the immediate supervisor of the Chief of Police, and all policies, directives and orders from the City Government to the Chief of Police shall be made by or transmitted through the (Mayor) (City Manager) as the executive head of the City Government. The Chief of Police shall report directly to the (Mayor) (City Manager) and not to the City Council, to individual members thereof, or to (any other committee or commission).

Powers and Duties of the Chief of Police

The Chief of Police shall direct the administration and operations of the Police Department, and in addition to policies transmitted to him by the (Mayor) (City Manager), shall establish such other policies, directives, rules and regulations for the administration and operations of the department as he sees fit. The Chief of Police shall serve as appointing authority for appointment to any position within the department other than his own, and shall have the power to suspend or dismiss any employee, consistent with the provisions of the (State law or City Charter).

BUDGETING

(Other ordinances should relate to municipal budgeting and fiscal management. Any such ordinance should provide for annual budgets to be submitted by each department, and that approval of expenditures should not require a second action by the full City Council, as long as the department's expenditures do not exceed monthly or quarterly allocations.)

PERSONNEL MANAGEMENT

(Other ordinances should relate to municipal personnel management, disciplinary action, and employee benefits in general. However, specific salaries for each position should not be set out in ordinance form. Salaries should be mentioned only in the annual budget or by resolution.)

CITY MANAGERS AND MAYORS

Most American cities have chosen one of two forms of municipal government—the *city manager system* and the *strong mayor system*. The relationship of the police, especially the chief, to the executive* in each of these forms is slightly different.

The principal difference between these two forms is the method of selecting of the executive head. Most mayors are selected by popular election and, as a re-

---

*In this chapter, the term "executive" will be used to designate the government chief executive (mayor, city manager, governor, county executive, or supervisor) to whom police report.

sult, often feel that they must reflect public opinion to a greater extent than a manager. The disadvantage of the strong mayor–council form (i.e., with the mayor independently elected and bearing responsibility for the executive branch) is that there is no assurance that the mayor will have even minimal qualifications. However talented and skilled mayors without governing experience may have been in whatever careers they pursued prior to election, the task of leading a city generally is best mastered by someone who has been prepared for it by training and experience. Unless new mayors bring these attributes to the job, a considerable amount of their time is bound to be spent learning from their own mistakes. The advantage of the strong mayor–council system is that mayors hold the mandate of the electorate and have complete executive control during their incumbency. When the mayor is competent, the system is probably superior to a city manager form of government in which the manager is of equal competence.

The advantage of the city manager system is that managers may be better schooled than mayors in the technical aspects of their jobs. City managers are professionals who bring to their positions considerable training and a great deal of experience in making municipalities run. Further, because each city can set precise selection standards for appointed offices but not for elected offices, each city should be able to hire the particular individual who best fits its needs. The major disadvantage of the city manager concept is that managers are often forced to keep themselves in check to satisfy a majority of council members. On occasion, managers must also relay the policies of the majority of the council to city department heads as if these policies were their own ideas. Managers understand this before they take their jobs, and this system works beautifully until deep philosophical differences appear. These often lead to managers' voluntary or forced resignations. Regardless of the loss of technical expertise that may result from such resignations, they must be understood in terms of our representative democracy. Like the military and police chiefs, city managers are ultimately accountable to elected officials.

POLICE COMMISSIONS AND OTHER FORMS OF CONTROL

Police commissions of varying structure and responsibility are found in some parts of the United States. One of the versions of the police commission concept is the small group of part-time officials (usually an odd number) appointed by the city council or mayor. The police commission is often given responsibility for the promulgation of rules and regulations and for the administration of personnel rules, with duties similar to those of a civil service commission. In some cases the police commission is an appeal body only for disciplinary and personnel matters, and in other instances it has direct statutory control over the entire operations of the department.

On occasion, multiple-member commissions have been converted into single-member "commissions." In the nineteenth century, New York City's Board of Police Commissioners elected one of its own to serve, in effect, as the department's chief. Since then, the commission has evolved into a single mayorally appointed commissioner who serves as the executive head of the agency. Although New York City police commissioners have most often come into their positions from the ranks, they hold civilian positions. In other cases, the term "police commissioner" is simply used in place of the title "chief of police," or there may be a civilian "commissioner" in addition to the chief.

Multimember police commissions are hard to justify except, perhaps, as appeal or review boards. Although civil service or personnel regulating committees exist in many jurisdictions, they, too, are hard to defend. True, they introduce citizen participation into the process, but, most obviously, they also represent an additional and diffuse bureaucratic layer that makes it more difficult to assign accountability for decisions and actions. When they are appointed in a representative fashion, they speak for constituencies that often are in conflict. Strong-minded and politically astute chiefs regularly figure out how to exploit these conflicts in ways that have reduced their commissions to irrelevance. Since commissioners typically are not experienced in police matters and have little involvement in the direct delivery of police services, they often are at the mercy of their chiefs, hearing only what chiefs want them to hear (see, e.g., Christopher et al., 1992).

DIRECTORS OF PUBLIC SAFETY

Some public safety departments—which generally comprise police, fire, and emergency medical services—are old enough to predate the expansion of the city manager movement. The position of director of public safety in Pittsburgh, for example, is a charter office that was established in 1901. Thus, while many public safety director positions have recently been created as means of overcoming the inadequacies of incumbent chiefs of police by appointing someone to supervise them, this is not universally true. Where it is true—as where public safety directorships are created to compensate for inadequate chiefs of police and civil service systems that prevent such chiefs' removal—the device is understandable. But it is a poor substitute for more acceptable corrective action, such as the use of disciplinary or personnel remedies that already exist, or the failure to mobilize political strength—or courage—sufficient to separate chiefs from jobs they perform unsatisfactorily. Needless to say, when public safety departments are created for this purpose, they add a bureaucratic layer that would not be necessary if competent people were chosen to head agencies in the first instance.

This is not to say that public safety departments are valueless. The public safety concept may be very useful at the state or regional level of government. Often, state and regional authority is unclear and widely dispersed, with the result that governors or executives of small jurisdictions are burdened with a multiplicity of departments that must be supervised and coordinated in the absence of a consolidation or grouping of functions. In such cases there is ample justification for establishing a department of public safety that combines state police, the state fire marshal, beverage control, weights and measures, civil defense, motor-vehicle inspection, and related functions. Regionally, these departments may provide multiple services for adjoining small jurisdictions or a single regional park or transportation commission or authority. Even at the local level, public safety departments may serve as a valuable means of streamlining and consolidating into a single operation the support services (communications, etc.) used by several critical agencies.

POLICE AS A CRIMINAL JUSTICE AGENCY

What should be clear is that, in the broadest sense, confusion about control of the police in the United States is an inevitable result of the constitutional principle of decentralized power. Given their druthers, the wide range of American police jurisdictions simply have not all chosen precisely the same mechanisms to oversee their police. Still, many of us, especially scholars and politicians, have added to the confusion through the ways in which we have chosen to view the police.

Regardless of the formal arrangements for controlling them, the police typically are defined as a criminal justice agency. As we discussed in Chapter 2, it is unrealistic to think of police solely—or even mostly—in terms of criminal justice, but this particular police role and the governmental relations that go with it complicate questions about who oversees the police.

Take, at the extreme, an individual who is arrested by a state police officer after the arrestee's drunk driving has caused a fatal crash on an interstate highway. The officer, a representative of the executive branch of state government, may be required to book his or her prisoner at a municipal or county police station. From there, the officer will bring the prisoner to a local court and will work with a local prosecutor on the case. The officer also is likely to have to report to and work with a county or city coroner. If the prisoner has not made bail, he or she is likely to be lodged in a jail operated by an elected county sheriff. Should the offender be indicted on felony charges, the officer will find himself or herself assigned to assist a local prosecutor in a case heard before a state court. Should the individual be convicted, the officer may be interviewed by a state probation officer—a representative of the judicial branch—responsible for recommending a sentence to the judge.

In short, during what is probably the most exciting part of their work—catching criminals and aiding in their prosecution—police officers answer to many officials other than the executive branch leaders to whom their chiefs report. But thinking of the police primarily as a component of a neatly defined criminal justice system may cause us to lose sight of the fact that this "system" involves many conflicting, competing, and overlapping sources of influence and authority. Further, it obscures the role of police as mainstays of many other important systems, as evidenced by the successful merger of police departments and non–criminal justice agencies into public safety departments. The police are, for example, a major component of the machinery set in place to keep highways and roads safe and uncongested. Because many of their decisions about deploying officers have a great effect on the economy and even on real estate values, the police also are deeply entrenched in their jurisdictions' local economies. Their work with injured and sick people, the mentally and emotionally disturbed, the homeless, and victims of domestic abuse also make the police part of the health and social welfare systems. Only when we view the police as an executive agency charged with wide responsibilities and ultimately accountable to the heads of their governments' executive branches do we begin to envision them realistically.

POLITICAL INFLUENCES ON POLICING

Even when we understand where the police fit in the governmental big picture, theory is not always precisely implemented in practice. Despite the neat executive branch organizational charts in civics books, there exists considerable debate about how directly elected officials should be a part of police administration. Politicians have themselves contributed to this confusion. First, and predictably, their personalities and hence their interactions with others vary dramatically. Regardless of the form of government, some strong and charismatic executives appoint weak chiefs; some weak executives appoint strong and charismatic chiefs. Some chiefs have built their own power bases independent of the people who appointed them. Some councils are in their executives' pockets; others are not. Some mayors have won their offices on strong law and order platforms; others have run as reformers who pledged to eliminate police brutality or corruption. As should be obvious, the permutations are endless.

Second, and more directly at the root of the problem, some officials have led the police in ways that more closely resemble warlords' oversight of private armies than anything related to democratic policing. The history books are replete with accounts of manipulations of the police for the narrow interests of elected officials and their cronies (see Fogelson, 1977; Johnson, 1981; Walker, 1977). These experiences so turned off well-meaning police chiefs that in their view, even the words "politics" and "politicians" implied something sinister. In 1936, August Vollmer, who was O. W. Wilson's mentor and his era's most influential police figure, put to paper his thoughts about the "professional politician":

> He may be a grafter—he usually is, and the fact is common knowledge—but as a rule he is a colorful figure with a profound understanding of human nature. The crooked politician does not hesitate to brag that he places men on jobs where they are not really needed, and, in order that this giving of employment to the poor be widely spread, he tells it to every gossip in his ward. Such a statement would ruin his standing in a "silk stocking" ward; but his working-class supporters say, "He's a swell guy. He puts everybody to work."
> . . . the politician who "fixes" cases for his constituents with the police, prosecutor, or judge adds much to his popularity and prestige. He impresses his followers by his familiarity with important personages in government offices, especially when he calls them on the telephone in the presence of the man who is seeking favor, addresses them by their given names, and instructs them to drop the case against his friend. This type of politician nullifies the efforts of law enforcement officials, and makes efficiency in governmental agencies impossible; in the resultant disintegration, the gangster finds ample opportunity to operate. (Vollmer, 1972:70–71)

In their desire to avoid doing anything that smacked of improper political influence on the police, many elected officials went to the opposite extreme. In ill-advised efforts to show that they had nothing in common with the hacks described by Vollmer, these officials abandoned even their legitimate roles as overseers of the police. Former New York City Deputy Mayor Edward K. Hamilton has suggested that this movement of politicians away from police administration began around the end of Prohibition—which greatly influenced Vollmer's views and which had clearly been the most corrupting police experience in this century. From the early 1930s until the great social upheavals of the early 1960s, Hamilton wrote, the prevailing sentiment in the nation's city halls was that close association with the police could only get a mayor into trouble. Since the country was relatively quiet and crime-free during those years, police administration appeared no more challenging than running more technical, but less politically sensitive, municipal services (like fire and sanitation). As a result, mayors had nothing to gain by immersing themselves in police matters. Conversely, mayors who did become closely identified with the police had to worry that they might be accused of improper political manipulation or that they might be smeared by any police corruption scandals that might arise. Rather than run these hazards, politically astute mayors reasoned that it was better to distance themselves from the police.

Similarly, most city managers view the administration of the police department with more concern and apprehension than they feel toward other city departments. Part of the reason is that the majority of managers achieve their positions through a combination of academic training and a period of apprenticeship in lower-level administrative positions. They are thus shielded to some extent from the rough-and-tumble politics that many mayors have experienced in their careers. Moreover, most city managers have backgrounds in general public administration, fiscal management, or engineering but seldom in law enforcement. As a result, they tend to be more aloof from the affairs of the police department than many mayors, who often are elected because of prominence within a community or because of past experience in city councils or ward politics. Most of these areas are likely to place them in closer contact with police or with policy decisions affecting police.

Many city managers therefore believe in giving police department heads a wide latitude for action except in regard to policies that affect all city departments, such as those concerning promotional procedures, personnel management, budgeting, and other administrative matters. On the other hand, most city managers refrain from attempting to make policies in such traditional police matters as scheduling, assignments, beat layouts, departmental rules and regulations, operations, internal record keeping, and communications procedures.

NAVIGATING IN POLITICAL WATERS

Over the last 60 years, the idea of "good government" came to include a police department that had been immunized against dirty political influences. In many places, the result was a situation in which police departments were granted a great degree of independence from *any and all* political influences over their operations. Indeed, in some jurisdictions, police chief executives even were awarded civil service tenure, from which they were removable from office, in essence, only if they were caught in criminal activity.² Thus insulated, these chiefs joined the nine members of the U.S. Supreme Court in a select group of public officials who had no bosses. As a result, and even where police autonomy did not proceed to such an extreme, former Police Chief Allen H. Andrews notes, there has developed:

> . . . a widely and firmly held belief among city officials that the police are excessively independent of city hall. In my opinion, the belief is factually based: The police do not see themselves as part of city hall or city government. Most heads of other municipal departments would unhesitatingly agree that the police chief is given far more autonomy and independence than they are. Most police chiefs probably would concur privately, while urging that political restrictions and interferences are still excessive in too many localities. (1985:7)

Ironically, adoption of community- and problem-oriented policing models designed to bring police closer to their clientele is likely to exacerbate the perception that police have grown independent of central political authority. The decentralization inherent in these policing arrangements inevitably turns line police officers and their supervisors into advocates for the interests of the small communities they serve. If they are to be effective at playing this role—*and they must be effective if community- and problem-oriented policing is to succeed*—they must vigorously champion their constituencies' demands for scarce resources, and in so doing, they may occasionally appear to be short-circuiting traditional organizational and political arrangements.

Improper and Proper Political Influences on Police Policy and Operations

In large measure, the difficulty of defining the appropriate place of the police vis-à-vis elected officials is attributable to the difficulty of distinguishing between *improper* and *proper* political influences on police policy and operations. In his essay on the subject, for example, Allen H. Andrews included "pressures for differential enforcement policies in different neighborhoods in order to adapt to varying customs and traditions" among the political influences he regarded as improper (Andrews, 1985:6). Yet police scholar and O. W. Wilson protégé Herman Goldstein has written of "the desirability of establishing new channels by which residents of a small area can—when there is no compelling reason to apply a policy uniformly through a city—have a voice in determining the services affecting their neighborhood" (Goldstein, 1977:148). The problem illustrated by these two competing views, obviously, involves deciding *which* reasons to apply policies uniformly are "compelling" and which are not. Further, since the philosophy embodied in Goldstein's statement is at the core of the burgeoning movement to community-oriented policing, the dilemma of whether and how to tailor policies to individual neighborhoods is not likely to be resolved anytime soon. Instead, it is likely to become a larger and larger component of the work of police at virtually every organizational level and to add to the difficulty of the administrator's job.

Similarly, Andrews objects to political interference in duty assignments and promotions (1985:6), while Patrick V. Murphy concludes from his successes as police chief in Syracuse; Washington, D.C.; Detroit; and New York that the issue is not as clear-cut as Andrews suggests:

> The chief has to realize that, as a practical matter, the mayor sees appointments to desirable city jobs as opportunities to pay some rewards—rewards that may help him build a political coalition so that both he and the chief can survive in office. By the same token, the mayor must recognize the importance of allowing the chief to preserve ultimate control over personnel matters: It gives the chief the ability to motivate his people to work for him because they know he can reward them. (Murphy, 1985:34)

Murphy is, of course, correct, but so is Andrews. The nature of American politics is that those who share candidates' philosophies and who work hard during elections to see that candidates get a chance to implement their views expect a piece of the action. Sometimes, this may dictate that they are themselves put into policy-making positions or that they seek highly placed appointments for qualified people who share their views. On other occasions, as Murphy acknowledges, winning candidates' political allies may seek to secure deputy chiefs' uniforms for their ignorant brothers-in-law (Murphy, 1985:34).

Lawyers are happiest when courts' decisions give them a "bright line" that distinguishes between appropriate and inappropriate behavior. No such bright line differentiates improper political influences on police from those that are acceptable and in accord with democratic principles. What history has made clear, however, is that it is unwise for executives to back off from all involvement in police matters. The breadth of most states' laws and the limited resources of the police dictate that police exercise some selectivity in their enforcement policies. Unless police decisions in this regard are informed by the wishes and philosophies of people elected to office by their constituents, decisions about whether and where and how stringently laws will be enforced may be the exclusive results of the whims of individual chiefs.

The absence of a bright line to clearly distinguish legitimate political influences on police discretion from pernicious political manipulation should not cause police officials to throw up their hands. There are, after all, few spheres of government activity for which an absolutely clear road map precisely points out the one correct path. Instead, as in their private lives, public officials typically apply some general criteria to all the important professional decisions laid before them. The first yardstick that should be used by police executives who have been asked by elected officials or other political operatives to resolve policy or operational issues in certain ways—or to carry out decisions already made by others—is a relatively simple question: *Who benefits and who loses by the course of action I am now urged to take?*

If the answer to this question is that the public interest is served and that nobody loses by the decision urged, the appropriate course of action is clear: do it. Conversely, if the decision urged will serve narrow partisan interests at the expense of the public interest, the imperative to avoid doing it is equally clear. As Patrick Murphy's comments suggest, however, few political decisions are so simple. Instead, they most often involve such combinations of benefits and losses as the following:

There may be minor losses to the general public or to police operations, but some partisan interest will be served. A high ranking vacancy in the department has been created by the retirement of a senior official, for example. The mayor has asked the chief to appoint to this position Jones, an officer who has been recommended by one of the mayor's staunchest political supporters. Jones has never performed the particular work involved in this new position, but the chief is confident that Jones, a fast learner, could do the job well. At the same time, one of the other candidates—Smith—has long worked directly for the retired official, and has historically been considered the logical and most knowledgeable successor to this new job. Indeed, the chief himself has always anticipated that he would appoint Smith to the position if it became vacant. Consequently, the chief also knows that many people in and out of the police department—most especially, the competing candidates—will recognize that a political endorsement was the edge that won Jones the job. The chief fears also that the appointment of Jones would cause Smith to retire from the department, which would mean that Jones would have to learn the *ins and outs* of the new position without the assistance of an experienced chief assistant. The chief voices these concerns to the mayor, who says, "I don't want to tell you what to do, but I'd really appreciate it if you could make this happen."

There will be both benefits and losses to the general public and/or to police operations, and some partisan interest will be served. For example, with great support from downtown interests, a candidate for mayor ran on a platform that included a promise to improve the city's tax base and to restore its declining downtown area. Now that she has won, the mayor meets with the police chief and tells him that she wants to retain his services. She then asks the chief to develop a plan for redeploying officers from poor and crime-ridden inner-city areas to the city's downtown shopping and tourist district. Doing this, the mayor asserts, will enhance the city's revenues and viability by assuring tourists and shoppers that downtown is a safe and pleasant place to shop and, consequently, by encouraging merchants to stay in town. The chief knows that the officers the mayor seeks to move from the city's most volatile neighborhoods are badly needed where they are, and that the transfers proposed by the mayor will have negative effects there. The mayor agrees, but asks the chief to consider whether failing to clean up downtown by establishing a great police presence there will eventually cause the whole city to slide into the same condition as the inner city.

Political pressures, of course, do not always originate in the executive branch. Individual council members may wish to influence the department or to obtain favors. This practice presumably is forbidden in some states, such as California, which limits the authority of individual council members by prohibiting them from doing anything except making collective decisions with the rest of their council colleagues. In other cases, a similar kind of control is established by city charter or as a result of the council's own less formal deliberations. In any event, and regardless of whether they have legitimate or less admirable purposes, the chief of police must sometimes decide how to deal with and when to discourage direct contacts by individual council members. Certainly, the chief should be open to suggestions from the people's elected legislators. At the same time, the chief should be alert to attempts to short-circuit the executive and, if only in the interests of his or her own job security, to the risk of giving rise to the perception that he or she is taking part in such attempts.

This issue is a delicate one, and the manner in which it is handled often determines whether a chief of police remains in his or her position. Some jurisdictions have legislated *bright lines* to govern contacts between council members and employees of the executive branch. The Alexandria, Virginia, ordinance shown in Box 3-2 is a good example of this mechanism. It essentially prohibits council members from muscling in on administrative prerogatives and, except for inquiry, requires council members to deal with the executive branch through the city manager.

Participation in Partisan Politics

An additional bright line can be stated: *Professional administrators owe it to their departments to refrain from partisan political campaigning in any form.* "Such activity," noted the Christopher Commission in its report on the Los Angeles Police Department, "politicizes the Chief, and ultimately the Department" (Christopher et al., 1992:220). A police chief who supports a candidate for local office in any overt way acts wrongly and, of course, runs the risk of being turned out of office if the candidate loses.

The incidence of purely political turnover of the chief's job seems to be receding. Some areas of the country have nonpartisan local government, and several states, such as California, operate under "little Hatch Acts," which effectively discourage partisan political campaigning.

Although police administrators are well advised to stay away from politi-cal campaigning, they should not go so far as to avoid speaking out to the pub-lic and to politicians about the issues themselves. Because sentiment on impor-tant public policy issues is so frequently divided along party lines, however, police chiefs who go into such forums must anticipate that those who hold op-posing views will characterize their views as matters of political expediency rather than as reasoned professional analyses. Chiefs of police and police labor unions, for example, have sometimes aroused the enmity of a majority of the city council because they openly supported the position of a minority of the council with views closer to their own. This problem can be ameliorated to some extent if police chiefs take great pains to speak about issues and to avoid giving any indication that the personalities involved have affected their judg-ments. Indeed, perhaps the worst thing that any chief can do in such a situa-tion is to give any hint in his or her statements that those who support the other side are unknowledgeable or less than well-intentioned. To speak out so strongly that one appears to be suggesting the defeat of opposing council members in the next election, for example, may spell the beginning of the end of a career in police leadership.

Resignation: The Ultimate Bargaining Chip

Although only some political imperatives are what Patrick Murphy has called "'deal breakers'—the minimal conditions without which [chiefs] simply [would] not accept the job" in the first place (1985:33), it should be clear that even routine politics forces hard choices on police administrators. No ready formula can resolve either the examples we cited above or the myriad other il-lustrations one could easily compile. Nor, except when apparent criminal con-duct is involved, can anybody precisely describe courses of action for chiefs who find themselves in violent disagreement with the recommendations urged upon them. When these choices do cross the line—as when appointments of unqualified people are forced on the chief or when the chief's authority to dis-cipline officers is compromised—the historic remedy has been for the chief to resign in protest.

The threat of this ultimate form of dissent is no doubt a powerful bargain-ing chip, especially when a chief with high status in the community or on the national or international police scene is concerned. It would certainly embar-rass and injure politically any executive who lost a chief with a reputation like that of Patrick Murphy, Lee Brown, or Joseph McNamara, for example, over what the chief saw as improper political interference. At the same time, as Her-man Goldstein has pointed out:

> A police chief, unlike others in equivalent positions of responsibility, is not free to quit his job with confidence that he can obtain employment in a community that is more in accord with his concepts and operating policies. A decision to resign means, for him, returning to a subordinate position in the same agency, retiring, or seeking employment outside the police field and he may also suffer a substantial financial loss. Boxed in this manner, many chiefs surrender to the pressures brought to bear on them. (1977:154)

Thus, a police chief's resignation is to negotiation with local officials as the hydrogen bomb is to international relations: it makes the point that one is upset enough to engage in the most drastic action, but it causes severe damage on both sides and also puts an end to further constructive dialogue. Further, it may do little to resolve the issue that led to the confrontation in the first place. In both nation-to-nation and police-to-politician relationships, the best way to deal with collisions of ethics, interests, pocketbooks, and egos is to avoid them.

PREVENTING POLITICAL BLOODSHED

Before candidates for chiefs' jobs accept them, they should have candid discussions with their executives about the degree of autonomy each expects the chief to enjoy and the extent to which directives—or *requests*—from political officials will impinge on it. It is far more difficult to violate ground rules that have been laid out in advance than to add new conditions to general understandings that had only been vaguely defined. Given the empowerment of previously remote interests that has accompanied community policing models, a clear understanding of where everybody stands is now more important than ever.

Setting the Ground Rules

One of the most important of such ground rules should govern the manner in which policy disagreements between executives and chiefs are to be handled. All such disputes should be matters of written public record. When executives turn down their chiefs' recommendations, they should be willing to document in writing their reasons for doing so. Conversely, when chiefs disagree with executives—especially in far-reaching matters such as that illustrated in our redeployment example—they should be willing to say so and to publicly articulate the reasons for their judgments. Such documentation serves two purposes. First, it establishes a system of accountability. It clearly leaves a record of who is responsible for what and, it is hoped, will also keep out of the relationship between police and the rest of government many suggestions for which people do not wish to be held accountable. Meeting a request to "give me a memo on that so that I can see your logic" is a real challenge when suggestions are inappropriate or simply lacking in logic. As the old saw has it, sunlight is the best disinfectant.

The second, and related, purpose of written documentation is that it allows writers the opportunity to carefully review and articulate their own ideas before they put them into the public forum. What may sound viable at a luncheon with a convincing advocate may not stand up to thorough and objective examination. The formulation of a written position that considers both sides of an issue, as well as the probable consequences of specific courses of action, is the best way to start such a process.

When a disagreement between chiefs and managers involves major policy (and not superficialities, in which case city administrators should not have been concerned anyway), executives have the right to prevail. Still, there should be a method for fully hearing both sides of issues about which chiefs are particularly adamant.

The importance of a mechanism for airing and resolving differences between police chiefs and executives on the merits, rather than solely on executives' gut feelings and rank, cannot be overemphasized. When the operation of a police department is proceeding smoothly, it is easy for a city administration to lapse into the widespread but oversimplified belief that the chief is to "run the department" as long as he or she performs in a satisfactory way and that the only alternative is to fire the chief when he or she is perceived to have done less than a good job. As indicated earlier, there are times when positions or actions by department heads must be specifically overruled by executives. Despite the processes that may have been set up to resolve differences between the executive and agency heads, in the end, executives should be expected to use their own best judgment to resolve serious differences between their own thinking and that of the department heads.

Such resolutions, of course, relieve department heads of responsibility for the consequences or the immediate effects of the actions. At the same time, executives must realize that unless they have appointed hacks, the people who run their agencies are far more technically competent and experienced in their disciplines than are they. Executives, therefore, should allow department heads to have broad authority over their respective domains. Executives should also pay very close heed to the recommendations of department heads—especially when their recommendations appear contrary to the executives' own views and, hence, to their own personal and career interests.

A practical means for resolving specific disagreements between a chief and an executive is an advance agreement between the two to present the chief's differing point of view to the city council or a council subcommittee (perhaps in executive session) as a form of appeal or as a vehicle for further discussion. The executive who is party to this should be expected, of course, to present his or her opposing views and, ultimately, to make the decision after the perspectives and recommendations of the council have been made plain to both disputants. This kind of arrangement should be discussed well before the development of problems themselves, preferably during the hiring interview at the time the chief of police is selected.

Personnel Matters

Once the rules of engagement for policy disagreements have been resolved, there must be discussion and agreement about which policy and operational areas are off-limits to executives. In some cases, both chiefs and executives are, in essence, locked out of important policy turfs. Where there exist strong civil service commissions or very stringent civil service regulations, chiefs and executives frequently have little or no authority over personnel selection or, in many instances, promotions. Further, civil service commissions frequently have appellate authority over discipline and dismissals as well. We know of many cases in which the executive and city council have given their blessings to the police chief's decision to terminate an officer, only to be overruled by the civil service commission. It is hard to do much about these limits—especially when they involve *state* civil service directives that *cities* retain police officers they would rather fire.

Regardless of whether such indefensible arrangements exist, and no matter who is involved in investigating and reviewing allegations of police misconduct, police chiefs should have the exclusive power to decide whether and how to discipline officers. This authority may be appealed to the courts by officers who claim that they have been unjustly treated, and in some jurisdictions, civil service commissions or similar bodies have the power of review. Whether through courts or such administrative proceedings, therefore, chiefs must be prepared occasionally to be overturned upon appeal. At the same time, they should insist that the authority of their jurisdictions' civilian complaint review boards or police commissions be limited to making findings of fact and recommendations as to whether officers' conduct violated departmental policies or rules. Neither elected officials nor such boards should be permitted to prescribe specific penalties for violations of departmental regulations. Choosing and exacting penalties or other corrective actions in disciplinary cases is an administrative matter that should be handled by the chief.

There are several reasons for this requirement. One is partly symbolic: chiefs sit atop their police departments' organizational charts, and if they are to command respect as more than mere figureheads, they must be equipped with sticks as well as carrots. More important, as the operating managers of their organizations, chiefs are best positioned to determine precisely what corrective action is appropriate in specific cases. While *ombudsmen*,[3] or civilian complaint investigators, may make recommendations as to whether officers violated the rules (or whether the rules themselves may have been inadequate), chiefs are best qualified by experience and position to identify and implement the best correctives. Especially if they have risen through the ranks within their agencies, chiefs have good institutional memories of how severe particular problems are and should be able to diagnose with some accuracy whether improper police behavior may be corrected by retraining for the officer involved, more widespread review and revision of training and policy, punishment, counseling, or some combination of all four. Like juries, those charged with investigating police conduct may determine what happened and whether it was wrong; but like judges, police chiefs should insist on reserving the exclusive authority to determine what to do when others have found wrongdoing.[4]

Personnel Deployment

Still, there are important areas in which agreements between chiefs and executives should be reached. Andrews and others have argued that decisions related to personnel deployment should be the exclusive province of the chief, and to a great extent, this is true. But it is very difficult to see how such authority can be absolute. Where executives have won election on promises to change police priorities, as in our example, or, increasingly, to divert to other activities officers assigned to enforcement of laws involving homosexual conduct, chiefs must be prepared for considerable general input along these lines. The parameters of this relationship should be negotiated in advance. At a minimum, police chiefs should expect that they will be authorized to develop and implement redeployment plans that respond to politicians' promises of broad philosophical shifts (e.g., to community policing, to more foot patrol, to more street-level narcotics enforcement, or to reduced emphasis on undercover operations in gay bars).

Labor Negotiations

Both prospective and incumbent police chiefs should take pains to see that their personnel deployment and disciplinary prerogatives are not given away during collective bargaining with police employee groups. Police chiefs histor-ically have not had much success in becoming a part of the formal manage-ment team in collective bargaining (see, e.g., Juris and Feuille, 1974). This has left chiefs in the awkward position of running organizations in which working conditions, disciplinary processes, and other important matters have been ne-gotiated by *management representatives* who know little about policing and who bear little responsibility for seeing that it is done well.

The consequences of such illogical arrangements often have limited police chiefs' ability to use their personnel well. In some jurisdictions, negotiators have agreed to provisions on officers' working hours that have made it ex-tremely expensive—or even impossible—for police chiefs to redeploy person-nel in response to crises or the needs of local communities. Again, as policing moves more and more into a community orientation, the disadvantages of such provisions are bound to become more evident and to serve as a greater in-centive for keeping them out of labor contracts.[5] In other cases, negotiated pro-cedures for investigating and adjudicating alleged police misconduct make re-sponsible administration extremely difficult.

In one big city, for example, allegations that have been made to the city's independent civilian complaint review board cannot be investigated or dealt with by the police department until the review board has completed its work. Since the review board is severely underfunded and understaffed (a conse-quence of the same smart union's lobbying), investigations are placed in a queue three or four years long. During that time, the chief can take no action to investigate or to make sure that officers involved in obvious and repetitive wrongdoing are placed where they cannot hurt anybody. This is so because the city's labor negotiators agreed to the union's positions that concurrent investi-gations are a hardship that would border on double jeopardy. Similarly, labor contract provisions apparently are rooted in the belief that suspending or transferring to nonstreet assignments officers accused—with great apparent justification—of outrageous misconduct pending the outcome of civilian re-view board investigations would indicate an unreasonable presumption that they were guilty before the review board has finished its work.

Since it literally takes years for the board to close cases, one consequence of all this is a terrible irony. As the chief knows, making a complaint to the board dooms it to a long period in the purgatory of the board's crammed in-boxes. At the same time, when the chief encourages citizens to bring com-plaints of misconduct to his or her internal investigators rather than to the re-view board, critics claim that the chief seeks only to perpetuate an alleged former pattern of in-house whitewashes of wrongful police conduct. As a re-sult, the entire process of investigating and disposing of cases of excessive force has been nullified through collective bargaining, and several officers with long and well-documented histories of brutality and abuse continue to patrol the city's streets.

More commonly, negotiators give away police departments' authority to retain records of citizens' complaints against officers unless the conduct alleged has been substantiated by investigation. This may sound like a reasonable policy, but it is not. In most police departments, a small number of officers somehow manage to become the subjects of a great number of complaints. In its report on the Los Angeles Police Department, for example, the Christopher Commission related that more than 1,800 officers were subjects of allegations of excessive force or improper tactics during the period 1986–1990; but 44 of these officers were subjects of 6 or more complaints (Christopher et al., 1992:36). During 1988 and 1989, 756 civilian complaints were lodged against Kansas City's more than 1,100 officers—but 29 officers accounted for nearly half of these (Kansas City Police Department, 1991). Since there is no objective physical evidence to substantiate the great majority of citizens' allegations against police, most of the complaints against such officers cannot be resolved. Nobody would argue that police officers should be disciplined for allegations that cannot be proved, but there is a legitimate use for this information. Without authority to use prior records to determine whether misconduct allegations are parts of apparent patterns of behavior, police administrators must treat each complaint against an officer as an isolated incident. This is a policy that can end in perpetuation of grossly excessive police use of force. It should be avoided, and even if they are barred from direct participation in labor negotiations, police chief administrators should make it plain to their superiors and to management's representatives at the bargaining table that their authority to deploy and to discipline cannot be bargained away.

DEVELOPING GOOD RELATIONSHIPS

Once the big issues have been resolved, police chiefs must deal routinely with their executives. Some of the problems that develop in these relationships can be attributed to faulty personal communication. This topic is explored in greater detail in Chapters 4 and 5, but several principles should be discussed here.

Communications

The police chief should report regularly to the executive through a combination of oral and written communications. When conversations result in policy changes, they should be reduced to writing. Written verifications of oral commitments are, unfortunately, a necessary evil in any well-run organization. However, the tone and content of memos from the chief should not give the supervisor the impression that the latter's memory is faulty or that the chief is "building a case" against the executive or manager.

It is sometimes difficult for chiefs promoted from within their departments to establish a friendly rapport with their executives. Where they once were executives' distant associates—if they enjoyed any relationships with their new bosses at all—new chiefs who have worked their way through the ranks suddenly find that they are important members of the executive cabinet. This situation obviously runs smoothest when day-to-day interaction is relaxed and informal, but the distances that previously existed are not always easy to bridge. To help do so, it may be useful for the new chief to make his or her first few official contacts with the executive in the presence of other, more experienced department heads. Informal staff luncheons and meetings often are useful for this purpose.

Police administrators should use a positive approach in their communications with their executives; they should emphasize successful activities rather than negative ones. However, when a deficiency or problem must be discussed, the chief should offer a solution (or perhaps several alternatives) along with the problem.

Bad news should not be delayed until it gets out of hand. For example, when the police administrator fails to notify the executive of a festering grievance (perhaps stemming from a questionable policy established by the executive) until a committee from the police association is en route to the city council, the manager is placed in a vulnerable position that may not be deserved.

Some difficulties between the executive and the chief may arise because the problems or needs of the department are not communicated by the executive beyond his or her own level to the city council or the legislative body. When this happens, and then when there is a subsequent feeling on the part of the city council that the facts should have been transmitted to the council by the chief, it is tempting for the police administrator to think about short-circuiting the usual line of communication through the executive. This can be a special problem during the budgeting process. The budget prepared by the chief of police must be reviewed by the executive, who then makes his or her own recommendations in the light of the demands and needs of other city departments and the state of revenues. The executive may or may not convey to the council the police chief's recommendations as to the amount of money to be spent for various programs in the budget. In some cases, the struggle for control over the budgeting of programs is at the heart of control over the entire fiscal apparatus of the municipality.

When Not to Communicate

In the city manager form of government, it is important for the police administrator to remember that the manager does not expect the chief always to confide totally in him or her. The chief should understand that what is said to the manager may have to be reported to the city council. It is unfair to disclose a confidence to the city manager and then expect him or her to refrain from discussing it with the city council.

There is no easy formula to help determine what kind of exceptional news should be reported to the executive. Reporting expectations are frequently related to the size of the jurisdiction: big news in a small town may be small news—or no news at all—in a big town. Generally, a police administrative matter or internal problem should be discussed immediately with the executive if it is likely to draw press or public attention or to be embarrassing to the administration. Operational situations, such as a single crime or a series of crimes or accidents, should have a high threshold. In most communities, headline news items, as well as operational situations that have captured the attention of a substantial number of citizens, ought to be communicated above the departmental level.

Dealing with Supportive Citizens

Long before the advent of community-oriented policing, police chiefs and key members of their departments were visibly supported by well-meaning citizens. This pattern, which is likely to increase with the move to community-oriented policing, is commendable but not without pitfalls. During budget hearings, for example, certain council members may oppose suggestions for expansion of the budget for what the chief believes to be essential police purposes. Citizens who support the department head's point of view can then endanger the chief's standing with these same council members by being over-aggressive, shifting the emphasis from the issue itself to one of personal or partisan conflict. In such cases, chiefs are well advised to attempt to coordinate their supporters and to educate them about politics as the art of compromise and negotiation, rather than as a form of angry confrontation. Where this is not possible, chiefs should take pains to soothe damaged egos or, in extreme cases, to subtly distance themselves from the most volatile and provocative of police supporters.

There may also be attempts by misguided members of the department to influence members of the city council on an individual basis. The temptation to engage in this practice is likely to expand with the adoption of community- and problem-oriented policing, but this practice should be discouraged and, if necessary, should be dealt with by disciplinary action. In one extreme instance of this kind, a supervisor in a police department asked his priest to influence a recalcitrant councilman during the next confessional dialogue between the priest and the councilman. Fortunately, the priest had better sense than the supervisor. It may be acceptable for police officers to help mobilize citizens so that they may more effectively apply political pressure at the appropriate spots, but individual officers should not do so themselves.

Avoiding Unnecessary Issues

The great number of influences brought to bear on the police may place the chief at some time or other in opposition to influential persons in the community. In consequence, some hostility may be created that can result in a temptation to expand an issue or to meet it head on, merely as a show of force. Such temptation should be resisted. Chiefs should avoid issues when the main thing to be gained is a moral victory; they have little else to gain and much to lose by tackling such issues. If they lose, they may find themselves out of office; if they win, they have gained nothing beyond the development of hostility that may never be dissipated.

The Trap of Inflexibility

Police resistance against "politics" is sometimes so strong that even when political figures in the legislative body have engaged in their rightful duties, police are unable to view such action favorably. The police must not build up such a "sales resistance" to outside influence that it cuts them off from worthwhile proposals. Constant guarding against pressures and frequent denial of requests tend to establish a behavior pattern that prompts the police to say "no" when they might better say "yes." They must guard themselves against putting on such a thick, defensive armor that they cannot distinguish between influence and wise suggestions and advice.

The Power Structure

Communities differ in the composition of the so-called power structure. The term is meaningless when it refers to the sum total of the business community, the heads of all civic organizations, the press, and the elected and appointed officials of the community. On occasion, however, the prime source of power can be much more specifically identified with a group, such as a single civic organization, citizens who share a special interest such as membership in a club, and so on. For example, the power structure in some rural communities is found in the volunteer fire department. In some big cities we know, members of the clergy have enormous influence on public opinion and, accordingly, on the politicians who hold office through the electoral process.

When the power structure in a community is concentrated in an identifiable organization that the police executive may conscientiously join (such as the Rotary club, the Kiwanis Club, the Lions, or—even though he or she may lose face temporarily in some quarters—the volunteer fire department), he or she should make an effort to participate actively in the organization. A few veteran police chiefs have stated facetiously (but not without some truth) that public opinion in the community is controlled by bartenders and hairdressers. Regardless of who exercises the power of opinion, chiefs of police should make certain that they are aware of who the *movers and shakers* are and of what they think and why.

Where appropriate, the police should also attempt to build bridges to the followings of opinion molders, especially when they are on one side of contentious public debates. Visits to—and, perhaps, opportunities to speak at—services conducted by influential ministers, priests, or rabbis, for example, should be a part of police chiefs' schedules. Gatherings of gay and lesbian groups, who are often locked in adversarial relationships with organized religion, also offer an opportunity for chiefs to find out what they are thinking and how the police may best serve their interests.

The City Hall Regulars

The police administrator may meet or come into contact with city hall habitués who, because of personal idiosyncrasies or because they represent unethical interests, have a particularly troublesome influence over policy makers. In some cases government officials can be misled into thinking that the city hall habitués and/or lobbyists truly do represent the majority of citizens. The department and the community can suffer from the consequences. For example, some of the habitual city hall visitors may have a more-than-average tolerance for gambling and the "open city." Their repeated suggestions can cause the police to reduce enforcement pressure or the number of personnel assigned to vice activity. Similarly, city hall lobbyists can influence council members to reduce expenditures to the point of endangering the safety of the community. The city policy makers, and particularly the police administrator, must be careful to distinguish between what the community as a whole should have and what representatives of special interests would have.

The Power of the Press

Many chiefs and many police personnel fear the media. Typically, they resist the efforts of reporters who seek to cover the police as an agency of government rather than merely as a group of people whose swashbuckling efforts occasionally merit spectacular headlines. This is a mistake. Limiting journalists' opportunities to doing no more than what former Los Angeles police reporter David Johnston has called "bang-bang" reporting (Johnston, 1983) may increase the prestige and mystique of the police in some quarters. Over the long haul, however, such a policy has great costs.

Police work, as veteran officers know, only rarely involves the kinds of stories that earn tabloid headlines or prominent spots on the late-night television news. But when the only information the public receives about their police concerns this bloody shoot-out, that gory car chase, or drug raids managed—if not staged—for the cameras, the public view of the police becomes unrealistic. When this view is mixed with the police images created by entertainment media, the result is a portrayal that gives citizens unrealistic expectations of the police. Members of the public exposed only to television cops and headlines about police exploits cannot help but be disappointed when they come into contact with real officers and the limits on their abilities to perform superhuman tasks and to root out crime. On this score, chiefs should not forget that, at the time they enter police departments, new officers' prior exposure to policing consists largely of the same hyped-up images that are held by the rest of the public. Consequently, new officers also are likely to hold unrealistic expectations of what their work will involve and to be disappointed by what they find.

To avoid this, police chiefs should cultivate relationships with the media that go beyond the occasional press conference or report on sensational events. Off-the-record discussions of police problems and proposed plans to deal with them help to ensure journalists' understanding and approval. In addition, such advance information helps to gain journalists' assistance in informing the public and winning public support, in meeting opposition to the plans, and in avoiding unanticipated press criticisms that sometimes spring from ignorance of the purpose and nature of police policies and operations. Although police chiefs have occasionally been burned by police reporters after confiding in them, such violations are quite rare. This is true, on the most pragmatic level,

Police administrators should encourage personnel to be open and skilled in dealing with the media. Here, a field commander briefs a reporter on his plans for keeping the peace at a demonstration.
Patsy Davidson/Image Works.

because reporters are cautious about alienating valuable sources in this way. Police reporters who betray the police chiefs they have been assigned to cover cut off their tap of information and, hence, their own livelihoods. Further, it is rarer still that such violations have any negative effects on either policing or the public interest generally. Instead, all they generally do is to educate public officials as to which journalists cannot be trusted to keep confidences.

In small and medium-sized jurisdictions, especially, community newspapers often have a strong influence in determining whether chiefs are retained or dismissed. There are instances in which local newspapers have become hostile to police chiefs or departments because the police have criticized and rebuked the press for inaccurate reporting of crime news. The police administrator should never allow such situations to escalate to the point of hard feelings and should personally make frequent contacts with the publisher or editor to discuss sensitive or political issues relating to the department.

On a more routine basis, the police interaction with the media, particularly in response to their questions about police policies and operations, should be as open as possible.

Openness

Openness is a policy that should extend to relations with the public as well as to contacts with the media. Police departments that keep reporters informed and occupied with productive story opportunities reduce the chances that a press corps with too little to do will spend its time digging for dirt and turning it into embarrassing negative stories. When reporters are led by administrators' cold shoulders to believe that police departments—or any other official agencies—are closed, their writings will reflect this view and will create distrust among the public. *Open* police departments are trusted by reporters and, hence, also are likely to be trusted by the media's readers, listeners, and viewers.

In the same way, police agencies that attempt to remain open to the citizenry tend to have fewer problems in coping with demands for greater citizen participation, while departments with a more traditional approach may frequently be targets for demands of this sort. In addition, open police departments build a reservoir of goodwill that may be necessary to see them through crises of public confidence.

Closed departments can often be identified by the following characteristics:

1. Holding to a traditional "institutional-style" philosophy that stresses equal and impartial law enforcement. The honest, incorruptible, institutional-style department may even resist attempts by the executive and members of the city council to influence basic police policies, maintaining that such efforts are "political" and are thus to be resisted.
2. Having a press policy that basically is one of noncooperation.
3. Striking a defensive attitude and failing to give deserved punishment to police officers in cases when citizens' complaints against them are sustained.

The closed institutional-style department is not without its benefits. Some reasonably effective police organizations have developed under these conditions, achieving high morale and carrying out good work as far as the members of the department are concerned, even though much of the community is dissatisfied. But when the lid blows off the community's dissatisfaction, the results are likely to be bloody.

Rather than operate in the closed fashion described by the characteristics above, police administrators should move toward comprehensive citizen-participation programs. Without compromising the authority of chiefs, these programs should allow citizens the opportunity for meaningful input into police policy and for substantial interaction with police in the design of plans to address community problems. The community-oriented policing models described later in this volume offer more concrete suggestions in this regard.

SUMMARY

Police administration would be a simple task if police agencies existed in a vacuum. They do not, and to pretend otherwise is a grave mistake. Police departments, as James Q. Wilson found in his classic study of police behavior (Wilson, 1968), are direct reflections of the social and political environments in which they function. If police are to serve these environments most appropriately, they must keep a finger on their pulses and must respond to their elected officials and to the people who pay their salaries. Conversely, if police are to help improve the quality of life in their communities now and in the future, they must not be hesitant to speak out on public policy issues.

QUESTIONS FOR DISCUSSION

1. Now that you have read Chapter 3, consider and discuss again the advantages and disadvantages of each of the following arrangements for accountability of police chief executives:
   a. Civil service tenure, with removal only "for cause"
   b. Serving at the pleasure of the mayor or some other government chief executive
   c. Direct election of police chiefs, as in the manner of choosing county sheriffs
   d. Fixed, renewable, contractual terms that overlap mayors' terms of office
   Have your views changed at all?
2. What is the basis of the principle of *home rule* and the consequent decentralization of U.S. policing? Would we be better off if police were more centralized at the federal or state level? Why or why not?
3. Many argue that community-oriented policing, like older community control models, is doomed to fail because there is no real *community* in the places that most need it. Is this argument valid? If so, what can be done to address this problem? What role can police play in doing so?
4. Define and put in writing some standards or principles that help to distinguish between proper and improper influences on policing.
5. Large police departments seem split on whether to appoint their press officers from the ranks or seek professional journalists for this job. Discuss the advantages and disadvantages of each of these arrangements.

NOTES

1. Jerome Skolnick (1975:290) asked of the proposal to implement community control policing in Berkeley, for example, "Does a city the size of Berkeley [113,165 people in 15.75 square miles] really require five police boards consisting of seventy-five people, and will these ever be able to agree on anything?"
2. After serving for a year as Los Angeles's police chief (1923–1924), August Vollmer concluded that the city was so thoroughly corrupt that the police department could aspire to integrity only if its chief were granted civil service tenure. In 1936, the Los Angeles City Council wrote Vollmer's Prohibition-era recommendation into law. This law was not honored until 1950, when Los Angeles's famous reform chief, William H. Parker, took office. From that point until a 1992 referendum, Los Angeles police chiefs enjoyed civil service protection in their jobs. The other major U.S. city that long granted its police chief civil service tenure was Milwaukee; see Skolnick and Fyfe (1993).
3. The concept of the ombudsman originated in Scandinavia and has spread with considerable success to other parts of the world. Most generally, the ombudsman provides regular monitoring of *all* services provided by a government, rather than just police, and investigates and monitors complaints against government officials. See, e.g., Gellhorn (1967).
4. It is not worth more than a note to point out that requests that chiefs overlook or treat leniently rules violations by specific officers with political connections should be ignored because they fail the acid test we discussed earlier: *Who benefits and who loses by the course of action I am now urged to take?*

5. Through the lobbying of strong local police labor groups, such provisions have also worked their way into state law. A New York law, for example, provided that most local police departments can assign officers only to one of three platoons (day, evening, or night). These departments were effectively prohibited from assigning patrol officers to work alternate hours (say, 8 P.M. to 4 A.M.) on the basis of analyses of crime and other police hazards. New York Unconsolidated Laws, title 3, chap. 11, para. 971 (1910).

SOURCES

ALTSHULER, ALAN W. *Community Control: The Black Demand for Participation in Large American Cities* (New York: Pegasus, 1970).

ANDREWS, ALLEN H. "Structuring the Political Independence of the Police Chief," pp. 5–19 in William A. Geller (ed.), *Police Leadership in America: Crisis and Opportunity* (New York: Praeger, 1985).

CHRISTOPHER, WARREN, et al. *Report of the Independent Commission on the Los Angeles Police Department* (July 1992).

FLANAGAN, TIMOTHY J., and KATHERINE M. JAMIESON (eds.). *Sourcebook of Criminal Justice Statistics—1987* (Washington, D.C.: U.S. Government Printing Office, 1988).

FOGELSON, ROBERT M. *Big-City Police* (Cambridge, Mass.: Harvard University Press, 1977).

GELLHORN, WALTER. *Ombudsmen and Others* (Cambridge, Mass.: Harvard University Press, 1967).

GOLDSTEIN, HERMAN. *Policing a Free Society* (Cambridge, Mass.: Ballinger, 1977).

HAMILTON, EDWARD K. "Police Productivity: The View from City Hall," pp. 11–34 in Joan L. Wolfle and John F. Heaphy (eds.), *Readings on Productivity in Policing* (Washington, D.C.: Police Foundation, 1975).

HUDNUT, WILLIAM H. III. "The Police and the Polis: An Executive's Perspective," pp. 20–29 in William A. Geller (ed.), *Police Leadership in America: Crisis and Opportunity* (New York: Praeger, 1985).

JOHNSON, DAVID H. *American Law Enforcement: A History* (St. Louis: Forum Press, 1981).

JOHNSTON, DAVID. "The Cop Watch," *Columbia Journalism Review,* 22:51–54 (Winter 1983).

JURIS, HERVEY, and PETER FEUILLE. "Employee Organizations," pp. 202–226 in O. Glenn Stahl and Richard A. Staufenberger (eds.), *Police Personnel Administration* (Scituate, Mass.: Duxbury, 1974).

Kansas City Police Department. *Recommendations of the Task Force on the Use of Force* (internal report, January 1991).

MURPHY, PATRICK V. "The Prospective Chief's Negotiation of Authority with the Executive," pp. 30–40 in William A. Geller (ed.), *Police Leadership in America: Crisis and Opportunity* (New York: Praeger, 1985).

SKOLNICK, JEROME H. "Neighborhood Police," pp. 288–291 in Jerome H. Skolnick and Thomas C. Gray (eds.), *Police in America* (Boston: Little, Brown, 1975).

——— and JAMES J. FYFE. *Above the Law: Police and the Excessive Use of Force* (New York: Free Press, 1993).

TROJANOWICZ, ROBERT, and BONNIE BUCQUEROUX. *Community Policing: A Contemporary Perspective* (Cincinnati: Anderson, 1990).

VOLLMER, AUGUST. *The Police and Modern Society* (Montclair, N.J.: Patterson Smith, 1972 reprint of original 1936 manuscript).

WALKER, SAMUEL. *A Critical History of Police Reform: The Emergence of Professionalism* (Lexington, Mass.: Lexington Books, 1977).

WILSON, JAMES Q. *Thinking about Crime,* 2d ed. (New York: Vintage Books, 1983).

———. *Varieties of Police Behavior* (Cambridge, Mass.: Harvard University Press, 1968).

PART TWO

Leadership and Administration

4

The Police Chief Executive As Leader

KEY WORDS AND PHRASES

Zone of acceptance (indifference)
Sources of authority
Weber's types of authority
Hawthorne effect
Motivational theory
Models of leadership
Leadership behavior categories
Police leadership styles
Leadership continuum
Leadership Grid
Situational leadership

Contingency theory
Path-goal theory
Institutional leadership
Leadership skills
Hierarchy of needs
Theory X and Theory Y
Immaturity-maturity theory
Dual-factor theory
Police stress
Transformational leadership

Leadership is a process of getting people to work toward some common objective. Executive leadership involves many processes that define organizational objectives and that move organizations toward desired goals. While there are many definitions of the concept of leadership,[1] each generally includes some notion of power, authority, cooperation, collective action, and persuasion. Leaders motivate others for joint action; they rally individual interests toward collective goals; and they provide some degree of connection or cohesiveness among many organizational personnel, all of whom are attempting to attain their own goals, as well as those of the organization.[2]

Especially in local governments, police executives are in pivotal leadership roles. They oversee an important community service; they are linked to other community services that directly affect the quality of residential and business life; and they are continually in the public's eye. In addition, municipal budgets for police services tend to be one of the largest municipal expenditures.

This chapter considers police executive leadership from several perspectives. First, it examines trends in thought which have centered debate on the internal leadership responsibilities of the police executive, sometimes at the expense of the police executive's external institutional leadership role. This is followed by a review of several theories of leadership and of individual and group motivation that are most affected by police executive leadership. Finally, the chapter considers the police executive in a leadership role in the broader administrative, social, and political communities, each of which continually shapes police policies and the range of goods and services that the police produce.

DEFINING LEADERSHIP

Much is written about leadership—its styles, its practices, and its impacts. Two factors are common to most definitions of leadership: Leadership is a group dynamic, and leadership involves the exercise of influence. Leaders are generally given the authority to influence individual and group behavior. By authority is meant "the power to make decisions which guide the actions of another. It is a relationship between two [or more] individuals" (Simon, 1976:125).

In organizations, leaders organize individual behavior toward a common purpose. As a consequence, leaders must understand both individual and group needs, as well as the factors that will motivate people toward production. This is often a subtle process; leaders encourage, praise, punish, teach, and reward individuals and groups in a complex process of influencing behavior. This influence process puts the leaders and the group in a continual negotiation over the work to be performed and the pace at which it will be accomplished.

This process also recognizes that not all persons and groups are motivated in exactly the same manner. Individuals and groups differ in both their willingness to work together and their willingness to be influenced by the leader. This is what Herbert Simon referred to as the employee's "zone of acceptance." (Simon, 1976:110–122), or the amount of influence a person will "accept." Chester Barnard, an executive with AT&T in the 1930s and a keen observer of the management and leadership process, recognized that individuals and groups may be indifferent to certain requests made by the leader:

> The phrase "zone of indifference" may be explained as follows: If all the orders for actions reasonably practicable be arranged in the order of their acceptability to the person affected, it may be conceived that there are a number which are clearly unacceptable, that is, which certainly will not be obeyed; there is another group somewhat more or less on the neutral line, that is either barely acceptable or barely unacceptable; and a third group unquestionably acceptable. This last group lies within the "zone of indifference." The person affected will accept orders lying within this zone and is relatively indifferent as to what the order is so far as the question of authority is concerned. Such an order lies within the range that in a general was anticipated at time of undertaking the connection with the organization. For example, if a soldier enlists, whether voluntary or not, in an army in which the men are ordinarily moved about within a certain broad region, it is a matter of indifference whether the order be to go to A or B, C or D, and so on; and going to A, B, C, D, etc. are in the zone of indifference.

FIGURE 4-1. Leader Influence in Organizational Behavior

> The zone of indifference will be wider or narrower depending upon the degree to which the inducements exceed the burdens and sacrifices which determine the individual's adhesion to the organization. It follows that the range of orders that will be accepted will be very limited among those who are barely induced to contribute to the system. (Barnard, 1968:168–169)

Barnard's *zone of indifference* and Simon's *zone of acceptance* recognize that individuals make decisions to join organizations and then to produce once in them. These decisions are influenced, generally, by the individual's goals and objectives. Organizations seek to influence individual decisions about production in many ways. Through systems of inducement, reward, punishment, self-fulfillment, and the like, organizations continually seek through their leaders to broaden the individual's zones of indifference and acceptance.

The leaders' challenge, then, is to understand the boundaries of these zones and to work with individuals and groups to better integrate individual and organizational goals. Figure 4-1 depicts these relationships as confronted by leaders.

Of course, groups and individuals influence the leader's behavior as well. It is this interactive influence-exchange process between the leader and groups that is often referred to as the "art" of management or leadership.

Sources of Leadership Authority

In organizational settings, persons can be formally charged with leadership roles, or they can assume these roles informally. When we think of leaders, we typically think of individuals with formal titles such as "chief of police," which give these persons the formal responsibility to lead.

In this sense, we say that the leader has the *authority* to lead; he or she has been granted this authority and has the *power* to exercise this authority in performing the duties as police chief. Here "authority" refers to the legitimate right to lead and influence people, while "power" refers to the capacity or ability to lead.

Power without authority is short-lived within organizations. As noted above, in defining their zones of indifference and acceptance, individuals are actually granting legitimacy to the power of the organization to guide their actions. Without such legitimacy, power quickly erodes or must be continually exercised to gain compliance. Leaders seek to exercise legitimate authority in organizational settings.

The German sociologist Max Weber (1947) distinguished among three forms of authority in organizations: traditional, charismatic, and legal-rational. Traditional authority is established through custom (e.g., king, queen, father, etc.). Charismatic authority is established through the personal appeal of an individual to a group of followers (e.g., Martin Luther King, Gandhi, John Kennedy, Winston Churchill, etc.). Legal-rational authority, according to Weber, stems from one's formal position in an organization and from the legal responsibilities and duties that are attached to that office (e.g., police chief, mayor, president, etc.). For Weber, legal-rational authority is a necessary condition for organizational survival; unfortunately kings and prophets die, while "bureaucrats," persons whose authority stems from their organizational position, simply succeed one another through a system of evaluation based on competency. Such a theory is the intellectual root for civil service systems, for example. Leaders, according to Weber, exercise their leadership by virtue of their position and their competence.

Within organizations there are sources of authority other than a formal leader such as the chief of police. French and Raven (1959:150–167) identified five sources of power and authority in social relations:

Reward power. Power stemming from the ability to give people something of value in exchange for their loyalty and willingness to cooperate (e.g., monetary rewards, social recognition, and the like)

Coercive power. Power stemming from the ability to take away or threaten to take away something of value to the individual for failing to comply or cooperate (e.g., a good work assignment, a promotion, a salary increase, and the like)

Legitimate power. Power stemming from the belief that the person exercising the power is doing so lawfully and rightfully, generally in connection with his or her position of accepted authority (e.g., the boss is making decisions within his or her sphere of authority)

Referent power. Power stemming from a person's identity or psychological attachment to an individual, group, or value of importance to that individual (e.g., authority granted to a sports team by virtue of the person's need to be part of the team)

Expert power. Power stemming from a recognized skill or knowledge in another which the individual values (e.g., authority granted to a mentor who is valued by the person as a knowledgeable person)

French and Raven's distinctions among the various sources of power have been further elaborated by Yukl (1981:12–17) into eleven different sources of influence which leaders exercise (see Table 4-1). These forms of influence all attest to the interactive nature of leadership in organizational settings.

Collectively, a consideration of power, authority, and influence in an organization points to the very real limits on a leader's behavior and action. It recognizes that there are often several competing sources of authority within organizations and that individuals and groups respond to these sources differently. It recognizes that there is no "one best way" to lead.

TABLE 4-1. **Yukl's Forms of Leadership Influence** 89

1. *Legitimate request.* A person complies or is influenced by another's request because the person believes that the agent has an "official right" to make the request.

2. *Instrumental compliance.* A person complies or changes his or her behavior based on an agent's promise (implicit or explicit) to help the person obtain a desired objective or outcome.

3. *Coercion.* A person complies or is influenced because of the agent's threat (implicit or explicit).

4. *Rational persuasion.* A person complies or is influenced because the agent has convinced the person that compliance is the best possible way for the person to obtain his or her goals or objectives.

5. *Rational faith.* A person complies because of his or her belief in the system of authority or leadership, without any explanation being made by the agent requesting the compliance.

6. *Inspirational appeal.* A person complies because the agent has convinced him or her that compliance is necessitated by some superordinate goal.

7. *Indoctrination.* A person complies because he or she has been subjected to a process of internalizing the values sought by the agent.

8. *Information distortion.* A person complies or is influenced by information provided by an agent which is distorted or falsified, but which nevertheless persuades compliance.

9. *Situational engineering.* A person complies or is influenced because his or her attitudes and/or behavior is affected because the agent is manipulating the person's social or physical environment.

10. *Personal identification.* A person complies or is influenced because he or she admires the personal qualities of the agent.

11. *Decision identification.* A person complies or is influenced because the agent has let the person participate in the decision-making process, which has increased the person's identification with the final decision.

Source: Adapted from Gary Y. Yukl, *Leadership in Organizations* (Englewood Cliffs, N.J.: Prentice Hall, 1981), pp. 12–17.) Adapted by permission of Prentice Hall, Upper Saddle River, N.J.

THE EVOLUTION OF
LEADERSHIP THOUGHT AND PRACTICE

The history of leadership thought and practice has involved a continuing struggle in defining the relationships among the leader, the worker, and the work to be done. Early philosophies of leadership behavior and management emphasized the ascendence of the leader above all other considerations. Leaders were virtuous, they were keenly intelligent, they were morally better than others, and, at times, they were divinely inspired. By contrast, workers and the work performed were simply factors to be manipulated toward the leader's ends. Since workers had few of the qualities of the leaders, they were easily dismissed as one of the factors of production. In a sense leaders were seen as having progressed morally and socially further on the evolutionary ladder. The "unwashed masses," by contrast, were inferior socially, educationally, morally, and certainly economically.

As time passed, this social Darwinian view of leadership yielded to concerns for the needs of the workers and the need for closer harmony between those being led and those doing the leading (Perrow, 1986:49–78). Workers, too, were motivated by things other than fear and the need to eat. They had aspirations that could be appealed to by the effective leader. And, perhaps, more importantly, they could resist the actions of the leader.

Finally, modern-day concepts of leadership also include concern for the situations and the work to be done in the selection of any particular leadership style. The context within which work occurs has also come to be considered important for leadership. The culture of the organization, its symbols and values, and the way in which the leader reinforces or challenges those contextual factors are all seen as part of the leadership process.

Leadership as a Historical Process

Although people have led and managed other people since the time of earliest recorded history, the development of modern leadership and management theory was slow to emerge. The reasons for the slow growth are varied. Part of the problem, no doubt, is that modern leadership theory is based on social enlightenment and democratic idealism, both of which were in short supply before the eighteenth century. Businesses themselves were uncomplicated and did not require complex solutions to simple problems. Further, the existing sciences in the seventeenth and eighteenth centuries were relatively unconcerned with matters outside their specialties; there were no sociologists or psychologists available to express opinions on management and leadership subjects. Finally, there has always been—until recent years—an inexhaustible supply of cheap labor.

Nonetheless, the history of management thought[3] has evolved from the development of early nation-states (such as ancient Greece, Egypt, and China) through the medieval period, when the mercantile class arose to compete with feudal governance and when "merchant states" such as those found in Venice flourished. Spurred by the Industrial Revolution, management and leadership theory and practice grew at a quickening pace—trying to keep up with an ever-more complex work world. And today management and leadership thought has expanded beyond the traditional organizational and leadership structure that governed the industrial era. Today's leaders are challenged to decentralize the organizations, get closer to their customers, and emphasize a system of management that is creative and imaginative (see, for example, Morgan, 1993; Peters and Waterman, 1982).

Leadership is a significant managerial task. Today it is less assumed that all managers are leaders. And it is now commonplace to spread leadership from individuals to groups and teams both within and outside organizations.

Ancient Leadership Systems. Ancient societies often exhibited well-developed managerial and leadership systems. Early Babylonia, for example, codified law under the Code of Hammurabi, thus making the relationship between person and state explicit and thereby providing the basis for organized and commercial society. Hammurabi, then king of Babylonia, unified many of the cities dotting the Tigris and Euphrates rivers. As a strong trade and mercantile class had emerged in early Babylonia, the Code of Hammurabi also had much to do with specifying business relationships.

Ancient Egypt and China were also known for the development of advanced bureaucracies which, among other things, accounted for the management of the construction of the Great Wall and the Great Pyramids. In Egypt ideas about centralized organization and the documenting of government transactions contributed to the practice of state leadership. In China whole classes of public bureaucrats emerged as early as the eleventh century B.C.:

> The Constitution of Chow, probably written about 1100 B.C., is a directory of all civil servants to the emperor, from the prime minister down to the household servants, with their jobs and duties carefully listed. (Peters and Waterman, 1982:11)

The Roman Empire was one of the greatest tributes to decentralized global leadership. An empire spanning at least three continents, Rome ruled a far-flung enterprise. Decentralized management, local leadership with allegiance to Rome, and military intervention to ensure some degree of compliance characterized the system of governance of the Roman Empire. While this system ultimately collapsed, leading to the Dark Ages, Roman governance spread leadership from the Holy Roman Emperor to a wide array of local decision makers. These developments in ancient societies paved the way for a number of management and leadership developments during the Middle Ages.

Leadership in the Middle Ages and the Renaissance. During the feudal Middle Ages, leadership stemmed from the "divine right of kings," a philosophy that suggested that kings ruled by the power vested in them by the deity. State-church relationships reinforced the divinity of monarchs throughout Europe and elsewhere. Feudal society and the leadership it produced centralized authority but decentralized operations, created allegiance and dependence systems as a means of governing, and produced distinct hierarchical relationships across a wide range of individuals and occupations, most notably the feudal lords and the serfs. But within feudal society a merchant class was developing, a class of individuals who would ultimately force monarchs to concede vast amounts of their authority and leadership over the affairs of civil society.

The signing of the Magna Carta in 1215 was a major watershed in the transformation of leadership from the ruling classes to then-emerging business classes. As medieval Europe emerged into the Enlightenment, social and political theorists challenged assumptions about the leadership role of government.

During the sixteenth century, Niccolo Machiavelli, a former diplomat who was intimately familiar with the inner workings of government, lost favor with the Florentine government, headed by the Medici princes. Having fallen from grace, Machiavelli sought to regain favor by writing *The Prince* and *The Discourses* (1950), two treatises on leadership and the exercise of power. Although Machiavelli never did regain his status in the Florentine court, his work has greatly influenced modern-day thought about management, organization, politics, and leadership.

Throughout the Renaissance, utopian writers such as Rousseau, Sir Thomas More, and others questioned the right of the state to lead. While such thinking touched only lightly on managerial thought and practice, it provided fertile ground for later theorists to expand on the relationships between those who led and those who did the leading.

The Industrial Revolution has had the most profound impact on modern-day management and leadership practice and theory. Before the Industrial Revolution the only large-scale organizations that existed were the military and the church, both hierarchically organized, rule-laden, and rank-centered. Most business were small-scale enterprises, many being family-owned where leadership passed from one generation to another. By the early 1700s, a major transformation of the workplace was under way.

The Industrial Revolution and the Transformation of Leadership. Until the Industrial Revolution, industry involved little mechanization, low-skilled workers, little organization across workers, and a *cottage industry* model of producing one piece of work at a time. Between 1700 and 1785, however, the Industrial Revolution spawned more complex organizations. Indeed, it led to the factory system with power-driven machinery and complex human interaction. The factory system called for the expansion of leadership and managerial practices to oversee the complexity it introduced. People and machine interactions, assembly-line production modes, and increased needs for skilled workers all strained the single-person leadership systems that had grown up in what were essentially family-run businesses. Coupled with an ever-widening maritime network of trade and exchange, the eighteenth century ushered in an era of expanded leadership thinking.

At the technical level, this leadership thinking was most closely associated with better integrating the worker with the machines driving industry. The early work of Frederick Taylor and Frank and Lillian Gilbreth created a scientific foundation for management and leadership. *Scientific management*, as it is known, had several underlying principles, each of which had implications for the role of leaders:

First. Develop a science for each element of a man's work, which replaces the old rule-of-thumb method.

Second. Scientifically select and then train, teach, and develop the workman, whereas in the past he chose his own work and trained himself as best he could.

Third. Heartily cooperate with the men so as to insure all the work is being done in accordance with the principles of the science which has been developed.

Fourth. There is an almost equal division of work and the responsibility between the management and the workmen. The management take over all work for which they are better fitted than the workmen, while in the past almost all of the work and the greater part of the responsibility were thrown upon the men. (Taylor, 1911:36–37)

While the scientific management era of leadership has been criticized for its absence of concern for the worker, much of the leadership thought at this time actually helped workers earn a better life. And, more important, management and leadership theorists of this era were much more likely to account for the needs of the worker than were their earlier counterparts. In creating the "shop system" and time-motion studies, among other things, for example, Taylor felt that he could actually increase cooperation between labor and management to the betterment of each:

> Taylor frequently stated that management was negligent in performing its functions—that in actuality it placed the burden of methods and output on labor, disclaiming any responsibility for itself. Taylor declared this was wrong. Management should do the work for which it was best suited—planning, organizing, controlling, determining methods and the like—and not push it off on labor's shoulders. . . . Under these conditions of harmonious cooperation, emphasis would be on increasing the whole and on the relative size of one's particular share, with a resultant increase in production, sales, job opportunities, wages, profit and general well-being. (George, 1972:93)

From Leader to Worker: Shifting the Focus of Leadership in the Twentieth Century. Management and leadership study up until the early 1900s was almost entirely focused on the managers rather than on the workers. As previously stated, labor was just one of several factors to be manipulated by management.

From the early 1920s through the 1960s, there occurred a shift in emphasis in leadership and managerial thought. This shift was from managers to workers.

In the 1920s, before the great stock market crash of 1929, American industry had adopted most of the mechanization of the Industrial Revolution, as well as the general practices of scientific management. Production lines, such as those created by Henry Ford, dotted the country. At the same time a group of researchers from Harvard University was conducting several industrial studies to better understand the dynamics of this revolution in industry.

Elton Mayo, a Harvard psychology professor, was interested in the social and psychological relationships within work settings. Together with a team of researchers from Harvard's Department of Industrial Research, Mayo and colleagues changed the face of leadership and management practice.

In a series of studies conducted in Cicero, Illinois, at the Western Electric Hawthorne Plant, Mayo and others found that group dynamics and individual social-psychological attachments to the workplace were powerful forces shaping industrial relations. Mayo's original studies examined the effects of fatigue on workers' production:

> A six girl team started on their unique manufacturing career in April 1927. As the account goes, the conditions of work were changed one at a time to study their effects on production, some of these changes being rest periods of different length and number, shorter work days, shorter work weeks, soup or coffee at the morning coffee breaks, and so on. With each change the effect was consistent: output increased, and at the same time the girls felt less fatigued. (George, 1972:136–137)

During this period, the now famous "illumination studies" were also under way under the supervision of Mayo and his colleagues (Roethlisberger and Dixon, 1939). These studies, originally cast to determine the effects of the physical environment, found that increases in illumination of the work setting being studied were accompanied by increases in output. This was no surprise, but it was also found that when lighting was decreased, output continued to increase; indeed, even when lighting was *significantly* reduced, the experimental group continued to increase production. At the same time, production in the control group also increased, even though lighting was held constant for this group throughout the experiment.

These studies and others like them led researchers to conclude that factors other than manipulations in the physical environment accounted for production in both the control and the experimental groups. Those factors were social and social-psychological; they involved individual attachments to the work group and the fact that these work groups felt special in that they were being studied by the scientists. Such scientific evidence of the importance of group dynamics ushered in an era of management and leadership study focused on people and work groups.

Much of *motivational theory* (as discussed below) finds its beginnings in the work of Mayo and his colleagues. Since that time, elaborate theories of individual and group motivation have emerged as part of a field of organizational psychology. Much of this theory and research assesses the dynamics of the workplace and the role of the leader in shaping and being shaped by those dynamics.

MODELS OF LEADERSHIP

Leadership has been studied from several perspectives. Our current understanding and models of leadership have themselves evolved over the years. Historically, leadership is associated with the personalities and personal traits of leaders. Many years of research have been devoted to studying the traits of leaders in the hope of distilling the "essence" of leadership and then modeling those traits in others.

More recently, leadership study has included a concern for the context within which leadership occurs. While the personal traits and characteristics of leaders are not regarded as unimportant, the forces shaping leadership have come to be viewed as situational and dynamic. In other words, where leaders were once thought to possess "natural" qualities that allowed them to lead, more-current thinking suggests that leaders actually "adjust" their style of leadership to the situations they face. Of course, such ability to be flexible and "adjust" may be an important individual characteristic in situational models of leadership as well.

Executive Leadership as a Personal Trait

Leadership in complex organizations has often been associated with the individual traits of the leader. Two streams of thought give credence to trait explanations of exemplary leadership. First, early organizational theorists such as Max Weber saw the legitimacy of leaders' being rooted in traditions and of the charismatic charm of the leader. Either historical leaders were "born" to their leadership role, as was the tradition of monarchical ascension to the throne, or they were "personalities" whom people followed because of their beliefs and pronouncements:

> In the case of charismatic authority, it is the charismatically qualified leader as such who is obeyed by virtue of personal trust in him and his revelation, his

heroism or his exemplary qualities so far as they fall within the scope of the individual's belief in his charisma. (Weber, 1975:328)

The "great men" of the industrial age in England and the "robber barons" of America's Industrial Revolution were hailed as great leaders, in part because of their personal characteristics and traits.[4] The "great-person" approach to explaining leadership traits is intuitive, often relying on qualitative judgment. As such, these explanations are illuminating for their ability to generate general "classes" of leaders, rather than to detail leadership traits (see Bennis and Nanus, 1985). In other words, this approach may identify people most of us would view as great, but it does not tell us much about *what* made them great.

A second approach to leadership study is found in many efforts aimed at identifying those qualities of leaders which distinguish them from nonleaders. *Stogdill's Handbook of Leadership* (Bass, 1981) is a compendium of leadership trait information gleaned from a survey of leadership studies conducted between 1904 and 1970. In all, Stogdill surveyed some 287 research studies and categorized the traits depicted in Figure 4-2. While Stogdill's work identified leadership traits across research projects, there is much disagreement in the literature about what the trait studies have actually produced (see, for example, Smith and Peterson, 1988; Yukl, 1981). Nonetheless, trait studies attempt to point out those characteristics of successful leaders. More recently, situational and contextual factors thought to affect leadership are used more and more to explain the successful exercise of leadership.

Historically, leadership in police organizations has been most associated with the traits of individuals thought to be good leaders. As policing has an essential "personal" quality—meaning that police officers more often than not relate to their organizational and work-group life on a very personal level—the individual and combined personal traits of leaders are often used to illustrate leadership and to look for its potential in others. Many police agencies today, for example, include "leadership potential" as part of the assessment of individuals for promotion. Such potential, however, is rarely empirically assessed. Rather, subjective evaluations are made. The subjective evaluations more often than not search for such personal qualities as confidence, presentational skill, demeanor, and the like as evidence of potential leadership capability.

Such a posture on leadership suggests that leading people is as much a personality issue as it is a set of techniques to motivate and sustain progress toward some organizational goal. Personal charisma, a take-charge attitude, physical stature, and other personal characteristics have been used in police circles to separate good leaders from others.

Interestingly, trait-based leadership discussions almost always focus on the positive aspects of leader behavior—good motivator, personal courage, loyalty, and the like. Any negative aspects of leadership are generally absent in such discussions. Leaders are to be admired for their strong and endearing qualities, not for their ability to restrict individual and group behavior among police officers.

At other times, as suggested above, police leadership has been identified with great individuals—people who were admired for their leadership ability. In the administrative lore of American policing, such persons as August Vollmer of Berkeley and William Parker of Los Angeles, among others, surface as examples of this leadership model.

FIGURE 4-2. Factors Affecting Leadership Style
Adapted from Patrick J. Bettin, Peggy S. Hunt, Jennifer L. Macaulay, and Susan E. Murphy,
"Shidō: Effective Leadership in Japan," pp. 83–92 in Kenneth E. Clark, Miriam B. Clark, and
David P. Campbell (eds.), Impact of Leadership *(Greensboro, N.C.: Center for Creative*
Leadership, copyright 1992. All rights reserved).

Leadership Behavioral Styles and Contexts

Another avenue of leadership thought is to attempt to identify a cluster of behaviors, thoughts, and actions, all of which contribute to the style of leadership
exhibited by any particular leader. This method of analysis is useful primarily
because it breaks down the complex and rather abstract phenomenon we call
leadership into a set of individual components that can be more easily identified and, perhaps, modified by training, experience, and feedback on performance. In addition, dissecting leadership in this manner also makes it possible
to more systematically vary one's leadership style according to the dictates of
particular situations. As police managers know, leadership behavior that
works well in the routine of day-to-day operations may produce disaster in
large-scale emergencies that require immediate obedience to quick and unilat-
eral command decisions.

Kurt Lewin. In the late 1930s, Kurt Lewin headed one of the first academic
studies of leadership style, examining three different styles of leadership used
in a boys' club: *democratic, autocratic,* and *laissez-faire* (Lewin, Lippett, and
White, 1939). For Lewin and his colleagues, the most significant question was:
"What style of leadership is most effective for what type of outcome?" Democratic leadership, for example, includes subordinates as meaningful participants
in decision making; this was found to be effective when the morale of the club
was at question. The autocratic style, in which the leader gives direction with
no opportunity for subordinates' input, appeared to be most effective when
production of model airplanes alone was considered (Lewin, Lippett, and

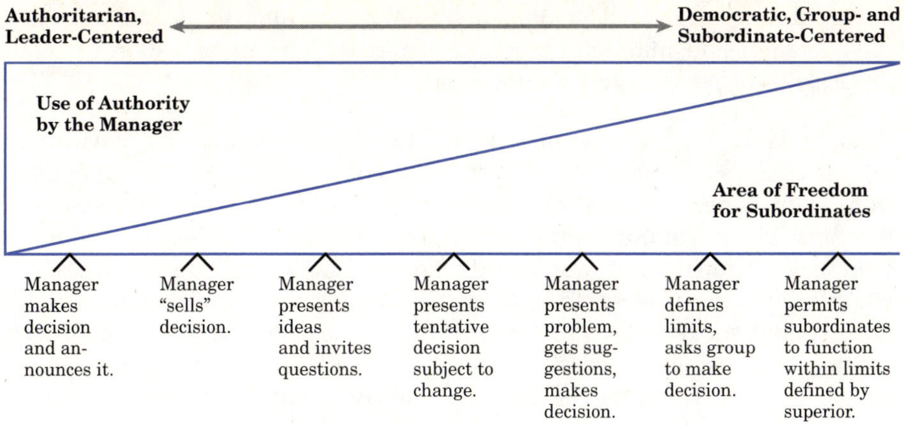

Authoritarian, Leader-Centered						Democratic, Group- and Subordinate-Centered

Use of Authority by the Manager

Area of Freedom for Subordinates

Manager makes decision and announces it.	Manager "sells" decision.	Manager presents ideas and invites questions.	Manager presents tentative decision subject to change.	Manager presents problem, gets suggestions, makes decision.	Manager defines limits, asks group to make decision.	Manager permits subordinates to function within limits defined by superior.

FIGURE 4-3. Authoritarian-Democratic Continuum
Reprinted by permission of Harvard Business Review. *An exhibit from "How to Choose a Leadership Pattern" by Robert Tannenbaum and Warren H. Schmidt,* Harvard Business review, *May/June 1973. Copyright © 1973 by the President and Fellows of Harvard College; all rights reserved.*

White, 1939:271–299). From these early beginnings, there has emerged an extensive literature of leadership behavior.[5]

Building on the work of Lewin and his colleagues, Tannenbaum and Schmidt (1973:162–180) envisioned leadership on a continuum that ranged from Lewin's conception of *authoritarian,* leader-centered behavior to *democratic,* group- and subordinate-centered behavior. According to Tannenbaum and Schmidt, selecting the appropriate leadership behavior involves consideration of three sets of forces that, respectively, affect managers, subordinates, and the organization itself.

Under this logic, forces affecting the manager include such personal characteristics and abilities as his or her personality, value system, and ability to handle ambiguity. Forces affecting subordinates include workers' general competence, willingness to assume greater responsibility, work experience, and the like. Among forces affecting the organization itself are its existing policies, practices, and procedures: in other words, the deck of cards dealt to managers and subordinates by their employer. Collectively, according to Tannenbaum and Schmidt, these factors shape the selection of a leadership style. Figure 4-3 presents the authoritarian–democratic leadership continuum.

Ohio State. During the 1940s and into the 1950s, important leadership studies were conducted by Stodgill and colleagues at Ohio State University (Stogdill and Coons, 1957). These studies concluded that leadership style varied along two important dimensions. The first of these dimensions was *consideration,* or the care for others demonstrated by leaders' behavior toward them—the "other orientation" of the leader. The second dimension was called *initiating structure,* or the degree to which the leader provides goals, objectives, and structure for those doing the work. Knowing a leader's level of consideration and initiating structure, these researchers suggested, would enable us to predict the type of leadership style that would emerge. Logically, therefore, using training or other developmental methods to alter the leader's level of consideration and initiating structure would help an organization to create precisely the type of leadership it wanted.

Rensis Likert. At the same time, Rensis Likert of the University of Michigan reported on his examination of the behaviors of a large number of supervisors from many types of organizations (Likert, 1961). Likert's analysis concluded that supervisors who differentiated their role from that of their subordinates, who were oriented less toward production and more toward employees, and who supervised tasks less closely were the more successful supervisors. Stated more simply, supervisors who involved themselves in managing rather than in the details of their employees' work and who made it clear that they were concerned with their employees were more likely to have encouraged workers' productivity and loyalty than were those supervisors who spent their days looking over employees' shoulders and carefully measuring and comparing employees' productivity.

The Managerial and Leadership Grid. The idea that supervisory and leadership style could be specified on three dimensions—one representing the supervisor's orientation toward the work, another her orientation toward the employee, and a third, the motivations (positive and negative) underlying the choice of any particular style—provided an inspiration for another means of identifying and analyzing variations in leadership styles. Using the findings of Stodgill and Likert, Blake and Mouton (1964), subsequently revised by Blake and McCanse (1991), designed a management and organizational development assessment instrument to identify any given manager's location on two 9 point scales, one measuring *concern for production* and the other measuring *concern for people.* The original *Managerial Grid* proposed by Blake and Mouton in 1964 proposed:

> . . . in essence that effective managers are those who show extremely high concern for both the maximizing of task performance and for those with whom they work, rather than trading off one dimension from the other. (Smith and Peterson, 1988:10)

In the revised *Leadership Grid* (Blake and McCanse, 1991), managers' scores on both the production and people concern scales represent one of five dominant leadership styles, with two additional management styles resulting from motivational shifts on the part of the managers:

1. *Country Club Management* (1,9): high concern for people, low concern for production;
2. *Impoverished Management* (1,1): low concern for both people and production;
3. *Middle of the Road Management* (5,5): balanced concern for both people and production;
4. *Team Management* (9,9): high concern for production and people;
5. *Authority-Compliance Management:* high concern for production, low concern for people;
6. *Paternalism/Materialism Management* (9+9): an adaptation of Country Club and Authority-Compliance Management where managerial rewards come

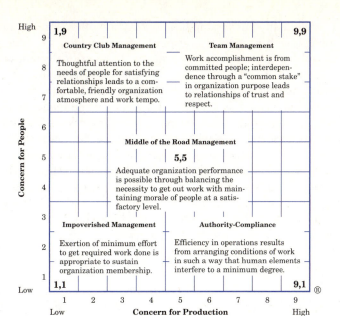

High
9

1,9
Country Club Management
Thoughtful attention to the needs of people for satisfying relationships leads to a comfortable, friendly organization atmosphere and work tempo.

8

7

Team Management
Work accomplishment is from committed people; interdependence through a "common stake" in organization purpose leads to relationships of trust and respect.

9,9

Concern for People

6

5

Middle of the Road Management
5,5
Adequate organization performance is possible through balancing the necessity to get out work with maintaining morale of people at a satisfactory level.

4

3

Impoverished Management
Exertion of minimum effort to get required work done is appropriate to sustain organization membership.

Authority-Compliance
Efficiency in operations results from arranging conditions of work in such a way that human elements interfere to a minimum degree.

2

1

1,1

9,1 ®

Low

1   2   3   4   5   6   7   8   9
Low   Concern for Production   High

Opportunistic Management

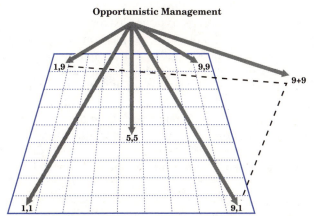

In opportunistic management organization performance occurs accoding to a system of exchanges, whereby effort is given only for an equivalent measure of the same. People adapt to the situation to gain maximum advantage from it.

9+9: Paternalistic Management

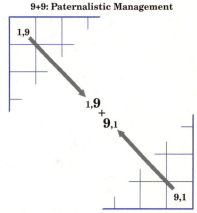

In 9+9 paternalistic management, reward and approval are granted to people in return for loyalty and obedience; failure to comply leads to punishment.

FIGURE 4-4. The Leadership Grid
From The Leadership Grid® figure, Paternalism Figure and Opportunism from Leadership Dilemmas—Grid Solutions, *by Robert R. Blake and Anne Adams McCanse (Formerly the Managerial Grid by Robert R. Blake and Jane S. Mouton). Houston: Gulf Publishing Company, (Grid Figure: p. 29, Paternalism Figure: p. 30, Opportunism Figure: p. 31). Copyright 1991 by Scientific Methods, Inc. Reproduced by permission of the owners.*

to those who exhibit loyalty to the manager, and where the absence of such loyalty is punished by the manager; and,

7. *Opportunism Management:* where the manager adjusts her/his style of management to gain maximum advantage to increase personal gain.

The Blake and McCanse leadership/management styles are presented with the *Leadership Grid Figure* in Figure 4-4.

While the Leadership Grid appears to offer a precise method of identifying the leadership style of any particular manager, its value is sometimes minimized by the tendency of trainers to uncritically allow managers to place themselves on its scales. This practice, obviously, introduces the bias inherent in any self-rating instrument. To use the grid more precisely, a manager's style should be assessed by those who work for the manager, as well as by those to whom the manager reports. Since many managers may believe that they function as *team managers* when in reality they do not, the Managerial/Leadership Grid is best thought of as an analytic device rather than as a precise diagnostic tool. When used appropriately, the Managerial/Leadership Grid can be used to better understand how management styles emerge and what drives the selection of any particular style. The grid is based on many years of research and refinement, and is an important tool for conceptualizing and understanding the styles managers adopt and enact.

Police Leadership Studies

Studies of police leadership style have occupied much of the professional discussion among academics and senior managers in police circles for some time. These studies have examined police leader characteristics, styles of communication, and the social and political context of police leadership.

Several trait- and behavioral-based studies of police leadership have been conducted since the early 1970s. Pursley (1974), for example, compared a sample of 132 police chiefs whom he classified as either traditional or nontraditional. The 58 traditional police chiefs in Pursley's study exemplified the authority-obedience management style of Blake and Mouton, although Pursley did not use the grid in his study method. These chiefs closely structured and controlled the work of subordinates; they delegated very little and tended to centralize their authority and decision making. The 74 nontraditionalists studied by Pursley, by contrast, were younger, better educated, and more flexible in their management style; they delegated to subordinates and were more likely to represent the Blake and Mouton team management leadership style.

In two studies, Kuykendall (1977, 1985) examined police executive leadership styles using the Blake and Mouton grid. In a sample of 25 San Francisco police executives in his first study, and later in a study of 225 police managers from four states, he found that most seemed to gravitate toward the team management style outlined by Blake and Mouton. He reported also, however, that they were likely to switch styles, depending on whether they were setting goals and objectives or implementing them. This research suggests that leadership style is modified by the central task to be achieved: more open in the definition of goals and objectives and more constrained during the implementation of those goals and objectives. By contrast, Swanson and Territo (1982) found that a sample of police leaders was most likely to employ this authority-obedience management style and occasionally to shift from it to what Blake and Mouton called impoverished management. Their findings are consistent with our previous consideration of the manner in which military organizational models have influenced modern-day policing.

Bernard Cohen (1980) conducted a study of 556 managers from the New York City Police Department that distinguished managers who were "tradition"-oriented from those oriented to "reform." Tradition-oriented managers, he reported, were generally older, less educated, more oriented to the rank-and-file officers beneath them, and less committed to managerial goals than were the reform-oriented managers. Cohen's dichotomy among these New York City police executives also suggested that the reform-oriented managers were more independent, more likely to be better evaluated, and more mobile within the police department than were the tradition-oriented managers. In some respects, Cohen's study actually reflects demographic changes within the New York City Police Department at the time. During the years in which he conducted research there, younger and better-educated people were reaching command ranks in the department. Cohen's characterization of major differences among New York's police leaders is consistent with a study of "police culture" in New York City which concluded that two cultures of policing have emerged: one emphasizing "street-level" concerns and the other "management" concerns (Reuss-Ianni, 1983).

In addition to the focus on police managers, James Q. Wilson (1978) has suggested that styles of police leadership are subtly affected by the communities in which police leaders find themselves. Communities ultimately select their police executives, and in doing so they search for leaders whose values are compatible with the leadership of their communities. This does not mean that the ultimate style of the police agency is directly affected by the community. Rather, as Wilson suggests:

> . . . the prevailing police style is not explicitly determined by community decisions, though a few of its elements may be shaped by these decisions. Put another way, the police are in all cases keenly sensitive to their political environment without in all cases being governed by it. . . . Thus, police work is carried out under the influence of a *political culture* though not necessarily under day-to-day political direction. . . . The most important way in which political culture affects police behavior is through the choice of police administrator and the molding of the expectations that govern his role. (Wilson, 1978:232–233)

For Wilson, three types of police agencies and, hence, three types of leadership styles emerge. The *watchman* style, most associated with large, urban inner cities, was seen as a rather laissez-faire mode of operation, emphasized through the behavior of police administrators and line-level officers. By contrast, Wilson argues that *legalistic* departments are led by the political ethos surrounding middle-class communities. These departments emphasize law, order, structure, and administrative efficiency. Finally, some police agencies emphasize the *service* interventions of local policing. These agencies were most likely to be found in upper-class communities, where problems of order and crime were relatively minor and where the political ethos demanded a less visible and more service-focused police force.

Wilson's typology of police leadership has been subjected to empirical analysis by Langworthy (1986), who, while unable to statistically confirm Wilson's argument, concluded:

> This does not argue that local governments have no effect on police agencies—clearly they do as they hire and fire the chief, pay salaries, and control the bud-

gets, but it does say that there is not a systematic relationship. (Langworthy, 1986:135–136)

Others (Rubinstein, 1973; Skolnick, 1966; Skolnick and Bayley, 1986; Skolnick and Fyfe, 1993) have argued that police agency styles do emerge through the interaction of the police leadership, the local community culture, and such variables as the size and complexity of the population to be served. All this research gives credence at least to the general idea that police leadership varies by community context.

Situational Leadership and Contingency Management

Still another approach to studying leadership has been to examine the situational contexts within which leadership is exercised. Contextualizing leadership in this way abandons the idea that there is one best way to manage. Instead, leadership is perceived as varying with the conditions it encounters. Under such arrangements, leaders are challenged with knowing the conditions they are encountering, the skills and abilities of those who are being led, the goals to be achieved, and the resources that can be brought to bear on accomplishing any particular objective. By contrast to other approaches, leadership is in a dynamic state, constantly in flux and always presenting a vast array of potential avenues to pursue.

To some extent the analyses of Stodgill, Likert, Tannenbaum and Schmidt, and Blake and Mouton all acknowledge (sometimes begrudgingly) that factors external to the leader have an impact on the choice and effectiveness of leadership style. Nonetheless, trait- and behavioral-based descriptions are relatively "closed-systems" approaches to understanding leadership dynamics; in other words, little outside the relationship between the leader and the worker is taken into consideration as affecting the choice and usefulness of any particular leadership style.

Situational leadership models are reflected in a shift from understanding leadership as a dynamic and ever-changing state.

Fielder's Contingency Theory

Fielder's (1967) *contingency theory* is a personality theory of leadership, but it incorporates several ideas about what shapes a leadership style. Perhaps the most important of these factors is "situational favorability," or those conditions that allow more or less leadership to be exercised in any given situation. Among the factors affecting situational favorability are the relationship between the leader and subordinates, the leader's position of power, and the amount or degree of structure in the tasks to be performed. Leaders with strong employee relationships, recognized authority, and structured work to be performed will, in all likelihood, exercise a different leadership style from leaders with weak or nonexistent employee relationships, low authority, and undefined or unstructured work. This contingency model ultimately suggests that it is easier to change the nature of the work than to change the personality of the leader. In other words, effective leadership behavior will ultimately rest on an assessment of the situation in which it is to be exercised.

Hershey and Blanchard's
Situational Leadership Model

A situational leadership model that emphasizes tasks and relationships as well as the maturity of the workers has been advanced by Hershey and Blanchard (1977). *Maturity* in this model is defined for the leader as the ability to set appropriately high goals, and for the worker to have the requisite experience and willingness to pursue those goals.

Hershey and Blanchard's situational leadership model asserts that task-oriented behavior on the part of the leader will steadily decrease as the job maturity (e.g., skills, experience, and psychological maturity) of the workers rises. Similarly, relationship-oriented behavior on the part of the leader will at first be high (consultive, supportive, nurturing, etc.) when workers' maturity is low, but it will gradually recede as workers become more independent by virtue of increased maturity. Figure 4-5 presents a diagram of the relationships between relationship and task behavior as modified by the maturity of persons being led. Reduced to the simplest terms, this model holds that managers' work becomes much easier as workers become more skilled and mature. The

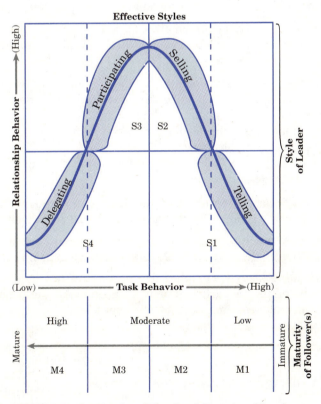

FIGURE 4-5. The Hershey/Blanchard Situational Leadership Model
From Paul Hershey and Kenneth H. Blanchard, Management of Organizational Behavior: Utilizing Human Resources, *3d ed. (Englewood Cliffs, N.J.: Prentice-Hall, 1977) p. 170.*

key to effective management over the long term, therefore, is to recruit the most mature and stable workers possible and to see that they are thoroughly trained to do their jobs.

As shown in Figure 4-5, leadership styles progress from "telling" styles, where communication is one way, task specific, and authoritative; through "selling" and "participating," where leader behavior is more open to communication, supportive, and encouraging; and finally to "delegating," where leadership is management "at a distance," recognizing that the competence of the workforce is at its highest. Telling leaders emphasize high-task and low-relationship behavior in the face of workforce immaturity. Selling and participating leaders emphasize high-relationship and gradually lower-task behavior in the face of a maturing workforce. And delegating leaders emphasize low-task and low-relationship behavior, preferring to "manage by exception" in the face of a mature workforce.

Path-Goal Theories of Leadership

Path-goal theories of leadership find their intellectual roots in the "expectancy theories" of the 1960s (e.g., Vroom, 1964). Essentially, path-goal theories suggest that subordinates will do what leaders want if they (the leaders) ensure that:

1. The subordinates understand what to do
2. The subordinates see the attainment of their own personal goals in attaining the organization's goals

The leader's role under the path-goal theory, then, is to ensure that subordinates are given tasks that maximize their own and the leader's goals. Variables of key interest to this model are the motivation, ability, and job satisfaction of subordinates and the leader's capacity to assess these factors and choose great paths for subordinates to follow.

House and Mitchell (1975) derived four types of leadership using the path-goal approach to leadership:

Directed leadership emphasizes the setting of standards and performance objectives, generally in the face of work that is not well defined.

Supportive leadership emphasizes social, group, and psychological support for subordinates in the face of work that is stressful and frustrating.

Participative leadership emphasizes consultative relationships with employees and employee participation in decision making in the face of work that needs employee commitment to be completed.

Achievement-oriented leadership emphasizes high goals and employee confidence and competence in the face of challenging and nonroutine work.

Multiple-Linkage Models of Leadership

One of the most comprehensive assessments of leader effectiveness is that of Yukl (1981), who examined an extensive number of contextual or situational variables thought to affect group and individual behavior. Yukl identified several factors that influence group performance. They include:

TABLE 4-2. Yukl's Leadership Behavior Categories

1. *Capacity.* Intelligence, alertness, verbal facility, originality, judgment

2. *Achievement.* Scholarship, knowledge, athletic accomplishments

3. *Responsibility.* Dependability, initiative, persistence, aggressiveness, self-confidence, desire to excel

4. *Participation.* Activity, sociability, cooperation, adaptability, humor

5. *Status.* Socioeconomic position, popularity

6. *Situation.* Mental level, status, skills, needs and interests of followers, objectives to be achieved, and so on

Source: Bernard M. Bass (ed.), *Stogdill's Handbook of Leadership* (New York: Free Press, 1981), p. 66.

> *Role clarity,* or the extent to which subordinates understand their jobs
>
> *Task skills,* or the degree to which subordinates have the requisite knowledge, skill, and ability to perform their jobs
>
> *Resources and support services,* or the degree to which subordinates have the proper tools to do their jobs
>
> *Task-role organization,* or whether the work unit is efficiently organized
>
> *Group cohesiveness and teamwork,* or the extent of cooperative interactions among subordinates within a work group. (Yukl, 1981:154)

The first four factors (role clarity, task skills, resources and support services, and task-role organization) most directly affect the performance of individual subordinates, while the performance of the group as a whole is most related to the last two of Yukl's situational variables (task-role organization and group cohesiveness and teamwork). Of course, the interaction of all five factors affects the interaction performance of individuals and groups. But these interactions are influenced by a set of intervening variables that Yukl has grouped into three categories:

1. Factors that affect one or more of the six individual and group factors, such as ability to reward (extrinsic and intrinsic) or work group size
2. Factors that affect all the individual or group productivity factors, such as the introduction of technology
3. Factors that affect the leader's ability to lead, such as rank, power, authority, and the like

From this analysis, Yukl derives a set of leadership behaviors that are situationally determined. These leadership behaviors are presented in Table 4-2.

Situational and Contingency Leadership in Policing

The role of situational and contingency leadership practices for police executives is rather straightforward. Such contingency is the case for police executive leadership in policing today. Police chief executives must provide leadership on complex and important social, political, and economic issues. They are

Police chiefs must be effective leaders of their communities as well as their departments. This chief knows that, and is a highly visible participant in a community
meeting.
Alan Carey/Image Works.

responsible for creating a climate of policing within any community which is
tough on crime and at the same time vigorously safeguards and honors democratic principles and constitutional guarantees. They must work with a wide
array of community, special-interest, political, and business groups, many of
whom place competing demands on the local police. They must balance the interest of police labor groups with those of political leadership and a community wanting more services from the police with less tax investment. In the
end, they must lead, not follow, the crime control debate, and they must do so
with, rather than against, the community. As Lee P. Brown has argued:

> Not only must a police chief assume leadership in fostering his community's
> sense of responsibility for crime prevention, he must also take the lead in ad-
> dressing broadened social service needs that could, if neglected, produce
> greater crime problems. He must articulate the principles that define the pub-
> lic's involvement, establish processes and structures to ensure appropriate po-
> lice-community collaboration, and recognize both the limits and the possibili-
> ties of that interaction. (Brown, 1985:71)

Sociologist Albert Reiss adds that :

> A central issue in modern policing is the role that police executives and their
> organizations shall have in responding to, and in shaping, social change given
> its ubiquity and accelerating rate. Historically the police served status quo in-
> terests. But, is it possible that conditions are now so altered that the police may
> be regarded as agents of social change in communities? (Reiss, 1985:65)

EXECUTIVE LEADERSHIP IN POLICE ORGANIZATIONS: GENERAL CONCERNS

Executive leadership in police organizations is a matter of urgent concern in American policing. As the chief executive officer of a police agency, the police executive is ultimately responsible for the management and direction of one of the most important of municipal services—the safety of the community. Such a responsibility calls for strong leadership in the midst of often-competing expectations of what the police should do, an aggressive media, political interests, and the interests of rank-and-file police officers.

For the past 30 years or so, crime and fear of crime have been the dominant issues on the domestic agenda. Since the mid-1960s, several government reports have identified crime and the fear of criminal victimization as significant public concerns. From the mid-1960s throughout the early 1980s, reported crime did, in fact, rise in the United States. And, correspondingly, the public's fear of crime also rose. During the 1980s criminal victimization actually declined in many American cities, but the public's fear of crime was unchanged. In fact, people continued to believe that crime was out of control and that they were likely to become crime victims. As Wilson and Kelling (1982) may have been the first to suggest, these fears probably have been based on the frequently inaccurate assumptions that incivility on the streets and neighborhood deterioration are sure indicators of crime and danger.

Fear of violent crime has also risen quite dramatically during the 1990s. The reports of drive-by shootings in urban areas, the nightly newscasts of crime and violence, and the continuous portrayal of "police" and "crime victim" shows in the media have created a public perception of pervasive violent crime. Public concern with actual victimization and the more generalized fear of crime it produces has focused many police chief executives on perceptions of safety as well as on actual risk. In attempting to address issues of crime, police chief executives have come to realize that they must be concerned with the public's fear of crime, as well as with the actual incidence of crime. Whether leading a drug march, addressing a civic group, or designing programs to help victims of crime, it is clear that police executives must help organize and lead businesses and residents toward safer communities (see Davis, 1985).

Today's police executive must also address an equally compelling public concern: Who will police the police? The past decade has witnessed a continual public outcry for greater oversight of policing at all levels of government. Police scandals in recent years have rocked the FBI, state police agencies, and local police. All too often, this outcry has been fueled by events in which police have misused or abused their authority. Police assaults on citizens, corruption scandals, and similar events have continually cast attention on the need for citizen oversight of the police. Public demands for greater police protection against crime and for greater restraint of police powers have, by consequence, occupied much of the police executive's time.

> Few municipal functions are simultaneously as sensitive and as seemingly as insensitive to the citizenry, as routine and as unpredictable, as rule-bound and as discretionary, as supervised by external oversight and as unsupervisable (even invisible) in daily detail as policing. The turbulence of crime and the

Leadership is not always pleasant. Holding badges seized from two of twelve police officers just arrested on corruption charges, New York Police Commissioner William Bratton keeps a stiff upper lip at a press conference.
AP/Wide World.

cloud of fear it spreads over the land, combined with the shrinking social services available to those of few means in a society that has created a public expectation of cradle-to-grave governmental assistance, make policing, in even its smallest details, of enormous interest and concern to the community at large, the news media, and politicians. (Andrews, 1985:5)

Institutional Leadership. Such public concerns place a great burden on police chief executives to assume an institutional leadership role. *Institutional leadership* refers to the leader's role in defining for the organization and for others the role of the organization and for bridging relationships between the organization and its wider environment.[6]

As institutional leaders, police chief executives spend much of their day-to-day activity dealing with individuals and groups external to the police department. As the most visible spokesperson for their police departments, police chief executives, through their public actions, mediate among differing expectations about police services, set the tone for the style of policing a community might receive, and shape public confidence in the safety of persons in their homes and their places of work and play. Police chief executives in most municipalities are often as visible to the public as the mayor, city or town council members, or city managers. This institutional leadership role of the police chief executive has been the least explored and yet is perhaps the most crucial of police executive functions.

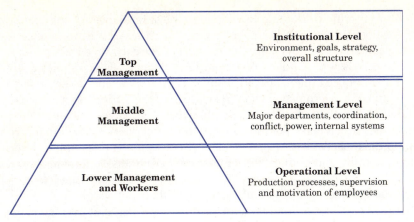

FIGURE 4-6. Levels of Leadership in Police Organizations
Reprinted by permission from Richard J. Daft, Organization Theory and Design,
*3d ed. (St. Paul, Minn.: West, 1989), p. 30. Copyright © 1989 by West Publishing
Co. All rights reserved.*

Internal Leadership. At the same time, police executives have an important
internal leadership role. Here the focus is on "keeping an eye on the store":
monitoring the internal behavior of police officers and the quality and quantity
of services they deliver to the public at large. Given the vast discretion of police officers, and the corresponding problems in exercising that discretion, police executives are continuously reviewing the actions of officers and of the department to ensure that these actions are lawful and publicly acceptable. Too,
police executives must be concerned with the quality of their departments' internal work environments. Officer morale, the availability and quality of
equipment, and the support apparatus for police service delivery are all internal leadership concerns of the police executive. In these circumstances, the police executive is generally exercising leadership at the managerial level within
the police organization (see Figure 4-6).

Leadership at the technical level of police agencies is generally not the
province of the police executive, except perhaps in the smallest of police departments. Technical leadership should be provided by first-line supervisors,
generally corporals and sergeants in today's police departments. All too often,
police executives, as well as the authorities who have appointed them, have
tended to attempt the technical oversight of the police department, while abdi-
cating responsibility for institutional and managerial leadership (see Mayo,
1985; Sherman, 1985). This has often created a crisis in confidence in the leadership abilities of police executives.

Competing external and internal demands for police executive leadership,
then, are at the core of the leadership problems faced within America's police
departments. Too much emphasis on external leadership, for example, may
create the internal perception that the police executive cares little for the workforce. Too much concern for internal leadership issues may create the external
perception that the police agency runs for the convenience of the police and
that the needs of the community are secondary. At times, police executives are
criticized for capitulating to political pressures. At other times, they are criti-

cized for ignoring or defying legitimate political influences or for abandoning their responsibilities to the public at large. Such duality in the police executive's leadership role obviously complicates police executive leadership.

The discussion of police executive leadership is also complicated by the structure of police organizations and by a general reluctance to endorse the police executive's external leadership role. Much of the leadership debate has been clouded by the often-close association between police agencies and military organizations that has resulted in focusing on supervisory oversight and control of subordinate behavior. Also, much less attention to the role of police executive as a community and political leader has emerged in this discussion. As a result, assessments of police leadership have generally been relegated to a debate about the qualities of individual leaders and their impact on "police morale," rather than a full consideration of the methods, theories, and management practices that strengthen police executive leadership. Criticisms based on morale— "Morale is lower now than it has ever been"; "The chief has really hurt the morale of the department with this latest step"—are hard to refute, since it is virtually impossible to systematically measure, or even to define, morale.

Police Leadership and the Military Model of Organization

Today, police organizations often resemble the military, both symbolically and functionally. Police uniforms are military in nature; police policies and procedures often emphasize compliance within the rank-and-authority system by identifying superior and subordinate officers and by including provisions for "conduct unbecoming of an officer," for example; police communications systems are replete with the tactical jargon of the military ("target hardening," "command post," and the like); and police rank systems have completely adopted the names and often the authorities of military rank structure (e.g., sergeant, lieutenant, captain, major, chief). Not only do the ranks resemble the military, but the insignia of these ranks are almost identical; in many police agencies, police chiefs wear four or five stars on their collars, symbolically linking them to their military counterparts, generals.

As Chapter 1 indicated, when Sir Robert Peel formed the Metropolitan Police of London in 1829, the model of organization on which his brainchild was based was that of the military. Military organization—with all the trappings of rank, centralized power, and authority and control—was thought to be an essential element in leading and controlling the police in civil society. And given that the police had the ultimate power to use force in society, such leadership and control were seen as necessary aspects of civilian oversight of law enforcement activities. The military model of strict, top-down leadership, then, was viewed as essential for civil policing in England as well as in the United States.

Military leaders were often characterized as stern, structured, and confident individuals who demanded loyalty and discipline and who would control the reins of power within the military service. In adapting this model to civil policing, the police also adopted the presumption that rank and authority would provide the police with the leadership necessary to direct and control police behavior. That is, having derived their structure and command systems from the military, police organizations often confused leader behavior with rank and assignment.

Formal ranks, with their accompanying authorities and powers, were almost taken *carte blanche* from the military into police work. As will be seen in this chapter, the fit between actual leadership and formal rank is loose at best. Nonetheless, early reformers of the police argued successfully that the police would be best led through a military rank system emphasizing top-down control.

Since the early days of Sir Robert Peel, leaders in policing have assumed their roles by virtue of their rank assignment, as much as by any other method. The rank structure in police organizations has presumed to equate leadership with formal rank in the police agency.

Given this confusion between formal authority and leadership, there has often been a great tension within police organizations between those who are formally charged with leadership responsibilities and those who are not. That is to say, police *leadership* has often been confused with police *rank*. Leaders have been designated not necessarily because they have been uniquely capable of leading but because they have held high ranks. Such thinking tends to ignore the many and varied bases of police leadership or authority.

More important, policing—while resembling the military in a rather symbolic way—is quite distinct from the military both functionally and operationally.[7] While the police wear uniforms, carry firearms, and have rank and insignia systems that resemble those of the military, civil policing differs from military operations in many fundamental ways, each of which complicates police leadership. For example, police officers enjoy considerable operational discretion, largely because they patrol alone or in pairs, without direct supervision. By contrast, military units typically function as teams, squads, or platoons. In such settings, individual discretion is subordinated to the group and is directly supervised by field commanders.

Similarly, civil policing, unlike its military counterparts, is less likely to have a clear definition of mission and objectives, finds it harder—if not impossible—to separate *enemies* from allies, and is governed by a tighter set of constitutional rules and procedures. In a democracy, the *means* of policing is as important as its *ends.* In other words, whether the criminal is brought to justice is no more important than whether this is accomplished within the limits of the Constitution; whether the neighborhood is orderly is no less important than whether police help to achieve order without unreasonably treating people whom some may view as disorderly or as simply undesirable. Such niceties are a far lesser concern for the military.

These and other very real distinctions between civil policing and the military determine the types and success of leadership exercised. The extent to which military leadership styles apply directly to democratic policing is much less direct than has been traditionally assumed. And, in fact, the military has more than recognized that rank alone does not ensure effective leadership. Civil police agencies are learning the same lesson.

LEADERSHIP SKILLS FOR EFFECTIVE MANAGEMENT

Our discussion of the various conceptions of leadership, styles of leadership, and contextual factors shaping leadership in police organizations points to the

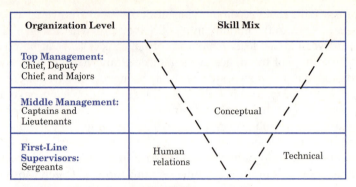

FIGURE 4-7. Police Leadership Skills
From Charles R. Swanson, Leonard Territo, and Robert W. Taylor, Police Administration: Structure, Processes and Behavior (*New York: Macmillan, 1988), p. 169. Adapted by permission of Prentice Hall, Upper Saddle River, N.J.*

fact that leaders must possess several skills in order to be effective. These skills include the ability to envision the police organization and its future, to communicate that vision to those inside and outside the organization, and to understand the work processes necessary to realize the vision of the organization, its clients, and its workforce. Generally speaking, these are considered the conceptual, human relations, and technical skills of managers.

Conceptual and Technical Skills

While it is obvious that all effective managers must possess some of each of these skills, the general argument is that as one moves from the direct technical supervision of the work to be performed, there arises a need to emphasize conceptual over technical skills. At the same time, middle managers must attempt to balance all three skills, often translating the vision of the broad organization into the technical actions of individual workers. The lower in the organization one is, the more important are technical skills. First-line supervisors such as sergeants must be technically proficient to supervise and lead street-level police officers, a skill that is less important to chiefs. Sergeants must also have some human relations skills to encourage teamwork and individual productivity.

Effective leadership, then, is predicated in part on adjusting the "mix" of skills most necessary to the particular organizational level of that leader. To be effective institutional leaders, police executives most often must emphasize conceptual and communication skills in pursuit of their duties. Figure 4-7 shows the mix of skills thought important in any police administrative structure.

LEADERSHIP, MANAGEMENT, AND MOTIVATION

Leadership is a concept closely tied to the idea of individual motivation. Leaders motivate people toward some purposeful end. Organizations, as well as the persons within them, pursue goals and objectives. Individual goals and organizational goals are not always the same. Successful leaders seek to link organizational and individual goals in ways that attempt to satisfy each. Balancing a concern for workers and for production, as outlined in Blake and Mouton's approach to defining managerial and leadership styles, illustrates the need to link individual and organizational goals.

Cooperation

If successful, leaders actually build "systems of cooperation." Such systems of cooperation provide individuals with a sense of identity with and participation in the organization, and at the same time permit them to pursue their own goals. Such cooperative systems generally recognize that collective action can produce results that exceed the contributions made by individuals alone. By cooperating, then, individuals have a stake in greater organizational performance, which, in turn, ultimately makes it possible for them to attain their personal goals.

The literature on management and leadership is replete with mention of cooperation as a central organizational need. Indeed, nearly 60 years ago, Luther Gulick wrote that the "dominance of an idea" within an organization was sufficient for the coordination of work (Gulick, 1937). Gulick recognized that, to the extent that workers shared a common belief, a compelling idea was all that was needed to coordinate work. Religious organizations that draw people into cooperative systems because of their beliefs illustrate Gulick's point, as does much current research on organizational culture and management by values (see, e.g., Ott, 1989) reflect this orientation. In fact, according to Peters and Waterman (1982:279–291), the ability of business organizations to instill a "corporate value system" often distinguishes between successful and less successful businesses:

> Every excellent company we studied is clear on what it stands for, and takes the process of value shaping seriously. In fact, we wonder whether it is possible to be an excellent company without clarity on values and without having the right sorts of values. (Peters and Waterman, 1982:280)

Organizational leaders have come to the realization that they lead complex systems, where human interactions produce customs, beliefs, myths, heros, villains, and a host of other values that guide individual and group behavior. Understanding the *culture* of the organization provides the leader with a deeper understanding of the attachments people have to the organization and to their own goals. As such, this information provides the leader with a deeper understanding of individual motivation.

> Organizations are mini-societies that have their own distinct patterns of culture and sub-culture. Thus one organization may see itself as a tight-knit team or family that believes in working together. Another may be permeated by the idea that "we're the best in the industry and intend to stay that way." Yet another may be highly fragmented, divided into groups that think about the world in very different ways, or that have different aspirations as to what their organization should be. Such patterns of belief or shared meaning, fragmented or integrated, and supported by various operating norms and rituals, can exert a decisive influence on the overall ability of the organization to deal with the challenges it faces. (Morgan, 1986:121)

Theories of Individual Motivation

In 1938 Chester I. Barnard, an AT&T executive and Harvard professor, emphasized the motivational role of leaders as they developed systems of cooperation:

> Executive responsibility, then, is the capacity of leaders by which, reflecting attitudes, ideals, hopes, derived largely from without themselves, they are compelled to bind the wills of men to the accomplishment of purposes beyond their immediate ends, beyond their times. (Barnard, 1968:283)

Individuals and groups are motivated by different things. *Motivational theories* recognize differences among people in terms of their motivation and in the means available to managers to lead people toward the fulfillment of their own and the organization's goals. Many motivational theories focus on the psychological and social-psychological needs of people in a social setting, including those at work. These theories attempt to explain how individual behavior is influenced by internal personal drives, desires, and wants. Such internal drives motivate; they create the need for a person to act in a particular way.

In contrast to the internal personal drive approach, theories emphasizing external factors as shaping individual behavior have also been used to explain motivation. These theories attempt to predict individual motivation from factors external to the person—for example, as stemming from rewards and punishments. Behavior, then, is conditioned through a complex series of reinforcements, some of which discourage certain behaviors while others encourage other behaviors.[8]

Maslow's Hierarchy of Needs.   For years, psychologists have sought to develop a theory of motivation. One of the earliest to develop a general theory of motivation was Abraham Maslow (1943), who theorized that people had a "hierarchy of needs" that defined individual motivational issues. Essentially people seek to satisfy these needs, one at a time, moving from the most basic of needs to others which express personal fulfillment issues. Figure 4-8 diagrams the needs hierarchy as envisioned by Maslow.

Maslow recognized that, in a given group of human beings, a certain percentage seem to be driven by some inner force rather than by a supervisor or a leader. These people seem to do their best even under adverse circumstances. Other individuals tend to react more strongly to conditions surrounding their place in society or their work. Their productivity can be affected by these factors. When times are right and conditions are good, they are highly productive. When things are bad, however, they are demoralized and unproductive.

Maslow's theory of human motivation suggests that individuals proceed to satisfy needs in the following order. First, individuals must take care of their most basic *physiological* needs. Such needs are generally taken to be the starting point in motivational theory. Individuals must satisfy their needs for food and water, shelter, sleep, physical warmth (temperature), and the like. If individuals cannot satisfy these basic needs, they will spend most of their time and psychological energy trying to do so, perhaps to the detriment of the needs of the organization. Exhausted, underfed, tired workers are not easily motivated.

FIGURE 4-8. Maslow's Hierarchy of Needs

Once people have satisfied their basic physiological needs, Maslow suggests they shift their attention (motivation) to satisfying *safety needs.* As Maslow suggests:

> The healthy, normal, fortunate adult in our culture is largely satisfied in his safety needs. The peaceful, smoothly running, "good" society ordinarily makes its members feel safe enough from wild animals, extremes of temperature, criminals, assaults and murder, etc. . . . a safe man no longer feels endangered. (Maslow, 1943:382)

Much of management and organizational leadership practice has focused on people attempting to satisfy their physiological and safety needs as an economic motivational issue. That is, it has generally been argued that wages and benefits are the most significant sources of an individual worker's motivation. And to the extent that workers are attempting to satisfy their psychological and safety needs (e.g., putting food on their tables, having a place to live, and being secure in their homes), economic incentives have been seen as the primary, if not singular, source of employee motivation. The early "production line" envisioned by Frederick Taylor tied workers' wages to the rate of production, under the theory that workers would be motivated to higher levels of production if their economic well-being were directly tied to production.

Maslow recognized that economic motivation alone did not explain individual motivation. Other factors, often beyond the crass "dollars-for-work" formula, were seen as also affecting an individual's motivation to work. *Social needs,* for example, according to Maslow also affect people's motivation. Human beings are social animals. They seek a sense of belonging, an attachment to some other or to a social grouping. For Maslow, humans have a love need. The social attachments that people have in the work-group setting have profound impacts on their lives. While work is considered a "secondary social relationship," as opposed to "primary social relationships" found in the family, much of a person's time is spent in social relationships at work. Such relationships generally result in people forming rather strong social groupings at work. The office coffee break, the relationship that patrol partners have with one another, the bowling league, and other social arrangements attest to the powerful social forces that are present in the workplace. To the extent than an individual is part of the social fabric of the workplace, that person is said to be fulfilling the social needs outlined by Maslow.

Having satisfied social needs, Maslow suggests that the individual will move to satisfy *self-esteem needs,* or those needs identified with self-respect and respect for others. Self-esteem is reflected in the individuals' sense that they are competent and confident in their role and that others recognize and acknowledge their competence and confidence. "Satisfaction of the self-esteem need leads to feelings of self-confidence, worth, strength, capability and adequacy of being useful and necessary in the world" (Maslow, 1943:386).

Finally, at the apex of Maslow's needs hierarchy, individuals seek to satisfy *self-actualization needs,* or those psychological needs to become everything one can possibly become. Self-actualization recognizes that people will strive for self-fulfillment, to reach their potential in their personal and work-related lives. Such motivation suggests that people derive a source of identity from their work, beyond that of simply being competent.

Maslow also proposed that these elements in the hierarchy are not equally influential on the individual at any given time. Instead, as the needs on a lower level are satisfied, the next succeeding level, or *salient,* becomes the next objective until the final level—that of self-actualization—is reached. Further, as the needs on a given level become more satisfied, the needs on the next-highest level grow stronger.

McGregor's Theory X and Theory Y

While Maslow's theory of human motivation seeks to identify the various needs people try to satisfy, other organizational theorists such as Douglas McGregor (1960) built their theories of human motivation on more general systems of human nature. For McGregor, managerial assumptions about human nature dictated much of the style of leadership used by managers. That is, McGregor's analysis starts with a specification of the conventional management practices of the time, as well as the underlying assumptions about workers which were part of that conventional wisdom about management. McGregor conceived of human nature, as well as the appropriate styles of leadership to guide that human behavior, on a behavioral and leadership continuum on which his Theory X and Theory Y represent the extremes.

McGregor's *Theory X* paints a dismal picture of workers and their motivation for work and a stern role for managers—controlling indolent and capricious workers. In contrast, McGregor's *Theory Y* is more optimistic in its definition of workers and their motivation, while casting a role for managers which is supportive rather than controlling. Table 4-3 contrasts McGregor's two models of motivation and associated leadership styles.

The predominant management style throughout recorded history has been

TABLE 4-3. McGregor's Theory X and Theory Y

THEORY X ASSUMPTIONS

1. People inherently dislike work and will avoid it as much as possible.

2. Therefore, most people must be controlled, directed, and threatened in order to produce.

3. People prefer to be directed because they do not like responsibility and want security above all.

THEORY Y ASSUMPTIONS

1. People naturally enjoy work.

2. Most people can exercise self-control and be self-directed if they are motivated to achieve a goal.

3. The average worker not only will accept, but will actively seek, responsibility.

4. The capacity of the average worker is only partially utilized.

consistent with the assumptions of Theory X. As shown in Table 4-3, Theory X assumes that the average human being has an inherent dislike of work and must be closely controlled if adequate productivity is to be achieved. Management's role, then, is to closely oversee the work performed, control worker behavior, and actively intervene in the work process, generally through the use or threat of punishment. After all, this model of motivation assumes that workers are inherently passive and unlikely to willingly participate in activities supporting the goals of the organization.

Theory Y, on the other hand, stresses greater worker participation in the definition and conduct of the work to be performed. Theory Y assumes that human beings will exercise self-direction and self-control to further objectives to which they are committed and, under proper conditions, not only will accept but will seek responsibility. Managers, then, are responsible for creating a climate of trust and support within which motivated workers can produce. In some respects, McGregor's Theory X and Theory Y correspond with the leadership styles in Blake and Mouton's managerial grid, most particularly the authority-obedience and team management styles.

Argyris and Immaturity-Maturity Theory

Industrial relations studies conducted from the early 1930s through the early 1950s concentrated almost entirely on the psychological and social-psychological development of workers in the work setting. Marking what is called the *human relations era* of management and leadership thought, these studies suggested that workers were complex individuals with needs, wants, and desires and that leaders needed to focus on individual and group needs if effective leadership were to be exercised.

TABLE 4-4. Argyris's Immaturity-Maturity Continuum

Childhood ⟶	Adulthood
Bureaucratic Life ⟵	⅃
Dependency on others	Independence of action
Subordinate role	Equal or superordinate role
Restricted time horizon	Broad time horizon
Passive or response behavior	Self-initiated behavior
Little self-awareness	Self-aware
Fleeting and erratic interests	Focused and committed interests
Fixed and role behavior	Flexible and adaptive behavior

Source: Chris Argyris, "The Individual and Organization: Some Problems of Mutual Adjustment," *Administrative Science Quarterly*, 1, 2:1–24 (1957). By permission of *Administrative Science Quarterly*. Copyright © 1957.

Another theme that emerged in the writings of the human relations theorists was that individual and organizational development were at times at cross-purposes. In other words, the organization's needs for obedience, compliance, and internal predictability sometimes conflicted with individual workers' needs for increased self-esteem and self-actualization.

After studying individual personality growth and worker behavior in many industrial settings, Chris Argyris (1957) concluded that in many instances workers were being asked, if not compelled, by organizations to reverse the processes in their lives which led them from being passive, dependent individuals and to become active and independent individuals. Bureaucracies, according to Argyris, were often more comfortable with immature individuals rather than with mature people. Argyris identified a personality development continuum along which a person's degree of maturity could be traced. The personality factors are presented in Table 4-4.

As shown in Table 4-4, individuals develop from immature to mature states across several dimensions. They move from a state of dependence on their environment and others to a state of independence in which they actually affect their environment and others. Mature people are less likely to accept subordinate roles in life; they are socially aware and exercise self-control; and they have diverse behaviors and strong interests and hold longtime perspectives. In short, they grow from infancy to adulthood with all the social and psychological development that these states generally imply.

Bureaucracies, on the other hand, according to Argyris, often seek to make their workers dependent. These organizations would prefer passive, dependent, predictable, and subordinate workers. Moreover, organizational leaders often expect the same subordination of personality growth among people they are charged to lead. In some respects, Argyris raises a question similar to that posed by McGregor's theorizing: Namely, what are the underlying assumptions *and expectations* of individuals in the workplace that guide the actions of leaders?

Herzberg: Dual-Factor Theory

Until the late 1950s, the factors affecting human motivation were seen as hierarchically arranged in a way that either supported or detracted from a person's motivation to work. The work of Maslow, McGregor, and Argyris is illustrative of this approach. In 1959, Frederick Herzberg and his colleagues published their theory that factors that created workers' job satisfaction were different from those that created dissatisfaction. For Herzberg, motivating factors (called *motivators*) were more *intrinsic* to the work performed. That is, Herzberg's findings suggested that people were most positively motivated by the content of the work they performed and by the satisfaction they derived from performing the work. In other words, motivation to do a job well came from liking one's job rather than from liking one's salary.

In contrast to motivators, *hygiene factors* were most associated with the organization and with *extrinsic* conditions surrounding the contexts within which work was performed. Herzberg and his colleagues found that factors associated with the organization itself—most often policies, procedures, supervisor practices, and the like—were much more the source of job dissatisfaction, and hence detracted from individual motivation, than were aspects of the actual work performed.

Ironically, police work itself is most often the only source of motivation for police officers. That is, a "job well done" can be a continuing source of personal motivation. Yet police management, governed by civil service rules and regulations, appears to concentrate little on improving motivators, relying almost entirely on hygiene factors. Unfortunately, many of the hygiene factors that affect police job dissatisfaction either are beyond the direct control of police managers (e.g., salary levels and other conditions of work) or are not thought important to police morale (e.g., policy and procedures).

This situation results in continuous turmoil in the morale of police departments. Without motivators and with little success or interest in changing hygienes, police managers and police personnel struggle daily with work attitudes and motivational issues.

Linking Motivational Theories

The motivational theories of Maslow, McGregor, Argyris, and Herzberg are related on several levels. Maslow's physiological, safety, and social needs are closely associated with Herzberg's hygiene factors in the sense that these needs are generally satisfied through the conditions of employment and the workplace, rather than through the self-esteem and self-actualization needs most reflective of Herzberg's motivators.

Similarly, Argyris's theories of personality development from immaturity to maturity have much in common with McGregor's Theory X and Theory Y. The major factor stimulating those who adhere to Theory X is their perception that workers are so immature that they must be carefully controlled by management. Theory Y holds that the manager interested in productivity is best advised to treat his or her workforce as mature and independent partners in a joint enterprise. In addition, the McGregor and Argyris motivational schema are consistent with those developed by Maslow and Herzberg in that each identifies multiple factors shaping individual motivation and the emphasis in leadership necessary to use that motivation toward organizational and individual goals.

Motivational Theory Applications in Police Organizations

Up to this point, we have discussed organizational behavior generally. What we are concerned with in a text on police administration, of course, is the effect of management on the behavior of a group of individuals organized to do a unique kind of work—policing.

Students of industrial psychology have long known that the productivity of workers can be influenced enormously by the kind of management in the organization. This is particularly true in organizations in which much physical activity and repetitive action are factors in production.

Police work, however, is much different from production-line activity. It typically is carried out by people who work alone or with a single partner, far removed from their supervisors. To a greater degree than in most organizations, the demand for police work is dictated by external factors, like the socioeconomic status of the people in the neighborhoods to which police are assigned, the proclivities of criminals, and even the weather. However, despite the role of the environment in shaping the nature and volume of police business, it is also clear that police officers and police work groups are greatly affected by police management.

As previously discussed, there has always been a close connection between leadership and motivation. Individuals face two important decisions in working: what organization to join and what level of effort to expend within that organization (Simon, 1976). As common sense would suggest, the motivation to join an organization and then to produce within it is affected by the perceived and real leadership of that agency.

Now, as in the past, people join police agencies with a strong sense of social purpose and with the belief that their jobs will be economically secure. Once they become part of the agency, they must conform to the policies and practices as well as the informal norms of the workplace. Through a process of occupational socialization the police recruit learns to become a police officer. The values learned by police recruits in interaction with senior officers more often than not shape the recruits' views of police-citizen interactions, police officer–police administration interactions, and interactions with fellow officers (see, e.g., Bennett and Greenstein, 1975; Van Maanen, 1973).

While officers generally start their careers with positive social values and commitments, they all too often end those same careers cynical and distanced from the communities they serve.

> Policemen generally perceive themselves as performing society's dirty work. As such, a gap is created between the police and the public. Today's patrolman feels cut off from the mainstream culture and unfairly stigmatized. In short, when the policeman dons his uniform, he enters a distinct subculture governed by norms and values designed to manage the strain created by an outsider role in the community. (Van Maanen, 1973:407)

This social distancing of the police from the communities they serve is the consequence of several workplace factors, each of which contributes to what has been called the police officer's *working personality*, and it comes about in a process first described by Skolnick (1966). Essentially, the police officer's working personality is influenced by danger, authority, and efficiency. Danger and authority shape police officers' stance toward police work in that these factors are often external pressures that influence police decision making. That is to say, police officers are ever vigilant in identifying behaviors that (1) pose physical danger to themselves and (2) challenge their authority. These forces shaping the police officer's working personality are generally external to the officers themselves; they are generated through interactions with the community.

Police Stressors

The concern of police administrators and the general public with *efficiency* makes this a factor shaping the police officer's working personality, as well. Police agency concerns with measurable *activity*—arrests, clearance rates, traffic and pedestrian stops, and the like—put pressure on officers to "produce" (see, e.g., Rubinstein, 1973). At the same time, much of what the police do may be perceived by the public as "nonproductive." For example, preventive patrol may give the appearance that the police are simply "riding around." Pressures for production from within the police agency and pressures from outside the department to *look productive* are often a great source of stress for police officers. Such stress obviously affects the officers' motivation to work.

While there is some equivocation about whether police work is the most stressful of occupations, few would disagree that it is stressful. And while many factors influence police officers' stress, those that stem from the police organization and its leadership are most often noted in studies of police stress as being more important than the stressful aspects of the work itself (Gaines and Van Tubergen, 1989; Kroes, 1976; Terry, 1983). Among major sources of police stress stemming from the police organization and police leadership are:

- Lack of administrative support
- Poor equipment
- Inadequate training and career development
- Burdensome policies and procedures
- Lack of opportunity to participate in police policymaking
- Insufficient resources (Crank and Caldero, 1991; Farmer, 1990; Kroes and Hurrell, 1975)

As the theories described above would suggest, managerial style frequently is cited as a major cause of police stress. And while it is more difficult to change the sources of police stress which emanate from the community, effective police leadership can affect internal, organizational sources of stress.

The major criticisms of police leadership style directly reflect the theories discussed above. In adapting the military organizational form to policing, it is frequently charged, police managers adhere to McGregor's Theory X. In addition, it is argued, police management ignores the self-esteem needs described by Maslow. As well, the civil service arena in which police departments typically function is strongly oriented toward what Herzberg called hygiene factors, and it offers few motivators. Finally, at least in their internal administration and relations, police departments seek dependence and passivity in police officers, qualities directly contrary to those most police agencies expect their officers to display in the field. In short, police organizations emphasize the control of police behavior almost to the exclusion of any other values (see Bittner, 1970; Manning, 1977; Klockars, 1985). Such a control focus creates the impression, if not the reality, that police management's (leadership) role is to restrict rather than to facilitate police work.

More specific management and leadership practices within police agencies also cause police stress. Such issues as failure to support line personnel, managerial indifference, and an overreliance on rules and regulations have had debilitating impacts on line-level police officers. Motivation to produce within the police department has been correspondingly affected, causing officers to play it safe, to avoid "making waves," and to diminish their commitment and esprit de corps.

The sources of these leadership problems, according to Herman Goldstein, include personnel systems that seem to work against the goal of identifying and developing managers with the greatest leadership potential. Among the weaknesses of such systems, Goldstein states, are the following:

> *The absence of leadership potential as a criterion in recruit selection.* Given that most police agencies promote from within the department, they typically do not hire police officers with a view toward their leadership potential, once they receive promotions. This severely restricts the "pool" of leadership skills available within police agencies.
>
> *Promotion procedures that do not seek or promote leadership quality.* All too often, police promotional systems rely on assessments of past performance, pencil and paper tests and ability to memorize policies and procedures as the measures of "promotability" within the police agency. Such practices generally fail to identify or reward leadership ability.
>
> *Minimal or no training for new leadership responsibilities.* Police leadership training is at best minimal. Survey after survey has revealed that police agencies typically provide very little leadership training to newly promoted leaders. What training is provided pays little attention to the "dynamics" of leadership, or the situational or contextual factors that shape the exercise of leadership on a day-to-day basis.
>
> *General absence of lateral mobility.* Police organizations, being rank centered, continue to promote leaders from within the agency. At the same time these leaders must "climb-the-ladder" of rank before they assume leadership responsibilities. Unlike industry which has introduced competition for leadership positions by virtue of interviewing and hiring those from outside the particular organization for leadership positions, police departments largely cut off such competition for leadership positions, thereby reducing the impact of leadership within the organization. (Goldstein, 1977:225–226)

Police organizations can learn much from private-sector organizations about leadership. Current proposals to increase police officer discretion in decision making as part of a problem- or community-oriented policing strategy (see Chapter 15) will require that police leaders share power inside and outside

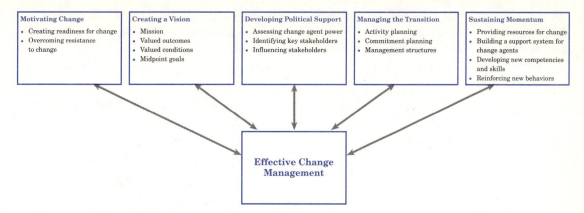

Motivating Change	Creating a Vision	Developing Political Support	Managing the Transition	Sustaining Momentum
• Creating readiness for change • Overcoming resistance to change	• Mission • Valued outcomes • Valued conditions • Midpoint goals	• Assessing change agent power • Identifying key stakeholders • Influencing stakeholders	• Activity planning • Commitment planning • Management structures	• Providing resources for change • Building a support system for change agents • Developing new competencies and skills • Reinforcing new behaviors

Effective Change Management

FIGURE 4-9. Role of Leader in Transformational Change
From Thomas G. Cummings and Edgar F. Huse, Organizational Development and Change, *4th ed. (St. Paul, Minn.: West, 1989), p. 108. Copyright © 1989 by West Publishing Co. All rights reserved.*

the police organization. Such a shift in policing will also require that police leaders help their organizations "transform," in part, by better understanding the motivation of the individuals and groups they lead.

Transformational and Group Leadership in Police Organizations

As previously discussed, leadership in police agency settings has typically been associated with the effort and work of individual police leaders. And while leadership in any organization is most dependent on individual officials' performance, more and more emphasis today has been placed on group leadership processes and the transformation of police agencies from bureaucratic monoliths to reflexive, thinking, and changing organizations.

As police organizations continually change, police chief executives find that they have become *transformational leaders.* Transformational leaders differ from those whose personal style or charisma is what inspires others to follow them. Transformational leaders are focused on change and on how to muster organizational resources to achieve change.

Transformational leaders, then, are institutionally focused. They have a vision of a new institutional order or practice, and they communicate this vision to others within the organization. In framing this vision, they also help others to see the worth of the vision and to recognize their own motivation for change (see, e.g., Seltzer and Bass, 1990; Tichy and Ulrich, 1984). They seek group sponsorship for change activities, and they build teams for changing organizational structures, processes, and cultures. Figure 4-9 depicts the role of the organizational leader in transformational change.

At its most general level, organizational transformation, including the leadership necessary for such transformation, is often triggered by major events in the organization's environment or by significant internal disruptions that threaten the life of the organization. In policing, both specific external events and general pressures from outside often have pushed police agencies toward organizational transformation:

- Miami resident Arthur McDuffie leads the police on a pursuit on his motor- cycle. When apprehended, he is beaten and dies a few days later. The sub- sequent acquittal of the officers who beat him sparks the Liberty City riots.
- The Philadelphia Police Department mounts an assault on a rowhouse oc- cupied by a radical group called MOVE. The assault results in the destruc- tion of two city blocks, the displacement of 200 neighborhood residents, and the death of 11 MOVE members.
- Four Los Angeles police officers are videotaped in the beating of Rodney King, a motorist who had been pursued by the Los Angeles Police Depart- ment and the California Highway Patrol. The acquittal of the police offi- cers sparked one of the worst riots in the U.S. history.
- Televised hearings in New York City indicate that, on a regular basis, offi- cers from several inner-city precincts engage in robbery, drug dealing, and brutality.

Each of these instances resulted in intense public pressure to investigate the police and change the managerial and operational practices of these agen- cies. In each case, the chief of police was replaced, ushering in a "reform" movement—in short, a process for organizational transformation.

Organizational transformation can also be motivated by major paradig- matic shifts in thought and practice that affect any particular organization. This is change by revolution rather than by evolution. In modern-day policing, the "quiet revolution" spoken of by George Kelling (1988)—wherein the Amer- ican police are transforming from a military, top-down, centralized organiza- tion to one emphasizing customers, services, and organizational flexibility—is an illustration in changes in the police paradigm. Community- and problem- oriented policing have profound implications for traditional policing. Table 4-5 shows the types of transformational changes implied by community- and problem-oriented policing in American law enforcement.

Transformational change in organizations, including police departments, is distinguished from other changes by the fact that transformational change is actively pursued by senior-level executives and managers. As Cummings and Huse (1985:419) have indicated, "A key feature of organizational transforma- tion is the active role of senior executives and line managers in all phases of the change process."

POLICE EXECUTIVES AS COMMUNITY LEADERS

Police administrators historically have been admonished to engage the com- munity while at the same time being somewhat distant and aloof from the in- fluences thought ultimately to corrupt police departments. "Politics" and a fear of political corruption, after all, are what led the police to adopt a reform ideology and more stringent administrative practices during the 1930s and throughout the 1950s (see Chapter 1).

TABLE 4-5. **Transformational Changes from Traditional to Community-Based Policing**

FROM	TO
Narrow focus on crime control programs	Broad focus on service to the community
Emphasis on serious crimes	Emphasis on community problem-solving
Reactive approaches	Reactive and proactive approaches
Rapid response to calls for service	Variable response depending on need
Dealing with incidents in a fragmented way	Dealing with broader community issues
Being remote from community, depersonalized	Being connected with community, interactive
Technology-driven	Needs-driven and technology-assisted
Efficient—"doing things right"	Effective—"doing the right things"
Centralized structure	Decentralized structure
Specialization of roles	Generalist and specialist roles
Standardization, uniformity	Flexibility, innovation, diversity
Autocratic style—"command and control"	Participative style—individual responsibility and discretion
Operational management of status quo	Strategic leadership of change
Focus on short-term procedures	Focus on longer-term impact of strategies
Focused patrol officer role—narrow duties	Enhanced patrol officer role—generalist duties
Training emphasis on fitness and defense	Balanced emphasis on defense and community relations
Performance based on "quantity" of arrests, tickets, etc.	Performance based on "quality" of achievements of community goals

Source: Implementing Community Policing: A Workbook for Implementing Change (Ontario, Can.: Ministry of the Solicitor General, 1991). Used by permission of Ministry of the Solicitor General, Ontario, Canada.

Police leadership in regard to community engagement, then, has been a "mixed message" to most police executives. Too much "engagement" has created the fear of too much politics; too little engagement has created the fear that police departments will become unaccountable to the communities they serve. Former Chicago Police Superintendent Richard J. Brzeczek articulates the delicate balance in police executive relationships with political processes:

> The fact that the police chief executive typically is not elected does not, except in the most basic, civics class view of the world, mean that the chief is, or should be, removed from nonpartisan politics—or, unfortunately, that he is exempt from partisan political pressures. The chief would be irresponsible in the extreme to attempt to run the police department without a healthy respect for the needs and preferences of the polis. . . . In attempting to strike a proper balance between the chief's political responsiveness (congruence between the chief's objectives and those of the public and the public's elected representatives), on the one hand, and his professional autonomy from the world of party politics, on the other, what should be the proper lines of authority between the chief and his elected superior(s)? (Brzeczek, 1985:48–49)

Balancing the political pressures shaping any community's demand for police services with the political independence of the police department is a major community leadership challenge for the police executive.

Every police executive is responsible for leadership in two broad areas. He or she must provide leadership within the department and, as the head of the force, must represent it in relations with the administrative head of the jurisdiction and, through the administrative head, with the municipal council and the public. In other words, the chief must provide the leadership on law enforcement issues for the entire community.

Promoting Programs

Promotion of programs aimed at particular community and/or crime issues is one avenue through which the police executive exercises leadership. Programs and objectives that experience the least difficulty are those that are both non-controversial and inexpensive. Few adults would question the police chief's advocacy of educational programs against drug abuse among schoolchildren or the chief's interest in prevention of street crime. The next level of difficulty is the program that has commendable objectives—such as the reduction of armed robberies by increasing the size of the patrol force or the recruitment of officers with high qualifications—but that encounters resistance from the city government and taxpayers because it is too expensive and results in increased taxes through higher payroll costs.

The third level of difficulty may be the program that affects the interests, profits, or convenience of a special group or of the public at large but that is not necessarily expensive. An example of this is the installation of metered parking, which is self-supporting but nevertheless controversial. Finally, of course, the highest level of difficulty is the program that not only has controversial objectives but also is considered too expensive by the people who control the budget.

The police administrator has important responsibilities in winning support for departmental programs, even those of the first level. The chief's task is much easier, of course, when the city administration or legislative body approves the program; he or she then has only to convince the public (and, at times, the members of the department) of its merits.

Part of this leadership responsibility is to provide positive educational information, but some effort must also be expended in addressing outside influences that conflict with the public good. Moreover, in introducing controversial programs, the police should enlist the support of influential groups at the start. An influential citizen or group committed to a policy or plan will not ordinarily oppose it later.

Developing Long-Standing Community Relationships

More important, police leadership is predicated on developing a long-standing relationship between the police department and the civic and business leadership of the community. General community support is based on understanding and on an open and continuing dialogue. Everyone should be kept informed about the nature and purpose of police policies and plans, because those who do not understand will not approve, and those who do not approve are likely to resist and sometimes actively oppose the plan's implementation.

Public understanding, in turn, must be based on facts, and the first step is to disseminate those facts that were used to reach department-level decisions so that they may be used to help others to reach an understanding of the police purpose and method. The facts gathered by the police must also be interpreted by them in order to ensure that correct conclusions are drawn from their consideration. The police likewise have a responsibility to interpret their acts and policies for the public so that all may know the logic and reasoning on which they are based.

At times, the police executive may introduce programs that are not well supported by other governmental decision makers. When this happens, the police executive is faced with the dilemma of what to do if his or her immediate supervisor is not exercising enough leadership or is opposing programs that the chief feels are in the public interest. Such a community leadership role may at times place the police executive in an awkward position: whether to pursue a program that is beneficial to community safety or to defer to the political process that in all likelihood appointed the police executive in the first place. Such a circumstance points to the need for some degree of political independence of the police executive (Andrews, 1985).

While the relationship between the police executive and political leaders is extremely important, police executives find that more and more of their time is being spent with local civic and business leaders, generally in local neighborhood settings. As part of the community policing efforts in many police agencies (described in Chapter 15), police executives are now taking a more active role in shaping the community's understanding of crime and public safety problems and in working with community and business leaders to address those problems.

Raymond C. Davis, who pioneered community-oriented policing when he was chief of the Santa Ana (California) Police Department, suggests several ways that police executives can organize the community for better policing (Davis, 1985). First, he says, police executives can better understand their own departments, the real versus imagined service capabilities, and the demands that the community places on police service. Second, in gathering information from the community, the police executive should be inclusive—gathering information and input from as wide a range of organizations and interests as possible, not just from those who traditionally support the police. Third, the police executive should be careful to tailor programs to specific communities and to their specific needs, avoiding programs that seek uniformity but miss a community's problems altogether. Fourth, the police executive must set the tone for law enforcement within any given community by being actively engaged in the policy debate with community and business leaders. Finally, the police executive should not be bound by traditional definitions of "police problems" but rather should be focused on bringing all the resources of the government to bear on the community's quality of life.

> People problems are community problems and ultimately police problems; the chief must be in the forefront of positive efforts to resolve them. Police crime prevention activities must address the spectrum of problems affecting the quality of life of a community. Overcrowded housing, health problems, traffic problems, summer jobs for youth, and nearly every determinant of public stability can affect the crime rate and the role of the police. Programs dealing with crimes against the elderly, victim assistance programs, youth employment programs, crisis intervention centers, school programs, and juvenile diversion and counseling programs are just some of the activities needing the involvement, aid, and support of the police. (Davis, 1985:93)

Ultimately, the effectiveness of the police executive in the community will hinge on building partnerships with community organizations, civic associations, and business groups and on opening police agencies up to public input and review. Lee P. Brown, former police chief executive officer in Atlanta, Houston, and New York City, has suggested that three principles should guide police executives in their leadership role in the community:

1. The police department must collaborate with the community in planning, operations, and performance evaluation.
2. All segments of the police department must be involved in improving the department's relationship with the community.
3. The police department must share its power with the community. (Brown, 1985:71)

In fulfilling the community leadership role, opening the police agency to civic inspection, sharing power, and transmitting a set of democratic values throughout the police organization, the role of the police executive in community leadership is to act as a "statesman" (Sherman, 1985). Such a role requires the vision to get beyond the day-to-day practicalities of policing; the moral and social responsibility to address social, political, and economic conditions that produce public safety problems as well as the police responses that address those problems; and the candor to shape the values of policing and of democratic governance. Such statesmanlike behavior is the essence of community leadership.

SUMMARY

This chapter has provided an overview of leadership in police organizations. We began with a consideration of the varied ways leadership has been defined and studied. As institutional leaders, police executives should continuously scan the external environment, looking for support and recognizing external forces that pose conflict for the police organization. These executives then translate that external demand and support into organizational goals and objectives, and they communicate these goals and objectives throughout the police organization. As institutional leaders, police executives seek to merge organizational and individual goals by building systems of cooperation both inside and outside the police department.

Initial considerations of leadership as a set of personality traits have generally yielded to more complex discussions of leadership as a process that is as much affected by the context or situations in which it is exercised as it affects those contexts and situations. As noted, discussions of police executive leadership have generally been complicated by the military model on which most police departments are organized and by the rank and command systems within these organizations. Typical discussions of police leadership tend to follow trait-based models of leadership. The situational and contextual models of leadership appear to be less well developed in policing.

Leadership is closely tied to individual and group motivation. Police officers make two important decisions regarding work. First, they choose the organization in which to work. Second, they make decisions about whether or not to produce and what to produce. Police executives are continuously in the process of adjusting their leadership style in light of differing and ever-changing motivations among police officers and police work groups. Understanding motivation provides the police executive with a better likelihood of reaching those to be led. Assumptions about power, authority, responsibility, and capability all undergird the models of leadership behavior and individual motivation. Successful leaders understand those assumptions, treating leadership as a continuously changing and evolving process.

Police executives also have a significant external community leadership role. Police departments have come to realize that the community creates significant pressures for police services and, at the same time, carefully evaluates the quality of those services. Police executives have come to realize that the community has a legitimate role in police policy making. Sharing power with the community is a formidable challenge to the police administrator of the twenty-first century.

In moving to a more dynamic police agency–community interaction, police executives will need to function as transformational leaders. They must help clarify the vision for change within the police department, while at the same time providing support and direction in the department's pursuit of that vision. They must also provide resources and moral support for organizational changes leading police agencies from the traditional approaches of service delivery and neighborhood and business interaction to more of a partnership model, where the police and community and business leaders share in defining public safety problems and in resolving them.

QUESTIONS FOR DISCUSSION

1. What are the different sources of leadership authority, and how are these differing sources of authority accepted by those being led? How do zones of acceptance and zones of indifference affect the acceptance of authority? What other factors affect the acceptance of a particular form of authority?
2. How has the definition of leadership evolved over the years, and how is leadership characterized today? What are the differences in leadership definitions that are trait- and situationally-based?
3. How is leadership defined under the scientific management and human relations approaches to motivation and leadership? What assumptions does each make about the leader and about those following the leader?
4. How has leadership been studied, what is known about good versus bad leadership, and how do these definitions apply to police leaders?
5. What are the major leadership issues confronting police management today, and what roles should police leaders be playing to address those issues? What are the differences and similarities in the police leader's role as institutional and internal leader?

NOTES

1. An excellent discussion of the development of the concept of leadership is found in Smith and Peterson (1988:1–14).
2. Among many fine reviews of leadership theory and practice are C. I. Barnard, *The Functions of the Executive* (1968); H. A. Simon, *Administrative Behavior* (1976); and Bennis and Nanus, *Leaders: The Strategies for Taking Charge* (1985).
3. For a good general overview of the history of management thought, see C. S. George, Jr., *The History of Management Thought* (1972).
4. There have been many works devoted to the "great man" approach to defining leadership. Most are tied to evolving theories of managerial social Darwinism emerging during the Industrial Revolution. For example, see Richard Hofstadter, *Social Darwinism in American Thought, 1900–1915* (1945); Robert S. McClosky, *American Conservatism in the Age of Enterprise* (1951); Reinhard Bendix, *Work and Authority in Industry* (1956), particularly chaps. 2 and 4; and Melville Dalton, *Men Who Manage* (1959).
5. Laissez-faire leadership, in which the leader leaves subordinates to their own devices, has generally been shown to be ineffective in all settings except those involving highly trained professionals working in very specialized areas.
6. For a brief review of the various levels of organizational leadership necessary in complex organizations, see Parsons (1960) and Thompson (1967).
7. Discussions of the "myth" of the military model as applied to civil policing are included in Bittner (1970) and Skolnick and Fyfe (1993).

8. The idea of conditioned behavior is perhaps best elaborated in B. F. Skinner's classic *Beyond Freedom and Dignity* (1971).

SOURCES

ANDREWS, ALLEN H., JR. "Structuring the Political Independence of the Police Chief," pp. 5–19 in William A. Geller (ed.), *Police Leadership in America* (New York: Praeger, 1985).

ARGYRIS, CHRIS. *Personality and Organization* (New York: Harper & Row, 1957).

BARNARD, CHESTER I. *The Functions of the Executive,* 13th Anniversary ed., (Cambridge, Mass.: Harvard University Press, 1968).

BASS, B. M. (ed.). *Stogdill's Handbook of Leadership* (New York: Free Press, 1981).

BENDIX, REINHARD. *Work and Authority in Industry* (Berkeley: University of California Press, 1956).

BENNETT, RICHARD R., and THEODORE GREENSTEIN. "The Police Personality: A Test of the Predispositional Model," *Journal of Police Science and Administration,* 3:439–445 (1975).

BENNIS, WARREN G., and B. NANUS. *Leaders: The Strategies for Taking Charge* (New York: Harper & Row, 1985).

BITTNER, EGON. *The Functions of Police in Modern Society* (Rockville, Md.: National Institute of Mental Health, 1970).

BLAKE, ROBERT R., and ANNE ADAMS MCCANSE. *Leadership Dilemmas—Grid Solutions* (Houston: Gulf Publishing, 1991).

BLAKE, ROBERT R., and JANE S. MOUTON. *The Managerial Grid* (Houston: Gulf Publishing, 1964).

BROWN, LEE P. "Police-Community Power Sharing," pp. 70–85 in William A. Geller (ed.), *Police Leadership in America* (New York: Praeger, 1985).

BRZECZEK, RICHARD J. "Chief-Mayor Relations: The View from the Chief's Chair," pp. 48–55 in William A. Geller (ed.), *Police Leadership in America* (New York: Praeger, 1985).

COHEN, BERNARD. "Leadership Styles of Commanders in the New York City Police Department," *Journal of Police Science and Administration,* 8:125–138 (1980).

CRANK, JOHN P., and M. CALDERO. "The Production of Occupational Stress in Medium-Sized Police Agencies: A Survey of Line Officers in Eight Municipal Departments," *Journal of Criminal Justice,* 19:339–349 (1991).

CUMMINGS, T. G., and E. F. HUSE. *Organization Development and Change,* 4th ed. (St. Paul, Minn.: West, 1985).

DALTON, MELVILLE. *Men Who Manage* (New York: Wiley, 1959).

DAVIS, RAYMOND C. "Organizing the Community for Improved Policing," pp. 84–95 in William A. Geller (ed.), *Police Leadership in America* (New York: Praeger, 1985).

FARMER, RICHARD E. "Clinical and Managerial Implications of Stress Research on the Police," *Journal of Police Science and Administration,* 17:105–218 (1990).

FIELDER, F. E. *A Contingency Theory of Leadership Effectiveness* (New York: McGraw-Hill, 1967).

FRENCH, J. R. B. P., and B. RAVEN. "The Bases of Social Power," pp. 150–167 in D. Cartwright (ed.), *Studies in Social Power* (Ann Arbor, Mich.: Institute for Social Research, 1959).

GAINES, LARRY K., and N. VAN TUBERGEN. "Job Stress in Police Work: An Exploratory Analysis into Structural Causes," *American Journal of Criminal Justice,* 13:197–214 (1989).

GEORGE, C. S., JR. *The History of Management Thought,* 2d ed. (Englewood Cliffs, N.J.: Prentice-Hall, 1972).

GOLDSTEIN, HERMAN. *Policing a Free Society* (Cambridge, Mass.: Ballinger, 1977).

GULICK, LUTHER. "Notes on the Theory of Organization," in Luther Gulick and L. Urwick (eds.), *Papers on the Science of Administration* (New York: Institute of Public Administration, 1937).

HERSHEY, P., and K. H. BLANCHARD. *Management of Organizational Behavior: Utilizing Human Resources,* 3d ed. (Englewood Cliffs, N.J.: Prentice-Hall, 1977).

HERZBERG, FREDERICK, B. MAUSNER, and B. SNYDERMAN. *The Motivation to Work* (New York: Wiley, 1959).

HOFSTADTER, RICHARD. *Social Darwinism in American Thought, 1900–1915* (Philadelphia: University of Pennsylvania Press, 1945).

HOUSE, R. J., and T. R. MITCHELL. "Path-Goal Theory of Leadership," in K. N. Wexley and G. A. Yukl (eds.), *Organizational Behavior and Industrial Psychology* (New York: Oxford University Press, 1975).

KELLING, GEORGE L. "Police and Communities: The Quiet Revolution," *Perspectives on Policing,* 1:1–8 (June 1988).

KLOCKARS, CARL B. *The Idea of Police* (Beverly Hills, Calif.: Sage, 1985).

KROES, WILLIAM H. *Society's Victim, the Policeman: An Analysis of Job Stress in Policing* (Springfield, Ill.: Thomas, 1976).

———, and J. J. HURRELL, JR. (eds.), *Job Stress and the Police Officer: Identifying Stress Reduction Techniques* (Washington, D.C.: U.S. Department of Health, Education, and Welfare, 1975).

KUYKENDALL, JACK. "Police Leadership: An Analysis of Executive Styles," *Criminal Justice Review,* 2:89–102 (1977).

———. "The Grid Styles of Police Managers," *American Journal of Police,* 4:38–70 (1985).

LANGWORTHY, ROBERT H. *The Structure of Police Organizations* (New York: Praeger, 1986).

LEWIN, KURT, R. LIPPITT, and R. K. WHITE. "Patterns of Aggressive Behavior in Experimentally Created Social Climates," *Journal of Social Psychology,* 10:271–299 (1939).

LIKERT, RENSIS. *New Patterns of Management* (New York: McGraw-Hill, 1961).

MACHIAVELLI, NICCOLO. *The Discourses* (New York: Random House, 1950).

———. *The Prince* (New York: Random House, 1950).

MANNING, PETER K. *Police Work: The Social Organization of Policing* (Cambridge, Mass.: M.I.T. Press, 1977).

MASLOW, ABRAHAM H. "A Theory of Human Motivation," *Psychological Review,* 50:370–396 (1943).

MAYO, LOUIS A. "Leading Blindly: An Assessment of Chiefs' Information about Police Operations," pp. 397–417 in William A. Geller (ed.), *Police Leadership in America* (New York: Praeger, 1985).

MCCLOSKY, ROBERT S. *American Conservatism in the Age of Enterprise* (Cambridge, Mass.: Harvard University Press, 1951).

MCGREGOR, DOUGLAS M. *The Human Side of Enterprise* (New York: McGraw-Hill, 1960).

MORGAN, G. *Images of Organization* (Newbury Park, Calif.: Sage, 1986).

———. *Imaginization: The Art of Creative Management* (Newbury Park, Calif.: Sage, 1993).

OTT, S. *The Organizational Culture Perspective* (Pacific Grove, Calif.: Brooks/Cole, 1989).

PARSONS, TALCOTT. *Structure and Process in Modern Societies* (New York: Free Press, 1960).

PERROW, CHARLES. *Complex Organizations: A Critical Essay* (New York: Random House, 1986).

PETERS, T. J., and R. H. WATERMAN, JR. *In Search of Excellence: Lessons from America's Best-Run Corporations* (New York: Warner Books, 1982).

PURSLEY, ROBERT D. "Leadership and Community Identification: Attitudes among Two Categories of Police Chiefs," *Journal of Police Science and Administration,* 2:414–422 (1974).

REISS, ALBERT J., JR. "Shaping and Serving the Community: The Role of the Police Chief Executive," pp. 61–69 in William A. Geller (ed.), *Police Leadership in America* (New York: Praeger, 1985).

REUSS-IANNI, ELIZABETH. *Two Cultures of Policing: Street Cops and Management Cops* (New Brunswick, N.J.: Transaction Books, 1983).

ROETHLISBERGER, F. J., and W. J. DIXON. *Management and the Worker* (Cambridge, Mass.: Harvard University Press, 1939).

RUBINSTEIN, JONATHAN. *City Police* (New York: Farrar, Straus and Giroux, 1973).

SELTZER, J., and B. M. BASS. "Transformational Leadership: Beyond Initiation and Consideration," *Journal of Management,* 16:693–703 (1990).

SHERMAN, LAWRENCE W. "The Police Executive as Statesman," pp. 459–466 in William A. Geller (ed.), *Police Leadership in America* (New York: Praeger, 1985).

SIMON, HERBERT A. *Administrative Behavior*, 3d ed. (New York: Free Press, 1976).

SKINNER, B. F. *Beyond Freedom and Dignity* (New York: Knopf, 1971).

SKOLNICK, JEROME H. *Justice without Trial* (New York: Macmillan, 1966).

———, and DAVID H. BAYLEY. *The New Blue Line* (New York: Free Press, 1986).

———, and JAMES J. FYFE. *Above the Law: Police and the Excessive Use of Force* (New York: Free Press, 1993).

SMITH, P. B., and M. F. PETERSON. *Leadership, Organizations and Culture* (Newbury Park, Calif.: Sage, 1988).

STOGDILL, R. M., and A. E. COONS. *Leader Behavior: Its Description and Measurement* (Columbus: Ohio State University, Bureau of Business Research, 1957).

SWANSON, CHARLES, and LEONARD TERRITO. "Police Leadership and Communication Styles," in Jack R. Greene (ed.), *Police and Police Work* (Beverly Hills, Calif.: Sage, 1982).

TANNENBAUM, R., and SCHMIDT, W. H. "How to Choose a Leadership Pattern," *Harvard Business Review,* 162–180 (May–June 1973).

TAYLOR, FREDERICK W. *Principles of Scientific Management* (New York: Harper and Bros., 1911).

TERRY, W. CLINTON. "Police Stress as an Individual and Administrative Problem: Some Conceptual and Theoretical Difficulties," *Journal of Police Science and Administration,* 11:156–165 (1983).

THOMPSON, J. D. *Organizations in Action* (New York: McGraw-Hill, 1967).

TICHY, N. M., and D. O. ULRICH. "The Leadership Challenge: A Call for the Transformational Leader," *Sloan Management Review,* 26:59–64 (Fall 1984).

VAN MAANEN, JOHN. "Observations on the Making of Policemen," *Human Organization,* 32:407–418 (1973).

VROOM, V. H. *Work and Motivation* (New York: Wiley, 1964).

WEBER, MAX. *The Social and Economic Theory of Organizations* (London: Oxford University Press, 1947).

———. *The Theory of Social and Economic Organization,* A. M. Henderson and T. Parsons (eds. and trans.) (New York: Macmillan, 1975).

WILSON, JAMES Q. *Varieties of Police Behavior: The Management of Law and Order in Eight American Cities* (Cambridge, Mass.: Harvard University Press, 1978).

———, and GEORGE L. KELLING. "Broken Windows: The Police and Neighborhood Safety," *Atlantic Monthly,* 249:29–38 (March 1982).

YUKL, G. A. *Leadership in Organizations* (Englewood Cliffs, N.J.: Prentice-Hall, 1981).

5

The Police Chief Executive as Administrator: Theory, Practice, and Strategies

KEY WORDS AND PHRASES

Science and art of administration
Bureaucracy
Division of labor
Management by values
Hierarchy of authority
Span of control
Level of organizational analysis
Open versus closed system
Boundary spanning
Organizational complexity
Impersonal authority

POSDCORB
Mechanistic vs. organic organizations
Organizational environment
Images of organization
Strategic management (process and elements)
Organizational technology
Organizational complexity
Management by objectives
Total quality management

Chapter 4 examined the role of the police executive as an institutional leader—charged with creating the internal organizational climate for productive work, while at the same time creating an external climate that supports and critiques the efforts of the local police. An important role for the police executive, then, is to link the internal police production process with the external demand for police services. This is generally accomplished through the establishment of an administrative regime—a policy, procedure, and decisional structure to guide organizational actions.

The police executive's role as administrator is essential for the efficient and effective management and operations of police organizations. The executive sets the internal tone or style of the police organization as well as the style of policing in any particular community. The selection of a police chief can be one of the most important decisions a community makes; that person must help translate the community's wants, desires, and concerns into the actions of police officers which ultimately affect the level of safety and civility in a community.

Today's police chief executive must manage the often-conflicting expectations of police performance, and do it within tightly defined fiscal constraints and within the cautious and watchful eye of the public and the news media. The police executive's administrative ability ultimately shapes the police organization internally, while at the same time shaping external support and respect for the police.

Given that police expenditures account for a large portion of any city's budget, the efficient and effective management of police organizations is high on the agenda of local mayors, city councils, and city managers. In fulfilling an administrative role, the police executive must apply the best practices of management to the day-to-day challenges of police work. As such, the police chief executive must apply both the art and the science of administration. These are the subjects of this chapter.

This chapter considers the administrative role of the police chief executive. It begins with a study of elements common to all organizations, followed by a consideration of the principles of management that are thought to create a science of administration. This discussion is followed by an examination of several tools available to administrators, as well as the managerial roles of administrators, including police executives. Finally, the chapter concludes with a brief discussion of several critical issues confronting police managers.

THE SCIENCE AND ART OF ADMINISTRATION

When we think of police administration, we think of policy and procedure and the internal management structures and practices that develop, support, interpret, and enforce those policies and procedures. The central role of the police executive as administrator is to create an organizational climate and structure that provide police and civilian personnel with a clear sense of what they are to achieve and how they can achieve it. Simply put, the police executive as administrator is charged with the responsibility to create an organizational order that supports department members, monitors activities, and judges results.

Administrative and managerial practice has come a long way over the past few centuries. Central to nearly all managerial writing and thought is the need for order, control, feedback, and measurement. Police administrators should seek to provide such order, control, feedback, and measurement in ways that facilitate the provision of police services.

It is often argued that administration, including police administration, is a *science*. That is, it has been suggested that successful administrators practice *principles of administration* gleaned from several scientific and practical observations of administrative behavior. Once applying these principles, police administrators can take some confidence that their organizations will function efficiently and effectively. This science of administration is quantitative, structured, and precise. Much of its emphasis comes from the traditional theories of organization and administration.

On the other hand, administration has also been described as an *art*, implying that effective administrators are born, not taught, and that individual personality and intellectual capacities explain effective administration far more fully than do scientific principles. Here the police administrator is asked to interpret and understand the complex meaning of the organization and its members and to craft programs to help channel the efforts of all toward a clearly defined organizational mission. The *art of administration*, then, is interpretive, qualitative, and ongoing. Much of the emphasis on this art comes from the human relations and contingency theories of organizational leadership discussed in Chapter 4.

Clearly, both positions have merit—administration requires the rigor of systematic application, mediated by an intuitive understanding of work, work groups, and the needs of the organization. The successful administrator knows how to organize, coordinate, and facilitate work and the organization's objectives. At the same time, the successful administrator must temper the techniques of administration with an understanding and appreciation for the *human enterprise*—meaning that all work is accomplished through people, who themselves have goals and objectives.

WHY DO WE NEED ORGANIZATIONS AND ADMINISTRATION?

Any discussion about the science and art of administration should, of necessity, ask: "Why do we need organizations and administration, anyway?" There are several answers to this question, the most important of which emphasize that formal organizations need to coordinate work by means that are generally external to their members—by some form of authority structure, a division of labor, and a system of rules, regulations, and compliance.

Organizations as Formal Social Systems

The word "organization" refers to a group of people engaged in activities to achieve a goal or mission. Most human activity involves some form of organization. Many of our human associations, however, are informal and voluntary. Under these circumstances, individuals tend to guide and orient their behavior toward others through some form of mutual adjustment. Such ongoing adjustment allows the social organization to maintain stability and purpose. Family organizations are good illustrations of the social organization, mutual adjustment system. They continuously define and redefine relations among participants, and they are guided by a general understanding of purpose.

Formal organizations, by contrast, are defined as those organizations that are "formally established for the explicit purpose of achieving certain goals" (Blau and Scott, 1962:4). Typical descriptions of formal organizations also include ideas about specialization, size, the complexity of activities pursued by the organization, and the environment in which the organization finds itself.

Formal organizations, also called bureaucracies, are seen as rather stable social institutions in that they typically go on even when personnel come and go. Historically, as societies became more complex, such organizational stability gave formal organizations a greater chance of accomplishing their missions. They were less dependent on the individual personalities of their leaders; they had an ongoing definition of purpose and activity; and, perhaps most important, they had developed a system of transferring leadership from one person to another.

Formal organizations are seen as a necessary component in modern society. They provide social system stability, they help organize society as it grows more complex, and they ensure that specific goals and objectives will be accomplished.

Because formal organizations are created to achieve specified missions and objectives, and because they need to structure the work activities of those who join them, the need for administration arises. That is, as organizations become formalized, so too does their administrative apparatus. Whereas in the family administration is generally left to the parent(s) or elders, in formal organizations administration and management are generally the responsibility of an administrative group.

Division of Labor and Coordination of Work

The need for administration, a central component in formal organizations, is best understood within the context of two important issues confronting formal organizations. The first is related to the division of labor in organizations, and the second is related to the coordination of work, if labor is to be divided.

The Division of Labor: Organizational Specialization. The *division of labor*, or specialization, in organizations refers to the range of tasks that any employee performs. When employees perform many tasks, specialization is low; when employees perform but a few tasks, specialization is high. The degree of specialization in any organization is influenced by many factors. The skills of the workers, the type of technology available to the organization, the constancy of demand for a particular product, the size of the organization, and the clarity of methods to achieve organizational objectives all influence the level of specialization.

Little agreement exists about the optimal degree of specialization in modern organizations, yet it is clear that modern organizations have become increasingly more specialized. This is, in part, due to the complexity of information that organizations seek to use and the number and complexity of functions they seek to perform. It is often also due to the size of the organization.

In most modern organizations, including those of the police, specialization tends to be rather high. Police departments have not only detectives and patrol officers but also juvenile, homicide, major crimes, and sexual violence detectives, as well as traffic, foot, tactical, and motor patrol officers. Even police agencies are specialized—the Federal Bureau of Investigation, the U.S. Border Patrol, the police functions within the U.S. Departments of the Treasury and Customs, state police agencies, county sheriffs, and even private security agencies all specialize in some form of police work or another.

Increased specialization generally requires the coordination of specialties to ensure that the overall goals of the organization are met—hence, the need for some method to manage or coordinate work. As organizations become specialized, those pursuing specialized functions may fail to see the broader goals and objectives of the organization. This is called *suboptimization*, meaning that the subgoals (specialties) of the organizations appear to be more important than the overall goals of the organization.

In policing, investigators may come to define the police organization in terms of investigations, while patrol officers may define the organization according to patrol functions. But, in reality, both functions (investigations and patrol) are important to the accomplishment of the police department's overall missions—the protection of life, rights, and property and the investigation of crime. In formal organizations with specialization, the coordination of specialties through some form of administrative process is a necessary element in ensuring that the broadest goals of the organization will be pursued and accomplished.

Students of organizational behavior have also recognized that specialization can produce efficiencies in the work process as well as increased effectiveness and greater impact on what is produced. To achieve such efficiencies and effectiveness, however, organizations must coordinate specialties. In police organizations rapid response and follow-up criminal investigations benefit from some specialization; patrol officers and detectives develop experience in handling different aspects of work in the police department. Still, detective and patrol officer functions need to be coordinated so that they complement rather than compete with one another. This is usually accomplished by having an administrative unit, like an office of operations, oversee both of these police functions.

Formal organizations, then, often spawn specialization through the division of labor. This division of labor in turn requires some administrative or coordinative process to ensure that the needs of the specialist do not overshadow the needs of the organization as a whole.

Moreover, when formal organizations take on any size at all, their ability to internally communicate requires some coordinative mechanism as well. Chester Barnard referred to organizations as systems of cooperation, but he acknowledged that "under most ordinary conditions, even with simple purposes, not many men can see what each is doing or the whole situation; nor can many communicate essential information regarding or governing specific action . . . " (Barnard, 1968:106). The division of labor in formal organization, then, creates other problems, such as communications and goal problems, for the organization. These problems are thought to be resolved through an administrative structure that increases the capacity of the organization to manage more complex communication and to keep an eye on the larger goals of the organization.

Coordination of Work in Formal Organizations. If the division of labor increases the need to coordinate work, how should this coordination be accomplished? In a discussion about administrative practice, Luther Gulick (1937), an early student of administrative behavior, asked a simple yet fundamental question about the need for coordinating work (administration): "How might work be coordinated?" Gulick answered that work could be coordinated in one of two ways, either (1) by the dominance of an idea or (2) by the creation of a system of authority to oversee and otherwise coordinate the enterprise.

If people were guided by a single idea, workers would "know" what was expected of them and would coordinate their efforts toward a shared goal. There would be little need for another method of coordinating the work, and there would be little need for administration. Today this is called *management by values*, or *mission-driven government*.[1] It emphasizes the reduction of rules, regulations, and procedures while increasing the visibility of the organization's mission and values as tools to guide individual and group behavior.

At the time of Gulick's writing (1937), he saw an ever-more complex world within which the dominance of an idea alone seemed unlikely as a significant method for coordinating work. Gulick argued that the scope and complexity of formal organizations would reduce the ability of a salient idea to coordinate activity.

Even today, in policing, for example, what constitutes public safety might have a wide interpretation both within and outside the police organization. Such variation in interpretation might lead one group to pursue a different meaning of public safety than another. Much of the discussion surrounding community policing, for example, is in clarifying its meaning so that it might become a guide for police behavior (see Greene, 1989; Greene and Mastrofski, 1988).

Given that many organizations employ many specialists, it is not clear that a single dominant idea could emerge within such organizations. Who, for example, should define police work—detectives or police officers?

Lacking such a shared goal, Gulick suggested that some *hierarchy of authority* would be needed "so that the work may be coordinated by orders of superiors to subordinates, reaching from the top to the bottom of the entire enterprise" (Gulick, 1937:6). This hierarchy of authority, or what the police refer to as the "chain of command," has become the most dominant method within complex organizations for coordinating work, although there is little agreement about what the optimal hierarchy of authority might be. Figure 5-1 presents the hierarchy of authority for the Philadelphia and Los Angeles police departments, two of the largest departments in the United States.

The idea of a hierarchy of authority to better coordinate work is related to another organizational concept referred to as the *span of control*, or the number of subordinates reporting to any one supervisor. Where hierarchy of authority defines the "tallness" or "squatness" of an organization, the span of control defines its breadth. The optimal span of control has been an elusive figure, although conventional wisdom often suggests a range of from five to seven subordinates reporting to any one supervisor.

The span of control in any organization depends on at least two major factors: (1) the complexity or criticality of the task to be performed and (2) the preparation and skills of those performing these tasks. Where the tasks to be performed are not too complex or critical and the skills of the workers are good, the span of control can be rather broad. Where the tasks to be performed are complex and/or critical and the skills of the workers are moderate or low,

FIGURE 5-1. Los Angeles/Philadelphia Police Department Organizational Charts
From the Los Angeles Police Department and the Philadelphia Police Department (May 1994).

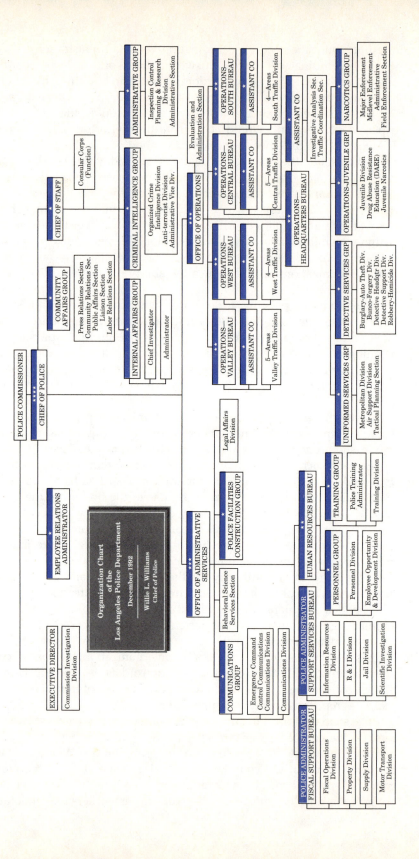

Philadelphia

Police Commissioner

Legal Counsel

Executive Officer

Public Affairs

D/C Operations

C.I.B.

D/C Administration & Training

D/C Special Operations

Research & Planning Unit

Management Services Bureau

Strategic Planning Bureau

Human Resources Bureau

Personnel
E.A.P.
E.E.O.

Supplemental Police Services Bureau

Special Patrol Bureau

Tactical Division

Park Division

Traffic Division
A.I.D.
Transit Unit
Traffic District
Taxi Unit
School Crossing Guards

Highway Patrol
A.C.T. Unit
Mounted

Stakeout Unit
Airport District
Canine Unit
Tactical Response Unit

Emergency Management Bureau

Operations Bureau North

East Police Division
North Police Division
Northeast Police Division
Northwest Police Division

East Detectives
North Detectives
Northeast Detectives

Operations Bureau South

South Detectives
Southwest Detectives
Central Detectives
North Central Detectives

South Police Division
Southwest Police Division
Central Police Division
North Central Police Division
West Police Division

Civil Affairs Bureau
Civil Affairs Division
Civil Affairs Unit
Conflict Prevention & Resolution

Emergency Response Bureau
Emergency Response Division
Ordnance Disposal
Marine Unit
Sanitation Unit

Detective Bureaus

Headquarters Division
Major Crimes

Homicide Division
Juvenile Aid Division
Sex Crimes

Headquarters Investigation Division
Mayor's Security
Organized Crime & Intelligence

Headquarters Investigation Unit
Criminal Investigations
Dignitary Protection
Background Section

Administration Bureau
Building Maintenance
Safety Director
Administrative Analysis
Automotive Services Division
Finance

Information Systems Bureau
Director Technical Services
P.C. Support
Information Systems Division
Data Processing
Project Management

Department Advocates
Special Investigation Bureau
Integrity Control Officer
Special Operations Division
City Wide Vice

Narcotics Strike Force
Strike Force Unit
Narcotics Offender Processing
Narcotics Field Units
Narcotics Response Unit
Divisional Squads
Juvenile Enforcement Teams

Narcotics Unit
Forfeiture Section
DEA Task Force
Organized Drug Gang Task Force
Special Investigations Narcotics
BNI Task Force

Internal Investigations Bureau
Ethics Accountability Division
Internal Affairs Division
Surveillance Unit
Police Shooting Team
Special Project Drug Screening
City Solicitor Liaison

Community Relations Bureau
Community Relations Division
Police Recruitment
Police Athletic League
Community Relations Unit

Communications Bureau
Documents Processing
Reports Control
Permits and Licenses
Graphic Arts Unit
Print Room
Police Radio
Mobile Communications
D.P.R.
Mail Room

Training Bureau
Advanced Training Division
Advanced Training
External Training
Recruit Training Division
Recruit Training
Educational Psychologist

Staff Services Bureau

Scientific Services Division
Laboratory Services
Criminalistic Laboratory
Chemistry Laboratory
Special Services
Mobile Crime Unit
Polygraph Unit
Questioned Documents
Firearms Identification Unit

Field Support Division
Offender Processing
Building Security Unit
Criminal Records Unit
Detention Unit
Identification Unit
CCTV

Court Evidence
Audio Visual
Traffic Court Unit
Evidence Unit
Court Liaison

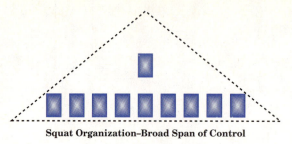 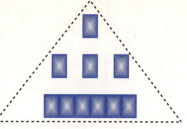

Squat Organization–Broad Span of Control   **Tall Organization–Narrow Span of Control**

FIGURE 5-2.   Span of Control and Organization Structure

then the span of control would be expected to narrow. Figure 5-2 presents a depiction of the relationship between span of control and hierarchy of authority.

Formal organizations with their corresponding complexity and division of labor produce a need for coordination of work. Such coordination is generally reflected in what we call administration. The basic methods of administration have been the creation of a system (hierarchy) of authority with a mediating span of control.

In addition to the hierarchy of authority and span of control, formal organizations, like their informal counterparts, are composed of common elements. Successful administrators understand these organizational elements and use them in constantly designing and refining their organization.

ELEMENTS COMMON TO ALL ORGANIZATIONS

Organizations are first and foremost social entities. As social beings, people are born into, affiliate with, and work in organizations. Much of modern life is experienced through some type of social organizational grouping. Whether the organization be a family, a community, a club or association we might join, or an organization we work in, there are common elements to all forms of social organizations.

Patterns of Interaction and Social Meaning in Organizations

All social organizations have goals, members, roles, a shared language, shared values, a system of authority, some division of labor, and some system to ensure group identity and compliance or conformity with group expectations. More important, the idea of social organizations:

> . . . refers to the ways in which human conduct becomes socially organized, that is, to the observed regularities in the behavior of people that are due to the social conditions in which they find themselves rather than to their physiological or psychological characteristics as individuals. (Blau and Scott, 1962:2)

Members enter familial organizations through birth; they are generally assigned some role in the family authority system (e.g., daughter, son, elder);

142

they generally have some level of authority attached to their assigned role (e.g., father, mother, or child); they share a common family language and value system that is learned; and there is generally some system for punishment and reward. While there are no policy and procedure manuals within most families, rules are generally understood and enforced through some sanction system.

Similarly, in more formal, work-based organizations, policies and procedures govern much of organizational life, creating social conditions that influence the individual's behavior and attachment to the organization. It is the social organization, more than the individual's characteristics, that shapes beliefs and behavior in organizational settings. Social organizations create the context or conditions for social interactions and for the meanings people attach to these interactions.

> The many social conditions that influence the conduct of people can be divided into two main types, which constitute the two basic aspects of social organizations: (1) the structure of social relations in a group or larger collectivity of people, and (2) the shared beliefs and orientations that unite members of the collectivity and guide their conduct. (Blau and Scott, 1962:2)

Social relations within organizations can be seen even by the casual observer. The regular and frequent interactions among people in social settings provide some clue to the existence of a social organization. These patterns of regular behavior tell us much about status, authority, and specialization within the organization.

But interactions alone do not create a bond among people in a social organization. Rather, the sentiments that people attach to their interactions with others and the shared beliefs that emerge through these interactions significantly define the social structure and culture of the organization.

Social organizations, then, are characterized by a frequent and regularized pattern of interaction which is observable within the organization, supported by a belief and value system that conditions the meanings people attach to organizational life as well as their participation within the organizational setting. Interaction provides a sense of structure, while beliefs provide a sense of shared meaning or culture.

Levels of Analysis in Complex Organizations[2]

Organizations are complex phenomena. They involve individuals, groups, and groups of groups. All too often when we speak of organizations, or of organizational theories, we fail to identify which level of analysis we are applying.

Individuals are the basic building blocks of the organization. Herbert Simon and James March (1958) suggest that individuals make two important decisions regarding their participation in organizational settings. The first is whether or not to join the organization, and the second is whether or not to produce. Such individual-level decision making is generally the province of psychology. Maslow's hierarchy of needs (Chapter 4) illustrates this approach.

Generally speaking, individuals in organizations also find themselves in groups. These groups occur through the division of labor by time, function, geography, production process, and the like. Individual interactions within groups, the realm of social psychology, has told us much about why people derive satisfaction from the workplace. Economic incentives notwithstanding, the Hawthorne studies and the work of Elton Mayo (see Chapter 4) have shown that group norms and group identities also influence an individual's attitudes and behavior in the workplace.

Finally, the interactions among groups of people within an organization also constitute a level of organizational analysis. This is the level at which much of traditional organizational and administrative theory has been aimed.

Formal versus Informal Organizations

Organizations can also be distinguished by their degree of formality and structure. Informal organizations, while sharing the basic characteristics of all organizations, arise through the social interactions of individuals or through family groupings. They tend to be relatively unstructured, but individuals within them more or less conform to the expectations of the group. Entrance to these organizations is also relatively informal, much of it being through birth or through some voluntary association. Rules and regulations are unlikely to be written, but expected behavior is known. Informal leadership and direction often emerge in these organizations rather than being explicitly defined and charged.

In contrast, formal organizations are explicitly established to achieve clear and identified goals and objectives. Entrance to these organizations is less ascriptive and more likely to be governed by some formal and explicit selection process. Rules and regulations are written and enforced within a formal sanction system. Often formal organizations are larger and more complex than informal organizations, and their size and complexity greatly contribute to the need for explicit regulation and formal administration.

In seeking to achieve specified goals and objectives, formal organizations often divide work, responsibility, and authority among organizational members, initiate monitoring and review systems, and track organizational accomplishments. Table 5-1 compares and contrasts informal and formal organizations on several organizational dimensions.

Distinguishing between informal and formal organizations should not be construed to imply that both cannot be present at the same time. Informal organizations exist within all formal organizations. Where people live, affiliate, or work together, informal patterns of interaction and shared beliefs arise as a natural consequence of human interaction.

More important, given that informal and formal organizations coexist, an understanding of organizational dynamics must integrate both into one complete picture of organizational life. As Blau and Scott have suggested:

> It is impossible to understand the nature of organization without investigating the networks of informal relations and the unofficial norms as well as the formal hierarchy of authority and the official body of rules, since the formally instituted and the informally emerging patterns are inextricably intertwined. (Blau and Scott, 1962:23)

Organizations as Closed versus Open Systems

Much has been made of the idea of organizations as closed versus open systems. Early approaches to organizational and administrative theory, discussed

Organizational Dimension	Formal	Informal
Guidelines for entrance	Universal standards	Group and individual standards
Basis of authority	Organizational rank	Varied, knowledge, skill, prestige
Guidelines for promotion	Universal standards	Craftsmanship, experience
Communication style	Structured and written	Unstructured and oral
Communications pattern	Horizontal/downward	Vertical
Guidelines for work	Rules and regulations	Group and craft norms
Ascendent goals	The organization's	The individual's and group's
Discipline enforcement	By written sanctions	By informal group sanctions
Basis for individual participation	Economic	Social
Individual allegiance	To the organization	To self and the group

below, treated organizations as being rather sealed off from their environments. These theories and approaches tended to emphasize the internal dynamics of the organization rather than its external relationships.

Closed models of organization tend to emphasize the structure of work and authority among and across work groups within organizations. Organizations are seen as deliberately structured social systems, with definable goal and activity systems, identifiable boundaries separating them from their environments, and an internal authority and rule system.

Closed organizational systems are not dependent on their environments; they are independent from them. These systems are focused internally on the structuring of relationships, authority, and communications within, not outside, the organization. They are modeled after the perpetual-motion clock—once set into motion, the clock works through a system of internal interlocking parts that have clear definitions and functions. Such closed models presume that the environment is stable and predictable and has little impact on the organization as a whole. The role of management is to oversee and administer the internal "clockworks" of the organization with little concern for environmental interruptions.

Open-system approaches to organization and management, by contrast, view the organization as in a continuous interaction with its environment. These theories and models of organization see the organization as importing energy from the environment (*input*), transforming that energy within the organization (*transformation*), and exporting the finished product to the environment, where it is ultimately consumed (*output*). Open-system approaches insist that the organization needs the environment to survive and that, while the en-

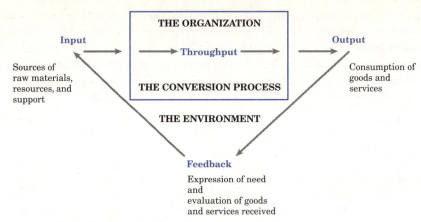

FIGURE 5-3.   Open-System Model

vironment creates uncertainty for the organization, without it the organization would simply die.

Perhaps most important, the boundaries anticipated in the closed-system models of organization are permeable in the open-system models. That is, in the open-system approach it is anticipated that the organization is in a continuous dialogue with its environment, particularly regarding its input and output transactions.

Figure 5-3 diagrams the open-system model and its associated organizational subsystems. As seen in Figure 5-3, the *boundary-spanning activities* of the organization occur at the input and output stages of the model. Such activities might include securing resources, personnel, and materials; building effective public relations; and providing direct and visible services to a visible clientele. The transformation process concerns the internal structure of work within the organization, and includes systems of production, maintenance, adaptation (meaning the capacity to change), and management of the systems subcomponents.

Organization Size and Complexity

Formal organizations also vary by size and complexity. The size of the organization has many implications for organizational design and administration. As size increases, many organizational dimensions change. Organizations with increasing size typically are associated with more levels of management and administration (hierarchy of authority), more formal and more ordered policy and procedure systems and communications processes (formalization), greater division of labor (specialization), and more centralization of authority. These organizational characteristics are related to increasing complexity within larger organizations.

Organizational complexity refers to both the height and the breadth of the organization. Vertical complexity refers to increased levels of authority within the organization. As previously discussed, this increased vertical complexity is largely due to a decreased span of control. As the organization more closely controls work through a narrow span of control, vertical complexity increases.

Organizational complexity is also related to the division of labor within an organization; such specialization increases the horizontal complexity of the organization. Horizontal complexity produced through specialization increases the need for work coordination and hence for a more complex hierarchy of authority. Together the vertical and horizontal complexity of the organization define its formal structure.

Centralization and Decentralization

The concepts of centralization and decentralization form the polar ends of a continuum that defines authority to make organizational decisions. In a completely centralized organization the chief executive, and only the chief executive, is empowered to make organizational decisions. In such organizations all decisions must be passed up the chain of command so that they can be decided. Once decided, the decisions are then passed down the chain of command to the level where they are implemented or executed. Such organizations enjoy a degree of control by virtue of their centralized authority, but control often comes at the expense of the timeliness of decision making.

In contrast to a fully centralized organization, a fully decentralized organization results in decisions being made by organizational members as they are confronted with a problem. Under such a system, management's role is to guide decisions, not make them. Such organizations might gain considerable value from timely decisions, but this may come at the expense of consistency.

Obviously, organizations are generally a mixture of both centralized and decentralized decision and authority systems. Such a mixture can be derived from the focus of decision making—strategic versus tactical, for example. In policing, police managers make most decisions about organizational issues (strategic), while police officers make most decisions about field situations (tactical). Or such centralized/decentralized decisions (authority) can be affected by the function of decision making, such as personnel, budgetary, assignment, workload, or evaluation decisions.

Centralization is greatly affected by organizational size. As organizations become larger, they tend to become decentralized. For example, in big-city police departments having multiple smaller administrative units such as precincts, districts, or command areas, the commanders of these smaller organizational units often become the "local police chief," making decisions about much of the service and management occurring in their area.

Elements common to all organizations make up the basic building blocks of administration. As police administrators consider their organizations, they invariably make choices about hierarchy of authority, span of control, division of labor, and the like, which produce organizational complexity. Such complexity, in turn, requires adaptive administrative systems to guide and coordinate work.

THEORIES OF ORGANIZATION AND MANAGEMENT

Discussions of management and administration are implicitly embedded with "images" of organizations. That is to say, whenever we think of "administration" or "management," we generally are thinking about the design and implementation of processes to control, direct, facilitate, or otherwise guide individuals within an organization toward some organization goal. Organizational administration is considered to be purposive (focused on some goal to be achieved) and rational (concerned with the relationship between means and ends or with the paths by which organizational goals are achieved).

Two schools of thought have greatly influenced our understanding of organization and management. The first, that of *organizational theory*, has generally concentrated on understanding the dynamics of organizations, most particularly the relationships created by organizational size, complexity, rationality, technology, specialization, and authority. Organizational theory attempts to describe and predict the behavior of individuals and groups within organizational settings as well as the behavior of organizations as they interact with their wider environments.

The second stream of thought influencing management practice stems from *administrative theory*, which has generally focused on discovering and outlining universal principles of administration—principles applying in any organizational setting. Administrative theory proposes that a science of administration exists such that the correct application of its principles will yield positive results for those charged with managing complex organizations.

Taken together, organizational and administrative theories have outlined the rich texture of organizational life while at the same time prompting administrators on the dos and don'ts of proper management. Each of these theories, briefly taken up below, provides the police executive as administrator with the context and tools of administration. Neither organizational nor administrative theories tell the administrator what to do in each and every case. Rather, both provide the administrator with an understanding of the dynamics of organizations and the major ways that administrators can guide organizations toward their intended goals and objectives.

Traditional Organizational Theory: Max Weber and Bureaucracy

The work of Max Weber (1947) most exemplifies this approach to understanding organizations. Weber was concerned with understanding the role of authority in formal organizations as well as with the way organizations should be structured for maximum efficiency and effectiveness. For Weber the authority to oversee and administer the "bureaucracy" (his term) was a weak point in much of the formal organization occurring at that time. That is, in postindustrial Germany, Weber observed that the organizations of the day seemed to rise and fall mainly on the authority their leader exercised, and on the acceptance of that authority by the leader's followers.

Weber's analysis concluded that the basis for organizational authority had to somehow transcend the personal characteristics of the leader that inspired the acceptance of authority, called *charismatic authority*, or the position occupied by the leader by virtue of family lineage, such as the passage of the throne from the king to another in the royal family. This was referred to as *traditional authority*.

For organizations to become stable social institutions, Weber reasoned, they needed to develop an authority system rooted in law, not tradition or charisma. This authority Weber called *legal-rational authority.* Legal-rational authority was independent of the officeholder. Weber argued that bureaucrats should be hired using universal standards and that the authority they exercised was tied to the office they held within the organization, rather than to them as individuals.

Such a system ensured that the authority of the "manager" would go on, even if different people occupied the formal position of manager. In police departments such legal-rational authority is reflected in the job descriptions and duties of all personnel. For example, the duties and responsibilities of a chief of police generally include setting the police department's policy and procedure, setting standards and monitoring organizational and individual performance, and representing the police department within city government. While different chiefs of police may place different emphases on one or more of these duties, all are charged with these roles and have the appropriate authority to ensure that these responsibilities will be accomplished.

Weber's "bureaucracy" is fundamentally rooted in the idea of *impersonal authority*, the exercise of authority that is attached to an official office or position. As Weber suggested:

> In the case of legal authority, obedience is owed to the legally established impersonal order. It extends to the person exercising the authority of office under it only by virtue of the formal legality of their commands and only within the scope of authority of the office. (Weber, 1947:328)

The type of organization Weber built around this system of impersonal authority had seven fundamental characteristics:

1. A continuous organization of official functions and bound by rules;
2. A specific sphere of competence. This involves (a) a sphere of obligations to perform functions which has been marked off as part of a systematic division of labor. (b) The provision of the incumbent with the necessary authority to carry out these functions. (c) That the necessary means of compulsion are clearly defined and their use is subject to defined conditions;
3. The organization of offices follows the principle of hierarchy; that is, each lower office is under the control and supervision of a higher one;
4. The rules which regulate the conduct of an office may be technical rules and norms. In both cases, if their application is to be fully rational, specialized training is necessary;
5. In the rational type [of organization] it is a matter of principle that the members of the administrative staff should be completely separated from ownership of the means of production or administration;
6. In the rational type case, there is also a complete absence of appropriation of his official position by the incumbent; and,
7. Administrative acts, decisions, and rules are formulated and recorded in writing. . . . (Weber, 1947:330–332)

Weber's "ideal organization," then, called for the logical ordering of offices from the top to the bottom of the organization; organizational authority was to be vested in the office, not the officeholder; a system of rules, regulations, discipline, and disciplinary appeal processes was to define and enforce expected organizational behavior; employees were to leave their personal lives at the organization's door—once they entered, they were acting in their official capacity as outlined by the organization, not as individuals; and the basis of promotion and reward must be technical proficiency and production.

While Weber's writings were not widely circulated before 1947, his work is one of the most systematic outlines of bureaucratic organizations. Much of what Weber wrote about has found its way into modern police organizations and their administration. Weber's work also paved the way for the development of modern organizational theory. And while Weber's theories of organization have received criticism for their seeming indifference to the social and social-psychological dynamics of organizational life (the art side of management and administration), much of Weber's work supported the work of those who had been laboring on theories of administrative organization and scientific management.

Administrative Theory and Scientific Management

In the wake of the eighteenth-century Industrial Revolution in England and its counterpart in the United States, industrial and mercantile organizations that had formerly been small-scale, single-proprietorship institutions began to grow in size and complexity. Before the 1800s industry was, generally speaking, small-scale, with local agriculture dominating much of the marketplace. By the late nineteenth century the family farm had been replaced by the factory. Waves of immigration from Europe provided a cheap labor force for the "workhouses" of the American industrial era.

Accompanying this rapid growth was the need to devise systems of administration and management which could accommodate not only a difference in the workplace (from the farm to the factory) but also a difference in the scale and complexity of activities undertaken. The managers of the industrial era were in search of systems for production, inventory, and financial control that were very different from those in practice before the Industrial Revolution. For example, whereas before the Industrial Revolution production was primarily an individual unit–based activity, the introduction of the factory system, including power-driven machinery, challenged managers to design and implement systems for accelerated mass production. Such systems necessitated the expansion of their managerial concepts as well:

> Management under the factory system was characterized by strict military control and organization. The owners were classified as merchant manufacturers, and they were more interested in selling their product than in developing a basic system of good management. Necessity, however, forced their attention to some of the more obvious management concepts and practices. And out of this attention grew some of the generally accepted managerial concepts. (George, 1972:52)

At the same time that managers were struggling to better understand and manage their organizations, economists, social philosophers, and industrialists were writing on their experiences with larger- and larger-scale organizations. Such writings were aimed at defining a set of managerial concepts, practices, and tools with universal application.

The early writing of Adam Smith (1793) laid the groundwork for the Industrial Revolution in England. Smith's work took up many issues of concern to managers of the day. His topics included how labor should be divided and how production could be made more simple. Time studies, routinely conducted in most large-scale manufacturing organizations today, can trace their intellectual roots to the work of Adam Smith and the early English industrialists.

By the mid-1800s and into the 1900s the literature on management had burgeoned.[3] Much of this managerial thought outlined what administrators were to do as the central feature of their role. Several authors during this era developed management and administrative theories using their experience as managers, and most sought to apply some form of the scientific method to their analyses. Of the many who wrote on these matters, the works of Henri Fayol, James Mooney and Alan Reiley, Luther Gulick, and Frederick Taylor were to have a profound impact on the then-emerging "science of administration." Taken together, they established a foundation of experience and theory that continues to guide thinking about organizational administration.

Henri Fayol: A General Theory of Administration

In 1888 Henri Fayol, a French industrialist, became the managing director of a mining firm on the verge of bankruptcy. When Fayol retired from the company in 1918, it was a soundly functioning organization enjoying financial stability. While Fayol was an excellent leader and manager in his own right, he attributed much of his success in the mining company to the system of management he had developed over a long career. In 1916 Fayol published *Administration industrielle et générale. General and Industrial Management,* the English translation of Fayol's work, was later published in 1929. Although Fayol's work did not reach wide circulation until the late 1940s, administrators and administrative theorists were conversant with his theories.

A central contribution that Fayol made to administrative thinking was his analysis of the various functions within organizations that required integration, the roles and responsibilities of managers that were derived from these various functions, and the resultant organizational "principles" that emerged from these responsibilities. Like others of his era, Fayol was searching for a general theory of administration—one that could apply to all organizations, irrespective of their products.

Fayol's general theory of administration recognized that several functions occurred simultaneously within organizations, each of which was important to the long-term survival of the enterprise. According to Fayol, the industrial enterprise could be divided into six major arenas:

1. *Technical,* or the manufacturing and production processes associated with industrial organizations
2. *Commercial,* or those organizational functions associated with buying, selling, and exchange

3. *Financial*, or the processes generally associated with the use of capital resources
4. *Security*, or the protection of persons and property associated with the enterprise
5. *Accounting*, or those processes associated with calculating costs, maintaining statistics, balancing sheets, and taking stock
6. *Managerial*, or those functions associated with planning, organizing, commanding, coordinating, and controlling the efforts of others in the pursuit of organizational objectives

For Fayol the managerial functions were the most important to the survival of the industrial organization. These managerial functions gave life to the organization and provided it with a sense of direction, purpose, and effect. Fayol's five managerial functions challenged managers to: (1) analyze their company's future and design a plan of action (planning), (2) build an organizational structure to achieve the plan (organizing), (3) maintain a sufficient level of activity among organizational personnel to achieve organizational goals and objectives (commanding), (4) unify or otherwise intertwine the efforts of individuals and groups toward higher-level organizational purposes (coordinating), and (5) set standards to ensure that work is accomplished according to the organizational plan (controlling). Managers who pursued such responsibilities, according to Fayol, would be more successful than managers who did not.

But management alone was not the solution to better organizational achievement. Fayol believed that certain principles of organization and administration were necessary to guide the organization. For managers to be effective they were told to observe the following "principles of administration":

1. Division of work (specialization belongs to the natural order).
2. Authority and responsibility (responsibility is a corollary with authority).
3. Discipline (discipline is what leaders make it).
4. Unity of command (men cannot bear dual command).
5. Unity of direction (one head and one plan for a group of activities having the same objective).
6. Subordination of individual interest to the general interest.
7. Remuneration (fair, rewarding of effort, reasonable).
8. Centralization (centralization belongs to the natural order).
9. Scalar chain (line of authority, gang-plank principle).
10. Order (a place for everyone and everyone in his place).
11. Equity (results from combination of kindness and justice).
12. Stability of tenure of personnel (prosperous firms are stable).
13. Initiative (great source of strength for business).
14. Esprit de corps (union is strength). (Fayol, 1949:19–20)

Fayol's principles are relatively straightforward. To be successful, managers should divide labor into specialized functions, authority and responsibility should be commensurate, discipline should be evenly applied, people should report to only one supervisor, the goals of the organization should be paramount in the workplace, lines of authority and the work routine should be orderly and clearly defined, and people should be fairly treated. Fayol's 14 principles were meant as a general guide for managers in the structuring of organizations and in their administration.

Henri Fayol's work also had great import for the idea of management as a separate and distinct discipline. Schools of business and public administration have much to thank Fayol for in his arguments for creating a discipline of management and administration. Throughout his work Fayol argues that management should have a distinct and separate body of knowledge and that this knowledge had universal application—hence, his principles of management. Second, Fayol's work represented the most complete theory of management available at that time. And third, Fayol's insistence on the training and preparation of managers lent credence to the status and importance of this occupation. Management, as a science, had a scientific body of knowledge, a set of laws, theories, and axioms to guide managerial behavior and to be learned through formal training and education.

James D. Mooney and Alan C. Reiley: *Onward Industry!*

In 1931, James D. Mooney and Alan C. Reiley published a classic organizational treatise entitled *Onward Industry!* This work, developed independently of Fayol's work in France, sought to identify and formalize principles of administration for general application. Mooney and Reiley:

> ... conceived of the idea that the principles of organization employed by all of the great leaders throughout history must surely be the same. ... What [was] found was that all sound organizational structures, including the Catholic Church, were based on a system of superior-subordinate relationships arranged in a hierarchical fashion, which [they] called the *scalar principle* [emphasis added]. [Their treatise] was a precise and classic treatment of the traditional managerial organization based on scalar processes, functional definitions of jobs, and fundamental coordination. (George, 1972:138)

Mooney and Reiley concluded their analysis of the historic elements in effective organizations by developing four organizational principles. The *coordinative principle* required unity of action, meaning that everyone in the organization should pursue the same objectives. The *scalar principle* required the creation of a hierarchy of authority with a clear and direct line of responsibility running from the top to the bottom of the organization. The *functional principle* required that organizations specialize function through the division of labor. Finally, the *staff principle* required that employees be divided into two major groupings: line (who have direct responsibility for the conduct of work) and staff (who provide support services to those actually doing the work).

The importance of Mooney and Reiley's work lies in the general framework for organization and management they outlined. While their approach tended to emphasize structure and control, as well as the engineering of relationships within organizations, their framework can be credited as the forerunner of organizational charts, tables of organization, and the formalized aspects of organizations we see daily. The similarity between the work of Mooney and

Reiley and that of Fayol also lent great credence to the idea that these "principles of organization" had universal application.

Luther Gulick

Luther Gulick approached the question of principles of administration in a slightly different fashion than Fayol, but he generally arrived at the same result. In the 1930s Gulick and his partner Lyndall Urwick were attempting to apply scientific principles to then emerging disciplines of management and administration.

Elaborating on Fayol's managerial duties, Gulick, in a paper entitled "Notes on the Theory of Organization," defined the following managerial responsibilities:

> **P**lanning, this is working out in broad outline the things that need to be done and the methods for doing them to accomplish the purpose set for the enterprise;
> **O**rganizing, that is the establishment of the formal structure of authority through which work subdivisions are arranged, defined and co-ordinated for the defined objective;
> **S**taffing, that is the whole personnel function of bringing in and training the staff and maintaining favorable conditions of work;
> **D**irecting, that is the continuous task of making decisions and embodying them in specific and general orders and instructions and serving as the leader of the enterprise;
> **C**oordinating, that is the all important duty of interrelating the various parts of the work;
> **R**eporting, that is keeping those to whom the executive is responsible informed as to what is going on, which thus includes keeping himself and his subordinates informed through records, research and inspection;
> **B**udgeting, with all that goes with budgeting in the form of fiscal planning, accounting and control. (Gulick, 1937:12)

Gulick's POSDCORB, derived from his managerial principles, became the standard definition of management responsibility. Gulick acknowledged that his principles were, in part, derived from Fayol. He also suggested that the seven managerial responsibilities he outlined might also themselves be subdivided as specialties within complex formal organizations.

> If these seven elements may be accepted as the major duties of the chief executive, it follows that they may be separately organized as subdivisions of the executive. The need for such subdivision depends entirely on the size and complexity of the enterprise. In the largest enterprises, particularly where the chief executive is as a matter of fact unable to do the work . . . it may be presumed that one or more parts of POSDCORB should be suborganized. (Gulick, 1937:13).

Gulick's suborganized POSDCORB is reflected in departments of planning, personnel administration, finance and budgeting, accounting, records, and communications. Each can be found in any large-scale organization, including those of the police.

Frederick Taylor: Scientific Management

Frederick Winslow Taylor is generally considered the "father of scientific management" in the United States. Taylor, an engineer from Philadelphia, elevated management from a rather despised and misunderstood occupation to one emphasizing scientific methods and improved results. As an engineer, Taylor was primarily interested in properly aligning the forces of production (people and machines) so that they might achieve optimal results.

Taylor developed his *Principles of Management*, published in 1911, through a series of analyses and papers he published concerning the creation of a "shop system"—a system of production aimed at maximizing efficiency. Using a scientific methodology that included work sampling, time-motion studies, and performance and output evaluations, Taylor first set about the business of understanding how work was performed. Next, he developed uniform methods for work, based on his prior analyses. Here he was concerned with setting the standards of the workplace such that a continuous flow of material and work effort would produce maximal results. Third, Taylor's system needed to be able to distinguish between workers, so that the right worker could be assigned to the right task. Here he also employed scientific analyses to study the proficiency of various workers at various tasks. Finally, Taylor recognized that such a coordinated work-flow process would also require coordinated supervision to ensure that the entire process would be maintained over time. Such a coordinated supervisory process actually had two fundamental elements: improved supervision and improved incentives for workers to produce. Taylor reasoned that ultimately workers needed to see a benefit in the coordinated work in which they were participating.

Taylor's four principles of scientific management, derived largely from his "shop studies," are well known. First, Taylor advocated that workers should be selected, trained, and matched with the work to be done in a scientific manner. Workers should be both physically and mentally well suited to their work. Second, the work itself should also be scientifically analyzed; rule-of-thumb methods for work estimation should be abandoned. For Taylor the effective manager should know as much about the work to be performed as the knowledge, skills, and abilities of the workers. Third, Taylor was concerned that a strong relationship exist between those who plan and those who do the work. By establishing such a relationship, scientific planning was not to be wasted on poor analysis or poor communication with those who would ultimately be responsible to carry out the planned work. Finally, Taylor's system of scientific management called for the sharing of responsibility—by labor and management—for the work process and work product. For Taylor, management and labor should do the work for which they were suited, with each bearing responsibility to the other for completing work in an efficient and timely manner (see Taylor, 1911:36–37).

The aims of scientific management summarized by Taylor also included many benefits to the workers. Taylor suggested that workers guided by his principles would be assured of continuous employment, earn higher incomes, have better living conditions due to higher incomes, work in healthier and "more socially agreeable conditions," be more justly treated particularly "through the elimination of discriminations in wage rates," and build a spirit of teamwork and common understanding that contrasted greatly with the conflict between labor and management at that time (Person, 1929:16–17).

Human Relations, Environmental Uncertainty, and the Art of Administration

Discussions of classic organizational theory and administrative science have often been criticized for failing to consider the wants, desires, and needs of the workers in organizations. These "bureaucratic" organizations, it is often said, are unresponsive to those inside as well as outside the organization. And many such theories of organization and administration have been criticized as being closed-system approaches to defining and managing complex organizations.

While the more traditional orientation to organization and management stressed the "science" and "principles" of administration, much work in psychology and social psychology has identified a more subtle and qualitative aspect of organizational life. Much of the thinking in this area can be grouped under the rubric "human relations," meaning the relationships of individuals and groups within organizations.

As we saw in examining police leadership (Chapter 4), individuals come to work for many reasons—some economic and some social and psychological. It follows then that the "art" of administration must take into account the variation in individuals and group dynamics within organizations if it is to be successful. While the reader is referred to the general discussion of motivational theory provided in Chapter 4, a discussion of managerial and administrative theories emphasizing "organic" as opposed to "mechanistic" ideas about organizations is presented here.

Mechanistic versus Organic Organizations.   Much of the classical approach to organizational and administrative theory portrays organizations as specialized, rigidly defined, formal social systems that emphasize strict adherence to a hierarchy of authority, the proliferation of rules and regulations to govern the behavior of organizational members, the centralization of authority, and the downward communication of policies, procedures, and decisions affecting every aspect of the organization.

Research and evaluation emphasizing what McGregor (1960) called "the human side of enterprise" suggested an alternative to this mechanistic view of formal organizations—the organic organizational model. Under this model, tasks are less specialized and contribute to the common tasks of the organization as a whole. Moreover, these tasks are less rigidly defined, allowing for adjustment and redefinition through interaction with employees. The organic organization is also said to be less control-centered, relying less on the formal hierarchy of authority and more on internal communication and the diffusion of knowledge and authority throughout the organization.

Environmental Uncertainty and Contingency Management.   In Chapter 4 contingency leadership was discussed as a process of continuous adjustment wherein the police leader adjusted her or his leadership style to conform to the nature of the tasks to be completed and the knowledge, skills, and abilities of those who are being led. The "one best way" to lead was abandoned under this approach in favor of a leadership approach emphasizing situational adjustment and continuous modification.

The art of organizational design and administration is also affected by the situational nature of organizational dynamics, most particularly by environmental considerations. Previously we discussed the open-system approach to defining organizations. This approach places great emphasis on the environment as both a source of input to the organization and a consumer of the organization's output.

Such an open-system approach suggests that organizations, including police departments, confront ever-shifting and changing environments and that the role of organizational administrators is to adjust the organization in light of such environmental change (See Lawrence and Lorsch, 1969). An organization's environment can be seen as defined by its rate of change (stable or unstable) and by its complexity (simple or complex). As the organization's environment becomes unstable (high rate of change) and more complex, it creates greater uncertainty for the organization. In contrast, an organization confronting a stable (low rate of change) and simple environment has low uncertainty—or, conversely, more certainty about its future.

The idea of environmental uncertainty is closely linked to organizational design and administration. As shown in Figure 5-4, the interaction of environmental change and complexity produces differing organizational structures, depending on the amount of environmental uncertainty present. In stable, simple organizational environments, the mechanistic approach, previously described, accommodates the environment. In the unstable, complex environment, where environmental uncertainty is highest, the organic model of organization, described above, is more useful.

FIGURE 5-4. Contingency Framework for Environmental Uncertainty
From Richard L. Daft, Organization Theory and Design, *3d ed. (St. Paul, Minn.: West, 1989), p. 63. Copyright © 1989 by West Publishing Company. All rights reserved.*

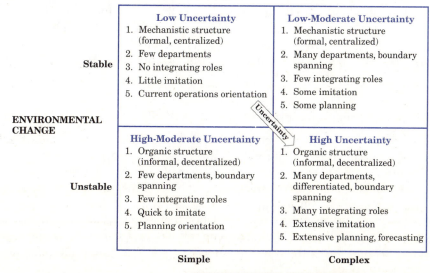

The environmental uncertainty continuum has direct application to policing and to police management. Each major department within the police agency can be seen as having some level of uncertainty posed by the environment. And, indeed, the police organization in its entirety can also be confronted by a shifting environment in terms of complexity and stability. Just as Lawrence and Lorsch found that sales and research departments faced different environments than did production and engineering departments within the same company (Lawrence and Lorsch, 1969), police patrol, detective, juvenile, homicide, SWAT, and community relations functions (departments) also confront different levels of environmental uncertainty. Consequently, they might be organized and administered differently, according to this approach to organizational design and management.

IMAGES OF ORGANIZATIONS

The idea of an organization is an abstraction. When we refer to "organizations," we are referring to a *social construct*—a definition for a social phenomenon that is abstract and not tangible. In reality you can't touch organizations, you can't see them, and you certainly can't understand them without considering many factors.

As abstractions, organizations represent many things to many people. Some people see organizations as authority systems, with offices arranged in ascending order (hierarchy of authority). Others see organizations as communications systems with linkages both horizontally and vertically within the organization. Still others see organizations in the intersection of small groups, each pursuing their independent objectives within the larger framework of the organization as a whole.

Gareth Morgan (1986) has studied these "images of organizations." For Morgan the images or metaphors we use to describe organizations tell us much about aspects of formal organizations we admire or detest. These metaphors also help us to distinguish many of the crucial functions or features within them. Morgan identifies eight images of organization that improve our understanding of organizations and of organizational behavior. These images also correspond to the various theories of organizations and administration we have previously considered.

Organizations as Machines

Much of the criticism of the closed-system approaches to organizations and management suggests that formal organizations have become too much like machines. This has been a continuing criticism of scientific management.

The machine image of organization emphasizes the interlocking structure of rules, regulations, policies, and procedures within organizations. It suggests an "assembly-line" mentality wherein labor (personnel) is just one more element in the assembly line. Management controls and manipulates the work process, creating tasks that are repetitive and that emphasize efficiency and mechanical application.

The taking of 911 reports by patrol officers, for example, is a repetitive process. Officers, mobilized by the citizenry through a system of telephone–radio call–police response have generally reduced the police to what Wilson (1968) called "report takers." Today's problem-oriented policing approach reflects an attempt to broaden police officer responsibilities to reduce much of the repetitiveness associated with the 911 system of police response.

The machine analogy for organizations, including police departments, cannot be abandoned entirely, as some might suggest. Rather, elements of the machine orientation—following the rule of law, for example—provide an operating structure for guiding and shaping police officer discretion.[4]

Organizations as Organisms

More consistent with the open-system approach to organization, the image of organizations as organisms casts attention on the dynamic relationships that characterize the organization and its environment. Organisms "live" in these environments; they are shaped by and shaping the environment in an interactive way.

Organisms also have needs of their own. They must satisfy those needs by "managing the environment." Much of contingency theory (discussed in Chapter 4) operates on the premise that the style of management, organization, and leadership depends on the type of situation (environment) confronted by the organization. Much of contingency management seeks to develop a good fit between the type of environment encountered by the organization and the internal structuring of the organization.

Gary Cordner (1978) describes police organizations as essentially "sealed off" from their environment. That is, police organizations, according to Cordner, have historically pursued their goals and structured their internal organization independently from the environments they confront. In recent years, court rulings and citizen complaints about individual police actions, as well as the overall effectiveness of the police to curb crime, have resulted in the environment exercising pressures on police organizations to reform.

Organizations as Brains

The brain metaphor emphasizes that organizations must have the capacity to think and learn. They develop communications systems that import knowledge and information from the environment, and they use that information for organizational purposes. Thinking organizations are seen as evolutionary in that they absorb and use new information and knowledge continuously. In some sense organizations as "brains" correspond both to the human relations approaches to management and to Gulick's first principle of coordinating work—the importance of a shared idea.

Since police departments process and use much information, the brain metaphor has some obvious implications for police management. Police information systems development, planning and research, and problem-solving activities and support systems all imply a thinking and intelligent police organization. Such organizational intelligence is a central feature of the administrative process, or should be. But beyond thinking of the administrative process as the brain controlling the rest of the organizations, Morgan suggests that we should think of the entire organization as a brain:

> The brain thus offers itself as an obvious metaphor for organization, particularly if our concern is to improve capacities for organizational intelligence. Many managers and organizational theorists have grasped this point. . . . In contrast, it is far less common to think of organizations *as if they were brains* [emphasis added], and to see if we can create new forms of organization that disperse brainlike capacities throughout the enterprise, rather than just confine them to special units or parts. (Morgan, 1986:79)

Morgan points out in addition that the brain analogy of organizations also implies that organizations have emotions. Just as the brain is divided into analytic and creative functions, so too are organizations.

Much of the problem-oriented policing movement can be seen as extending police thinking, learning, and reacting throughout the police organization (Goldstein, 1990). Problem solving, as a police activity, requires police officers to scan their environments, analyze problems and service needs, respond to those needs with programs targeted to achieve results, and analyze the results of their efforts (Eck and Spelman, 1987; Goldstein, 1990). Such activities, diffused throughout the police organization, are illustrative of Morgan's "thinking organization."

Organizations as Cultures

The cultural model of organizations emphasizes the underlying values, beliefs, and attitudes of organizational members. Culture, it should be remembered, is the meaning that people attach to their interactions within social and formal organizations. Cultures produce language, symbols, heros, villains, and myths. Understanding the culture, or multiple cultures, of an organization such as the police tells us something about what binds people together.

The occupational culture of policing has often been associated with a mixed set of values and attitudes. Upon entering police service, police recruits tend to express values of civic assistance, support for public safety, and the protection of the innocent from those who would victimize them. After some time, the police are said to become more cynical and distant from the public they serve. Perhaps after seeing people at their worst over many years, the police simply distance themselves from the pain and suffering they encounter on a daily basis. On the other hand, several analyses of the police in the United States and elsewhere suggest that other forces significantly and negatively impact on the occupational culture of the police. As Skolnick and Fyfe suggest:

> Social scientists have studied the police in the United States, in Europe and in Asia. The fundamental culture of policing is everywhere similar, which is understandable since everywhere the same features of the police role—danger, authority and the mandate to use coercive force—are everywhere present. This combination generates and supports norms of internal solidarity or *brotherhood*. Most police feel comfortable, and socialize mainly, with other cops, a fea-

ture of police culture noted by observers of police from the 1960s to the 1990s. (Skolnick and Fyfe, 1993:92)

The social isolation of the police from the rest of society is believed to be most affected by police concerns with danger, authority, and efficiency and with their use of force to gain compliance (see Bittner, 1971; Klockars, 1985; Skolnick, 1975). Because the public, or at least some segment of it, poses a danger to the police, because the police dislike the questioning of their authority, because the police often feel that they are criticized regarding the efficiency of their actions, and because the police must often use coercive force to gain citizen compliance, they tend to withdraw from society—forming their own cultural grouping, the "thin blue line" culture.

Recently, researchers studying police culture within the New York City Police Department have concluded that at least two cultures of policing exist within modern police departments (Reuss-Ianni, 1983). The first, the "street-cop culture," is most identified with the operational aspects of the police department. The *street-cop culture* emphasizes returning to the good old days; strengthening the authority of the police, believed to have been eroded over the past 20 years; reducing the rules, regulations, and bureaucracy, believed to interfere with good police work; and returning loyalty as the basis for internal police support.

In contrast, the "management-cop culture" within modern police departments emphasizes administrative regularity, efficiency, and public accountability. Like Weber's bureaucrats, the *management-cop culture* stresses order, efficiency, and the proper exercise of administrative and legal authority.

Organizations as Political Systems

Organizational life has a political dimension. That is, nineteenth- and twentieth-century organizations have been designed to distribute power and authority unevenly throughout the organization. There are those who rule organizations, and there are those who are ruled within organizations. The hierarchy of authority, or chain of command, in police departments clearly outlines power and authority positions within organizations.

Such uneven distribution of power and authority invariably leads to the creation of an internal politic within organizations. Such politics are the grist of ongoing relationships within organizations, but they are rarely talked about, except informally. As Morgan notes:

> The political metaphor can be used to unravel the politics of day-to-day organizational life. Most people working in an organization readily admit in private that they are surrounded by forms of "wheeling and dealing" through which different people attempt to advance specific interests. However, this kind of activity is rarely discussed in public. The idea that organizations are supposed to be rational enterprises in which their members seek common goals tends to discourage discussion. . . . Politics, in short, is seen as a dirty word. This is unfortunate, since it often prevents us from recognizing that politics and politicking may be an essential aspect of organizational life. (Morgan, 1986:142)

Organizations, particularly larger ones, can also be seen as a set of inter-locking and shifting coalitions of smaller groups. The detective and patrol offi-cer coalitions are obvious. So are the managerial, supervisory, and work-level coalitions. These coalitions sometimes subtly and other times overtly influence police policy and operational decision making. As such, these coalitions repre-sent political forces within the police agency.

Police executives also find themselves in political relations with those ex-ternal to the police agency. Community, business, and elected political leaders are continuously attempting to influence some aspect of the police depart-ment's policies, procedures, or operational tactics. Police administrators have long recognized the political dimensions of their jobs. As Richard J. Brzeczek, former commissioner of the Chicago Police Department, has written:

> It is no wonder that police and politics are intertwined in many ways. The ob-jective for the mayor and the police chief should not be to deny this interde-pendence but to clarify its proper scope. Policing and police administration should avoid party or partisan politics but should embrace politics and politi-cal action in the highest sense of those terms. (Brzeczek, 1985:48)

Organizations as Psychic Prisons

Organizations have a dominant role in shaping modern life. When viewed as psychic prisons, organizations are often seen as trapping people psychologi-cally, increasing individual stress, and generally dehumanizing people. The routine of organizational life can wear people down. Such stresses ultimately affect job satisfaction, attachments to the organization, and indeed the psycho-logical and physical health of employees.

In police work the routines of policing, coupled with police officer con-cerns about the support of their superiors and the quality of the equipment they use, often produce morale problems. Such problems can be associated with organizations as psychic prisons.

Beyond the routinizing impact that organizations may produce on behav-ior, the "group think" they produce may be more important to their long-term survival. As Morgan points out:

> False assumptions can become enmeshed in cognitive traps. False assump-tions, taken for granted beliefs, unquestioned operating rules, and numerous other premises and practices can combine to create self-contained views of the world that provide both a resource for and a constraint on organized action. While they create a way of seeing and suggest a way of acting, they also tend to create ways of not seeing, and eliminate the possibility of actions associated with alternative views of the world. (Morgan, 1986:202)

When the Philadelphia Police Department bombed an inner-city row house occupied by a group of social dissidents called MOVE, such group think was in place. For months the city of Philadelphia and its police had been as-sailed by neighborhood complaints about MOVE members fortifying the home, harassing neighbors, brandishing guns, and generally making neigh-borhood life miserable. The Philadelphia police and fire departments devised a plan for assaulting the MOVE headquarters which ultimately resulted in burning down two city blocks, displacing over 250 people, and costing the lives of 11 MOVE members. More recently, the group think of federal authorities and their handling of the Branch Davidians in Waco, Texas, confirms the powerful and sometimes devastating influence of such group processes within law enforcement organizations.

Organizations as Structures in Flux and Transformation

Much of what has been written about organizations shares a common, yet not always explicit, premise that organizations seek stability. These approaches to defining organizations see change as a disruptive force in organizations, which while unavoidable nevertheless creates problems for the organization undergoing such change. In fact, much of management thought and practice, including the ideas associated with contingency theory, tend to treat change as having a destabilizing effect on organizations.

An alternative view, that of seeing organizations as continuously evolving, changing, and transforming, suggests that the dynamic relationship between organization and environment results in a continual, not episodic, change process. Organizations interact with their environments; they are changed by *and they change* those environments. Such interactive change fuels other change cycles such that the organization and its environment are in a constant state of mutual adjustment.

> All organizations are successful in creating identities of one kind or another, for in many respects the whole process of organizing is the realization of an identity. But some identities are likely to be more robust and enduring than others. As organizations assert their identities they can initiate major transformations in the social ecology to which they belong. They can set the basis for their own destruction, or they can create the conditions that will allow them to evolve along with the environment. (Morgan, 1986:245)

In policing, this process of organizational-environmental interaction and change is quite evident. For example, the crime-fighter image that the police have traditionally held as their central purpose has given way to a more service- and problem-oriented definition of police services. In the 1940s and throughout the 1950s police agencies convinced their publics (the environment) that they were crime fighters. That definition of police work was well entrenched by the 1980s.

Since the early 1970s and into the 1990s the environment of policing (the public, public officials, community leaders, and the like) has consistently pressured the police to adopt a broader, yet unspecified, definition of their role in crime prevention and crime control. This pressure has resulted in the adoption of community- and problem-oriented policing strategies in many of America's police departments today.[5]

The interaction of police department and environment, then, is a continuous process. Changes in police policies concerning domestic violence, use of force, and vehicle pursuits illustrate the continuous change process under way in American policing.

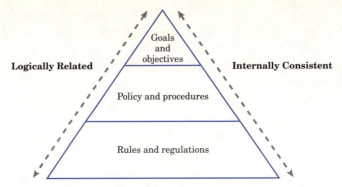

FIGURE 5-5. Relationships among Goals and Objectives, Policies and Procedures, and Rules and Regulations

Organizations as Instruments of Domination

Organizations can also exploit their hosting communities, their employees, and others in pursuit of their own ends. Characterizing organizations as instruments of domination reveals the dark side of organizational life.

Policing is not always viewed as being consensual and law abiding. The imagery that pictures the police as an "iron fist" cloaked in a "velvet glove" (Institute for the Study of Labor and Economic Crisis, 1982) sees the police as a repressive force in society. Such a repressive force, it is argued, invariably enforces the status quo, which favors those in political and economic power. The police role then is to manage the underclass.

POLICE ORGANIZATIONS AND ADMINISTRATION

Traditional organizational and management thought has portrayed organizations as pyramids where the workers occupy the base of the pyramid and administrators the top. In between the workers and the administrators are levels of supervisors and middle managers, each of whom translates policy and procedure from the top of the organization into work behaviors at the bottom of the organization. In a similar fashion, in an otherwise rational organization, the behaviors of individual workers (in this case police officers) should be logically related to the supervisory and policy and procedural apparatus of the police organization. Figure 5-5 depicts this classical orientation to defining organizations.

Police organizations, largely because of their close affinity to military organizations, have generally embraced the common characteristics of classically defined organizations. That is, they are governed from the top down; they rely on complicated systems of policy and procedure; they are rank-centered, meaning they give great meaning to the various ranks within the department (e.g., chief, captain, lieutenant, sergeant, and the like); and they tend to be control-centered, meaning they generally seek to more directly control the actions of the workers (patrol officers and detectives) who occupy the base of the police organization.

165

CHAPTER 5
The Police Chief
Executive as
Administrator

The Evolution of Police Organizations and Administration

As suggested in Chapter 1, police organizations have gone through several eras of development over the past 75 to 100 years. The growth of metropolitan and big-city police agencies, coupled with their common histories of corruption and inefficiency, spawned a reform era lasting to the present day.

Preceding the turn of this century and extending into the 1920s and 1930s, police organizations, particularly those in big cities, were closely aligned with the "political machines" of that era.[6] There was near-universal agreement then that the police were in need of significant reform. American policing had become a national disgrace; several reform commissions outlined massive corruption, patronage, illegal behavior on behalf of the police, and political interference with the policy making and day-to-day functioning of the police. The police were as lawless as the people they were thought to control.[7]

Part of the police reform was achieved by tightening organizational controls over police officer actions, thereby reducing discretion, and by wresting power from political elites and giving authority for police administrators back to police chiefs. By reducing the discretion of police officers, a "professional," rule-driven model of policing and of police management was advocated. At the same time, efforts to redistribute power to police managers argued for a more centralized and bureaucratized system of police management. As Hunt and Magenau point out: "Growth in the size and scope of metropolitan police organizations has combined with internal management and external political/reform interests in regulating police activities and restricting working-level discretion" (Hunt and Magenau, 1993:40).

Such reforms greatly altered the administrative structures and management of police agencies. Whereas in the past police officers had been directed by those in political power or by their own corrupt instincts, turn-of-the-century reformers saw the police as controlled by strong-willed and technically proficient police managers, with elaborate policy and procedural systems, supported by a professional work ethic. Such reform continued throughout the first half of this century.

Finally, police technological advancements, including improved communications and computer-aided dispatch, gave greater illusion, if not reality, to the idea that police administrators had tight control over police agencies. Such innovations also changed the dynamics of interaction between the police and the public. As Reiss notes:

> Early organizational casualties of this technology were the walking beats and the station house—the basic units of a decentralized command system with the walking beats organized around the station houses or police precincts. With the closing of station houses, citizens could no longer lodge complaints and adjudicate matters in their neighborhood. These could only be handled by the dispatch of officers to phoned mobilizations or travel to a central station. Officers were no longer needed to patrol a walking beat since a single officer

could handle a number of walking beats from the dispatched patrol car....
[This] model had miscalculated what citizens expect of their police. Many, it
turned out, did not expect a rapid response time and were willing to wait until
the police could handle their problem.... More important, the insulation of
the police from their public came at a high price. (Reiss, 1992:52–53)

In recent times, police organizational structure and administrative practice
have come under great criticism and reflection. Whereas in the past police organizations and their administrations were criticized for not adequately structuring and supervising the work of police organizations, today the criticism is
that police management has lost touch with the operational needs of the police
and the community. So concerned were police administrators with the means
of defining and controlling police behavior, they have lost sight of the ends of
policing—namely, community safety and neighborhood quality of life. Goldstein (1977, 1990) has suggested that the police have inverted means over ends,
the consequence being that little attention is being devoted to solving and
ameliorating community crime and order maintenance problems.

Proponents of the new policing (see, for example, Skolnick and Bayley,
1986; Sparrow, Moore, and Kennedy, 1990; Trojanowicz and Bucqueroux, 1990)
generally argue for some form of decentralized management and service delivery, a flattening of the police organizational structure and a loosing of organizational control, and greater interaction between the police and the communities they serve. Whereas in the past policing was thought best controlled
through the rule of law and administrative rules and regulations, newer emphases in policing suggest that the police should be guided by community
norms and sentiments as well (Mastrofski and Greene, 1993).

Organizations of any size require administration. They require some form
of a guidance system that can: (1) help define goals and objectives, (2) structure
and provide order for the work and communication process, (3) monitor work
and the production process, and (4) correct deviations in the work process. In
police departments this orientation is reflected in the setting of policy and procedure; the formal communications process, often referred to as the "chain of
command"; and the oversight to work provided primarily by first-line supervisors, most often sergeants.

SYSTEMS FOR ORGANIZATIONAL MANAGEMENT

Police administrators have several systems to provide direction and to monitor
their organizations. These systems focus on various aspects of the organization, each of which provides the administrator with a better grasp of the organization, the behavior of its members, and the effects of its efforts.

Strategic Management and Organizational Goals

Typically, administrators in law enforcement have risen to their positions
through the chain of command. Moreover, given that police departments are
heavily dominated by operational considerations, many police administrators,
while having extensive operational experience, lack strategic management ex-

perience. This probably explains the general tendency among police chiefs to focus on the tactical and operational side of the police department, more than on the strategic management side.

Strategic management is, perhaps, the most important responsibility of the police executive. It involves the total governance of the organization—that is, the way in which the organization is defined, directed, monitored, and evaluated. Strategic management is an open-system approach to organizational administration. The strategic management process is highly analytic, seeking to build the organization's strategy on a firm information base.

The strategy of the police organization is the broad plan for how it will deal with its environment to accomplish its goals. This strategy is based on the organization's mission and objectives, which are derived from the environmental demands for a wide range of police services as well as from an understanding of the police department's capacity to deliver such services. The strategic management process involves the determination of the organization's strategy, called *strategy formation*, as well as the implementation of strategies once they have been determined.

As an open-system, analytic approach, strategic management first assesses the organization and its environment to better match demands and capacity. This typically begins with two important assessments, one outside (environmental assessment) and the other inside (capacity assessment) the organization.

Environmental assessments tend to focus on understanding the demands exerted on the police department for services. Of particular concern in environmental assessment are *opportunities and threats* posed by the environment. Opportunities might include demand for police victim assistance, anticipated changes in the legal code, or major shifts in the population requiring new or modified police services. Threats, by contrast, might be represented by issues of privatization of police services, fiscal cutbacks in the municipality, or deep resentment of police practices or tactics. By analyzing the opportunities and threats created by the environment, the police administrator is in a better position to define the mission of the department and its major goals and objectives.

In addition to assessing the environment, police administrators must also take stock of their own organization. What are the strengths and weaknesses of the organization? What does it do well, and what does it do poorly? What do departmental members think they should do, and what values guide their behavior and attitudes? Answers to these questions, and others like them, provide the police administrator with a better understanding of the capacities and capabilities of the police organization.

Fitting environmental and organizational analyses into a strategic plan is accomplished by defining the organization's mission and major objectives. Many police departments today have mission and value statements that define for them and for others what the organization thinks is important and what services it should provide.

Once the police administrator has a defined and accepted mission and goals statement, the process of strategic planning can begin. The development of a strategic plan requires that the police agency explicitly define how it will accomplish its mission and objectives. This typically requires that organiza-

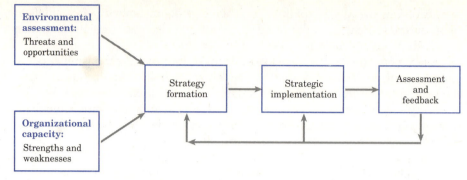

FIGURE 5-6. Strategic Management Process

tional administrators, managers, supervisors, and line-level workers come to some agreement on how goals and objectives should be accomplished. It is not unusual in the stage of forming strategies that police administrators attempt to gain a wide range of participants in this process. This participation is necessary for two primary reasons. First, broad-based participation in the formation of the organization's strategies helps to ensure that as much information as possible will be available to inform this developmental process. Second, such participation is expected to increase the normative sponsorship—or acceptance—of the completed strategic plan. That is, when people within the organization feel they have had some stake in defining the organization's strategy, they are more likely to carry out the plan and to take ownership of the plan at the implementation stage of strategic management.

Strategic plans must be implemented through the organization—through its structure, its technology, its personnel, its culture, and its technology. Moreover, new strategies for the police organization must also be monitored to ensure that they are being properly implemented and to assess their impact. This entire process is generally referred to as *strategic implementation.*

Taken together, strategy formation and strategic implementation are dominant responsibilities of police administrators. "The primary responsibility of top managers is to determine an organization's goals and strategy, and therein adapt the organization to a changing environment" (Daft, 1989:490). Figure 5-6 depicts both the strategy formation and strategic implementation issues in strategic management.[8]

Organizational Technology

"Organizational technology" refers to those processes by which the organization transforms inputs into outputs. In policing, the dominant organizational technologies have been deterrent patrol, rapid response, and follow-up criminal investigations. Despite several major studies questioning the efficacy of these technologies,[9] they persist in much of modern-day policing.

The technologies of the police are deeply rooted in the call-response system—911. This technology places heavy emphasis on the citizenry to define and demand police services. The 911 technology, while shaping the formal organization of the police, shapes the informal organization of policing as well (see Manning, 1992).

An alternative technology, that of problem solving, has been suggested as a replacement for the 911 response system.[10] Problem-oriented policing suggests that the police be more analytic with the information they collect, as well as more targeted in their responses to crime and disorder problems. Analytic thinking and measured crime control responses differentiate problem-solving policing from traditional reactive policing:

> Fundamental to the idea of problem-solving, for example, is the activity of thought and analysis to understand the problem that lies behind the incidents to which the police are summoned. . . . This is not the same as seeking out the root causes of the crime problem in general. It is a much shallower, situational approach. It takes seriously the notion that situations might be criminogenic and that crime can be prevented by changing the situations that seem to be producing calls for service. (Moore, 1992:20–121)

Viewed as an important shift in organizational technology, problem-solving policing requires that the police manager reconsider: (1) how communications and records systems that are individually focused can be made problem-focused; (2) how incidents can be aggregated for police interventions, (3) how police interventions can be targeted for particular problems, and (4) how the police organization will know when a particular problem has been either resolved or significantly ameliorated.

A police organization based on a problem-solving technology might look considerably different from one based on the traditional technologies underpinning police service delivery and management. In a separate assessment of community-based policing and the need for change in police organizations, Skolnick and Bayley (1986) concluded that patrol would require significant re-orientation—a technology change—for this innovation to be successful.

Organizational Size, Structure, and Complexity

As we have previously discussed, the size, structure, and complexity of an organization are interrelated. Large-scale, complex organizations have been typically associated with centralized, formalized, and complicated organizational structures. But as we have also seen, the environment of the organization also has an effect on the organizations' structure and methods for doing business (technology).

In policing there has been an ongoing discussion about the level of specialization (horizontal complexity) and the scope of the chain of command (vertical complexity) necessary to do "good policing." Many have argued that the highly centralized and certainly specialized modern American police might become decentralized and despecialized, thereby increasing the responsiveness of the police to community crime and order maintenance problems. Whether police are viewed as generalists or specialists and whether they are controlled through narrowly defined authority systems or loosely coupled supervisory systems are issues not yet resolved. Nevertheless, changes in the structure, size, and complexity of police organizations are within the reach of most police administrators.

Many police agencies have moved to systems of management emphasizing teams and leadership groups, rather than relying on the traditional top-down approach to management associated with classical management. Still other police agencies have used special task forces or short-lived project or matrix organizations to accomplish temporally defined projects. Once these projects have been completed, these temporary organizations have been reformed for other emerging projects.

There are many organizational configurations. Morgan (1989:64) has described six dominant types:

1. The rigidly organized bureaucracy, represented by traditional organizational and administrative theory
2. The bureaucracy run by a senior executive's group, distinguished by some limited sharing of authority for strategic organizational decisions
3. The bureaucracy using cross-departmental teams and task forces, characterized by team membership within a traditional departmental (specialized) structure
4. The matrix organization, giving equal authority to the functional departments within the larger organization, thereby breaking down the hierarchy of authority
5. The project-based organization, distinguished by its ability to continually reform itself as new problems arise, drawing from the specializations that are thought necessary to address particular problems
6. The loosely coupled organic network, characterized by its absence of a structured and formal authority, preferring to decentralize authority and function to small groups who are more guided by "the salience of an idea"

The organization types are configured along the mechanistic-organic continuum previously discussed, the rigidly organized bureaucratic organization being the most structured and the loosely coupled organic network being the least structured. Figure 5-7 shows a schematic of each type of organization structure produced according to Morgan's analysis.

Organizational Communications

Communications are often referred to as the lifeblood of an organization. Communications link those responsible for the organization as a whole (administrators) with those doing the work of the organization. Communications also define, symbolically and pragmatically, how the organization "thinks." Communications within police organizations occur on several levels.

First, organizational communications include some of the previous considerations of the 911 and associated call-response systems. These systems shape what police officers respond to in their everyday work routine. Changes in definition or emphasis within the response systems can dramatically change how

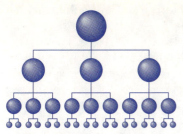

Model 1. The Rigid Bureaucracy

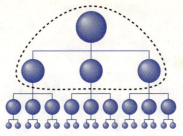

Model 2. The Bureaucracy with a Senior "Management" Team

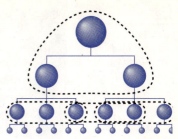

Model 3. The Burueacracy with Project Teams and Task Forces

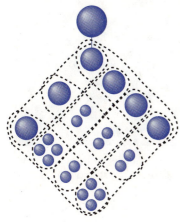

Model 4. The Matrix Organization

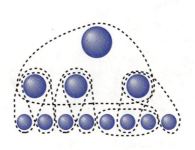

Model 5. The Project Organization

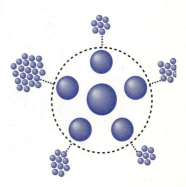

Model 6. The Loosely Coupled Organic Network

Model 1.	Model 2.	Model 3.	Model 4.	Model 5.	Model 6.
The rigidly organized bureaucracy	The bureaucracy run by a senior executives' group	The bureaucracy that has created cross-departmental teams and task forces	The matrix organization	The project-based organization	The loosely coupled organic network

◄──►

MECHANISTIC BUREAUCRATIC
Organized for stability

ORGANIC NETWORK
Organized for flexibility and change

FIGURE 5-7. Morgan's Schematic Illustrations of Six Organizational Models
From Gareth Morgan, Creative Organization Theory: A Resourcebook *(Newbury Park, Calif.: Sage, 1989), pp. 64–66. Copyright © 1989 by Sage Publications, Inc. Reprinted by permission of Sage Publications, Inc.*

police respond to calls for assistance as well as the importance they attach to those responses. For example, changes in police responses to "domestic and family violence" situations have generally resulted in these incidents being viewed by many police officers as more serious than they were previously held to be. What is of importance to an organization can be reflected in the priority that the issue, topic, or event receives in the formal communications system of

Although computers certainly have facilitated police crime analysis and decision making, they must be regarded as a complement to, not a substitute for, sound management and programs.
Bob Daemmrich/Image Works.

that organization. So changing the system of organizational communications can have a dramatic effect on organizational and individual performance.

Second, changes in the formal reporting of incidents and events can increase the learning and responsiveness of the police as well. For example, the use of solvability factors—facts known at a crime scene that indicate whether the case will be successfully concluded—has been associated with more efficient investigator decision making, as well as with greater patrol officer involvement during the preliminary stages of criminal investigations. Similarly, crime analysis and the recent efforts in problem solving shape how information is collected and used within police organizations, as well as how that information is communicated to police officers and the citizenry. So changing the form of communications, such as increasing the analytic capacity of the police to investigate crime, can enhance organizational effectiveness.

Third, changing the content of police communications, as well as the symbolic content of those communications, can alter police officer investment in the quality of the work performed. For example, police shorthand for minor law violators or others who are seen as disruptive to police practices is less than complimentary (Van Maanen, 1978). Moreover, the officers' sense of compassion and the situations also conspire to shape the officers' language and orientation toward others (Muir, 1977). The internal language of policing tells us much about what is valued by the police organization and by the police culture. Where the language of policing distances the police from the public, administrators are likely to confront other organizational and service delivery problems. Where the language of policing supports police officer and community interaction, it is anticipated that a more consensual communications linkage is formed. The new language of community policing, for example, stresses cooperation, partnership, and the coproduction of crime control activities. This language is significantly different from the crime-fighting language of traditional policing.

Management by Objectives

Over the years many management systems have been designed and implemented in both the public and private sector. Most of these programs have tended to build upon the functions of management as envisioned in administrative theory, modified by the experiences gained from the human relations managerial movement. They also tend to emphasize rational planning and the role of management in setting goals, monitoring work, and evaluating results.

Management by objectives, or MBO, was first espoused by Peter Drucker in 1954. MBO is viewed as an interactive process wherein management and the workers define quantifiable objectives that will guide the activities of work units. These objectives are tied directly to the organization's mission, and they are meant to provide organizational subunits and individual workers with a clearer picture of what is expected of them and how they fit into a larger organizational framework. Such a process, it is anticipated, increases the level of job satisfaction among workers because they clearly understand what they are to do and they have had some voice in determining those objectives. This process also is anticipated to improve the organization's capacity to plan, implement, and monitor programs toward larger organizational missions and purposes.

The MBO process attempts to build organizational consensus about the objectives individuals and work groups should be pursuing. MBO first identifies the goals and objectives of the organization as a whole and its subunits. This has been a traditional responsibility of management. Under MBO, subunit participation is encouraged to build agreement within the organization. Second, MBO stresses the setting of unit objectives within the broader framework of the organization's mission and overarching goals. Subunit objectives, also determined in a consensual fashion, form the basis for establishing strategies of action to achieve these objectives. This is the third stage of the MBO process. Finally, MBO evaluates the selected subunit strategies in light of the objectives set for each subunit.

> The primary advantage to be realized from MBO is the development of a systematic planning, monitoring and improving approach to managing your organization. It forces you to regularly look at what your organization is doing and how it can be changed to better accomplish your mission. (Brocka and Brocka, 1992:207)

MBO, and variations of it, has found its way into police management as well. The language and practice of management teams, strategic plans, and program objectives have some root in the MBO process. That is, it is relatively commonplace in many police agencies to follow the tenets of MBO, whether or not they announce an MBO program. Goals are defined, strategies agreed upon and set, and results monitored (Moore and Stephens, 1991).

Total Quality Management

Total quality management (TQM) is a rather significant departure from traditional approaches to planning, organizing, directing, and so forth. TQM has, perhaps, been most associated with the work of W. Edwards Demming and his classic work, *Out of Crisis* (1986).

For Demming and others, modern-day organizations commit "seven deadly sins" (Walton, 1986:36):

1. They lack a constancy of purpose, meaning that they have no long-term goals;
2. They tend to emphasize short-term results rather than long-term effects;
3. Their systems of evaluation destroy teamwork and encourage rivalry because they do not value the work of groups, but only of individuals;
4. They tend to move their managers around so swiftly (in the private sector they move from one organization to another) so that management has little commitment to long-term results;
5. They tend to focus on the quantifiable statistics which are available, which tend to ignore the longer-term and qualitative impacts of the organization;
6. They have excessive medical costs, attributable to workers using sick and other compensatory time to avoid work; and
7. They have excessive costs of warranty due in part to the declining quality of their product and in part to the willingness of lawyers to pursue product claims.

Although Demming was concentrating primarily on private-sector organizations, public organizations like the police have similar problems. Policing has been characterized by a short-term focus on many of these dimensions. For example, the American police have been criticized for a lack of constancy of purpose stemming from the role conflicts between fighting crime, maintaining order, and providing service. The management of the American police have tended to focus on yearly and quarterly results, individual not group performance ratings, and job-hopping among managers. These same agencies are also said to rely too much on Uniform Crime Statistics as the visible measure of their performance. And, of course, police agencies enjoy their share of increased absenteeism and litigation.

To address the decline in the American business firm, and indeed its parallel in the public sector, TQM has been advanced as a process for continuously improving the quality of products, thereby ensuring the long-term viability of the enterprise. TQM advocates have argued that American management has excluded the worker from participation in decision making and that management, or rather the system of management, is the greatest source of problems in organizations. TQM advocates suggest that workers need to be able to work smarter, not harder. Smart workers will require an investment and commitment by management.

Demming has outlined 14 points, which summarize the TQM approach to organizational management. While others have embellished on Demming's list, the points remain central to much of the work that occurs under the rubric "total quality management." Demming's 14-point program admonishes managers to:

1. Create constancy of purpose for improvement of product and services—an organizational culture must guide the corporate culture and provide a focus to the organization.
2. Adopt the new philosophy, emphasizing quality in product, service, and decision making.
3. Cease dependence on inspection to achieve quality; inspection measures but does not correct the problem.
4. Minimize total costs by working with a single supplier.
5. Improve, constantly and forever, every process.
6. Institute training on the job; training applies to all levels of the organization.
7. Adopt and institute leadership, which emanates from knowledge, expertise, and interpersonal skills, not level of authority.
8. Drive out fear—fear stems from insecure leadership that must rely on work rules, authority, punishment, and a corporate culture based upon internal competition.
9. Break down barriers between staff areas; everyone must work as a team working toward the good of the team.
10. Eliminate slogans, exhortations, and targets for the work force. Programs or campaigns that command a task but leave the worker powerless to achieve the objective constitute management by fear.
11. Eliminate numerical quotas for the work force and numerical goals for management.
12. Remove barriers that rob people of pride of workmanship; eliminate the annual rating system.
13. Institute a vigorous program of education and self-improvement for everyone.
14. Put everyone in the company to work to accomplish the transformation—to do this, top-management commitment is required. The transformation is everybody's job. (Adapted from Brocka and Brocka, 1992:65–68)

TQM has begun to take hold in American policing. It has been the subject of organizational reform in the Madison, Wisconsin, Police Department (Couper and Lobitz, 1991), where it has changed the organizational culture and structure of this medium-sized police agency. As important, elements of TQM have found their way into number of reforms within American police agencies.

Nonetheless, the TQM movement in policing, as well as other public agencies, has been cautious. Part of the problem in implementing TQM methods in the public sector is the inability to precisely define and monitor organization outputs and to separate those outputs from other governmental agency actions. For example, the quality of life in any neighborhood is affected by the combined policies of many government agencies. Identifying individual agency contributions to neighborhood quality of life has been elusive.

SUMMARY

This chapter has focused on the complexity in roles of police executives as administrators. Police executives function as administrators when they plan, organize, control, direct, and budget for police services. They are guided in their behavior by a knowledge of various elements of organization which can produce differing organizational structures and communications systems.

Moreover, these administrators are guided by existing theories of organization and administration which provide a general outline of the roles and functions of an effective administrator. The "science" of administration, implied by organizational and administrative theory, must be tempered by the administrator's understanding of individual, group, and intergroup dynamics within an organization and by the organization's interactions with a wider environment. Moreover, examining the various competing "images of organization" provides the administrator with contrasting views of individuals and groups.

The open-system approach to organizations and administration provides a dynamic conceptualization of organizations. Understanding that the organization imports energy, material, and support from the environment, transforms that energy into goods and services, and then exports those goods and services to the environment for consumption provides the administrator with a better understanding of the forces (internal and external) which shape the police organization.

Police administrators have at their disposal several management systems with which to better administer their organizations. Strategic management and goal setting, and adjustments to the organization's technology, size, structure, complexity, and communications, can all alter the shape and functioning of the police organization. And use of managerial planning, monitoring and evaluation systems like management by objectives and total quality management can provide managers with a system for managing the police enterprise.

QUESTIONS FOR DISCUSSION

1. How is administration defined? What various definitions have been given to the responsibilities and duties of administrators?
2. What are the distinguishing characteristics of a closed- and open-systems approach to management and administration, and what organizational elements form the system?
3. What elements are common to all social systems, and how are they changed when we define a social system as a formal organization?
4. Describe four "images of organization." What do they mean, and how are they visible in police organizations?
5. What management systems are available to police managers in administering police organizations? How do these systems differ, and how do they impact the police organization?

NOTES

1. For a review of the shift from rule-based government organizations toward those emphasizing mission and value statements, see Osborne and Gaebler (1993); and

for a review of the belief and value systems that shape government organizations, see Wilson (1989).

2. Adapted from Daft (1989).
3. For an excellent review of the early writers on management in England and the United States, see George (1972), especially chaps. 4 and 5.
4. For an assessment of how the rule-making process can shape police officer discretion, see Davis (1973) and Walker (1993).
5. For an assessment of this transformation, see Greene (1993).
6. For several excellent histories of the police, see Fogelson (1977), Johnson (1979), Lane (1967), Miller (1977), Monkonnen (1981), and Walker (1977).
7. For a review of police lawlessness, see Kappler, Sluder, and Alpert (1994).
8. For a review of some of the issues confronting police managers seeking strategic interventions, see Moore and Stephens (1991).
9. For a review of these studies, see Greenwood and Petersilia (1975), Kelling et al. (1974), and Pate et al. (1976).
10. The problem-solving approach to policing recognizes that the police will still have some emergency response responsibility and that response will be relatively unpredictable. But "hot spot" analysis (see Sherman, Gartin, and Buerger, 1989) and other progressive police crime control tactics (see Sherman, 1992) suggest an emerging shift in the dominant technology underpinning modern-day policing.

SOURCES

BARNARD, CHESTER I. *The Functions of the Executive*, 13th Anniversary ed. (Cambridge, Mass.: Harvard University Press, 1968).

BITTNER, EGON. *The Functions of Police in Modern Society* (Washington, D.C.: National Institute of Mental Health, 1971).

BLAU, PETER M., and W. RICHARD SCOTT. *Formal Organizations: A Comparative Approach* (San Francisco: Chandler, 1962).

BROCKA, BRUCE, and SUZANNE BROCKA. *Quality Management* (Homewood, Ill.: Irwin, 1992).

BRZECZEK, RICHARD J. "Chief-Mayor Relations: A View from the Chief's Chair," in William A. Geller (ed.), *Police Leadership in America: Crisis and Opportunity* (New York: Praeger, 1985).

CORDNER, GARY W. "Open and Closed Models of Police Organizations: Traditions, Dilemmas and Practical Considerations," *Journal of Police Science and Administration,* 6:22–34 (1978).

COUPER, DAVID C., and SABINE H. LOBITZ. *Quality Policing: The Madison Experience* (Washington, D.C.: Police Executive Research Forum, 1991).

DAFT, RICHARD L. *Organizational Theory and Design,* 3d ed. (St. Paul, Minn.: West, 1989), pp. 24–26.

DAVIS, KENNETH CULP. *Discretionary Justice,* 2d ed. (Chicago: University of Illinois Press, 1973).

DEMMING, W. EDWARDS. *Out of Crisis* (Cambridge, Mass.: M.I.T. Center for Advanced Engineering Study, 1986).

ECK, JOHN, and WILLIAM SPELMAN. *Problem-Oriented Policing in Newport News* (Washington, D.C.: National Institute of Justice, 1987).

FAYOL, HENRI. *General and Industrial Management* (London: Pitman, 1949).

FOGELSON, ROBERT M. *Big City Police* (Cambridge, Mass.: Harvard University Press, 1977).

GEORGE, CLAUDE S. *The History of Management Thought,* 2d ed. (Englewood Cliffs, N.J.: Prentice-Hall, 1972).

GOLDSTEIN, HERMAN. *Policing a Free Society* (Cambridge, Mass.: Ballinger, 1977).

GOLDSTEIN, HERMAN. *Problem-Oriented Policing* (New York: McGraw-Hill, 1990).

GREENE, JACK R. "Civic Accountability and the Police: Lessons Learned from Police and Community Relations," pp. 369–394 in Roger G. Dunham and Geoffrey P. Alpert (eds.), *Critical Issues in Policing: Contemporary Readings*, 2d ed. (Prospect Heights, Ill.: Waveland, 1989).

———, and STEPHEN D. MASTROFSKI (eds.). *Community Policing: Rhetoric or Reality?* (New York: Praeger, 1988).

GREENWOOD, PETER, and JOAN PETERSILIA. *The Criminal Investigation Process, Vol. 1: Summary and Policy Implications* (Santa Monica, Calif.: Rand, 1975).

GULICK, LUTHER. "Notes on the Theory of Organization," pp. 3–13 in Luther Gulick and Lyndall Urwick (eds.), *Papers on the Science of Administration* (New York: Institute of Public Administration, 1937).

HUNT, RAYMOND G., and JOHN M. MAGENAU. *Power and the Police Chief: An Institutional and Organizational Analysis* (Newbury Park, Calif.: Sage, 1993).

Institute for the Study of Labor and Economic Crisis, *The Iron Fist and the Velvet Glove*, 3d ed. (San Francisco: Crime and Social Justice Associates, 1982).

JOHNSON, DAVID R. *Policing the Urban Underworld: The Impact of Crime on the Development of the American Police, 1800–1887* (Philadelphia: Temple University Press, 1979).

KAPPLER, VICTOR E., RICHARD D. SLUDER, and GEOFFREY P. ALPERT. *Forces of Deviance: Understanding the Dark Side of Policing* (Prospect Heights, Ill.: Waveland, 1994).

KELLING, GEORGE L., TONY PATE, DUANE DIECKMAN, and CHARLES BROWN. *The Kansas City Preventive Patrol Experiment: A Summary Report* (Washington, D.C.: Police Foundation, 1974).

KLOCKARS, CARL B. *The Idea of Police* (Beverly Hills, Calif.: Sage, 1985).

LANE, ROGER. *Policing the City: Boston, 1822–1885* (Cambridge, Mass.: Harvard University Press, 1967).

LAWRENCE, PAUL R., and JAY W. LORSCH. *Developing Organizations* (Reading, Mass.: Addison Wesley, 1969), pp. 23–30.

MANNING, PETER K. "Technological and Materials Resource Issues," pp. 251–280 in Larry T. Hoover (ed.), *Police Management: Issues and Perspectives* (Washington, D.C.: Police Executive Research Forum, 1992).

MARCH, JAMES G., and HERBERT A. SIMON. *Organizations* (New York: Wiley, 1958).

MASTROFSKI, STEPHEN D., and JACK R. GREENE. "Community Policing and the Rule of Law," pp. 80–102 in David Weisburd and Craig Uchida (eds.), *Police Innovation and Control of the Police* (New York: Springer-Verlag, 1993).

McGREGOR, DOUGLAS. *The Human Side of Enterprise* (New York: McGraw-Hill, 1960).

MILLER, WILBUR R. *Cops and Bobbies: Police Authority in New York and London, 1830–1870* (Chicago: University of Chicago Press, 1977).

MONKKONEN, ERIC. *Police in Urban America, 1860–1920* (Cambridge, Eng.: Cambridge University Press, 1981).

MOONEY, JAMES D., and ALAN C. REILEY. *Onward Industry!* (New York: Harper and Bros., 1931).

MORGAN, GARETH. *Images of Organization* (Beverly Hills, Calif.: Sage, 1986).

———. *Creative Organization Theory: A Resourcebook* (Newbury Park, Calif.: Sage, 1989).

MOORE, MARK H. "Problem-Solving and Community Policing," in Norval Morris and Michael Tonry (eds.), *Modern Policing* (Chicago: University of Chicago Press, 1992).

———, and DARREL W. STEPHENS. *Beyond Command and Control: The Strategic Management of Police Departments* (Washington, D.C.: Police Executive Research Forum, 1991).

MUIR, WILLIAM KERR. *The Police: Streetcorner Politicians* (Chicago: University of Chicago Press, 1977).

OSBORNE, DAVID, and TED GAEBLER. *Reinventing Government* (New York: Plume, 1993), chap. 4, pp. 108–137.

PATE, TONY, ROBERT A. BOWERS, and RON PARKS. *Three Approaches to Criminal Apprehension in Kansas City: An Evaluation Report* (Washington, D.C.: Police Foundation, 1976).

PERSON, H. S. (ed.). *Scientific Management in American Industry* (New York: Harper and Bros., 1911).

REISS, ALBERT J., JR. "Police Organization in the Twentieth Century," in Michael Tonry and Norval Morris (eds.), *Modern Policing* (Chicago: University of Chicago Press, 1992).

REUSS-IANNI, ELIZABETH. *Two Cultures of Policing: Street Cops and Management Cops* (New Brunswick, N.J.: Transaction Books, 1983).

SHERMAN, LAWRENCE W. "Attacking Crime: Police and Crime Control," pp. 159–230 in Norval Morris and Michael Tonry (eds.), *Modern Policing* (Chicago: University of Chicago Press, 1992).

———, P. R. GARTIN, and M. E. BUERGER. "Hot Spots of Predatory Crime: Routine Activities and the Criminology of Place," *Criminology*, 27:27–55 (1989).

SKOLNICK, JEROME. *Justice without Trial: Law Enforcement in Democratic Society* (New York: Wiley, 1975).

———, and DAVID H. BAYLEY. *The New Blue Line: Police Innovation in Six American Cities* (New York: Free Press, 1986), pp. 210–229.

———, and JAMES J. FYFE. *Above the Law: Police and the Excessive Use of Force* (New York: Free Press, 1993).

SMITH, ADAM. *An Inquiry into the Nature and Causes of the Wealth of Nations* (London: A. Strahan and T. Cadell, 1793).

SPARROW, MALCOLM K., MARK H. MOORE, and DAVID M. KENNEDY. *Beyond 911: A New Era for Policing* (New York: Basic Books, 1990).

TAYLOR, FREDERICK. *Principles of Scientific Management* (New York: Harper and Bros., 1911).

TROJANOWICZ, ROBERT, and BONNIE BUCQUEROUX. *Community Policing: A Contemporary Perspective* (Cincinnati: Anderson, 1990).

VAN MAANEN, JOHN. "The Asshole," in Peter K. Manning and John Van Maanen (eds.), *Policing: A View from the Streets* (Santa Monica, Calif.: Goodyear, 1978).

WALKER, SAMUEL. "Historical Roots of the Legal Control of Police Behavior," pp. 32–58 in David Weisburd and Craig Uchida (eds.), *Police Innovation and Control of the Police: Problems of Law, Order and Community* (New York: Springer-Verlag, 1993).

———. A Critical History of Police Reform: The Emergence of Professionalism (Lexington, Mass.: Lexington Books, 1977).

WALTON, MARY. *The Demming Management Method* (New York: Perigee Books, 1986).

WEBER, MAX. *The Theory of Social and Economic Organization*, A. M. Henderson and Talcott Parsons (trans.) (New York: Free Press, 1947).

WILSON, JAMES Q. *Varieties of Police Behavior* (Cambridge, Mass.: Harvard University Press, 1968).

———. *Bureaucracy* (New York: Basic Books, 1989), chap. 4, pp. 50–71.

6

Police Research

Research is the systematic study of an issue or a phenomenon. In their private lives, most people conduct research before they make important decisions. Big purchases usually are preceded by the use of research techniques such as the old automobile manufacturer's suggestion that prospective buyers "ask the man who owns one." Smart buyers also read consumer publications for their ratings and let their fingers do the walking through classified directories and advertisements to find the merchants who will give the best prices and the lenders who will extend the most favorable financing.

Research also is a fundamental part of police administration. Without research, line and staff operations, as well as capital investments, can be based only on hunches rather than on analyses of what is likely to work, what is likely to fail, and what equipment best suits the needs of departments and the communities they serve. Thus, knowledge of basic research principles and their applicability to policing is at least as integral to the chief's job as is knowledge of criminal investigative techniques and strategies.

Certainly, police chiefs' other responsibilities make it unwise for them to learn the intricacies of investigation and research as well as those who actually do these jobs. Where both investigation and research are concerned, however, police chiefs must know enough to be able to distinguish between good work and bad work and to act accordingly. They should also know what research resources are available to them, both inside and outside their agencies.

ORIGINAL AND SECONDARY RESEARCH

A good first step in the process of learning about research is gaining an understanding of the distinction between original research and secondary research. *Original research* seeks answers to questions that previously had been mysteries to everybody, and through the collection and analysis of previously nonexistent data, it actually creates new knowledge. Original research in any field usually is conducted only by highly trained specialists and, particularly in the physical sciences, may be so deeply technical that it can be understood only by other research specialists. Other original research, such as surveys of public opinion or such private behavior as sexual practices, produces information of clear and immediate interest to a broad audience.

Secondary research, by contrast, is more common and consists of attempts to reexamine existing data in order to answer questions not considered by original researchers or otherwise to learn what others may already know about a particular subject. Spending a day consulting books in a library or searching the files of a computer service for information is a good example of secondary research, as is a reexamination of data originally collected and analyzed for some other purpose.

The well-known Minneapolis Domestic Violence Experiment (Sherman and Berk, 1984a, 1984b) was original research. Those who designed and conducted it collected and analyzed new data in an effort to determine whether there was one best way for police to attempt to resolve violent domestic quarrels. Until the Minneapolis Experiment, nobody had collected such data, and nobody had carefully and systematically attempted to answer the question at issue.[1]

Today, several years after the Minneapolis Experiment and a few similar studies, this work is available for secondary research. Such work might be conducted by police staff members asked by their chief to pull together and summarize the research and literature on police interventions in domestic violence in order to assist in police development. Such researchers would not collect and analyze previously nonexistent data. Instead, they probably would begin their work by going to a library or a reference service to find out whether someone, somewhere, has already studied this subject in a systematic way. No doubt, they would also confer with other police departments in order to determine whether they have altered their policies in response to the original research that had already been conducted. In short, their product would be a compilation of knowledge that, while new to themselves and their chief, was not new to others who study or perform police work.

Most original police research is conducted in a small number of the larger police departments. Police in Dade County (Florida), Dallas, Houston, Kansas

City (Missouri), Madison, Minneapolis, Newark, New York City, Oakland, and Rochester have been studied extensively in research projects that have created new knowledge with implications for policing throughout the United States. Usually, this research has been conducted in collaboration with universities or other nonprofit research organizations and has received the financial support of state law enforcement planning agencies or the federal government itself. At the federal level, support for police research most often originates with the National Institute of Justice, the research arm of the U.S. Department of Justice.[2]

As should be clear, most of the research conducted by police agencies is secondary work, and, most generally, police departments are *consumers* of original research rather than participants in it. Since only a small number of departments serve as the settings or laboratories for original research, most police officials never participate directly in this process. Some of the distrust of research and researchers, therefore, may be attributable to a belief that research does not apply to their agencies or that their own histories of satisfactory performance without reliance on the research of others are demonstrations of its irrelevancy.

Such views and the antagonism they reflect are mistakes. Over the last three decades, especially, research has changed policing for the better, and it is clear that future improvements in policing also will be based heavily on research findings and conclusions.

TYPES OF RESEARCH

Beyond the division between original and secondary work, research in the police field may be categorized in several ways. One important distinction is that between research in technology and equipment and research relating to the behavior of human beings. Another is whether research is oriented toward improvement of administration and management or toward operational improvement. Finally, police research can be classified according to its position on a scale embraced by basic research on one extreme and applied research on the other. These categories can be depicted in matrix form (see Figure 6-1).

FIGURE 6-1. Matrix Illustrating the Dimension of Police Research

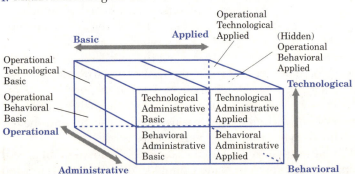

Basic versus Applied Research

As used in this matrix, *basic research* refers to pure, or nondirective, research—to experimentation or some other study without knowing precisely what the final result or objective may be. It can also mean the invention of a new solution to or concept for solving an existing problem. *Applied research* refers to the testing or evaluation of products or methods already in use or to testing to determine whether fully developed ideas may be applied to specific police use.

Technological versus Behavioral Research

As conceptualized in Figure 6-1, *technological research* involves the physical sciences, equipment, or products. *Behavioral research*, on the other hand, relates to studies in the social sciences and in the ways in which humans conduct themselves and relate to each other. Again, there is no sharp defining line between the two; most technological research involves consideration of the human beings who will use the technology or be affected by its use. Recent studies conducted in many police agencies on the issue of whether to change police side arms from revolvers to semiautomatic pistols, for example, involve technological questions that are complicated by a variety of behavioral considerations. Are the benefits of the semiautomatics' larger ammunition capacity outweighed by the danger that officers might fire shots indiscriminately? Because of their greater complexity, do semiautomatics require more frequent cleaning and maintenance than revolvers? If so, can officers be expected to assure that it is done?

Virtually every study of police technology involves similar, heavy consideration of the technology's interface with the people who must employ it. Indeed, *purely* technological research is a rarity in policing. Other public services—fire fighting, waste removal and disposal, public health—face problems that are primarily technological. Accordingly, they have advanced greatly as the scientific community has applied itself to their disciplines. The biggest challenges in policing, however, are person-to-person problems rather than scientific hurdles. Thus, like other public sector *human services*, policing has enjoyed great advances suggested by the findings of behavioral research. Research that focuses only on technology without addressing these behavioral questions is without meaning.

Operational versus Administrative Research

A somewhat clearer, but still not entirely distinguishable, line generally may be drawn between operational research and administrative research. *Operational research* embraces the direct delivery of police services. Its subjects include line activities such as patrol, investigation, and the prevention of crime and disorder—the purposes for which the police exist. At the other end of the scale, *administrative research* refers to studies of management and of the services that support operations.

From Figure 6-1, one may derive eight possible mission areas. These eight, with examples of research topics or programs that fall mostly, but usually not entirely, within them, are as follows:

1. *Technological-administrative-basic.* Experimentation with new concepts for automatic vehicle locators (which are essentially supervisory in nature); exploration of administrative uses for newly discovered computer or operations research techniques.
2. *Technological-administrative-applied.* Development of computer formats; application of management-systems engineering; testing of office equipment.
3. *Behavioral-administrative-basic.* Experiments in innovative management; exploration of ways to enhance employee motivation; theorization on career development systems.
4. *Behavioral-administrative-applied.* Development of improved promotional examinations and standards; application of improved supervisory methods.
5. *Operational-technological-basic.* Development of concepts for nonlethal weaponry; analysis of newly discovered scientific phenomena for possible application in the criminalistics laboratory or other criminal investigative processes.
6. *Operational-technological-applied.* Study of effects of existing weaponry; testing of operational equipment, such as personal radios, mobile computer terminals, and computerized fingerprint recognition systems; evaluation of locks, hardware, alarms, and other security systems.
7. *Operational-behavioral-basic.* Identification of causes of criminality and ways to ameliorate them; victimization studies; biomedical research; development of tactics for dealing with new police problems.
8. *Operational-behavioral-applied.* Evaluation of the effect of various field operations; conduct of studies of innovative operational methods; evaluation of programs intended to improve police relations with the community.

DIRECTIONS FOR TECHNOLOGICAL RESEARCH

At the present time, there are a number of promising applications for technology in the police field. They include enhanced use of video and audio recording technology; improved computer capabilities that make complete and more rapid record and name checks a reality and that allow access to cooperative information and electronic mail networks; and recent advances in identification methods such as fingerprinting, voiceprinting, and DNA analysis. In addition, there have been long and continuing efforts to apply technology to police weaponry, as in the development of nonlethal alternatives to deadly force.

Although these technological advances appear promising, we should keep in mind the experiences hinted at above. Over the years, policing has enjoyed an array of technological advances, each of which was widely anticipated as an immediate solution, a magic bullet, to some major police problem. It is difficult, however, to recall any technological advance that made a police problem go away or that was not soon counteracted by those whose conduct it was designed to affect. The booming business in vehicle radar detectors is an excellent example.

Thus, police administrators should retain a large and healthy degree of skepticism about the ultimate value of current and future technological trends.

Computer technology, for example, promises great things. It can quickly match fingerprints, speed communications, and enable quick analyses of workload so that personnel deployment can be promptly altered when necessary. Despite this promise, computers are only as good as the data fed into them. Where fingerprints are concerned, for example, the most sophisticated computers are useless unless clean and identifiable latent prints are found at crime scenes and can be matched to prints already in criminal information files. As experienced investigators know, this happens far less often that we would like. In other areas of concern, the quality of the information fed into computers is lacking because machinery has outstripped the sophistication, expertise, and training of police staffs. Further, the extent to which we can make good use of the results of computer analyses for deployment purposes is limited by the personal expertise and ingenuity of the administrators and supervisors who must interpret them. In recent years, it has not been unusual to find that police computers have gathered dust because this expertise and ingenuity were in short supply.

Most generally, policing—like teaching, social work, and other human services (occupations to which not all police enjoy comparison)—is a business that depends most heavily on successful personal interaction. To maintain order on the streets, police officers must win the respect and voluntary compliance of citizens. No amount of technology can mute the resentment and even the violence that have been caused by inappropriate police conduct during interaction with citizens. No investigative tool will ever be as valuable as a sharp investigator's ability to draw information from crime witnesses, victims, and suspects or to cultivate regular informants. However dazzling and however expensive, no video training program can substitute for role-play training. In the former, trainees interact with narrowly programmed screen images in darkened rooms that are, in effect, video arcades. When role-plays are done well, trainees interact directly with flesh-and-blood human beings in realistic settings. Managers and supervisors who win their officers' respect and confidence will always be more valuable than any computer in efforts to make police operations more efficient and effective.

The moral is this: Police administrators should encourage and insist on technological advances, but they should not expect any to change their lives or to be a substitute for the good, sound, interpersonal ability that comes with a competent and well-trained staff. Nor is it likely that any technological research will advance policing as much as behavioral research designed to directly affect police interaction among themselves and with their clientele.

POLICE RESISTANCE TO BEHAVIORAL RESEARCH

Many police historically have been resistant to research, particularly when it involves questions of behavior rather than hard-and-fast technology. In the view of many, studies of human behavior and interaction are "touchy-feely" exercises, more in keeping with the needs and images of teachers and social workers than with the work of street officers. To some degree, this mind-set exists in all police departments, even those that have long boasted research and planning units: the mere existence of such a unit is no guarantee that it actually does anything.

Police resistance to research, thankfully, has dwindled in recent years as the benefits of this process and the costs of ignoring it have become apparent. Still—and despite the establishment of the Police Executive Research Forum, a membership organization devoted to conducting, disseminating, and discussing research—policing is an action-oriented discipline in which many practitioners continue to regard research as an ivory-tower exercise that has little value in the "real world." Consequently, a discussion of the reasons for police resistance to research is worthwhile.

Oversimplification and Unreasonable Expectations

Pure technological research frequently results in cut-and-dried solutions to specific questions. This is so because the principles of the hard sciences are immutable, producing precisely the same results every time a set of conditions is created. Combining the same ingredients in precisely the same way always produces a soft drink that tastes precisely the same; exposing water to temperatures below 32° Fahrenheit always produces ice; and dropping an ice cube into a warm soft drink always produces the same fizz.

Except for the work that leads to the development of new police tools or laboratory methods, however, most of the research that may be useful to police officials is inherently less precise than this. As suggested above, this is so because police research—even most of that which may be classified as technological—includes the study of human behavior rather than the application of rigid laws of physics or chemistry. As we know, all human beings and the conditions in which the police encounter them are somewhat different—as are all police officers. Consequently, it is very difficult to predict with absolute accuracy how people will react to certain police actions or whether all officers may be capable of carrying out police actions as precisely as policy makers might like. Attempting to separate a husband and wife involved in a noisy dispute will usually—*but not always*—produce calm, and assigning a foot patrol officer to a small beat in a commercial area will deter most—*but not all*—would-be robbers.

It is shortsighted to distrust or reject behavioral research because of this relative imprecision. Behavioral research may never provide the neat, clean, and absolute results of research in the hard sciences, but it can greatly increase the chances of success in many areas of police concern. Further, even when decisions based on such research do not provide the desired results, they can be defended as the most rational and logical action in the circumstances.

The problem of hostage taking—certainly, one of the most critical types of human behavior the police confront—is a prime example. Adherence to the principles and strategies devised by those who have studied hostage taking and how to deal with it won't always prevent bloodshed, but these strategies have provided a far better approach than the former practice of "storming the gates" and hoping for luck. In the few incidents where bloodshed occurs even though police have precisely followed research-based hostage procedures, they have the consolation of knowing that they had done the best they could under the circumstances. In short, research should not be rejected merely because it does not provide absolutely foolproof solutions to police problems. There are few panaceas in policing, but research can help provide a method for addressing many problems.

A Failure to Communicate

A second reason for the rejection of behavioral research—*and researchers*—by the police is that the language and concerns of police and researchers some-times vary widely. On occasion, this occurs because researchers are charlatans and/or are more interested in publishing spectacular findings than in under-standing the operational implications of their work. During the years when two of us (Fyfe and Walsh) worked in the New York City Police Academy, for example, a team of academic researchers asked for and was granted permis-sion to give several hundred recruit officers a pencil-and-paper psychological examination designed to measure such personality characteristics as authori-tarianism, prejudice, and propensity to either help or hurt others. When the re-searchers' analyses ultimately showed that the officers were less authoritarian, less prejudiced, less violence-prone, and more interested in helping others than were other people their age, the researchers expressed disappointment and gave up their work without preparing the publication they had planned.

Clearly, these researchers had been interested only in publishing findings that suggested that new police officers were trigger-happy junior fascists. Needless to say, it was a long time before any researchers were again trusted at the academy. More important, these researchers ignored their responsibility to disseminate these important findings, which undoubtedly set back the cause of attempting to improve policing. Attempts to reform the police by recruiting a "better class of people" may be fruitful when new officers are, in fact, more prone to violence than others their age. But when the best data show that those recruited are considerably more humane and less violent than the general run of the population, such attempts may divert us from more profitable strategies such as organizational reform or changes in policy and training.

Practitioners are not without sin on this score, and they also have been known to manipulate research for narrow interests. In their private discus-sions, behavioral researchers often talk about the difference between organiza-tional research and real research. In their view, *real research* is designed to de-velop new information and analyze data objectively and fully, regardless of where it may lead. The type of *self-serving research* scholars denigrate, by con-trast, usually is designed to avoid causing administrators to be embarrassed. Some of it makes unwarranted leaps in logic under the guise of science in order to defend against charges that existing practice is inappropriate. In other cases, it consists of pseudoscience that purports to demonstrate the need for some new program or strategy inspired more by a desire to achieve some par-tisan political goal than by a wish to accomplish any legitimate police objec-tive. Much of the official research that was part of recent federal administra-tions' desire to abolish the exclusionary rule (which prohibits the use of unconstitutionally seized evidence in criminal trials), for example, was accu-rately regarded by most knowledgeable researchers as a transparent overstate-ment of the rule's effects on the efforts of police and prosecutors.[3] In a similar way, both adherents and opponents of the death penalty have bolstered their arguments with statistics concerning its purported deterrent effects. In most cases, however, the numbers on either side of the death penalty debate mean little because they include general homicide rates and overlook the fact that only a small percentage of homicides—aggravated murders, such as contract murders, killings of police officers, and killings during the course of robberies or other crimes—are capital offenses. Capital punishment has nothing to do with reckless vehicular homicides by drunk drivers or deaths that result from bar fights, because these offenses are not punishable by death in any state. Yet when either side of the issue presents statistical evidence of the merits of their argument, their numbers usually include both capital murders and homicides not subject to capital punishment.[4]

Communication between researchers and practitioners sometimes fails for reasons that have nothing to do with such hidden agendas. Many practitioners place great stock in Mark Twain's advice that "there are lies, damned lies, and statistics." Almost reflexively, such practitioners reject as sophistry much quantitative research. Conversely, many police researchers appear to be fixated on methodological sophistication and purity, without regard to whether their work addresses meaningful questions or can be interpreted by those who must attempt to put it into practice. Analytic techniques such as PROBIT, LOGIT, rotated varimax factor analysis, time series analysis, and ARIMA modeling all have been used in studies of police work and behavior. Unless those who perform such analyses apply them to the *right* questions and, subsequently, translate them and their meanings into language understandable by the police chiefs and other officials authorized to act on them, however, the analyses are meaningless.

Another problem is that practitioners sometimes may overestimate researchers' knowledge about operational problems. In doing so, practitioners forget that most researchers bring to their work expertise in the process of formulating and investigating research questions rather than extensive training in the substance of police work or any other discipline. Quite often, and no matter how much they may deny it, this occurs because administrators are somewhat intimidated by researchers. Veteran police administrators who meet with Ph.D.s from this or that university or research institution sometimes assume that such researchers may regard practitioners' statements and interpretations of their problems as simplistic or unnecessary. This is a mistake: police should carefully discuss policy and operational problems with researchers to make sure that methodologists understand all the issues and that they design their studies in ways that are as useful to practitioners as possible. Researchers usually bring to their work sophisticated methods rather than great knowledge of the issues they study. If police research is to be meaningful, police officials must collaborate in it by providing substantive knowledge to which researchers' methods can be applied.

A similar point is made by two experienced researchers who have participated in large-scale observation studies of police patrol officers at work. According to Stephen Mastrofski and Roger Parks, statistical studies that describe police behavior may be useful, but they are not nearly as valuable to either practitioners or scholars as studies that also describe and analyze *why* police do the things that observers record. To understand the *why* of police behavior, Mastrofski and Parks advise other researchers, one must go beyond statistics. Researchers must also ask the officers involved to explain their interpretations of the situations observed and the reasoning that led them to attempt to resolve them as they did (Mastrofski and Parks, 1990). In the same way, police administrators should make sure that, before beginning their work, researchers are thoroughly grounded in the reasoning that has defined current practice and that may help them to design their studies to test whether current practice is the best way to do things.

Perceived Lack of Relevance

The Kansas City Preventive Patrol Experiment and the Minneapolis Domestic Violence Experiment are only the most obvious illustrations that most police research is conducted in one site (or a very small number of sites) at a time. This focus on single places has two major causes. First, most researchers work with extremely limited resources and cannot obtain the funding to test their sometimes controversial ideas in more than one place. Second—and even when resources allow—it is very difficult to manage or interpret the meanings of findings in more than one major research site at a time.[5]

Since every American police jurisdiction differs in some ways from every other jurisdiction, one consequence of this pattern of single-site research is summary rejection of work—especially that which results in surprising findings—on grounds that it was conducted in a place that has nothing in common with one's own. Thus, comments such as the following have followed every major police research study:

Of a finding that 38 percent of the Chicago police officers who were shot had shot themselves or were shot by other officers, either accidentally or intentionally (Geller and Karales, 1981):

That's because cops in big cities aren't raised around guns or are more prone to suicides and heavy drinking. I don't have to do any fancy research to know that officers in rural areas like mine are stable, God-fearing people, taught by their fathers to handle guns properly. We don't compare to those folks.

Of the Kansas City Preventive Patrol Experiment's finding that random preventive patrol in marked police cars had no obvious effect on crime or on citizens' perceptions of the adequacy of police patrol coverage (Kelling et al., 1974):

They can't tell me that patrol makes no difference. That may be true in Kansas City, but I can tell you that the citizens here would notice right away if we cut back on the number of patrol cars in their neighborhood. This is not Kansas City.

Of findings that citizens' satisfaction with police responses to their calls for service was not affected by delaying responses to nonemergency calls rather than following the former practice of attempting to dispatch cars immediately to all calls for service (Pate et al., 1976; Spelman and Brown, 1981):

That may work in other places, but you can't tell me the taxpayers in this town won't go through the ceiling if I tried to pull that on them. I know them better than that. They're a tougher bunch than you'd find in most cities.

Certainly, there are great differences across jurisdictions, and, certainly, no finding in any one place—or in any small number of places—should be accepted as a prescription on how to do business elsewhere. In fact, all the above findings have either been replicated or found valuable application in other places. Thus, assuming that the methods employed are sound,[6] research should not be rejected out of hand merely because it was conducted elsewhere. Instead, it should be carefully reviewed with an eye toward determining precisely how it might be applied in one's own jurisdiction.

In conducting such reviews, one should keep in mind two factors. First, *policing varies from place to place at the top much more than at the bottom.* Beyond question, police chiefs in large jurisdictions have very different—but not always more difficult—jobs than their colleagues in smaller jurisdictions. Big city chiefs rarely take part in line activities, but it is not unusual for chiefs in smaller jurisdictions to do so. Regardless of jurisdiction size, the politics—and the personalities of politicians—vary from jurisdiction to jurisdiction in ways that have great effects on the chief's job. So, too, do laws, labor agreements, and regulations that define chiefs' powers, authority, and responsibilities. Although these factors filter down to the work of line police officers and detectives, their effects at that level are far less than they are at the top of the department.

Regardless of politics, in the biggest cities and the most isolated rural areas, a traffic stop is a traffic stop, a homicide investigation is a homicide investigation, and a domestic dispute investigation is a domestic dispute investigation. Regardless of geographic area or jurisdiction size, the skills required to successfully accomplish these tasks—as well as virtually all the universal tasks performed by street officers and detectives—are the same, or very close to the same. Consequently, research that deals with police line operations generally has far more relevance across jurisdictions than may be immediately apparent. Led by their own working experiences at the top of their organizations—where they deal with local politics, local politicians, local laws, and the like—to believe that their jurisdictions are one-of-a-kind, police chiefs tend to overlook the commonality of policing at the line level. Instead, as a general rule, they should view research that suggests ways of changing police line operations as potentially much more relevant than, for example, work that presumes to tell them precisely how to get along with their particular mayors or city councils.

The second factor to keep in mind is that *most original police research is conducted in larger places only because data accumulate there more quickly than in smaller places.* Since police officers only rarely use their firearms, for example, researchers who want to conduct statistically meaningful studies of *how* officers use their guns must do their work either in one large jurisdiction or in a very large number of small jurisdictions. For obvious reasons, it is easier to study five years' worth of police shootings in one department of 25,000 officers than to do so in 1,000 departments of 25 officers each or in 10 departments of 2,500 officers each. The same issue pervades statistical studies of any other area of police operations, from response time, through crime reporting practices, to domestic violence. Consequently, it should come as no surprise that most police research takes place in the bigger jurisdictions. Rather than reject it on these grounds, one should refer back to the first of our two admonitions—*policing varies from place to place at the top much more than at the bottom*—in order to see how it may apply at home.

In doing so, one should consider carefully how well a research site matches with one's own jurisdiction on the factors that do make a difference at the line level of policing. With obvious dependence on the specific issue studied, these include:

- Demographic characteristics:
  Population age
  Population ethnic composition
  Population socioeconomics
  Crime rates
  Population density
- Size of geographic area patrolled
- Laws or regulations that specifically address the subject studied
- Agency characteristics:
  Level of training related to subject studied
  Management and supervisory arrangements that may affect findings

Other items could be added to this list, and it is not possible to derive any clear formula for determining the extent to which each might—or should—affect the interpretation and application of research findings. To stay atop relevant research findings and, insofar as possible, to use them in formulating policies and practices, it might be advisable to create a departmental research utilization committee, on either a permanent basis or a case-by-case basis. Members of such a committee could be chosen on the basis of individual expertise, as well as on the basis of how adoption of research findings might affect the operations of their units. Membership on such a committee should not be limited to police officials but, wherever appropriate, should also include concerned citizens, other government officials, and scholars whose substantive interests and/or research skills may be put to good use.

Belief that Experience Is the Best Teacher

Police sometimes denigrate research on grounds that *real-world* experience is the best teacher. This logic holds, with some degree of accuracy, that nobody who has not walked a beat, staffed a patrol car, or investigated crimes can understand police work or problems. Unfortunately, not everybody has the opportunity to share in the most valuable experiences; consequently, not everybody has the opportunity to learn by experience what is most likely to work. Further, not everybody who enjoys the most valuable real-world experiences sees them in the same way or draws the same lessons from them. One great value of research is that it systematically tries to identify the best lessons of experience and to spread their benefits among *everybody*. Most highly skilled and successful detectives, for example, have been taught by experience that they should devote their efforts to some cases rather than to others. Yet unless researchers identify and document the manner in which such detectives make their investigative decisions, other detectives will have to learn this process the hard way, through trial and error, if they learn it at all.

By systematically identifying and analyzing the most important lessons learned by the most experienced and successful people, research can make this process far more efficient and effective. The Rand Corporation's studies of criminal investigation, for example, confirmed something that many police already believed: the chances of solving some reported crimes were so slight that investigating them served only to divert detectives from work on more promising cases (Greenwood et al., 1977; Greenwood and Petersilia, 1975). Later, the Rochester Police Department built on this work by carefully studying the records of 500 solved cases. The result was a list of "solvability factors" that distinguish cases likely to be solved from those in which even the most skilled investigative efforts are unlikely to result in clearance by arrest. According to the Rochester Police Department, these solvability factors are as follows:

1. Witnesses to the crime
2. Knowledge of a suspect's name
3. Knowledge of where a suspect can be located
4. Description of a suspect
5. Identification of a suspect
6. Property with identifiable characteristics, marks, or numbers, so it can be traced
7. A significant modus operandi (MO)
8. Significant physical evidence
9. Description that identifies the automobile used by the suspect
10. Positive results from crime scene search
11. Belief that a crime may be solved with publicity and/or reasonable additional investigative effort
12. Opportunity for but one person to have committed the crime (Rochester PD, n/d)

Obviously, an understanding of the department's interpretation of these factors is necessary before they may be applied. The Rochester police have provided this for officers in the manual that describes these factors. Once trained in the application of these factors, the patrol officers who conduct preliminary investigations of reported crimes are instructed in the means of identifying whether these factors exist in each case. If no factors can be identified, the presumption is that the case will be closed without further investigation.

These factors may seem obvious to readers with great policing experience, but they had not been systematically identified prior to the Rochester research. Before this research, decisions to close cases could be made only on the basis of *hunches*. Hunches and other best guesses, however, are hard to explain to victims who question why the crimes against them are not investigated as thoroughly as were the crimes against their neighbors or their relatives in other jurisdictions. Consequently, prior to the work of Rand and the Rochester Police Department, American police typically avoided such uncomfortable questioning by investigating—or at least *purporting* to investigate—all cases, regardless of how hopeless. Building on prior studies and what some detectives *already knew*, the Rochester research systematized this information and made it available to *all* officers, creating a logical and empirically based set of standards for investigation. Equally important, the Rochester research provided police with a defensible explanation for closing cases unlikely to result in arrest or the recovery of stolen property.

More recently, computer technology has made it possible to build on this investigative research by constructing *artificial intelligence* systems. These seek to harness the knowledge of experienced detectives by employing the rules of thumb they use in their attempts to identify suspects. One of the first departments to use such a system is the Baltimore County, Maryland, Police Department. There, lengthy research has resulted in a protocol that requires investigating officers to enter into a computer a long list of the characteristics of reported burglaries and the locations in which they occurred. These are then matched against the characteristics of offenders in prior crimes, reducing considerably the number of likely suspects. Certainly, this system does not always provide a solution, but it is a good example of the manner in which collaboration between researchers and practitioners can make available to everybody the lessons learned by a few ("Artificial Intelligence," 1991:17).

BEHAVIORAL RESEARCH CONTRIBUTIONS TO POLICING

As suggested above, the most fundamental distinction in original research is between *basic* and *applied* work. Basic research typically starts with a clean slate and looks at the fundamental issues underlying an area of study. As such, and unlike applied research, basic research rarely is useful in addressing immediate day-to-day problems. Instead, when done well—or when researchers are startled by important discoveries they did not expect—basic research results in the construction of testable theories and perspectives that, over the long haul, may have an enormous impact on practice. The most significant basic research in the physical sciences has resulted in discoveries and theories so astounding that many years of additional work were necessary before society could figure how the new information may be useful. Even then, development of the first uses for new theories and information usually is only the first step in an endless process. Think of what has happened to commerce and the travel industry since it was discovered that Earth is round; the uses to which Ben Franklin's experiments with lightning, a kite, and a key have been put over the last two centuries; the implications, good and bad, of Einstein's deceptively simple theory that $E = MC^2$.

Basic research also has been involved in the definition of and approaches to policing's grand problems: What, as Robert Peel asked, should be the role of the police in society? If we began from scratch, how would we organize the police? What do we know about human behavior that might be useful in deciding whether we should organize the police to prevent crime or to respond to it after it has occurred, or both?

Studies of Police Patrol Officers and Their Work

James Q. Wilson's *Varieties of Police Behavior* (Wilson, 1968) is a good example of basic police research. After studying police work in eight jurisdictions, Wilson concluded that the popular definition of the police as law enforcers was misleading and incomplete and that we would be better advised to think of the police role in terms of order maintenance. Certainly, this reconceptualization may have bruised some egos: the label "law enforcer" has a much nicer ring than does "order maintainer." As Chapter 2 suggests, however, most of the police and scholars who have thought about Wilson's point over the years since his studies have come to see that it has considerable validity.[7] In addition, police have come to see that Wilson's research and subsequent redefinition of the police role have great implications for the manner in which police are deployed and how police performance is evaluated. The administrator who thinks of officers as law enforcers is prone to measure their efforts by counting the number of arrests they make and the number of summonses they issue and, at the extreme, to be less concerned with questions of whether these activities actually accomplish anything. The administrator whose primary concern is order maintenance, by contrast, is far more apt to be worried about whether the streets actually are orderly and civil and to be less interested in being able to show how often officers have arrested or ticketed in order to help achieve this state.

Basic research like Wilson's lays a foundation for more applied work. Wilson's finding that police and police work varied so much from place to place challenged the popular notions that *police were all the same* and that politics played no part in determining the nature and quality of police service. This revelation encouraged others to look more carefully at the relationships among police, politics, and the public (see, e.g., Goldstein, 1977; Lundman, 1980; Manning, 1977; Sherman et al., 1973; Skolnick and Bayley, 1986). Recent implementations and tests of community- and problem-oriented policing (Eck and Spelman, 1987; Goldstein, 1979, 1986; Trojanowicz and Bucqueroux, 1990), for example, are the results of a logical evolution that began with basic research by Wilson and others concerning the belief that the job of the police is much broader than pure law enforcement and is greatly affected by the nature and politics of the community.

Applied research, as suggested above, generally does not have the grand scope of basic research. Instead, it typically is directed at narrower issues—but it may have a great immediate and long-term impact on some aspect of police operations. Like basic research, it grows on itself as it creates more and more knowledge. Two lines of applied research are the most influential illustrations: the first involves the deployment of police patrol officers; the second involves the use of deadly force by police officers.

Patrol Research

Beginning with Robert Peel's London Metropolitan Police, "preventive patrol" was seen as the primary police responsibility. The presence on the street of officers in distinctive uniforms, it was reasoned for nearly a century and a half, prevented a great deal of crime and resulted in the apprehension of a large number of criminals caught in the act by vigilant officers.

In the early 1960s, however, sociologist Albert Reiss studied police patrol operations in high-crime neighborhoods in Boston, Chicago, and Washington, D.C. Reiss (1971:95–100) reported that:

- Patrol officers spent only two-tenths of one percent of their time intervening in criminal incidents that they had observed during the course of their rounds.
- Handling criminal matters accounted for only three percent of all time on patrol.
- Criminal matters accounted for only 20 percent of all patrol officers' time in service.
- In Chicago, 93 percent of all police interactions with citizens originated with citizens' calls for service.
- In Chicago, only one percent of all interactions with citizens began with observations made by patrolling officers.

Given the large share of police resources devoted to preventive patrol, these were surprising findings. But they apparently were not unique to these three cities. Jonathan Rubinstein described another set of research results:

> According to a survey conducted by the Los Angeles Police Department in 1965—then the most mobile force in the country and widely regarded as the most professional—the entire department working at maximum efficiency had at most one hundred opportunities each week to discover a burglary in progress and only two chances of catching a robber in the act. The department's analysts thought these estimates to be inflated because no department ever works at peak efficiency. There are always men absent, others taken for special assignments, and even more who do not work precisely to the norms established by those who develop patrol schedules. In addition, these estimates represented only 12 percent of the burglaries and 2 percent of the robberies *known* to the police. Using these admittedly inaccurate and inflated figures, the chance of each patrolman capturing a burglar occurred once every three months and a robber once every fourteen years. (Rubinstein, 1973:347)

Then, in 1966, James S. Press found that great increases in the number of patrol officers in one New York City precinct resulted in decreases in "outside" crimes that officers could see without leaving their patrol cars but had no apparent effect on other offenses (Press, 1971:11). This finding placed in doubt the former conventional wisdom that police strength had great effects on crime rates.

Later the Rand Corporation reported that:

> It is intuitively reasonable, but as yet unverified, that preventive patrol affects some types of crime more than others. Such information, along with predictions of where and when various types of crime are likely to occur, would be useful in allocating preventive patrol efforts spatially and temporarily. The relative effectiveness of various tactics of preventive con-patrol (e.g., conspicuous or covert presence, continued presence or intermittent saturation of an area, one or two-man cars, etc.) also are not known. In short, between one-third and one-half of all patrol time is devoted to preventive patrol and the police cannot specify with confidence what effect it has on crime and criminal apprehension. (Kakalik and Wildhorn, 1975:264–265)

In 1973, Rand completed a study of crime in the New York City subways and reported that saturating trains and stations with patrol officers did reduce serious crime there. The bad news was Rand's estimate that each crime which was deterred cost $35,000. In addition, some crime had apparently been "displaced" to nearby streets, which experienced increased crime (Chaiken et al., 1974:v).

The Kansas City Preventive Patrol Experiment.   In 1974, the Police Foundation completed a controlled scientific experiment designed to test the effects of variations in random preventive coverage. Of their work in Kansas City (Missouri)—probably the single most important police study to date—the researchers reported:

> Three controlled levels of routine preventive patrol were used in the experimental areas. One area, termed "reactive," received no preventive patrol. Officers entered the area only in response to citizen calls for assistance. This in effect substantially reduced police presence in that area. In the second area, called "proactive," police visibility was increased two to three times its usual level. In the third area, termed "control," the normal level of patrol was maintained. Analysis of the data gathered revealed that the three areas experienced no significant differences in the level of crime, citizens' attitudes toward police services, citizens' fear of crime, police response time, or citizens' satisfaction with police response time. (Kelling et al., 1974:iii)

Kelling and his colleagues were careful to point out that their research did not justify the conclusion that police had no effect on crime or that police personnel strength should be reduced. Still, this study caused a firestorm in the law enforcement community, especially among those who apparently saw it as a flawed attack on the value of police patrol operations (Davis and Knowles, 1975; Larson, 1975). When the dust began to settle, however, the Kansas City Preventive Patrol Experiment spawned a variety of studies.

If random preventive patrol—merely assigning officers to patrol large beats however they saw fit—had little effect on crime, it was reasoned, perhaps officers should be deployed more systematically. The concept of *directed patrol*—in which analysis of crime and other police hazards serves as the basis for directing officers to be present at certain times and places—was born, implemented, and tested in several jurisdictions (Cordner, 1981).

Such directed patrol systems, however, assume that officers will be *free* to patrol specific areas at predetermined times. If analysis of local crime patterns indicated, for example, that purse snatches were common at commuter train stations during rush hours, officers would have to be posted at such locations if a directed patrol program was to be meaningful. If, as tradition held, however, such officers also were required to respond immediately to all calls for service, it rarely would be possible for them to conform to their directed patrol assignments. Thus was raised the question of whether it was, in fact, necessary for officers to respond immediately to all calls.

Response Time Studies.   The Police Foundation studied this question and found that only a small proportion of calls to police required an immediate response by officers in order to protect life or property or to apprehend criminals. This same study reported that the traditional measure of *response time*—the time elapsed between police receipt of a call and the arrival on the scene of officers—was deceptive because it ignored the fact that citizens often waited

for considerable periods of time before calling the police. One implication of
this particular finding was that instead of expending great efforts on shaving
seconds off the time it took them to arrive after becoming aware of the need for
their services, police should attempt to educate citizens about the need to call
for help promptly (Pate et al., 1976). Perhaps most important, this study reported that citizens' satisfaction with police response was far more dependent
on knowing when police would arrive than on whether they promised to arrive immediately (see also Spelman and Brown, 1981). In other words, whether
the police promise about arrival time was kept was more important than
whether the police tried to arrive immediately.

Differential Response. This, in turn, led to the development of systems that
prioritized calls in terms of those requiring immediate assistance, those to
which response could be delayed (as long as the caller understood that response would be delayed), and those that might permit some other response
altogether (e.g., a telephone report of a crime or a response to the scene by a
community service officer or police aide for purposes of taking a report). When
researchers who evaluated these systems reported that they had been successful (see, e.g., Cohen and McEwen, 1984), differential response programs were
implemented on a widespread basis. These programs subsequently allowed
patrol officers relatively large blocks of uncommitted time so that, barring
emergencies that truly required immediate response, they could be free to adhere to directed patrol assignments.

Alternatives to Random Patrol. Further, administrators and researchers reasoned, if it was true that random patrol by uniformed officers in marked cars
had little effect on crime or citizens' satisfaction, other ways of deploying officers might have a greater impact. Thus, soon after the Kansas City Preventive
Patrol Experiment, there followed research on the deterrent and apprehension
effects of assigning plainclothes officers to patrol covertly (Caiden, 1977) and
expanding the use of foot patrol (Police Foundation, 1981). Ultimately, this trail
of research led to a broad rethinking of just what the police patrol officers
could accomplish and to the reconceptualization of their role in what we have
begun to describe as community- (Trojanowicz and Bucqueroux, 1990) and
problem-oriented policing (Goldstein, 1986).

Research on Police Use of Deadly Force[8]

When the colonists came to this country from England, they brought with
them a common-law principle that authorized the use of deadly force to apprehend any and all fleeing felony suspects. The *fleeing felon rule* had its origins in
the Middle Ages, before there were organized police forces and at a time when,
because firearms had not yet been invented, *deadly force* generally required ordinary male citizens to attempt to arrest fleeing felons by engaging them in
close combat and by subduing them with clubs, swords, or knives. These were
life-or-death situations for the felony suspects involved, since prisons had not
yet been invented either: at the time, all felonies were capital offenses, punish-

able by execution after trials before courts that did not honor present legal niceties. In such circumstances, it was reasoned, deadly force was appropriate, necessary to protect those responsible for arresting felons (who also were in life-or-death circumstances), and not disproportionate to the punishments arrestees were likely to receive after having been brought to justice.

As our laws and our society evolved, however, the use of capital punishment shriveled, and it became possible for police to use deadly force—their firearms—against people who were at great distances from them, who presented no demonstrable danger to anybody, and who were suspected of such nonviolent property crimes as bicycle and vehicle theft, use of stolen credit cards, and commercial burglaries. In this environment, the justification and necessity for the fleeing felon rule came into question: the police were allowed to kill people merely suspected of offenses for which conviction would mean only a short prison term or probation. Perhaps the most eloquent statement on this point was a query presented by a participant in the American Law Institute's 1931 proceedings:

> May I ask what we are killing [the suspect] for when he steals an automobile? . . . It cannot be . . . that we allow the officer to kill him because he stole the automobile, because the statute provides only three years in a penitentiary for that. Is it then . . . for fleeing that we kill him? Fleeing from arrest . . . is punishable by a light penalty, a penalty much less than that for stealing the automobile. If we are not killing him for stealing the automobile and not killing him for fleeing, what are we killing him for? (American Law Institute, 1931:186–187)

As the states modified their criminal laws, many narrowed the range of fleeing suspects police were authorized to shoot. By the 1960s, about half the states limited police use of deadly force to situations in which the lives of officers or other innocent persons were in imminent danger or in which shooting was the only possible way to apprehend suspects who were fleeing from such violent crimes as murder, robbery, rape, and assault. In the remaining states, statutes continued to include the *any fleeing felon rule.*

Samuel Chapman. Even where statutes had been modified, however, critics suggested that, because of the breadth of the law and the difficulty of enforcing the criminal law against police officers accused of using excessive force, police departments should promulgate their own more specific, internally enforced administrative rules to control officers' shooting discretion. In 1963, Samuel Chapman and Thompson Crockett published the results of a survey of Michigan police departments: few had any written policies related to deadly force, and most relied on sketchy "oral policies." As a result, according to Thompson and Crockett:

> "[W]hen to fire" is frequently trusted to the "judgment" or "discretion" of officers as individuals. . . . The consequence is that while officers know *how* to care for and use their firearms, many have little or no understanding of *when* the

weapon may be employed. This paradox is similar to teaching an employee how to maintain and drive an automobile while neglecting to instruct him on the subject of motor vehicle regulations. (Chapman and Crockett, 1963:41; emphasis in original)

Chapman reiterated his call for restrictive administrative policies on the use of deadly force in a 1967 report to the President's Commission on Law Enforcement and Administration of Justice, which includes a model deadly force policy that in later years served as the basis for policy reform throughout the country (Chapman, 1967). In his 1967 report, Chapman reported finding the following departmental deadly force policies, each from a different agency and each quoted in its entirety:

[Referring to the police side arm] Never take me out in anger, never put me back in disgrace.

Unnecessary and careless handling of firearms may cause accidents, and the drawing, aiming, or snapping of firearms within Police Headquarters, or in other places, is forbidden.

Leave the gun in the holster until you intend to use it.

Shoot only when absolutely necessary to apprehend a criminal who has committed a major felony.

Never pull a sidearm as a threat, and if it is drawn, be prepared to use same.

It is left to the discretion of each individual officer when and how to shoot. (Chapman, 1967)

Even though another presidential commission found that many of the violent disorders of the 1960s had been started by controversial police shootings (National Advisory Commission on Civil Disorders, 1968), police generally resisted the call to formulate deadly force policy. This was so even among the largest police agencies: the New York City Police Department had no written deadly force policy at all until 1972, and the Los Angeles Police Department's 1972 policy related to shooting at fleeing felons was little more than a set of general advice to follow state law and use "sound judgment":

556.60 *Fleeing Felons.* By statute, an officer is authorized the use of deadly force when it reasonably appears necessary to prevent the escape of a felon. Such force may only be exercised when all reasonable alternatives have been exhausted and must be based only on facts or what reasonably appear to be the facts known to the officer at the moment he shoots.

It is not practical to enumerate specific felonies and state with certainty that the escape of the perpetrator must be prevented at all cost, or that there are other felonious crimes where the perpetrator must be allowed to escape rather than shoot him. Such decisions are based on sound judgment, not arbitrary checklists. (Los Angeles Police Department, 1972)

Until it was changed in June 1975, the Cleveland Police Department's policy was equally vague:

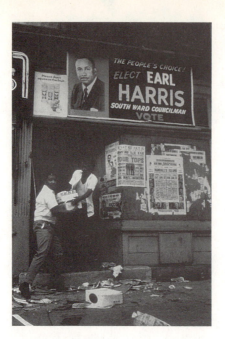

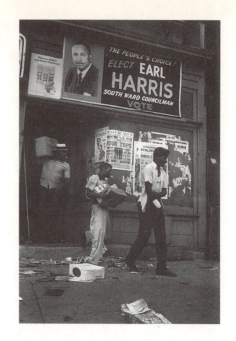

The riots of the 1960s marked a watershed in American policing, and called into question many police practices that had previously gone unchallenged. This sequence of pictures was taken by a *Life* Magazine photographer during the 1967 Newark, New Jersey, riot. It shows two men stealing beer from a liquor store that had been broken into the previous day. Two police officers arrive, one of whom uses his shotgun to shoot a

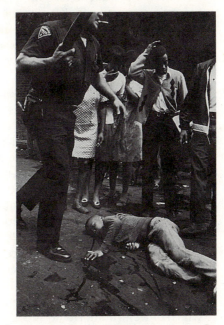

fleeing looter. The officer then stands over the looter, who died within three minutes. In the last photo, the second officer rushes to aid an innocent twelve-year-old bystander who was hit in the neck and thigh by the first officer's shotgun blast. Though seriously wounded, the boy recovered.
Life *Magazine,* © *Time, Inc.*

Officers and members should use only such force as necessary to effect the arrest and detention of persons. (Milton et al., 1977:48)

The administrative literature of the time also ignored the topic. The last two editions of this book (Wilson and McLaren, 1972, 1976), the 1971 edition of the International City Management Association's *Municipal Police Administration* (Eastman and Eastman, 1971), and the 1977 and 1982 editions of the successor *Local Government Police Management* (Garmire, 1977, 1982) include no discussions or recommendations whatever related to deadly force policy.

The reluctance of police to formulate administrative policy probably can be traced to several sources. First, there existed no real *state-of-the-art* or professional debate related to deadly force. As far as can be determined, only one study of officers' use of deadly force existed at the time, and it had found that Philadelphia police used their guns with great restraint during the 1950s (Robin, 1963). Thus, despite the riots of the 1960s, deadly force was not much of an issue, and there was perceived to be no need to fix something that was not broken. Second, and unquestionably, many police administrators feared that administrative restrictions on deadly force, such as a prohibition on shooting at fleeing felons, would increase crime rates and danger to the police and the public. Third, many administrators knew—then, as now—that restricting officers' authority to use firearms during a period of rising concern about crime and violence would expose them to charges that they had *handcuffed* their own officers. Fourth, chiefs were reluctant to establish restrictive deadly force guidelines because they knew that these standards could be used against them and their departments in civil litigation emanating from a police shooting.

The Police Foundation Study. This began to change in 1977, when Catherine Milton and her colleagues at the Police Foundation published a study of deadly force in seven major U.S. cities (Milton et al., 1977). Among this study's most important findings was the discovery that the rates at which police officers shot civilians varied across these cities with little relationship to rates of crime, violence, or other factors that one might expect to affect how frequently police resorted to their weapons. Table 6-1 presents data from the foundation study and shows that police in Birmingham were more than four times as likely to shoot people in 1973 (rate = 25.0) as were officers in Washington, D.C. (rate = 6.0). Certainly, this difference and others shown in the table could not be explained by the differences in crime and violence among the cities: Birmingham is certainly not four times as dangerous to police officers as Washington is to its officers. What did differ among the cities, however, was the extent to which officers' authority to shoot at fleeing suspects was limited.

These and other results of the study led Milton and her colleagues to several conclusions and recommendations. One was that fairly enforced internal administrative policy apparently did have an effect on the number of police shootings. Another was that police departments whose officers shot people more often than did officers from other similar agencies might benefit from

TABLE 6-1. **1973 Rates of Police Shooting per 1,000 Officers**

City	Rate	City	Rate
Portland (Oreg.)	4.2	Kansas City (Mo.)	12.2
Washington, D.C.	6.0	Detroit	21.8
Indianapolis	7.2	Birmingham	25.0
Oakland	9.6		

Source: Milton et al., 1977:30. Reprinted with permission of the Police Foundation.

studying what those agencies did to minimize the use of deadly force. A third was for more comprehensive research to determine whether these preliminary findings would hold up under closer scrutiny.

Fyfe's New York Study. In 1979, one of the authors of this book published the results of his study of the effects on police shootings of a restrictive deadly force policy in New York City. Fyfe's study found that the 1972 imposition of a policy that stated the NYPD's philosophy of shooting only to protect life sharply reduced shootings by officers. In 1971, for example, NYPD officers shot and killed 87 people; in 1973, after the imposition of the policy, 66 people were fatally shot by police, a number that by 1975 had further decreased to 42. Equally important, this study also reported that officer injuries and deaths declined after the policy was established and that there were no apparent negative effects on rates of crime, public safety, or the aggressiveness of officers (Fyfe, 1979).

Working with the information in the Milton and Fyfe studies, the National Organization of Black Law Enforcement Executives (NOBLE) introduced a resolution at the 1980 meeting of the International Association of Chiefs of Police calling on the IACP's member departments to formulate policies restricting the use of deadly force to life-threatening situations. After a rancorous debate, the NOBLE resolution was voted down, and the IACP instead urged its members to formulate policies that were "consistent with their jurisdictional law" (IACP, 1980). In other words, as late as 1980, the country's major professional police organization supported the rule authorizing police officers to shoot any fleeing felony suspects. It did so, in part, on the understandable grounds that the existing research had not yet adequately demonstrated the wisdom of abandoning the any fleeing felon rule or of otherwise adopting more stringent shooting guidelines than were provided in state law.

Matulia's IACP Study. In 1982, IACP staff member Kenneth J. Matulia published an exhaustive, federally funded study of police use of deadly force in 54 U.S. cities with populations of more than 250,000 (Matulia, 1982, 1985).[9] The study found startling variations in rates of justifiable homicide by the police in these places, as Table 6-2 demonstrates.

More specifically, Table 6-2 demonstrates that police in New Orleans (7.7 justifiable homicides per 1,000 officers) and Birmingham (rate = 7.5) were almost ten times as likely to kill citizens as were officers in Newark (0.8), a city that seemed at least as violent. Jacksonville police killed nearly three times as often (6.5) as did Miami police (2.5), and Long Beach officers killed people nearly twice as often (6.4) as did police in adjoining Los Angeles (3.5). This information helped to convince police leadership that practice regarding this most critical police decision—the decision to shoot—was far from uniform and led to several important findings. Among these, Matulia reported:

- Comprehensive administrative deadly force review policy and procedural controls seem to be related to a lower [justifiable homicide rate]. . . .
- State laws have less impact on the use of deadly force than do departmental guidelines.
- The majority of existing firearms training systems are deficient in: assuring policy understanding, officer survival tactics, comprehensiveness, job relatedness, attendance control, and assuring that only qualified officers are certified to carry firearms. (Matulia, 1985:13)

These findings led the IACP to reformulate its views on deadly force policy and to establish the Model Policy excerpted in Box 6-1. This policy and the research that led to it were enormously influential. To reiterate, in 1963, Chapman and Crockett had found that deadly force policy was skimpy and vague, and Chapman reported the same findings in 1967. As of 1980, Matulia reported, 8 of the 54 largest U.S. municipal police departments still permitted police to shoot to apprehend unarmed, nonviolent, fleeing property crime suspects (Matulia, 1982:161); not surprisingly, most of these cities appeared at or near the head of the list of justifiable homicide rates reported in the same study. But a Police Executive Research Forum (PERF) survey of the 1982 policies of 75 large departments showed that only one continued to follow the any fleeing felon rule (PERF, 1982), and the Commission on Accreditation for Law Enforcement Agencies (CALEA) established a requirement that candidates for accreditation go beyond merely prohibiting shootings of unarmed fleeing suspects:

1.3.2 A written directive states that an officer may use deadly force only when the officer believes that the action is in defense of human life, including the officer's own life, or in defense of any person in immediate danger of serious physical injury. . . .

1.3.3 A written directive specifies that use of deadly force against a "fleeing felon" must meet the conditions required by standard 1.3.2. (CALEA, 1983:1–2)

Then, in its 1985 *Tennessee v. Garner*[10] decision, the U.S. Supreme Court cited this PERF study as evidence that its ruling that the any fleeing felon rule was unconstitutional would make little difference to American police because they had already taken it upon themselves to do away with it. It was reasonable, the majority wrote, for police to use deadly force to defend life or to apprehend armed and dangerous felony suspects, but shooting nonviolent fleeing property crime suspects was a form of unreasonable seizure that violated the Fourth Amendment and that therefore must be forbidden. Immediately af-

TABLE 6-2. **Rates of Justifiable Homicide by the Police per 1,000 Officers, 1975–1979**

Rank	City	Rate per 1,000 Officers	Rank	City	Rate per 1,000 Officers
1	New Orleans	7.7	29	San Jose	2.4
2	Birmingham	7.5	30	Phoenix	2.2
3	Oakland	6.7	31	Seattle	2.2
4	Jacksonville	6.5	32	Philadelphia	2.1
5	Long Beach	6.4	33	Albuquerque	2.1
6	Houston	5.8	34	Cincinnati	2.0
7	Oklahoma City	4.9	35	Columbus	2.0
8	St. Louis	4.5	36	Rochester	1.9
9	Tucson	4.2	37	Fort Worth	1.8
10	Nashville	4.1	38	Minneapolis	1.8
11	Indianapolis	4.0	39	Chicago	1.7
12	Detroit	4.0	40	Washington, D.C.	1.7
13	Wichita	3.6	41	Denver	1.6
14	San Antonio	3.5	42	San Francisco	1.6
15	Dallas	3.5	43	Toledo	1.5
16	Kansas City	3.5	44	New York	1.4
17	Los Angeles	3.5	45	Akron	1.3
18	San Diego	3.3	46	Portland, Oreg.	1.2
19	Cleveland	3.2	47	Charlotte	1.0
20	Memphis	3.1	48	Austin	0.9
21	Tulsa	3.1	49	Buffalo	0.9
22	Tampa	3.0	50	Newark	0.8
23	Louisville	2.7	51	St. Paul	0.7
24	Baltimore	2.6	52	Boston	0.6
25	Omaha	2.5	53	Honolulu	0.5
26	Miami	2.5	54	Sacramento	0.4
27	El Paso	2.5			Mean = 2.8
28	Norfolk	2.4			

Source: Derived from Matulia, 1985:B-2. Copyright held by the International Association of Chiefs of Police, 515 N. Washington Street, Alexandria, VA 22314. Further reproduction without express written permission from IACP is strictly prohibited.

terward, the one holdout department cited in the PERF study changed its policy to conform to the Supreme Court's new rules.

Thus, during the little more than two decades after Samuel Chapman—then a graduate student and former police officer—had begun his studies of deadly force policy, there occurred revolutionary change in police thinking about when it was appropriate to take lives, and this change encouraged the Supreme Court to strike a centuries-old legal principle.

The consequences of this collaboration between researchers and police practitioners have been significant on the street, as well. The data collected by Geller and Scott for their recent comprehensive review of deadly force suggest that despite increasing violence in the United States generally, police kill fewer people today than they did in the early 1970s (Geller and Scott,

BOX 6-1.   Excerpts from the International Association of Chiefs of Police Model Policy on Police Use of Deadly Force

The following excerpts relate primarily to control of officers' discretion in carrying, displaying, and discharging firearms. The IACP's Model Policy also contains provisions for weapons specification and investigations and review of firearms discharges. These topics are discussed further in Chapter 15.

As you read this policy, contrast its thoroughness with the provisions of your state's laws concerning police use of deadly force, as well as with some of the earlier policy statements cited in this chapter.

Defining Deadly Force. "Deadly force" as used in this policy is defined as that force which is intended to cause death or grave injury or which creates some specified degree of risk that a reasonable and prudent person would consider likely to cause death or grave injury.

The Value of Human Life. The value of human life is immeasurable in our society. Police officers have been delegated the awesome responsibility to protect life and property and apprehend criminal offenders. The apprehension of criminal offenders must at all times be subservient to the protection of life.

Shoot to Stop. Members shall not fire their weapons to kill, but rather to *stop* and incapacitate an assailant from completing a potentially deadly act as described in the following sections of the policy. For maximum stopping effectiveness and minimal danger to innocent bystanders, the officer should shoot at "center body mass."

Defense of Life. An officer may use deadly force to protect himself or others from what he reasonably believes to be an immediate threat of death or (near death) critical bodily harm.

Significant Threat. An officer may use deadly force to effect the capture or prevent the escape and the officer has probable cause to believe that the suspect poses a significant threat of death or serious physical injury to others.

Juveniles. No distinction shall be made relative to the age of the intended target of deadly force. Self-defense and imminent threat shall be the only policy guideline for employing deadly force.

Warning Shots. A police officer is not justified in using his firearm to fire a warning shot.

Risk to Innocent Bystanders. Officers are prohibited from discharging firearms when it appears likely that an innocent person may be injured.

Shooting at or from Moving Vehicles. Officers should not discharge a firearm at or from a moving vehicle except as the last ultimate measure of self-defense or defense of another when the suspect is using deadly force by means other than the vehicle.

Shots to Destroy Animals. The killing of an animal is justified (1) for self-defense, (2) to prevent substantial harm to the officer or another, or (3) when the animal is so badly injured that humanity requires its relief from further suffering.

A seriously wounded or injured animal may be destroyed only after all attempts have been made to request assistance from the agency (humane society, animal control, game warden, etc.) responsible for disposal of animals. The destruction of vicious animals should be guided by the same rules set forth for self-defense and the defense and safety of others.

Safe Handling of Firearms. Except for general maintenance, storage or authorized training, officers shall not draw or exhibit their firearm unless circumstances create strong reasonable cause to believe that it may be necessary to lawfully use the weapon in conformance with other sections of this policy.

Secondary Weapon. A secondary (back-up) on-duty handgun is authorized but only upon meeting specific department approval.

Off Duty Weapon. Officers are encouraged, but not mandated, to carry a handgun when off duty. An officer who elects *not* to carry a handgun while off duty shall not be subjected to disciplinary action if an occasion should arise in which he could have taken police action if he were armed. (Exception) Off-duty officers while operating a department vehicle shall be armed with an approved weapon.

Firearms Training. The departmental firearms training program will include comprehensive instruction of (1) departmental policy on use of deadly force, (2) the legal requirements, (3) moral responsibilities of carrying a firearm, (4) firearm safety, and (5) firearm proficiency.

The firearms proficiency training will as closely as possible reflect those circumstances and conditions that our officers are most likely to confront in real-life deadly force situations.

All aspects of the firearms training program will include the officers' on-duty, off-duty and secondary weapon.

Source: Matulia, 1985:63–77.

1992:539–548).[11] The more sophisticated training that has accompanied restrictive deadly force training (combined, no doubt, with widespread use of bullet-resistant vests) has also had great effects on officer safety. In 1971, U.S. police were feloniously killed at a rate of 38 per 100,000 officers. That figure has steadily decreased since then and was 12 per 100,000 in 1991 (Geller and Scott, 1992:549–550).[12]

SUMMARY

As this overly brief discussion suggests, research has had an enormous impact on police patrol operations and deadly force policy and practice. Building on itself sequentially, behavioral research has transformed policing. Given the rapid advancement of computer analytic capabilities and techniques and the constant emphasis on police efficiency and effectiveness, it is sure to continue to do so.

Police officials can ignore the need to stay abreast of the latest original research only at great risk. If they do not know about the latest developments in the police field, they may deprive their constituents, their officers, and themselves of the best and most systematic thinking on how things might be done better. If they do not take steps to become knowledgeable consumers of research, they may misinterpret and lose the benefits of what they read.[13] At a minimum, if they do not conduct their own secondary research to see that their decisions, policies, and practices are informed by the successes and mistakes of others, they will lose the benefits of cumulative police experience in this country and abroad. Professionals cannot afford to do that.

QUESTIONS FOR DISCUSSION

1. How can chiefs and other police practitioners best prepare themselves to be intelligent consumers of research? Is it necessary that they become sophisticated statisticians and researchers themselves?
2. How would you establish a research capability in the police agency that employs you or that serves the community in which you reside?
3. After receiving instruction on a new computerized fingerprint identification system, a veteran investigator said, "This is nice, but I don't think it's nearly as useful as a good snitch. You know, with all these bells and whistles, the old ways are still the best." How would you respond to this observation?
4. What are the implications for your agency of the Kansas City Preventive Patrol Experiment's finding that random preventive patrol had little effect on rates of crime or public perceptions of safety on the streets in that city?
5. A 1990 study found that five years after the *Garner* decision, only 4 of the approximately 31 states whose fleeing felon laws violated the Supreme Court's new rules had changed their laws to conform with *Garner* (Fyfe and Walker, 1990). What do you make of this? Why did the remaining states not change their laws? What does it mean for police officials' ability to rely on their states' laws as a guide to policy and action?

NOTES

1. This is not to suggest that the Minneapolis Experiment produced a *definitive* answer to this question. As several writers have noted, the Minneapolis Experiment had several weaknesses that severely limit the meaning and value of its findings. See Berk and Newton (1985), Fyfe and Flavin (1991), and Hirschel et al. (1992).

2. Other federal agencies that have funded police-related research, often involving evaluations of programs conducted jointly by police and other institutions or agencies, include the National Institutes of Health, the National Science Foundation, the Bureau of Justice Assistance, and the Bureau of Justice Statistics.

3. A Justice Department study reported, for example, that 4.8 percent of California felony cases rejected for prosecution during the period 1976–1979 were dropped primarily because of "search and seizure problems." Most readers interpreted this to mean that nearly 1 in 20 cases brought to prosecutors (4.8 percent) were lost because of the exclusion of evidence and, consequently, that the exclusionary rule had a considerable impact on California prosecutions. These readers were misled. In fact, only 16.5 percent of all cases were rejected by prosecutors; 4.8 percent *of these*—or *0.77 percent of all cases*—were rejected because of search and seizure problems. Thus, artful phrasing and the use of an unorthodox denominator (cases rejected rather than all cases) misled many people to overestimate the effects of the exclusionary rule. Indeed, lost in the same study was the fact that loss of cooperation by victims or witnesses led to more than 10 times as many rejections as did search and seizure problems. See National Institute of Justice (1982), Davies (1983), and Fyfe (1983).

4. See, for example, the work of death penalty advocate Isaac Ehrlich (1975) and death penalty opponent Hans Zeisel (1982).

5. Thankfully for researchers, a third major reason for working in only one site at a time seems to have diminished in recent years. In our experience, as well as in the experience of other researchers, it appears that the reluctance of police chiefs to open their departments and their records to researchers has diminished greatly over the past decade or so.

6. Police officials' backgrounds and training usually do not prepare them to make assessments of the soundness and appropriateness of sophisticated research methods and statistical techniques. Thus, where such questions arise, they should be referred to someone trained in statistics and research methods. As a general rule, however, research that is published in professional *refereed* journals may be presumed to be reasonably free from major methodological defects. Refereed journals remove all identifiers from the manuscripts they receive and then send the manuscripts to anonymous scholars for "blind peer review," in which referees are not told whose work they are reviewing and authors are not provided with referees' names. In better journals, these reviews result in rejection of most manuscripts and in revision of some few that eventually see publication.

7. Wilson also bruised some egos by pointing out that, far from being autonomous and independent of politics, police and their behavior were directly affected by local political environments, philosophies, and concerns. This may not sound like a surprising revelation today, but at the time of Wilson's work, this reality frequently was denied by politicians and the public, who clung instead to the fiction that professionalism required that police be above politics. As the work of Wilson and others has since suggested, however, insisting that police be free of all political influences frequently has meant that they are beyond any accountability. See, e.g., Goldstein (1977), Hamilton (1975), Murphy and Plate (1977), Powers (1986), and Skolnick and Fyfe (1993).

8. This discussion is drawn heavily from Fyfe (1988).

9. Matulia reported no data for Atlanta, Milwaukee, and Pittsburgh. Throughout this chapter, whenever possible, the second (1985) edition of Matulia's work is cited because it remains available to interested readers.

10. 471 U.S. 1 (1985).

11. Surprisingly, there is no single comprehensive and accurate source of data on either fatal police shootings or the use of deadly force.

12. Research has also had great effects on policies and practices related to off-duty officers' duties, responsibilities, and weapons use. These are discussed further in Chapter 14.

13. An excellent quick-reference book for police administrators interested in becoming more sophisticated consumers of behavioral research is the Police Executive Research Forum's *Using Research: A Primer for Law Enforcement Managers* (Eck, 1984).

SOURCES

American Law Institute. *ALI Proceedings,* pp. 186–187 (statement of Professor Mikell, 1931).

"Artificial Intelligence, Real Results," *Law Enforcement News* (Apr. 30, 1991:17).

BERK, RICHARD A., and PHYLLIS J. NEWTON. "Does Arrest Really Deter Wife Battery? An Effort to Replicate the Findings of the Minneapolis Spouse Abuse Experiment," *American Sociological Review,* 50:253–262 (1985).

CAIDEN, GERALD E. *Police Revitalization* (Lexington, Mass.: Lexington Books, 1977).

CHAIKEN, JAN M., MICHAEL W. LAWLESS, and KEITH A. STEVENSON. *The Impact of Police Activity on Crime: Robberies on the New York City Subway System,* Report R-1424-NYC (New York: New York City Rand Institute, January 1974).

CHAPMAN, SAMUEL G. *Police Firearms Use Policy,* report to the President's Commission on Law Enforcement and Administration of Justice (Washington, D.C.: U.S. Government Printing Office, 1967).

———, and THOMPSON S. CROCKETT. "Gunsight Dilemma: Police Firearms Policy," *Police,* 6:40–45 (May–June 1963).

COHEN, BERNARD. *The Police Administration of Justice,* report to the New York City Police Department (New York: New York City Rand Institute, 1970).

———, and JAN M. CHAIKEN. *Police Background Characteristics and Performance* (Lexington, Mass.: Lexington Books, 1973).

COHEN, M., and J. THOMAS McEWEN. "Handling Calls for Service: Alternatives to Traditional Policing," *NIJ Reports* (Washington, D.C.: National Institute of Justice, 1984).

Commission on Accreditation for Law Enforcement Agencies, Inc. *Standards for Law Enforcement Agencies* (Fairfax, Va., 1983).

CORDNER, GARY W. "The Effects of Directed Patrol," pp. 37–58 in James J. Fyfe (ed.), *Contemporary Issues in Law Enforcement* (Newbury Park, Calif.: Sage, 1981).

DAVIES, THOMAS. "A Hard Look at What We Know (and Still Need to Learn) about the 'Costs' of the Exclusionary Rule: The NIJ Study and Other Studies of 'Lost' Arrests," *American Bar Foundation Research Journal* (1983:611–690).

DAVIS, EDWARD M., and LYLE KNOWLES. "An Evaluation of the Kansas City Preventive Patrol Experiment," *Police Chief,* 22:24–27, 30 (June 1975).

EASTMAN, GEORGE D., and ESTHER M. EASTMAN (eds.). *Municipal Police Administration,* 7th ed. (Washington, D.C.: International City Management Association, 1971).

ECK, JOHN E. *Using Research: A Primer for Law Enforcement Managers* (Washington, D.C.: Police Executive Research Forum, 1984).

———, and WILLIAM SPELMAN. *Problem Solving: Problem-Oriented Policing in Newport News* (Washington, D.C.: Police Executive Research Forum, 1987).

EHRLICH, ISAAC. "The Deterrent Effect of Capital Punishment: A Question of Life and Death," *American Economic Review*, 65:397 (1975).

FYFE, JAMES J. "Administrative Interventions on Police Shooting Discretion: An Empirical Examination," *Journal of Criminal Justice*, 7:309–324 (Winter 1979).

———. "Enforcement Workshop: The NIJ Study of the Exclusionary Rule," *Criminal Law Bulletin*, 19:253 (May–June 1983).

———. "Police Use of Deadly Force: Research and Reform," *Justice Quarterly*, 5:165–205 (June 1988).

———, and JEANNE M. FLAVIN. "Police Arrest Decisions and Domestic Violence," paper presented to Law and Society Association, Amsterdam (June 1991).

———, and JEFFREY T. WALKER. "*Garner* plus Five Years: An Examination of Supreme Court Intervention into Police Discretion and Legislative Prerogatives," *American Journal of Criminal Justice*, 14:167–188 (Spring 1990).

GARMIRE, BERNARD L. (ed.). *Local Government Police Management*, 1st ed. (Washington, D.C.: International City Management Association, 1977).

———. *Local Government Police Management*, 2d ed. (Washington, D.C.: International City Management Association, 1982).

GELLER, WILLIAM, and KEVIN KARALES. *Split-Second Decisions: Shootings of and by Chicago Police* (Chicago: Chicago Law Enforcement Study Group, 1981).

———, and MICHAEL S. SCOTT. *Deadly Force: What We Know* (Washington, D.C.: Police Executive Research Forum, 1992).

GOLDSTEIN, HERMAN. "Improving Policing: A Problem Oriented Approach," *Crime and Delinquency*, 25:236 (April 1979).

———. *Policing a Free Society* (Cambridge, Mass.: Ballinger, 1977).

———. "Toward Community-Oriented Policing: Potential Basic Requirements and Threshold Questions," *Crime and Delinquency*, 33:1–30 (1986).

GREENWOOD, PETER W., JAN M. CHAIKEN, and JOAN PETERSILIA. *The Criminal Investigation Process* (Lexington, Mass.: Heath, 1977).

———, and JOAN PETERSILIA. *The Criminal Investigation Process*, vol. 1: *Summary and Policy Implications* (Santa Monica, Calif.: Rand, 1975).

HAMILTON, EDWARD K. "Police Productivity: The View from City Hall," pp. 11–34 in Joan L. Wolfle and John F. Heaphy (eds.), *Readings on Productivity in Policing* (Washington, D.C.: Police Foundation, 1975).

HIRSCHEL, J. DAVID, IRA W. HUTCHISON, CHARLES W. DEAN, and ANN-MARIE MILLS. "Review Essay on the Law Enforcement Response to Spouse Abuse: Past, Present, and Future," *Justice Quarterly*, 9:247–284 (1992).

International Association of Chiefs of Police. Official resolution adopted by the membership pursuant to Article VII, Section 4, of the IACP Constitution (St. Louis, Mo., September 1980).

KAKALIK, JAMES S., and SORREL WILDHORN. *Aids to Decision-Making in Police Patrol* (Santa Monica, Calif.: Rand, 1975).

KELLING, GEORGE L., TONY PATE, DUANE DIECKMAN, and CHARLES E. BROWN. *The Kansas City Preventive Patrol Experiment: A Technical Report* (Washington, D.C.: Police Foundation, 1974).

LARSON, RICHARD C. "What Happened to Patrol Operations in Kansas City? A Review of the Kansas City Preventive Patrol Experiment," *Journal of Criminal Justice*, 267–297 (1975).

Los Angeles Police Department. *Policy Manual* (March 1972).

LUNDMAN, RICHARD J. "Police Patrol Work: A Comparative Perspective," pp. 52–65 in Richard J. Lundman (ed.), *Police Behavior: A Sociological Perspective* (New York: Oxford University Press, 1980).

MANNING, PETER K. *Police Work: The Social Organization of Policing* (Cambridge, Mass.: M.I.T. Press, 1977).

MASTROFSKI, STEPHEN D., and ROGER B. PARKS. "Improving Observational Studies of Police," *Criminology*, 28:475–496 (August 1990).

MATULIA, KENNETH J. *A Balance of Forces* (Gaithersburg, Md.: International Association of Chiefs of Police, 1982; 2d ed., 1985).

MILTON, CATHERINE, et al. *Police Use of Deadly Force* (Washington, D.C.: Police Foundation, 1977).

MURPHY, PATRICK V., and THOMAS PLATE. *Commissioner: A View from the Top of American Law Enforcement* (New York: Simon & Schuster, 1977).

National Advisory Commission on Civil Disorders. *Report of the National Advisory Commission on Civil Disorders* (New York: Dutton, 1968).

National Institute of Justice. *The Effects of the Exclusionary Rule: A Study in California* (Washington, D.C.: U.S. Government Printing Office, 1982).

PATE, TONY, R. A. BOWERS, A. FERRARA, and J. LORENCE. *Police Response Time: Its Determinants and Effects* (Washington, D.C.: Police Foundation, 1976).

Police Executive Research Forum. *Survey of Police Deadly Force Policies*, unpublished report (Washington, D.C., 1982).

Police Foundation. *The Newark Foot Patrol Experiment* (Washington, D.C., 1981).

POWERS, RICHARD G. *Secrecy and Power: The Life of J. Edgar Hoover* (New York: Free Press, 1986).

PRESS, JAMES S. *Some Effects of an Increase of Police Manpower in the 20th Precinct of New York City*, Report R-704-NYC (New York: New York City Rand Institute, October 1971).

REISS, ALBERT J., JR. *The Police and the Public* (New Haven: Yale University Press, 1971).

ROBIN, GERALD D. "Justifiable Homicide by Police Officers," *Journal of Criminal Law, Criminology and Police Science*, 225–231 (May–June 1963).

Rochester (N.Y.) Police Department. *Preliminary Investigations Manual* (n.d.).

RUBINSTEIN, JONATHAN. *City Police* (New York: Farrar, Straus and Giroux, 1973).

SHERMAN, LAWRENCE W., and RICHARD A. BERK. "The Minneapolis Domestic Violence Experiment," *Police Foundation Reports*, 1 (April 1984).

——, and ——. "The Specific Deterrent Effect of Arrests for Domestic Assault," *American Sociological Review*, 49:261–272 (1984).

——, CATHERINE H. MILTON, and THOMAS V. KELLY. *Team Policing: Seven Case Studies* (Washington, D.C.: Police Foundation, 1973).

SKOLNICK, JEROME H., and DAVID H. BAYLEY. *The New Blue Line* (New York: Free Press, 1986).

——, and JAMES J. FYFE. *Above the Law: Police and the Excessive Use of Force* (New York: Free Press, 1993).

SPELMAN, WILLIAM G., and DALE K. BROWN. *Calling the Police: A Replication of the Kansas City Response Time Analysis* (Washington, D.C.: Police Executive Research Forum, 1981).

TROJANOWICZ, ROBERT, and BONNIE BUCQUEROUX. *Community Policing: A Contemporary Perspective* (Cincinnati: Anderson, 1990).

WILSON, JAMES Q. *Varieties of Police Behavior* (Cambridge, Mass.: Harvard University Press, 1968).

WILSON, O. W., and ROY CLINTON MCLAREN. *Police Administration*, 3d ed. (New York: McGraw-Hill, 1972).

——, and ——. *Police Administration*, 4th ed. (New York: McGraw-Hill, 1976).

ZEISEL, HANS. *The Limits of Law Enforcement* (Chicago: University of Chicago Press, 1982).

7

Police Planning

KEY WORDS AND PHRASES

Planning unit personnel
Kurt Lewin
Force-field analysis
Systems and procedures
Field operations analysis
Operations research
Completed staff work
Crisis management
Ivory-tower plans
Administrative plans

Value-driven policing
Management plans
General orders
Special orders
Operational plans
Regular operating procedures
Unusual activity plans
Creating procedures
Tactical plans
Computer technology

Planning is the careful development of methods to achieve desirable goals or conditions. Generations of management students have been taught that organizational planning is the primary administrative function and the basis from which all else proceeds. More than a half-century ago, for example, public administration pioneer Luther Gulick built on a World War I–era analysis of French management writer Henri Fayol (whose 1916 work was translated into English and distributed in the United States in 1949) to create an acronym—PODSCORB—useful for describing the functions of management:

Planning

Organizing

Directing

Staffing

COordinating

Reporting

Budgeting (Gulick, 1937:13)

Writing specifically for students of police management—many of whom committed his acronym to memory in preparation for promotional examinations—Richard L. Holcomb invented an even more colorful acronym, POST-BECPIRD:

Planning

Organization

Staffing

Training

Budgeting

Equipment

Coordination

Public Information

Reporting

Directing (Holcomb, 1961:77–78)

Further, according to Holcomb, planning is a five-step process that includes the following:

1. The need for the plan must be discovered.
2. A statement of the objective must be formulated.
3. Relevant data must be gathered and analyzed.
4. The details of the plan must be developed.
5. Concurrences must be obtained from organizational units whose operations may be affected by the plan. (Holcomb, 1961:79)

Two observations can be made about Holcomb's conceptualization. First, it is incomplete in the sense that its step 5 prescribes only the need to obtain concurrence from other "organizational units." In fact, planners must try to conduct a *global* survey of the potential effects of their proposals and to do everything reasonable to ensure that unintended negative consequences do not befall people, groups, or other interests inside or outside the agency.

Second, if planning is to be successful, each of the steps identified by Holcomb must include research. It is not enough to simply wait for the need for plans to become apparent, because it then may be too late to formulate and implement plans for a problem that has already reached the crisis level. Hence, step 1 of Holcomb's model requires that all organizations constantly and proactively scan the horizon for problems likely to affect their constituencies and themselves.

This responsibility is particularly critical where police agencies and other providers of emergency service are concerned. In many organizations, most planning is for the short range and helps accomplish a task that can be scheduled for convenience. Such plans typically can be forgotten or stuck up on a shelf once the job is complete, to be reactivated the next time the organization chooses or needs to do the same job. In policing, such plans might include arrangements for entrance examinations, promotion ceremonies, meetings with the public, and routine purchases of replacement equipment such as cars and radios.

Plans of this type are not the crucial part of policing, however. The success of the police enterprise depends heavily on the worth of plans designed to help people through sudden crises that may arise at unpredictable and inconvenient times, during which they must know in advance precisely what to do in order to avoid disaster. These plans cannot be forgotten, because when the crises for which they are designed suddenly arise, they must be implemented unhesitatingly. Motorists who suddenly find themselves skidding on ice patches in their new cars are in big trouble unless they are instantly able to activate advance planning for such dilemmas. Similarly, unless training has provided police officers with advance plans for dealing with the sudden crises they will invariably face at some unpredictable times during their careers—such as the violent emotionally disturbed person, or the motorist who flees when the officer signals him or her to stop, or the outraged participants in a domestic dispute—they will be forced into on-the-spot decisions that are very likely to make matters worse rather than better.

In police departments and most other organizations, the close relationship between planning and research is generally reflected in the existence of a single central unit that bears the primary responsibility for both of these functions. Almost all large corporations, for example, have invested heavily in *R&D*—research and development—units, while police departments usually call these entities *research and planning units*, or vice versa (for brevity's sake, we will refer to them simply as "planning units"). While the existence of such a unit is necessary, it should not provide an excuse for people in other agency units to wash their hands of responsibility for planning. Planning must go on throughout the agency, and everybody, at every level, should be encouraged to plan.

STEPS IN PLANNING

The research concepts presented in the previous chapter are useful in understanding the actual planning process. Planning begins with research—finding facts and analyzing them to determine present and future needs—and then procedures and resources are developed to meet these needs. The plan is the detailed outline of the procedure to be used. The following steps must be taken in its development:

1. The need for the plan must be recognized. An apparent need must be verified by a more intensive investigation and analysis.
2. The objective must be stated, and the general method of operation (the manner in which the objective is to be attained) must be determined.
3. Data necessary in the development of the plan must be gathered and analyzed. Included will be answers to the questions of "what," "where," "when," "who," and "how."

4. The details of the plan must be developed: personnel and equipment must be provided and organized, procedures developed or applied, schedules drawn up, and assignments made.
5. Planning reports must be prepared, utilizing the concepts mentioned in the description of completed staff work.
6. Planners should participate in a staff capacity during implementation, if this is requested by persons carrying out the plan.
7. Plans must be reviewed, and modified if necessary, to accommodate changes in need and technology.

STAFFING AND ORGANIZING THE PLANNING FUNCTION

Police experience with formalized planning units suggests that the best position for them is as close as possible to the chief of police, particularly when inadequate attention has been given to planning functions in the past. During the infancy and development of a planning unit, strong support from the chief of police, as well as regular access to the chief, is needed to ensure department-wide acceptance and understanding. Not all subordinate management personnel will be immediately sympathetic to the need for such a unit. Further, locating the planning unit in a subordinate bureau or division may tend to isolate it from the decision-making process.

On the other hand, if the planning unit is well established and functions without the need for continuing support from the chief, the chief should be able to delegate the planning effort to a deputy who is sympathetic to the planning process and who also has the ear of the chief. In such circumstances, the planning function can be made a part of an administrative services unit.

Planning Unit Personnel

The success of the planning unit, even in a small department, depends heavily on the qualifications of its staff members. They must have a sound knowledge of police administration bolstered by good judgment, initiative, enthusiasm, and persuasiveness. They must have imagination in order to conceive fresh solutions to problems that may be rooted in traditional, stultified practices. Since a part of their task consists of gaining concurrences on plans, they must be personable and must work well with other people, particularly operational personnel. If they are to be effective, they must also be willing to revise their own ideas and creations as necessary and to deal well with criticism.

Planning staff must be especially able to cope with criticism that involves emotions, rather than rational objections to their proposals and concepts. Virtually every change or new direction suggested by a planning unit carries with it implicit criticism of what has gone on before. Those responsible for existing policy or practice may see suggestions for change as attacks on themselves or their abilities. Consequently, it must be understood, they are likely to react in ways that go beyond cool and analytic professionalism. It is as important to

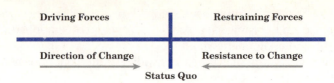

FIGURE 7-1. Kurt Lewin's Force-Field Analysis

anticipate such reactions and mitigate them in an understanding way as it is to develop intellectually defensible plans. Thus, the effective planner must be part politician.

Force-Field Analysis. Psychologist Kurt Lewin's conception of *force-field analysis* illustrates this point. According to Lewin, the state of any human activity can be described by a vertical line that is locked into its position by opposing *driving* and *restraining* forces (see Figure 7-1). For our purposes, it may be useful to think of this vertical line as representing the current state of some police policy issue, such as an agency's receptivity to community- or problem-oriented policing or officers' attitudes about affirmative action.

In order to produce change, this vertical line must be moved to the right, in the direction of change, by the driving forces. This can be accomplished by either or some combination of two strategies. First, the driving forces can be strengthened to the point where they simply overpower the restraining forces. Alternatively, advocates of change can try to reduce the resistance offered by the restraining forces.

The temptation, especially in hierarchical organizations like police agencies, is to overcome resistance through power, by strengthening the driving forces and trying to roll over resistance. When this is done, however, the restraining forces typically increase their resistance, turning the change process into a pushing contest that increases animosity and the degree of tension on the vertical line, or day-to-day working environment. In such circumstances, this vertical line may move, but it will do so only under great pressure. Worse, as soon as the pressure of the driving forces is released—which, given the press of other business, is bound to happen eventually—this vertical line is likely to snap back under the increased pressure of the restraining forces. Like a spring under great pressure, when it does so, it is likely to come back so far and so fast that the cause of change will be retarded rather than advanced, and our vertical line will end up moved to the left rather than the right.

For these reasons, planners and change strategists should concentrate as much as possible on reducing, rather than bulldozing, resistance to their proposals. Instead of simply mandating that those who have long followed old policies change to follow new policies, for example, planners should anticipate their resistance and reduce it by inviting them to enter the change process as early as possible and to participate in dialogues in which they have both input and a chance to see why the new policies are better than the old.

In too many police agencies, this does not occur. Instead, administrators and their planning units formulate plans in a vacuum and mandate adherence to them. Then, to overcome resistance, they try to make *examples* of a few who question or challenge their authority. Subsequently, they appear stunned when their middle managers and line personnel regard those disciplined not as examples but as *martyrs*. In the end, they often find that the backlash caused by their insensitivity has made things worse than they were when they first started their plans.

Effectively developing and implementing new plans, therefore, should include careful consideration of sources of likely resistance and strategies to reduce their resistance with as little tension as possible. In the simplest language, planners must figure out whose ox is likely to be gored by an anticipated plan. Once they do so, rather than merely expressing regrets, they should work with the ox's owner to save it or to replace it with another.

Civilian Planners. In small departments, the formal planning function may be the part-time task of one or more sworn personnel. As departments increase in size, however, posts in the planning unit may be filled more effectively and economically by civilians than by police officers. For example, methods and forms analysts, programmers, and data-processing personnel all need special background and training. The skills they require are relevant in a broad range of activities beyond law enforcement and, conversely, are rarely found among police personnel. Junior members of the planning unit may be drawn from universities and colleges that offer courses in public or business administration or criminal justice. In recent years, particularly, many universities have developed programs that apply modern information technology—computers—to administrative and policy problems and have become extremely fruitful grounds for recruiting planning staff. Such staffers must, of course, work closely with staff who have had considerable policing experience.

In addition to the permanent staff of the planning unit, members from various branches of the department may be assigned on a temporary basis to work on problems in their fields. This is especially important when large numbers of officers will be affected by a plan, since their acceptance of it is necessary for its successful operation. A representative who understands the point of view of the operating units can anticipate objections to, and recognize the weaknesses of, proposals before they become incorporated into plans.

Organization of Responsibilities

A recommended structure for a planning unit in a large department is depicted in Figure 7-2. Although no subdivision of the planning unit is normally suggested below the division level in medium-sized departments, some of the responsibilities and functions may merit temporary subdivisional status during developmental stages. For example, a data-processing section may be formed within the planning division during a period of heavy staff work. Later, the

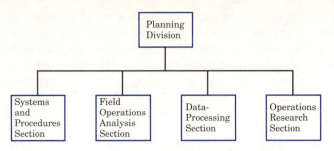

FIGURE 7-2. Organization of Planning Unit in Large Department

section may be discontinued if the programming and planning workload declines.

Systems and Procedures. The systems and procedures section is concerned with the preparation of departmentwide directives and general orders, special orders, and memorandums. It performs the research necessary for the preparation of drafts for review by the chief and his or her staff, and it should also bear responsibility for proactive and timely problem identification. To this end, it should keep pace with social and economic trends, court decisions, legislative edicts, and other matters that may eventually affect police operations. A particularly important responsibility here is to constantly monitor changes in the jurisdiction's population and to evaluate the implications for such changes in agency policy and operations. Doing this requires that planners get out of their offices and interact closely with other department entities—especially patrol and community relations units—with the field operations analysis unit, and with the public. If, in cooperation with line and inspections units that also bear responsibility for looking at the future in this way, it does these jobs well, this section can protect the agency's credibility and avoid embarrassment and sudden unpleasant surprises.

This section should also have the responsibility for indexing and cataloging department publications and supplying these indexes to department personnel. It also reviews each order issued at any level in the department in order to eliminate any conflicts or inconsistencies with other directives. The systems and procedures section should also be concerned with the development of procedural manuals and with forms control. The latter is an extremely important function that ensures clarity, uniformity, and brevity in recording and communicating all kinds of information. Specific tasks include cataloging and indexing every form in use in the department and devising flowcharts to show where the forms originate, who sends them, where they go, and what use is made of them. In addition, the office conducts a continuing review of forms to make sure that they conform to department policy and to determine whether combining, computerizing, or eliminating forms would be feasible and economical. All orders for forms from any unit in the department must go through this office so that it may review the number ordered and restrict this number to no more than can be used in one year.

The section should maintain a "suspense file" on requests for changes in order to study these suggestions before a new design is ordered. When the forms-control unit prepares a new form or redesigns an old one, it submits the proposed form to the units that will be using it for comments or concurrence. When the form finally leaves this section, all aspects of its design and content have been completed, and it should be ready for reproduction or printing.

The development of procedural manuals is a continuing process closely allied with forms control and with paperwork simplification. A constant check is necessary to prevent duplication of files and inefficient methods of originating or routing records and other material.

Field Operations Analysis.   The field operations analysis section—frequently called the *crime analysis unit*—analyzes crime and other incident reports in order to isolate information that may help to identify criminals or emerging police problems, such as patterns of criminal activity or disorder. Such information is helpful in planning the operations of a division or district and in promptly mobilizing all appropriate resources to address the problems identified. A department with a canine or tactical unit, for example, can most sensibly plan assignments and procedures for these special groups when the nature of offenses can be clearly delineated and computer-mapped from day to day.

Field operations analysis tasks may be separated into two categories: (1) long-range or strategic operations analysis, intended to predict trends (e.g., in crime or in population growth or composition) and the manner in which they will probably affect personnel and other resource requirements; and (2) short-range or tactical operations analysis, including preparation of crime-analysis bulletins and computer maps for day-to-day use. In some large departments, this short-range activity has been placed in field operations or patrol bureaus, while long-range activity has been retained in the central planning unit. No matter what the arrangement, interaction between field units and central planners should be constant.

Data Processing.   Today's decision-making process depends heavily on computer handling of data, the storage and retrieval of information, and the generation of reports. Although the advent of reasonably priced personal computers has made it possible for operational units to conduct many of their own analyses, the central data-processing function should be located within the planning unit during its infancy in the department for the same reason that planning itself should be placed under the control of, or as close as possible to, the office of the chief. Much of the initial work in the data-processing area will require continuous effort by the personnel of the planning division, with constant review, revision, and updating of techniques. Ultimately, however, some of the routine processes can be transferred to another division in the department, with only the design and development phase of future projects remaining a responsibility of the planning unit.[1]

Remember that a computer is a tool rather than a magical device or instant problem solver. Although far more sophisticated, the computer should be considered in much the same light as a typewriter or calculator. Further, as the need for computer use begins to increase in many of the divisions of the department, there will be growing justification for placing computer operations in service bureaus rather than in a planning division.

Operations Research. There should be a section responsible for operations research and for general planning and development activities not described in references to the work of other sections.

More than a quarter of a century ago, the influential report of the President's Commission on Law Enforcement and Administration of Justice was most emphatic in recommending the establishment of an operations research capability in larger police departments:

> As an important mechanism for innovation within police agencies, it is urged that police departments of one thousand or more employees establish an operations research group comprising professionally trained scientists, mathematicians and engineers, including at least one person with a broad statistics background, and at least one with electronics competence. (President's Commission on Law Enforcement and Administration of Justice, 1967:61)

Given the rapid growth and decreased cost of computer technology, this recommendation today holds great relevance for agencies of all sizes. The work of an operations research section, or of the person responsible for it on a full- or part-time basis, should obviously involve the use of operations research techniques. The term "operations research" has been adopted by business management and military management to mean a systematic, method-oriented, basic inquiry into the structure, characteristics, functions, and relationships of an organization. Its techniques provide the administrator with a scientific basis for solving problems in terms of the best interests of the total organization. Some of the techniques that have potential police use are linear programming, game theory, statistical analysis, and simulation. In the application of an operations research technique, for example, there must be the collection of relevant and pertinent data. The analysis of the collected data must be so detailed and valid as to provide a model of the real-time situation. Next, there must be a manipulation of the model to estimate what will occur under varying circumstances. Selection of the optimum course of action can then result from the testing. A continuing check must be made on the validity of the model in the light of any new data that are developed.

The operations research section should furnish the administrator with current and regular reports on significant management problems, including information needed to direct and control programs and projects. To carry out this responsibility, the section should develop a management-information system. Such a system would:

- Identify management problems.
- Identify controls that are needed to manage more effectively.
- Aid the planning, monitoring, and progress of programs and projects.

- Provide timely progress reports to identify areas where actions may be required.
- Identify areas where utilization may be improved.
- Improve the quality and content of data on which management decisions are based.
- Identify the factors that influence the decisions.

Various types of basic reports should be developed by the system, such as management-analysis reports, master-employee reports, and program- or project-status reports.

This section should conduct studies to determine the most economical types of equipment for efficient performance and the most economical schedules for replacement. Operations research techniques are ideally suited to this kind of problem solving.

THE PLANNING PROCESS

The role of the central planning unit should be carefully described in writing. Ideally speaking, the planning unit should view its role as carrying out the chief's responsibility for planning rather than the sergeant's. Emphasis should be on management rather than operations; on long-term strategies rather than short-term tactics; on staff coordination rather than direct involvement. In actual practice, of course, things are not nearly so clear-cut—hence the reason for suggesting carefully defined, written policy statements.

The staff planning process involves a state of mind rather than adherence to a rigid set of principles to guide the activity. It can utilize the application of the scientific method—the statement of a problem, development of a hypothesis, testing, and the conclusion. The process can certainly involve tests of efficiency: Is the operation in question being handled in the best way possible? Can it be done in any other way? Can it be done at a lower overall cost? With greater efficiency? With greater safety? The process also is concerned with the general application of the "policy planning" method, which is to describe past practice, the current status of the problem, and good practice in general; to analyze alternatives (including, if appropriate, past attempts at solutions); and to make specific recommendations for future action.

Roles of Planning Units: Two Examples

Two of the nation's largest police departments—in New York City and in Los Angeles—vary considerably in the roles of the central planning units and in the details provided in formal statements of their central planning units' roles. While reading the two statements of roles and duties in Boxes 7-1 and 7-2, consider their impacts on the operations and other units of each department, as well as the degree to which each concentrates organizational power in one of-

BOX 7-1. Central Planning in New York City

According to the New York City Police Department's *Administrative Guide*, its Office of Management Analysis and Planning bears the following responsibilities:

MISSION

- Evaluate policy, develop programs, provide management control, and coordinate planning efforts within the department.

FUNCTIONS

- Provide members of the department with needful information, and scrutinize all directives and orders on matters of policy and procedures to prevent conflict.
- Analyze, evaluate and propose department policy.
- Provide advice, direction, and analysis assistance to all command levels.
- Monitor and evaluate major department projects and programs.
- Administer and coordinate the department's funding activities.

POLICY & ANALYSIS DIVISION

- Analyze department policy for compatibility and impact on department objective and evaluate productivity proposals.
- Conduct high priority issue analysis and cost-benefit analysis of major department programs and enforcement activities.
- Conduct labor policy analysis in the labor negotiation context.
- Provide the department with long-range planning capability, and coordinate, assist and review input of decentralized planning efforts of the department.

MANAGEMENT SERVICES DIVISION

- Provide a professional internal management consultant for improvement of the department's managerial, operating, and economic performance.
- Raise the level of sophistication of the crime analysis methods used by the department.
- Conduct regular and special analysis of crime statistics and data to determine trends and patterns.
- Compile crime data for dissemination to units in the department and other authorized agencies.
- Develop, monitor, and evaluate major new or existing programs and review high priority projects.
- Administer employee participation in the planning process.

REPORTS & PROCEDURES DIVISION

- Revise the department manual and review, edit and publish intradepartmental directives to promote coordination and prevent conflict.
- Develop and coordinate the reports control, forms control, and the records retention procedures of the department.

Source: New York City Police Department, *Administrative Guide* (1974).

fice. Consider also the extent to which each of the departments' chief executive officers is dependent on the commanders of these units.

Completed Staff Work

The concept of *completed staff work* plays an important part in the production of planning and research reports. Completed staff work is the study of a situation and the statement of recommended action in such a form as to allow the administrator to make a prompt and effective decision. The concept has been distilled to the following elements:

1. A brief statement of the problem or topic

BOX 7-2. Central Planning in Los Angeles

The Los Angeles Police Department *Manual* states:

680.01 Planning and Research Division—Organization. Planning and Research Division is composed of:

- Office of the Commanding Officer.
- Procedures and Directives Section.
- Planning Section.

680.05 Planning and Research Division, Office of the Commanding Officer—Special Duties. The Office of the Commanding Officer, Planning and Research Division, is responsible for the following special duties:

Emergency Control Center Division. Preparing the Emergency Control Center Division for activation, including:

- Reviewing and implementing forms and systems used in the Emergency Control Center (ECC).
- Training personnel for ECC operations.
- Assigning personnel to staff the ECC when it is activated.

Research Information Center. Maintaining the Research Information Center (RIC), including:

- Coordinating control of all Department staff research.
- Making all final determinations on what action constitutes staff research and issuing administrative DR numbers for all staff research.
- Receiving, indexing, and filing all Staff Research Control Forms 1.15, and staff research reports for ten years from the date of their receipt in the RIC;
- Providing information from these files upon request, and:
- Conducting administrative audits to ensure compliance with staff research control functions.

680.10 Planning and Research Division—General Functions. Planning and Research Division is responsible for the following functions:

- Coordinating control of all Department staff research.

- Processing requests for Department directives.
- Amending, maintaining and distributing the Department manual.
- Developing new forms and examining existing forms to determine the need for revision or elimination.
- Preparing and maintaining Department maps, charts, graphs, and special purpose visual aids.
- Conducting research pertaining to actual or proposed legislative changes.
- Responding to inquiries concerning the effect of existing law and legal decisions on Department procedures.
- Researching, reviewing, and reporting on legislation, decisions, and City Attorney's and District Attorney's opinions.
- Conducting research and preparing special project reports as directed.
- Researching and preparing Environmental Impact Reports required of the Department, and analyzing Environmental Impact Reports that may affect the Department.
- Researching and analyzing short-term and long-term matters which affect Department operations.
- Maintaining a repository of research and management information, including copies of staff reports, research projects, studies, and surveys that affect the policies, procedures, operations, and management of the Department.
- Responding to selected inquiries from other agencies regarding Department procedures, policy, and operations.
- Investigating, analyzing, and preparing the Department's budget proposals, in the format requested by the Mayor and City Administrative Officer, on requests for alterations and improvements and capital projects.
- Investigating and handling requests for interim alterations and improvements of police facilities.
- Coordinating the development and implementation of capital projects, including those funded through approved ballot measures.
- Handling correspondence and communications with the Building Services, Department of General Services, regarding alterations and improvements which have been approved in the

BOX 7-2. **Central Planning in Los Angeles** *(continued)*

budget, and minor modifications to existing buildings and grounds.

- Providing staff support for the Police Facilities Committee.
- Coordinating Department space allocations and maintaining the Department's Space Master Plan.
- Coordinating, monitoring, and assigning product evaluations to the following commands:
  - Training Division for lethal weapons, nonlethal control devices, protective equipment, and related products.
  - Motor Transport Division for vehicles and related products.
  - Specialized divisions for products which are to be used specifically in their specialized assignments.
  - Planning and Research Division for all other products.

680.15 Planning and Research Division—Special Duties. Planning and Research Division is responsible for the following special duties:

Department Directives. Maintaining the distribution list of Department directives.

Legal Bulletins. Preparing and publishing periodic legal bulletins and notices pertaining to case and statute law.

Law Library. Maintaining the Department's law library.

Home-Garaging Program. Providing staff support for the Home-Garaging Committee; reviewing, processing, and maintaining a file of all Home-Garaging Approval Summaries, Home-Garaging Vehicle Authority Applications, Home-Garaging Vehicle Logs, and Home-Garaging Employee Authorizations.

Management Bulletins. Preparing Management Bulletins.

Product Evaluation Manual. Maintaining and distributing the Product Evaluation Manual.

Emergency Broadcast System. Conducting monthly Emergency Broadcast System checks in conjunction with the Los Angeles County Sheriff's Department.

Cellular Telephones. Coordinating cellular telephone billing and providing concerned command officers with monthly telephone bills.

680.20 Planning and Research Division—Special Liaison. Planning and Research Division maintains special liaison with:

Emergency Operations Organization. Regarding the control and operations of the Emergency Control Center.

City Attorney's Office. Coordinating activities relative to requests for legal opinions, legal information, and case law interpretation.

Source: Los Angeles Police Department, Planning and Research Division, *Manual of the Los Angeles Police Department* (1991).

2. Elaboration of the problem or topic, containing factual information and detailed explanations, if necessary
3. Analysis of alternative courses of action and their consequences, taking into account the comments of other staff members and supervisors affected by the work
4. Final conclusion and recommended action, ready for approval or disapproval
5. Enabling directives or general orders, ready for signature
6. Appendix items, if appropriate, consisting of detailed reports that bear on the work but that are not essential to the conclusion, detailed statements of concurrences or objections of staff, exhibits, and examples or mock-ups

Items 3 and 6 in the above list mention review by members of the staff or supervisors who are affected by the plan. A proposed action given review in this way is said to have been "staffed." This process stimulates the development of ideas by middle management, including alternatives perhaps not envisioned by planning officers. It exposes the plan to the reality of applied use and helps to identify inaccuracies. It encourages acceptance of the plan when it is adopted. Finally, the process cultivates the sense of unity of purpose and encourages members of the department to act as a team.

Initiation of Planning

The work of the planning unit may be initiated in several ways. Much activity, it is hoped, will be generated by ideas coming from the chief, who, by virtue of his position, should have the most global view of the agency's activities and external relationships. At the same time, however, the chief and other high-level staff should do everything reasonably possible to see that both recognition of the need for planning and *meaningful and welcomed* participation in it permeate every department level. In addition, of course, much planning effort will be initiated by the planning staff as a purposeful activity. Some of the input should come from the staff inspections unit. An increasing number of requests for work will be made by other divisions, especially when the planning staff has demonstrated the usefulness of its products. In short, all agency units and levels should provide the planning unit with input and suggestions.

The inspections function has an important bearing on the planning process. The first step in planning is the determination of needs, and some form of inspection is a great aid in this process. As suggested earlier in this chapter, the need for the plan must be recognized before the plan can be developed, and this recognition may occur at any level in the organization. Attention may be called to the need by failures resulting in injury to officers, prisoners, or private citizens or by sudden decreases in effectiveness as measured by percentage of stolen property recovered or of cases cleared by arrest. It may be recognized by the operating divisions in the routine performance of their duties. Often, however, the recognition of the need for a plan results from the use of inspectional devices that will ensure an examination of all aspects of the department's operations.

Although the central planning unit should constantly scan the horizon, the discovery of needs in their own fields also is the responsibility of the operating units. Unit heads cannot shift this responsibility any more than chiefs can, but they may charge their subordinates to be on the alert for evidence of such needs. Evidence may be found at any level of authority, but when the operating unit fails to discover it, the final responsibility rests with the chief. For this reason, and because operating personnel may be unwilling or unable to recognize or anticipate needs and problems, the chief should charge personnel assigned to conduct inspections to be alert for situations requiring new plans.

Once the usefulness of planning has been demonstrated, the planning unit may have some difficulty in coordinating requests for service when they originate directly from operating units. Requests should therefore be channeled

Operating units must be encouraged to participate in the planning process. This officer examines a weekend's crime reports in an attempt to identify patterns and trends.
Spencer Grant/Stock, Boston.

through the chain of command so that intermediate and higher levels may be informed and so that they may have the opportunity to coordinate requests.

RESISTANCE TO FORMAL PLANNING

Even though the need for planning is generally recognized, some in policing, both at the top and at the bottom, have long resisted it. The sources of this resistance are understandable but should be addressed because those who devote great energy to the development of plans that are ignored on the line or buried at the top of the agency are likely to give up. Policing is, after all, an action-oriented occupation that provides instruction in and rewards its members for responding coolly to crises that befuddle both other officials and ordinary citizens. In some departments, in fact, the top officials have earned their positions not because of their general administrative skill but precisely because they have proved themselves to be their organizations' best crisis managers. Because it is an operating style that has served them well, such administrators often believe that the best way to accomplish the police mission is to encourage officers and managers to work in a similar reactive manner.

Police Work as Crisis Management

The mind-set that may develop in policing, therefore, is that planning should be minimized—if used at all—and that each crisis, whether operational, administrative, or purely political, should be dealt with on an ad hoc basis. A major problem with this approach is that it disregards the lessons of history and causes decision makers to reinvent the wheel every time they face a crisis. More important, this approach means that some of the most crucial police decisions will be made in hurried and emotional circumstances, when the chances of mistakes are highest.

Line officers also may be prone to hold a negative view of the value of planning. Yet regardless of whether they realize it, good line officers do implement a plan each time they deal with a critical event. Typically, they apply their training and their experience to each new situation they encounter and, almost instinctively, deal with it from start to finish by employing a quickly formulated plan. Some evidence of the effectiveness of their planning ability is the fact that these officers satisfactorily handle the overwhelming majority of the problems they confront.

Ivory-Tower Plans

The success of these line officers also is evidence of the need to include their input in the formulation of formal plans by headquarters units. Too often, this does not occur, with the result that formal police plans are regarded with disdain by those assigned to implement them in the field.

In most large police departments, no official has more access to the chief or develops a closer working relationship with him or her than does the planning unit commander (see Boxes 7-1 and 7-2). In too many cases, this close relationship has tended to develop into an unhealthy overcentralization of authority and simple clout. On occasion, this occurs because heads of formal planning units engage in *empire building*—conscious efforts to expand and broaden the natural power that emanates from their office. On other occasions, the planners' empire is the result of an unintentional, simple evolution based on mutual trust and familiarity. In still other cases, growth is less welcome and occurs only because tasks that have no clear and logical home are dumped on the planning unit, with the consequence that none is done well. Regardless of how it happens, the growth of planners' autonomy usually is accompanied by shrinkage in operating units' authority to design their own programs and to determine their own fates. This, in turn, is sure to breed within operational units a top-to-bottom disdain for planning units and their work. To avoid this, both departmental chief executives and staff planners themselves must conscientiously attempt to keep their relationship from becoming one that freezes everybody else out of the planning process.

In this attempt, agencies must constantly keep in mind that the planning process is intimately tied up with operations and that operating personnel should participate in planning to the fullest extent possible. The planning unit should therefore consider stimulation of the planning process throughout the department to be a first responsibility. It should not attempt to relieve operating units and personnel of their obligation to participate in planning, for to do so would result in impractical proposals or loss of confidence in the success of the plan.

Although agency heads are responsible for establishing planning protocols and the formulation of plans may be made the responsibility of one person or of a large planning division, all units in the department that may be affected by plans must be actively involved in preparing and finalizing them. Participation in the development of a plan will stimulate interest in its operation and promote an understanding of its purpose and application. It is essential that those who are affected by plans consider them practical and acceptable. Those who contribute to the development of plans usually find them workable and sound and give sympathetic support to their implementation. In addition, their participation will lead to further awareness on the part of operating personnel of the need to recognize or seek out areas where planning is needed. This, in turn, will keep the planning function alive at a level below that of the central planning unit.

Plans relating to personnel management, for example, should be prepared with major input from the personnel officer or with his or her assistance and guidance. Also, the experience of line officers in detecting needs and in establishing objectives and standards for selection, promotion, training, rating, discipline, and welfare should be considered if the plans are to be satisfactory. Likewise, the finance officer may develop and operate the mechanics of a budget and of accounting and purchasing procedures; but present and future personnel, equipment, supplies, and building needs, as well as their specifications, can be identified and interpreted only in the light of the experience of operating personnel. Plans relating to records-division operations should be developed through major input by the records-division staff, or under their guidance, and special operating procedures should be developed by personnel engaged in the work to which they apply. The chief, in turn, needs the experience of the entire department in predicting the probable results of any proposed modification of organization, policy, or procedure.

Planning is closely and fundamentally related to such other administrative tasks as inspections and training. The inspection process can serve to reveal the flaws that generate the need for remedial planning. Since the end result of planning is very often the introduction of new techniques, success in implementing them depends on training and indoctrinating members in the new methods.

In short, for plans to be meaningful, the total resources of the department must be utilized in their preparation. Where relevant, plans must reflect the experience of line officers, the findings of statisticians, the conclusions of the crime and methods analysts, the counsel of staff inspectors, and the advice of every organic unit that may make use of them.

Fighting the Last War

Failure to involve operational units in planning and in regular review of existing plans tends to result in unquestioning reliance on plans that, too late, are found to have become useless. This scenario often involves the development of an elaborate plan after some unexpected crisis has caught a police department unawares and ill-prepared. The new plan, developed by a central unit or a task force of senior officials, is put away, and for years no similar crisis occurs. During this period, some of those who have created the plan retire, and others assume that it would be a simple matter to initiate the plan in order to resolve new crises. Then, suddenly, a similar crisis occurs and the department pulls its plan from the drawer, dusts it off, and finds that it has become useless because everybody involved in its development has long since retired and because it has not been modified to keep pace with changing conditions.

The 1977 blackout in New York City illustrates the need for institutionalized planning and regular review of plans. In 1964, for the first time in 21 years, New York City suffered major civil disorders. After assessing the damage and its response to it, the NYPD overhauled its emergency mobilization plans, leaving intact a provision that required off-duty officers to respond for duty at their "resident precincts," the police patrol headquarters for the neighborhoods in which they lived. This provision made sense in 1964, as it had in 1943, because, despite a 1960 law that, for the first time, authorized officers to live outside the city limits, most police officers still lived within the city. In addition, this provision was left in place because, owing to a 1964 crime wave on the subways, New York City officers were temporarily required to travel to and from work in uniform.

Over the next decade, however, a very high percentage of New York City officers (perhaps half) moved to the suburbs. For these officers, "resident precincts" were the department's few small facilities on the edges of the city, far from the inner-city neighborhoods in which disorders were most likely. In addition, in the years after the 1964 opening of the Verrazano-Narrows Bridge, thousands of officers and their families moved to Staten Island, a quiet and formerly isolated "suburb within the city." Further, the requirement that officers commute in uniform had long been rescinded, and virtually all officers stored their uniforms not at home but in their lockers at work.

This was the situation in 1977, when lightning struck a power station during a storm at 9:35 P.M. on an intensely hot summer night. Suddenly, and without warning, all of New York City was thrust into darkness. This had happened once before in New York City, in November 1965. On that earlier occasion, the atmosphere in the city was festive: citizens helped officers direct traffic, neighbors partied by candlelight, and, taking only a little literary license, a Doris Day movie memorialized what had been a real communal affair. Nine months later, it was long said, New York City's birthrate hit its all-time high.

This was not true of the 1977 blackout. Almost immediately, looters and arsonists began to trash the city's most blighted neighborhoods. Eight thousand off-duty officers reported quickly to their resident precincts—almost all in a few isolated, outlying facilities. There, they met their neighbor officers—people they might have seen in supermarket aisles but, generally, people with whom they had never before worked.

Nothing was going on in these outlying precincts, however, and so officers had to be bused to the action. But many of the buses first had to be driven out to these precincts from their garages in the center of the city. These round-trips were made through New York's usual traffic and were aggravated by the fact that the blackout had knocked out all the city's traffic lights and streetlights. By the time most of these officers finally did arrive where they had been needed, it was too late for them to be of much help. Worse, the few who did get to the distressed neighborhoods quickly were not equipped with uniforms, helmets, and batons. Instead, dressed in the jeans, shorts, T-shirts, and sneakers officers wear at home on hot summer nights, they were virtually indistinguishable from the looters they had been mobilized to police. According to researchers Robert Curvin and Bruce Porter:

> "I was overjoyed to hear I was getting a busload of guys from Staten Island," said Captain Driscoll [the commander of a riot-torn Brooklyn precinct], "But when they walked in the door, they looked like a tennis team." Near Fordham Road in the Bronx, one merchant reported seeing a policeman try to corral looters while he brandished a toilet bowl brush. (Curvin and Porter, 1979:69)

During the 36-hour blackout, 1,616 stores were looted of $150 million in merchandise. The Fire Department received more than 3,900 alarms and ignored 1,600 because it was so heavily burdened with major blazes. Although it is not clear how much difference a more rapid police mobilization would have made, the most severe losses to theft and arson occurred in the riot's earliest stages.

The most important moral of this story is that planning is a *dynamic* process rather than a *static* process. The plan to deal effectively with the 1964 disorder was not developed until after the smoke from that ordeal had cleared. In 1977, this plan was of little use because the department had neglected to consider whether and which changes in the city and in itself would affect implementation of the plan. Instead, like the generals who are said always to be planning for the *last* war they fought, the department tried in 1977 to implement a plan for the last disorder it had faced. That disorder had been isolated in 2 neighborhoods—Harlem and Bedford-Stuyvesant—but the 1977 blackout affected 31 neighborhoods.

A second moral is that *tactical* plans should be reviewed regularly at all levels and by all units of an agency in order to determine whether they have remained feasible. The 1977 blackout led to such a critique. As a result, the mobilization procedure requires that off-duty officers respond to predetermined locations where emergency equipment (batons, helmets, clearly identifiable garb) is stored. In addition, there now exists a plan for mobilizing officers to citywide disorder, as well as to disorder in just a few areas. Finally, the department mandated an annual review and critique of its disaster and disorder plans.

Even this thoroughness, however, has not guaranteed success or that carefully devised plans will be implemented or followed. A recent report by Richard H. Girgenti, the New York State Commissioner of Criminal Justice, was extremely critical of the NYPD for its 1991 failure to promptly end four nights of civil disturbance in the Crown Heights section of Brooklyn. This event began with a clash between Crown Heights's blacks and ultraorthodox Hasidic Jews, who, in the best of times, live side by side very uneasily. "At the core of the Crown Heights community," Girgenti observed in his report, "is a deep-seated conflict between blacks and [the Lubavitcher sect of Hasidic Jews] which is imbued with racial prejudice, anti-semitism, and religious intolerance" (Girgenti, 1993:43).

Four days before this disorder began, the Chief of Department, Robert Johnston, an expert in controlling civil disorder, had retired. Johnston's retirement set off a series of promotions, transfers, and temporary assignments that ran right down the chain of command.

To replace Johnston, the department's commissioner elevated Chief of Patrol David Scott, another veteran commander of large-scale uniformed police operations at demonstrations and disorders. After his promotion, Chief Scott left town on a previously scheduled vacation. During Scott's absence, Joseph Borrelli, the Chief of Detectives, was made acting Chief of Department. Borrelli, a long-term detective commander whose career included the successful conclusion of many of New York's most notorious criminal cases, had little experience in commanding major patrol operations. Scott was succeeded as Chief of Patrol by Mario Selvaggi, a veteran patrol commander who had rarely been assigned to Brooklyn during his long career and who knew little of the peculiar tensions between its African American and Hasidic residents. Several hours before the disorder began, the commander of the Crown Heights precinct was transferred and replaced.

Thus, when Crown Heights exploded, "a leadership vacuum existed at the highest levels of the Department [and] the Department lacked a critical analysis of what was happening in the streets and whether the police response to these events was effective" (Girgenti, 1993:19). By Girgenti's assessment, the police response was not effective.

Contrary to requirements, the department's disorder plans had not been annually reviewed. Acting Chief of Department Borrelli decided to leave it "to experienced patrol commanders to operate as they saw fit, explaining that decisions regarding the strategy and tactics to be used in particular situations normally 'are left to the uniformed command' " (Girgenti, 1993:248). The uniformed commanders, however, were waiting for direction from above, while the police commissioner "viewed Borrelli as 'the person there who was in charge of everything'" (Girgenti, 1993:21) and assumed that field commanders were effectively handling the situation. As a result:

> . . . the Crown Heights disturbance represented the most extensive racial unrest in New York City in over twenty years. It differed from most disturbances throughout the turbulent 1960s, however, as the violence was directed at one segment of the population. (Girgenti, 1993:9)

In the end:

> Over 150 police officers and at least thirty-eight civilians were injured during the disturbance. Most of the injuries resulted from assaults.
> Twenty-seven bias crimes were identified in the [Crown Heights] Precinct, including twenty-one anti-semitic, three anti-black, and three anti-white incidents. The underlying crimes included one homicide, fourteen robberies and assaults, seven instances of harassment or menacing, and five involving criminal mischief. Twelve other assaults and forty crimes involving property damage by groups were identified, but did not meet the Department's criteria for classification as bias-related. (Girgenti, 1993:10)

As the Crown Heights incident makes clear, therefore, the planning process must include provisions for adherence to paper prescriptions and some means of ensuring that the expertise for carrying out plans is always available.

TYPES OF PLANS

Plans may be classified in several ways, but it probably is most useful to conceive of them as falling into five broad categories: administrative, management, operational, procedural, and tactical.

Administrative Plans

Administrative plans are, in essence, the agency's constitution: its organization chart, the statement of its relationship to the community and other officials and institutions, and the statement of its responsibilities and authority and the division of these responsibilities among departmental units. In recent years, the trend toward *value-driven policing*, in which agencies establish and abide by formally stated organizational values, or ideals, had led to the creation of a whole new variety of administrative plans.

The Baltimore County, Maryland, Police Department was one of the first to subscribe to value-driven policing. In September 1987, the department announced in a special order that it was beginning study of the agency's values. A few months later, a Values Committee, including representatives from each rank, began to derive a statement of values toward which the agency could strive.

After two years of work interrupted by the normal press of police business and the difficulties of convening a multimember committee, the department issued the following statement of its first principles:

> AS PUBLIC SERVANTS . . .
>   We shall preserve and advance the principles of democracy and freedom in our pluralistic society.
>   We are accountable to higher authority and the community we serve.
> AS MEMBERS OF THE POLICE DEPARTMENT . . .
>   We aspire to professionalism in all aspects of our operations.
>   We shall maintain the highest standards of integrity.
>   We shall treat each other with mutual trust, fairness, and dignity, as we strive to accomplish the Police Department's mission.
> IN SERVICE TO THE COMMUNITIES OF BALTIMORE COUNTY . . .
>   We are committed to fair and impartial enforcement of the laws, reduction of fear, prevention of crime, vigorous pursuit of offenders, and compassionate assistance to victims of crime. . . .
>   We are committed to community policing. (See Behan, 1993:37–52.)

Management Plans

Management, or *strategic, plans* are, in effect, attempts to anticipate where a jurisdiction will be in the future and to ensure that official resources are marshaled accordingly. These plans necessarily involve the effects of broad social, economic, and environmental trends on the organization. At present, for example, police agencies should be concerned with the long-term effects on their operations of such social issues as AIDS and the apparent shift of the U.S. economy from manufacturing to a more highly automated, service-oriented mode.

Both these issues present complex questions that require much analysis before even the most general plans may be put into place. Some of the effects of AIDS on policing are relatively easy to predict—it already has created among police a greater awareness of the need for increased caution in handling persons who have suffered bleeding wounds, for example—but others are not so clear. What should be done with officers who test HIV-positive? How many are there likely to be? How intensively should police agencies attempt to determine the manner in which HIV-positive officers have acquired the virus?

Recent shifts in the society and the economy have created similar dilemmas for police administrators and planners. What is the significance to police in a highly industrialized jurisdiction of the displacement of factory workers by more highly trained technicians and engineers? What changes in policing should follow shrinkage of the lower-middle and working classes and the increased disparity between the well-trained people who design work and those who do it? It is often said, for example, that the rapid growth of the computer industry will divide the society into two groups: geniuses who create computers and those capable only of pushing computer buttons and passing the resulting printouts on to their bosses. Certainly, we would all like to think that this is an overstatement, but somewhere under the morass of the great social and economic changes we continually experience, there are major implications for police and those they serve. Managerial, or strategic, planners try to identify these implications.

Other management plans involve shorter time horizons and describe the future courses of action involved in the organization and management of personnel and matériel and in the procurement and disbursement of money. Such planning relieves the chief and his or her command group of burdens that otherwise would require so much of their time that they would be unable to carry out their functions of direction, coordination, and control.

Management plans usually affect an entire agency, rather than just some subunits, and often are issued in the form of general orders or special orders.

General orders usually address long-term concerns such as the formulation of general policies to deal with recurring situations. Police department policies on the use of deadly force, inquiries from the press, and disciplinary action, for example, often are issued as general orders.

Special orders usually are designed to assist in dealing with specific unusual events that affect an entire department or almost all of it. These may include parades, festivals, major sporting events, visits of dignitaries, and political conventions.

Allocation of Personnel. The most important and most expensive police resource is personnel. Consequently, the most important management planning tasks involve the allocation of personnel. In very small departments, resource allocation often becomes one of the major personal tasks of the chief at budget time, when he or she must convince the city administration of the need to increase the size of the agency. The degree of success in this undertaking is often regarded as the hallmark of the ability of an administrator. In a department of any size, the task of justifying increased personnel should not be trusted to chance or guesswork but instead should be supported by factual information related to increased demand for police services or through comparisons with other agencies of comparable size. Because there are so many variables that may affect the number of police officers across jurisdictions of similar size, however, the latter technique is the least desirable expedient and should be carried out only when there is an absence of other information. No matter how this task is conducted, however, administrators should take care not to let it consume so much time that it diverts them from properly overseeing the line operations of their agencies.

The preferred method for determining personnel requirements is to base estimates on actual and projected workload requirements. This sort of system can be worked out manually in a very small department and through the application of machine processing in the larger agency. The technique is often carried out by the data-processing personnel assigned to the planning division, sometimes because the personnel in that unit developed the technique in the first place.

Staffing Plans. Plans must be made to reflect the distribution of personnel among the various units of the department. Forms in table format should be prepared that will enable the chief to know at a glance from day to day the number of personnel actively working in each unit. In this way, it will be possible to detect any dangerous depletion of personnel in one unit owing to relief days, illness, and transfer. The plan for the allocation and distribution of patrol personnel is depicted graphically in the form of beat maps. The planning unit can participate in beat studies and the preparation of beat maps.

Personnel Plans. Procedures must be established to ensure implementation of the department personnel program, described in detail in Chapter 9. For example, the steps in the recruitment procedure should be completely outlined, from the announcement of acceptance of applications to the final appointment of the successful candidates. Procedures and forms must be devised to ensure an accurate record of the accomplishments of individual employees. A rating form should be developed and procedures adopted to ensure a periodic evaluation of all officers. A career development plan is an essential part of the police personnel program. The plan should list requirements and opportunities.

Training Plans. Recruit, in-service, career development, and roll-call training should be planned, as should curricula, schedules, lesson plans, and examinations. In-service training programs must be integrated into the work schedule. Guides and checklists should be prepared for field instructors to ensure complete coverage of all training subjects by explanation and demonstration and to assist them in supervising the patrol work of recruits.

Community Relations Plans. In addition to establishing sound and constructive relationships with all other departments involved in the administration of the city government, it is desirable that plans be made to organize community agencies and individual groups and societies for cooperative efforts with the police department. The public information officer or community relations unit must play a role in the development of these plans.

Comprehensive Law Enforcement and Criminal Justice Plans. Many of the aspects of comprehensive state law enforcement plans can have a direct effect on local police management, and management planning efforts resulting in funding must obviously avoid conflict with the state plan. Regions, counties, and cities (particularly larger agencies) also contribute proposals for specific projects that often become a part of the state comprehensive plan. In other cases, they may be required to submit comprehensive, generalized plans for their own regions or agencies.

Management Planning through Consulting. Police-management surveys conducted by consulting firms can usually be described as general plans for the improvement of the department. In most cases, consultants emphasize management improvement. Consultants' reports tend to stress recommendations for the enhancement and development of management functions such as leadership and direction, planning, and personnel management.

Although many consultants bring to their work a strong combination of analytic skills and substantive knowledge of police issues, the expertise of others may lie primarily in the study of organizations *generally*, rather than in the study of police organizations in particular. This should certainly not be a disqualification. Instead, it might even be a reason to select such a consultant over one whose work concentrates solely on police: anyone who can successfully advise major corporations on how to organize and operate in the most profitable ways surely has some information that would be valuable to police agencies. Thus, as Chapter 6 suggested with regard to researchers, the general analytic skills of some external consultants are a reason for police staff to work closely with them in order to assure that their work product is of maximum value to the particular concerns of the community and the agency under study.

Budget Plans. Future needs for personnel, equipment, and capital improvements must be estimated and justified if appropriations are to be obtained. Budgeting involves planning in order to ascertain future requirements; surveys must be conducted to determine the need for replacing worn and outmoded equipment or to meet increased demands in transportation, communications, weapons, laboratory, traffic control, maintenance, accounting, and jail.

Other Fiscal Plans. Accounting procedures must be established and expenditure reports provided to assist in making administrative decisions and in holding expenditures within appropriations. Specifications must be drawn for equipment, and purchasing procedures must be established to ensure a check of deliveries with the prescribed specifications. Plans and specifications must be drafted for the construction of new buildings and for the remodeling of old ones.

Operational Plans

Operational plans usually are based on an analysis of agency workload and prescribe each unit's efforts to handle it. In Chapter 6, for example, we pointed out that a long line of research on the effectiveness of police patrol activities had led to the development of alternatives to the former tradition of simply assigning officers to random preventive patrol. The operating unit documents that describe implementation of these alternative programs from year to year are among operational plans. Thus, as cases in point, the criteria patrol commanders should use in deploying officers across patrol beats or the rules the communications division uses in placing calls for service on a *differential response* queue would be part of an agency's operational plans. So, too, would a patrol commander's report to a police chief executive on how he or she intended to deal with an increased workload during a forthcoming fiscal year in which budgetary constraints made it likely that the patrol unit would have fewer personnel and matériel resources.

If the current trend toward community- and problem-oriented policing continues, this area of police planning is likely to become more decentralized in the future. The greater involvement of field personnel in the creation and implementation of operational plans designed for local problems is sure to create an exciting and challenging time for central police planners. Especially in large agencies, central planners will have to ensure that, without seeming to oversee field personnel in the manner of Big Brother, they remain apprised of what works and what does not. This will require that field units report on their successes and their failures so that, taking care to avoid stifling innovation or embarrassing individuals, central administrators and planners can take part in circulating information about innovations that have succeeded and those that have not. One way to accomplish this would require central planners to serve as facilitators or coordinators in periodic conferences in which field personnel could discuss, evaluate, and attempt to generalize from each other's experiences in attempting to devise and implement operational plans for their communities.

Plans for the operation of line units include *regular operating procedures*, which are designed to meet routine, everyday, year-round needs, and *unusual activity plans,* designed to deal with intermittent, and often unexpected, variations in activity. Often, these procedures and plans are based on a type of research called *field operations analysis.*

Regular Operating Procedures. Operating units must have specific plans to meet current needs. Each unit's personnel must be distributed throughout the hours of operation and throughout the area of jurisdiction in proportion to need. The most desirable shift hours must be determined, the patrol and traffic forces must be distributed among the shifts, and the jurisdiction must be divided into beats for each shift. Assignments must be devised to allow certain officers to meet intermittent needs and yet provide for their productive use during the hours when they are not so occupied. Schedules must take into account such factors as relief days, lunch periods, and the hours, nature, and location of regular work. Supervision becomes more difficult when regular assignments are interrupted in order to deal with short-time, periodic needs; nevertheless, plans must be made to ensure that suitable supervision is provided.

Specialized assignments must be worked out by the supervisors in both the detective and youth divisions to provide approximately equal workloads, taking into consideration variations in the importance of cases and the average time required to investigate them. Assignment of officers to a unit should be on the basis of need, and within units assignments should be made on the basis of special ability and interest, as well as in proportion to need. The planning unit may also participate in organizing the nature and extent of specialized assignments, but such activity is very close to the basic raison d'être of operational commanders, and so they should remain free to fill the assignments.

Programs must be developed to meet particular needs in each field of activity. For example, the traffic unit needs programs of enforcement, public education, and engineering. Each of these may comprise several individual parts; for example, the public education program will require diverse approaches, depending on whether it is directed at pedestrians, motorists, schoolchildren, churchgoers, elderly people, or people residing in a given district. A large department may have a safety-education unit to plan such programs. The youth division needs operational plans intended to eliminate certain delinquency-inducing factors in the community. Programs designed to make better citizens of delinquent and predelinquent children and minors or to promote better relationships between officers and adolescents will be required. This division will also need plans to obtain assistance from all community agencies in the diagnosis and treatment of certain delinquents.

Unusual Activity Plans. Regular operating programs of the field units are based on the assumption, proved valid by experience, that the nature, frequency, time, and place of occurrences that call for police action are reasonably predictable. At the same time, such predictions are possible because the hazards that result in these occurrences do not change quickly: street layouts, obstructions to vision, the nature of business enterprises, and the character of the residents in a given area remain fairly stable over a relatively long period of time. When the offenses that occur within the area are plotted by means of computer maps or simple pin maps, the concentration of accidents and of each class of crime will be found in approximately the same position from one year to the next. The police are thus able to plan with considerable consistency a program of prevention and enforcement in any field of police activity based on an average need.

Criminal activity and unusual situations and circumstances have no respect for averages, however, and create irregular, out-of-the-ordinary, short-term demands for service. In the investigative units, the unusual need is nearly always met by the temporary adjustment of regular assignments, and it will seldom be necessary to augment the strength of these units. For example, a sudden surge of burglaries may result in a caseload beyond the capacity of the detective, or detectives, assigned to handle this type of crime. Some of these cases may be given to other investigators whose current load may be lighter than usual.

Unusual needs in the traffic and patrol units may also be met by such internal adjustments, except on occasions, such as large community events, that create demands beyond the capacity of personnel normally adequate for the regular operating programs. The patrol unit may encounter unusual criminal activity, such as a series of robberies, burglaries, or other crimes committed by one or more persons, usually during the same hours of the day, on the same days of the week, and in the same section of the city. Plans must be made to meet these situations without loss of time through last-minute readjustments of assignment schedules.

A mobile reserve unit or task force should be available to strike at or otherwise meet such out-of-the-ordinary needs in jurisdictions where they occur frequently; this condition is likely to be found in cities or urbanized counties of more than 200,000 inhabitants. Such a task force is described in Chapter 16. A task force may receive planning assistance in the form of an operations analysis carried out by a unit attached to the field operations bureau. In some cities, the planning unit has the responsibility of analyzing the crime situation so that it may detect areas in which patterns of criminal activity demonstrate the need for this kind of operation.

Field Operations Analysis. As suggested earlier in this chapter, the terms "field operations analysis" and "crime analysis" are used by many police departments to describe the identification of crime trends and patterns (as well as traffic-accident and enforcement patterns) through the statistical treatment of information and through an examination of actual investigative reports. This technique is an effective service for patrol officers in helping them concentrate their activity at the proper locations and times and on the appropriate subjects. It has a very practical use for a detective during the interrogation of a suspect in the search for crimes that may be attributable to that suspect. There is a close relationship between crime analysis and the modus operandi search. The latter usually results from a request by a detective to the records unit (or modus operandi unit within that unit, if one exists) to search the files in an attempt to link an unknown offender's method of operation with the patterns and habits of persons who are known to the police. Often the crime analyst will discover characteristic patterns connecting seemingly isolated cases. He or she can then initiate a modus operandi search or alert field investigators as to the potential value of the search.

In too many cases, crime analysis is not carried out at all, even though it is applicable to medium-sized and larger departments. In others, an examination of crime or traffic reports is not conducted until a problem situation arises. In sophisticated, large departments, however, various formal systems are used to analyze crime or traffic trends and patterns.

In a small department, crime analysis can be carried out by a physical examination of crime reports to identify crime patterns and to establish crime trends. A common method is to assign the activity to a report-review officer who also administers the report follow-up system. The officer can categorize crime reports and then produce spot or computer maps, crime-analysis bulletins, and other information that may be of value to patrol officers and investigators.

Some cities carry out crime analysis at the level of the field operations bureau or in the planning unit itself. The treatment of crime analysis in a planning unit should focus on strategic analysis as opposed to the tactical analysis carried out by field operations personnel.

Procedural Plans

Procedural plans are the nuts and bolts of police plans; they provide guidance for routine and not-so-routine operations and, especially in large departments, may be quite voluminous. The Los Angeles Police Department's *Manual*, for example, includes three long chapters, or "volumes," of procedural plans. The first, "Management Rules and Procedures," consists of 110 pages, with three small-type columns per page and a numbering system for its sections that begins with 105 and ends with 880.30. In this volume are subchapters on:

Supervision

General management procedures

Planning and accounting

Records and reports

Supplies and maintenance

Uniforms and personal equipment

Personnel management

Disciplinary procedures

These subchapters range from general plans that describe command protocols at unusual events through the manners in which uniforms are to be worn to the procedure for certifying that the names of officers killed in the line of duty may be inscribed on the department's Police Memorial.

The second, and longest (149 pages) LAPD "volume" of procedural plans is entitled "Line Procedures." It includes separate subsections on:

Communications

Field activities

Traffic control

Traffic accidents

Booking, custody, and disposition of property

Booking and custody of prisoners

Follow-up investigation

Outside police agencies (Los Angeles Police Department, 1991)

Procedural prescriptions certainly are critical to the good order of any police agency, and care must be taken to develop and enforce them. At the same time, however, administrators must avoid the tendency to overemphasize the way things get done and to overlook the problem of seeing that things actually do get done. This tendency toward *ritual* rather than *results*, toward excessive *red tape*, can be overcome through several steps.

First, before the establishment of any new procedure, a clear statement of what it is expected to accomplish should be developed. This is not an easy task, because calls for new procedures often begin with only a general sense that "something should be done" about a vaguely defined problem. Before planners proceed, these vague problems and troubling situations should be carefully diagnosed and made explicit as clear problem statements.

Second, consensus about the validity of the resulting problem statement should be obtained from as many as possible of the people affected by it. This process should go as far down the organizational ladder as practicable because line personnel may have a very different view of the issue than do administrators or planning staff. If subsequently compelled to abide by procedures they regard as unrealistic, uninformed, or dictatorial, line personnel are likely to do so grudgingly or, worse, to avoid becoming involved in the whole area of activity concerned. Embarrassed by citizens' complaints that traffic enforcement agencies had notified them that police officers had placed parking tickets on their vehicles while the vehicles were stolen and missing, for example, some police departments have created procedures requiring that officers conduct stolen-property checks before issuing citations. Often, these procedures prove unworkable—heavy radio traffic or a large volume of such requests for information delays response—with the result that some officers ignore the regulation and that others simply stop issuing parking tickets.

Third, this problem statement should serve as the target for planners throughout the development of related procedures. On occasion, when one is deeply immersed in a project, the forest is lost for the trees: the task of achieving the original objective becomes obscured by minutiae. Posting the problem statement prominently and reviewing it frequently help to avoid this.

Fourth, planners should not try to anticipate every situation in which the problem may arise and to develop an alternative procedure for each. Because policing is an infinitely variable undertaking in which no two situations are precisely alike, this is an impossible task, and attempts to answer every possible "What if . . . ?" question lead only to hopelessly complex and unusable plans. Instead, procedures should leave some reasonable amount of discretion to line personnel. The hallmark of professionalism, after all, is not blind conformity to rigidly programmed procedures but the ability to apply a set of guidelines to a range of generally similar situations.

Fifth, the resulting procedure should be reviewed at every level affected by it, and every level must have an opportunity for meaningful comment. These comments should be considered carefully, and the procedure modified accordingly.

Sixth, the procedure should be field-tested and evaluated. No procedure should be considered inviolable, and pride of authorship should be a distant priority behind a desire to address problems satisfactorily. During this period of initial evaluation, care should be taken to see that the problem has been properly defined and that the new procedure does not create more problems than it solves.

Seventh, the procedure should be modified as indicated by the evaluation conducted in the preceding step.

Eighth, the procedure should be promulgated as an order or as an amendment to the agency manual. This step involves much more than sending a few sheets of paper out of headquarters. Unless new procedures are accompanied by explanations of intent and by instruction in implementing them, the effort devoted to creating them is made worthless. Where comparatively minor procedural changes are concerned, promulgation might consist of no more than brief memos and/or explanations by supervisors at roll calls. In the case of complex new procedures or procedures that reflect major shifts in philosophy or police priorities, however, formal training is fundamental to success.

In years past, for example, many police departments followed a general philosophy that did not distinguish between simple domestic disputes and actual domestic violence and that treated arrests at "domestics" as signals of officers' failure to resolve them in the least drastic ways. As the distinctions between loud arguments and criminal violence became clear, police agencies established procedures that defined arrest as the appropriate way for officers to respond to criminal domestic violence (Buzawa and Buzawa, 1990). Such a sea change in operating philosophy could not be successfully implemented without accompanying training that addressed both the reasons for the change and the skepticism of officers who might not otherwise believe that the agency really meant what the new procedure said.

Ninth, the process of evaluation should be continuous. Times change: with them, objectives change, and problems assume new dimensions. On happy occasions, problems may even disappear. Consequently, procedures must be continually assessed for relevance and viability.

To summarize, the process of creating procedures includes nine steps:

1. Identifying goals and articulating them in clear problem statements
2. Obtaining consensus on the validity of goal statements
3. Maintaining a clear focus on the problem statement
4. Avoiding the tendency toward overprescription and excessive rigidity
5. Reviewing preliminary plans at every affected level
6. Field-testing and evaluating preliminary plans
7. Modifying preliminary plans as necessary
8. Issuing the resulting plans
9. Continually evaluating plans and modifying them as appropriate

During this entire process, pain should be taken to ensure that problem statements and resulting procedures are not simply means of shifting blame for unavoidable embarrassments from the agency's top level to its lowest levels. In any organization, there is a danger that administrators may respond to complaints about service by imposing unworkable procedural requirements on line personnel.

This is sometimes done by administrators who have no expectation of enforcing the requirements until something goes wrong. In the case of the parking-ticket-on-stolen-car problem discussed above, for example, officers can maintain acceptable levels of parking enforcement without fear that anybody is checking to see that they have checked to determine whether each ticketed vehicle is stolen—as long as they are not unfortunate enough to ticket a stolen car.

When this happens and the car owner complains that police were more interested in raising revenue than in recovering taxpayers' stolen cars, administrators engage in the "CYA" exercise of disciplining offending officers for violating usually meaningless procedures. A far better solution is to scrap the procedural requirement until the technology for instant checks of every illegally parked car becomes available and, in the meantime, to bite the bullet by apologizing and explaining the reasons for such unfortunate incidents to offended motorists.

Tactical Plans

Tactical plans are developed for specific types of emergencies. Some tactical plans provide guidance for dealing with generic problems involving single officers or small groups of officers. This may assist in relatively routine encounters between individual officers and citizens, such as traffic stops, responses to reported crimes in progress, and the mediation of disputes, as well as more stressful events such as hostage and barricade situations. Other tactical plans—*contingency plans*—may involve widespread disorders and disasters or problems at particular locations, such as prison riots, plane crashes on the local airport's runway, or demonstrations at such politically sensitive locations as city hall or abortion clinics.

Planning for Police-Citizen Encounters. In recent years, this type of tactical planning—designed primarily to help individual officers get safely through the one-on-one encounters that fill their working days—has assumed great importance. This development is, in part, a result of the expansion of government liability for failing to properly prepare street officers for the sensitive situations that are part and parcel of their work. The best way to minimize government's exposure to vicarious liability under *Monell v. New York City Department of Social Services*[2] is to make sure that officers are adequately trained to deal with the most sensitive and trying aspects of their work. More generally, however, the growth of tactical planning is a result of the recognition that the line officer's work cannot safely be left to intuition, good sense, or any other innate characteristic of police officers, no matter how individually gifted.

With appreciation of the value of tactical planning at the level of the line officer has come a variety of commercial training programs and texts that recently have made such phrases as "officer safety," "officer survival," "edged weapons," "kill zones," and "zone of safety" a part of police jargon. Before police administrators invest in any of these programs or expose officers to them, however, several issues should be kept in mind.

First, no matter how carefully and competently designed, no externally developed police literature or training material—*including this book*—can precisely fit the needs of every U.S. police and law enforcement agency. Second, some commercially available tactical training material has been criticized for creating a sense of paranoia among officers through the use of overly graphic and unrealistic filmed scenarios (see, e.g., Geller and Scott, 1992:335–340).

Before encouraging officers to follow the principles outlined in any such material, administrators, planners, and trainers should carefully review the material. If it is plainly unrealistic or otherwise inappropriate, it should not be used at all. Where it may offer recommendations that do not precisely conform to local law, policies, or conditions, it should be edited or used only with appropriate cautionary comments.

Perhaps the best solution to the problem of developing tactical plans for officers' street-level confrontations is the development of a departmental tactical manual or set of periodically issued tactical bulletins. These can be designed by planners and trainers—with the *meaningful* input of field personnel—issued to officers, and accompanied by explanatory training.

Such operational plans should be clearly and concisely stated so that no confusion exists in their application. They should be developed for operational areas in which it is highly likely that officers will encounter situations that challenge their safety, the safety of citizens, and the good order of the jurisdiction and the agency. Among the operational areas that should be included in this category are the following:

- Vehicle stops, including high-risk stops and vehicle pursuits
- Use of force, including use and display of firearms
- Responses to reported or suspected crimes in progress
- Encounters with mentally and emotionally disturbed persons
- Field stops and interrogations of suspicious persons
- Arrests, search, and transportation of suspects
- Intervention into disputes
- Domestic violence, including sexual abuse
- Barricade and hostage situations
- Interactions with crime victims
- Death notifications
- Interactions with specific racial, ethnic, and sexual minorities
- Hate crime investigations

Each of these areas of planning calls for continuous study and research, and frequent modifications of plans may be necessary. In doing so, it must be recognized that it is not possible to outline in exact detail the actions to be taken in every possible situation. Human conduct is subject to infinite variation and cannot be predicted with accuracy; therefore, some freedom to make quick decisions on the spot is desirable. Planning should be so complete, however, that nothing that can be decided in reflective study is left to the impulsive decision of an individual officer.

Contingency Plans.   Every police department should develop and maintain contingency plans for the handling of such things as floods, blizzards, airplane crashes, explosions, and other disasters, both natural and man-made. As Box 7-2 suggests, one of the most important contingency plans is that which relates to civil disorders and riots. Another essential plan concerns barricaded persons and subjects who are holding hostages. Input from operational personnel is most important in the development of these plans. Procedures must be prepared to meet varying degrees of emergencies while at the same time providing continuing police coverage of areas not affected by an emergency. These should actually be a series of plans to cope with progressively intensified need, but they should be outlined and presented in such a way that a simple request

In the largest police agencies, sophisticated command and control facilities help top staff to monitor the implementation of contingency plans at large-scale police operations. *Mark Lennihan/AP/Wide World.*

for a plan by its number will set it into action immediately. For example, Plan 1 may call for the utilization of five patrol cars and a sergeant's car from the district of the occurrence, but when the emergency increases or is originally of great proportions, a call for Plans 2, 3, and so on, will automatically send additional cars from adjacent and other districts, without ever unduly reducing the strength of any one district.

In the formulation of such plans, arrangements must be made for the establishment of a command post (usually the first patrol car on the scene) at a location to which other cars can readily report. The command post should keep a log of vehicles reporting and should handle all radio communications with the central complaint room.

Proper handling of a large-scale disaster or civil disorder may require total mobilization of the department for protracted periods. Obviously, plans must be carefully developed, comprehensive, and thoroughly understood. They should be distributed in the form of general orders to ensure departmentwide circulation and comprehension. There may be a need for several variations of the full-scale mobilization plan to cover the differing demands of the several kinds of disasters or disorders that may affect the community, but any such plan should establish the nature of the emergency command structure, the method of initiating and terminating the plan, clarification of authority and responsibility for summoning outside assistance, and provision for coordination and liaison before and during emergencies.

Certain specific locations, such as airports, docks, and munitions plants, are sites of potential disaster. Plans to meet these possible emergencies must be available at all times. They must be specific in terms of outlining the actual roads and arteries that are to be closed to traffic, which hospitals are to be alerted, how the scene is to be isolated, and which other agencies are to be called on for assistance. The mission must be clearly understood—e.g., to control traffic, isolate the scene, preserve life, or protect property.

Specific emergency plans can operate under a *move-up system*, which is based on the application of general emergency plans to specific situations, i.e., prescribing certain situations that call for the activation of one or more of the specific emergency plans. As pointed out earlier, such a system would be designed to increase the resources devoted to emergencies without unreasonably depleting any district or area that is not involved in an emergency of its police coverage. Strength is drawn from the task force and from ever-widening circles of districts within the city.

Procedures for coping with specific situations at known locations should also be planned. Included in this category are plans for dealing with attacks against buildings equipped with alarm systems and against police or other public buildings by violent dissidents and mobs. Plans must also be made for blockades and jail emergencies and for special community events, large public meetings, athletic contests, parades, political rallies, and protest demonstrations.

Finally, as Box 7-2 suggests, all plans, tactical and operational, should include provisions for regular training of personnel at all levels affected.

Summary: Types of Plans

Obviously, these five types of plans are not categories that are carved in stone. The divisions among them are sometimes fuzzy, and there is obviously some overlap among them: plans to address some problems might be classified into two or more of these categories. Since it is difficult to classify plans[3] no matter where the lines among the types are drawn, the types should not be treated as categories for memorization but as a useful checklist or means of making sure that critical planning areas have been addressed.

THE IMPACT OF COMPUTER TECHNOLOGY ON PLANNING

The great majority of reports produced by police computers are statistical in nature and are intended to present routine administrative or crime-reporting information for immediate use rather than to provide long-range management information for making policy decisions or on-line operational support for field personnel.

Unfortunately, the use of computers in many departments has been prompted by jurisdictions' desire to enter what is now a fashionable field. In many agencies there exists sophisticated computer capability that lays dormant because no staff member is capable of using it or because the only staff member capable of doing so has left policing or moved on to other duties. This situation has certainly not been helped by the aggressive sales policies of computer manufacturers, who will not usually turn down the opportunity to sell or install their hardware even when there is reasonable doubt about the practical value of the equipment. Before investing in sophisticated hardware and the programs required to run them (discussed further in Chapter 8), police administrators should make certain that the human end of this resource equation is adequately prepared to use its electronic end.

In addition, experience has taught that even when implemented as anticipated, computerization has caused unanticipated problems. One of these involves major privacy concerns and a new planning problem for police agencies. Rapid computerized availability of information concerning vehicle registrations, vehicle and professional licenses, arrest and conviction records, and intelligence histories, for example, has sometimes led to abuses such as unauthorized access to confidential information or the illegal sale of such information by corrupt employees. In all cases, the sensitivity of information planned for inclusion in police computers must be carefully analyzed, and plans must be put in place to limit access according to a purely and tightly controlled "as needed" basis.[4]

Properly employed, computer technology can affect the planner in several major areas.

1. The planner may use the technology directly as a tool in management planning related to human and material resources, including applications of operations research techniques described earlier.
2. The planner's involvement with data-processing and computer technology may consist of design input into operational or real-time computer systems, such as computer-assisted dispatch and alternate response models.
3. The planner may have to control and coordinate requests from various divisions for adopting procedures utilizing data processing. Among the most frequent of these requests in U.S. policing agencies are those that involve criminal intelligence, an area of special sensitivity and concern for privacy.
4. The planner who acts in a staff capacity may sometimes be asked to generate material for day-to-day crime or operations analysis. This is especially true when the staff planner has been involved already as the system designer and has an appropriately programmed computer located physically within the planning unit.
5. The computer should ease the planner's work and, as computer literacy develops around the agency, should result in greater assumption of the planning function by operational units. To this end, chiefs and their staffs should encourage all personnel to become computer-literate and to devise means by which the computer can aid them in their work.

The first three of these areas are logical responsibilities of a central planning unit, but the use of planning personnel to generate routine crime analyses should be avoided unless the only usable computer is operated by the planning unit.

SUMMARY

It has long been virtually impossible for police patrol officers to plan their workdays. The work of these officers is, by and large, driven by factors beyond their control. Consequently, they never know precisely what they will encounter from day to day and moment to moment. It is predictable, however, that during the career of any individual officer—or during a single week in the work of a large agency's patrol officers—the routine will be interrupted by crises of predictable types. Individual officers never know when they will have to decide what to do about a fleeing motorist, but it is predictable that they will have to do so at some time during their careers. Police chiefs in large agencies never know which of their officers will be faced with such a situation during a given week, but it is predictable that one or more officers will face such a decision at some time during the week. Perhaps the most critical police planning is that which helps line personnel to deal with these crises, to mobilize plans that have been laid out in advance. In formulating such plans, police staff play much the same role as football coaches who lay out the X's and O's that guide those on the line. And, like good coaches, police planners must ensure that training accompanies their scribbles.

In a more general way, planning is important to the police administrator for precisely the same reasons that it is important to other executives in the public and private sectors. Leading a police agency or any other group of people is a complex—and competitive—endeavor. Good administrators must be able to harness the work of their people in the most efficient and effective ways, and they must also be able to explain to skeptical citizens, officials, and officers why the plans they have authorized and implemented ensure efficiency and effectiveness. Since unpredictability is at the heart of line police work, however, some administrators doubt the value of planning, preferring instead to encourage officers and officials to focus almost exclusively on crisis management. This style of operation, good football coaches know, is a recipe for disaster and should be avoided at all costs.

QUESTIONS FOR DISCUSSION

1. The economies and populations of U.S. cities change regularly, in ways that may have a great effect on police policy and operations. Consider some examples of this phenomenon and the mechanisms police agencies might use to stay ahead or, at least, apace of such change. What arrangements should be made to determine what police should do about the changes they may identify?
2. Prepare a Lewinian force-field analysis chart, and identify the driving and restraining forces that have determined the current state of affairs related to the following issues in the police agency that employs you or that serves the community in which you reside:
   a. Affirmative action efforts designed to increase the representation of women and minority males among police officers at all ranks.
   b. Progress in the adoption of community- or problem-oriented policing models.
   c. Support and encouragement for higher education among employees.
   Now, regardless of your personal feelings on these issues, devise strategies to produce change in each of these areas. As you do, try, wherever possible, to reduce resistance to change rather than simply to overpower it.
3. Even though the New York City Police Department has successfully defused hundreds of potentially explosive demonstrations and disorders over the last generation, it has not been immune from criticism about its handling of several major

events such as the 1977 blackout and the 1991 civil disturbance in Crown Heights. What types of plans and related mechanisms might have produced better results in the situations described? Are such plans and mechanisms in place in the police agency that employs you or that serves the community in which you reside?

4. A veteran police supervisor complained that many procedural plans are so detailed that they make it impossible for line personnel to respond flexibly to emergencies. As a result, she asserted, "We're more concerned about going by the book than with making sure the job gets done, and this lets things get out of hand too often." Presuming that her perception is accurate, what are its likely causes? How would you go about developing plans that strike a better balance between the need for consistency and the need for flexibility?

5. The state has decided to build a new 2,000-inmate maximum security prison on a large vacant piece of land at the edge of the jurisdiction served by the police agency you head. Plan for this: What impact will this construction project have on your operations? What will completion of the project mean to your agency? What relationships and understandings will need to be arranged and formalized?

NOTES

1. This is the arrangement in both the New York City Police Department (NYPD) and the Los Angeles Police Department (LAPD), whose planning units are described in Boxes 7-1 and 7-2.

2. *Monell v. New York City Department of Social Services*, 436 U.S. 658 (1978). With this case, the Supreme Court ruled that municipalities could be held financially liable for constitutional violations caused by their employees if it could be shown that such violations were the results of inadequate supervision or training. This case and its implications are discussed further in Chapters 2 and 15.

3. In his text on police planning, for example, Wilson (1957) presented an alternative classification of plans into five categories: procedural, tactical, operational, extradepartmental, and management. Swanson, Territo, and Taylor (1993) use a four-category classification: administrative, operational, procedural, and tactical. Neither of these two classification schemes nor the categorization used in this book is better than any of the others. All three simply are alternative ways of comprehensively describing the issue areas that should be addressed by planners.

4. See Burnham (1983) and Marx (1988, pp. 208–211) for discussions of the impact of computers on privacy.

SOURCES

BEHAN, CORNELIUS J. "Values," pp. 37–52 in John W. Bizzack (ed.), *Issues in Policing: New Perspectives* (Lexington, Ky.: Autumn House, 1993).

BURNHAM, DAVID. *The Rise of the Computer State* (New York: Random House, 1983).

BUZAWA, EVA, and CARL BUZAWA. *Domestic Violence: The Criminal Justice Response* (Newbury Park, Calif.: Sage, 1990).

CURVIN, ROBERT, and BRUCE PORTER. *Blackout Looting!* (New York: Gardner Press, 1979).

FAYOL, HENRI. *General and Industrial Management,* Constance Storrs (trans.) (London: Sir Isaac Pitman, 1949 translation of original 1916 French-language manuscript).

GELLER, WILLIAM A., and MICHAEL S. SCOTT. *Deadly Force: What We Know* (Washington, D.C.: Police Executive Research Forum, 1992).

GIRGENTI, RICHARD H. *A Report to the Governor on the Disturbances in Crown Heights,* vol. I: *An Assessment of the City's Preparedness and Response to Civil Disorder* (Albany: New York State Department of Criminal Justice Services, 1993).

GULICK, LUTHER. "The Theory of Organization," in Luther Gulick and Lyndall Urwick (eds.), *Papers on the Science of Administration* (New York: Institute of Public Administration, 1937).

HOLCOMB, RICHARD L. (ed.). *Municipal Police Administration,* 5th ed. (Chicago: International City Management Association, 1961).

Los Angeles Police Department, Planning and Research Division. *Manual of the Los Angeles Police Department* (1991).

MARX, GARY T. *Undercover: Police Surveillance in America* (Berkeley: University of California Press, 1988).

Monell v. New York City Department of Social Services, 436 U.S. 658 (1978).

New York City Police Department. *Administrative Guide* (1974).

President's Commission on Law Enforcement and Administration of Justice. *Task Force Report: The Police* (Washington, D.C.: U.S. Government Printing Office, 1967).

SWANSON, CHARLES R., LEONARD TERRITO, and ROBERT W. TAYLOR. *Police Administration,* 3d ed. (New York: Macmillan, 1993).

WILSON, O. W. *Police Planning,* 2d ed. (Springfield, Ill.: Thomas, 1957).

8

Financial Management and Budgeting

KEY WORDS AND PHRASES

Expenditures

Personnel costs

Operational cost

Financial management

Efficiency

Effectiveness

Budget

Budget cycle

Fiscal guidelines

Padding

Audit

Object/line item

Capital outlay

Performance budget

Outcome budget

PPBS

Zero-based budget

Expenditure control budget

Managing resources and expenditures is a major concern for the average American family, as well as for government agencies and private industry. Most of us worry about staying within the budget, protecting income, and getting the best return from investments and purchases. Since the 1970s, local governments have been experiencing financial problems resulting from declining revenues, reduction in federal revenue sharing, and voter-initiated tax and expenditure limitations. All of this has contributed to a shortage of income for public services at a time when demand for these services is increasing. As a result, elected and appointed public officials are under constant pressure to control expenditures and to maximize the use of existing revenues. In some instances, this has led to police budgetary decisions being decided by uninformed and overtly political debates that have little to do with rational discussions of public need and a lot to do with political, institutional, and occupational self-interest (Murphy, 1993: 8).

Politically imposed cost-saving measures often involve downsizing the police department. This is because the usual police department budget consists of 80 to 85 percent personnel costs and 15 to 20 percent operational costs. Doing more with less has become a reality, rather than just a slogan, for a number of police departments, and police administrators are being challenged to demonstrate the cost-effectiveness of their operations. These conditions have led to an increased awareness of the importance of financial issues and the need to improve the financial management of police organizations.

Financial management consists of planning, controlling, and using an organization's financial resources in an efficient and effective manner. *Efficiency* measures the cost of a unit of work, output, or objective. *Effectiveness* refers to the extent to which an organization achieves its desired objective. The basic underlying principle of financial management is to achieve maximum results with minimum cost. *Budgeting* involves setting financial objectives, identifying the required resources, and linking these resources to employee productivity and organizational objectives (Brock, Palmer, and Price, 1990). A *budget* is a formal statement of the financial resources required to carry out a specific set of organizational activities during a given time period. Simply put, it is the selection of ends and the means to achieve those ends (Lee and Johnson, 1983).

A properly developed budget can make a major contribution to the management of an organization because it has the potential of being used as both a strategic planning device and a financial working document that will assist the chief administrator in accomplishing the agency mission. This is because the budget plays a central role in every organizational activity. It is used to obtain revenues for recruiting, selecting, training, and compensating personnel; delivering services; purchasing equipment; maintaining the buildings that house the organization; and implementing new programs. In creating a budget, strategic decisions must be made about program objectives, cost, and continuance by department heads, governmental executives, and legislative bodies.

Budgets also reflect the fiscal and political reality of the organizations that create them. The difficulties associated with public budgetary systems have led some to describe them as onerous, omnipresent, useless, demeaning traps that direct managers' attention to yesterday's priorities (Osborne and Gaebler, 1992:117). However accurate this assessment, the fact remains that budgets are a critical factor in organization survival. A police department would be unable to function and would cease to exist without the resources obtained through the budgeting process.

THE BUDGETING PROCESS

Police agencies obtain their resources from public revenues that represent at best a finite source of income. Agency budgets, however, are more than just financial statements. They are an integral part of the government's managerial accountability process, serving as both a fiscal plan and a managerial control device. Budgets reduce all organizational activities such as hiring, training personnel, patrol, and equipment purchases to a basic unit of analysis, the dollar. This permits the monitoring of expenditures and the evaluation of performance by providing a basis for comparing the cost of an activity or expenditure to its benefit.

Conforming to Government Fiscal Procedures

State statutory requirements normally control all governmental budgets. Administrative law, formulated by the state budget office, may even specify what numbers are placed on specific budget line items. Since all police departments are part of either a local, county, or state government, their budgetary process must conform to the format established by the political subdivision's fiscal management system. Mayors, city managers, county executives, governors, city councils, and legislatures dispense public funds according to their fiscal policies and the needs of their citizens. As a result, budgeting is a strategic, managerial, financial, and political activity that involves intense competition for funds among governmental departments. Indeed, winning a substantial slice of the budgetary pie is a major, if informally recognized, measure of a police chief's success. More than any other aspect of police management, the police department's budgeting process must conform to the governing body's fiscal procedures.

The Budget Cycle

The entire *budget cycle*, from start to finish, consists of a series of events that are repeated at about the same time every year. Some government authorities require a significant amount of advance planning, including presentation of preliminary budgets, estimates of expenditures, and adherence to schedules before final approval of the budget. This process may vary, but it generally involves the following activities:

1. Establishment of fiscal guidelines
2. Preparation of the budget
3. Budget approval
4. Budget implementation
5. Budget evaluation and auditing

Establishment of Fiscal Guidelines. The executive head of the government or his or her chief financial officer must take a leadership role in budget development and preparation. This may take the form of an executive policy statement and/or memorandum that will contain fiscal policy, expenditure guidelines for department heads, and a budget activity schedule. In this manner, executive policy becomes an integral part of each subunit's budgetary process. The budget schedule establishes a time line for the process. This schedule usually involves a period of six to eight months within which deadlines are set for a series of activities, such as initial and final submissions, administrative review, and legislative hearings that will result in the budget's being adopted by a specific date. This date is often established by law.

Upon receiving the governing executive's budget message and schedule, chiefs of medium-sized and large departments issue their own sets of instructions to bureau and division heads and to their fiscal staff units. These instructions usually reiterate the overall scheduling requirements, establish timeliness for the preparation of the department's budget, and define the responsibilities

of those involved in the budget's preparation. Typically, executive managers of
smaller agencies simply maintain the schedule.

Preparation of the Budget.   The creation of a department's budget begins
with identifying the resources and expenditures needed for the continuance of
operations and development of new programs for the coming *fiscal year* (a 12-
month accounting period which is designated by the governmental authority
and which normally runs from July 1 through June 30 or from October 1
through September 30). The budget is prepared using either an independent
administrative process or a process that calls for multilevel managerial participation. The method selected will reflect as much the complexity of the process
as the department's managerial philosophy.

In a large department, budget preparation can be an extremely complex
process because of the numerous subdivisions, programs, grants, and personnel classifications. It is usually prepared in separate bureaus staffed by civilian
experts trained in finance. The principal operational commanders have limited
involvement except for developing staffing and equipment requests for their
subdivisions. Medium-sized departments typically employ a small staff consisting of a middle manager assisted by one or two civilians. In small agencies,
budgets are normally prepared by the chief of police (Moore and Stephens,
1991; Whisenand and Ferguson, 1989:177–178).

In traditionally managed bureaucratic departments, budget preparation
proceeds from the top down. The chief, administrative staff, and/or senior-
level managers determine organizational goals, define measurable objectives,
and prepare all budget requests. Little if any consultation with lower-level
managers and supervisors takes place, and when it does, it usually is limited
to one-sided information gathering.

In departments that practice more participatory philosophies such as total
quality management, budgetary preparation is a *mission-driven* process that
takes place at all levels of the organization, flowing from the bottom to the top.
This approach begins with lower-level managers preparing resource requests
in accordance with the department's fiscal guidelines and their unit's quality
standards and objectives. As each organizational level completes its unit's budget request, the proposal is discussed, negotiated, modified, and approved by
the next level. This process continues until the final budget proposal is submitted to the chief and his or her executive team for review. The advantage of this
approach is that all levels are involved in the establishment of department objectives; the identification of quality standards, resources, and expenditures;
and the resource allocation process. It establishes managerial accountability
and an awareness of the need for sound fiscal practice with unit managers (Osborne and Gaebler, 1992). However, it demands a high level of competence and
commitment from the individuals involved. The several budgetary systems
currently in use are discussed later in this chapter.

An important activity during the budget preparation stage is determining
the cost of providing services and programs during the next fiscal year. Unless
reliable cost information is developed, a department can experience substantial cost overruns and underfunding. Cost information is also needed by administrators responsible for analyzing the efficiency of operations and moni-

Policing is expensive: How much does it cost to field the officers assembled for this patrol district's rollcall at just one eight-hour shift?
George Godoy.

toring the expenditure of budgeted resources. Lastly, cost information provides a more inclusive and descriptive measure of the resources used by a department in the delivery of its services (Chabotar, 1982).

Determining cost involves the identification and analysis of all available data that permit a reasonable estimation to be made about the cost of a service or program and its impact. Costing is not an exact science. Conclusions regarding the efficiency or inefficiency of police operations are judgmental. They depend on the evaluator's experience, priorities, available resources, and estimation of the public's expectations and needs (Chabotar, 1982:27). Recent attempts by many police departments to evaluate the quality and effectiveness of their service delivery through citizen surveys represent a positive approach to improving the level of information available to administrators making these decisions.

In their financial management handbook for local governmental officials, Groves and Valente (1986:187–189) recommend the following six steps to identify the full cost of a municipal service:

1. Determine the purpose of the study.
2. Determine the time period for the study.
3. Identify the resources used in providing the service.
4. Choose appropriate units of measurement.
5. Collect cost information.

6. Use cost information.

This costing method can be used by police administrators for a variety of studies. For example, it can be used to find the full cost of patrol services, the average cost to process one felony arrest, the cost of a 16-hour community foot patrol assignment, or the cost of adding two additional investigators to the sex crimes unit.

The purpose of the study (e.g., finding the cost of patrol services or the cost associated with creating a gang task force) determines the type of data to be collected and the appropriate time for data gathering. Determining the annual cost of a service (e.g., patrol, investigations, etc.) requires obtaining cost information for an entire fiscal year or for a representative sample period that is typical of the year's activity. The cost of creating a special unit will involve estimations of all costs associated with start-up, staffing, administration, operations, and evaluation during the projected fiscal year in which the unit will be created and placed into operation.

All resources used in providing the service must be identified. These include personnel, equipment, time expended, administration, and facilities used. Both direct and indirect costs must be determined in order to estimate total cost. *Direct cost* is attributable to the production of a particular service or activity; *indirect cost* is also attributable to the production of a service but is jointly shared with many other services (Chabotar, 1982). (See Box 8-1 for types of costs associated with police services.)

The next step in the costing process is to decide how work output and unit cost should be measured. A *unit of output* is one instance of the service provided, and the *unit cost* is the average cost of providing one unit of service. For example, if the department wants to know the average cost of a work unit of traffic enforcement, it may decide to use the number of traffic citations issued by the unit as an output measure. It can then determine the unit cost (direct and indirect) in dollars to produce one citation by dividing the total operating cost of the traffic squad by the number of citations produced. The important thing to remember, however, is that whatever measures are selected, they must serve the purposes of the study.

How much cost data should be collected depends on the level of detail required by the analysis and the difficulty of obtaining information from the department's record system. *Cost information* can be located in expenditure records, past budgets, and such nonfinancial records as maintenance records and mileage reports. *Cost analysis* focuses on expenses to provide a service, rather than just expenditures generally. Expenditures are cash outlays made when a resource is purchased or expended (Chabotar, 1982:17–41)—the purchase cost of a patrol vehicle or the salaries of the officers who staff it, for example. However, expenses would include the cost of resources used to provide the service (patrol) over a given time period. Costs associated with the patrol unit would include gasoline, maintenance, officer training, patrol supervision, and administration, in addition to the cost of the vehicle prorated for the period of its use and the officers' salaries.

This discussion of cost analysis is concerned with the budgetary process. However, cost studies are a management tool that can be used to evaluate the

BOX 8-1. Costs Associated with Police Service Delivery

PERSONNEL COSTS

Salaries and Wages

Salaries and wages of personnel, including expenses for overtime, holiday and vacation pay, sick and funeral leave, personal leave pay, administrative leave pay, shift differential, hazardous assignment pay, educational incentives, and all other forms of compensation that are granted. Special pay differentials are either a separate cost category or included as part of salaries and wages.

Fringe Benefits

Items may include life, health, disability, and other types of insurance; pensions fund contribution; workman's compensation; uniform allowance; unemployment insurance; and similar benefits.

NONPERSONNEL COSTS

Materials & Supplies

Items and commodities which are consumed or used in providing the service, including office supplies, repair and maintenance, and small tools with a limited life expectancy. These items must be attributable to the service being provided and be a significant cost element to warrant assignment. (Items costing less than $150.00 to $500 are typically considered supplies.)

Fixed Assets

Real property (the land and anything affixed to the land), machinery, and equipment readily identified with the cost of the service being evaluated. A fixed asset must have a useful life greater than one year. A portion of the purchase price of a fixed asset may be taken (computed) annually as a Direct Cost. An example would be the percentage of a patrol car's value taken as a direct cost in a given year until the total cost less the salvage value of the vehicle is reached. The annual cost of a fixed asset is also called its "annual depreciation."

Travel & Transportation

Includes all cost related to travel, meal and hotel allowances, etc., needed to deliver a specific service. Since these expenses are regularly reported as the basis for reimbursement and easily identified, they are usually considered as direct costs.

Contractual Services

Utilities, insurance and bonding services, communications service and repair (could include lease of equipment), rents and leases, legal services, accounting services, and any other service for which a contract is drawn. If the costs of the contractual service are consumed by and directly attributable to a given police service, its costs are direct. If the costs of the contractual service cannot be readily allocated to a specific service, the costs must be allocated to multiple services and considered indirect.

Miscellaneous Costs

Printing and binding, memberships and dues, advertising, and any other cost not otherwise classified. Whether these costs are direct or indirect depends on the ability to assign a specific cost to a specific service.

INDIRECT COSTS ASSOCIATED WITH POLICE SERVICE DELIVERY

Overhead

Costs associated with acquiring, operating, maintaining, or use of a physical asset which is used in the provision of an organization's services. These costs are used in common by many programs of the department. Examples are, building repair and maintenance, utilities, rent, etc. The basis for allocating these costs to a particular service varies, but in all cases the basis is chosen so that the costs are equitably distributed to the service in relation to the benefits received.

General & Administrative (G&A) Expense

Costs necessary for the overall management and operations of the jurisdiction or department which are not directly attributable to particular services. For example, cost of chief executive and senior management staff, personnel, central unit support, data processing and the costs of other individuals and offices needed for the provision of all police services, not just the one being costed. That portion of G&A expense attributable to a specific service is usually determined based on direct cost.

Source: Kent John Chabotar, *Measuring the Costs of Police Services* (Washington, D.C.: U.S. Department of Justice, National Institute of Justice, 1982:21–22).

efficiency of a variety of functions. Their utility depends on how well they are understood and how relevant they are to the individual managers responsible for the organizational areas covered by the report.

Budget Approval.   Once the department's budget is prepared, the chief and the senior administrative staff review it to determine if it meets the department's guidelines and needs. It is important that all justification statements for increases in expenditures or new programs be clearly written and contain sufficient supporting data to ease the decision-making process.

After this final internal review, the department's budget is submitted to the mayor, city manager, county commissioner, or governor. Depending on the size of the governing authority, there may be several layers of administrative and legislative review before the budget is finally approved. Governmental administrative units and/or financial officers will review it, consult with the department's chief executive about requests and changes, and then forward it with a recommended funding level to the chief executive of the government. The department's budget will then be consolidated into the government unit's budget and will be presented to the legislature (city council, board of aldermen, etc.). The legislature will review the budget and usually will hold a series of public hearings before final approval.

The heads of government departments usually must appear at these hearings to present, defend, or explain any or all of their budgetary requests and operational policies for the coming year. The department's chief executive should be prepared to make a professional presentation at the budgetary hearing. This would include the use of such devices as charts, overheads, video tape, computer graphics, and slides to clarify important factors. Resource requests should be supported with data that link them to reasonable and measurable objectives. Lastly, flexibility must be built into the system so that it is possible to comply with final allocation decisions without endangering basic services. Occasionally, a chief of police may be able to persuade decision makers, through the strength and forcefulness of his or her personality and the elected officials' willingness, to transfer financial resources to the police department. However, successful budgetary hearings demand trust, logic, sound documentation, reason, and clarity of communication. At this point, the budget has evolved into a communication device that is no more effective than the arguments contained within it or made in its behalf ("The Budget as a Communication Tool," 1988).

It is not an uncommon practice for some administrators to submit a budget that requests more resources than they believe necessary. This is referred to as *padding* the budget. The justifications usually offered to support this practice include the rationale that higher authorities will cut back honestly estimated requests and this is the only way to obtain sufficient operating resources. There is a fine line in some cases between padding, which involves a budget submission containing requests known to be unnecessary, and a simple statement of actual needs when it is known that the government is unable or unwilling to finance the necessary resources. In either situation, the police administrator knows the budget request will not be met; but while the latter course may be acceptable and desirable, the former is not.

Misrepresentation of data is closely related to padding, and often the intent is the same: to make a strong case for greater resources. Whereas the padded budget may not contain an actual falsification of supporting facts and figures, the deliberate misrepresentation does. When discovered, this activity should result in punishment for the unit head involved. Lastly, both padding and misrepresentation violate the trust that must exist between the appointed police administrator and the governing body. These activities damage the reputation of the administrator, help to create an atmosphere of distrust, and strain the relationship between the department and its governing unit. The adoption of the budget by the legislative body sets the stage for the implementation of the budget during the coming fiscal year.

Budget Implementation.   Implementation is, perhaps, the most critical phase of the budgetary process. The revenues allocated to the department by the legislature determine exactly what is available to be spent and for what purposes. The chief executive is responsible for managing these resources in an effective and efficient manner. The department's share of the budget is usually subdivided into a system of accounts identified by category or program such as personnel costs, operating expenses, and capital expenditures. Funds in these accounts must only be spent for their identified purpose. If an account's funding is insufficient, it may be difficult to gain approval to shift funds from another account in the department or to obtain additional funds from the governing authority until the next budgetary period.

Since budgetary implementation requires the expenditures of revenues, the department's management information system should include an accounting system that records all purchase requests, orders, invoices, and payments. This system must be consistent with the one used by the dominant governmental authority. State governments normally provide a "purchasing manual" through the office of the state budget director or controlling audit authority that will provide purchasing guidelines. A department directive should specify who in the department is responsible for requesting and approving purchases.

Police departments cannot operate like the rest of us, who use credit cards to purchase what we want now, with the intention to pay for it with future income. No purchases should be made without sufficient funds to cover them. All future purchases must be identified in the department's budgetary preparation process and the necessary funds must be set aside for this activity. This is accomplished by *encumbering,* or committing, funds by item in the budget that will be used to pay for the goods or services when they are supplied or used. If the goods or services are not purchased or are purchased at a lower rate than originally identified, the unused portion of the allocation can be unencumbered and kept in the budget as an *unencumbered balance.* However, the funds that are paid out (*expended)* for goods and services received must be removed from the department's budget.

Accounting software, such as spreadsheets and database management systems for mainframe and small personal computer systems, has made financial records management an easier task for all departments, no matter what their size or resources. Computers provide managers with instant access to financial accounts. Computers can be programmed to facilitate data entry as well as to produce financial reports for senior command staff and the chief administrator.

These reports are necessary for monitoring the status of the budget items. As purchase requisitions and orders are processed, their deduction from a computerized budget account can be processed immediately by authorized personnel. A system of periodic account reporting and administrative review assists in reducing the potential for overspending, at the same time that it provides a warning of potential deficits. This is a significant enhancement of administrative control over the implementation process.

Budget Evaluation and Auditing. Police administrators generally conduct a comprehensive review of their current budget accounts before the end of the fiscal year. This is usually the first step in the planning and preparation process for the next year's budget. This internal managerial review should ensure that all weekly, monthly, and/or at least quarterly reporting and recording procedures were followed, the status of all accounts is correct, and resources are sufficient for the department to meet its objectives and provide services during the remaining part of the fiscal year. Any identified discrepancies should be investigated and corrected. The identification of a need for additional resources will become the subject of the next round of the budgetary process.

Periodically, or as determined by law, the department's fiscal activities and accounts should be subject to an audit conducted by accountants not employed by the governmental authority. This ensures financial accountability and control. The integrity of financial management in the public sector differs from that in the private sector. The private-sector standard of evaluation is primarily profit, whereas public officials, legislatures, and citizens want and need to know whether government funds are handled properly. Financial auditing contributes to public accountability by assessing whether a department's financial statements present correctly its financial position and the results of its operations and by determining whether its internal financial controls are in compliance with laws and regulations. Although external audits are noted for the identification of error and/or fraudulent manipulations, they are also a managerial tool for evaluating a department's expenditure and record-keeping procedures (U.S. General Accounting Office, 1994).

BUDGETING SYSTEMS

Five different budgeting systems are in use today. None of these systems adequately meets the needs of the differing political, economic, administrative, and legal perspectives involved in public budgeting. Systems vary from place to place, depending on the resource and service delivery values that dominate the process within a governmental subdivision. Each budgetary system has its own set of advantages and disadvantages.

Object/Line Item Budgeting

The *object/line item budget* is the oldest, most frequently encountered, and simplest method. The term "object/line item" refers to the manner in which expenditures are classified within the budget. Each significant expenditure is given a separate line in the budget document. This system uses the previous year's budget as its standard of comparison for estimating increases or decreases in the projected fiscal year. In its simplest form (usually in smaller agencies), the budget is divided into three basic categories: personnel services, operating expenses, and capital outlay.

1. *Personnel services* are composed of a listing of salaries and benefits subdivided by each of the department's position classifications, such as chief, captain, lieutenants, sergeants, police officers, administrative assistants, clerical workers, etc.
2. *Operating expenses* may include repair and maintenance, supplies and equipment, contractual services, equipment leases, service contracts, building and vehicle leases, travel, etc.
3. *Capital outlay* covers expenditures that can be prorated beyond the budgetary year to the entire useful life of the item such as buildings, vehicles, computers, and remodeling of existing facilities.

In the budgets of some medium-sized and large departments, it is not uncommon to find that the line items have been grouped into subcategories such as divisions, bureaus, or units. Each functional component would then have its own separate budget. In addition, some object/line item budgets will contain a set of columns listing the dollar amount of the previous fiscal year's allocation for each item, the current year's award, and the department head's recommended request. This information permits legislative expenditure decisions to be based on a comparative analysis during the final budgetary adoption process. The law enforcement operating budget of the Palm Beach County, Florida, sheriff's office, shown in Table 8-1, is an example of this budgetary form.

The advantages of this system are that it is reasonably simple and easy to understand and prepare. It provides governmental oversight staff and legislative bodies with strong control over expenditures. And it allows administrators and legislators to shift or eliminate items they consider excessive or inappropriate without endangering allocations for essential services. As a result, the object/line item budget achieves its primary function, financial expenditure control. This is often accomplished, however, without consideration for program goals, objectives, and service demand.

The principal shortcomings of this system are that it does not help in program costing and formulation, policy determination, or evaluation of performance objectives. Its focus is on expenditures, with no relationship to results. An object/line item budget is practically useless for providing administrators with information they need to identify all the expenditures associated with a specific program and/or activity with anything approaching accuracy. For example, if the chief executive wished to know the total costs of the agency's burglary reduction program, there would be no way to determine it. Each of the program's expenditures would be listed in line items that record all the department's expenditures for that category, e.g., vehicle fuel, overtime, office supplies, etc. In order to facilitate program costing, the chief administrator would be required to maintain an internal budgetary system arranged differently from the object/line item budget to overcome this shortcoming. In some agencies the object/line item budget can get very specific, which in turn increases it complexity. As a case in point, there might be a line item for a variety of items such as fax machines, personal computers, utility sheds, and the like.

Another disadvantage of this budgetary system is that it has the potential for relegating budgeting to a mechanical process instead of treating it as a dy-

TABLE 8-1. Palm Beach County Sheriff's Office Law Enforcement Budget

Object Code	Description	History FY 93–94	Current Budget FY 94–95	Anticipated Expenditures FY 94–95	Sheriff Recommended FY 95–96
011	Executive salaries	98,752	102,518	89,508	106,957
012	Regular salaries	49,385,089	52,672,658	51,385,868	55,234,190
013	Other salaries	173,631	180,153	238,784	167,117
014	Overtime	1,749,626	1,613,625	2,351,732	1,887,177
015	Special pay	1,838,536	1,560,072	939,322	1,998,706
021	FICA	3,930,834	3,914,714	4,054,270	4,147,130
022	Retirement	12,509,424	13,342,230	13,323,040	14,337,314
023	Life & health insurance	3,286,362	3,596,286	3,176,452	4,578,549
024	Worker compensation	1,324,992	1,310,249	1,310,254	2,232,059
025	Unemployment compensation	28,944	20,000	20,000	50,000
10	Personal services	74,326,190	78,312,505	76,889,230	84,739,199
031	Professional services	634,192	559,936	665,998	631,675
032	Accounting services	0	9,026	9,026	4,000
033	Court reporting	242	825	164	425
034	Contracted services	763,744	625,199	562,926	992,894
035	Investigations	60,639	110,000	100,992	100,000
040	Travel expenses	463,264	602,726	602,726	283,932
041	Communication services	418,260	515,750	548,388	652,544
042	Freight	76,354	96,576	96,122	105,374
043	Utilities	1,066,019	1,140,751	926,694	1,116,587
044	Rentals and leases	74,534	134,666	84,650	125,094
045	Insurance	2,084,589	1,470,912	1,470,912	1,996,598
046	Repair and maintenance	2,254,813	2,616,889	2,148,517	2,483,494
047	Printing and binding	178,310	249,183	187,844	305,559
049	Other charges/obligations	66,433	98,238	115,119	111,665
051	Office supplies	241,828	263,434	242,782	325,097
052	Operating supplies	2,274,211	2,433,591	2,203,311	2,706,038
054	Books/memberships/training	86,157	104,169	104,169	545,218
30	Operating expenses	10,743,589	11,031,871	10,070,340	12,486,194
062	Buildings and improvements	36,058	224,456	224,456	91,592
063	Improvements-nonbuilding	2,454	146,900	146,900	141,200
064	Equipment/furniture/machine	838,068	773,229	773,229	921,222
60	Capital outlay	876,580	1,114,585	1,144,585	1,154,014
071	Principal	5,575	0	0	0
072	Interest	9,294	0	4,413	0
70	Debt service	14,869	0	4,413	0
091	Transfers	2,245,640	3,576,819	3,576,819	3,465,620
099	Contingency		200,000	200,000	200,000
90	Non-operating	2,245,640	3,776,819	3,776,819	3,665,620
	Total function 21	88,206,868	94,265,780	91,885,387	102,045,027

Courtesy Palm Beach County, Florida, Sheriff's Office.

namic managerial planning function. It encourages administrators to increase or decrease their resource requests incrementally, based on past allocations rather than on cost-benefit or cost-effective evaluation. This can be accomplished simply by adding or subtracting a standard 10 percent, depending on whether past appropriations were considered sufficient or too much or too little. In addition, many object/line item budget systems do not permit funds in one category to be reallocated to another category. This encourages unit heads to spend as much as they can without saving resources that might be used in another manner (Osborne and Gaebler, 1992). As a result, fiscal control can become the organization's primary managerial imperative instead of commitment to its mission and goals. The need to focus on accomplishment helps to create performance budgeting.

Performance Budgeting

The need for a *performance budget* was first suggested for the federal government in the 1949 Hoover Commission Report. This system allocates resources according to the needs of specific activities and projects, instead of just identifying items requiring expenditures. It works well with organizations that are divided into various specialized subdivisions performing discrete activities. For example, in a large police department the separate organizational divisions and subunits would be considered activities in this type of budget.

The performance budget uses the work unit (patrol, traffic enforcement) and cost per unit (dollars per hour of patrol, dollars per citation issued) as the basis for evaluating activities. Activities are funded if they produce the output desired. All expenditures for an activity must be justified by a performance report that identifies the activity's purpose and the quantification of its contribution to unit or department objectives. These reports are used in determining allocation levels.

Rosenbloom and Goldman (1993:302) point out that this budget at a minimum involves the following objectives:

1. *Formulation* and adoption of a plan of activities and programs for a stated time period. In other words, what is the agency intending to do, why, how much of it, and when?
2. *Funding*, that is, relating program costs to resources, or determining what kind of agency performance can be obtained within the confines of the resources available.
3. *Execution*, or the achievement of the authorized plan within the time frame, and resources allocated to it.

In order to accomplish these objectives, managers are required to clearly plan their programs and to identify and define units of work, their cost, and related resource allocations. This can be a complex and time-consuming task that requires the identification and recording of performance data as well as a knowledge of cost-benefit analysis procedures not normally possessed by police operational managers. Hiring a professional staff to identify, analyze, and interpret the data needed may be beyond the present resources of all but the largest police departments. In addition, there exists within policing a debate about what constitutes appropriate measures of performance. For example, how do we measure crime prevention? If crime does not occur, can it be attributed to police activity or to some other factor? The fact that policing has developed few widely accepted and useful measures of performance clouds the budgetary process.

The major advantage of this budget, however, is that it integrates organizational planning and evaluation with the budgetary process and provides flexibility in the allocation of resources to serve program needs. However, the requirements of this type of budgeting may be beyond the capabilities of some police departments. In addition, it does not provide legislators the same level of participation and control as the object/line item budget.

Program or Outcome Budgeting

The *program*, or *outcome, budget* is similar to the performance budget except that, instead of focusing on activity outputs, it focuses on the results or objectives to be achieved with funding—for example, the quality, or effectiveness, of the services produced. Budget accounts are assigned to programs based on their need and the quality of their effectiveness or potential outcomes. Many medium-sized and large police departments use a form of program budgeting in their financial management systems. Program budgeting subdivides all department expenditures such as administrative, personnel, equipment, and overhead by each of the department's programs. It provides administrators as well as governmental officials with a basis for relating resources to the achievement of specific program goals. It is hoped that this budget form will provide more information to both administrators and legislators on which to base resource allocation decisions.

In developing this budget, a fairly common practice is to select as a program area the broadest grouping as it relates to the organization's mission and objectives. Subprograms should consist of essential elements of program categories that produce similar outcomes. Examples of program areas are narcotics control, traffic, juvenile gang control, and driving-under-the-influence enforcement. An example of a subprogram within a program area is accident reduction (within the traffic control program area). Further subdivisions are usually identified as elements or tasks (such as gathering physical evidence, writing reports, or interviewing witnesses) and are grouped under the program descriptor workload.

A program budget includes:

1. A statement of need based on legal mandates, administrative directives, organizational mission, and objectives
2. Identification of the organization's program structure
3. A description of each program and its objectives
4. A work plan for the achievement of program objectives
5. Identification of a program time line
6. Identification of the resources needed to fund the programs

The planning effort required to produce this budget form establishes managerial accountability and performance direction for the department's personnel. This is so because it links resource allocation and expenditures to identifiable objectives that the managers help to develop and agree to achieve.

The development of a program or outcome budget, like the performance budget, takes time, effort, and advanced administrative skill, and it too raises the problem of identifying measurable performance outcomes. Program or outcome budgeting, however, provides the department's chief executive with an excellent explanatory instrument on which to justify requests for resources.

The Planning, Programming, Budgeting System

The planning, programming, budgeting system (PPBS) is a formalized version of program budgeting developed by the Rand Corporation for the federal government in the 1960s. This budgetary system is designed to unite the activities of planning and budgeting by requiring that administrators identify a program's cost and budget during its planning stage. The basic activities associated with this budgetary process include:

1. The identification of program goals in operational terms. For example, instead of identifying the goal of a program as crime prevention, it would be presented as preventing x number of burglaries, y number of armed robberies, etc.
2. Analysis of the total cost of programs over one and several years.
3. Analysis of the cost-effectiveness of using alternative ways of achieving goals. In the example above, how much does it cost to prevent x number of burglaries by using target harding measures as compared with a residential educational effort?
4. Development of a systematic way of considering the comparative costs and benefits of all department programs. For example, what is the cost of a community policing program compared with the cost of standard patrol operations in a particular area?

PPBS divides police activity into programs—e.g., patrol, investigations, juvenile, and traffic—and computes the budget on the basis of the expenditures for each program. Its purpose is to have managers analyze the performance and impact of their programs and then connect the findings to the current year's budget. This creates a process that requires managers to identify and support their program activities. It provides senior administrators with the information they need to determine tradeoffs among programs or activities with similar objectives. PPBS was primarily designed as a managerial planning instrument for the analyses of broad policy decisions and identification of desired outputs.

However, PPBS has fallen short of expectations. Because of its primary focus on long-range planning, it defines budgeting in terms of cost calculations based on the planning and programming steps and does not provide an operating tool for line managers. Consequently, it has the tendency to direct managerial focus toward planning new programs and/or major increases in ongoing programs while not encouraging continual program evaluation. The intense political environment of the budgetary process and the dynamics of police service demand and delivery in many communities prevent the use of this system.

Zero-Based Budgeting

Traditionally, public budgeting systems evaluate the allocation of future resources in light of current and past expenditures. Previously approved budget allocations become the starting point for the beginning of the next year's process. *Zero-based budgeting* attempts to prevent this by requiring administrators to reevaluate and justify each year's budgeting activities in a self-contained fashion, with little or no reference to past years (Lynch, 1985). They must determine whether current programs are efficient and effective and which programs should be eliminated to fund a higher priority or reduce the current budget (Pyhrr, 1973:254).

Police departments using this system would identify the purpose of their various programs, develop alternatives to achieve this purpose and determine performance data in order to justify the allocation of resources. Programs and subprograms are identified in much the same way as a regular program budget. Originally this process required the justification of each expenditure from a starting point of zero funding. However, during the budget formulation process, it is not uncommon for the chief governmental executive to establish several levels of expenditure for operating agencies to use as targets. For example, department heads may be asked to describe what level of services could be provided for 85 percent, 100 percent, and 115 percent of the current funding levels for each activity being contemplated. Another way of stating this is *–15, zero, and +15 resource funding*.

Administrators using this system are required to develop decision packages that permit the evaluation and ranking of programs competing for resources. A decision package contains a statement of purpose, costs, benefits, the impact at various funding levels, and any consequences of nonperformance (see Box 8-2). Rank is assigned to programs in order of priority and consequences. An intent of zero-based budgeting is to fund high-priority new and existing programs at the expense of obsolete and/or redundant programs without significant reduction of service. Decision packages should provide all the information policy makers need to determine at what level, if any, resources will be allocated to a particular program. The packages should be formulated at the lowest level of the organization responsible for a discrete activity, function, or operation. As a result, the first critical step in establishing a zero-based system is to identify the lowest organizational level or decision unit for which a budget will be prepared (Taylor, 1978).

Zero-based budgeting requires that all managers be fully trained in the process before implementation because it shifts the responsibility for the justification of expenditures from top administrators to unit managers. The intent

BOX 8-2. Decision Package Elements

Decision package: Data gathered for budget analysis

- *Purpose.* Define the activity and explain what the activity is, including what the activity is engaged in.
- *Cost.* Specify the direct and indirect costs of the activity.
- *Alternative courses of action.* Identify other activities that would meet the purpose.

- *Measures of performance.* Provide data that estimate the impact of static funding, increased funding, and decreased funding for the activity.
- *Consequences of not performing the activity.* Explain what happens when total funding is removed and the activity is not performed.
- *Benefits of performing the activity.* State the positive results the activity will bring to the agency.

of zero-based budgeting is to significantly impact the middle and lower levels of management in terms of planning, efficiency, and cost effectiveness.

The advantage of this system is that it provides organizational direction combining planning with budgeting and decision making. The process of identification, evaluation, and justification of all programs is expected to increase the quality of decisions. It also enhances administrative flexibility in reallocating resources to higher-priority programs. However, these decisions tend to remain political ones, no matter how thorough the budgetary information. In addition, in large agencies this process can mean numerous decision packages that bury executives in an avalanche of data, impossible to review in a timely manner (Lynch, 1985).

A New Direction: Expenditure Control Budget

The above discussion of the various budgeting systems suggests that police executives should have a clear understanding of the realities of their economic and political environment as well as of the needs of the communities they serve. Needs usually point to the problems that should be solved. Moore and Stephens (1991:96) make the argument that in organizations that focus on identifying and solving problems for the community, managers should be involved in thinking about projects to be undertaken. These projects become claimants on the organization's resources. To the extent that projects propose solutions to problems that are important to those who oversee police departments, they may result in the allocation of more resources to the department.

This argument suggests that police executives should consider a mission-driven, decentralized, and results-oriented budget system. Budgetary development should be a *bottom-up* activity that involves all levels of the department. The managers responsible for implementing the budget should have a part in its creation as well as control over its execution. This should give them ownership for their product and a desire to make it work because they are financially accountable for their efforts.

In their now-famous work, *Reinventing Government*, David Osborne and Ted Gaebler (1992:117–124) support this argument by claiming that current object/

line item budget systems trap managers in yesterday's priorities, which quickly become tomorrow's waste. They suggest a new form of governmental budgeting, called an *expenditure control budget,* which enables organizations to focus on their missions without being controlled by past spending categories. This budgetary process grew out of the experience of the city of Fairfield, California, and has been adopted by a dozen American cities and several foreign nations.

It replaces the dominant line item with a general fund budget that operates much like a family budget. In our personal financial systems, what we save or don't spend, we keep—we do not lose it. This budget creates a general fund for each governmental subdivision. The general fund for each department is determined by a formula that gives it the same amount as last year, increased to account for inflation and growth factors such as population, service demand, etc. If a major new program is proposed and accepted, new funds would be appropriated.

Osborne and Gaebler claim that the critical difference between this budget system and the others is the way it encourages department managers to view their allocations. Since they are permitted to keep what they save, they focus on cost-efficient activities. The resources they save can be reinvested in their operations. These reinvested resources can be used to test new ideas and to provide a reserve fund for changing conditions. In addition, the budget process is simplified. The time-consuming budget cycle described earlier in this chapter is reduced to determining the allocation and then having people manage it for the long haul (Osborne and Gaebler, 1992:122–124).

SUMMARY

Fiscal management is a demanding administrative function. Budgeting involves the identification of expenditures and resources relating to organizational programs and services. Budgets are political as well as managerial documents. The budgetary process holds the attention of administrators, politicians, leaders of interest groups, and citizens interested in "who gets what and how much" from public revenues (Wildavsky and Hammond, 1978). Budget systems have been developing throughout this century. None meet all the needs of the individuals involved in the process. The object/line item budget has been the favored approach because it places the locus of power for allocating funds in the hands of legislatures. Performance budgets are attempts to encourage and reward success, but they present several problems. One of the most significant problems is the great sophistication required to define programmatic "success." Program budgeting also focuses on outcomes, but it defines them in advance, as goals to be achieved by the units of an organization. Planned program and zero-based budgeting systems are managerial approaches that attempt to control the political impact of budgetary decisions by strengthening the executive's position. The expenditure control budget is a new direction that is representative of the entrepreneurial spirit challenging the traditional approach to managing government. Only time will tell how much of an impact it will have.

A major policy concern for the financial management of police organizations is the necessity to identify and prioritize objectives and to match them with resources. The basic question that administrators face in light of today's fiscal realities is not "What do I want to accomplish?" but "What can I accomplish given the economic reality within which the department operates and the resources it presently has?" If for no other reason than this, it is important that administrators use a fiscal management system that involves every manager and supervisor in systematically identifying the worth and cost effectiveness of the programs and activities.

QUESTIONS FOR DISCUSSION

1. Calculate the annual cost of staffing a two-officer patrol car around the clock, seven days a week, in your community. Include in your calculation all salaries and fringe benefits for the officers involved, as well as the costs of supplying, maintaining, and fueling the car; the costs of such support services as supervision and communication; and any other costs suggested by Box 8-1.

2. Is there more than one way to conduct the calculation discussed above? If so, do these different calculations result in different figures? Why? Which of the different calculations results in the most accurate and most reliable figures?

3. Compare the costs you have calculated with the costs of other means of achieving the same purposes that a two-officer car serves to fulfill. What are these purposes? Are there more effective or more efficient means of achieving them?

4. Are any purposes served when a police chief submits budget requests knowing that politicians are unwilling to grant them?

5. On occasion, legislators who have enacted statutes or regulations authorizing elaborate enforcement programs veto the funds to carry out these programs. Why? How should police chief executives respond to this type of conduct?

SOURCES

BROCK, HORACE R., CHARLES E. PALMER, and JOHN E. PRICE. *Accounting Principles and Applications,* 6th ed. (New York: McGraw-Hill, 1990).

"The Budget as a Communication Tool," *MIS REPORT* (Washington, D.C.: International City Management Association), vol. 20, no. 2 (February 1988).

CHABOTAR, KENT JOHN. *Measuring the Costs of Police Services* (Washington, D.C.: U.S. Department of Justice, National Institute of Justice, 1982).

GROVES, SANFORD M., and MAUREEN GODSEY VALENTE. *Evaluating Financial Condition: A Handbook for Local Government* (Washington, D.C.: International City Management Association, 1986).

International Association of Chiefs of Police. *Managing the Small Law Enforcement Agency* (Arlington, Va.: International Association of Chiefs of Police, 1990).

LEE, ROBERT D., JR., and RONALD W. JOHNSON. *Public Budgeting Systems,* 3d ed. (Rockville, Md.: Aspen, 1983).

LYNCH, THOMAS D. *Public Budgeting in America,* 2d ed. (Englewood Cliffs, N.J.: Prentice-Hall, 1985).

MOORE, MARK H., and DARREL W. STEPHENS. *Beyond Command and Control: The Strategic Management of Police Departments* (Washington, D.C.: Police Executive Research Forum, 1991).

MURPHY, CHRISTOPHER. *Thinking Critically about Police Resources* (Halifax, Canada: Atlantic Institute of Criminology, 1993).

OSBORNE, DAVID E., and TED GAEBLER. *Reinventing Government: How the Entrepreneurial Spirit Is Transforming the Public Sector* (New York: Penguin Books, 1992).

PYHRR, PETER A. *Zero-Based Budgeting* (New York: Wiley, 1973).

ROSENBLOOM, DAVID H., and DEBORAH D. GOLDMAN. *Public Administration: Understanding Management: Politics and Law in the Public Sector*, 3d ed. (New York: McGraw-Hill, 1993).

TAYLOR, GRAEME M. "Introduction to Zero-Base Budgeting," pp. 271–284 in Albert C. Hyde and Jay M. Shafritz (eds.), *Government Budgeting* (Oak Park, Ill.: Moore, 1978).

U.S. General Accounting Office. *Government Auditing Standards* (Washington, D.C.: GAO, 1994).

WHISENAND, PAUL M., and FRED FERGUSON. *The Managing of Police Organizations*, 3d ed. (Englewood Cliffs, N.J.: Prentice-Hall, 1989).

WILDAVSKY, AARON, and ARTHUR HAMMOND. "Comprehensive versus Incremental Budgeting in the Department of Agriculture," pp. 236–251 in Albert C. Hyde and Jay M. Shafritz (eds.), *Government Budgeting* (Oak Park, Ill.: Moore, 1978).

9

Personnel Management I: Hiring and Entry-Level Training

KEY WORDS AND PHRASES

BFOQs
KSAs
Civilianization
Employment discrimination
Griggs v. Duke Power Co.
Entrance standards
Residency requirements
Education

Recruitment
Lateral entry
Screening and selection
Cyclical hiring
Americans with Disabilities Act
Psychological testing
Assessment center
Probation

This first of two chapters devoted to police personnel management introduces readers to the subject and discusses issues, problems, ideas, and strategies related to hiring and preparing new people for their work. Chapter 10 will pick up where this chapter leaves off, focusing mainly on issues involving the management and training of employees beyond the entry, or *vestibule,* level.

Our heavy emphasis on the people who do policing is understandable. Capital assets—factories, machinery, and the like—are many industries' most valuable and expensive resources. Facilities and hardware—training academy buildings, cars, radios, police stations, computers, laboratories—also are critical to the success of police missions, but the money spent on them is dwarfed by the single most valuable and expensive police resource: *personnel,* the men and women, sworn and civilian, who do police work.

The reasons for this balance between human and capital resources is also easy to explain: policing is a highly demanding service industry in which most problems involve person-to-person issues rather than technology. To a greater degree than is true of most other work, therefore, the success of policing depends on the quality of personnel and their ability to interact with others, rather than on the sophistication of their equipment.

271

CHAPTER 9
Personnel
Management I:
Hiring and
Entry-Level Training

Consequently, personnel management is a most important police administrative responsibility. It should be shared by three separate entities:

1. *The central personnel office.* This office typically handles personnel matters for an entire jurisdiction and all its agencies.
2. *The chief and his or her agency personnel office or officer.* The agency personnel office should keep the chief advised on personnel issues, while the chief bears the responsibility for ensuring that the mayor, city manager, or other government chief executive is aware of personnel-related matters. The chief and the agency personnel office must also encourage, cajole, and demand participation in personnel management on the part of line units.
3. *Individual commanders and supervisors.* They are closer than any other representatives of management to field personnel.

ENLISTING LINE EMPLOYEES IN PERSONNEL MANAGEMENT

Even closer to field personnel than supervisors or commanders are their colleagues, other line officers. In most police agencies, the front line is a tightly knit group in which there are few secrets and everybody seems to know everything about everybody else. Regardless of official performance measures, for example, patrol officers typically share a very accurate consensus of who the best and worst officers are, who can be counted on in times of trouble, who is likely to generate trouble for his or her colleagues, and who may be less than dependable because of some permanent personality disorder or temporary personal problem (see, e.g., Rubinstein, 1973). Such officers also know firsthand the consequences of personnel policies and practices that may hinder, rather than further, the attainment of agency goals. Typically, these officers also are full of ideas—some good, some bad—about how personnel practices may be improved.

Divisions between Line and Staff

Unfortunately, it has generally been very difficult for police administrators to enlist the assistance of line officers in the personnel management task. This is a waste of a great resource, and every effort should be made to draw line personnel into meaningful discussion about how best to harness their talents and deal with their problems.

There are a variety of reasons for the general historic absence of line participation in personnel management. In quasi-military organizations, the division between staff and line is sharply drawn, based on the belief that line employees should have no part in administrative tasks. In many agencies, this assumption is exacerbated by the belief among line officers—accurate in some agencies—that the department's management regards them as inferior and untrustworthy adversaries (Reuss-Ianni, 1983). Similarly, there exists in many agencies a sense that line personnel are held accountable after the fact for having failed to participate in the more negative aspects of personnel management—usually by *whistle-blowing,* or calling official attention to misconduct and troubled officers—but are denied input into such more positive administrative functions as deciding who should be promoted or selected for desirable or specialized assignments.

The costs of such divisiveness are too high to be tolerated. Since police administrators bear the ultimate responsibility for the effectiveness of their agencies, it is up to them to initiate and persist in efforts to eliminate schisms of this sort. Such efforts should begin with an assessment of factors that contribute to the polarization between what Reuss-Ianni terms "street cops" and "management cops." One cause of the divisiveness may be the existence and enforcement of an unrealistically rigid rulebook. Such a volume breeds antagonism because, rather than serving to accomplish legitimate organizational goals, it usually holds officers to an impossible standard of conduct that is overlooked except in cases in which something goes wrong. As the discussion of rulebook expansion in Chapter 12 will make clear, the tendency for police manuals to evolve into such documents is great. To guard against this, no new rule should be enacted without first ensuring that it cannot be used in a *rulebook slowdown,* during which employees bring the work of the organization to a halt by adhering closely to its own regulations. Existing rules should be examined for the same purpose, and the comments of line personnel on both existing and proposed new rules should be sought out and carefully considered. In other words, as a prerequisite to harnessing line officers' expertise in personnel matters, it must be understood at all levels that *management cops* do not have a monopoly on good ideas about solutions to new problems or alternative approaches to old problems. There exists an enormous reservoir of talent and expertise at the line levels of police agencies. Administrators who fail to harness it lose effectiveness in the short run and divide their agencies in the long run.

Line officers and supervisors, in turn, must realize that personnel management cannot be sloughed off on somebody "downtown" or on the staff of a police training center. Line officers who value the well-being of the people with whom they work should see personnel management as a fundamental part of their responsibilities. The line officers are closer to the problems and issues than anyone else and, just as a cooperative citizenry brings the police information about community conditions requiring police attention, line officers must bring personnel problems and issues to the attention of those specifically charged to deal with them. But line officers will not do so unless their cooperation is sought out and encouraged.

The Dangers of Policing

An important point should be made on this score. Policing has long been regarded as an extremely dangerous occupation. Certainly, nobody would minimize the physical risks associated with police work, either in its more sensitive and specialized varieties or in such "routine" work as patrol or traffic duty. Yet experience indicates that the greatest dangers of policing are accidents and psychological and spiritual stressors, rather than assaultive criminals. As Fig-

273

*CHAPTER 9
Personnel
Management I:
Hiring and
Entry-Level Training*

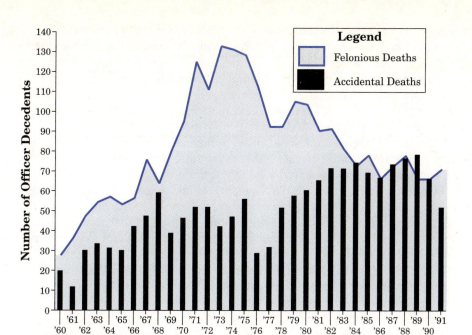

FIGURE 9-1. American law enforcement officers killed feloniously and accidentally, 1960–1991.
Source: *William A. Geller and Michael S. Scott*, Deadly Force: What We Know *(Washington, D.C.: Police Executive Research Forum, 1992, p. 234), derived from FBI annual reports. Used with permission.*

ure 9-1 indicates, after peaking in the 1970s, the number of U.S. law enforcement officers killed feloniously has fortunately declined in recent years (from 134, 132, and 129 in 1973, 1974, and 1975, respectively, to 71 in 1991). At the same time, the number of officers killed accidentally (often in traffic accidents, drownings, and falls) has increased significantly. In 1960, for example, 20 officers died as the result of line-of-duty accidents, but during the years from 1980 to 1991, the average annual number of accidental police line-of-duty deaths was 69.8 (felonious deaths during those same years averaged 78.2). Further, according to Devallis Rutledge, it is likely that an additional two U.S. police officers kill themselves every week (Rutledge, 1988:108).

There are many reasons for the decrease in felonious killings of the police. Police tactics for dealing with potentially violent persons have become more sophisticated in recent years, and such equipment as bullet-resistant vests saved many police lives that otherwise would have been lost to assailants' bullets and knives. The data suggest, however, that there is now a need to apply the same sort of expertise and equipment to the problem of accidental deaths.

The suicide data reflect a problem of another sort. Although there is some variation in police suicide rates across jurisdictions, data collected by Geller and Scott (1992:232–238) show that, in every jurisdiction where information was available, the police suicide rate is higher than the public suicide rate.

Some might not be surprised by this finding. After all, police officers have readier access to guns, the tools with which most kill themselves, than do most of the public. On closer examination, however, the high police suicide rate is an extremely troubling commentary on the nature of police work and the support provided to those who do it. No matter how rational it may seem to those who kill themselves, suicide is the ultimate self-destructive act, the expression of terminal hopelessness, alienation, and maladjustment. That it should occur more often among police officers—who, almost without exception, were carefully tested and screened for signs of psychological maladjustment when they entered their profession—suggests that something has affected these officers *after* they joined the police service.

Here is the point at which the assistance of line personnel can make a difference. In 1978, Fyfe found that virtually every New York City officer who had recently committed suicide had demonstrated evidence of alienation and withdrawal that had been observed, but ignored, by colleagues and local supervisors. The unwillingness to be seen as *busybodies* may be understandable, but in the end it did nothing to keep officers from taking their own lives. Similarly, many police officers who end their careers with acts of brutality or corruption are later described by coworkers as having been emotionally disturbed, undependable, untrustworthy, isolated, or racist long before their dismissals.

Especially in larger agencies, it is very difficult for personnel offices to learn that such officers are among the ranks unless these officers' line colleagues care enough to call attention to them. Encouraging this behavior requires administrators to ensure that any information provided will be treated confidentially and sensitively, and that the department is interested in *helping* its people rather than in hurting them. This is no small challenge, and only a few departments have been truly successful in meeting it. A frequent complaint among line personnel is that their departments provide no mechanisms for dealing with the personal or psychological problems of in-service officers, or of calling suspected corruption to official attention without being labeled and stigmatized as an informer. Where this problem exists, it requires a change in organizational culture, which should begin with the recognition of a major inconsistency in the practice of many agencies. It makes little sense to expend great effort in conducting psychological and character screening of officer candidates and subsequently to ignore the potential effects on their psyches and sense of integrity of the very work for which they were so carefully screened.

POLICE PERSONNEL MANAGEMENT TASKS

The tasks included under the heading of police personnel management include the following:

1. *Establishment of entrance standards.* This task requires a *position classification* system that defines the duties of each position in the agency and that goes on to specify the *knowledges, skills, and abilities—KSAs—*required for each. At the entry level, the central task generally is to establish standards that identify people who can be *trained* to master the job's KSAs, rather than to find people who already possess them.

2. *Recruitment.* Recruiters should seek to create an agency that parallels the service population as closely as possible by race, ethnicity, and gender, and they should recruit as broadly as possible. A major issue here is whether, and at what levels, the agency may permit *lateral entry*—the hiring of new employees at advanced ranks based on prior experience elsewhere and/or other job credentials.

3. *Screening and selection.* In attempting to achieve the goal of a representative police agency, care must be taken to avoid charges, valid or not, that standards have been "lowered" in order to achieve arbitrary quotas.

4. *Entry-level training.* Entry-level training should be regarded as an important extension of the screening and selection process. If candidates do not do well in training, it is highly unlikely they will do well in the job for which they are being trained.

5. *In-service and specialized training.* Beyond the entry level, training should be a continuous process that keeps all personnel up to date on how to deal with new problems and issues and that refreshes their ability to use critical, but rarely employed, skills (e.g., using firearms and tactics, dealing with barricade and hostage situations).

6. *Position classification and assignment.* Every position in the department should have a specified set of duties, and every effort should be made to find the most qualified individual for each job.

7. *Career development for persons at all levels.* Agencies should continue training to broaden employees' experience and expertise throughout their careers.

8. *Evaluation and monitoring.* All personnel should be formally evaluated by their immediate supervisors on a regular basis and should be held to performance standards that are clearly stated and defined. The monitoring function also requires that, without turning the agency into an organization that intrudes unjustifiably on officers' personal lives, line supervisors must recognize that some *private* conduct by officers—abusing alcohol or drugs, consorting with criminals, committing domestic violence—does affect employees' performance and the effectiveness and credibility of the agency. Line supervisors are likely to be the first officials to become aware of conduct of this type. When evidence is strong, they should not hesitate to initiate corrective action; in other cases, they must be encouraged to bring their suspicions to the attention of officials who may look into them further and must be held accountable if they do not.

9. *Promotion.* Closely related to the task of career development is that of promotion, or the selection and training of persons for advanced ranks or positions. Because the number of advanced ranks typically is very small in relation to the number of eligible candidates, the criteria used in promotion are bound to be seen by many as arbitrary, and every effort should be made to ensure that this perception is inaccurate.

10. *Personnel information system.* A personnel information system should document each employee's career history, accomplishments, and failings and should be readily accessible on a *need-to-know* basis.

11. *Compensation plan.* This should include a clear salary range for all positions that is objectively and recognizably related to the difficulties of the work performed and the qualifications required to perform them. It should pro-

275

CHAPTER 9
*Personnel
Management I:
Hiring and
Entry-Level Training*

vide for significant salary differentiation among ranks—without which there is little incentive for officers to assume the responsibilities that go with increasing rank. Pension and fringe benefits should also be specified in the compensation plan.

12. *Labor relations.* The task here is two-pronged: Management has to deal both with individual employees and with representatives of labor.

Tasks 1 to 4 are discussed in this chapter, while tasks 5 to 12 are treated in Chapter 10.

EVOLUTION OF
POLICE PERSONNEL MANAGEMENT

In the nineteenth century, personnel management in most urban police departments was highly politicized and corrupt. In general, it was conducted by officials who saw their police departments largely as a means of keeping themselves and their cronies in power and on the municipal payroll, rather than as organizations designed to protect and serve ordinary citizens.[1] (See Box 9-1.)

Civilianization

The civil service reforms of the early twentieth century have helped to shape current police personnel policies and practices. The move to *civilianization* has also had a major effect on the profiles of U.S. police agencies. This trend began in the 1960s, with the recognition that police departments might be more efficient and less needlessly exclusive if nonenforcement jobs were filled by people who were specially trained for them and/or who would not have the same high salary requirements as sworn police officers.

Civilianization has not been without critics, however. In some cases, attacks on civilianization seem to reflect the antagonism one might expect from self-interested police union leaders anxious to preserve their empires or from hard-liners who instinctively resist any change whatever. Still, an important point should be kept in mind by those who consider civilianization as a cut-rate alternative to exclusively sworn police departments: police officers are hardly overpaid, and the expectation that competent people can be found to work high-pressure jobs around the clock and on weekends for significantly less compensation than officers receive often is inaccurate. In any discussion of the civilianization of such positions as emergency phone operators and radio dispatchers, therefore, the question of competence must be given careful attention. In other words, the idea of finding competent and dedicated people to work 24/7 for only a small percentage of a sworn officers' wage may be a pipe dream. Indeed, where costs are concerned, it may be wiser to increase civilian salaries to levels close to those of officers and to regard civilianization primarily as a means of saving on the generous pension benefits that officers enjoy.

Employment Discrimination

The major changes in personnel policies, practices, and compositions of U.S. police agencies have been wrought by the employment discrimination legislation and litigation of the past generation. Title VII of the Civil Rights Act of

BOX 9-1. The Governor's Start in Public Service

In 1898, Wisconsin Governor George W. Peck told the Fifth Annual Convention of the National Association of the Chiefs of Police of the United States and Canada (now the International Association of Chiefs of Police) of his first job in the public service:

Twenty-five years ago (1873) I went from the City of New York where I was assisting "Brick" Pomeroy to make the greatest and meanest paper there was in this country to LaCrosse to assist him there, and took the editorship of the LaCrosse Democrat. Soon after I got there, there was an election for mayor of the city, and of course the paper took a prominent part in the campaign. Being its editor, I did more, I think, probably to elect the mayor of the city (the democrat who was elected) than any man in the city. I lied for him twenty-four hours out of the day, twelve hours through the newspapers and twelve or thirteen hours about the city in saloons and elsewhere.

At that time the only patronage that the mayor of the city had was to appoint a chief of police. It was customary during a campaign to abuse the administration that was in power, and particularly to abuse the chief of police, to swear that he was in the pay of the gamblers and the houses of ill fame, and to prove it on him. I went through that campaign and when the mayor was elected he came to me and said, "What can I do for you?" And I said, "Nothing, except maybe something that has got a salary." He said, "How would you like to be chief of police?" I said, "What does a fellow have to do to be a chief of police?" "Why," he says, "I don't know, just be chief of police." I said, "How much is the salary?" He said, "It is $1,200." "Good," I said, "I will take it in a minute." So he appointed me chief of police and the council, that did not know me from Adam, confirmed me. Nobody in the town knew me because I had been there only a short time, and after they got to know me they were sorry that they did. I had promised the gamblers during the campaign that they were perfectly safe. I had promised the good people of the city that the gamblers would be sent to hell if I got a good chance at them. So that I was on an equal footing with everybody.

The first day that I was chief of police every friend that I had in town, about twenty of them, got drunk. At 8:30 I went down from my house where I had given the news to my wife that I had been appointed to $1,200—I did not remember what the office was, but it was

$1,200—I went down, and the first man I met was my most intimate friend, and he was drunk, and I said, "Frank, what is the matter with you, why are you full?" And he said, "I tell you, we are celebrating." And I said, "Well, hold on, you don't want to get full the first night." So I walked him around town for half an hour and got him sober and took him home. That was my first duty as chief of police. Then I met another friend downtown who was full and I walked him an hour and sobered him up and took him home. I kept that up till four o'clock in the morning and then went home and told my wife that I was overworked.

The next morning I went down to the office and called in an Irish policeman that had been there for many years, and I said, "Tom, I don't know anything about this business, what do you have to do?" And he said, by God, all you have to do is look wise. He says, "Chief, what you want is to get a hat that turns down on the side and look out from under it." He said, "Look out this way and that way and look wise." So I went and got a hat that turned down on the side and looked out from under it. I thought that was the way the Hawkshaws, the detectives, did. I wanted to be a great detective, and when I got out of the office I wanted to start in New York a secret detective agency. So I looked wise, but the boys played it on me. I was hazed from Genesis to Revelation.

The first thing that they did was to get a Norwegian who weighed about 300 pounds and have him pretend to get drunk, and have me arrest him. That Norwegian was soberer than I am this minute, and yet he appeared to be drunk, and the boys all went away and left me to arrest the Norwegian. I went up to him and took him by the leg, and I could hardly lift the leg, and finally the Norwegian, after I had hit him on the bottom of the foot for awhile, got up and took me under his arm and carried me down to the ferryboat and was going to take me over into Minnesota. . . .

That was about a sample of my experience as chief of police for a year. They got me out just as soon as possible. I was not a real success, I am sure. I had more fun though than any chief of police in the world, but I was not a success as a Hawkshaw, and after my term of office expired and I got away from the town and went to Milwaukee, I felt a great relief.

Source: Dilworth, 1976, pp. 22–26.

The last generation's equal employment legislation, litigation, and personnel practices have dramatically changed the membership of both police academy training classes and training staffs. Today's police agencies are more representative than ever of the populations they serve.
Jesse Mobley/Image Works.

1964 and the amendments added to it by the Equal Employment Opportunity Act of 1972 prohibit employers, including the police, from discriminating against individual job applicants or incumbents on the basis of race, color, religion, sex, or national origin.

In its 1971 decision in *Griggs v. Duke Power Company,* the U.S. Supreme Court established the test for employment discrimination which has since led to a major overhaul of virtually all police entrance requirements. Griggs, a black employee with the Duke Power Company, had been denied a promotion to a supervisory position on the grounds that he did not possess a high school diploma, a credential the company required for such a position. Griggs's lawyers argued that he had been a highly satisfactory employee. They also demonstrated statistically that the high school diploma requirement discriminated against black employees because far fewer black than white employees possessed such diplomas. This was not enough to show that discrimination was unconstitutional because, as the Court reasoned, it was possible that the high school diploma requirement was *job-relevant,* in the sense that those who possessed such a credential made better supervisors than those who did not. The Duke Power Company was not able to show that this was so, however, and Griggs prevailed against the company. Very briefly, the disparate impact test that emanated from the case is as follows:

279

*CHAPTER 9
Personnel
Management I:
Hiring and
Entry-Level Training*

1. A plaintiff who alleges discrimination must show that he or she has been excluded from employment or promotion by an employment standard that discriminates against the protected class of which he or she is a member. This is quite often judged by the yardstick of a *four-fifths rule*, which requires that the acceptance rates for minorities and women must be 80 percent, or four-fifths, as high as the rates for whites and men.

2. Upon proof that a standard discriminates against a protected class (a showing that the four-fifths rule is not operative, for example), the burden shifts to the employer to prove that the discriminatory standard is a job-relevant *bona fide occupational qualification* (*BFOQ*) that distinguishes between people who can perform satisfactorily and those who cannot.[2] If this cannot be proved, the standard is unconstitutionally discriminatory.

Thus, the Court distinguished between standards that discriminate against protected groups but that are necessary for successful job performance and standards that cannot be shown to serve such a purpose. One example of the former is offered by the fire service, which generally requires firefighter candidates to pass stringent tests of upper-body strength. This requirement clearly had a disparate impact on female candidates, few of whom have been able to pass this segment of fire department entrance examinations. Still, this standard generally has been upheld by the courts because fire departments have been able to prove that it is a job-relevant BFOQ; hauling hoses, wielding axes, climbing ladders, and carrying fire victims to safety are the core of the firefighter's job, and anyone without the upper-body strength adequate to perform these tasks cannot be a successful firefighter. Thus, especially when it can be shown that in-service personnel meet the standard set by entrance examinations, the standard has held despite its disparate impact on women (see, for example, *Evans v. City of Evanston*, 1989, and *Zamlen v. City of Cleveland*, 1989). (See Box 9-2.)

The police generally have had a much more difficult time demonstrating the job relevance of their traditional entrance requirements. Originally, of course, police agencies could not meet the challenge of *Griggs* because, never having hired anybody who did not meet their standards, they had no basis for comparing, for example, the performance of male and female officers, short and tall officers,[3] officers who did well on written entrance exams and those who did not, officers who excelled at strength and agility tests that measured gymnastic performance—but did not relate directly to police work—and those who did not fare well on these tests.

When Fyfe and Walsh joined the New York City Police Department in the early 1960s, for example, the police entrance examination—typical of tests of the time—included an obstacle course, a standing broad jump, pull-ups, a sit-up while holding a weight on one's shoulders, and one-handed dumbbell presses. These certainly were valid measures of physical agility and strength, but it would be difficult to defend them as job-relevant; they involve abilities that are rarely, if ever, required in field police work. When, for example, is a patrol officer required to accomplish a 5-foot, 10-inch standing broad jump while wearing gym clothes and sneakers? Or to do a sit-up while holding an 80-pound weight and being gripped at the ankles by another person?

BOX 9-2. Women in Policing: 1969

Prior to *Griggs* and Title VII, the New York Police Department, like most others, hired two classes of sworn personnel: patrol*men* and police*women*. At that time, policewomen accounted for less than 1 percent of the department's personnel and did not work in line patrol assignments. Instead, they were hired in anticipation that they would work as youth officers, matrons, investigators, and office workers. Until two policewomen successfully sued the department for the right to compete for promotion, they remained in entry-level positions throughout their careers.

Then, in 1969, the news media reported that a Louisiana police department had begun to hire and assign policewomen in the same manner as policemen. The inquiring reporter for the New York Police Department's magazine asked officers for their views of this revolutionary new development and received the following comments:

Ptl. Paul DiStephano (1 Precinct)

"The idea of a woman driving a radio car is enough to make you want to quit the job and join the Fire Department. I also shudder at the thought of what would happen when we went on our first burglary run on some tenement roof together. She'd probably get her heel caught or worry about getting her dress dirty. At family disputes she wouldn't do much better. She'd naturally gravitate towards the wife's side of the argument. A patrolman, on the other hand, is much more objective and is a better arbiter."

Polw. Dorothy Mobley (Police Academy)

"A woman is just as capable as a man, so I don't believe the opportunity to patrol in a radio car should be eliminated just because she is a woman. I realize that such an assignment can be dangerous, perhaps too dangerous for policewomen in some commands, but it's not necessarily true for all. In any case I'm willing to give it a try."

Polw. Margie Jones (Police Academy)

"Patrolling in a radio car is a man's job and I don't feel a policewoman should have any part in it. The women in the Louisiana Police Department might very well be a tougher breed of female than those of us up north, but most likely it's that their police work is easier. There are other areas where a woman can easily be just as effective, or maybe more so, than a patrolman. Dealing with youngsters is certainly one of them. No, I'm not ready to ride in a radio car. I'm having a bad enough time preparing myself emotionally for the day when I'll have to search a woman DOA."

Ptl. James Miller (18 Precinct)

"It's a bad arrangement. A woman just isn't built to handle situations that confront policemen. They're not physically equipped to do a job that sometimes demands muscle. As part of a radio car crew, I don't think they could really contribute anything towards quality police work on the streets."

Ptl. George Hall (60 Precinct)

"A woman's place is definitely not in a radio car—it's in an office. I'll even go a little further than that—a woman belongs at home, taking care of the kids. If I were ever thrown into a radio car with a policewoman, I'd be in double trouble. You see, I chauffeur bosses and I don't relish the thought of driving a woman sergeant all day long. Heaven forbid. It's bad enough that I have to go home and listen to the wife—and we've been married 27 years."

Ptl. Edwin Westman (43 Precinct)

"I don't think it's a good idea. A cop would be excessively pressured by the added responsibility of having to constantly look out for her welfare. And worrying about her all the time, his mind might stray from the job's requirements. Besides, a policewoman's talents would be wasted riding in a car on regular precinct patrol. She's much better suited for more specialized work like plainclothes."

Source: Spring 3100, The Magazine of the New York City Police Department, December 1969, p. 48. Reprinted by permission.

281

CHAPTER 9
Personnel
Management I:
Hiring and
Entry-Level Training

History and recent hirings have since provided opportunities to test the validity of former police employment standards, but there remains little or no evidence that traditional entrance requirements resulted in a more able police service than exists today. Indeed, a convincing argument that such standards are irrelevant could be based on the poor fitness levels of many incumbent officers. In most agencies, many satisfactory and highly regarded officers who passed stringent strength and agility tests at the time they joined their employers' ranks could not, if asked, pass the same tests again. Consequently, most police strength and agility testing has undergone dramatic revision in recent years. In addition, such former objective entrance standards as minimum heights, weights, and eyesight scores had virtually disappeared from police job announcements by the mid-1980s (Fyfe, 1986a). (See Box 9-3.)

ENTRANCE STANDARDS

Unwavering adherence to two principles should guide the formulation of entrance standards and every other personnel management task: (1) The best personnel must invariably be selected for appointment and promotion. (2) Doubt in reference to appointment, promotion, or separation from service must be resolved in favor of the department.

The death of most former objective but unvalidated standards does not mean that no standards can be developed. Instead, the standards that are used must have *predictive validity:* they must be statistically valid as predictors of success in the job sought, and they must be related to the job. Thus, for example, a height requirement of 5 feet, 9 inches might not have predictive validity, but a requirement that officers be tall enough to drive a patrol car or to fire a weapon over the roof of a car may be more defensible. A requirement that, on completion of training, candidates press x amount of pounds might not be predictively valid; but a requirement that, within a given time period, candidates run to a closed car, open it, and drag a dummy from it without having the dummy's head hit the ground probably would be acceptable as a job-relevant test of a candidate's ability to pull an injured person from a burning car.

As noted earlier, the establishment of entrance standards through position classification should serve to identify people who can be trained to master the job's KSAs, rather than to find people who already possess them. All this must be done in the context of affirmative action or specific court orders, which may require that departments give preference in hiring to minorities over equally qualified whites or males. It must also be done in the knowledge that every decision to hire or promote an individual implicitly denies the job in question to other candidates, and this is bound to engender antagonisms.

Residency Requirements

As Box 9-3 suggests, preservice residency requirements—demanding that appointees live in their employing jurisdictions—were long opposed by police professionals. President Johnson's Commission on Law Enforcement and Administration of Justice (1967:130–131) was especially critical of these requirements which, according to a 1962 International Association of Chiefs of Police study, existed in 75 percent of the departments surveyed (O'Connor, 1962). The

BOX 9-3. O. W. Wilson on Police Entry Standards, 1963

In the second edition of this book (1963), O. W. Wilson described what should be expected of candidates for *patrolman*—then the prevailing title for the job most agencies have since retitled *police officer:*

Residence requirements. [A]dvantages are derived from the appointment of an out-of-town man; he has no local entangling alliances, and his background and standards of living sometimes make him more content than the city-bred man with the conditions of police service. . . .

Advantages of youth. Important advantages are gained by recruiting young men into police service. The older the man, the greater the likelihood that he has experienced failure in some field of activity. Successful police forces cannot be built of men who have been unsuccessful and who, as a consequence, may have established undesirable patterns of thought and conduct. . . . The disadvantages of the immaturity of youth should be discounted. Time and experience quickly correct the immaturity of otherwise well-qualified men. . . .

Height and weight. . . . Many capable men of somewhat less than average height are lost to police service when standards rule out their application because of this one factor. . . . It seems an unjustifiable waste to close the door to men who cannot meet the height requirement but who are qualified in all other respects.

It should not be forgotten, however, that the patrolman is frequently called upon to display both strength and agility, and it is desirable that the standards for all police officers be worked out in such a way that there will be more officers in the upper height range. The small man is at a disadvantage in dealing with a crowd or with an unruly individual. The larger man is better able to observe in a crowd, and his size tends to instill a respect not felt toward the smaller person. One good-sized policeman, when asked whether there was any advantage in being so large, replied that it saved a lot of fighting.

A height above 6 feet 4 inches should alert the physician to the possibility of abnormality because a greater height is frequently the result of an early glandular disorder, which may have had other lasting effects on the physical or psychological well-being of the individual.

Flexibility in application of standards. The following table establishes a scale of percentage scores for the factors of

Scoring Table for Height, Weight, and Education

Percentage Score	Age	Height (less than 6 feet 4 inches but more than)		Education
100	21	6 feet	1 inch	Master's degree in criminology
98	22	6	0	
95	23	5	11	Master's degree
90	24	5	10	A.B. or B.S. degree
85	25	5	9 1/2	3 years college
80	26	5	9	2 years college
75	27	5	8 3/4	1 year college
70	28	5	8 1/2	High school graduate
65		5	8 1/4	
60	29	5	8	
55		5	7 3/4	3 years high school
50	30	5	7 1/2	
45		5	7 1/4	
40	31	5	7	2 years high school

BOX 9-3. O. W. Wilson on Police Entry Standards, 1963 (*continued*)

age, height, and education and permits a more flexible standard of qualifications, which is preferable to arbitrary, fixed minimum standards for each factor. A candidate who is twenty-one years of age, 6 feet 1 inch in height, and has a master's degree in law enforcement or police administration would make a perfect score of 300. It is recommended that the minimum qualifying score be set at 240. At this point, a man who is twenty-six years of age, 5 feet 9 inches tall, and has attended college two years would qualify. A younger man can qualify with less height or less education; an older man would have to have greater height or higher educational qualification. The table permits applicants who have college education to qualify even though they are slightly under the customary height standard; it also permits younger applicants to qualify even though they have not graduated from high school. Thus it avoids that elimination of well-qualified candidates who are slightly under the customary minimum standards.

Intelligence. An intelligence quotient of 112 is advisable as a minimum standard in police service. . . .

Experience has shown that the appointment of men with an intelligence quotient below 105 is ill-advised; promotions to supervisory and command positions must be denied to policemen of inferior intellect if impairment of service is to be avoided, whereas, when the intelligence of the entire body of the force is high, competent leadership within the department is assured, and the department can safely promote through the ranks to the very top position.

The physical and medical examination. . . . The practice of summarily rejecting a candidate because of flat feet should be reappraised. Studies indicate that congenital flat feet are a foot *type* and are a normal characteristic for

some races. . . . Congenital flat feet do not prevent active, heavy work and do not require medical attention. Acquired flat feet, on the other hand, may lead to chronic difficulties that impair the value of an officer's services.

A relaxation of visual acuity requirements seems justified. Former standards of 20/20, and 20/30 vision correctable to 20/20, should be changed to permit a 20/40 vision with a 20/20 binocular conversion (Wilson, 1963:137–147).

Now consider the following:

1. Where did female officer candidates fit into Wilson's thinking?
2. Identify the disparate impacts of the employment standards Wilson describes on males in such presently protected groups as racial and ethnic minorities and older people.
3. What evidence could be mustered to argue that the standards Wilson describes are job-relevant BFOQs? Is there any evidence, for example, that gradations in height as fine as those presented in Wilson's table distinguish between capable and incapable police candidates?
4. What is the opposite side of Wilson's contention that out-of-town candidates are desirable because they may have no "local entangling alliances"? What is it about out-of-towners, apparently from rural areas, that may make them more content than "city-bred" candidates with "the conditions of police service"?

sentiment that prevailed among professionals at the time of the President's Commission was that these requirements artificially limited the talent pools from which police departments could draw. Such requirements might have been necessary during the Depression, it was argued, because jobs were then scarce; in such circumstances, use of residency requirements to preserve jobs for hometown workers may have been justifiable and understandable. More recent data suggest that these sentiments have become practice: Peter and Deirdre Strawbridge's survey of 72 large U.S. police departments found that only 25 (34.7 percent) still retained preservice residency requirements (Strawbridge and Strawbridge, 1990:17–22).

During the 1960s, the imposition of postemployment residency requirements was also seen as an unnecessary hardship, particularly in cities in which housing was extremely expensive or, ironically, where crime rates were so high that officers could not reasonably be required to raise their families in them.

Things have changed since then. The nation's employment picture is no longer so rosy that attempting to preserve local jobs for local residents can readily be criticized as parochial protectionism. Further, in many cases, out-of-town recruitment and the absence of residency requirements have created urban police departments consisting largely of white suburbanites who bring to their work little understanding of or sensitivity to the cultures and problems of the inner-city minority citizens they serve. In the eyes of some, the great writer James Baldwin suggested, such officers are "occupying soldier[s] in a bitterly hostile country" (Baldwin, 1962:66–67).

Much of the estrangement described by Baldwin can be, and has been, overcome by careful training and humane policing. In our racially and socially diverse society, however, it has become clear that *representativeness* in police agencies is highly desirable. Unfortunately, when communities are policed by people who do not look like them, the likelihood of antagonism and mutual suspicion is greatly increased. In many of the places in which preservice and postemployment residency requirements have endured or been operational-ized, they have been seen as a vehicle for enhancing representativeness and police familiarity and commitment to local communities.

This view may seem somewhat cynical in what most of us would like to think of as a color-blind society, but it is simply a recognition of where we are at this point in our history. Before rejecting it out of hand, one should consider what the state of police-community relations would be like if white suburbs were policed largely by black and brown people who commuted to work from the inner city and who had little or no familiarity with suburban lifestyles. If white suburban kids were questioned or chased off street corners by black commuter police, if white suburban traffic violators were ticketed by black commuter police, if white suburban couples' domestic disputes were mediated by black commuter police, frictions and suspicions not unlike those that frequently characterize inner-city police-community relations would almost certainly be much greater than they are at present, especially if controverted incidents—such as shootings by officers—were to occur.

The question of postemployment residency requirements raises an additional issue. In many large cities, a great number of police officers drive home on paydays and, instead of recirculating their salaries into the economies of the municipalities that employ them, they add their paychecks to the economies of the suburbs in which they live. This one-way flow of money from cash-strapped cities to more prosperous suburbs, many municipal officials have argued, has contributed to the financial decline of the cities and is a reason for demanding that officers live where they work.

Police employee groups have long fought residency requirements. The legal aspect of their battles, however, seems to have ended in 1976 when, in *McCarthy v. Philadelphia Civil Service Commission*, the U.S. Supreme Court rejected a Philadelphia firefighter's argument that his employer's limitations on his ability to live where he chose were unconstitutional. This appears unlikely to change. In addition to the economic and community relations arguments, a key part of the logic underlying residency requirements for emergency service

285

CHAPTER 9
Personnel
Management I:
Hiring and
Entry-Level Training

employees such as police and firefighters is the difficulty that might be encountered trying to mobilize out-of-towners in sudden emergencies.[4]

Where residency has become a social and economic issue, several compromises to the creation of hard-and-fast prohibitions have been put in place. These include the granting of partial or absolute preference to local residents in both appointment and promotion decisions. Further, the understanding in many agencies in which high-level *exempt* ranks may be filled at the chief's discretion (rather than according to civil service regulations) is that these top jobs are available to in-town residents only. It is not unusual for senior officials to move into town to accept such appointments.

Age Standards

As Box 9-3 suggests, the longtime traditional minimum age for entry into most police agencies was 21 years. More recently, however, there has developed a movement toward recruitment of people as young as 18 into police service. After all, it is reasoned, persons of this age may serve in the military and have the right to vote. Thus, according to the data collected by the Strawbridges, a few major cities have begun to hire teenagers as probationary officers (Strawbridge and Strawbridge, 1990:17–22).

While there do not yet appear to be any systematic studies comparing the performance of such young officers to that of older colleagues, this practice raises troubling questions. How, for example, does a teenager go about resolving a dispute in a barroom that he or she is not legally permitted to patronize? Will older domestic disputants take seriously the mediation efforts of inexperienced teenagers? Equally important, are teenagers sufficiently mature and self-confident to resist any pressures from older peers to engage in wrongful conduct? In its recent report on police corruption in New York City, the Mollen Commission concluded that it was not a good idea to hire teenagers and urged—successfully—that police attempt to recruit more mature individuals (Mollen et al., 1994). As a general suggestion, therefore, it seems appropriate to reiterate an old saw: If it ain't broke, don't fix it. Unless dire problems in recruiting more mature people are encountered—and in the absence of any court findings that barring persons under 21 from policing is discriminatory—there are few reasons to recruit teenage police officers. This does not seem an undue hardship on potential police personnel; it merely postpones, but does not cancel, their plans for police careers.

Conversely, as Box 9-3 suggests, it long has been believed in some quarters that applicants who had not selected policing as a career early in their lives were motivated by failures in other endeavors, rather than by deep interest in police work (see, e.g., Leonard and More, 1993:456). However, an interest in law enforcement can develop at any age, and as litigation and legislation suggest, only one factor seems to militate against hiring those between, say, 30 and 50 years of age for general patrol service. This is the question of the jurisdiction's ability to absorb an older employee into the pension or retirement system, given the simple mathematical probability that older recruits are more likely than young recruits to become disabled through disease during their careers. Weighing against this potential cost, however, is another cold mathematical fact: people who enter policing at comparatively advanced ages are likely to die sooner and to collect pensions for fewer years than are people who enter policing young and who retire after meeting minimum pension eligibility requirements.

Therefore, the major question is whether an older person is fit by health, character, and experience to become a police officer, rather than merely how old he or she is. Under the federal Age Discrimination in Employment Act (ADEA), individuals whose eyesight, hearing, and general health have deteriorated to the point where they cannot perform the police job lack the BFOQs necessary for the job. In such cases, rejection is in order regardless of the candidate's age. But, under ADEA provisions, employers cannot use age itself as a BFOQ unless it can be shown that, simply by virtue of their age, older persons cannot perform the job. Thus, if an individual meets all entry requirements, there is no reason for rejection purely on grounds that he or she has enjoyed more birthdays than other candidates.

Vision Standards

In the past, as Box 9-3 demonstrates, police entry requirements for uncorrected vision were very stringent. The theory was that, regardless of how much officers' vision could be corrected by glasses or contact lenses, uncorrected vision was critical because, in the heat of combat with dangerous adversaries, officers were likely to lose their glasses or lenses. Cases in which this has occurred, however, are so rare that current standards generally focus on corrected vision rather than on uncorrected vision.

Education

Despite historic complaints about the low level of police educational requirements and attainment (Carter, Sapp, and Stephens, 1989a, 1989b; Fosdick, 1920; National Advisory Commission, 1973; National Commission on Law Enforcement Observance, 1968; President's Commission, 1967; Saunders, 1970; Sherman et al., 1978; Tamm, 1962; Vollmer, 1972), higher education requirements for entry into the police service are a rarity, usually found only in prosperous suburban police departments. Only 4 of the 72 urban agencies surveyed by Strawbridge and Strawbridge, for example, required new officers to have completed education beyond the high school level (Strawbridge and Strawbridge, 1990:17–24).[5]

This is unfortunate. Any reasonable assessment of the police task demonstrates that it is on a par with other public service careers that require a baccalaureate degree or more for entry. Like schoolteachers, police officers exercise considerable discretion and work out of the sight of their supervisors. Like prosecutors, police officers make decisions that can affect citizens' lives, liberties, futures, and reputations. To a far greater degree than any other civil servants, police officers work in a tinderkeg in which their wrongful decisions can start riots or unseat political administrations. Yet instead of being viewed as on the same plane with other public service positions in which incumbents bear such heavy decision-making responsibility, police typically are lumped together with firefighters and sanitation workers. Certainly, firefighting and sanitation work are important functions, but the only real similarities between them and policing are irregular hours, danger, and uniforms. Firefighting and sanitation work require technical and procedural knowledge, strength, and great deals of courage, but at the line level neither of these jobs requires individual discretion comparable to that necessary for effective street-level policing. Indeed, it is difficult to argue that doing the job of a police patrol officer or investigator *well* requires any less skill, judgment, or knowledge of human behavior than is required of agents of the FBI, DEA, or Secret Service. Yet the educational attainment required of entering state and local police officers generally is far less than that required of these federal agents.

There is, of course, considerable resistance to a college educational requirement for police. Many oppose such a requirement, arguing that it has a disparate impact on minorities and that it cannot be shown to be job-relevant.[6] Resistance also comes from within police ranks, where many argue that non-college-educated officers have done very well.

The research on the relative effectiveness of college-educated police officers shows mixed results largely, it is safe to say, because of varying methodologies and, most important, because of the continuing absence of a clear definition of police effectiveness.[7] Further, and regardless of the direction of its findings, important questions lie beyond the reach of the research to date:

1. In many U.S. jurisdictions, there is great dissatisfaction with police service. We have no way to determine how well police would be doing, or how high their occupational prestige would be, if they had traditionally been viewed as an occupation that demanded higher education. Instead, all we can do is compare their standing and prestige—and probably their influence—to public-sector occupations, such as the FBI, DEA, Secret Service, schoolteachers, social workers, prosecutors, and public defenders, in which higher education is a given.

2. Opinion and experience are divided regarding the effects of higher educational requirements on minority recruitment. In his consultant report to the National Advisory Commission on Higher Education for Police Officers, Gwynne Peirson argued that increased educational requirements would increase the attractiveness of police careers to a broad pool of highly qualified minorities. The issue, as Peirson framed it, was that a college requirement for entry into police work would redefine the occupation as a profession and, consequently, would make it attractive to well-educated people, including minorities, who would not otherwise consider it as a career (Peirson, 1978).[8]

3. As former Attorney General Ramsey Clark suggested nearly a quarter of a century ago, about half of all college-age people—the cohort from which most police are recruited and the group that will serve as the major clientele of entering police officers for many years to come—actually were in college at the time Clark wrote. It made sense, Clark reasoned, that new police should be at least as well educated as the contemporaries whose conduct they would be expected to affect (Clark, 1970:128–129).

4. People who enter policing after college usually make a conscious choice among many alternatives in response to a vocational call. It is not clear

287

CHAPTER 9
Personnel
Management I:
Hiring and
Entry-Level Training

that this is so among many non-college-educated people. Because fewer career options are available to these candidates than to their college-educated peers, logic would suggest some noncollege candidates are likely to apply for police careers not because they have any particular calling or great interest in policing but simply because it is the best job they can get. While nobody can be faulted for such a motivation, logic also suggests that both dedication to organizational goals and the potential for leadership and contributions to the discipline are likely to be greater among those who choose an occupation than among those who have few other options (see Kappeler, Sapp, and Carter, 1993; Mollen et al., 1994).

RECRUITMENT

This discussion of entry standards should illustrate that, in trying to mold a representative and effective department, experienced police recruiters confront major obstacles. Many women, people of color, and well-educated individuals—who have much to contribute to policing—do not regard police work as an appropriate career. In addition, some percentage of applicants for police careers are drawn to the job for all the wrong reasons, and once hired they usually show themselves to be "badge-heavy," brutal, or corrupt. Since such candidates are frequently among the most enthusiastic clients of recruiters, it is easy to overlook hints of their unsuitability. This is an unfortunate mistake, and recruiting officers and those involved in screening should guard against it.

Targeting Candidates

Several targets should be high on recruiters' lists. Local residents should be made aware of recruiting efforts through public service announcements on radio and television and in the print media, as well as through the presence of recruiting booths and personnel at, for example, shopping areas and malls. Leaders of such groups as Boy Scouts and Girl Scouts and athletic associations frequently remain in touch with their alumni, and they should be contacted personally for suggestions about well-qualified individuals. College and university campuses and military installations are filled with young people about to embark on life careers. Their placement and career offices are excellent sources of information about how to best go about recruiting. In addition to participating in career days at such institutions, for example, some police departments have conducted their testing procedures right on nearby campuses and military bases.

Lateral Entry

One problem for most police recruiters has been the traditional legal requirement that all new sworn police personnel enter at the same level: the lowest and most poorly paid. Prevailing personnel systems typically do not grant credit for prior police service or for participation in pension and retirement systems in other jurisdictions, and they virtually dictate that police officers spend their entire careers within a single agency. As the President's Commission on Law Enforcement and Administration of Justice pointed out, this has resulted in a police service in which some officers' particular skills and abilities may be in oversupply in some agencies and absent in others. It also has made it very difficult for police officers who, for personal or professional reasons, wish to move to other areas or other agencies.

289

CHAPTER 9
Personnel
Management I:
Hiring and
Entry-Level Training

Eliminating barriers to entry at advanced levels—so that, for example, a highly qualified but underutilized sex crimes investigator with 10 years' service can move to another agency without loss of rank and pension credits—is primarily a problem of laws enacted at the urging of employee groups who resent increased competition for limited advancement opportunities. Police administrators—even those who do not readily *perceive* that these laws are damaging—should speak out against them and should work for statewide retirement systems for police.[9] As the President's Commission and others have suggested, a system that places artificial boundaries on professional mobility and that limits competition for specialist, supervisory, and management positions to those holding the rank immediately below that sought has "stifled the professional development of the police" (President's Commission, 1967:142). However traditional and long-standing, laws that limit police mobility and cross-fertilization serve only to limit both competition for police leadership positions and the ability of the police service to use all its human resources to maximum benefit.

Where provisions for lateral entry do exist—or where personnel simply move from one agency to another—there often is a temptation to regard the new employee as a finished product and to place him or her directly into service. This is a mistake, and care should be taken to ensure that new personnel at all levels are given training and orientation in the agency's policies and peculiar problems. Before any lateral entry provisions are implemented, care should also be taken to put to rest the fears of incumbent employees. While they may resist changes that expand the pool of talent that may enter their agencies at other than the traditional entry level, they should also understand that lateral entry is a two-way street that increases their career options and ability to move and advance in other agencies.

SCREENING AND SELECTION

Screening and selection of probationary employees are daunting tasks. They put those charged with personnel management in the unenviable position of attempting to predict who will succeed in some of the most unpredictable and stressful work in or out of government. In addition, in attempting to achieve the goal of a representative police agency, care must be taken to avoid charges, valid or not, that standards have been *lowered* in order to achieve arbitrary quotas. Although *morale* is amorphous and difficult to measure, experience has made it plain that few things are more divisive and more damaging to the morale of both majority officers and those in protected classes than the charge that minority or female officers are poorly qualified and hold their jobs only because their employers have bent the rules and principles of affirmative action. Where such charges are valid—and, in some places, they have been valid—everybody suffers.

The goal of screening and selection is to identify and hire persons who can be trained to do the job for which they are being hired. Even though many departments hire only candidates who have passed through state or regional civil service procedures and who have been trained by academies operated at those levels of government, the admonition above applies to inexperienced officers as well as to those who join new employers through lateral entry procedures. *No new employee is a finished product, and all must receive some form of entry-level training from their new employers.*

While employers should be concerned with fair play and elimination of arbitrariness in their screening and selection procedures, the nature of police work dictates that they not take chances on questionable candidates. All doubts about whether an individual is fitted for police work must be resolved in favor of the agency and of the public its members are sworn to protect. Many reasons for this should be evident: unsuitable officers may unnecessarily hurt citizens, other officers, and themselves; abuse their offices for personal profit; discredit their departments; and cause civil liability. Even disregarding such calamities, taking chances on borderline candidates frequently results in the employment of marginal performers whose cost to the public treasury far outweighs their contribution. Tenuring a police officer who can then work a career of 20 or more years (in which he or she may do incalculable damage) and then retire on a generous pension is, even in the lowest-paid police agencies, a million-dollar marriage for life. Before such a step is undertaken, great care should be exercised. On this point, it should not be forgotten that new employees' training and probationary periods are critical parts of the screening process.

Cyclical Hiring

Recent history demands a cautionary note on screening. The volatile social, political, and economic conditions that have prevailed in many big cities over the last several years have created pressures that have severely damaged police administrators' ability to put only the best people into police uniforms. As crime and community decay have increased in these places, police strength has sometimes been greatly increased without thought to whether there exists the capacity to adequately screen, train, and socialize large numbers of new officers. Although it profits "law-and-order" politicians to *put more cops on the streets*—and although such personnel increases may enable an increase in police visibility—administrators should avoid the temptation to do too much too soon and should champion regular hirings even though it may slow expansion of the ranks. This is so because the negative consequences of cyclical hiring—which usually involves long hiring freezes or minimal hiring followed by quick and dramatic increases in personnel—are quite serious. Hiring freezes and near cessations usually occur because of fiscal problems. Typically, these financial imperatives usually also cause personnel charged with conducting employee investigations and entry-level training to be transferred to field duty; there is no sense in supporting personnel processing units when they have nothing to do.

291

CHAPTER 9
Personnel
Management I:
Hiring and
Entry-Level Training

Then, when hiring suddenly is authorized, central personnel offices and police agencies must immediately gear up—but they rarely do so successfully. On short notice, they must assemble and train staffs of personnel investigators who, in limited time periods, must conduct and evaluate background checks of candidates. Then, the combination of investigators' lack of expertise and heavy caseloads greatly increases the chances that unsuitable candidates will enter police ranks. Training also suffers because curricula must be hurriedly brought up to date and because instructors must be quickly recruited—or *drafted*—and trained. After completing their classroom training, new officers are then assigned to work with inexperienced field training instructors and are then assigned to field commands. There, rather than being a small minority that is slowly socialized into the department's field culture and operating style, they often shape the agency's culture in their own image, without the benefits of mellowing and mature older hands. Often, they also are led by young and inexperienced supervisors and commanders who have been promoted hurriedly to keep departmental spans of control within reasonable limits and who, because of the same problems associated with mass hirings, often are ill-prepared by training and experience for their new responsibilities. When, as usually happens, hiring stops and the years roll by, personnel and training staff are returned to field assignments and the agency's capacities in these specialties are depleted. Worse, the officers hired in this manner find that their career opportunities are limited, because advanced ranks have been filled with young personnel promoted at the same time they were hired. This breeds discontentment and polarization between the "street cops" and the "management cops" (see Reuss-Ianni, 1983). Further, at least three jurisdictions that have engaged in this kind of boom-and-bust hiring in recent years—Miami, Washington, D.C., and New York—have suffered subsequent corruption scandals.

No matter how alluring the notion of rapidly increasing the size of their agencies, therefore, police administrators and their political leaders should push for steady, regularized hiring that reduces divisiveness and ensures that the agency's capacity to properly conduct its personnel management is kept at a high level. Colleges and universities could not effectively operate if they went for years with few or no entering students and then suddenly found themselves overwhelmed with an enormous entering class; neither can police agencies.

Selection Criteria

Once a pool of candidates who can meet an agency's age, residency, vision, and educational requirements has been identified and recruited, some process for selecting those most suitable for police work must be implemented. In addition to the strength and agility tests discussed earlier in this chapter, these typically include: (1) written examinations, (2) medical examinations, (3) psychological testing, (4) interviews and/or assessment centers, and (5) character and background examinations, including determinations of involvement in drug sales or abuse.

Written Examinations. Screening and selection methods must all test for BFOQs. The first step in this process typically is a written examination. Regardless of their substance, written examinations are, first and foremost, tests of reading comprehension and skills that are generally better taught in suburban and middle-class schools than in schools in inner cities and other less-than-prosperous neighborhoods. No matter how much science and good faith are involved in efforts to eliminate class and cultural biases from the substance of police entrance examinations, therefore, the statistics almost invariably demonstrate that, on average, middle-class, white, and suburban candidates typically perform better on the entrance exams than do minority candidates and others who, through no fault of their own, have enjoyed only limited educational opportunities (see, e.g., Glastris, 1994). Since it is usually impossible to demonstrate the job relevance of written examinations, police agencies have recently begun to regard these as *qualifiers* only, rather than as determinants of the order of candidates' standing on eligible lists.[10]

Medical Examinations. Police traditionally have hired only persons who are in excellent medical condition. In recent years, however, traditional police tests of candidates' medical conditions have been complicated by the federal Americans with Disabilities Act of 1990 (ADA). The ADA includes extensive prohibitions on discrimination against those who suffer disabilities or those who, by marriage, for example, are related to or associated with disabled persons. *Disabled persons,* according to the ADA, generally include those who have actual or perceived physical or psychological impairments that make them less able than average persons to perform one or more major life activities (e.g., walking, speaking, hearing, breathing, learning, or caring for themselves). Disabled people may not be kept out of a job if they meet all the stated requirements of the job description and would be able to perform all the *essential functions* of the job with some reasonable accommodations. Such accommodations might include the purchase or installation of special equipment and/or the minor restructuring of the job, working schedules, policies, or work environment.

Among the specific provisions of the ADA are those that:

1. Prohibit inquiries about medical conditions or medical tests before job offers are made. Offers can, however, be made contingent on successful completion of medical examinations.
2. Prohibit discrimination in access to job application sites.
3. Prohibit discrimination in advertising and recruitment efforts.
4. Prohibit discrimination in tenure, seniority, and fringe benefits.

5. Prohibit discrimination against persons whose associations with persons needing special care, in anticipation that their duties and responsibilities to such persons will consume too much time or endanger them to the degree that they will not be able to perform satisfactorily. Thus, a mother with an invalid child could not be denied employment by a police department on grounds that her family responsibilities *might lead to* excessive and unpredictable absenteeism. On the other hand, if her responsibilities to the child did in fact cause excessive and unpredictable absenteeism, her employers apparently would have a strong case that she had not met job requirements. The test, in other words, is the real effect of such an association, rather than an employer's feelings about what effects might be expected.

293

CHAPTER 9
*Personnel
Management I:
Hiring and
Entry-Level Training*

The ADA does not protect drug abusers; homosexuals; bisexuals; persons who engage in aberrational sexual behavior, compulsive gambling, theft, or pyromania; persons whose disorders have been caused by drug abuse; or persons whose disabilities are only temporary.

In sum, the ADA has an apparent great impact on the hiring and personnel practices of all employers. Although interpretations and applications of the ADA are still at an early stage, its major effects on the police appear to fall into three areas:

1. The order in which police selection and screening devices typically have been employed usually must be rearranged so that medical, psychological, and physical agility examinations come at the end of the process rather than at the beginning. In this manner, offers of employment to qualified candidates can be made contingent on successful completion of these tests.
2. Job announcements, descriptions, and applications should be carefully reviewed to ensure that they conform to the ADA requirements concerning the description of each position's essential functions.
3. All staff involved in recruiting, hiring, and personnel processing and decision making generally should be retrained to ensure that they understand and conform to all ADA requirements.

Psychological Testing. Because the police officer's job involves great temptations and opportunities for abuse, as well as exposure to psychologically stressful situations and persons, it is extremely critical to ensure that everything possible be done to screen out the psychologically unfit or vulnerable. As suggested above, it also is critical that efforts to determine whether exposure to police work has caused psychological problems that may affect employees' ability to perform continue throughout their careers. If police work is so stressful that candidates must be extensively screened before they are exposed to it, it follows that police agencies must also monitor carefully the psychological status of people who, day after day, perform this work. The fact that they may have survived initial screening says little or nothing about whether police personnel will go unaffected by years of exposure to life-and-death situations and problems that defy solution. Further, the psychological strains of police work and their effects upon the emotions and psyches may affect civilian employees as well as sworn officers (see Box 9-4).

Perhaps because of the apparent long-term unwillingness of the police to admit that "macho" police personnel might be vulnerable to psychological stresses—or, indeed, to acknowledge that officers even had emotions—psychological screening has become widespread only over the last generation. A 1961 International Association of Chiefs of Police survey of 300 police departments found that only 50 of 300 police departments—16.7 percent—administered any type of psychological or psychiatric examinations (O'Connor, 1962). In 1986, the International City Management Association reported that 71.2 percent of 910 respondents to a survey of police departments in cities with populations of 10,000 or more employed such testing (Fyfe, 1986a:6). The more recent research of Strawbridge and Strawbridge (1990) suggests that the trend to increased use of psychological and psychiatric testing and screening continues: of the 72 large departments they studied, 68 (or 94.4 percent) used psychometric tests or psychological interviews in their screening procedures.

Police departments that do not have access to a psychologist or psychiatrist who serves as a full-time staff member of the central personnel office or the agency personnel office typically engage such mental health professionals on a consulting or contract basis. This is a satisfactory arrangement only so long as such consultants are knowledgeable and sensitive about the nature of police work and its demands on officers and the civilian personnel who support them most closely.

In their screening efforts, mental health professionals typically use interviews in combination with one or more pencil-and-paper psychometric examinations.[11] While most such examinations can be computer-scored, their results must be interpreted by professionals. Whether full-time staff or consultants, these professionals must clearly understand the intricacies of policing if their efforts are to be fully useful.

Further, both written psychological examinations and interviews and other face-to-face exercises are *instruments* designed to predict what is likely to happen in the future. Although they have been developed with a great degree of expertise, the predictive value of such examinations and exercises is less than total. Consequently, they are best viewed as means of identifying and screening out the most extreme cases, rather than as precise means of determining who is and who is not suitable for a career in policing. Statistical comparisons between the experiences of departments that use these methods and those that do not use them may demonstrate that, in the aggregate, such procedures are effective. But no responsible mental health professional would suggest that these procedures are capable of identifying every unsuitable candidate or person likely to be severely affected by exposure to the stresses of policing.

Interviews and Assessment Centers. No useful purpose is served by the practice of attempting to screen candidates by interviewing them when they file their applications. In years past, interviewers often had authority to eliminate candidates they regarded as inadequate, a power that was sometimes abused to exclude racial minorities or persons aligned with the wrong political party. As the courts have consistently reiterated since *Griggs*, however, the police

BOX 9-4. Holding the 911 Line

Trying to stay calm through 10 hours of emergencies

It's a new day. I walk down to the basement of the public-safety building, pass through a secured entrance and walk slowly down a long, quiet corridor. My stomach tightens a bit as I approach a final locked door. It's starting all over again, and I'm a little anxious. I get some supplies from my locker. A headset, Rolodex file and "bible"—a notebook bursting with maps, charts, policy and procedure updates that will help guide me through this day. I go down the wheelchair ramp, into the deepest, most secluded corner of the building. I'm in the Phoenix Police Communications Center, known as "911." A vitally important place, one filled with tremendous responsibility, sadness, frustration and few rewards.

It's a dim, noisy and unassuming room. Four posters, one on each wall, seem out of place. They're scenic posters of beautiful places—the snow-covered mountains of Austria, an icy lake in Norway, a quaint fishing village in some faraway country. I suppose the posters are there to make us feel serene in the otherwise chaotic setting. There are four rows of small, unadorned and rather dingy cubicles, five in each row. I find one that's unoccupied and set up camp. I'm surrounded by a computer terminal, tape recorder, multiline phone console, cup of coffee and a small photograph of my son. It's 0800 hours. I take a deep breath, say a little prayer and hope that I don't make any mistakes that might get me on the 6 o'clock news. This will be my not-so-happy home for the next 10 hours.

"911, what is your emergency?" It's my first call of the day. The woman is crying but calm. She has tried to wake her elderly husband. With the push of a button I connect her to the fire department. They ask if she wants to attempt CPR, but she says, "No, he's cold and blue . . . I'm sure he's dead." I leave the sobbing widow in the hands of the fire dispatcher and disconnect from the call. I'm feeling sad, but I must move on. I have more incoming calls to take.

It's busy this morning. The orange lights in each corner of the room are shining brightly, a constant reminder that nonemergency calls have been holding more than 90 seconds. My phone console appears to be glowing, covered with blinking red lights. It's almost hypnotic, like when you sit in the dark and stare at a lit Christmas tree, or gaze into a flickering fireplace. But then I remember that each light represents a person—a person with a problem, someone in crisis.

A loud bell is ringing. It means an emergency call is trying to get through but the lines are jammed. All operators are already on a call. I quickly put my caller on hold. He's just reporting a burglary that occurred over the weekend.

Fortunately, most of the 120,000 calls each month are routine. There are those who are lost and need directions; some are victims of thefts, burglaries, assaults, and need to make police reports; others are angry and need to complain; some are lonely and need to talk. There's the ever-present pressure to treat each caller with the respect and dignity that we all deserve. This can be especially difficult when a citizen yells insults and calls us obscene names. We try not to let it affect us—to remain in control. We must keep answering those blinking lights.

"911, what is your emergency?" This one's serious. A bad traffic accident, head-on collision. "Yes, sir, we'll get right out there." I get officers started and advise the fire department. Now everyone in the vicinity of the accident is calling. "Yes, ma'am, we're on the way." "We'll be out shortly, sir, thanks for calling." My supervisor comes out of his office to advise us of something. He always looks serious, but this time it's different. He looks worried and upset. He tells us that two of our detectives were involved in the collision. He doesn't know who they are or how badly they're injured. My heart stops momentarily because my husband is a detective. I quickly call the office and confirm that he is safe. I'm relieved but still stunned. I look around the room at my friends and know we're each praying silently that the officers are OK. But there's not much time for sentiment. There are more calls to take, more decisions to make and more pressures needing attention.

This is not a fun place. But I glance around at my co-workers and am proud to be part of this team. They are dedicated men and women who are doing their best to serve the public, in spite of the adversities. Some operators have been here 20 years, others only a few months. Some are burnt out, tired or just waiting for something better to come along. Most of us are trying to keep a sense of purpose and oddly, a sense of humor in what we do. We have to, because the things we hear are often frightening or even gruesome. We must sound unaffected and keep our callers calm.

"911, what is your emergency?" It's just a boy on a pay phone getting his kicks by calling me vulgar names. He hangs up before I have a chance to educate him on correct 911 usage. We get a lot of trivial calls, pranksters, hang-ups, citizens complaining to us about a noncrime situation, something they should handle themselves. People call us because they don't know where to turn. Everyone must be treated fairly and with respect. It's a difficult balance to maintain.

My supervisor again comes out to advise us. His face shows a sadness I've never seen in him. "The officers were killed in that accident." A quietness descends over the room. I suppose the bells

are still ringing and the lights flashing but I don't hear or see them. The typing stops; talking ceases. I just want to get out of here and cry, but I have to stay and do my job. I have to keep going. I can break down on my long drive home tonight; for now I have phones to answer, people to help.

I answer a call. It's an irate man calling from his cellular car phone. He says he's in a hurry to get to work and there's a major traffic jam blocking his way. "Get some damned officers out here to direct traffic; I pay my taxes and I expect you people to do your jobs. Listen, lady, I'm gonna be late for an important meeting!"

I bite my lip to keep from saying what I want to. "Yes, sir," I say, "there was a serious accident in that area and officers are on the scene. Please be patient, we're doing the best we can."

must attempt to obtain as many candidates as possible. Consequently, no one person or subjective process can be permitted to reduce the pool of candidates before they have had an opportunity to demonstrate their mettle on more objective criteria.

Thus, the purposes of personal interviews at the time of filing applications are only to answer any questions candidates may have and to provide them with information, preferably written, that describes the department and its working procedures, so that candidates may read them at their convenience. Literature given to applicants usually does not devote enough attention to the hazards and unpleasant aspects of police service. Although police administrators are obliged to make police work as reasonably safe as they can, it should not be oversold as a safe occupation without hazards. Police work is more dangerous than many other vocations, and police officers are regularly subjected to unpleasant experiences and conditions. Literature provided to applicants at preliminary interviews should also include clear statements of entry requirements and should discuss the qualities desired in recruits. Most unqualified applicants, reading these requirements, will take themselves out of consideration.

At the other extreme, care should also be taken to avoid exaggerating the disadvantages of the service. This is a real temptation because many personnel administrators believe that presenting a pessimistic outlook will encourage less-determined candidates to withdraw, thus avoiding the problem of dealing with dissatisfied personnel who have come to feel that they were hired under false pretenses.

297

CHAPTER 9
Personnel
Management I:
Hiring and
Entry-Level Training

Thus, oral interviews should be used as screening devices only insofar as they serve to determine whether candidates who have already met other requirements for entry into the agency possess the basic personality and behavioral characteristics necessary to represent officialdom in a variety of crisis situations. This is admittedly a vague mandate, and considerable subjectivity is involved in the interview process. For this reason, interviews should be handled with care, should be conducted by well-qualified boards—rather than by individuals—and should not result in an irrevocable decision to reject candidates. Interviewers must be well trained, must agree in advance on the questions they will ask, and must be willing to permit candidates to ask questions.

Somewhat more objectivity is built into the *assessment center* process consisting of performance tests in which individuals are asked to perform one or more job-related tasks under the observation of assessors. These tests are more frequently used for promotion than for entrance, probably because entrance screening generally seeks to find people from other disciplines who can be trained to do the police job and whose expertise in policing generally is minimal. Candidates for promotion, by contrast, can more reasonably be expected to possess considerable knowledge about the issues, problems, and methods related to the jobs they seek.

The interview or assessment may also include a polygraph exam, a practice that seems more frequent in the southeastern United States than in other parts of the nation. Of the 17 southeastern departments surveyed by Strawbridge and Strawbridge, 15 (88.2 percent) reported using polygraphs in the screening process, but only 31 of 51 (60.7 percent) of reporting departments from other areas of the country did so (Strawbridge and Strawbridge, 1990:17–22).

Character and Background Examinations. It is, of course, critical that police personnel possess high character and great ability to resist the temptations to corruption, brutality, and other misconduct to which policing is prone. Achieving this purpose through preemployment investigation typically is a two-stage process:

1. *Screening through criminal records sources,* such as the National Criminal Investigation Center and similar state systems. In many agencies, search results that include the discovery of conviction records for felonies or some misdemeanors (usually involving violence, drugs, or evidence of dishonesty or sexual misconduct) are excluders, as are extremely bad traffic records. Arrests not resulting in conviction should also be carefully scrutinized for evidence that outcomes favorable to candidates had nothing to do with whether candidates had committed the acts charged; a rapist who is acquitted because his victim ceases cooperating with prosecutors may not be a convict, but he is still a rapist and an inappropriate candidate for a police career.
2. *Checks with noncriminal sources of information,* such as job references, neighbors, and credit agencies, concerning candidates' reliability, discipline, and

trustworthiness. Wherever possible, these checks should be done formally through the official mechanisms prior employers have put in place for this purpose, and such informal channels as former supervisors or coworkers who may be personally known to investigators should be regarded as secondary, rather than primary, sources. These checks should be as thoroughly documented as possible.

Drugs.   Another commonly used aspect of background and character examinations is the determination of whether and to what extent candidates may have histories of illicit drug use. Certainly, it would be most desirable if drug use were such an aberration that exclusion on the basis of any drug history would not be a major issue. Over the last several decades, however, formerly rigid policies of exclusion for any drug history whatever have been modified by many, if not most, police employers. Among the factors that should be considered in setting policy for deciding which drug activities should serve as excluders are the following:

1. *Did the candidate sell, or merely use, drugs?* Regardless of the area of the country or the extent of drug use among the general public, it would be difficult for any police agency to knowingly hire any officer or civilian employee who has sold or otherwise profited from drugs.
2. *How frequently did the candidate use drugs?* Many prominent people and officials have admitted to youthful experimentation with drugs. There is a substantial difference between rare, or even once-in-a-lifetime, activities of this type and apparent regular use or addiction.
3. *What types of drugs did the candidate use?* By statute or prosecutorial policy, several U.S. jurisdictions have effectively decriminalized possession or cultivation of small amounts of marijuana for personal use. This reflects a view of this illicit substance that is quite different from that involving cocaine, heroin, and other "harder," presumably more addictive, drugs. Especially in places where such de jure or de facto legalization has occurred, the circumstances and places in which marijuana is obtained or used also differ in ways that personnel administrators might want to take into account in setting policy. In every U.S. jurisdiction, cocaine, heroin, and the like become available for use only following contact with felons. This is not always true where experimental marijuana use is concerned.
4. *How long ago did the candidate use drugs?* It should be unthinkable for a police agency to hire an active drug user, but it has happened.[12] While it is hard to conceive of circumstances that would justify hiring such a person, we do live in a society in which several top officials, including President Clinton, have admitted to *past,* youthful, experimentation with drugs. If such experimentation is not a disqualifier for such high office, it is difficult to argue that it should exclude one from entering a police agency.

ENTRY-LEVEL TRAINING

Entry-level, or *vestibule,* training is the single most critical phase in the career of any police officer or civilian employee. During these months, new officers *begin* to learn the principles, procedures, and skills required to perform in the field. They should also learn that their entry-level formal training does not provide all the answers, that they must continually attempt to build on the knowledge gained in formal training, and that they must adapt what they learn to their own characteristics and abilities. To some degree or other, new civilian personnel—especially those in communications and other activities involving direct contact with the public—also learn the same lessons.

299

CHAPTER 9
*Personnel
Management I:
Hiring and
Entry-Level Training*

Problems with Training Relevance

As suggested earlier, the traditional charge against entry-level training is that it does not adequately reflect the realities of the work for which it is presumed to prepare officers. Where this complaint is accurate, it may generally be attributed to one or both of two major problems. First, training is *intentionally irrelevant.* Second, the training academy has become an *isolated ivory tower.*

Intentional Irrelevance.   In a few agencies, the reality of the field may include an absence of supervision and standards so egregious that training curricula cannot formally describe what new officers will find after they have graduated from training. The lesson plans of police departments that have been found to be corrupt or brutal have rarely acknowledged this ugly truth. Instead, their curricula usually have been exercises in hypocrisy written and taught by staff who have sought training positions as a way of insulating themselves from the misconduct they found when they joined their agencies, or who attempt to convey reality through winks, off-the-cuff remarks, changes in tone, and other between-the-lines techniques. Of such an agency, Jonathan Rubinstein wrote:

> There is no way to prepare a policeman for the situation he discovers on the street. There are some open discussions at the police academy about the possibilities for graft, but most instructors restrict themselves to repeating the traditional homilies about "not selling your soul for a bowl of porridge."
>   . . . The moralizing to which the recruit is subjected in the academy mercifully stops when he gets to the district, but he quickly finds that even the frank advice of helpful teachers has not prepared him for what he finds. Although his experience depends greatly on the kind of district he is sent to, one thing he finds everywhere is bribery. (Rubinstein, 1973:401, 405)

The Ivory-Tower Problem.   A second problem, however, can exist even in agencies that are generally well run. Training staff may not interact regularly enough with administrators, line personnel, and community members in a way which ensures that training remains current and in touch with emerging problems and issues.

Ensuring the Relevance of Training

Obviously, intentionally irrelevant training such as that described by Rubinstein reflects deep agencywide deficiencies. Where such training exists, the problem lies at the very core of the agency and cannot be corrected simply by improving training. Instead, only a major overhaul of the entire agency and its relationship to the community can correct such a condition. The ivory-tower problem, however, may occur even in well-intended agencies and regional training institutions, and should be addressed with the following strategies, described in detail below:

- Encouraging interaction between administrators and trainers
- Seeking and acting on feedback from line officers, supervisors, and the public
- Requiring after-action reports and reviews, and identifying their training implications
- Avoiding oversimplification and attempts to provide pat answers to complex problems

Encouraging Interaction between Administrators and Trainers. Training is of limited value if it does not teach precisely the agency's general philosophy and substantive policies and procedures. An unfortunate tendency among smaller agencies is to assume that new officers who come to their employ after having received entry-level training at regional or state police facilities (or occasionally during the course of employment in other police agencies) are "finished products" who need no further grooming or training before they assume field duties. This is a mistake. No American community is precisely the same as any other, and no American police agency's policies, procedures, rules, regulations, and expectations of officers are precisely the same as any other's.

For this reason, every agency must realize that it has a responsibility to supplement any training delivered by regional or state authorities with a program tailored to its own needs and expectations. To accomplish this, the agency's training officer—a position that should be described and assigned in *every* agency, regardless of size—should conduct careful reviews of entry-level training provided to employees by other officials. When conflicts between training curricula and agency policy are discovered, they should be pointed out to training officials so that accommodations can be negotiated. When training curricula do not address the needs of specific jurisdictions (e.g., in terms of describing and responding to the need to serve particular local populations or to deal with police problems unique to the community), agencies themselves must provide employees with the necessary supplementary training.

In larger agencies, disjunction between policy makers and trainers sometimes is caused by simple lack of communication. In one such agency, for example, police trainers taught officers to hogtie violent arrestees and emotionally disturbed persons by using handcuffs and plastic cords and by then drawing their ankles up toward their wrists by use of a cord restraint. When several persons died of *positional asphyxia*—suffocation caused by the pressure of one's own weight on the rib cage, lungs, and diaphragm—while restrained in this manner and placed or transported in prone positions, civil rights suits were brought against officers and the department. In the course of this litigation, it was discovered that the policy makers who, years earlier, had drawn up the department's regulations on leg and arm restraints had recognized the dangers of hogtying and had specifically forbidden it. During the intervening years, however, the department's trainers apparently took it upon themselves to expand the hand and ankle restraint policies to include hogtying. There was no official authorization for this training, but, amazingly, no administrator had monitored training carefully enough to put an end to it until hundreds of officers were instructed in this dangerous technique and several deaths had resulted.[13]

301

CHAPTER 9
*Personnel
Management I:
Hiring and
Entry-Level Training*

In short, trainers may be expert in their subject and the methods of teaching it, but as the courts regularly remind us, trainers are merely representatives of the chief administrators who are ultimately responsible for what is taught to officers and other employees. Thus, in both small and large agencies, administrators are duty bound to make certain that they understand and approve what is being taught to the people who serve under them.

Seeking and Acting on Consumer Feedback.   Police training, especially at the entry level, must also be informed by the insights of the officers who put it to use—as well as by the insights of the sergeants, lieutenants, and captains who supervise and command them and the public they serve. Trainers should regularly meet with field personnel to identify training deficiencies and to develop means of correcting them. In several agencies, *focus groups* of randomly selected officers have proved very successful at this task and can begin their work with a few simple questions from trainers:

- How are you doing out there?
- Where did we let you down? Are you running into problems for which training did not adequately prepare you?
- If we have let you down, have you got any suggestions about what might be done to help you to address these problems?
- Would you be willing to work with us in developing such training?
- Do you see any new problems starting to develop that trainers should be thinking about?
- Would you please keep us advised about new problems that may arise so that we can work together to develop training for them?

It is excellent practice to put the same sorts of questions to supervisors and field commanders. They are the department representatives who live most closely with new officers' successes and failures, and, when asked, they invariably have many constructive suggestions about the content and methods of training new officers. In addition, merely participating in training in this way gives them a stake in the training enterprise and reduces the chance that they may explain away their officers' mistakes by claiming that trainers do their work inadequately. Making stakeholders of field supervisors in this way, of course, assumes that field supervisors' participation is meaningful and that the supervisors see concrete results coming from their suggestions and criticisms. Soliciting—and then ignoring—their input is certain merely to expand whatever schisms may exist between trainers and the field.

Especially in medium or large jurisdictions, a major component of entry-level training should acquaint new personnel with the cultures and folkways of the various groups in the service population. Regardless of the nature or breadth of new officers' background and experience, they are unlikely to have come in contact with the great variety of people—whites, blacks, Hispanics, Asians, Native Americans, Christians, Jews, Muslims, rich, poor, gays, addicts, radicals, racists, the blind, the deaf, the insane—who make up the populations of many U.S. jurisdictions. Police in such places inevitably interact with members of all these groups, usually during some sort of crisis. It is critical that they not make matters worse by inadvertently violating some cultural taboo or by failing to recognize that body language, tone of voice, and gestures may mean as much in communication as what is actually said. Box 9-5 presents a blue-ribbon commission's recommendations and comments concerning police training in Milwaukee; it is an appropriate checklist for any agency.

Requiring After-Action Reports and Reviews. The department's own experiences, in terms of both police situations that were satisfactorily resolved and those that ended unhappily, should be carefully scrutinized for policy and training implications. Whenever an officer fires his or her gun, is injured, uses force, draws a citizen's complaint, engages in a pursuit, has an accident, or satisfactorily resolves a seemingly impossible situation, trainers should seek to identify the incident's training implications. Every critical police incident should be seen as an opportunity to assess the value and relevance of training, and everybody who reviews such incidents should carefully consider and articulate the training (and policy) implications of these incidents. Regardless of how it happens to turn out, a badly handled incident may indicate a training need on the part of the officers involved and/or a more widespread deficiency that should be corrected if future disaster is to be avoided.

Avoiding Oversimplification. One of the major causes of artificiality in police training—especially at the recruit level—is the understandable desire of instructors to come up with a hard, fast, and foolproof solution to every potential field problem raised in training discussions. In their zeal to provide easy answers to trainees' "What if?" questions—as in, "I understand what to do if *A* happens, Sir, but what if *B* (or *C*, or *D*, or any combination thereof) happens? What do I do then?"—training staff may oversimplify very complex problems. It is important that instructors, training curricula, and trainees recognize that there may not be a hard, fast, and foolproof answer to every police dilemma. If there were a clear path to a happy ending in every crisis, police work would be a far less challenging task that could be performed by functionaries who exercised little or no discretion.

Certainly, it is critical that officers be provided with guidelines that bound their discretion as much as possible. At the same time, training and trainers must acknowledge that, like doctors and lawyers, field police officers work on *probabilities* rather than *certainties*. In their professional moments of truth, all face the same dilemma:

> There is no guaranteed solution to this problem, but my training and experience indicate that Approach A is more likely to work than Approach B; I will apply Approach A to the best of my ability and will hope that it does the job. If it becomes apparent that Approach A is not working, I will switch to B, and will consider still other alternatives. If nothing works, I will be saddened, but will know that I have done all that was appropriate and possible under the circumstances, that I have abided by the principles of my profession, and that I will be able to explain why I did what I did.

Training people to exercise discretion in uncertain environments is not an easy task. But this task must be mastered by skilled instructors who teach a curriculum that recognizes and deals realistically with the complexities and ambiguities of police work—and with the importance of being able to explain

BOX 9-5. Training Recommendations of the Milwaukee Mayor's Commission
Academy Training and Field Training

The content of recruit training and in-service training must clearly reflect the philosophy of community-oriented policing and the goal of appreciating diversity. Officers must be trained in the practical topics of their profession, but they must also be trained in styles of behavior which respect all people as individuals. The use of stereotyped examples in training promotes thinking in stereotypes. The duty of police officers is not to be moral judges, but to uphold the law and to provide protection and service to all.

The entire curriculum should be reviewed for sequence and for course content which reflects Department values and the philosophy of community-oriented policing. All segments of the community should be invited to participate in this review process. Periodic re-review should be utilized to keep materials up-to-date. . . . We have been told that the Training Academy has a small permanent staff, and that many courses are scheduled when other instructors from the Department are available. Instructors must be made available so that topics can be coordinated.

Training and in-service training on mandatory arrest in domestic violence situations must be reviewed, in conjunction with . . . other organizations working in this area. We received testimony suggesting that officers do not always follow domestic violence procedures. We have also been told that the MPD's policy on mandatory arrest is unnecessarily lengthy and complicated. All Department members should be trained to see domestic violence and abuse as violence, not as an acceptable part of any relationship.

Academy instructors must have teaching skills as well as subject matter expertise. They must be familiar with modern teaching methodology, and should provide students with objectives for the entire course and for each lesson. The Department should consider having courses team-taught by a professional instructor working in tandem with an MPD expert. Courses on community policing, victim issues, and valuing diversity should include community members as team teachers and evaluators of both the materials and the cadets. Personnel from other government agencies should make presentations on resources they can provide for officers, and should have the opportunity to evaluate cadet achievement of learning objectives.

As part of its community orientation, the MPD should offer community-based organizations the opportunity to have liaisons observe or participate in training, and to provide feedback to Academy staff both on the content and on their perception of recruit learning achievement. The Department should also consider having Academy classes visit community-based organizations, and should consider the possibility of internships with community-based organizations and other City departments during Field Training. At all times during Academy training, field training, and in-service training, instructors and students should remember that they themselves are members of many communities and may have valuable experiences and perceptions to share.

The goal of Academy training should be to help recruits succeed, while ensuring that those who are unfit for service are eliminated. The philosophy of Academy training should be that the police officer is part of the community, and each course in the curriculum should reflect that philosophy. Academy staff has the best opportunity to make a thorough evaluation of each recruit who has already passed the selection process. Academy staff has the responsibility to ensure that every recruit who has met these selection criteria learns what is needed to become a police officer, and learns a context of community orientation in which to place those technical skills. The staff has the responsibility to provide extra help to recruits who have difficulty with specific parts of the curriculum, if they are otherwise showing themselves to have the potential to be good officers. At the same time, the staff has the responsibility to the Department and the community to ensure that recruits who on a day-to-day basis demonstrate that they cannot master the curriculum or cannot master the desired behaviors of a police officer are eliminated from the training process.

BOX 9-5. Training Recommendations of the Milwaukee Mayor's Commission *(continued)*
Academy Training and Field Training

All recruits should be given a copy of the Law Enforcement Standards Board's [LESB] "Uniform Student Performance Objectives" before entering the Academy, as well as course outlines and objectives for each additional topic covered by the MPD, and for the overall objectives of the training program. Recruits should be able to monitor their own progress. The FPC [Fire and Police Commission] should develop an evaluation form for recruits to complete anonymously, covering Academy instructors and the entire training program, including how well instructors achieve the stated objectives of their courses, and how well the Academy meets the LESB objectives and the additional MPD objectives. The FPC should provide a summary of recruit evaluations to Academy staff and the Chief, so that they may monitor the need for change and use this information in performance evaluations of instructional staff. The FPC should also do follow-up evaluations one year and two years after each class graduates from the Academy, asking how they evaluate their training in light of their experience on the streets. Exit interviews with recruits who leave and with officers who leave within two years of Academy graduations should ask whether training was a factor in the decision.

The Field Training program should be longer than twelve weeks, and the Department should consider the community internships suggested above. Field training and the supervision that a new officer receives during the probationary period are critical to instilling the values and behaviors of community-oriented police work. No matter what a recruit has learned at the Academy, it is what he or she sees on the street, and sees condoned or criticized by supervisors, that will become the patterns of a career.

We recommend that the FPC and MPD develop a plan for periodic evaluations of the Academy by teams of outside specialists representing other police departments and academic criminal justice programs. We suggest these evaluations at two-year intervals, with no police department or academic institution represented at two sequential evaluations. Evaluators should have the opportunity to interview Academy staff, outside instructors, and cadets, to review lesson plans, examinations, and other materials, and to observe classes.

The MPD should investigate the possibility of giving cadets college credits through a local academic institution for their training period at the Academy, and should also consider an academic co-head for the Academy.

Source: From the Mayor's Citizen Commission on Police—Community Relations, *A Report to Mayor John O. Norquist and the Board of Fire and Police Commissioners.* Used by permission.

why one did what one did. The cost of failing to do this, especially at the recruit level, is training that is unrealistic and that causes frustration among new personnel who find that they have not been adequately prepared for their work.

Like all police training, entry-level training should not be conducted exclusively in classrooms or at firearms ranges. Instead, formal classroom instruction should alternate with exposure to the field, so that trainees get an opportunity to apply what they have learned in a formal setting and so that they can come back to the classroom to do remedial work on what their field experience has demonstrated that they did not adequately learn the first time.

Training for Crises

304 Training inadequacies often go unnoticed in the routine of day-to-day police operations. Indeed, the imperative to train officers and employees carefully

and continuously is often obscured by the passage of quiet, uneventful work-days in which nobody is hurt, no life-or-death decisions must be made, and nobody's patience or emotions are worn thin by the provocative actions of persons or groups. At its core, however, policing is the business of preventing and defusing crises, and no matter how sleepy a jurisdiction, police will inevitably be called on to perform this difficult task.

305

CHAPTER 9
Personnel
Management I:
Hiring and
Entry-Level Training

The most critical of all police training, therefore, is that intended to help personnel make decisions in crisis situations in which they do not have access to "the book," or to ready consultation with other officials. This requires careful analysis of the hazards that employees in various positions are likely to encounter during the course of their careers. It also demands that the steps described above be used in the development of training sufficient to ensure that personnel will handle these hazards in a systematic way, rather than in an ad hoc fashion that inevitably produces disastrous mistakes. In attempting to develop such training, it is useful to keep one important point in mind: *People call the police to emergencies because they assume that the police are capable of solving problems that nobody else can deal with.* Certainly, some problems prove impossible even for the police, but unless the police are carefully trained to respond to this public expectation, citizens will learn that calling the police is a waste of time because officers are no more capable than anybody else.

Training to Approach Crises. Training for critical police incidents frequently has ignored the fact that the manner in which police *approach* dangerous situations plays a great role in determining their outcomes. Instead, such training generally has focused on the *final frame,* or confrontation stage, of situations that actually begin earlier, when officers observe and decide to investigate suspicious circumstances or, more often, are made aware by their dispatchers or by citizens that they are about to confront potentially violent persons or situations (Binder and Scharf, 1980; Fyfe, 1986b, 1988). By concentrating more intensely on the strategies and tactics used in structuring officers' confrontations with persons involved in crises, trainers may help officers to avoid putting themselves in harm's way and, thus, to reduce the chances that they or citizens will be injured in such situations. Almost by virtue of their fixed and two-dimensional format, for example, "shoot–don't shoot" training films and computer simulations make it impossible to train officers in the importance of proper approaches to emergencies. Instead, such programs often put trainees into the simulated final frames of situations that competent officers would have approached more carefully. Any training that focuses exclusively on decisions to shoot or refrain from shooting and that ignores tactics that may help officers avoid such decisions in the first place is only half complete.

Avoiding Paranoia. A related danger is the tendency to develop and/or present training material that makes it appear that every event in an officer's working life is a life-or-death tactical exercise. Some of the commercial training presently available to police, for example, is based on the rarest of situations and may encourage officers to believe that there lurks a hidden gun rather than simply a vehicle registration in every motorist's glove compartment; that every argument between husbands and wives involves deranged would-be cop killers; that, as one film suggested, every biker has turned his motorcycle's

The most critical police training prepares officers for the life-or-death situations all officers hope they never encounter. Role-plays such as this one are probably the most effective instructional method for this training.
Dan Chidester/Image Works.

handlebars into shotguns designed to kill unwary officers; or that, as another film would have it, every street drunk should be treated as a martial arts expert who has strapped concealed "edged weapons" all over his body. When material of this nature is presented to officers—especially to young and impressionable recruits—a great danger arises that they will adopt an operating style better suited to combat soldiers than to peace officers. Certainly, officers must be highly sensitive to the dangers of the streets, and they must be prepared to anticipate and deal with those dangers. But they should not be made paranoid by unrealistic training that presents their work as an occupation in which one is always no more than an instant from a gory death or a decision about whether to take another's life. Before any training material is delivered to officers or other personnel, therefore, administrators should make certain that the philosophy and content of the material are consistent with agency goals and experience.

Training for Life Off-Duty

Police training programs often fail to train officers for one of the most important challenges of becoming a police officer: learning how to be an off-duty cop. Even allowing for overtime, police officers spend most of the 168 hours in every week off-duty. During this time, they are in a strange sort of limbo. Generally required by law to take some sort of vague "appropriate police action whenever necessary," officers are never truly off-duty, in the same sense that they might have been able to forget their work before they joined the ranks of the police. The involvement of off-duty officers in arguments and other minor annoyances always is colored by the line that separates their status as private citizens from that of police officers sworn to uphold all laws. Unless this line is made clear by unambiguous policy and training, some off-duty officers inevitably turn disagreeable private matters into police situations that have negative consequences for all concerned, including their employers. In recent years, cases in which off-duty officers have resolved arguments with family, friends, neighbors, thoughtless motorists, and barroom drunks by suddenly invoking their police authority and making arrests—or even shooting their antagonists—have resulted in civil suits and substantial judgments against the officers and their departments and, occasionally, in arrests of officers (see, eg., Fyfe, 1980; Geller and Scott, 1992:161–167, 266–267; New York City Police Department, 1987).

307

CHAPTER 9
Personnel
Management I:
Hiring and
Entry-Level Training

The line between police officer and private citizen should be made clear by policies and training that:

1. Discourage or forbid officers from engaging in activities that bring discredit to their departments and damage the relationship between police and community.
2. Cause officers to understand that they hold a special place and status in the community. Therefore, they must not seek special privileges, and must be good neighbors and citizens of good reputation.
3. Require officers to identify themselves as police officers when they become subjects of police action.
4. Forbid officers from carrying guns in visible places unless they reasonably anticipate an immediate need to use their guns.
5. Forbid officers from carrying guns when they are or have been drinking.
6. Forbid officers from drinking so heavily that they are not in control of their faculties.
7. Forbid officers from using their law enforcement powers and/or guns to resolve personal disputes.
8. Discourage or forbid officers from engaging in traffic enforcement and other minor enforcement actions, unless the violations involved present a real, immediate, and serious threat to life and property.

In addition, training must ensure that officers understand that tactics and strategies which may be appropriate when they are on-duty, in uniform, readily identifiable to all, and equipped with a radio may be grossly inappropriate in circumstances when they are off-duty, alone, out of uniform, not readily identifiable, and not equipped with easy means of communication. This may seem obvious, but in the heat of off-duty crises—a stickup at a convenience store while an off-duty officer is on the cashier's line, a burglar's attempt to break into a neighbor's home—officers whose training has not specifically sensitized them to the differences between what may be appropriate when on-duty and in uniform and what may be appropriate when off-duty may revert to their training and do precisely the wrong thing. As a consequence, they may find themselves at a tactical disadvantage, or facing overwhelming odds, or mistaken for criminals by innocent citizens—as well as by responding on-duty officers. In short, being an off-duty police officer differs greatly from being either an on-duty officer or a civilian who has left work. Departments that do not adequately sensitize officers to these differences risk the safety of officers and the public.

External Training Resources

A great number of government agencies, universities, and private organizations offer training courses for police at every level. Many institutions—such as the FBI Academy in Quantico (Virginia), the International Association of Chiefs of Police, the University of Louisville's Southern Police Institute, and Northwestern University's Traffic Institute—have such a grasp of the field and access to so many resources that virtually any course they offer will provide major benefits for participants and their agencies. In addition, the longer-term residential courses offered by many of these institutions—most notably, by the FBI National Academy and the Southern Police Institute—have created large networks of alumni who usually serve as career-long resources to participants and their agencies. At the state and regional level, many agencies and police officer standards and training commissions also prescribe and offer training, as do some prosecutors and the training academies of large state, county, and municipal departments.

In their zeal to see that personnel are trained well, however, administrators should be careful to avoid courses offered by unqualified individuals or organizations. Police training is a big business that unfortunately has attracted a few commercial organizations more interested in turning a quick profit than in ensuring that the content of their courses is useful and realistic.

Before enrolling personnel in such courses—or in any external programs—administrators should carefully examine vendors' credentials and should check with other police agencies to determine whether they have permitted their personnel to participate in the courses in question. Where they have, of course, the relevant questions involve the value of the courses; where they have not, the salient question is, "Why not?"

Similarly, before making commitments to purchase and use such externally produced training materials as films, videotapes, and computer-aided simulations, administrators should ensure that these products are reviewed and approved by qualified in-house personnel. In many agencies, this process is conducted by a training committee consisting, for example, of field, training, and community relations personnel, as well as the agency's legal advisor and, where appropriate, representatives of the community or other affected institutions (e.g., mental health officials, prosecutors).

Two general recommendations emerge from this discussion of external training for police personnel:

1. *Policing is a public service, and, wherever possible, it is usually wise to give police business to nonprofit institutions that share a commitment to public service. In general, the safest course of action is to give first preference in external*

training to courses conducted by other police and government agencies, by universities, and by the traditional law enforcement membership organizations.

2. *The agency has an obligation to carefully review any training provided by external organizations and to supplement it with in-house training designed to ensure that employees know precisely what the agency expects from them.*

309

CHAPTER *9*
Personnel
Management I:
Hiring and
Entry-Level Training

Entry-Level Training and Probation as Screeners

Properly designed entry-level training and related probationary experiences are the best available predictors of a person's performance in a job. The traditional professions know this lesson well, and it is for this reason that they continue to screen candidates for full membership to their ranks long after such candidates have passed their entrance examinations. Regardless of how well they have performed during their undergraduate education and on entrance examinations, people who wish to be doctors know they must also excel in medical training and in internships and residencies. Similarly, regardless of their law school records, young lawyers do not learn whether their firms will admit them to partnership—or ask them to leave—until they have demonstrated their mettle for several years as lower-level associates. New professors also know they must demonstrate excellence for several years before their universities decide either to grant them tenure or to show them the door.

Ironically, many of the same police administrators and supervisors who complain that affirmative action and equal employment opportunity rules have watered down police employment standards treat an appointment as a probationary officer as an irrevocable ticket to a lifetime police career. If these officials truly wanted to emulate the traditional professions, one would expect they would rely very heavily on the screening value of entry-level training and probationary performance.

They do not. Instead, they treat probation as a mere formality and, in some cases, have even insulated probationers from the disciplinary standards and procedures to which all other personnel in their agencies are subject. When they do so, their actions—and inactions—betray the sentiment that police officers are a beleaguered breed apart from the rest of the population. Given the safeguards that typically protect employees once they have attained civil service tenure, this parochial view makes moot all the science and good faith that may have been expended on the screening and selection procedures that precede training and probation.

Failure to remove incompetent and otherwise unsuited probationers is a mark of weak leadership, and police chiefs who do not avail themselves of this opportunity to complete the selection process cannot legitimately complain that they are denied personnel control. Further, because performance in a carefully designed training program and during probation is so defensible as a predictor of long-term job performance and the ability to accept discipline, terminations during probation are far more likely to stand up under court challenges than would attempts to reinstate the less demonstrably relevant standards for which some old-line police administrators seem to pine.

Entry-level training should be a demanding part of the screening process. A third of the officer candidates who participated in this state police training program resigned or were separated.
AP/Wide World.

Thus, entry-level training should be regarded as an important extension of the screening and selection process, and the entire probationary period—especially during the trial on the job that takes place when new candidates are first assigned to the field—should be viewed as the final selection standard. If candidates do not do well in training or while they are under close scrutiny during their probationary periods, it is highly unlikely they will do well in the job for which they are being trained and tested.

There should be no hesitation in separating unsatisfactory probationers, and once supervising officers have studied the individual case and have reached a conclusion that a recruit is unsatisfactory, there should be no appeal from this decision. Failing to use these screeners as means of identifying unsuitable people who have somehow not been identified by more abstract employment marries the agency to people who, at best, will mature into merely marginal performers and who, at worst, will become even more unsatisfactory once locked into their jobs by civil service tenure. In short, no agency should regard a new employee as a *permanent* employee merely because he or she has passed some tests and been sworn into a probationary position.

Field Training.   Entry-level training in all agencies should include a *field training* component, in which new personnel work with qualified training officers in systematic, documented, and evaluated on-the-job training settings. There are several obvious needs for this training, one of the most significant of which is that it allows for direct observation and evaluation of behaviors that are not measurable in classroom settings.

Field training should be a structured training experience rather than simply "learning by doing" under the supervision of officers whose only qualification is long experience. Field training officers should be the department's most qualified personnel. They must themselves be carefully trained to provide trainees with thoughtful and constructive direction and feedback, to furnish their departments with thorough documentation of the strengths and weaknesses of individual trainees, and to offer suggestions about how to improve training generally.

311

CHAPTER 9
Personnel
Management I:
Hiring and
Entry-Level Training

Probation

As suggested above, probation—the last step in selection—is also the first true *job-related* test in the selection procedure. A major difficulty with reliance on probation is that it fails to take into account supervisors' human tendency to overlook the failures and weaknesses of young officer candidates they have come to know personally. Consequently, one of the great challenges to police administrators is to convince first-line and middle-level supervisors that they must begin the process of separating borderline and unfit candidates who have managed to slide through in the formal testing and entrance requirements.

The probationary period should last at least one year. Some weaknesses and incompetence may not be discovered in a shorter time, particularly when, as it should, recruit training may require six months or more. Special attention should be given to the supervision and rating of probationers. They should be observed closely during their training period and during class hours; notebooks, examinations, and classroom attitudes should be evaluated, and evaluations should be carefully recorded. When probationers are sent into the field, they should spend time with several different supervisors, usually patrol officers with several years' service who have demonstrated their ability to direct and guide rookies and who have enthusiasm and unquestioned loyalty to their jobs. Records of accomplishments and service ratings should be made at least quarterly and preferably every month. High standards must be maintained, and doubtful cases should be resolved in favor of the department.

SUMMARY

Policing is a labor-intensive business that has enormous effects on citizens' lives and liberties and on the livability and safety of our communities. Its success or failure depends, in greatest measure, on the capabilities of officers in the street. Working at their agencies' lowest levels, often alone and usually without direct supervision, field officers determine whom to arrest and how much force to employ in doing so, whom to ticket, whom to chase off the corner, whom to stop and question, how to resolve disputes, and how to handle challenges to their authority. In doing so, these officers also determine their agencies' public standing, reputation, and credibility. Ultimately, this means that they may also determine whether elected officials and police administrators will accomplish—or even continue to hold—their jobs. People who do not respect or trust the police rarely trust or grant legitimacy to the governments that employ them. When that happens in a democracy, the government is likely to be ousted at the polls. Thus, if only for reasons of self-interest and out of desire to achieve their broader goals and preserve their places in history, elected officials and police administrators have a compelling stake in fielding the best possible police officers. No slick PR operation, no community relations gimmick, no patronage or pandering can possibly right the wrongs done by incompetent or insensitive street officers.

To accomplish this, elected officials and police administrators must seek out the best possible people, and they must do everything possible to provide them with realistic and relevant training. They must also refrain from thinking of new officers as members of the police family from the day they are sworn in. New police officers are trainees—probationers who have no right to lifetime claims on police badges and authority until they have demonstrated that they are capable of making the transition from accomplished citizen to successful police officer. Those whose performance in classroom training, field training, and/or probation indicates that they cannot do so—or even that there is some doubt about their ability to do so—should unhesitatingly be separated from the service.

QUESTIONS FOR DISCUSSION

1. The issue of age limits on entering police officers was brought into sharp focus by a 54-year-old grandmother who has recently completed the Philadelphia Police Department's recruit training program and been assigned as a probationary patrol officer. Consider and discuss the question she has put to those who are skeptical about this career choice: *Why not?*

2. Would you recommend that residency requirements be employed by the police agency in which you work or that serves the community in which you reside? Why or why not?

3. A study of New York City police officers found that more than 90 percent were opposed to lateral entry (Fyfe and Pope, 1972). Perhaps surprisingly, they opposed allowing NYPD officers—themselves—to enter other departments at advanced levels just as strongly as they opposed opening NYPD's advanced ranks to officers from other agencies. How would you explain their attitude?

4. You have been appointed to a task force charged with addressing a personnel problem in a large police agency. The problem is that the department has had difficulty finding and retaining capable civilian employees to work in such positions as radio dispatchers and emergency telephone operators. A task force survey has reported that there apparently are four major causes of this problem:

   a. Low salaries, which average about 60 percent of a patrol officer's wages.

   b. Irregular hours, which make it especially difficult for single parents (who are numerous among candidates for these jobs) to travel to and from work and to adequately care for their children.

313

CHAPTER 9
Personnel
Management I:
Hiring and
Entry-Level Training

c. Perceived second-class status at work. Many dispatchers and operators, especially women and minority members, report that they are resented and treated poorly by uniformed police personnel.

d. Poor training. The best operators and dispatchers are rewarded for their performance by being assigned to undemanding, nonemergency, telephones and radio frequencies. This means that there are few skilled people available to train new hires, many of whom resign out of frustration with their attempts at trial-and-error learning.

Develop a plan to present to the chief to address this problem.

5. Written police entrance examinations have been attacked for decades as irrelevant and discriminatory tests of speed-reading ability rather than suitability for police work. How would you go about addressing this criticism? If the discriminatory effects of these exams could not be eliminated, what substitutes might be employed?

NOTES

1. Among the best analyses of the relationships between early U.S. police and politicians are Astor, 1971; Fogelson, 1977; Fosdick, 1920; Johnson, 1981; Miller, 1977; National Commission on Law Observance and Enforcement, 1968; and Walker, 1977.

2. There was a brief hiatus in the effects of *Griggs* on employment discrimination policy, practice, and litigation. Neither *Griggs* nor the 1964 or 1972 civil rights litigation required a showing that discrimination was *intentional*. Instead, their provisions required only a showing that, intentional or otherwise, employment standards discriminated against protected groups (e.g., women, persons of color, the elderly) before employers would be required to demonstrate that these standards were job-relevant, in that they distinguished between successful and unsuccessful job candidates. In 1989, however, a Supreme Court that had grown far more conservative than the 1971 *Griggs* Court ruled, in essence, that persons alleging discrimination would be required to show that it was intentional (*Wards Cove Packing Co. v. Antonio*). This case created an extremely difficult obstacle to demonstrating that discriminatory employment practices were serious enough to be a constitutional violation. What employer who chose to discriminate intentionally would admit to this or fail to cover up evidence of evil intent? The *Wards Cove* case was set aside when President Bush signed the Civil Rights Act of 1991, which, for all intents and purposes, reestablished the *Griggs* "disparate impact" test as the means of proving discrimination in employment practices. At the same time, however, because this act prohibits *norming* of test scores based on race and gender, it greatly complicates the task of producing representative public agencies.

3. Indeed, during the years of the Great Depression and through the massive hirings of New York City police and firefighters following World War II, there existed a small "stretching" industry. This business was operated by people who, through a series of exercises and actual physical stretching, would temporarily add an inch or more to the heights of candidates who, without such assistance, would otherwise have been too short to meet their prospective employers' height standards. When the stretching, exercises, and sleeping on a hard board ended, the candidate would return to normal height. But by then, he or she had already been measured and was locked into the job. While looking for his break on Broadway early in his career, the actor Jason Robards supported himself by working as a "stretcher." A similar small industry prepared people with poor eyesight for police and fire department testing

by guiding them in a series of long, grueling, and painful eye exercises. When the exercises stopped, eyesight returned to its previous poor state, and new officers could don their glasses once more, knowing that their eyes would never again be tested by their employers.

4. Before the Detroit Police Department established a residency requirement in the 1970s, it found that some of its officers were living not only out of town but also out of the country, in Canada.

5. Educational incentives such as pay differentials and assumption of tuition payments appear to be more common methods for encouraging higher education by police personnel. These, of course, apply to in-service personnel, rather than to recruits (see, e.g., Sherman et al., 1978).

6. One of the reasons that these requirements seem to be most prevalent in prosperous suburban police agencies is that their disparate impact on minorities in these places is minimal because their residents include few minority citizens.

7. See, e.g., Carter et al., 1989a, 1989b; Cohen and Chaiken, 1973; Hoover, 1983; and Kappeler, Sapp, and Carter, 1993, for research purporting to demonstrate that college-educated police officers are a particular asset. See Worden, 1990, which reaches a contrary conclusion.

8. Peirson was apparently well qualified to make this judgment. An African American and former Oakland, California, police officer, he held a doctorate in criminology from the University of California at Berkeley and served on the faculty of Howard University for many years before his death. He had also been one of the famed World War II Tuskegee Airmen.

9. The President's Commission on Law Enforcement and Administration of Justice suggested the development of a *nationwide* police retirement system (1967:142). In the years that have since passed, there has been no movement to such a system, and because of the extreme variations in police compensation and benefits across the states, such a system seems unlikely in the foreseeable future. In a few states (e.g., Florida), however, statutory arrangements for *pension portability* between police agencies appear to have operated with some success, and mobility between departments occurs with some frequency.

10. It is somewhat surprising that, regardless of content, the typical multiple-choice, pencil-and-paper police entrance examination is not more often the subject of *Griggs*-based suits alleging lack of job relevance. When is any U.S. police officer required to answer a written multiple-choice question in the course of his or her duties?

11. The Minnesota Multiphasic Personality Inventory (MMPI) is probably the most widely used psychometric examination, in or out of policing. Other frequently employed tests include the Sixteen Personality Factor Questionnaire (16PF), the California Psychological Inventory (CPI), and the Guilford-Zimmerman Temperament Survey.

12. One candidate for employment in a large southern agency was reported by his polygraph examiner to have been deceptive when asked questions concerning drug use and sales. Under intense questioning, he eventually admitted to having used marijuana 10 times during the 15 days immediately preceding his polygraph exam. The candidate continued to deny involvement in drug sales, but the polygraph examiner reported that he was deceptive on this point. When the candidate subsequently produced the results of another private polygraph examination which, not surprisingly, purported to show that he had not dealt drugs, he was hired despite his recent and frequent marijuana use and his deception concerning it. He went on

to a career marked by frequent misconduct, disciplinary actions, and civil rights suits, including one in which he was found to have wrongfully arrested, beaten, and shot and killed a man.

13. For discussions of positional asphyxia, see Appendix 15-1, this volume, Reay at al., 1988, 1992; and San Diego Police Department, 1992. (The San Diego Police Department is *not* the agency described in this discussion.)

315

CHAPTER 9
Personnel
Management I:
Hiring and
Entry-Level Training

SOURCES

ASTOR, GERALD. *The New York City Cops: An Informal History* (New York: Scribner, 1971).

BALDWIN, JAMES, *Noboby Knows My Name* (New York: Dell Publishing, 1962).

BINDER, ARNOLD, and PETER SCHARF. "The Violent Police-Citizen Encounter," *Annals of the American Academy of Political and Social Science*, 452:111–121 (November 1980).

CARTER, DAVID L., ALAN D. SAPP, and DARREL W. STEPHENS. "Higher Education as a Bona Fide Occupational Qualification," *American Journal of Police*, 7:1–28 (1989a).

———, ———, and ———. *The State of Police Education: Policy Direction for the 21st Century* (Washington, D.C.: Police Executive Research Forum, 1989b).

CLARK, RAMSEY. *Crime in America* (New York: Simon and Schuster, 1970).

COHEN, BERNARD, and JAN M. CHAIKEN. *Police Background Characteristics and Performance* (Lexington, Mass.: Lexington Books, 1973).

Evans v. City of Evanston, 881 F.2nd 382 (1989).

FOGELSON, ROBERT M. *Big-City Police* (Cambridge, Mass.: Harvard University Press, 1977).

FOSDICK, RAYMOND. *American Police Systems* (New York: Century, 1920).

FYFE, JAMES J. "Always Prepared: Police Off-Duty Guns," *Annals of the American Academy of Political and Social Sciences*, 452:72–81 (November 1980).

———. *Police Personnel Practices*, Baseline Data Reports, vol. 18, no. 6 (Washington, D.C.: International City Management Association, 1986a).

———. *The Metro-Dade Police/Citizen Violence Reduction Project: Final Report* (Washington, D.C.: Police Foundation, 1988).

———. "The Split-Second Syndrome and Other Determinants of Police Violence," pp. 207–225 in Anne T. Campbell and John J. Gibb (eds.), *Violent Transactions* (Oxford: Basil Blackwell, 1986b).

———. "Shots Fired: An Examination of New York City Police Firearms Discharges," Ph.D. dissertation, State University of New York at Albany (Ann Arbor, Mich.: University Microfilms, 1978).

———, and CARL E. POPE. "New York City Police Attitudes toward Promotional Criteria," unpublished master's thesis, School of Criminal Justice, State University of New York at Albany, 1972.

GELLER, WILLIAM A., and MICHAEL S. SCOTT. *Deadly Force: What We Know* (Washington, D.C.: Police Executive Research Forum, 1992).

GLASTRIS, PAUL, "The Thin White Line," *U.S. News & World Report*, 53–54 (Aug. 15, 1994).

Griggs v. Duke Power Company, 401 U.S. 424 (1971).

HOOVER, LARRY. "The Educational Criteria: Dilemmas and Debate," in Calvin Swank and John Conser (eds.), *The Police Personnel System* (New York: Wiley, 1983).

JOHNSON, DAVID H. *American Law Enforcement: A History* (St. Louis, Mo.: Forum Press, 1981).

KAPPELER, VICTOR E., ALAN D. SAPP, and DAVID L. CARTER. "Police Officer Higher Education, Citizen Complaints and Departmental Rule Violations," *American Journal of Police*, 11:37–54 (1993).

LEONARD, V. A., and HARRY W. MORE. *Police Organization and Management*, 8th ed. (Mineola, N.Y.: Foundation Press, 1993).

McCarthy v. Philadelphia Civil Service Commission, 424 U.S. 645 (1976).

MILLER, WILBUR R. *Cops and Bobbies: Police Authority in London and New York City, 1830–1870* (Chicago: University of Chicago Press, 1977).

MOLLEN, MILTON, et al. *Report of the Commission to Investigate Allegations of Police Corruption and the Anti-Corruption Procedures of the Police Department* (New York: City of New York, July 7, 1994).

National Advisory Commission on Criminal Justice Standards and Goals. *Police* (Washington, D.C.: U.S. Government Printing Office, 1973).

National Commission on Law Observance and Enforcement. *Report on Police*, vol. 14 (Montclair, N.J.: Patterson Smith, 1968 reprint of 1931 original).

New York City Police Department. "Civil Liability of Police Officers," *Legal Bureau Bulletin*, vol. 18, no. 2 (Mar. 5, 1987).

O'CONNOR, GEORGE W. "Survey of Selection Methods" (monograph) (Washington, D.C.: International Association of Chiefs of Police, 1962).

PEIRSON, GWYNNE. *Higher Educational Requirements and Minority Recruitment for the Police: Conflicting Goals?* (Washington, D.C.: Police Foundation, 1978).

President's Commission on Law Enforcement and Administration of Justice. *Task Force Report: The Police* (Washington, D.C.: U.S. Government Printing Office, 1967).

REAY, DONALD T., CORINNE L. FLIGNER, ALLAN D. STILWELL, and JUDY ARNOLD. "Positional Asphyxia during Law Enforcement Transport," *American Journal of Forensic Medicine and Pathology*, 13:90–97 (1992).

———, JOHN D. HOWARD, CORINNE L. FLIGNER, and RICHARD J. WARD. "Effects of Positional Restraint on Oxygen Saturation and Heart Rate Following Exercise," *American Journal of Forensic Medicine and Pathology*, 9:16–18 (1988).

REUSS-IANNI, ELIZABETH. *Two Cultures of Policing: Street Cops and Management Cops* (New Brunswick, N.J.: Transaction Books, 1983).

RUBINSTEIN, JONATHAN. *City Police* (New York: Farrar, Straus and Giroux, 1973).

RUTLEDGE, DEVALLIS. *The Officer Survival Manual*, 2d ed. (Placerville, Calif.: Custom Publishing, 1988).

San Diego Police Department. *Final Report of the Custody Death Task Force*, unpublished internal report (June 1992).

SAUNDERS, CHARLES B. JR. *Upgrading the American Police* (Washington, D.C.: Brookings Institution, 1970).

SHERMAN, LAWRENCE W., and the National Advisory Commission on Higher Education for Police Officers. *The Quality of Police Education* (San Francisco: Jossey-Bass, 1978).

STRAWBRIDGE, PETER, and DEIRDRE STRAWBRIDGE. "A Networking Guide to Recruitment, Selection, and Probationary Training of Police Officers in the Major Police Departments of the United States of America" (monograph) (New York: John Jay College of Criminal Justice, 1990).

TAMM, QUINN. "A Change for the Better," *Police Chief*, 5–6 (January 1962).

VOLLMER, AUGUST. *The Police and Modern Society* (Montclair, N.J.: Patterson Smith, 1972 reprint of original 1936 manuscript).

WALKER, SAMUEL. *A Critical History of Police Reform: The Emergence of Professionalism* (Lexington, Mass.: Lexington Books, 1977).

Wards Cove Packing Co. v. Antonio, 4393 U.S. 802 (1989).

Western Cities Magazine. "Forced Arbitration: Why Cities Worry," pp. 171–180 in James

J. Fyfe (ed.), *Police Management Today: Issues and Case Studies* (Washington, D.C.: International City Management Association, 1985).

WILSON, O. W. *Police Administration*, 2d ed. (New York: McGraw-Hill, 1963).

WORDEN, ROBERT. "A Badge and a Baccalaureate: Policies, Hypotheses, and Further Evidence," *Justice Quarterly*, 7:555–592 (September 1990).

Zamlen v. City of Cleveland, 686 F.Supp. 631 (1989), U.S. *cert. den.*, 111 Supreme Court Reporter 1388 (1990).

317

CHAPTER 9
*Personnel
Management I:
Hiring and
Entry-Level Training*

10

Personnel Management II: Human Resource Management

KEY WORDS AND PHRASES

In-service and specialized training
Position classification and assignment
Career development
Evaluation and monitoring
Promotion
Peter Principle
Personnel information system

Compensation plan
Labor relations
Labor union
Job actions
Strikes
Impasse resolution
Grievance procedures

In Chapter 9, we focused on general principles of police personnel management and on the tasks necessary to identify, recruit, screen, and train new officers and civilian employees. In this chapter, the focus shifts to the tasks necessary to manage personnel once they have been employed and have completed their probationary periods. These tasks include in-service and specialized training, position classification and assignment, career development, evaluation and monitoring, promotion, personnel information systems, compensation plans, and labor relations.

IN-SERVICE AND SPECIALIZED TRAINING

Police training is a *dynamic* process that should not end when employees graduate from the recruit academy or complete other entry-level training. Every police administrator should make certain that every employee has been carefully trained for the particular duties of his or her position and that every employee's training extends throughout his or her career. To do otherwise creates an enormous risk that employees will lose their ability to respond to crises that occur rarely but that demand great mastery of complex subject matter. Regardless of how intensely he or she may have been trained in a recruit academy to handle hostage situations, for example, an officer who is not exposed to such an event for 10 years is likely to make a bad situation worse if he or she has not been continually refreshed and updated on prescribed policies and procedures.

319

CHAPTER *10*
Personnel
Management II:
Human Resource
Management

Further, police training must be dynamic and ongoing because police problems and the accepted means of addressing them are dynamic and continually changing. Over the last 10 years or so, police procedures related to issues such as domestic violence, public nuisances, use of force, and the technology of criminal investigation have changed dramatically. More general operating philosophies have also changed considerably with the emergence of community and problem-oriented policing. Without continuous formal training during this period, there can be no assurance that the officers and civilian employees charged with implementing these changes are doing so appropriately.

Both of the major federal commissions that have studied the police in the last generation have recommended a minimum of 40 hours per year of formal in-service training for all police officers (National Advisory Commission, 1973:404; President's Commission on Law Enforcement, 1967:139–140). Certainly, following these recommendations is costly, but over the long term the costs of failing to provide adequate in-service training are likely to be far greater. On a routine basis, these costs include the diminished performance, service, and officers' sense of professionalism and self-worth that invariably accompany low levels of training. They also include the risk that inadequate training will cause officers to unnecessarily hurt themselves or others. This risk, of course, may also lead to civil liability for failure to properly train and supervise.

Particularly useful in the development of in-service training curricula and emphases is the process of learning from the agency's actual experiences, especially its glowing successes and its unambiguous failures. As suggested in Chapter 9, policy and training specialists should work with experienced field personnel to review such controversial actions as vehicle accidents, shootings, use of force, pursuits, assaults on officers, and injuries to officers for the purpose of identifying their training implications.

In addition to in-service training for employees who remain in their entry-level positions for long periods of time, therefore, police agencies must provide training beyond the entry level for personnel such as investigators, crime scene technicians, crime prevention and SWAT officers, and others who hold special assignments; for personnel who have been or will be promoted to advanced supervisory or management positions; and for in-service supervisors, managers, and executives (see e.g., Commission on Accreditation, 1994:chap. 33).

Specialized Training

Specialists should not be created unless it can be shown that they do the job substantially better than generalists. This is usually the case only if specialists know something that generalists do not, a state that can exist only when specialists are provided with unique training for their positions. For some particularly technical jobs that require special education and training prior to entry into a police agency—running a laboratory or serving as legal advisor, for example—training provided by the agency is likely to consist only of orienting already highly skilled new personnel to the organization and its administration. In other cases, specialized personnel should be given extensive training by their agencies. No criminal or accident investigator, narcotics officer, crime scene technician, or community relations officer should be presumed to be prepared for his or her new assignment merely by dint of success in a patrol assignment. Instead, they must be carefully taught both the theory and the practice of their new work.

Supervisory and Management and Executive Training

The principle that no employee should hold a position for which he or she has not been prepared by education and training applies to supervisors and managers, as well as to those at the entry level. Again, training at these levels should continue throughout managers' careers and should be specially designed for the duties of the position held.

Supervisory Training. The most important of all supervisory and management training is that provided when officers are promoted to sergeant. After the transition from civilian to recruit, no police career step is more significant than this move. It is at this point that officers cease being responsible only for their own performance and must assume responsibility for seeing to it that others do their jobs well. For the first time, they are entitled to give orders to other police personnel and, if they are to be successful, can no longer regard themselves as peers of the officers who do the job. Instead, they must come to view themselves as leaders and must recognize that their authority may be easily compromised if they succumb to the temptation to regard themselves merely as "officers with stripes."

Nobody is more important than the field sergeant to the success or failure of day-to-day police operations. The sergeant oversees and lives with the officers on the line. The sergeant translates departmental directives and policies into practice. The sergeant is police management's representative on the street, and his or her abilities and working style are much more significant to patrol officers than is that of the chief. Without training that provides new sergeants with substantive information on supervisory theory and practice—and that gets them to shift their perspective and mental set from that of the worker to that of the manager and leader—no police organization can say that its supervisors have been adequately prepared for their work.

Management and Executive Training. As rank increases and the pool of personnel at each level decreases, there is a temptation to disregard the need for continuing training. This is a mistake. Nobody in any position in a police organization is immune from or above the need for continuing professional training and development.

Large police departments sometimes meet this need by running their own internal management and executive development programs. With the partial support of local philanthropies, for example, the New York City Police Department's Executive Development Program offers an elaborate catalogue from which top career civilian employees and officers above the rank of lieutenant must choose and participate in workshops and seminars for at least five days annually. Many small and medium-sized departments are fortunate enough to be in states in which arrangements for training have been negotiated with state university systems.[1] Where such arrangements do not exist, establishment of such programs is a goal that should be sought. Often, such arrangements can involve interdepartmental collaboration or the assistance of such institutions as the FBI Academy, the International Association of Chiefs of Police, state chiefs' associations, the Police Executive Research Forum, and many nonpolice organizations that one might not normally regard as resources in attempts to develop management and executive excellence.

321

CHAPTER 10
Personnel
Management II:
Human Resource
Management

More specifically, as Chapter 4 has pointed out, the importance of conceptual skills increases and the importance of technical skills decreases as one moves up in rank. By the time one reaches the highest management levels, mastery of an organization's technical work—be it policing or watchmaking—is much less important than the conceptual ability to anticipate future organizational needs and to gather and deploy the resources necessary to meet them. Police chiefs need not know how to collect latent fingerprints, but they had better know how to forecast and meet the future need for skilled crime scene technicians. Presidents of watch companies need not know how to assemble high-quality watches, but their stockholders will be very unhappy if they have not hired and trained enough people who do. In other words, as one moves further up an agency's organizational chart, training programs designed for managers and executives, rather than specifically for police (or for watchmakers), become increasingly useful.

Many universities and other institutions recognize this and have responded to the need for high-level management training by developing programs that have application for executives in a wide variety of fields or that have focused more specifically on government management. Many local police executives have participated in the Federal Executive Seminar Center courses conducted in Charlottesville, Virginia, by the U.S. Office of Personnel Management. With faculty from Harvard University, the Police Executive Research Forum conducts summer management and executive training. Other universities conduct weekend executive training programs (sometimes degree-granting) that expose participants to the latest management thinking in both the private and public sectors and that teach means of applying it to one's particular work. Where such programs do not exist, expressions of interest often can stimulate their creation.

Preparing Candidates for Promotion. In some large departments, supervisory and management training includes courses designed to prepare eligible candidates for the competitive examination for the next rank. Such courses typically are based on the bibliographies for written promotional examinations and also include considerable information useful in participating in assessment center and decision-making exercises.

Although it is sometimes derided as a "cram school" approach, this strategy actually pays impressive dividends to agencies. Because they recognize that only some few of their number are likely to be promoted, students are highly motivated, eager to learn, and very competitive. Consequently—and assuming the validity of the testing process—those who are eventually promoted should come into their new jobs already having mastered a good percentage of the relevant body of knowledge. Those who are not promoted also will have absorbed a considerable amount of information that should be useful in their work. Finally, since those who participate in such training should do so during their off-duty hours, expenses to the agency are minimal.

POSITION CLASSIFICATION AND ASSIGNMENT

Because of the great variety of positions that may be held by individuals with specific ranks, assignment is a particularly sensitive administrative function. In many agencies, for example, *sergeants* may be assigned to patrol duties in very violent neighborhoods or in areas that officers regard as "country clubs"; they may be assigned to challenging and prestigious investigative or staff positions or to dull, routine supervisory work. If an administration is to be credible and productive, it is critical that such assignments be made objectively and on the basis of credentials, rather than because some officers know the right people or have other connections to power and influence. If a police agency is to avoid the perception that influence peddling and nepotism, rather than merit, determine the course of one's career, all *special* and *desirable* assignments should be advertised throughout the agency, with clearly stated eligibility requirements and instructions for applications.

CAREER DEVELOPMENT

The concept of career development involves two distinct efforts: (1) providing personnel with specific skills so that they might better perform their current jobs, and (2) attempting systematically to broaden the experience and expertise of employees to prepare them for future responsibilities. This second effort obviously is most relevant to personnel likely to proceed through an organization's ranks toward its top levels. When such upwardly mobile persons are identified—typically through quick rises through the ranks early in their careers—this may be accomplished through a program of systematic rotation of assignments, perhaps in conjunction with a *mentoring* program in which junior employees are tutored by more senior officials. In large agencies especially, this ensures that those who eventually rise to the top have a broad view of their departments and the manner in which the subunits relate to each other and to the accomplishment of organizational goals. Such a background is invaluable to those who must one day set organizational priorities and decide how to distribute scarce resources across departmental units.

But career development is also important for those whose career paths do not take them to the tops of their agencies. For such personnel, career development and assignment rotation often provide an enriching and broadening experience that avoids boredom and burnout and that keeps enthusiasm for the job at a high level.

323

CHAPTER *10*
Personnel
Management II:
Human Resource
Management

EVALUATION AND MONITORING

Getting the most out of each employee—and ensuring that each employee derives as much satisfaction and fulfillment as possible from work—demands assessment and feedback on his or her work. This can be done on a daily, informal, basis, but all personnel should also be formally evaluated by their immediate supervisors on a regular basis—and on performance criteria that are clearly stated and defined. The monitoring function also requires that, without turning the agency into an organization that intrudes unjustifiably on officers' personal lives, line supervisors must recognize that some *private* conduct by officers—alcohol or drug abuse, consorting with criminals, domestic violence—does affect employees' performance and the effectiveness, reputation, and credibility of the agency. Line supervisors are likely to be the first officials to become aware of conduct of this type. When evidence is strong, they should not hesitate to initiate corrective action; in other cases, they must be encouraged and held accountable for bringing their suspicions to the attention of officials who may look into them further.

Performance evaluation is the systematic audit of an employee's job-related performance by his or her immediate supervisor. Formal evaluation systems should be conducted in all police departments regardless of size (see, e.g., Commission on Accreditation, 1994:chap. 35). A majority of the larger police departments use a highly structured process that requires periodic performance evaluations of all employees based upon standardized criteria and forms. In smaller agencies the process tends to be less formal, but it should be thorough and well documented. The use of evaluation systems by police administrators is directly related to their concern for agency accountability, legal liability, and employee productivity, effectiveness, and efficiency. Police chiefs have painfully become aware that, in this era of litigation, their department's performance evaluation system can be an important evidential factor in a litigant's case. Suits brought under the Civil Rights Act of 1964 and the Equal Employment Opportunity Act of 1972 and its amendment, the 1978 Uniform Guidelines on Employee Selection, have placed managers in the position of justifying and documenting in court their employee-related decisions. This has created strong pressure for the development of organized and valid performance evaluation systems.

Unfortunately, performance evaluation has evolved as one of the more frustrating and controversial issues in personnel management. The design, implementation, and maintenance of an effective performance evaluation system is an essential but difficult task faced by the police administrator. For many years, authorities in the personnel field, in public as well as private management, have tried to devise foolproof systems for evaluating individual performance. Personnel technicians have believed that the ideal form could satisfy many purposes, such as serving as a guide for salary increases, promotion, transfer, and disciplinary action; increasing productivity and efficiency; and stimulating supervision. Achievement of these multiple objectives has simply not been possible, so that the *perfect* evaluation system and form still do not exist.

The problems associated with performance evaluation are not in the process and forms but in the commitment of the police agency and its managers to administer and properly conduct evaluations. The performance evaluation process requires that one individual assess the performance of another. This ensures that subjectivity will be a factor. Subjectivity can be controlled if the system is administered fairly, job-relevant performance criteria are used in evaluating performance, and supervisors are trained to use the system. However, the most expertly developed performance appraisal system can be rendered meaningless if the department's administrators have little commitment to the process and the supervisors assigned to rate employees are not held accountable for their evaluation practices. The key to the successful operation of a department's performance evaluation system is the leadership of the chief executive officer. It is the chief's responsibility to monitor the system to ensure that it is functioning in a fair and legal manner, while achieving the purposes for which it was designed (Commission on Accreditation, 1994: Standard 35-1).

The Purposes of Evaluation

The performance evaluation system is a managerial tool, and it should be designed to accomplish a set of specific objectives. Information obtained from police department evaluation systems is currently being used by administrators as the basis for employment decisions regarding probation, training, promotion, discipline, transfer, termination, special assignment, and merit increase. Performance evaluation directly benefits employees by letting them know what they are expected to do and how well their department thinks they have performed.

A properly developed and managed performance evaluation system should serve a department by helping to:

1. Identify employee performance-related strengths, weaknesses, and potential
2. Provide information necessary for personnel assignments, employee improvement plans, recognition, and promotion
3. Provide documentation to demonstrate the appropriateness of discipline
4. Provide information for career development
5. Provide information for the development of training programs
6. Provide information for merit salary decisions
7. Establish managerial and supervisory accountability for subordinate performance
8. Provide employees with feedback about their performance and contribution to the department's work effort
9. Provide information on which to evaluate unit effectiveness
10. Establish a basis for employee counseling
11. Provide information on which to demonstrate the adequacy of personnel practices to courts, external reviewers, and critics.

The literature on performance evaluation identifies six problems common to such systems: (1) validity, (2) rating error, (3) leniency, (4) central tendency, (5) halo errors, and (6) bias. Each of these is discussed in the following pages.

Validity. Plaintiffs in liability actions against police departments often attempt to establish a pattern of managerial neglect. A claim of negligence is likely to be sustained if the plaintiff can establish that a department has failed to engage in an ongoing process of ensuring officer competence (e.g., through training) and appropriate performance behavior (e.g., through supervision and evaluation). In such cases a department's formal evaluation process can become its first line of defense, provided it is a valid system.

However, in a study of performance evaluation systems that included 150 supervisors from 67 small and medium-sized municipal police departments, Walsh found that the majority of supervisors (93 percent, $N = 114$) were using forms and processes that their departments had copied from other law enforcement agencies. None of these departments had conducted a job analysis to identify performance criteria on which to base their evaluation system but, instead, used broadly defined traits to assess employee performance. Typical traits included on these forms were quality of work, dependability, job attitude, job knowledge, appearance, initiative, and leadership. As may be readily observed, these are subjective, general rather than specifically tied to documented incidents, and open to various interpretations by evaluators. This study concluded that the performance evaluation systems used by most of these departments would not pass a court-imposed test of their validity and that they were not an appropriate basis on which to make administrative decisions (Walsh, 1990).

Today, the courts scrutinize performance evaluation procedures as closely as they do employee selection procedures. The law requires that decisions affecting the status of employees must be based on valid job-related criteria. Status decisions are those that concern termination, transfer, demotion, retention, promotion, merit increase, and job assignment. Many administrators base these decisions on information obtained from their performance evaluation process. If the evaluation process is faulty, such decisions obviously may not be valid.

The issue of *validity* concerns whether or not a procedure (i.e., performance evaluation criterion) measures what it is intended to measure. In other words, *do the criteria that are used to evaluate an employee provide correct estimates of the employee's work effort?* The organizational and industrial psychology literature describes a variety of extremely technical and complex procedures for establishing validity. These are beyond the ability of all but the largest police departments to conduct. However, the one criterion of validity that all police administrators must understand is *content validity.* Section 1607.5:B of the (1978) EEOC Uniform Guidelines on Employee Selection Procedures states that content validity occurs when a selection procedure "representatively samples significant aspects of performance on the job" for which the individuals are to be evaluated. The EEOC Guidelines define a selection procedure as "any measure, combination of measures, or procedure used as a basis for any employment decision" (Section 1067.5:B).

In order to meet the criterion of content validity, standards used to assess employee performance must be job-related. Job-relatedness has been defined in a number of court decisions related to Title VII of the Civil Rights Act of 1964.

In *Griggs v. Duke Power Co.* (1971), the Supreme Court stated:

> What Congress has forbidden is giving these [evaluation] devices and mechanisms controlling force unless they are demonstrably a reasonable measure of performance. . . . What Congress has commanded is that any test used must measure the person for the job, not the person in the abstract.

This decision means that employers must be certain that their evaluation criteria measure an employee's actual job-related performance. These criteria should be based on the performance expectations of the position in which the employee is serving. In order for a police agency to meet this requirement, it first must identify and establish the duties and the performance expectations for each of the positions it is evaluating.

In *Brito v. Zia Co.* (1973), a federal circuit court ruled that Zia Company had violated the rights of a number of minority employees when they were discharged because of low performance appraisal scores. This ruling concluded that the performance appraisal system used was, in fact, an employment test. However, the performance evaluation system was found to be invalid because the company failed to prove that the appraisal instrument was related to important elements of work behavior in the job in which the employees were being evaluated. The court held that the basis for the evaluations were the "best judgments" and "opinions" of the supervisors rather than identifiable criteria based on quality or quantity of work. In addition, there was a lack of documentation to support the supervisors' judgments. In fact, two or three supervisors were found not even to have observed the workers on a daily basis.

Thus, the courts have made it plain that *evaluation criteria, like all other job standards, must relate to the important duties of the job the employee is doing.* In other words, a department should not be using the same evaluation criteria for a police officer performing traffic duty as for an officer in an investigative assignment. As specified in *Griggs,* the duties of a job and the type of behavior required to carry out these duties must be clearly established. Evaluators must have knowledge of the quality and/or quantity of work required for the duties of a specific position to be satisfactorily performed. But *Brito v. Zia* also instructs police managers to observe their subordinates as they perform their duties and to document their observations in order to support their employee evaluations. While not a Supreme Court decision, this case clearly states that subjective supervisory judgments alone are insufficient to sustain a test of validity; they must be supported by such objective criteria as descriptions of actual incidents of performance.

In 1975, the use of performance appraisals as the criterion for hiring was found invalid in *Albemarle Paper Company v. Moody.* The Supreme Court reasoned that the company had not conducted an analysis to define the critical requirements of the job but, instead, had attempted to validate the test by using supervisory rankings of employees. The basis of employees' rankings was un-

327

CHAPTER 10
Personnel
Management II:
Human Resource
Management

defined, however, making it impossible to determine what criteria of performance were being used by the supervisors. Since this case, a claim of validity by an employer cannot be sustained in court without establishing that a job analysis has been conducted prior to the development of the evaluation system. A *job analysis* is a systematic detailed study conducted to determine what the job entails, the conditions under which it is performed, and the knowledge, skills, and abilities (KSAs) representative of the "content" of a position (*Segar v. Civiletti*, 1981). It is a basic technique that assists an organization in identifying the critical and important elements of an employment position. Today, many law enforcement departments have evaluation systems, but only a limited number meet the standards imposed by this case.[2]

Another issue associated with police evaluation systems is the use of personal traits as performance measures. Criteria of this type are subjective and susceptible to the bias, partiality, and whim of the evaluator. In *James v. Stockham Valves & Fitting Co.* (1977), a circuit court ruled that traits can only be used if they are defined in terms of overt observable behavior. If a department is using trait evaluation criteria, its evaluators must be able to interpret and describe them as they relate to observed job performance. Thus, for example, an evaluation indicating that an employee lacks "judgment" or "maturity" must give examples of how the absence of this trait has shown itself in the employee's work.

In summary, the content validity of a performance evaluation system can be established if its measurement criteria are job-related and based on the actual observation of the employee's performance, and if a record of these observations is maintained. (See Box 10-1.)

Rating Error. A constant complaint of many police department employees is rater inconsistency. Often, two officers performing equal work receive different ratings if one employee is supervised by a lenient sergeant and the other by a more demanding supervisor. Rater inconsistency also can occur when a unit changes supervisors during the evaluation period, and everybody suddenly discovers that the level of performance accepted by one supervisor may not conform to the new supervisor's expectations. Rater inconsistency can lead to employee dissension and can affect morale. Leniency, central tendency, halo errors, and bias are among the more common types of errors that contribute to rater inconsistency and invalid performance reviews.

Leniency. It is not uncommon to hear administrators complain that their department's supervisors are too easy in their rating of employees. This occurs when supervisors give employees favorable ratings without considering the actual performance contribution of each person. These supervisors usually give their subordinates "above average" or "outstanding" ratings. Factors that contribute to leniency include: the rater's desire to avoid conflict, the application of subjective personal standards to the rating scale, friendship with subordinates, inadequate rater training, vagueness in the performance criteria, and lack of faith in the performance review system.

Leniency is unfair to the better performers, who may respond with resentment by adjusting their performance to the lowest acceptable performance

BOX 10-1. Job Standards? What Do You Mean, Job Standards?

A Midwestern police officer shot and killed a woman under controverted circumstances. The woman's survivors brought a suit against the officer, a sergeant who was at the scene, and the police department. Before the trial, it was discovered that the officer and the sergeant had long disciplinary records but had always received acceptable performance evaluations.

Anxious to determine how the department's performance standards and evaluation system worked, the plaintiff's attorney deposed the officer in charge of the department's Office of Professional Standards (OPS). The deposition included the following questions and answers. As you read it, consider how a jury might assess the department's performance in monitoring and evaluating officers, as well as its standards of conduct:

Q. Okay. Now, is there a rule of thumb when you were—what was your guide—to determine whether or not an officer should be terminated?

A. The extent of the situation.

Q. Okay. So the more powerful the facts or the more negligent or reckless the officer was, the more likely he was going to get severe punishment?

A. That's correct.

Q. Okay. What if—was there a rule of thumb, or did you have a practice, custom with regard to the number of complaints of citizen complaints? That none of them, let's say, amounted to termination, but there were a lot of them. Was there a point at which you'd say that was enough, he's gone?

A. Not under civil service law.

Q. Okay. Why do you say that?

A. Because there is no guideline for that under civil service.

Q. I mean, your own—I mean, you have a—you're not a slave to the civil service. You have a law enforcement—you have a police department to run. So you have some guy who's been getting into trouble repeatedly with citizens. At some point you've got to say, I can't take the heat anymore. Did you have—what was that threshold? That level?

A. Depending on the circumstances, once again.

Q. Was there a written regulation at the time of this incident regarding the kind and character and number of OPS or police complaints, citizen complaints against a police officer, that would automatically terminate the officer?

A. Not automatically. There was no automatic termination.

Q. Okay. Was there—was there a police a—is there a police regulation regarding guidelines for the OPS?

A. Yes, there is.

Q. And do those guidelines include what to look for in violations by police officers?

A. I don't understand that.

Q. Well, trouble signs such as lateness, repeated lateness or absenteeism, or arguments with citizens, abusive language with citizens, things like that you would look at?

A. No.

Q. Okay. What about complaints of excessive force? Are there guidelines that tell you how many—what kind of repeated violations or complaints, I should say, by citizens that this officer physically abused citizens? That was—

A. No.

Q. Nothing, okay, what about internal? That is, insubordinate, late, abusive to prisoners, things like that were—that a person got disciplined for over a course of time?

Is there—was there a point—would there be a point in which that officer would be terminated?

A. No.

Q. So, would I be correct that a police officer can be an abusive, loud mouthed, insubordinate to superior officers, and would never face termination but would just get suspensions and written reprimands?

A. He would receive written reprimands, dismerits [sic], and time off, things like that. And each one would be documented on the previous disciplinary. And when there was, in my estimation, enough to bring it before the civil service board for termination, I would.

Q. Okay. And what would that threshold be?

A. I think the best way to say that would be in the same light as most of the supreme court would do. They would wait for the best case to present, to bring forward. Bring a certa [sic] writeup and bring the case up so that they can have the best case. And that's what I would wait for.

Q. Okay. But there were no written guidelines.

A. No, there is not.

Q. How would an officer know what the rule of thumb was at [your department] about these kind of discipline problems?

A. They don't.

Q. How do they know?

A. If you like to use it, through the grapevine or whatever. They knew.

Q. They know. So, it's sort of like if you cross this line, you're in big trouble?

A. That's about right.

Q. Okay. And that line was—

A. At the time when I decided it to be.

level. It can be controlled through administrative review or supervisory evaluations, which should include a requirement that raters justify their employee ratings.

329

CHAPTER 10
*Personnel
Management II:
Human Resource
Management*

Central Tendency. This error reflects an unwillingness on the part of evaluators to assign extreme ratings. The result is that everyone receives a standard rating, even those who deserve very high or very low ratings. Central tendency, like leniency, undervalues the work of the good performer and rewards the marginal employee. It establishes the minimal performance effort as the supervisor's acceptable standard. Typically, supervisors who rate in this way do so because they wish to avoid interpersonal conflict with their officers. It is also an easy way out for evaluators who have failed to adequately monitor and record performance information during the rating period. This error is common in departments that have inadequate policy guidelines, rater training, and administrative monitoring of their performance evaluation process.

Halo Errors. Halo errors occur when the rater allows an overall personal assessment, either favorable or unfavorable, of the subordinate or one critical incident or performance dimension to influence the evaluation of all the relevant job dimensions. Halo errors are less likely to occur if the performance dimensions are clearly defined and if raters base their evaluations on observed performance information gathered day to day over the entire rating period.

Bias. Administrators must be extremely careful and monitor their rating systems to ensure that personal bias regarding employees' race, sex, ethnicity, sexual preferences, religion, seniority, and lifestyle do not influence their performance evaluations. Biased ratings obviously hurt the employees involved, and they can subject the department to Equal Employment Opportunity Commission investigations, lawsuits, monetary damages, and loss of reputation. Evaluation bias may also be influenced by occupational stereotyping. For example, some supervisors give high ratings to "hot-dog," aggressive officers, but rate "old-timer," senior officers low because they feel that patrol is a young person's job and that older employees would not still be patrol officers at the end of their careers if they possessed any ability and initiative.

All the above errors can be controlled by maintaining administrative review of the evaluation process and by providing a procedure for ratee grievances. Raters should be required by their department to monitor and record negative and positive incidents of employee performance during the evaluation period. The only basis for employees' ratings should be their performance on the job.

Evaluation Methods

The performance evaluation procedures employed by law enforcement agencies vary in complexity, comprehensiveness, and accuracy. The variety of evaluation methods currently being used in policing include: trait-rating scales, ranking procedures, critical incidents, and behaviorally anchored rating scales.

None of these measurement procedures is totally without problems, but the behaviorally anchored rating scale appears to have proved slightly superior to the other methods.

Trait-Rating Scales.   Trait-rating scales are the most commonly used evaluation method in law enforcement. These scales use a set of predefined rating factors such as *appearance, communication skills, quality of work,* and *dependability.*

Raters in trait-rating systems are asked to make and specify their judgment of employees' level of behavior or performance for each of the rating factors, by either checking a point on a numerical ranking scale or checking a box under a range of brief descriptive adjectives (typically, *inadequate, adequate,* and *superior*). In most departments that use the trait-rating scale, individual raters have the responsibility of making the appropriate connection between the trait being evaluated and the employee's performance. This connection depends almost exclusively on the subjective judgment and interpretation of the supervisor. Unfortunately, the standard evaluation criteria used (e.g., *quality of work*) are open to a variety of interpretations. The ambiguity of these rating scales can lead to errors in ratings which render them useless. Trait-rating scales are extremely vulnerable to rater error, and their validity has been questioned by the courts.

Ranking or Forced Distribution Method.   Rather than evaluating each employee individually, *rank ordering* rates the employee in comparison with his or her peers in the work unit. This procedure requires the rater to rank all employees in order of their performance from high to low, either for each rating dimension or for their total performance. Some departments direct evaluators to rank-order their employees according to a slightly modified bell-shaped percentage distribution by checking a set of categories similar to the following:

Top	10%
Very good	10%
Satisfactory	50%
Marginal	20%
Unsatisfactory	10%

Raters can easily use this method when they are evaluating a few employees, but the task becomes difficult with larger numbers of employees. This process also prevents comparison of employees in different units. In large departments, for example, members of presumably elite units are rated against each other, rather than against the norm for the department as a whole. Further, the ranking and forced distribution methods used by many law enforcement agencies employ trait-based performance criteria that require evaluators to rely on their subjective interpretations, rather than on anything concrete. Such a system is akin to asking baseball managers to rank-order the hitters on their teams without collecting data on their batting averages. Regardless of the presumed precision of the bell curve, such a system involves only a best guess rather than a scientifically derived appraisal.

Critical Incident Method.   In this process, supervisors rate their employees' performance based on incidents that are predetermined as critical to the individual's job. Critical incidents are considered accurate evaluators of effective or ineffective job-related performance. Raters must document their observation of an employee's performance of the critical incidents.

The critical incident method can be used by supervisors in conjunction with trait-rating scales and ranking procedures. Its major advantage is that it focuses on actual performance over the rating period and it is suitable for subordinate performance counseling. However, unless a job analysis has been conducted to identify a set of critical job-related incidents, this method will also depend on the subjective evaluations of the supervisor. Obviously, this method also provides little or no information about how well employees bear up under the burden of day-to-day routine operations.

331

CHAPTER 10
Personnel
Management II:
Human Resource
Management

Behaviorally Anchored Rating Scales. Behaviorally anchored rating scales (BARS) utilize performance criteria based on critical incidents. Some police departments use this method in an attempt to control rater subjectivity. While the development of the procedures can be time-consuming, the resulting scales are worthwhile because they require supervisors to focus on job-related performance rather than individual traits. The construction of a BARS system usually is a five-step process, which is described in Box 10-2.

Despite the variety of performance appraisal systems used by law enforcement agencies, most usually involve the following basic elements:

1. A set of predefined evaluation criteria for each organizational position
2. A specific time period for monitoring and evaluating performance
3. A requirement that the rater record his or her assessment on a standardized form

The employees' ratings then become part of their employment records. All the performance measurement strategies described above and used by police departments have one central feature in common: *They require close and ongoing administrative control and review to achieve their objectives.*

Administrative Considerations

Regardless of the system used for performance evaluation, evaluations should be based on a job analysis, and they should be carried out at least once every six months for employees in regular status. Employees in probationary positions should be rated more often, at least every two to three months during a probationary period of at least one year. The job analysis for each organizational position should be maintained on file in the agency. This information is a prerequisite for effective position assignment, salary administration, supervision, and training, as well as performance evaluation.

The performance evaluation system should be described in a manual and should contain rater instructions with illustrated examples. The manual should also contain a statement of the objectives of the system, and should stress that the employee is to be evaluated for performance *only* during the rating period. Lastly, it should contain procedures for supervisors to follow when establishing and/or updating performance standards.

In addition to the manual, all members of the department who have the responsibility of rating employees should receive training in the systems, procedures, and techniques of performance evaluation. This training should include instruction in the standards required by the Equal Employment Opportunity

BOX 10-2. **Five Steps to Construct a Behaviorally Anchored Rating Scale**

1. *Identifying job dimensions.* The first step is to identify a group of job dimensions. These can be determined by doing a job analysis or by gathering suggestions from a group of individuals who are knowledgeable about the positions in question (e.g., a group of employees or supervisors). A job dimension reflects an important and necessary task (or group of tasks) of the job. Each of these dimensions should be ranked according to its importance to the purpose of the job.

   To assist supervisors and employees in identifying important job dimensions, the following questions (derived from Arlington County, 1981:2) should prove helpful. Is the key element (job dimension):

   - A significant component of the job?
   - A recurring aspect of the job?
   - Position-based rather than incumbent-based?
   - Within the authority delegated to the position?
   - Purposeful/goal-oriented?
   - Required to fulfill the role that the organization has specified for the job?
   - Distinguishable from other key elements?
   - Practical to measure?
   - Specific enough to determine whether results are accomplished?

2. *Identifying critical incidents relating to the job dimensions.* Once the job dimensions have been identified, raters (e.g., a group of patrol supervisors) are requested to identify a set of specific observed examples of performance that range from satisfactory to unsatisfactory. These critical incidents are clustered according to the performance dimension they represent.

3. *Checking incident-dimension relationship.* These identified critical incidents are "scrambled," and another group of job-knowledgeable individuals are asked to reassign each critical incident to the performance dimension that best describes it. Those incidents that reach some percentage of agreement (usually 50 to 80 percent) between steps 2 and 3 are retained.

4. *Rating incidents.* The same group in step 3 rates each surviving critical incident in terms of its effectiveness or ineffectiveness to the appropriate job dimension. These ratings are averaged and the standard deviation is determined for each item. On the basis of the standard deviation criterion, incidents will be either included or discarded for the final scales.

5. *Creating the BARS scale.* Those incidents that remain after steps 3 and 4 serve as the final behavioral anchors for the performance dimensions. The resultant BARS instrument consists of a series of vertically listed scales (one per performance dimension) anchored by the incidents. Each incident is located on the scale according to its rating.

Commission as well as in the specific dimensions on which performance is based.

Each performance evaluation report should be reviewed and signed by the rater's supervisor. However, it is essential that the employee be given the opportunity to sign the performance evaluation form to indicate he or she has read it. The administrator must establish grievance procedures for employees to appeal their rating or for raters to appeal a change in rating by their superiors. In larger agencies, review panels should be created for this purpose, while chiefs of small departments can perform this task. Deadlines must be established for grievances to be filed and reviewed.

In smaller police departments, the chief of police should inspect the evaluation system at least once a year. The purpose of this inspection is to review the raters' compliance with the department's policy, the system's procedures, the rater's use of the forms, and the identification of rating error. The chief should also review employee improvement plans developed by supervisors to address deficiencies in employee performance. In medium and larger departments this task can be performed by a designated ranking officer or the central personnel division. However, the chief executive officer has final accountability for the system. Federal courts have upheld rating systems that include meaningful instructions for evaluators, upper-level review of performance ratings, and the opportunity for the employee to review and grieve the evaluation (see *Womack v. Shell Chemical Co., 1981*).

333

CHAPTER *10*
Personnel
Management II:
Human Resource
Management

The commitment of a department's supervisors is essential to the success of a performance evaluation system. Supervisors are the individuals directly responsible for the quality of the department's work. Line supervisors oversee the transformation of the department's goals, objectives, policy, and procedures into performance. The effectiveness and efficiency of this effort depends on the supervisor's ability to make accurate judgments about job performance and people.

Supervisors should be trained to understand that performance appraisal is not just the act of filling out a form or an unpleasant duty that must be performed. Instead, it should be stressed that performance evaluation is an ongoing process that is an essential feature of the supervisor's role. One benefit of a formal performance evaluation process is that it can force supervisors to communicate on a regular basis with their employees. The very fact that performance interviews take place may have beneficial effects on performance.

Supervisors should be directed not to limit their evaluation of an employee's performance to output measures. These measures are often referred to by police officers as "the numbers," activity, or stats. They include numbers of arrest, traffic citations, vehicle accident investigations, field interview reports, and the like, and they are relatively easy to document. They lack validity as performance measures because they depend so heavily on the nature of the area officers patrol or the shift they work. When stats are the only thing that counts, officers often adjust their work patterns to achieve them with a minimum of effort. Therefore, statistical measures should not be the only basis for supervisory evaluation. The manner in which employees accomplish their duties must also be considered. This will ensure that the employee's total work effort, rather than just his or her statistical output, is subject to the rater's assessment. In addition, numbers give no indication of how *well* employees do their jobs or whether they solve the problems they confront. As we have suggested throughout this book, knowing how many arrests an officer has made tells us little about the quality of those arrests or whether they involved situations that could—*or should*—have been handled less formally.

PROMOTION

Promotion in police service ordinarily means advancement to a position of leadership, and as one moves further up the ranks, promotion takes one further from line police services. It can be argued that while this system has pro-

Her smile is a clear indication of this officer's joy at this promotion.
Jill Freedman.

duced some excellent leaders, it also suffers great disadvantages. Most specifically, it often causes the most gifted personnel to abandon the direct delivery of police services to less competent officers, and it causes them to seek the raises and enhanced prestige that go with promotion to leadership and staff positions. Thus, it has been suggested that there should be ways for personnel to advance financially and in terms of prestige without being forced to leave line positions and to enter management (see, e.g., Goldstein, 1977:266–267).

There are precedents in other fields for such systems. Excellent baseball players, trial lawyers, surgeons, scientists, scholars, and teachers can all advance financially and professionally without leaving line work for management positions. In quasimilitary police organizations, however, the only route to greater prestige and income requires one to assume supervisory and managerial positions. Until an alternative organizational arrangement for police agencies is developed—which does not appear likely to happen anytime soon—this complaint will continue to be valid.

The Peter Principle

The combined effects of the classical hierarchical organizational model and civil service tenure cause most police agencies to suffer from another problem that has been the subject of extremely influential writing. Peter and Hull have pointed out that the normal tendency in bureaucracies is to promote employees until they reach a level they are incompetent to handle, and then to freeze them at that point for the rest of their careers (Peter and Hull, 1969). In police agencies, this *Peter Principle* typically follows seven steps:

335

CHAPTER 10
Personnel
Management II:
Human Resource
Management

1. An excellent police officer is rewarded for high performance by promotion to sergeant.
2. The sergeant excels as a field supervisor and continues the upward progression to lieutenant.
3. Having proved to be an outstanding administrative aide, the individual is promoted to captain and is assigned to a major field command.
4. As a commander, the individual proves to be a bust, never rising above mediocrity in anything.
5. The individual's career advancement has ended, but unwilling—or unable because of civil service regulations to assign this person elsewhere—superiors leave him or her in this command post for years.
6. There, the commander alienates personnel and the community and grows increasingly embittered because he or she hates the job and is headed nowhere.
7. Because this individual holds an important command slot, career opportunities for more promising junior officers are stifled.

The rigidity of police rank structures and civil service protections often presents a real challenge to administrators who are eager to avoid the Peter Principle situation. Sometimes, they can negotiate lateral transfers to positions more in accord with specific individuals' talents. Indeed, administrators often are surprised to find that employees caught in the last stage of the Peter Principle welcome such changes. In such negotiations, administrators must take care to avoid exacerbating employees' perceptions that their job changes are indications of failure. Instead, these moves are more accurately described as corrections of poor fits between otherwise successful people and the jobs they temporarily hold.

When such a graceful stepping aside is not possible, chief executives should keep in mind that their primary job is to render high-quality service to the community, rather than to provide jobs for personnel whose ineptitude quickly leads superiors, coworkers, and junior employees to regard them as "dead wood." Certainly, every effort should be made to reward past loyalty and performance, but these are no substitute for continuing contributions to organizational goals. When it comes time for administrators to request, or even demand, retirements, they should not hesitate to do so.

The First Promotion

The officer's first promotion is normally to a supervisory position (from patrol officer to sergeant). When patrol officers are to be promoted to the rank of sergeant, it is essential to choose those who possess the greatest potential leadership qualities. From among the group of sergeants will subsequently be drawn those for advancement to higher responsibilities of command. It is extremely important for the department to have at each level in the chain of command an adequate number of officers who are well qualified for advancement to higher positions.

Selection for promotion presents greater difficulties—and is even more important—than selection of recruits. Despite the firsthand knowledge of promotion candidates that supervisory and command officers may possess, present methods for detecting and accurately measuring the qualities necessary for successful leadership are seriously inadequate. Promotions should invariably be given to the officers who are best equipped to perform the duties of the higher position and not to those whose restricted leadership potential makes it unlikely that they will ever be qualified for advancement beyond the position under consideration. Neither should promotions be given as a reward for faithful service or acts of heroism, except when the recipient is the best-qualified candidate.

Length of Service.   Length of service in policing or in the rank immediately below that sought by candidates for promotion has been a traditional standard for promotion. Since length of service, per se, says little about quality of service or potential for success in the next higher rank, however, it is difficult to justify including this criterion among those weighted toward promotions. Indeed, there is even research evidence that length of service works *against* successful performance in command ranks. In his Rand Corporation studies, Bernard Cohen attempted to find predictors of the job performance of New York City police captains. He examined 31 separate variables that tested virtually every hypothesis one might offer—age, education, scores on promotional exams, departmental commendations and discipline, military experience, nature of assignments during one's career, and so forth. He found that only one variable was associated with success as a police captain: The longer one had served as a lieutenant, the lower one's subsequent performance ratings as a captain (Cohen, 1980). In addition, the use of seniority as a promotion criterion is also likely to work against efforts to advance women and minority officers who have only recently come to policing in significant numbers.

As a general principle, therefore, seniority should not be a weighted factor in promotion decisions. Instead, interviewers and assessors should attempt to determine whether, as is true in many cases, older candidates have gained better judgment, greater self-confidence and decisiveness, greater knowledge, and an improved ability to get along with people during their years in service; or, conversely, whether the passing years have resulted in diminished energy, initiative, enthusiasm, interest in work, and willingness to accept responsibility. The factor of length of service should be measured only in these terms.

Promotion-Potential Ratings.   As our discussion of the Peter Principle suggested, performance in one's current job may not necessarily indicate one's potential for success in the next-higher level. Consequently, performance evaluations should not be used as part of the promotion process. Instead, a separate rating should be made for the express purpose of evaluating promotion potential. At the time candidates for promotion go through the selection process, they should be given ratings to assess potential performance in the rank being sought. This is particularly true of the promotion from patrol officer to sergeant, when the nature of duties performed shifts abruptly from patrol tasks to supervisory responsibilities.

Identification of Promotion Potential. Among all the desirable characteristics of the good supervisor, the qualities of leadership rank first. Since these attributes ensure superior performance, promotions should be given to those who excel in leadership. Leadership has been discussed extensively in Chapter 4, but attention here is directed primarily at establishment of procedures helpful in evaluating leadership potential and performance.

337

CHAPTER 10
*Personnel
Management II:
Human Resource
Management*

Information Needed for Evaluation. Leadership potential in individuals being considered for promotion is best evaluated in terms of incidents, observed and recorded by their supervisors, that give evidence of the presence or absence of the desired qualities. Each leadership quality is composed of so many traits of such diverse nature as to make the evaluation and weighting of the component factors difficult. For example, the ability to get along with people depends on such characteristics as courtesy, tact, poise, voice, demeanor, facial expression, self-confidence, friendliness, helpfulness, consideration, unselfishness, integrity, and fairness—and several other factors that are not so easily recognized or defined. Analyzing and evaluating each of these component traits seems unnecessarily complicated and purposeless, since some important characteristics will be overlooked, false appraisals will be given to others, and inaccurate weights will be assigned to all.

"Sound judgment," for example, is the vaguely defined end result of personal traits, lessons learned, and other factors—so many and so varied that it is difficult to isolate, define, and evaluate them. The desired quality is most accurately detected and assessed by evaluation of incidents that demonstrate the ability to make situationally correct decisions. These incidents should be noted by supervising officers at the time of their occurrence. When suitably recorded, they form the basis for a fair and reasonably accurate appraisal.

Promotion-Potential Rating Form. In contrast to the performance evaluation, the promotion-potential rating is intended to have a role in the scoring process and is therefore based on a numerical grade. The rating should not take place until the candidate passes the written examination. The promotion-potential rating should be given a weighting of 10 to 20 percent of the total score. Training of raters is essential to the success of any evaluation system, especially when the rating will have an administrative use, such as in promotion. Explanation of the process to all personnel is also helpful in dispelling doubts and rumors.

Written Examinations. As a general rule, police departments—especially the larger ones and those under the influence of central personnel agencies—rely too heavily on written tests of knowledge in selection for promotion. The popularity of the written test for this purpose arises from a sincere desire to select personnel objectively, on the basis of merit, free of outside or departmental favoritism. The test fills much of this bill; it is easily administered, it provides a numerical score, and it seems fair in that candidates can blame only themselves for unsatisfactory results. Consequently, it should not be surprising that the use of the written test is so widespread. But—despite the great efforts recently devoted to ensuring that promotion examinations test for the appropriate KSAs—there remain great questions about their validity as a measure of merit or as a predictor of job performance.[3] In the end, therefore, the written examination should be only one of several factors considered in promotion decisions.

Trial on the Job.   Trial on the job is closely related to probationary performance and is sometimes used by administrators in small departments to determine the best-qualified of several candidates, each of whom is given an opportunity to act as supervisor for a temporary period. One difficulty with this procedure, however, is that acting supervisors face a real dilemma if there is a good possibility they may be among the unsuccessful candidates. Acting supervisors who feel it likely they will once again return to the ranks often tend to be too sympathetic and too considerate toward workers. Acting supervisors should therefore be placed in this category only when the administrator is reasonably sure, on the basis of other criteria, that they will remain there.

Perhaps because administrators are never quite sure about what to do with supervisors who fail during probationary periods, the probationary strategy has not been as widely adopted in promotion procedures as at the entry level. Nevertheless, during the supervisor's probationary period, the administrator can use probationary status as leverage to encourage the new supervisor to carry out activities that might seem unpopular, particularly to the new first-line supervisor. Once the new supervisor begins to mature in the role and realizes that it is possible to make constructive but sometimes unpopular decisions without losing respect, attitudes that can persist for the rest of his or her career may be solidified in a healthy way.

Exempt-Rank Positions.   Among the civil service reforms of the early twentieth century was a movement to insulate police departments completely from political influences. There were understandable reasons for doing this, because in many places the political influences on police were highly partisan and corrupting. In their attempts to protect and grant the police independence from crooked politicians, the era's reformers urged that police chiefs and their highest-ranking staff be granted civil service tenure. August Vollmer, the great police reformer, wrote that "the professional crooked politician" was "Public Enemy No. 1" (1972:70), and he argued that the only way to ensure impartial policing was to see that police chiefs could operate independently. Without a guarantee that a police chief could be removed from office only for cause, Vollmer wrote:

> An honest and aggressive executive is powerless when he is unable to reward the efficient and to dismiss incompetent subordinates; his prestige evaporates when his men recognize—and they will not be slow in forming the correct conclusion—that the actual head of the police department is the political boss. (Vollmer, 1972:85)

Similarly, the major blue-ribbon commission of Vollmer's time recommended that the chief "be surrounded with every protective civil service device imaginable" or corruption and inefficiency would be virtually inevitable

(National Commission on Law Observance and Enforcement, 1968:52). The problem with acting on this well-founded Prohibition-era sentiment, however, is that doing so has insulated police chiefs not only from improper political influences but also from appropriate mechanisms of accountability to elected officials. On occasion, this has allowed autocratic and unreasonable police administrators to force idiosyncratic views of policing on divided politicians and a confused public (see, e.g., Skolnick and Fyfe, 1993:134–172). In such situations, to paraphrase Vollmer, mayors and other elected government chief executives—presumably the commanders in chief of their police—have been powerless to reward the efficient and to dismiss incompetent subordinates and, thus, have been denied appropriate influence over police and criminal justice policy. When this has happened, the supposedly apolitical police chief typically has become a major political figure because he has had to answer to nobody, while the mayor has had to answer to the voters. In short, it is not a good idea to grant police chief executives the same sort of lifetime tenure that may be enjoyed by personnel who hold ranks below the policy-making level (see also Moore and Stephens, 1991:49–65).

339

CHAPTER *10*
*Personnel
Management II:
Human Resource
Management*

For the same reasons, especially in large police agencies that serve diverse populations, it is advisable to exempt the highest ranks from civil service protection. When new chief executives in any organization—the White House, a city hall, a corporate headquarters, the military—assume office, they generally attempt to assemble *cabinets* of close advisors and high-ranking assistants who share their views and philosophies, who are willing to work hard to see that these views and philosophies affect service delivery, and who owe their loyalty and their jobs to the people who have entrusted them with such great responsibility. Without the authority to do this—and to ask those who do not share their views to leave—chief executives may be compelled to retain policy-level officials who are antagonistic to their views and who, because tenure guarantees that they can be removed only for such cause as committing a crime, are free to quietly undermine their chiefs and their goals. In this sense, a police chief who cannot select top deputies is much like a president stuck with the last incumbent's cabinet members.

Thus, in many departments, deputy-chief positions and other high-ranking offices above the level of captain are filled through executive appointment rather than through formal civil service procedures. When an exempt-rank system is used, personnel ordinarily retain their permanent civil service status in the lower rank. For example, if the rank of captain is the highest civil service rank that may be reached through competitive examination, persons who hold higher rank should serve in such capacity at the pleasure of the chief executive, and they should return to their permanent civil service rank if they are subsequently demoted.

CREATING AND ADMINISTERING A PERSONNEL INFORMATION SYSTEM

A *personnel information system* should document each employees' career history and should include:

1. His or her application to the department
2. The results of preemployment screening and investigation
3. Syllabi of all training courses completed, along with records of the employees' performance in such courses
4. Copies of all field training assessments and performance evaluations
5. Copies of all citizen commendations, complaints, and comments, as well as the department's responses to them
6. Documentation of all departmental commendations and disciplinary investigations and action
7. Documentation of such other unusual events in the officer's career history as use of nonlethal and lethal force, civil suits, injuries, sick leaves, and vehicle accidents
8. Documentation of all educational attainment and special expertise
9. Copies of activity and performance reports
10. Records of assignments, transfers, requests for transfers, and promotions

In all but the very smallest departments, personnel information systems should be automated, so that quick retrieval of data concerning either individual employees or larger personnel and policy issues is possible. When this is not immediately possible, a cross-referencing system should be established so that, for example, officers with special language skills can be readily identified when the need for their assistance arises.

COMPENSATION PLAN

Police compensation plans include provisions for salaries, fringe benefits, and pensions. Such plans often are tied to those of other government uniformed services, namely, firefighting and sanitation. However convenient this latter arrangement may be for public financial officers, it has little basis in the substance of the work performed by these services.

A police agency's compensation plan should provide for salaries attractive enough to be competitive with those of both other area police agencies and other occupations that compete for the most talented people among the pool from which an agency draws its personnel. It should also stimulate innovation and excellent performance, and it should work against a "civil service mentality," the perception among employees that performance—whether good, bad, or indifferent—is irrelevant because a fixed paycheck is a guarantee no matter what one does. To avoid such a mentality, the compensation plan must reward performance and must distinguish among contributions to agency goals substantially enough to provide an incentive for the best personnel to work toward advancement and increased responsibility. In too many agencies, the salary differentials among ranks are so insignificant that, as their financial and familial responsibilities increase, many of the best personnel try to advance economically through off-duty moonlighting activities, rather than by competing for scarce promotions within their departments. Often, they do so in preparation for second careers that begin immediately after they have completed the minimal service necessary for retirement on a pension.

The Chief's Role

341

CHAPTER 10
Personnel
Management II:
Human Resource
Management

Administration of police compensation plans typically falls most heavily on central personnel agencies. This is understandable, because employee compensation is widely seen as an accounting function rather than as a role that involves great technical knowledge of policing (or whatever other work is being performed). Police administrators, however, must recognize that costs are involved in failing to provide municipal fiscal officers with input on how this greatest of all police expenditures is distributed.

Avoiding Salary Disincentives. The great breadth of duties that may be performed by those who hold a single position title, combined with the absence of any salary distinctions related to the difficulty of duties actually performed, may create a situation in which the most competent personnel systematically work themselves into the least demanding and least sensitive jobs. Two hypothetical examples illustrate this point and its effects:

> Everybody who holds the title "police officer" in a large and diverse county agency earns precisely the same salary, altered only by periodic and fixed "longevity increases." The center of the county is a poor, largely minority area, characterized by high rates of crime and violence and great police-community tensions. The center-county area is also a very difficult commute from the quiet outlying areas in which, regardless of race, most officers live. As a result, assignments to center-county have come to be regarded as something to be avoided. When officers exercise their periodic seniority- and merit-based bids for assignments and working hours, they almost invariably ask out of center-county, and request reassignment to the outlying areas closer to their homes. Consequently—especially during highly volatile night hours—center-county is policed almost exclusively by inexperienced young officers and those who have never received performance evaluations high enough to win reassignment to the duties and hours of their choice. Far less demanding and dangerous outlying areas, by contrast, are policed by the cream of the agency's crop, especially during daylight hours on weekdays, when police business is at its lowest.

> All the nonsupervisory personnel in the communications bureau of a large municipal department hold the title "dispatcher/operator," and make precisely the same salary regardless of working hours and duties, for which they also bid on the basis of seniority and performance. As a consequence, both 911 telephones and the busiest and most sensitive police radio dispatchers' seats are occupied by the inexperienced and the most marginal performers. Such less demanding assignments in the communications bureau as handling nonemergency phone lines and staffing rarely employed tactical and special radio frequencies are held by the bureau's best.

Obviously, neither of these circumstances should exist. Because police administrators and supervisors frequently are denied any authority to differentiate among personnel on the basis of the nature and difficulty of their work, however, both are common causes of police operational deficiencies. In many cases, they are the results of labor negotiations conducted by militant union leaders so anxious to maintain solidarity among their members that they reject any provisions that differentiate among employees. Because the absence of performance-based differentials in compensation hurts the public and the police and benefits only marginal employees, police administrators should do everything possible and ethical to see that such union leaders do not get their way.

Pay Grades. A series of *grades* based on the difficulty and/or unique qualifications required for specific assignments within broad position titles may help to reward excellence and achievement. To turn the most challenging assignments into goals to be sought after, rather than something to be avoided, these should include increments of at least 5 percent per grade (see, e.g., Lutz and Morgan, 1974). The following examples (which could easily be combined with differentiations based on performance and seniority) illustrate such a schema within a single *police officer* title:

> *Police Officer I:* 100 percent of base salary. For those who perform daytime patrol duty in low-activity areas, or clerical duty.

> *Police Officer II:* 105 percent of base salary. For those who perform daytime patrol duty in high-activity areas; nighttime patrol duty in low-activity areas; routine criminal investigations; duties requiring some degree of special training, such as crime scene technicians, computer or evidence specialists; officers who can speak, write, and understand a second language common among the community served.

> *Police Officer III:* 115 percent of base salary. For those who perform night patrol duty in high-activity areas; field and academy training instructors; specialized criminal investigators; SWAT officers.

> *Police Officer IV:* 125 percent of base salary. For those who perform especially dangerous duties or who are qualified for special duties by virtue of unique education or training acquired at their own initiative. Undercover officers; bomb and explosive technicians; hostage negotiators; attorneys; SCUBA divers; etc.

In many agencies, pay grade differentials also take into account educational attainment. Where affirmative action litigation or other resistance has been strong enough to avert postsecondary education requirements for entry and advancement, many departments have awarded salary increments based on educational attainment beyond the minimal requirement.

However logical it may seem to base salary on difficulty and sensitivity of assignment, a very important caveat is in order. Especially in jurisdictions already polarized by race and social class, the suggestion that officers who work in high-crime—usually minority—areas should be specially chosen and given more compensation than those who work in quieter areas may invite both constructive criticism by sincere and concerned citizens and exploitation by those who seek opportunities to polarize the public. On one side of this issue, residents of high-crime areas may find it objectionable that officers are awarded what can easily be portrayed as "combat pay" to work in their communities.

On the other side, representatives of more affluent and quiet communities may argue that such a plan systematically shifts the best police officers from their neighborhoods, which pay a disproportionate share of taxes, to low-income communities that contribute little to public services.

Obviously, this is a very tricky line to walk, and it should be explored cautiously. Chiefs who wish to reward personnel more realistically for the relative difficulty of their work should do so only in close consultation with community and political leaders, and they should take pains to ensure that the nature of a community served is only one among many factors that affect salary grade.

343

CHAPTER 10
Personnel
Management II:
Human Resource
Management

Executive Salaries

Because it may appear to be so self-serving, another issue that chiefs have trouble raising is that of the top range of police salaries. In contrast to the income of police executives, the income of lower-level officers vis-à-vis other workers who bear similar responsibilities and bring similar qualifications to work in the private sectors is not disproportionately out of line. Often, this is so because the unions or others who represent the interests of entry-level employees have been very successful in negotiating favorable labor contracts.

Yet even in agencies that provide the most generous compensation to managers and executives, those at the upper echelons of police organizations—typically unrepresented by labor organizations—are grossly underpaid in comparison with private-sector executives. Indeed, because they usually are barred from accepting overtime pay, it is not unheard of for some police chief executives to earn considerably less than many of the managers, supervisors, investigators, and officers they lead. Even when this is not so, it is rare for a police chief executive's salary among even the largest and most complex jurisdictions to be more than three times as high as the maximum salary for entry-level officers. In the private sector, however, it is not unusual for executives of organizations comparable in size and complexity to these agencies to earn 10—or even 50 or 100—times as much as line employees.

This is not an argument for the creation of a class of millionaire police chiefs. Unlike government and nonprofit organizations, the private sector consists of enterprises designed primarily to make money for owners rather than to provide a public service. It is understandable, therefore, that those who rise to the top of private organizations should be handsomely paid, while taxpayers should expect those who head public organizations to derive much of their satisfaction in such nonmaterial ways as their contribution to and impact on lives and public policy.

Still, the disparity between the salaries of police executives and those in the private sector is troubling because it may drive the most talented executives out of policing into better-paying lines of work. When those who are presented with the option to leave policing for far more lucrative work do so, the public often suffers, not only because it is losing them as individuals but also because their police positions are assumed by less-talented people who have no such options. Where salary disparity is great compared with the private sector, government officials must seek to correct the situation.

Working conditions like these have intensified police officers' sense that they are not valued by management, and have greatly strengthened their loyalty to unions and labor groups.
Jill Freedman.

LABOR RELATIONS

Increasingly, police administrators must deal with organized labor representatives who are specially trained experts in labor relations. In some police departments, administrators are faced with the problem of coordinating relationships with several unions; one or more organizations may represent sworn officers, and one or more may represent nonsworn civilian employees. The objectives of these employee groups often conflict with one another and lead to very difficult labor negotiations. Today, the relationship between employees and the police executive is increasingly defined and affected by the chief's actions and attitudes toward the employee labor organization and its interests.

Labor relations have not always been a primary area of concern for police administrators. Poor personnel management practices in the past by police administrators have contributed to the growth of police unions and employee use of such disruptive tactics as the "blue flu" (in which officers report sick with feigned illnesses), slowdowns, and strikes. In some police departments, the adversarial conduct of management and employees' unions has created a combative work climate that has affected the agencies' operations. It is important that law enforcement administrators and their employees' representatives create a working relationship in which each side can relate to the other in a responsible and productive manner. Police administrators take an active role in managing their departments' labor relations. If they fail to do so, they may find that they have lost some of their managerial control as a result of the collective bargaining process.

The Nature of Police Unions

345

CHAPTER 10
Personnel
Management II:
Human Resource
Management

A *labor union* is an organization in which employees participate, and which takes part in collective bargaining or negotiations to protect or promote the welfare, interests, and rights of its members (Swank and Conser, 1983). To many people the word "union" necessarily means affiliation with a traditional organized labor group such as the AFL-CIO or the International Brotherhood of Teamsters, but in modern labor relations practice, any group—such as a police fraternal and benevolent association which is also a recognized bargaining agent in law—is by definition a union. Most police officers are represented by local independent associations that originally were formed to provide benefits to officers who were sick or disabled, and to care for their families in the event of the officers' death or incapacity. However, as time passed, these associations became collective bargaining units for their members.

One of the important considerations for management in dealing with unions is to keep in mind that "union" means *oneness.* As a general rule, unions exert influence by eliminating differences among employees. The goal of the union leader is to create an employee monolith that speaks with one voice and that does not have competing interests within its ranks. To this end, unions generally seek to ensure that all members are treated as equals by management and to see that management mistreatment of one individual is regarded as an insult to all.

This makes sense from a union leader's point of view. It minimizes internal squabbling, aligns members' interests, and reduces opportunities for favoritism, vendettas, discrimination, personality conflicts, and other forms of unequal and high-handed treatment that have sometimes characterized management's approach to labor relations. However justified by past experience, this method of achieving employee solidarity ignores a reality: In terms of performance, ability, reliability, integrity, and willingness to accept discipline, not all workers—whether they are unionized or not—are equal. Pretending that they are reduces the administrators' ability to motivate excellent performers to even higher performance and to bring mediocre or poor employees up to standard.[4]

The Growth of Police Unions

Historically, unions originated with the medieval guild system. In colonial Boston, coopers and shoemakers formed a guild in 1648 to maintain standards and prevent competition. Beginning in the mid-nineteenth century, public employee and private-sector unions began to form and to grow in membership. In 1867, one of the first police fraternal associations, the Police Relief Association, was organized in St. Louis. In 1892, the Patrolmen's Benevolent Association of New York City was formed, and in 1915 the Fraternal Order of Police was organized in Fort Pitt, Pennsylvania. By World War I, there were hundreds of police associations, organized primarily for social and benevolent purposes.

In the years immediately following World War I, the emerging labor movement sought to organize police employees. In 1919, for example, 35 police employee organizations were affiliated with the American Federation of Labor (AFL). However, the drive for police unionization suffered a major setback during that same year. On September 9, 1919, more than 1,100 officers of the Boston Police Department struck to protest the police commissioner's firing of several police officers who had sought to organize the Boston officers with the American Federation of Labor. This was not the first time an American police department had been subjected to a strike by its officers. In 1889, the police officers of Ithaca, New York, had walked off their jobs in labor protests, and in 1918 Cincinnati officers had done the same thing (see, e.g., Reppetto, 1978).

The Boston strike is significant, however, because the events associated with it confirmed for the American police both their low status and their powerlessness. Boston police officers averaged an 87-hour workweek, received low wages, and had to put up with outrageously unsanitary working conditions. During the four days of the strike, there were massive looting, riots, and a number of deaths and serious injuries. The mayor of Boston brought in the state guard, with the support of then–Massachusetts Governor Calvin Coolidge, to restore order. Coolidge, stating that "there is no right to strike against the public safety by anybody, anywhere, anytime," ended the strike by firing all the officers involved in it. The Boston Police strike mobilized national opinion against the police labor movement, which most Americans came to see as a threat to their personal safety (see, e.g., Fogelson, 1977; Reppetto, 1978; Walker, 1977).

The aftermath of the debacle in Boston was that the police officer was denied labor's most effective weapon, the strike, and lost equity with private-sector blue-collar workers. For several decades, police labor agitation was dormant, although officers did continue to form local organizations, many of which associated with larger state and national groups.

By the 1960s, the federal government and various states had begun to recognize the right of public employees to engage in collective bargaining. At the same time, public tolerance of police membership in organized labor unions began to rise, and union locals affiliated with the national organizations had become widespread. By contrast with the large national membership in the International Association of Fire Fighters (an AFL-CIO affiliate that represents almost all unionized firefighters), police union membership is quite diversified. The local chapters, lodges, or associations fall into three main groups:

1. *Independent local police employee organizations* not affiliated with any larger group. Many state police agencies and large municipal departments are characterized by such organizations. The Los Angeles Police Protective League and the New York City Patrolmen's Benevolent Association are examples of this type of organization.

2. *Local employee organizations* loosely affiliated with a parent organization that is statewide or national in scope. Unions in this category include those in the Fraternal Order of Police (FOP), which represents about 150,000 members in some 1,400 lodges, located in 44 states. All sworn members of a department, no matter what their rank, can be FOP members.

3. *Organizations affiliated with traditional labor unions* or with groups that have most of the characteristics of traditional labor unions. Examples of the former include the International Union of Police Associations (or IUPA, founded by the executives of the now-defunct International Conference of

Police Associations and organized in 1978 as an affiliate of the AFL-CIO); chapters of the American Federation of State, County and Municipal Employees (or AFSCME, also an affiliate of the AFL-CIO); the Service Employees International Union (affiliated with the AFL-CIO); and the International Brotherhood of Teamsters. Teamsters-affiliated organizations include the International Brotherhood of Police Officers and the National Union of Police Officers.

347

CHAPTER 10
Personnel
Management II:
Human Resource
Management

Because of fear that a single national police union would result in excessive centralization of power, diversification within the police labor movement is often viewed as a positive situation. However, a major problem associated with the different police labor organizations is that the collective bargaining process can become very complex in large police departments that must negotiate with several different employee groups.[5] The reality is that employee organizations are a fact of organizational life, regardless of whether or not the administrator agrees with them. Therefore, it is important that management understand them, their leaders, and the needs of police employees. It is most appropriate that the police chief and his or her administrators attempt to create cooperative working relationships with employee representatives in order to reduce labor tensions within the department.

Why Unions Form: Concerns of Employees

It is often said that unions form because management has failed. Although this view is an oversimplification that does not apply to all agencies, it is a generally valid and valuable insight. Unions form primarily because employees believe that they have no other way to obtain improvements in salaries, benefits, work conditions, and management practice. These improvements are often grouped into two categories: *economic issues*—those relating to salaries, as well as most benefits—and *noneconomic matters*—working conditions and management practices.

In general, most employees and their unions want to achieve, maintain, or exceed parity in salaries and benefits (such as medical insurance, retirement, and overtime pay) with personnel in departments of similar size and with similar policing problems. The extent to which employees expect to exceed parity usually depends on their perceptions of the economic health of their local government and community as compared with others, and on the cost of living in the local area in relation to where they reside.

Failure of the municipality to meet employee expectations on economic issues can have disastrous effects on employee morale and can lead to deterioration in relationships with the municipality. Economic issues were the major incentives behind police labor unrest in many cities during the 1960s.

Matters related to management practice or those that affect working conditions have a far greater impact on the relationship between employee and police administrator, because of the latter's responsibility in determining policy on these matters. Among the more important noneconomic concerns of unions are seniority, disciplinary action, supervisory practice, claimed lowering of standards, civilianization, and lateral entry.

Seniority. Traditionally, unions have sought increasing dependence on seniority and have advocated its use to determine selection of days off, vacation time, and shift hours. Actually, the use of seniority for these limited purpose is not a problem for most chiefs and becomes a convenience in scheduling. Nevertheless, a seniority scheduling policy should not be incorporated into collective bargaining agreements and should simply be adopted through departmental directives.

However, unions also frequently seek to extend the seniority principle as a way to select officers for preferred assignments and as a quantifiable factor in promotions. As suggested above, use of seniority for these purposes is detrimental to good management and supervision and should be strongly resisted.

Disciplinary Action. Employees are concerned with what they perceive as unreasonable and arbitrary use of punitive discipline by management. Many collective bargaining contracts now contain language that protects officers against unreasonable actions, and several states have adopted versions of the police officer's bill of rights as state law (i.e., California, Florida, Illinois, Maryland, and Nevada). This procedural protection is provided to officers when they are subjected to disciplinary investigation that could lead to dismissal, demotion, suspension, reduction in salary, written reprimand, and/or transfer for the purpose of punishment (Aitchison, 1992). Among the more common elements to be found in procedural protection of police officers are the following:

1. Notification, prior to questioning, of the nature of the investigation, the charges being made (including possible criminal charges), and the scope of the inquiry
2. Notification that the employee has the right to consult with and have an employee representative present during a disciplinary interview
3. Notification of the names of investigating officers and those present at the interrogation
4. Limitations on the hour of day, location, and duration of questioning
5. Prohibition of involuntary statements by officers suspected of wrongdoing
6. Prohibition of the use of intimidation and offensive or coercive language by interrogators
7. Requirement that the complete interrogation is to be recorded and that there be no "off-the-record" questioning
8. Notification of constitutional rights in the event of criminal charges
9. Notification in writing when the investigation is complete; and when the disposition has been made, notification in writing as to the nature of the disposition
10. Prohibition of involuntary polygraph examination of officers

These protections should not pose problems for most police administrators, and adopting them would seem to be reasonable and enlightened. However, the exclusion of involuntary polygraph examinations has been more controversial, since the courts have held that police officers (1) do not have the right to refuse to answer questions providing they are narrowly and directly related to their official duties and the ongoing investigation (*Gardner v. Broderick*, 1968) and (2) may be compelled in most jurisdictions to submit to a polygraph examination (see, e.g., *Anderson v. City of Philadelphia*, 1987; *Eshelman v. Blubaum*, 1977; *Farmer v. City of Fort Lauderdale*, 1983; and *Faust v. Police Civil Service Commission of Philadelphia*, 1975).

349

CHAPTER 10
Personnel
Management II:
Human Resource
Management

Poor Supervisory Practice.   Examples of supervisory practices likely to produce union protests include making transfers or shift changes with little or no warning, reprimanding officers in the presence of other officers when it would be more appropriate to observe the etiquette of supervision by doing so in private, and giving orders in an abusive or intimidating manner.

Lowering of Standards.   Labor unions often object to efforts by police or city administrators to increase the number of persons who are recruited or selected for police officer positions. This resistance is often based on the perception that the higher numbers are the result of lowered standards. Unions generally explain their opposition on the grounds that the safety of both the community and existing police officers will be affected. The administrator, however, must recognize that opposition of this kind may be a subterfuge to disguise objections to recruitment of minorities and women.

Civilianization.   Unions have also objected to the expanded use of civilians, especially in positions traditionally filled by police officers. At times a union may acknowledge the protectionism that forms the basis for its position, but most typically the objection will be based on the claim that sworn officers can handle these positions with greater efficiency, understanding, and safety.

Lateral Entry and Promotion from Within.   Police officer resistance to lateral entry is so intense and pervasive that promotion from within the ranks is the near-universal practice in American police departments. Outside appointments, even at the chief level, are often opposed by the union on the grounds that personnel from within the agency deserve the opportunity for promotion and that an outsider would not be familiar with local conditions.

What Unions Expect to Gain

Union objectives sometimes parallel those of management. An interesting exercise occasionally performed by labor relations specialists is to ask a mixed group of union and management employees to separate into two groups—union and management—and then to ask each group to identify its objectives. Surprisingly, some striking parallels emerge, with both groups claiming to want improved salaries, better work conditions, increased professionalization, increased productivity, and higher morale.

Another exercise used by labor relations specialists is to ask a group of employees to list a number of items that dissatisfy them. At a later point—after a sufficient period of time so that participants cannot directly recall the list of dissatisfiers—the group is asked to identify job characteristics that would satisfy them. The two lists are often quite different. Low salaries and benefits usually appear near the top among dissatisfiers, with recognition of good work high among the satisfiers. The lesson to be learned here is that paying attention only to the dissatisfiers does not ensure the ultimate satisfaction of employees. Low salaries may make workers unhappy; but as labor disputes among even highly paid professional athletes indicate, high salaries do not ensure worker satisfaction.

Police Militancy

Partly as a result of internal concerns listed above—along with dissatisfaction with management, unresolved grievances, impasses in bargaining, and changes in the external environment—police employees and the unions that represent them have become increasingly militant. Juris and Feuille (1974) claim that this militancy is rooted in the police reaction to what they perceive as a hostile work environment, and low pay. In addition, Juris and Feuille conclude, the successes of other public employee unions and the influx of young police officers have also contributed to police militancy.

The combination of all these influences has led to the following forms of police militancy and political actions.

Political Action.   Involvement of employee organizations in support for or against political candidates, or making public statements criticizing officials such as the police administrator, the city manager, the mayor, or city council members. With increasing frequency, unions have held *votes of confidence* for police chiefs. Almost without exception, these actions turn out to be *votes of no confidence*, because relationships between the chief and the employees at this stage have generally deteriorated to the point where the employees want to see the chief replaced. A vote of no confidence is an awesome weapon which makes it very difficult for non-civil service chiefs to stay in office. Although large parts of the public may side with chiefs when no-confidence votes result from conflict between the public interest and what unions see as the interests of their members, city managers and mayors may not have the courage or political strength to support the chief even if the chief does not deserve the no-confidence vote.

Job Actions.   These typically include:

- Vigorous enforcement of minor or technical violations not usually enforced
- Failure to issue traffic or parking tickets (thus reducing government revenues)
- Rulebook slowdowns of the nature discussed earlier in this chapter, in which overly detailed procedures such as those involved in response to service calls or inspection of police vehicles are followed to the letter

Fortunately, most job actions result in adverse reactions from the public and usually achieve no objective other than to advertise employee dissatisfaction.

Strikes and Work Stoppages.   "Sick-outs" and "blue flu" are terms applied to massive use of sick leave by many or even all members of the employee organization. Strikes and work stoppages achieved considerable notoriety in the late

1960s and early 1970s, when there were sick-outs in Detroit (1967) and New York City (1962, 1966, and 1968) and strikes in Montreal (1969), Milwaukee (1971), and New York City (1971). Despite near-universal laws against police involvement in such actions, there has since been a limited but regular stream of strikes and work stoppages. In 1974, the U.S. Bureau of Labor Statistics reported 1,500 officers had engaged in 11 strikes, but by 1978 there were 42 strikes involving 5,843 employees (U.S. Department of Commerce and Department of Labor, 1978:5). In 1994, Los Angeles police officers staged a brief sick-out.

351

CHAPTER 10
Personnel
Management II:
Human Resource
Management

Law enforcement officers are generally forbidden by state law to strike. Some states, such as Florida, Indiana, and Wisconsin, have enacted statutes that give public employers the right to sue employee labor organizations that engage in illegal strikes. When a strike is illegal, the labor organization that conducts such a strike may be held liable for civil damages (Aitchison, 1992).

Prohibition against Strikes and Job Actions. Although engaging in political action and votes of confidence may seem to many police and city administrators to be disconcerting, unprofessional, and difficult to control, activities of this kind can be prevented by not giving employees cause and by incorporating prohibitions against these actions in collective bargaining agreements.

In addition to being barred from striking by state law, police officers should be forbidden to join a union local or chapter that endorses the right to strike, work slowdowns, or other actions as a means of achieving its demands. At the same time, the fact that an organized labor union wins a recognition election in a police department should not be read automatically as a sign that the local organization will endorse the technique of striking. As long as the chapter or local agrees to remain free of strikes and job actions, police officers should be permitted to affiliate—if they wish—with organized labor. Since police officers should be denied the right to strike, an alternative to the strike or slowdown seems desirable. Although it generally (and probably, reasonably) produces results more favorable to the labor side of disputes (*Western Cities*, 1985), compulsory arbitration for resolving impasses between management and police unions is a more acceptable solution than labor confrontations in which the department's reputation suffers.

Union militancy poses one of the greatest tests of a police chief's commitment to fair management practices in the face of great, and often grossly unfair, provocations. The only logical course of action is to take the high road, by continuing to display an attitude of trust and good faith and avoiding an escalation of bad feeling. The chief should also encourage union leaders to attend training courses and workshops that offer exposure to managerial concepts and should continuously try to cultivate an amicable and open relationship with the union officers and, if appropriate, with informal leaders in the ranks.

Recognition

In the absence of legislation that gives public employees the right to engage in collective bargaining, management is not obliged to recognize or otherwise deal with a union or employee association. When such enabling legislation exists, management has substantially fewer options in the face of a request for

BOX 10-3. Management Guidelines for Dealing with Unionization

1. To maintain a good faith doubt, the employer must not make public statements which indicate, in any way, that the employer believes or has knowledge that the union has a substantial amount of support.

2. The employer should demand proof that the union has majority support of the employees. Otherwise, an employer can be trapped into recognizing a clique rather than a union or become the object of an unfair labor practice charge if there is a rival union.

3. The employer must not look at or touch union authorization cards or the right to "doubt" may be surrendered and a charge of unfair labor practice be lodged against the employer. An impartial, outside person may be brought in to check the cards but the employer must be prepared to recognize the union based on the results. In general, however, the card check is not a satisfactory means of determining whether recognition should be granted since the employer has no way of knowing whether the signatures are valid or under what circumstances they were obtained.

4. The employer has the right to demand a certification election.

5. Existing departmental rules and regulations can limit the employer's flexibility to respond to a recognition campaign. A key example is a rule regulating solicitation and distribution of literature on departmental premises and/or during working hours. It is important to remember that this rule applies equally to labor and management. If there is a broad rule restricting solicitation, therefore, neither party may have the right to use handouts or bulletin boards or to make speeches on departmental property and time. The opposite is generally true if there is no rule or the rule is weak regarding solicitation. Under the latter circumstances, an employer is likely to be vulnerable to court proceedings or an unfair labor practice charge if there is an attempt to promulgate a restrictive solicitation rule during a recognition campaign.

6. Employers should be careful not to say *the wrong thing* when making speeches or other public statements. They should not say that recognition of the unions will result in strikes or a reduction in the work force. The employer can enumerate the disadvantages of a union or refute false statements by union organizers with *facts*, rather than threats or speculation about worst-case results of unionization.

Source: Ayres and Wheelen, 1977, pp. 123–124.

recognition. Employees then generally have the right to be recognized—to be represented by a union in collective bargaining or grievance arbitration (Ayres and Wheelen, 1977).

Since most American police officers are members of unions or other employee organizations, and because the vast majority of larger departments—about 82 percent in cities between 250,000 and 500,000 (Walker, 1977)—are unionized, it seems almost pointless to discuss ways to oppose the formation of a union. However, there may be valid reasons for not recognizing a particular effort to organize employees—for example, when there is "good-faith doubt" that a substantial percentage of the employees are in favor of the union or when there is a rivalry between two groups at the expense of one another. The guidelines suggested in Box 10-3 should prove useful in such situations.

When it is clear that employees want recognition and that a single union is unopposed, the most logical means of recognition is a voluntary agreement between the union and management. Recognition can then be considered to be part of the collective bargaining agreement.

353

CHAPTER 10
Personnel
Management II:
Human Resource
Management

Unit Determination

The question of who should be included in union membership is closely related to recognition. This issue is complicated in some cities by the decision of groups of supervisors—such as sergeants or lieutenants—to join (or not to join) the bargaining unit representing patrol officers. Although chiefs should not undertake union busting, they should find diplomatic ways to point out that supervisors and managers who belong to the same unions as those they supervise are in a conflicted position.

Collective Bargaining

Collective bargaining agreements are now a fact of life in many agencies at every level of government. Since the National Labor Relations Act does not recognize state governments and their political subdivisions as "employers," laws regulating collective bargaining agreements with police agencies have been developed on a state-by-state basis. Some states require local governments to recognize unions or other groups chosen by employees to represent them in negotiations concerning salaries and work conditions. There is, however, considerable variation with respect to administration of the collective bargaining process. The actual bargaining process may be carried out by designated specialists in collective bargaining by government officials and/or specified members of the police department's administrative staff.

What Can Be Negotiated?   A favorite expression of labor relations specialists is that *people can negotiate anything they want to have negotiated.* Realistically, collective bargaining does have practical limits on its scope. In some cases, the law obliges management to negotiate matters relating to salaries and benefits. A second category covers issues that might or might not be negotiated, depending on the views of one party or the other. A final category includes matters that are legally excluded from the bargaining process or that would lead to illegal contract terms. For example, if state law mandates that officers must complete 40-hour in-service training programs each year, union and management cannot agree to reduce that number of hours.

Management Rights.   Shared decision making is implicit in collective bargaining, and to the extent that decision making is shared, the rights of management are diluted. Some public employers—now in the minority—vigorously oppose most or all union aims. However, in the view of most employers, dilution of managerial prerogatives is justifiable to lessen employee dissension and to reduce the possibility of adverse employee actions. Other employers view collective bargaining more positively and recognize that the shared decision making in collective bargaining is a form of participatory management and that employees usually are better off because of higher salaries, increased benefits, and improved work conditions. A humanistic concern for employees is a key factor in successful management, and it is a characteristic consistently found in the best organizations.

Nevertheless, the police administrator should be able to adopt methods that will increase the effectiveness and efficiency of the agency without unreasonable interference from the union. This concept is illustrated by this summary statement from an analysis of police collective bargaining agreements conducted by the Police Executive Research Forum (PERF) and the National League of Cities:

> The elusive goal in effective labor-management is to reach an agreement that balances the interests of management (retention of decisionmaking options) with the interests of the employee organization (job security, wages, hours, and certain working conditions). This balance is not a fixed set of weights, applicable in every case; rather, it is a series of constantly changing variables with which to measure the perceived needs of the parties. Most important among the needs of the public manager is the ability to take the necessary action to deliver public services at the most efficient level possible. If the collective bargaining agreement prevents such action or requires further concessions, the public interest in efficient government may suffer accordingly (Rynecki, Cairns, and Cairns, 1978:5).

The PERF publication contains representative examples of clauses from collective bargaining agreements as well as a comprehensive analysis of the various categories and groups of the clauses. Approximately 75 percent of the jurisdictions represented in the survey had some form of management rights clause in their agreements. These ranged from weak nonspecific clauses to stronger versions that provide specification of management rights both in the number of items and in the detail afforded to each, incorporation of management's residual rights, and limitations on grievance arbitration machinery. Box 10-4 is an example of a strong management rights clause.

Preparation for Bargaining.   Local governments are notorious for being less well prepared for collective bargaining than employee unions are. Several months in advance, management should gather economic information to support its positions and to be able to assess the accuracy of information prepared by the union. At a minimum, the municipal administration should conduct surveys of salaries and benefits in comparable jurisdictions and should obtain consumer price index information directly from the source (rather than from an intermediary, such as a newspaper).

Police chiefs have increasingly refrained from participating in actual collective bargaining sessions. Consequently, central government administrations have assumed the leadership role in negotiations with unions. However, the chief has the obligation of making sure that comparative statistical data gathered by the city is accurate. One of the reasons that the police chief's staff may be given less responsibility in planning for negotiations by the jurisdiction's central administration is that police officers on the staff may be viewed as sympathetic to their fellow officers, and, of course, in some cases they may actually be members of the union. When such situations exist, other city employees, usually those in a central personnel agency, typically are asked to conduct surveys. When such nonpolice personnel conduct surveys, care must be taken to

BOX 10-4. A Strong Management Rights Clause

Except—and *only* to the extent—that specific provisions of this Agreement expressly provide otherwise, it is hereby mutually agreed that the city has and will continue to retain, regardless of the frequency of exercise, rights to operate and manage its affairs in each and every respect. The rights reserved to the sole discretion of the City shall include, but not be limited to the right:

a. to determine the organization of City Government;

b. to determine and change the purpose and extent of each of its constituent departments;

c. to exercise control and discretion over the organization and efficiency of operations of the City;

d. to set standards for service to be offered to the public;

e. to direct the employees of the City including the right to assign work and overtime;

f. to hire, examine, classify, promote, train, transfer, assign, and schedule employees in positions with the City;

g. to suspend, demote, discharge, or take other disciplinary action against employees for proper cause;

h. to increase, reduce or change, modify, or alter the composition and size of the work force, in-cluding the right to relieve employees from duties because of lack of work or funds or other reasons;

i. to determine the location, methods, means, and personnel by which operations are to be conducted, including the right to determine whether goods or services are to be made, provided, or purchased;

j. to establish, modify, combine, or abolish job positions and classification;

k. to change or eliminate existing methods of operation, equipment, or facilities;

l. to establish, implement, and maintain an effective internal security program;

m. to create, modify, or delete departmental rules;

n. to contract or subcontract out work; and to use non-sworn personnel in any manner.

Those inherent managerial functions, prerogatives, and policymaking rights whether listed above or not which the City has not expressly modified or restricted by a specific provision of this Agreement are not in any way, directly or indirectly, subject to the grievance and arbitration procedures contained herein.

Source: Rynecki, Cairns, and Cairns, 1978, 6–7.

---

ensure that they are sensitive to the subtleties that may be involved. For example, because of their ongoing interest in police salaries, police staff may know better than personnel staff that a comparison city may have established the beginning salary as step A but, in practice, may not start anyone below step C. Longevity steps and specialist pay may also be the source of improper comparisons. For these reasons, the police administrator should double-check comparative data to make sure that the information is correct.

On noneconomic issues, the administrator should conduct research on contract language in other jurisdictions. Fact gathering in the noneconomic area should be carried out continuously during the year and not be left as a last-minute activity.

A management bargaining team should be established to carry out preparatory work, and in some cities the team members, or most of them, also participate in the actual bargaining sessions. In medium-sized and large cities, the team often consists of a labor relations lawyer, a representative of the central personnel department, a member of the central fiscal management department, and a member of the police administrator's staff. A representative of the city manager, mayor, or other government chief executive also is included in cases in which the administration is not fully represented by one of the other participants. The most important requirement for establishing a workable structure for negotiations is that one of the team members (preferably the lawyer) be selected as the team leader and primary negotiator.

The Contract Workbook. A good way to prepare for negotiations is to develop a *contract workbook.* The basis for the workbook can be last year's contract, until such time as the union's current demands are known. On this point, it is particularly important to review items *tabled* in the last session, since they will likely be brought up again. Each separate demand or issue should have its own page in the workbook, with the present contract language at the top, followed by an inch or so of text describing the new union position. Next, a paragraph summarizing the position of the management bargaining team should be added—preferably in two versions. The initial portion should consist of the contract language which is hoped for or *ideal,* and the second portion should specify the language for the *bottom-line* position, beyond which management will go no further.

After the comments of the management bargaining team have been added to the pages, they should be reviewed by the chief of police, who should indicate whether there is agreement or disagreement and the reasons therefor.

The final step in preparing the contract workbook should consist of adding the opinions of the city manager or mayor to each page. Nothing focuses one's attention more than knowing precisely what the boss wants. At the conclusion of each negotiating session, the workbook, as amended, can be used to draft the final language of the contract. Obviously, the actual content of the workbook should be kept confidential and should not be disclosed to the union or made public.

Getting to Know the Union's Bargaining Team. An obvious but often-overlooked element in planning is the need to know the strengths and capabilities of the union's team members and to understand the relationship between the team leader, other team members, and the employees.

The Bargaining Process. The actual collective bargaining process usually begins with each party's agreeing to a bargaining schedule (which often sets up beginning dates and the date on which mediation or arbitration commences, if there is no agreement) and to the rules to be followed by both parties. Commonly, rules of this sort require each side to maintain confidentiality after initial proposals are presented to the other party. The rules may also specify the number of people who will engage in the bargaining sessions, along with their titles or positions. It is very important to establish clear guidelines to be followed in the event there is an impasse in negotiations.

The next step is for each side to formulate its initial proposals. For the union, this often means a series of meetings with the membership so that the bargaining committee understands what the membership wants. For management, the initial posture can be determined more easily, but the ease with which management's positions are established is in no way related to their importance. The point is that management should not just simply react to the proposals of the union. Instead, management should prepare a list of positive proposals that it believes should be agreed upon by the union.

It is very important for management to keep in mind that even though a contract provision can be modified or eliminated in the next bargaining session, this process is obviously more difficult. Once concessions are made, removing a benefit or favorable working condition is always hard. Bargainers should never damage their positions by giving in on issues in anticipation that poor provisions can be eliminated easily the next time around. It is far easier to deny a concession in the first instance than it is to reverse it later.

The Role of the Chief in Collective Bargaining.   Before collective bargaining became widespread, many chiefs found satisfaction and pride in acting as the leader in the quest for additional personnel benefits and salary increases. The emergence of formal collective bargaining has made a difference in such situations because the bargaining usually takes place between the employee organization and the governmental administration—sometimes directly with a city council or legislative committee. Consequently, there are several good reasons that chiefs should not participate directly and personally in bargaining sessions:

1. The level of rhetoric and emotion is often quite high, sometimes as a matter of role playing by both union and management, but occasionally with real emotion and hostility involved. This setting can be uncomfortable for the chief, who should not be in a position either to apologize for any of the participants or to discipline them.
2. The presence of the chief on the bargaining team does not allow management to have the opportunity to "catch its breath" by pausing long enough to find out what the chief's reaction might be.
3. The chief is usually expected to be decisive, which is difficult to do if he or she has to state continuously that a union position must be taken into advisement.
4. A certain amount of bluffing, along with deliberate withholding of the bottom-line positions, may be inherent in the bargaining process. At times, as in a poker game, this behavior can border on deception. It seems inappropriate for the chief to be a willing participant in such activity, particularly when the chief is expected to exhibit exemplary conduct in all other areas of management practice and to be forthright and truthful in dealing with employees.

An alternative, and usually effective, procedure is to permit a trusted associate to act as the chief's representative on the management bargaining team.

The Contract.   This document should be drafted carefully. Under ideal circumstances, it is a composite of the views of both management and labor. A common problem in contracts is the tendency to assume that the other party understands a generality or abstraction. The truth is that within a few days of the signing of a contract, the parties involved have begun to forget what was

357

CHAPTER 10
Personnel
Management II:
Human Resource
Management

understood and, instead, begin the process of deciding what they think—or would like to think—was meant. The rule in drafting contract language is to be specific, rather than general, and to be detailed, rather than vague. Model contract language is available from several sources, including the International Association of Chiefs of Police, the Police Executive Research Forum, and the International City Management Association.

Impasse Resolution. The most common method for resolving difficulties between union and management is, of course, the direct negotiation that takes place between the two parties during collective bargaining. When this fails, the alternative (except for illegal strikes or job actions) is to resort to one or more of the impasse-resolving procedures: mediation, fact-finding, or binding arbitration.

> *Mediation* occurs when labor and management agree to bring in a neutral third party—a mediator or conciliator—who usually attempts to continue the negotiations process (often through separate or joint meetings) and seeks voluntary agreement on the issues.
>
> *Fact-finding* is a more formal process, in which the third party acts very much in a judicial role. Evidence for the positions of the parties is presented to the fact finder, with examination and cross-examination of witnesses, and the recommendations by the fact finder are presented to both. However, these recommendations are not binding.
>
> *Binding arbitration* is the next stage in formality. It differs from fact-finding in that the parties voluntarily agree that the outcome of the arbitration will be binding as well as final. *Compulsory arbitration* is a form of binding arbitration that results from a legal mandate, rather than from a voluntary agreement between labor and management.

Although labor relations specialists consistently state that mediation is superior to fact-finding and that fact-finding is more desirable than binding arbitration, the inability of police unions to engage in legal strikes makes the escalation toward binding arbitration very tempting for them. In the private sector, mediation during a strike may be costly for both sides. In police collective bargaining, however, management can simply avoid coming to terms with the union unless there is some form of compulsory arbitration.

Critics of binding or compulsory arbitration argue that it strips away the motivation to reach voluntary agreement during direct negotiation between the parties. In addition, the solutions achieved by binding arbitration are not always accepted gracefully. A 1969 police strike in Montreal, for example, was a reaction to an unpopular arbitration decision. Usually, however, binding arbitration results in substantial awards to employees (*Western Cities*, 1985).

A final argument brought by critics is that binding arbitration sometimes causes the parties to adhere to extreme positions, in the hope that the arbitrator will split the difference. This last tendency has spurred interest in a form of binding arbitration known as *last best offer*. When an impasse is reached on an issue, each party is allowed to make a single final offer. The arbitrator must then pick one of the two offers but may *not* select an alternative that amounts to a compromise between the two positions. Because this form of arbitration culminates in an either-or decision by the arbitrator, the parties generally attempt to be more reasonable and more realistic than is usually the case under ordinary binding arbitration.

359

*CHAPTER 10
Personnel
Management II:
Human Resource
Management*

The last-best-offer technique, with mediation as the first-stage solution, is a reasonable and workable solution to the no-strike dilemma of the police union, and it should be given serious attention as a means for impasse resolution.

Contract Administration

After agreement has been reached, with subsequent ratification by union members and approval by the administration's executive head, publicity may be generated about key provisions, and supervisors and other personnel may be instructed about the provisions.

Grievance Arbitration

The contract should specify the means for addressing grievances of one party for the failure of the other to live up to one or more terms of the contract. The majority of the collective bargaining agreements reported on in the PERF study provided for some form of binding arbitration by a neutral third party, such as a person selected through mutual agreements, if a grievance cannot be resolved in earlier stages (Rynecki, Cairns, and Cairns, 1978:19). Some agreements stipulate that the arbitrator must be a member of the American Arbitration Association. Almost all require a grievance to be filed by the employee (or group of employees) within a specified period following the alleged contract violation.

Grievance Procedures Unrelated to the Contract

All police departments should have a formal grievance process for resolving employees' work-related problems not covered by the collective bargaining agreement. Actually, a carefully developed grievance process can also be used to address contract-related as well as general grievances. This permits employees to have an option in choosing the procedure established by management or the procedure described in the contract.

General grievance procedures should cover a wide range of circumstances, including the following:

1. Matters affecting personal status: performance evaluation, disciplinary action, the conduct of others, and personal disputes.
2. Matters affecting the benefits and the working conditions of groups of employees, such as salaries, overtime, working hours, and retirement. Most contract-related grievances pertain to this area, so the general grievance procedures should not conflict with or discourage the use of the procedures specified in the collective bargaining agreement.
3. Management, administrative, and supervisory methods and procedures.
4. Matters relating to police operations: complaints about patrol methods, extent of service which should (or should not) be rendered.

The Commission on Accreditation for Law Enforcement Agencies' *Standards for Law Enforcement Agencies* requires that grievance procedures be established by a written directive and contain the following elements:

1. *Scope,* or identification of matters that are grievable.
2. Time limitations for filing or presenting the grievance and for going through the various steps in the process
3. Description of the steps to be followed in the grievance procedure
4. Designation of the organizational component responsible for coordination of the procedure
5. Criteria for employee representation (Commission on Accreditation, 1994: Standard 25-1)

The commission also requires that each grievance be written. The written grievance should contain the facts on which it is based, a description of the specific wrongful act and the harm done, and a statement of the remedy or adjustment sought.

Other grievance procedures specified by the Commission on Accreditation (1994: Standard 25-1) require:

1. A written response by management to each grievance containing a notation of the time and date and the person receiving the grievance
2. An analysis of the facts or allegations to be made, if any
3. A written appeal procedure
4. A description of the grievance committee composition, functions, and criteria for appointment
5. Procedures for the maintenance and control of the grievance records
6. Annual analysis of grievances

Most grievance procedures provide for communication of complaints through regular command channels as a first step, with appeal to an alternative channel as a second step.

The grievance committee is a common element in many grievance procedures, but the structure and composition of such committees are by no means consistent. Most committees have rank-and-file representation, and the structure of the committee is often specified in collective bargaining agreements. The committee may have several responsibilities, including listening to grievances, rejecting unfounded complaints, consolidating and coordinating grievances, and preparing recommendations that are transmitted to the administration.

If the first step in the grievance procedure consists of communication through the chain of command to a certain level, it does not make sense to redirect committee reports to this same level. Grievance committee recommendations should therefore be directed to the chief of police and, if not acted on, to the highest level of government with the authority to remedy the grievance. Grievance committees ought to be welcomed by the chief of police; conditions that generate complaints should be investigated thoroughly and discussed by the chief and the committee, and, insofar as possible, they should be corrected.

Professional and Social Associations

361

CHAPTER 10
Personnel
Management II:
Human Resource
Management

All members of the department should be encouraged to join professional police organizations. Many employee associations exist primarily to influence the bargaining process or to induce changes in salary or working conditions. There are numerous other employee organizations, however, that attempt to carry out other objectives, such as philanthropic activities, juvenile-crime-prevention work, recreation, and legislative changes affecting police or public safety. For example, African American police officers' associations, particularly in large urban departments, have been concerned about discrimination against black officers by whites. They have also assumed a protective attitude toward black citizens whom they feel have been subject to abuse by white police officers, and they have engaged in many outreach programs involving troubled young people. Although their concern about discrimination and abuse has led to ill will in some departments, it should be viewed as a positive and healthy force.

Employee organizations should be discouraged from forming or continuing if they intend to engage in unprofessional activities and practices. For example, exerting pressure on merchants for various reasons and high-pressure solicitation for dances and benefits are undesirable practices. The police administrator can discourage improper activities by making clear and unmistakable declarations of policy, by publicizing the improper methods in the public media, and finally by taking disciplinary action.

SUMMARY

Police administration is, first and foremost, the art and science of managing people. Regardless of how much experience and training one may have in the substance of policing, therefore, chiefs who have not carefully schooled themselves in personnel management are not fully qualified for their jobs. At the same time, chiefs should realize that they cannot properly manage their personnel without assistance, and they should negotiate the external relationships and delegate the internal tasks necessary to accomplish this challenging task.

QUESTIONS FOR DISCUSSION

1. What steps should a police department take to develop a valid and defensible performance evaluation system? Should evaluations vary by rank and position? Should evaluations of personnel assigned to different units be compared?

2. Your department has been sued on grounds that the pencil-and-paper multiple-choice examinations it uses for promotion purposes are discriminatory. The plaintiffs have the evidence to prove this part of their claim. Black candidates historically have attained lower scores than have white candidates. The second part of the plaintiffs' claim is that these examinations are not job-relevant. Their complaint states:

   Promotional examinations presented in a written, multiple-choice format do not reflect the decision-making environments that successful candidates face when they are promoted: The important decisions made by sergeants, lieutenants, and captains are not presented to them in a written, multiple-choice format in an examination classroom.

Discuss the advice you would give the chief and the department's legal staff in dealing with this suit and with the promotional system.

3. How would you go about developing and validating a program of promotional and in-service training for sergeants in the police department in which you work or that serves the community in which you live? What would you do about candidates who fail the promotion-training course? How would you see that sergeants mastered the contents of their in-service training?

4. Within a few weeks after the hiring of a police chief from another city, a police officer in the chief's new department shot and killed a young man under controversial circumstances. Nasty demonstrations and a grand jury investigation of the officer followed. The chief stated that although the facts were unclear, the loss of the young man's life had been a tragedy and that he would attend the young man's funeral. The president of his department's union then told the press that his members were outraged at the chief's "failure to support his officers" and that he would call for a vote of his members' confidence in the chief if the chief went through with his plans to attend the funeral. "I'm sure it will be a near-unanimous no-confidence vote," the union president said, "and it will poison this chief's ability to run this department as long as he stays in town." The chief, an old friend, has called you for advice because you know his new city and department well. What would you tell the chief?

5. How would you enlist the field officers, supervisors, and commanders in the police department in which you work or that serves the community in which you live in an effort to assist in identifying officers whose personal problems may affect their work?

NOTES

1. Courses conducted by the University of Louisville's Southern Police Institute, Texas's Sam Houston State University, and Pennsylvania State University's POLEX (Police Executive Training Program) are prime examples.

2. For examples of department evaluation systems that meet these standards, see the Boulder (Colorado) Police Department's *Evaluation Procedures Manual* (December 1984) and the Metro-Dade (Florida) Police Department's *Performance Evaluation Standard Operation Procedures,* Revision 4 (February 1983).

3. Cohen's (1980) study of New York police captains, for example, found no association between written examination scores and subsequent performance.

4. An extreme example makes the point. In New York City during the early 1970s, the police department sought to reward and motivate excellence among patrol officers and field trainers by identifying the highest performers among them and rewarding them with a significant pay-grade differential. The department put in place a complex identification process that included nomination by peers, supervisors, and commanders; examination of career records; and a screening board composed of officials who had no connection to candidates. Under existing civil service regulations, the only manner in which the salary increment could be rewarded was to designate those chosen as *detectives,* a distinction that had formerly been the exclusive domain of investigators. Instead of greeting this as an appropriate method of recognizing and rewarding excellence, both the police officer and detective employee groups protested. The Patrolmen's Benevolent Association argued that awarding detective designation to patrol officers meant that some would receive 15 percent more salary than others who performed the same tasks. The Detectives' En-

363

CHAPTER 10
Personnel
Management II:
Human Resource
Management

dowment Association (DEA) sued to challenge management's rights to demean their rank by assigning it to "mere street officers," rather than to investigators who, the DEA alleged, did more important and critical work. Although management prevailed in court, the program eventually evaporated because of resistance by employee groups to what they regarded as imposed factionalization of both patrol officers and detectives. Thus, in the interests of maintaining oneness within their ranks, the unions effectively killed a program that would have significantly improved the lot of about 1,000 of their members.

5. Perhaps the best example of this complexity is the New York City Police Department. Labor organizations among just that agency's uniformed personnel include the Patrolmen's Benevolent Association, the Policewomen's Endowment Association, the Detectives' Endowment Association, the Sergeants' Benevolent Association, the Lieutenants' Benevolent Association, and the Captains' Endowment Association. Negotiating with these groups is further complicated by the existence of a complex "pay-parity" relationship among the uniformed services. Under this arrangement, salaries for entry-level police officers and firefighters are identical, and entry-level sanitation workers earn 90 percent of whatever this figure happens to be. Where police are concerned, the major features of this compensation plan are shown in the following table. In essence, this plan fixes all salaries on the basis of the first successful contract negotiation between the city and any of the bargaining agents for these ranks (or fire or sanitation unions).

RANK	PERCENT OF BASE SALARY
Police officer	100
Detective third grade	115
Sergeant or detective second grade	130
Lieutenant, sergeant on special assignment, sergeant in command of detective squad, or detective first grade	150
Lieutenant on special assignment, or lieutenant in command of detective squad	175
Captain	200

SOURCES

AITCHISON, WILL. *The Rights of Law Enforcement Officers,* 2d ed. (Portland, Oreg.: Labor Relations Information System, 1992).

Albemarle Paper Company v. Moody, 95 S.Ct. 2362.

Anderson v. City of Philadelphia, 668 F.Supp. 441 (1987).

Arlington County. *Employee Performance Appraisal Manual* (Arlington, Va.: Arlington County Government, 1981).

ASTOR, GERALD. *The New York Cops: An Informal History* (New York: Scribner, 1971).

AYRES, RICHARD M., and THOMAS L. WHEELEN (eds.). *Collective Bargaining in the Public Sector* (Gaithersburg, Md.: International Association of Chiefs of Police, 1977), pp. 123–124.

Boulder (Colorado) Police Department. *Evaluation Procedures Manual* (December 1984).

Brito v. Zia Co., 478 F.2nd 1200 (1973).

COHEN, BERNARD. "Leadership Styles of Commanders in the New York City Police Department," *Journal of Police Science and Administration,* 8:125–138 (1980).

Commission on Accreditation for Law Enforcement Agencies. *Standards for Law Enforcement Agencies,* 3d ed. (Fairfax, Va.: Commission on Accreditation for Law Enforcement Agencies, Inc., 1994).

Eshelman v. Blubaum, 560 P.2d 1283 (Ariz. 1977).

Farmer v. City of Fort Lauderdale, 427 So.2d 187 (Fla. 1983).

Faust v. Police Civil Service Commission of Philadelphia, 347 A.2d 765 (Pa. 1975).

FOGELSON, ROBERT M. *Big-City Police* (Cambridge, Mass.: Harvard University Press, 1977).

Gardner v. Broderick, 393 U.S. 273 (1968).

GOLDSTEIN, HERMAN. *Policing a Free Society* (Cambridge, Mass.: Ballinger, 1977).

Griggs v. Duke Power Company, 401 U.S. 424 (1971).

James v. Stockham Valves & Fitting Co., 559 F.2nd 310 (1977).

JURIS, HERVEY, and PETER FEUILLE. "Employee Organizations," pp. 202–226 in O. Glenn Stahl and Richard A. Staufenberger (eds.), *Police Personnel Administration* (North Scituate, Mass.: Duxbury, 1974).

LUTZ, CARL F., and JAMES P. MORGAN. "Jobs and Rank," pp. 17–44 in O. Glenn Stahl and Richard A. Staufenberger (eds.), *Police Personnel Administration* (North Scituate, Mass.: Duxbury, 1974).

MOORE, MARK H., and DARREL W. STEPHENS. *Beyond Command and Control: The Strategic Management of Police Departments* (Washington, D.C.: Police Executive Research Forum, 1991).

National Advisory Commission on Criminal Justice Standards and Goals. *Police* (Washington, D.C.: U.S. Government Printing Office, 1973).

National Commission on Law Observance and Enforcement. *Report on Police,* vol. 14 (Montclair, N.J.: Patterson Smith, 1968 reprint of 1931 original).

President's Commission on Law Enforcement and Administration of Justice. *Task Force Report: The Police* (Washington, D.C.: U.S. Government Printing Office, 1967).

PETER, LAURENCE J., and RAYMOND HULL. *The Peter Principle* (New York: Morrow, 1969).

REPPETTO, THOMAS A. *The Blue Parade* (New York: Free Press, 1978).

RYNECKI, STEVEN A., DOUGLAS A. CAIRNS, and DONALD J. CAIRNS. *Police Collective Bargaining Agreements* (Washington, D.C.: National League of Cities and Police Executive Research Forum, 1978).

Segar v. Civiletti, 25 FEP 1452 (1981).

SKOLNICK, JEROME H., and JAMES J. FYFE. *Above the Law: Police and the Excessive Use of Force* (New York: Free Press, 1993).

SWANK, CALVIN, and JAMES CONSER (eds.). *The Police Personnel System* (New York: Wiley, 1983).

U.S. Department of Commerce and Department of Labor. *Labor-Management Relations in State and Local Governments* (Washington, D.C.: U.S. Government Printing Office, 1978).

U.S. Equal Employment Opportunity Commission, "Guidelines on Employee Selection Procedures," *Federal Register,* vol. 43, no. 166, 1978.

VOLLMER, AUGUST. *The Police and Modern Society* (Montclair, N.J.: Patterson Smith, 1972 reprint of original 1936 manuscript).

WALKER, SAMUEL. *A Critical History of Police Reform: The Emergence of Professionalism* (Lexington, Mass.: Lexington Books, 1977).

WALSH, WILLIAM F. "Performance Evaluation in Small and Medium Police Departments: A Supervisory Perspective," *American Journal of Police,* 9:93–109 (1990).

Western Cities Magazine. "Forced Arbitration: Why Cities Worry," pp. 171–180 in James J. Fyfe (ed.), *Police Management Today: Issues and Case Studies* (Washington, D.C.: International City Management Association, 1985).

Womack v. Shell Chemical Co., 28 FEP 224 (1981).

11

Productivity and Performance Measurement

KEY WORDS AND PHRASES

Bureaucratic government
Open systems
Productivity
Efficiency
Effectiveness
Performance appraisal
Performance management

Job analysis
Good policing
Standards
Accountability
Uniform Crime Reports
Crime rates

Like any other municipal function, policing is largely supported by local tax dollars. The vast majority of police agencies in the United States are associated with municipal governments. Except for school systems, which are typically funded through separate school taxes, police departments often account for the largest expenditure in municipal government. Their size and visibility in municipal finance make police services the object of close and careful public scrutiny.

Further, the largest share of municipal expenditures for police services is related to personnel costs. Policing is labor-intensive; upward of 90 percent of police budgets is devoted to salaries, fringe benefits, and long-term retirement packages.

Policing is labor-intensive because it has been organized as an emergency response system that provides services typically carried out by one or two police officers in interaction with one or a few citizens. Such personal interaction is costly, not only in terms of police salaries but also in terms of the costs of training and such support as police radio communications, motor vehicles, computer assistance, and advanced weapons.

Policing also is among the most critical services provided by local governments. Police services undergird our general conception of an ordered society, in which people can live, work, and play in relative safety. Because the police are available 24 hours a day, 7 days a week, police services provide a lifeline to other municipal services. The police are called for just about everything: loud barking dogs, neighbor disputes, minor medical problems, general information about city services, weather and time, special events, travel directions, and information about school openings and closings. This, of course, is in addition to their more traditional crime prevention and criminal apprehension responsibilities.

The costs and importance of police services demand that municipal policy makers closely monitor police budgets with a view to increasing police productivity and measuring police performance. Such political and administrative oversight of the police is consistent with one of the most important ideals of democratic society—civilian oversight of government.

As the chief operating officer of the police agency, the police chief executive must continually monitor both the expenditure of police resources and the public safety effects produced by these expenditures. The police chief executive must also convince those who fund the police agency that resources are used properly and with the greatest efficiency and effectiveness. In short, the police chief executive must focus on police productivity, particularly in times of limited municipal resources.

This chapter considers the issues of police productivity and performance measurement as central to the role of the police chief executive. By defining productivity and measuring police performance, the police chief executive can increase the impact of policing on a jurisdiction's quality of life. At the same time, the police chief executive can assure others in government, and, most important, the citizens who pay all the bills, that police resources are being used to their greatest potential.

MUNICIPAL FINANCE AND POLICE-PERFORMANCE MEASUREMENT

From the late 1940s to the mid-1970s, the American economy prospered at both the national and local levels. Municipalities generally found themselves with an expanding "economic pie" so large that evaluation of municipal services, including those of the police, was an issue of minor concern. At that time, the job appeared to be getting done, money was freely available, and there was little interest in carefully auditing books and operations. Consequently, the efficiency, effectiveness, and productivity of government in general, and of the police in particular, were largely assumed and rarely evaluated closely (Greene, Cordner, and Bynum, 1986). During this period, the police and other government agencies typically increased their budgets incrementally, in what might be termed a *10-percent solution*: this year's budget plus 10 percent. Any demonstration that expenditures were linked to outcomes was rare. Instead, police departments relied on the *crime clock*[1] and arrest statistics, neither of which measures effort or outcome.

Since the mid-1970s, the American economy has experienced tremendous restrictions, recessions, and eco-spasms (Peterson, 1986). The oil embargo and double-digit inflation of the 1970s, the deficit funding of the 1980s, a huge national debt, and the current drive to downsize government have pressured federal, state, and local policy makers to better understand the impact of their investments, including those made for public safety. Simply put, local governments must get a maximum return on what they invest in public services. Without exception, they are all in search of the proverbial "biggest bang for the buck."

In the early and mid-1970s municipal finances nearly collapsed in some major municipalities. For perhaps the first time since the Great Depression, America's cities found it necessary to remove significant numbers of police officers from their payrolls. In New York, Philadelphia, San Francisco, Detroit, and other places, newly hired police officers were laid off. Faced with a choice of fiscal collapse or a reduction in the size of the government's work force, many cities chose to rethink municipal expenditures, including those for police services. Since then, policy makers at all levels of government have become acutely aware of the need to increase the productivity of government services.

Today the hue and cry is to "reinvent" government, to make it more responsive and less costly (Osborne and Gaebler, 1993: chaps. 5 and 7). Under the *reinvention model*, governments must fund performance, not effort. They must become entrepreneurial—meaning that they must compete in a marketplace that emphasizes a "bottom line"—the accomplishment of *results*, rather than merely how hard agencies may work. As Osborne and Gaebler observe:

> Entrepreneurial governments seek to change rewards and incentives. Public entrepreneurs know that when institutions are funded according to inputs, they have little reason to strive for better performance. But when they are funded according to outcomes, they become obsessive about performance. (Osborne and Gaebler, 1993:139)

Before the 1970s, police chief executives and other city managers were rarely held accountable for fiscal expenditure, productivity, or performance measurement. As the then–Police Foundation president, former New York City Police Commissioner Patrick V. Murphy, suggested in 1975:

> Up until now [1975] police administrators have not been held to close account for the use of resources. While there have been instances where they have been held responsible, fairly or unfairly, for police corruption, increased crime, or for the inept handling of mass public disorders, for the most part police chiefs have not been held accountable for the productivity and improvement of their departments by any well developed standards. (Murphy, 1975:36).

Without well-developed standards for measuring police agency productivity, police chiefs historically relied on such indirect measures as the crime rate or the number of calls for service the police agency handled in any given year. At the same time, police chiefs called for increased police resources to continue the "war on crime" that began in the 1930s and that escalated in the 1960s. Throughout these decades, police chiefs have tended to address concerns about productivity by calling for more police officers to combat rising and more publicly visible crime.

The rather dramatic changes in the economies and finances of local communities today demand that police chief executives ensure that the public safety objectives of their departments are achieved even in times of fiscal cutbacks. It is not enough for the police chief executive to lament the absence of resources for public safety. Rather, the police chief executive must continuously monitor and shift resources to provide maximum police services to the community. In contemporary jargon, police chiefs must "work harder smarter" rather than just harder, and they must accomplish more with less.

Measurement of police agency productivity and police officer performance continues to be confounded with vague statements about missions, roles, and responsibilities as well as imprecise measurement of efforts and outcomes. This is a problem for government in general, as well as for the police in particular. In fact, it is a problem most associated with bureaucratic governmental organizations:

> Because they don't measure results, bureaucratic governments rarely achieve them. They spend ever more on public education, yet test scores and dropout rates barely budge. They spend ever more on job training for welfare recipients, yet welfare rolls continue to grow. They spend ever more on police and prisons, yet crime rates continue to rise. (Osborne and Gaebler, 1993:139)

The continuing pressures of municipal finance on police chief executives highlight the need for better measures of productivity, including measures of police officer and police agency performance. Such measures are consistent with the *open-system* perspective on organizational management—they provide a clearer gauge of the impact of the services the police produce, as well as the costs of those services. They also provide for a *feedback loop* so that the police chief executives, municipal policy makers, and the general public can make informed decisions about the quantity, quality, cost, and impact of public safety services. Figure 11-1 portrays productivity and performance measurement in the context of open-system management.

FIGURE 11-1. Open System Approach to Diagnosing Individual and Group Performance
Source: *Michael I. Harrison,* Diagnosing Organizations: Methods, Models, and Processes *(Newbury Park, Calif.: Sage, 1987), p. 51. Copyright © 1987 by Sage Publications, Inc. Reprinted by permission of Sage Publications, Inc.*

ENVIRONMENT

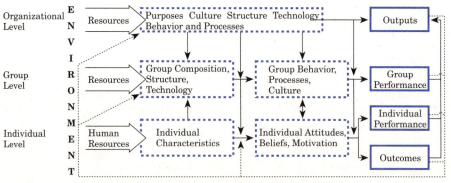

Note: Solid lines show main lines of influence; dotted lines show feedback loops.

DEFINING PRODUCTIVITY AND PERFORMANCE MEASUREMENT

Productivity

"Productivity" means many things to many people. Popular discussion of whether people or organizations are productive usually involves the extent to which they make fullest use of their resources in order to produce results. Increases and decreases in productivity are then gauged by the relationship of inputs to outputs—again, resources to results. Productive individuals or organizations minimize resources and maximize results. Unproductive individuals or organizations, by contrast, use maximum resources with minimum results. Thus, *productivity* is the relationship between results achieved and costs incurred.

Productivity is generally assessed for the organization as a whole. Within organizations, "performance measurement" (discussed below) is the term generally used to describe assessment of the efforts of individuals and groups working within the organization.

The evaluation of organizational productivity involves taking into account two related concepts: efficiency and effectiveness. "Efficiency" refers to means, and "effectiveness" refers to end results.

Efficiency means achieving a result or producing a product or service with the least expenditure of resources. As such, it is a measure of the cost of production, not of what is produced. In policing, ideas about efficiency are reflected in statements like "We respond to 70 percent of our calls for service in 3 minutes or less" and "Detectives have an average workload of 50 cases per month." In both instances, the central issue is how resources—in this case, patrol response and detective workload—are used.

By contrast, *effectiveness* is the extent to which a desired result is achieved, irrespective of cost considerations. Here the focus is on the impact of police department efforts and activities, not necessarily on their costs. Statements such as "Neighborhood safety has increased over the past year" and "Our community is one of the safest cities in America" reflect a concern for the *impact* of police activities and do not take into account the costs of the services that produce these results.

The concept of *productivity links concerns between efficiency and effectiveness by measuring the impact of services produced in light of their costs.* As one commentator on government productivity suggests:

> Productivity is a combination of the effectiveness and efficiency concepts. Productivity asks both whether a desired result was achieved (the effectiveness question) and what resources were consumed to achieve it (the efficiency question). (Kuper, 1975:3)

The purpose of measuring and assessing an agency's productivity is to improve the agency's functioning and effects. In policing, productivity measurement seeks to better understand:

1. How police services are produced
2. What the costs of these services are
3. How costs vary by type of service provided

4. What the impact of different services is on the problems they seek to address or the goals they seek to achieve

In the long term, productivity measurement should provide the police organization with a better understanding of the relationship between its efforts and its results. This information can then be used to improve organizational functioning in any number of areas. Most specifically:

1. The process of measuring current levels of productivity can indicate the existence of particular problems.
2. Over time, productivity measurement tracks the progress or lack of progress in improving productivity.
3. Productivity data collected by geographical areas within a jurisdiction can help identify areas in particular need of attention.
4. Productivity measurement for the agency as a whole can serve as the basis for developing and refining evaluations of specific activities.
5. Productivity measurement can provide agencies with the information necessary to set productivity targets.
6. Establishment of productivity targets can help to establish performance incentives for both managerial and nonmanagerial personnel.
7. Measurement of data can be used for in-depth productivity studies on ways to improve specific aspects of productivity.
8. Productivity measurement information can be a major way to account for government operations to the public.[2]

Productivity measurement, then, can provide police chief executives with powerful sources of information about their agency and its personnel. In an age of increased pressure to assure the taxpayer that government resources are being used efficiently and effectively, police chief executives who have not already been directed to do so would be wise to institute productivity measurement within their agencies. Failing to do so leaves the police largely unable to define their worth or to defend their police departments to the public and to those who oversee municipal expenditure.

Problems in Defining Success in Public Safety

All public agencies have problems specifying and measuring the impact of their efforts. Unlike their private-sector counterparts, which can measure profits and losses, public-sector agencies pursue rather broadly defined and symbolic missions and objectives. To turn a profit by making cars and trucks, for example, is a far more tangible goal than the police ideal of protecting and serving.

Government agencies like schools, health care facilities, social welfare agencies, and the police pursue goals called *commonweal goals,* meaning goals that affect all people in society, regardless of whether they use the services of those agencies directly. Such commonweal, or public, goals mandate that public agencies preserve the Constitution and democracy, educate the public, improve the public health, and provide and preserve public tranquility. These are tall tasks for any organization. Furthermore, they express a global intent for these government agencies—an intent that is difficult to specify with precision.

What constitutes "public tranquility"? What is an "educated" or "rehabilitated" person? What is a "healthy public"? All these are matters with latitude in interpretation far wider than is true of a corporate profit statement. Consequently, they often confound productivity measurement in the public sector. Such vagueness in the goals of most public agencies provides little direction for the measurement of productivity or performance.

The vagueness of government agency goals and objectives is related to the fact that much of what government does has a largely symbolic component (Edelman, 1964, 1977), meaning that government policies and programs represent ideals and images in the wider society as much as they represent tangible programs and practices. The phrase "to protect and serve" conjures up the idea of an omnipotent, caring government that seeks to help citizens in their day-to-day encounters with life. But such a vague, symbolic statement of government goals and objectives also clouds and confounds the productivity measurement issue. Broadly stated missions and objectives, with highly symbolic, emotional, and political content, like "to protect and serve," provide little guidance for productivity or performance measurement. Serving and protecting whom, at what cost, and with what impact are productivity assessment issues that have remained elusive in much of the police productivity discussion.

Symbolism in the goals and objectives of policing also produces an emotional response to issues of crime, order, and justice on the part of the public. Police missions and objectives have been a continual source of public discourse, and fear of crime has kept police issues in the forefront of the American agenda since the 1960s. The political landscape is littered with the sloganism of law and order. Public campaigns to "stamp out crime," "three strikes and you're out," and "retake the streets" are deeply emotional and political issues in America. The emotionalism and politicism associated with fear of crime also cloud productivity and performance measurement. The current trend toward "three strikes and you're out," for example, plays on fear and symbolism and ignores questions about the productivity of housing geriatric prisoners long beyond the time when they pose any danger to society.[3]

Moreover, we have not yet reached consensus on what police are to do. Are they specialized crime fighters or generalized service providers? Are they singly responsible for preventing crime and maintaining public order, or are the actions of other social and governmental institutions equally likely to increase or retard crime and disorder? The resolution of these questions is likely to have significant impact on the definition of police productivity chosen.

Public agencies having such symbolic and globally defined missions have often opted to measure effort as opposed to effect. That is to say, while it has been difficult for the police to estimate the impact on society's safety of what they do, they do know what they do. Typically, such secondary measures of productivity are used as proxies for the outcome measures that have eluded the police. A *proxy measure* is a substitute measure for performance.

Proxy measures of police performance and productivity are problematic because they often project an image of the relative success or failure of the police agency far removed from the actual level of department and individual performance and productivity. Meeting organizationally prescribed norms or quotas often becomes a substitute definition and measurement for achieving results.

For example, when police agencies count as measures of performance such things as the number of traffic citations they issue, they often fail to account for the fact that these numbers, in large measure, reflect some combination of the resources the police put to the task of writing traffic citations and the quota systems some departments persist in using to ensure that some purportedly acceptable number of citations is issued in any given month. Using such measures as proxies for productivity is self-serving and unconnected to the impact the police attempt to achieve in writing traffic citations: safer and less congested roadways. Herman Goldstein has correctly referred to this as a police *means-ends* problem. Because it is difficult to measure the effects of many police activities, he argues, the police have instead measured their productivity by counting the number of times they use the tools they have been provided to achieve their goals (Goldstein, 1979).

Thus, rather than determining whether the roads are safer and less congested, police historically have assessed their traffic productivity in terms of the numbers of vehicles stopped and summonses issued. These proxy measures, of course, beg the question of whether the enforcement involved accomplishes anything in the way of making the roads safer and less congested. In addition, because it is very easy to direct officers to issue more tickets, it is very easy to "increase productivity" in this manner. It is not so easy to show that anything police do has positive impacts on highway safety and congestion.

An associated problem in the measurement of police productivity is the general inability to disentangle the collective impact on crime and social disorder of many government services and varying social conditions. Even if crime and disorder go down in a particular community, it has been relatively impossible to attribute such decline to the actions of the police alone. James Q. Wilson states:

> There are no "real" measures of overall [police] success; what is measurable about the level of public order, safety and amenity in any given large city can only partially, if at all, be affected by police behavior. . . . Proxy measures almost always turn out to be process measures—response time, arrest rates or clearance rates—that may or may not have any relationship to crime rates or levels of public order. (Wilson, 1993:16)

Relying entirely on proxy measures can create an organizational system that defines "success" through secondary methods and then reviews that success through some of the process measures defined above. The result is that of a self-reflecting system, wherein the police department sees the image it wants to see and continually fails to assess the image of itself held by others, primarily its customers. This self-fulfilling image of success can be quite illusory. For example, for years police chiefs, adhering to the means-ends pattern described by Goldstein, have made public pronouncements about the number of arrests their officers had made for such problematic and highly visible crimes as drug trafficking and prostitution. But the public has been too smart to accept these figures as measures of success in dealing with the problems involved. Residents and businesspersons judge the productivity of their police departments not on how many arrests they make but rather on whether the problem persists. Few citizens know—*or care*—how many street drug dealers or prostitutes

This officer is distributing antidrug information to the kids on her beat. What measures should be used to assess the productivity of such efforts?
Kolvoord/Image Works.

the police arrest; but they know and care deeply about whether they and their children can use their streets without tripping over drug dealers and buyers, crack vials, used needles, and prostitutes and their customers. The police assess their productivity using *effort* as the criterion for performance evaluation, while citizens are far more interested in *effect*. In short, citizens are concerned with street conditions rather than with arrest numbers, and they are apathetic toward proxy measures that do not take conditions into account.

Performance Measurement in Policing

At the most general level, *performance measurement* is the scientific assessment of work-related tasks and behaviors and their attachment to desired organizational outcomes. It involves the measurement of effort, and it ties the activities of individuals and groups within organizations to the missions and objectives of those organizations.

Mastrofski and Wadman (1991:363) distinguish between *performance appraisal* and *performance measurement*. As they conceptualize it, the former refers to processes associated with evaluating an individual's job performance, and the latter refers to the evaluation of goal accomplishment. According to Mastrofski and Wadman, standards for police performance appraisal—how well an individual performs tasks—are better developed than are standards for performance measurement—whether the goal of the tasks actually is accomplished.

For nearly 30 years, national commissions, researchers, the courts, and academics have debated and refined standards and measures for assessing the performance of individual police officers. Beginning in the late 1960s with President Lyndon Johnson's Commission on Law Enforcement and Administration of Justice (President's Commission, 1967a, 1967b) and the Kerner Report (National Advisory Commission on Civil Disorders, 1968), and followed by both the standards pertaining to the urban police function promulgated by the American Bar Association (1973) and National Advisory Commission on Criminal Justice Standards and Goals (1976), a body of literature and prescription for defining police performance has been generated. This prescriptive literature has also been supported by a wide range of studies that examine police performance and that outline several approaches to improving performance appraisal systems within police agencies.[4] In addition, several court cases have significantly shaped the definition and measurement of police performance.

Many of the approaches advocated for improving police performance appraisal systems involve some form of job analysis coupled with a system of rating individuals in their work roles and activities. Knowledge about the nature and content of organizational jobs is vital for effective management. Job analysis provides a means to systematically study organizational jobs for two purposes:

1. To clarify the roles, responsibilities, and skills associated with each organizational job
2. To group similar tasked jobs under what are called "job classes"

Job analysis can also help to increase employee input in defining jobs, particularly if employees are consulted as part of the analysis process.

Job analysis refers to the assessment of jobs (not individuals in them) with particular concern for the knowledge, skills, and abilities (KSAs) necessary for an individual to successfully perform that job. Job-analytic approaches study classes of jobs. Such analyses typically result in statements about what the job incumbent must know and what range of skills and abilities he or she must have to fulfill the requirements of that job class (see Schneider and Greene, 1982:313–406). In policing, analyses are most often conducted for the position of patrol officer, first-line supervisors, and, frequently, general detective.

While there are a variety of job-analytic approaches, Mastrofski and Wadman (1991:366) have grouped them into four broadly defined categories:

1. *Task-based methods,* emphasizing current tasks and conditions of work
2. *Attribute-based methods,* emphasizing the physical and mental requirements of the job as well as specifying employee aptitudes thought to be related to these requirements
3. *Behavior-based methods,* emphasizing what the employee does
4. *Functional-job analysis,* which combines task-, attribute-, and behavior-based methods of job analysis

These methods yield varying information about individuals' performance in specified jobs. Task- and attribute-based job analysis techniques have been used for some time. These analyses typically focus on the frequency and criticality of tasks performed by workers, or on how often they are performed and how critical and/or dangerous they are. In policing, these methods generally involve observing officers in field settings and/or asking samples of police officers how often they perform certain tasks and how important it is to perform these tasks. At times, these analyses also ask supervisors to identify the frequency and criticality of tasks performed by their subordinates.

Attribute systems for job analyses employ methods similar to those of task-based systems. Typically either they ask job incumbents and or supervisors to identify the necessary attributes for successfully performing a particular job, or they deduce attributes from the tasks performed. For example, if police officers must take down crime victims' statements in an accurate and complete manner, they must have the necessary communication skills (e.g., listening, oral, and written skills) to function well in those tasks. Similarly, if some aspect of the job requires a level of physical strength, officers must possess the necessary physical attributes.

This is not to say that arbitrary physical or other attributes can be established to exclude persons from obtaining police positions. Rather, it means that attributes that are "job-related" can be used to separate those who can function in the job and those who cannot. Much of the litigation surrounding police hiring standards has challenged the job-relatedness of such standards as height, eyesight, and certain levels of physical ability.

In part due to challenges to the validity of job criteria developed through either task- or attribute-based systems, behavioral and functional job-task analyses focus on the long-term behaviors of employees and the use of several job-related criteria for defining any particular class of jobs. Behavioral and functional rating systems focus on job performance rather than on personality. While they are time-consuming to design and conduct, they are generally perceived to more directly engage the employee in defining the job, while at the same time providing feedback to the employee and the organization.[5]

Job analysis provides important information about the requirements of any job. Such information becomes the basis for employee selection, training, and evaluation. However, inappropriate or incomplete job analyses, or no job analyses at all, have led police agencies historically to select, train, and evaluate police personnel on criteria other than those needed for success in the job. Such practices have resulted in several court decisions requiring that police selection, training, and promotion be "job-related."[6]

Police performance appraisal through some form of job analysis is the foundation on which other individual and organizational performance assessments are made. Without appropriate job definition, an individual's performance in that job or the contribution that job makes to the broader goals and objectives of the police agency will be unknown and largely undeterminable.

Once a job analysis has been conducted and descriptions of jobs and their associated evaluative dimensions are clarified, a system for job rating must be developed. *Job rating* is the assessment of an individual within the context of a predefined job. Rating systems abound, and they have been described in some detail in Chapter 10.

PRINCIPLES OF GOOD POLICING

The idea of assessing productivity as well as the performance of police officers presumes that we know what *good policing* is. While it may be easy to specify the police behaviors and activities we don't want—corruption, brutality, perjury, false accusations, and the like—there is an absence of consensus concerning what constitutes good policing. Measuring the productivity of the police, then, is complicated by the absence of a clear definition of good policing (see Fyfe, 1993). To paraphrase an old saw, one person's good aggressive policing is another person's police harassment.

What Is Good Policing?

The most desirable processes and outcomes of municipal police services have been difficult to specify largely because there is little clear agreement about either. We share an abstract notion, for instance, that the police should enforce the law and that they should follow the law themselves while doing so; but it is often unclear how we want them to go about doing this or what we expect them to accomplish in doing it.

The literature on police includes several discussions related to the means and ends of policing described by Goldstein (1979). Even before Goldstein labeled the means-ends syndrome, Skolnick (1966) suggested that "law" and "order" in policing are in a constant tension, competing with each other as definitions of the police and of their role in a democratic society. In some cases—crowd scenes and demonstrations, for example—police can enforce the law only at the risk of destroying order. Klockars (1985:7–18) suggested that the police cannot be defined solely on the basis of their ends, primarily because they have been charged with achieving so many ends. Rather, he suggests that the police must be defined on the basis of the means they use to accomplish their work. And, for Klockars, the most common means used in policing is *coercive force.* Fyfe (1993) has written that measuring police success in terms of whether they achieve their ends is wrongheaded because so many factors other than whether the police have acted correctly affect the outcomes of their most pressing challenges. Despite the best police efforts, he argues, police situations often end unhappily for reasons beyond the control of the police; conversely, some situations end happily even though the police may have acted unreasonably and improperly. Thus, like Klockars, Fyfe suggests that, in measuring police performance, it is best to look directly at how they have performed rather than at how it may have happened to turn out. In policing, like medicine, the operation may be a success even though the patient has died; and, conversely, not even the most poorly performed operation can kill some patients.

Moreover, values associated with modern policing often stress the importance of the police in upholding democracy, maintaining an orderly society, and providing emergency crisis intervention services to the public. These values, while important in underpinning much of what the police do, often lose their operational impact because they are too broadly stated or because they can be seen as competing with one another.

> Many police officials and much of the public fail to understand the responsibilities of the police in providing equal law enforcement, in assuring due process, and in protecting the right of political dissent. Most bothersome is the fact that talk about supporting democratic values in the context of police oper-

ations has come to be equated, by many police and by some elements of the public, with a soft and permissive attitude towards criminals and toward unruly elements in our society. This situation is exacerbated when the loudest critics of the police, who vociferously defend constitutional rights, fail to acknowledge the complexity of the police task and seem totally unaware of the problems the police must handle on the streets, often under extremely difficult circumstances. (Goldstein, 1977:13)

The complexity of defining good policing has led one observer to suggest that policing is governed by two sets of standards, one involving *legality*, or "compliance with explicitly formulated schemes and regulations," and the other with *workmanship* or "maintenance of minimally acceptable levels of knowledgeable, skilled and judicious performance" (Bittner, 1983:2–3). Legal and administrative definitions of policing are most often associated with the "means" of the police, while standards of workmanship are almost invariably attached to the "ends" of policing. Legality is most often associated with defining and shaping expectations of police performance *before* the police act, while workmanship is most associated with *after-the-fact* assessments of police performance. Both legality and workmanship help shape any definition of good policing. Before the police take actions, we want to be certain that they understand the laws and the rules and that they must abide by them; when police actions end, our interest shifts to whether they have accomplished the purposes for which the laws and rules were intended.

The *craft of policing* also shapes expectations about good policing within the police community (Bittner, 1990, chap. 8; Brown, 1981; Manning, 1977). The experiential side of policing has much to contribute to better describing desired police outcomes. To do so, however, those who have mastered policing through their real-world experiences must translate what they have learned into a form that can be taught to others in formal training. As Bayley and Bittner (1984) put it, if practical experience is to be used as a better guide to good police work:

1. It must be used to illustrate the "problematic nature" of policing in formal training programs, that is, the uncertainty and vagueness of situations confronted by the officers who are policing the street.
2. Veteran police officers should be used to teach police recruits the workmanship of policing so that the "modeling" of good policing can be accomplished.
3. Training grounded in experience should recur throughout officers' careers in order to reinforce the craft norms of the police in deciding what is good police work.
4. Police departments should reward the master craftspeople in policing, not just those who passed civil service tests, so that the experiential values of good policing are officially recognized and explicitly supported. In other words, being a good police officer should count as much toward promotion as doing well on exams.

Standards for Good Policing

If policing has a legal and administrative dimension, as well as a craft or workmanship dimension, then good policing can be defined on the basis of both criteria, so long as they are not in conflict. The Community Relations Service of the U.S. Department of Justice (1987) has outlined what it considers to be "principles of good policing" in avoiding violence between the police and the public. Of primary concern to the Community Relations Service is the need for the police to adopt a conflict management approach, within which tensions and violence might be reduced. At the same time, the police need to adopt a stance of negotiation, rather than confrontation, and must identify and analyze situations most often associated with violence. In most places, these situations include arrest encounters, responses to disturbance calls, traffic stops and pursuits, investigations of suspicious persons, handling and transporting of people in police custody, interventions with mentally disturbed persons, and hostage or barricade situations.

Principles of good policing can emerge and help the police and the community to define the most desirable public safety outcomes through a mixture of policy and procedure changes, training, effective supervision, values clarification, and community outreach. Such an approach has the potential to improve the balance between administrative regulation and the craft norms of the police as ways of increasing police productivity measurement and police accountability. In short, this approach can bridge the gap between what Reuss-Ianni (1983) calls book-driven "management cops" and experienced "street cops."

MEASURING POLICE PRODUCTIVITY

The measurement of police agency productivity has slowly evolved. Where tradition long required measures of productivity that emphasize such *hard*, police-generated, evidence as arrest and crime statistics, productivity measurement has come to include *soft* indicators of police performance, such as public perceptions of neighborhood safety and the adequacy of policy presence, as well as public confidence in the police. Further, traditional means-oriented measures of performance, such as numbers of arrests, summonses, and field interrogations, have been augmented by more direct measures of the extent to which these efforts result in public order and safety. Especially in communities that have implemented problem- and community-oriented police models, police traffic safety productivity may be measured by determining whether accidents and congestion actually are reduced, rather than merely by counting the tickets issued by officers trying to achieve those goals. Finally, the process, or indirect, measures of police officer efforts have also been incorporated into many approaches to police productivity and performance measurement. As Bayley has indicated:

> With respect to direct performance measures, it is important to distinguish the "hard" from the "soft," meaning those that measure objective change in communities and those that measure subjective perceptions of changes. (Bayley, 1993:16)

Illustrations of Bayley's categories of "hard," "soft," and "indirect" measures are presented in Table 11-1. As can be seen, these measures stem from

TABLE 11-1. Police Performance Measures

379

CHAPTER 11
Productivity and
Performance
Measurement

I. Direct
  A. Hard
    Crime rates
    Criminal victimizations
    Ability of the public to undertake routine activities
    Real estate values
    Commercial activity in places of public accommodation
    Number of disorder situations interrupted
    Number of community "problems" solved
    Information volunteered to the police about crimes
  B. Soft
    Fear of crime
    Confidence in the police
    Commitment to neighborhoods
    Satisfaction with police action
    Complaints about police service
    Willingness to assist the police
    Community solidarity

II. Indirect
    Number of police officers
    Number of uniformed officers on the street
    Proportion of detectives to uniformed officers
    Ratio of supervisors to police officers
    Response times
    Arrests
    Clear-up rates
    Number of community crime-prevention meetings
    Number of Neighborhood Watch groups
    Speed in answering telephones

Source: David H. Bayley. "Back from Wonderland, or Toward the Rational Use of Police Resources," p. 15 in Anthony N. Doob (ed.), *Thinking about Police Resources* (Toronto: University of Toronto, Centre for Criminology, 1993).

whether they are observable (hard), are perceptual (soft), or measure police efforts rather than effects (indirect).

Traditional Productivity Measures

The police have employed measurement systems almost since the days of Robert Peel. In general, these systems have been attempts to quantify the activities of police officers and the police organization. Such quantified measures of police activity have become proxy measures for police agency productivity and police officer performance. Most of these measures have focused on the crime-fighting role of the police. They have been most visible in the Uniform Crime Reporting System and police agency reporting of arrest and clearance rates.

The Uniform Crime Reports and the Crime Rate. Perhaps the most well known source of information used to measure police agency productivity and, to a lesser extent, police officer performance is the FBI's *Uniform Crime Reports* (UCR) and its associated *Crime Index*, the latter of which is composed of the rate per 100,000 population of eight common violent and property crimes.[7]

The Uniform Crime Reporting System was created by the International Association of Chiefs of Police in 1927. In 1930, at the urging of J. Edgar Hoover, the U.S. Congress empowered the FBI to assume the responsibility for collating, analyzing, and disseminating these reports as a means of better accounting for crime. In addition to the Crime Index, the UCR itemize the annual number of crimes known to the police, the number of arrests the police make, police employment figures, and the number of killings and assaults of police officers. This information is reported jurisdiction by jurisdiction and is then grouped by population size.

Historically, police agencies have turned to the UCR as a measure of their performance. In most American cities, the rise and fall in crime is reported annually to the public. Typically, much hoopla is made when crime declines, and mayors, police chiefs, and other public figures compete to take credit for the decreases. And, of course, when crime increases, the police have typically asked for more resources to better wage their war on crime. Moreover, police departments often compare themselves to others on the basis of the UCR. Philadelphia, for example, claimed for many years that the UCR's figures demonstrated that it was the *safest city* among the ten largest urban American police jurisdictions. Dramatic increases in reported crime during the early 1980s when Philadelphia's city administration changed, however, suggested that Philadelphia's low crime rate was an artifact of creativity in police reporting practices, rather than an indication that Philadelphians were any safer than other big-city dwellers. (See Box 11-1.)

Even without such deliberate distortion by officials, there are several grounds for criticizing the UCR as a measure of crime and related police agency productivity. Those who have carefully studied the UCR state that these shortcomings include:

1. The UCR only records reported crime. The *National Crime Survey* (the NCS, which includes information collected by surveyors who go out and ask people whether they have been victims of crime) estimates that only 37 percent of all personal and household crimes are reported to the police. Most often, underreporting occurs because victims believe that police can do nothing to solve the crimes involved.
2. Conversely, the NCS and others have found evidence that statistics for some types of crimes may be affected by false reporting of events that did not occur. Some reported rapes are, in fact, means of explaining unwanted pregnancies; some vehicle larceny reports are insurance frauds.
3. Some crime reports are accidentally lost or misclassified by the police.
4. Under the UCR's hierarchy rule, the police record only the most serious crime involved in any incident. Thus, if someone is raped and robbed, only the rape appears in the UCR totals.
5. All Index crimes have the same value. In the absence of any weighting of the relative seriousness, or *disutility,* of the crimes included in the Index, a murder, a rape, a stolen bicycle, and a credit card fraud are all the same.

BOX 11-1. Crime Statistics: Cooking the Books

Philadelphia was not alone in practicing voodoo crime reporting. Two of the authors recall the time when New York City officers were encouraged to keep that city's crime rate artificially low by classifying reported Part I offenses in ways that would keep them out of the Crime Index. Thus, a crime in which an apartment door was broken and a television set was stolen would be classified as a non-Index (Part II) criminal mischief and petit larceny, rather than as a Part I burglary, which would add to the Crime Index figures. A mugging in which a person's wallet or purse had been forcibly taken during a street attack would be classified as a Part II simple assault and petit larceny, rather than the robbery it actually had been. This practice ended in 1966, when newly elected Mayor John V. Lindsay pointed out that New York was losing federal anticrime aid by understating the dimensions of its crime problem. At that point, the pendulum swung so far the other way that even unfounded events were classified as criminal investigations in order to reap all the federal benefits possible. More recently, in the mid-1980s, Chicago television station WBBM won several awards for a series that documented the police practice of wrongly declaring that crimes reported to them had simply never happened.

This kind of creative bookkeeping was a long and honored tradition in both cities. The President's Commission on Law Enforcement and Administration traced the manipulation of crime statistics in New York and Chicago back for a generation before its 1967 reports:

Although Chicago, with about 3 million people, has remained a little less than half the size of New York City with 7 1/2 million . . . , it was reporting in 1935 about 8 times as many robberies. It continued to report several times as many robberies as New York City until 1949, when the FBI discontinued publication of New York reports because it no longer believed them. In 1950 New York discontinued its prior practice of allowing precincts to handle complaints directly and installed a central reporting system, through which citizens had to route all calls.

In the first year, robberies rose 400 percent and burglaries 1,300 percent, passing Chicago in volume for both offenses. In 1959 Chicago installed a central complaint bureau of its own, reporting thereafter several times more robberies than New York. In 1966 [Lindsay's first year as New York's mayor] New York, which appeared to have had a sharp decline in robberies in the late fifties, again tightened its central controls and found a much higher number of offenses. Based on preliminary reports for 1966, it is now reporting about 25 percent more robberies than Chicago. (President's Commission, 1967b:26)

The effects of this tinkering with crime statistics are shown in the following chart.

Robbery and Burglary Trends for Chicago and New York, 1935–1966

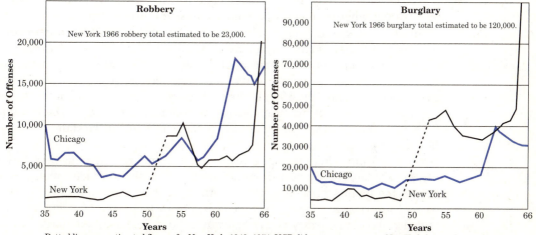

Dotted lines are estimated figures for New York, 1949–1951. UCR did not accept or report New York figures during those years.
Source: Uniform Crime Reports, 1936–1966. 1966 figures estimated from 11 months' report.

6. The eight Crime Index offenses provide no measure of such other important crimes as organized crime, white-collar crime, and narcotics trafficking.

7. The Index is based on each jurisdiction's *resident* population, and takes no account of the number of people who live in a jurisdiction as an accurate measure of the number of people—or places or other targets of crime—vulnerable to crime within it. Older central cities ringed by newer, large suburbs (New York, Chicago, Philadelphia, Detroit, Boston, San Francisco, for example) and tourist cities (such as Las Vegas and Miami) typically have relatively small resident populations that, every day, are swelled enormously by a great number of commuters and sightseers. Washington, D.C., as a case in point, has a resident population of less than 600,000; but the best estimates of its *daytime population*, including workers and sightseers, place this figure at about 1.5 million. Thus, Washington's crime rate per 100,000 residents is greatly affected by the fact that many of the cars stolen and pockets picked within its borders belong not to its 600,000 residents but to its 900,000 daily visitors.

Similarly, resident population is a misleading base for many crimes' rates. Burglaries, for example, are crimes against places—homes, stores, and offices—rather than people. Most cities, especially in their downtown areas, have a very high number of places vulnerable to burglary in relation to their resident populations. Nobody lives in Chicago's Sears Tower or New York's Empire State Building, but the burglary rates per 100,000 residents in each of these building's neighborhoods is skewed by the fact that each contains many offices that are inviting targets to burglars. Conversely, vehicle larceny rates per 100,000 residents in suburbs and outlying areas—where there typically are two cars for every three residents—are usually much higher than is true of cities, where there typically is one car for every three residents (see Black, 1970; O'Brian, 1985).

Arrest Rates. Arrest rates calculate the number of persons arrested for all crimes known to the police. They are generally reported as the ratio of arrests to reported crime. To the extent that they are subject to much of the same manipulation associated with the UCR statistics, arrest rates are questionable measures of police agency productivity and individual officers' performance. Further, many factors affect officers' decisions to take persons into custody. In addition to the seriousness of the crime, such factors as the relationship between the victim and the offender or the presence or absence of a lobby for action by the victim—as an individual or as a member of a specific class of victims, such as abused spouses—also influence police officer arrest decisions (see Black, 1973).

Perhaps more important, arrests are rare events for the police. That is to say, the availability of arrest situations for the police is extremely small in relation to the totality of their contacts with the public. Further, police agencies have typically specialized their functions to associate some assignments more with arrests than others. Officers in juvenile aid, community relations, foot patrol, and other *preventive* specialties within police agencies might produce few

All arrests are challenging and dangerous, but they may not be an adequate measure of officers' performance.
Jill Friedman.

arrests compared with members of *arrest-focused* units like gang, drug, or violent offenders units. Thus, while opportunities for arrests are rare occurrences for the police generally, those involved in preventive tasks, rather than in detective work or in other arrest-focused specialties functions, may have virtually no opportunity to make arrests.

Much research has reported that approximately 20 percent of police work, or even less, is actually devoted to law enforcement, including arrest situations (Reiss, 1971; Whitaker, 1982). And while Greene and Klockars (1991) have found that police crime-related activity accounts for nearly one-half of officers' time, it should be clear that crime and arrest statistics cannot readily be used properly and comprehensively to evaluate police agencies' productivity or police officers' performance.

Finally, arrests are a poor measure of police performance, particularly when they are compared with aggregate crime statistics, because the police arrest more people for minor violations than for serious violations. That is to say, in the aggregate, police arrest statistics include large numbers of arrests for lesser offenses, while the crime rate is, generally speaking, computed on the basis of serious crime. In many jurisdictions, police arrest statistics may readily be swollen by periodic crackdowns on street prostitution and drug trafficking, offenses that are not directly related to murders and other serious Part I offenses. Consequently, comparing arrests with offenses is like comparing apples and oranges; they simply do not reflect the same crime or public safety issues.

In short, the use of UCR or crime rates as the single or even dominant measure of police agency productivity raises serious questions about what is being measured and how police work is portrayed. Perhaps more importantly, arrest and crime statistics are much more likely to be influenced by persons or events other than those controlled by the police—those citizens who report crimes and the type of police and citizen encounters that produce arrest opportunities.

The Clearance Rate. The *clearance rate* is the ratio of the number of crimes reported to the police divided into the number of crimes for which the police believe they have a suspect:

$$\text{Clearance rate} = \frac{\text{crimes in which suspect believed identified}}{\text{crimes reported}}$$

The clearance rate has historically been used as a measure of the police ability to "solve crime," and it has been most associated with detective work (see Eck, 1982; Erickson, 1981) where, in many agencies, detectives and detective units refer to it as their "batting average."

Clearance rates are notoriously suspect in defining police productivity. First, clearance rates have little independent verification and are determined entirely by the police. This means that, for UCR and other reporting purposes, it is the police who determine whether a crime is "solved" or not. When individuals arrested for particular crimes are acquitted of the charges against them, it is rare that police clearance rates are adjusted.[8] Second, the police often clear multiple crimes by *writing off* cases to an individual arrested for a similar offense. Every urban police department has a long list of unsolved and unsophisticated apartment burglaries, for example. When an individual is arrested for committing a similar crime—such as kicking in an apartment door and stealing the television set—it is not unusual for the police to clear all the unsolved burglaries to that suspect. This is done even though the subject cannot actually be charged because, of course, no court would sustain the purported belief of the police that the suspect committed them all. More often than not, clearance rates reflect this negotiation. And while it is entirely possible that individual burglars account for a large percentage of burglaries, it is not at all clear that the police have a way of ensuring correspondence between the number of crimes they clear and the number of crimes committed by an arrested person.

Third, clearance rates are also potentially contaminated by what is referred to as the process of exceptional clearance. *Exceptional clearance* refers to situations where the police claim to know who committed the crime but are unable to prove it, generally because the victim of the crime is unwilling to publicly accuse the offender. In domestic violence cases, for example, it has been traditionally held that female victims of abuse are unwilling to prosecute their assailants. In such circumstances, as in many organized crime cases in which victims fear retaliation, the police have used the exceptional clearance as a method for "solving" the crime.

In addition, many crimes are not reported until they are cleared. Drug and prostitution offenses, for example, typically are unknown to the police until officers came into their police stations with persons under arrest for committing them. Hence, unlike most other crimes, these *officer-reported offenses* typically have clearance rates near 100 percent. Police departments that wish to make it appear that they are extremely productive, therefore, can pad their "batting averages" by lumping these offenses in with crimes against persons and property (which have much lower clearance rates) and deriving a single aggregate clearance rate.[9]

Clearance rates that are used as measures of police productivity are highly susceptible to internal manipulation by the police. Without some external referent, such statistics may reflect more the efforts of the police than their effects.

Ratios of Police to Citizens. An indirect, quantified measure often used to describe police productivity is the number of police officers per 1,000 residents. This measure is widely regarded as an indication of the adequacy of police services available in any jurisdiction.

In fact, the police-to-population ratio explains very little about police productivity. This ratio rarely adjusts for population density, variations in the presence of nonresident population discussed above, differences in city physical configurations or the level of reported crime, or victimization in any particular city. An example is illustrative: Knowing that Philadelphia and Los Angeles, respectively, have 3.8 and 2.8 officers per 1,000 residents tells us little about police productivity unless we carefully analyze several related factors. First, Los Angeles's population (about 3 million) is spread over 450 square miles, while Philadelphia's (about 1.7 million) is contained within 128 square miles. On the one hand, this may make it necessary to have more officers available to respond to calls in Los Angeles if response time is to remain within acceptable levels. On the other hand, the great number of densely populated areas in Philadelphia may make it necessary to assign a large number of officers to very labor-intensive foot patrol, which is impractical in much of Los Angeles. Second, it is probable that, as an older city with boundaries established long before its surrounding suburbs became much larger than the city itself, Philadelphia has a daytime population with a greater proportion of nonresident commuters than does Los Angeles. Third, the California Highway Patrol relieves the Los Angeles police of a good deal of the responsibility for policing the city's extensive freeway system, which remains its major mode of transportation. Such an arrangement does not exist in Philadelphia, where the police department includes its own highway patrol unit. Fourth, the major mode of transportation in Philadelphia is a subway system much more extensive than the system now under construction in Los Angeles. Policing this system places demands on Philadelphia police that will not exist in Los Angeles for several years.

Police-to-population ratios also are misleading in that they generally account for all sworn police personnel, whether they are assigned to patrol or other street-level duties or to organizational specializations that might reduce their ability to contribute in some direct fashion to public safety. Typically, upward of 20 to 25 percent of sworn police personnel hold administrative assignments and another 15 to 20 percent hold investigative functions of some type. Another 5 to 10 percent may function in such support services as radio communications, jail security, and the like. In some police departments, less than 40 percent of police personnel are actually assigned to street-level duties. Although there certainly is reason to question why some departments may have a comparatively high level of overhead personnel, such disparity in assignment and function limits the value of comparing ratios of police to population.

Evolving Measures of Police Productivity

Growing dissatisfaction with what is regarded as the "bean counting" involved in traditional measures of police productivity, performance, and measurement (Eck, 1984; Spelman, 1988) has gradually led the police to assess agency and officer performance on other dimensions and with differing sources of information. In Bayley's (1993) terms, some of these measures are hard, while others are soft. Nevertheless, these evolving measures of police productivity and performance emphasize changes in the environment of policing, as well as citizen acceptance and perceptions of the police.

Much of the evolution of police performance and productivity measurements rests in these assessments' shift in focus from the police organization to the environment. In the past, almost all police measures focused on what the police do. Today, much of the assessment of police agencies and personnel focuses on the impact of their actions on their most immediate clients—the citizenry of their communities.

This is a watershed in the measurement of police productivity. It clearly shifts the question from effort to effect, at the same time that it shifts the assessment of the police from themselves to their customers. As part of a larger movement toward "customer-driven government" (Osborne and Gaebler, 1993), client-based information has become increasingly more important to government agencies, including the police.

The most dominant forms of customer information regarding the adequacy and effectiveness of police departments come from victimization and customer satisfaction surveys and fear of crime and community quality of life assessments. Each of these sources of information asks community residents about their experiences with crime and the police, and each can provide a very different picture of police performance and productivity.

Victimization Surveys.   In 1967, the President's Commission on Law Enforcement and Administration of Justice reported on its attempts to obtain a clear picture of crime in the United States. The commission had contracted with the University of Chicago to survey 10,000 scientifically selected households and with the Bureau of Social Science Research and the University of Michigan to study victimization in Washington, Chicago, and Boston. Both surveys, the commission reported, found that a considerable amount of crime went unreported, particularly in crime-ridden neighborhoods in which citizens had become well aware that the likelihood of solving the crimes against them was low.

The results of this work stimulated the U.S. Department of Justice to launch a series of studies of crime victims in America's cities. These city-based victimization surveys, in turn, evolved into what is now called the *National Crime Survey,* a scientific assessment of criminal victimization in the United States.

Victim, rather than incident-based, information provides local police agencies with a better approximation of the true level of victimization in a community. Victim surveys have become a regular part of many police department assessments of their productivity and impact. The appendix at the end of this chapter provides an illustration of victim surveys used by local police agencies.

The most significant issues involved in the use of victim surveys by the police are:

1. The need to use scientific sampling methods so as to make the findings credible
2. The need to ensure anonymity, so that those asked to respond do not feel that they are subjects of police investigation
3. The continued use of such methods over time, in order to create an understanding of trends in victimization (U.S. Department of Justice, Bureau of Justice Statistics, 1992)

Victimization information and studies can be useful supplements to the more traditional arrest and crime statistics. Their use, however, is conditioned by the science behind them. Victim surveys conducted without appropriate sampling procedures produce rather useless information.

Police Task Evaluation. Police task and effort studies have been conducted for many years. The workload of the police, and indirectly their productivity, has been assessed by using police dispatch records and activity reports as well as by observing officers at work and using police surveys.[10] These studies generally point to a wide range of activities performed by the police, as well as a high degree of ambiguity in definition surrounding these activities. Much of what the police respond to is initially defined by citizens. Therefore, much of the assessment of police performance has a built-in bias toward reactive policing—policing in response to citizen requests for assistance.

More recently, attention to the day-to-day activities of the police, and particularly to their interactions with the public, has grown. The implications of this shift in focus on what the police *actually do* in community settings are many. First, the broad assessment of the police relationship with the community provides insight into the degree to which the public accepts police interventions, as well as more generalized assessments of police impacts.[11] Second, the current practice and philosophy of community- and problem-oriented policing is focused on the ability of the police to affect community conditions that generate crime and disorder and/or to solve community problems, as well as police understanding of cultural differences among communities (see Alpert and Dunham, 1988; Goldstein, 1990; Kelling, 1992). Third, current efforts to reconceptualize police performance and productivity also account for changes in the internal value set or culture of the police organization (Greene, Alpert, and Styles, 1992).

Fear of Crime and Community Quality of Life. Like crime and victimization, issues of fear of crime and the quality of neighborhood life are important issues in any municipality. Studies of police operations conducted by the Police Foundation in the late 1970s and early 1980s (Police Foundation, 1981; Pate et al., 1985; Wycoff et al., 1985) suggested that police tactics and deployment

One of the most important things police do is to make sure that the lives of vulnerable citizens are not altered by the fear of crime.
AP/Wide World.

plans had great effects on how community residents and businesspersons felt about their community and their use of public places.

The theory that undergirds efforts to reduce fear of crime was popularized in 1982 in Wilson and Kelling's important article "Broken Windows." This paper suggests that as communities become more fearful, they abandon public places. Such abandonment, in turn, leaves those public places to those who would violate the law. A continuing cycle of neighborhood deterioration ensues that, in the end, makes law-abiding citizens prisoners in their own homes, afraid to venture out into public places for fear of victimization.

Fear-of-crime surveys typically ask whether respondents are afraid to go out at night, avoid places because of fear of victimization, and take crime prevention precautions. Police use of fear-of-crime surveys began in Baltimore County, Maryland, in the early 1980s (Cordner, 1985). Since then, these surveys have become a feature of several police research projects, as well as part of the information some police agencies now regularly collect from the public.

Fear-of-crime surveys have the same needs and limitations as do crime victim surveys. The cornerstone of this approach to collecting environmental information is in the application of scientific research and sampling procedures.

Customer Satisfaction with Services Provided. In recent years, the police have begun to put a simple question to the users of its services: "How are we doing?" Such a question and the responses it elicits provide police chief executives with *benchmarks* to better assess agency and individual performance.

Traditionally, the police have asked little of their customers. The *professional model* of policing implied that as professionals the police should be somewhat aloof and distant from the public. The professional model also implied that the police "knew what was best" for their cities when it came to crime control.

Community- and Problem-Oriented Policing and Performance Measurement

Since the mid-1980s, American policing has been struggling with a shift in focus, emphasis, and tactics. Variously labeled community- or problem-oriented policing, this shift in focus conceptualizes police performance as the application of information about crime and disorder problems within specific community contexts. That is, under these approaches, the police are to better use information to solve community-based problems.

Problem-oriented policing is a process that:

1. *Begins with careful analysis of a problem that the police have been asked to confront.* In Chapter 2, for example, we analyzed the amorphous "crime problem" and determined that the parts of it that had been defined as responsibilities of local police generally consisted of street (or "peasant") crime, rather than complex financial and political crime.

2. *Identifies the most likely causes of the problem.* Although the causes of peasant crime are complex, it is clear that the terrible social conditions in the neighborhoods in which this crime flourishes must be a major causative factor. It is not enough to know this, however. While broad social conditions may lie at the root of most crime, many criminals are unwittingly assisted in their work by people who give them opportunities to do their dirty work. Purse snatchers, for example, may be victims of terrible social conditions (which certainly do not excuse their crimes), but they often are able to commit their acts only because some women are too nonchalant about their security while they walk on city streets. Although it certainly is not a cause of crime, what police themselves do—or do not do—may help criminals to flourish. Police who are not around at the times and places at which crime is most likely to occur, or who grow so distant from the public that they lose sources of information, make criminals' lives easy.

3. *Attempts to identify the people and institutions in positions to eliminate these causes or, at least, to reduce their negative effects.* In considering the problem of crime, we concluded that the police themselves had relatively little direct influence on social conditions and that the people and institutions best positioned to effect lasting change in crime were the taxpayers and the officials they elected to spend their money in ways that best improved the public's quality of life. At the same time, police officials who point out that much crime is attributable to the terrible influences of the inner city are not absolved from doing everything possible to combat crime on a day-to-day basis while they press for changes in these influences. Nor can high-ranking police officials assume that their experience and position give them a monopoly on insights into the crime problem within their agencies. Street-level police officers, investigators, and supervisors may not have ready access to the big picture the chief and staff see every day, but these personnel surely know what's happening on their beats. To a man—*or woman*—they also have some ideas concerning what to do about it.

4. *Enlists the support of these people and institutions in attempts to address the problem.* Support for attempts to address any problem is strongest only among those who have participated in the whole process of identifying, analyzing, and trying to address problems. In step 3, we noted that the people positioned to have an effect on the crime problem include ordinary citizens, government officials, and street-level police personnel. No anti-crime strategy or tactic is likely to succeed unless it enjoys wide support among these groups, and police administrators must be prepared to win such support. They must act as change agents, convincing sometimes apathetic citizens, jaded politicians, and burned-out police officers that their ideas and efforts are valued and, most important, necessary.

To do this, we would probably encourage the police chief and his or her staff at every level to seek opportunities to speak out about the need to find ways of changing the social conditions that apparently breed crime.[12] In addition, this would probably require considerable outreach to ensure that citizens are apprised of the benefits of working with police to prevent crime and to apprehend criminals. Internally, it might mean reducing the rigidity of chains of command that sometimes operate on the assumption that the ability to recognize and address problems exists only at the top level. The end product might be one or more task forces or committees of officials, citizens, and police charged with meaningful participation in the remaining parts of the process.

5. *Formulates both long-term strategies and short-range tactics that these people and institutions can employ to take corrective action.* Strategies are well-organized attempts to plan actions over an extended period of time, while *tactics* are attempts to deal in the short term with immediate crises or unacceptable conditions. There is a great temptation not to think of social problems in the long term, especially among police who have been socialized and trained to anticipate and respond to emergencies and other unacceptable conditions. Doing so, however, is shortsighted and simply ensures that crises will be regularly repeated; problems are most likely to be eradicated when their causes are eliminated. At the same time, an overly long view— "Until we realize that criminals are victims of society, we will always have criminals and there will be nothing the police can do to eliminate crime" simply is inaccurate and does nothing to help the honest people who wish to use their streets unmolested *tonight*. Thus, included in this step would be determination of the most appropriate means of deploying personnel and working with the public in crime prevention and apprehension efforts. These would probably include a crime analysis program that provides the information necessary to deploy police resources in ways most likely to prevent crime, as well as a program to educate citizens about crime prevention and to enroll their help in crime prevention and reporting. In short, police approaches to problems must include both long-term strategies to eliminate the cause of problems and short-term tactics to deal with immediate crises and conditions. Again, support for the strategies and tactics that evolve from this step are likely to be strong only among those who have participated in formulating them. Thus, participation should be as broad as reasonably possible.

6. *Implements strategies and tactics.* As suggested in Chapter 5, many environ-

mental, organizational, and individual factors affect how a job actually gets done. Since the history of program failure may be traced largely to failures of implementation, administrators should not take this step for granted, and must carefully monitor project implementation.

7. *Constantly monitors and reconsiders the state of the problem, progress toward alleviating it, and the effectiveness of strategies and tactics.* With our crime problem, we would want to know whether deployment, prevention, and apprehension tactics had any apparent effects. In the longer term, we would be most interested in determining the effects of our attempts to motivate actors to address broader social conditions beyond the direct jurisdiction of the police. In both cases, we would carefully consider whether experience suggested any modifications in our efforts, with a special eye to negative unanticipated consequences of our efforts.

Like it or not, this evaluative process *will* be extremely open. In addition to the police themselves, the individuals and institutions likely to comment on any significant anticrime effort include officials and those seeking office, ordinary citizens, organized public-interest groups of all stripes, police employee groups, and the courts. The earlier these potential critics have been invited into the process, the more likely it is that their criticisms will be constructive and informed. To the extent that they have been denied access to the process of formulating and evaluating strategies and tactics, their criticisms are likely to express their anger at having been left out of the process early on. More substantively, their criticisms will come from perspectives that, they will rightly point out, should have been considered early on. Hence, both to avoid Monday-morning quarterbacking and to enjoy the benefits of as many views as possible, it is best to invite as many people as possible to play on Sunday.

Management specialists describe such an operation as an *open system* that takes *inputs* (such as the crime problem), subjects them to a *process* (analysis,

FIGURE 11-2. Addressing Problems: An Open System Approach

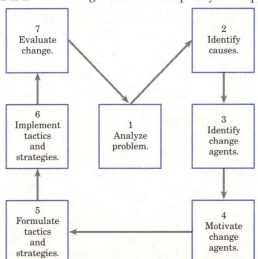

identification of causes and influential actors, formulation and implementation of strategies and tactics), evaluates *feedback,* and treats this feedback as input as the process continues with appropriate modifications. Figure 11-2 illustrates this graphically.

An Example. When citizens call to complain that strange cars are parked in front of their driveways, they usually are far more interested in having the cars removed than in seeing that they are ticketed. Thus, officers who respond to such apparently routine situations simply by ticketing cars and proceeding on their way do nothing to solve these complainants' problems except, perhaps, to deter future violations. On the other hand, officers who take the time to see that such vehicles are moved (and perhaps to issue tickets, as well) are far more responsive to the problems they have been asked to address. In such a routine case, the open system approach to solving problems would function thus:

1. *Analyze problem.* The complainant's problem, and the most immediate reason for the complainant's concern, is that he or she cannot get in or out of the driveway. This is not necessarily a law enforcement problem.
2. *Identify causes.* The most immediate cause is obvious: the car blocking the citizen's driveway. Also of considerable importance, however, is the question of what caused the car to wind up in front of the driveway. It may have been parked there intentionally; but it also may have been parked there by a stranger to the neighborhood who didn't notice the driveway. It may be disabled and may have been pushed to the curb by a driver who has gone for help. It may have been stolen and abandoned. In such a case, a parking ticket would serve only to anger both the complainant and the car owner. The quickest way to check these possibilities is to use the patrol car's radio or computer system to find out who owns the car and whether it has been stolen.
3. *Identify change agents.* Most often, this will turn out to be the car's owner, who can usually be located with a phone call or with knocks on a couple of nearby doors. In other cases, as when the car has been stolen or is disabled, the only person likely to solve the complainant's problem of being able to move in and out of the driveway may be a tow operator.
4. *Motivate change agents.* This usually is quite simple: "Mr. Jones, this is Officer Smith. Did you know that your car is parked in a driveway? Please get down here and move it immediately, or I will have it towed and it will take you hours and a lot of money and trouble to get it back." In cases of stolen, abandoned, or disabled cars, there may be no choice but to call tows immediately.
5. *Formulate tactics and strategies.*
6. *Implement tactics and strategies.* Much of steps 5 and 6 may depend on circumstances. If it is learned that the condition is a chronic one, in which neighbors routinely violate each other's access to driveways, enforcement action may be necessary to deter future violations. Is the driveway poorly marked or otherwise not readily identifiable as a driveway? If so, the complainant should be advised to correct this condition to avoid recurrence in the future.
7. *Evaluate change.* Listen to the police radio and cruise by the location from

Some officers do *good policing* instinctively; others may have much to learn from them.
Jill Freedman.

time to time to see whether the condition has recurred. If it has, more severe action (ticketing, towing) may be necessary to prevent return calls.

Problem-Oriented Policing: A Continuing Attempt to Define Good Police Work. In the above case, the officer's actions involved no mysterious new formula. Instead, they consisted only of what most veteran officers have regarded for years as good police work: finding a problem, analyzing it to determine how it could be alleviated, doing what had to be done to alleviate it, and checking later to see that the relief obtained was long-lasting. This simple process is what problem-oriented policing is all about. All veteran police officers can readily identify the best police officers among them, but, quite often, these same veteran officers are unable to describe with precision the characteristics of these good officers. Instead, one frequently hears comments to the effect that "Adams is a great cop because she has great *street sense*" (or *common sense*, or *judgment*, or *maturity*, or whatever). This knowledge may be very useful to Officer Adams's colleagues ("Oh, Adams? She's a terrific officer. You don't have to worry about anything when she's around"), but it does little to translate her skills into something that can be taught to other officers who may never have the opportunity to learn the skills by observing Adams at work.

In other words, problem-oriented policing is simply an attempt to formally articulate the principles and processes that veteran police officers have long recognized as the essence of high-quality policing. It puts into writing what we mean when we talk about good cops and good police work. This is important if we are to preserve and improve the quality of good police work, but it also is very difficult. Any casual observer could tell that Ted Williams was a great hitter, but students of baseball still try to determine precisely what he did to make him a better batter than anybody else who has played the game since his time. Much of Williams's success was due to innate ability, but, insofar as possible, the principles and processes he used to put his skills to best advantage have been handed down to thousands of other ballplayers. The result has been that hitting has become much more a science than an art and that the quality of the game at every level has improved. In much the same way, problem-oriented policing tries to change policing from an art that some fortunate few are *born* to do well to a science that many can be *taught* to do well. This can be accomplished only after the characteristics of good police officers and good police work have been isolated and translated into principles and processes that can be taught.

Opportunities for Improving Police Productivity

With current trends in public law enforcement shifting from traditional methods to some form of community- or problem-oriented policing, several opportunities to reshape police performance and productivity measurement present themselves. As previously indicated, several new measures of police performance and productivity are ever so slowly changing how police efforts and impacts are measured. Shifts away from the "bean counting" of calculating reported crimes, clearance rates, or arrests and toward the measurement of victimization and client satisfaction with police services are already occurring.

Moreover, problem-solving approaches are emphasizing the need to assess resolved or diminished problems as a central feature of a new police performance and productivity measurement system. Perhaps one of the most important potential shifts in measurement of police agency productivity and police officer performance is to examine the impact of police efforts on neighborhood crime and safety conditions. That is to say, there is considerable evidence, and agreement, that neighborhood circumstances conducive to crime and disorder are measurable and can be made objective. Research on community crime prevention has continually pointed to the idea of a *neighborhood context*: the presence of neighborhood cohesion and bonds, as well as street-level activities, which either discourage or promote criminal activity (Greene and McLaughlin, 1993; Rosenbaum, 1986; Sherman, 1986). Much of this research suggests that communities with social cohesion and information are better able to ward off crime and disorder than are disorganized and information-deprived communities. Such findings suggest that the police may play an important role in arming the community with information and strategies for its own self-protection, or that police may at least engage the community in what Skolnick and Bayley (1986) have called the "coproduction" of public safety services. If such community mobilization and crime prevention are possible, it is argued, the context of community life can be changed. This will, in turn, produce a change in the level of crime and disorder occurring within that community. By fixing the community's "broken windows," community viability can be increased, while crime and disorder can be decreased (Wilson and Kelling, 1982).

If such neighborhood contexts are measurable, they might provide an independent assessment of the impact of police services. For the police, this 395

CHAPTER *11*
Productivity and
Performance
Measurement

would require a shift from counting their individual and collective efforts to measuring the impact of those efforts in neighborhood settings. James Q. Wilson observes:

> The police ought to make the production of safer, more orderly neighborhoods (not lower crime rates or more drug arrests or more traffic tickets) one of their goals. They ought to design ways of assessing the conditions of neighborhoods before and after various police interventions. They ought to use that assessment to modify their deployments and tactics. (Wilson, 1993:161)

Shifting the focus of police productivity and performance measurement to the community and neighborhood level of analysis may lead to better assessment of how much and how well police are able to affect conditions leading to crime and disorder.

For several years, research has suggested that a community's fear of crime is influenced by many factors and that excessive community fear can undermine crime prevention efforts (Skogan, 1990). Early experiments have suggested that the police might indeed affect the level of community fear of crime through their physical presence and through problem-solving activities aimed at addressing the "signs of crime" that produce fear among community residents (Cordner, 1986; Pate et al., 1986). It has been argued that by opening storefront offices, providing neighborhood foot patrols, and actively engaging the community in crime prevention discussions and activities, the police can affect the level of community fear of crime as well as the social and physical context within which crime and neighborhood disorder flourish.

In addition to enabling community crime prevention by affecting the context of community life, which, in turn, either contributes to or discourages crime and disorder, police agencies pursuing community- or problem-oriented police strategies might strive for goals that emphasize "doing justice," "promoting secure communities," or "promoting noncriminal options," particularly for youth in crime-ridden communities (Alpert and Moore, 1993). By linking a broadly stated police department mission with such objectives, and by identifying alternative and current sources of productivity measurement, police departments in the future might radically alter their approach to productivity specification and measurement. Box 11-2 provides a glimpse of such measures as offered by Alpert and Moore.

CONCLUSION

This chapter has focused on the definition and measurement of police agency productivity and police officer performance. Productivity was defined as the relationship between resources and effects, and it involves the assessment of both the efficiency and the effectiveness of the police.

Police agency productivity has historically been assessed using such proxy measures as crime, arrest, and clearance rates, as well as measures of effort such as calls for service and the number of police officers per 1,000 residents. The historical use of these measures came about largely because of the difficulty in specifying police outcomes and impacts. The global and often sym-

BOX 11-2. Alpert and Moore's Framework for Police Performance Measurement

The mission of the police consists of many diverse activities, not objectives in themselves but which are directed toward the protection of life. Goals include doing justice, promoting secure communities, restoring crime victims, and promoting noncriminal options.

POLICE: GOALS, METHODS, AND PERFORMANCE INDICATORS

Goals
Doing justice. Treating citizens in an appropriate manner based upon their conduct.

Methods/activities
Balancing formal and informal social controls, responding to calls for service, patrolling tactics, issuing traffic tickets, conducting investigations, writing reports, making arrests, and assisting in criminal prosecutions.

Performance indicators
Nature and type of patrolling strategy, number of traffic tickets issued, known crimes that are cleared by audit or arrest, quality of reports, analysis of who calls the police, evaluation of policies emphasizing values over rules, time invested and quality of investigations, number of known crimes cleared by conviction, arrests and arrests cleared by conviction, cases released because of police misconduct, citizen complaints, lawsuits filed, and results of dispositions and officer-initiated encounters.

Goals
Promoting secure communities, enabling citizens to enjoy a life without fear of crime or victimization.

Methods/activities
Preventing/deterring criminal behavior and victimization, problem-solving initiatives, training for community differences, assisting citizens by reducing fear of crime and victimization.

Performance indicators
Programs and resources allocated to crime prevention programs, inter-governmental programs, resources, both time and dollars dedicated to problem-solving, rewards and monitoring of police, public trust and confidence in police performance, public attitudes toward police actions and public fear of crime, and home and business security checks.

Goals
Restoring crime victims, by restoring victims' lives and welfare as much as possible.

Methods/activities
Assisting crime victims to understand the criminal justice system, assisting crime victims with their difficulties created by the victimization, assisting crime victims to put their lives back together.

Performance indicators
Number of contacts with victims after initial call for assistance, types of assistance provided to victims, including information, comfort, transportation, and referrals to other agencies.

Goals
Promoting noncriminal options, by developing strong relationships with individuals in the community.

Methods/activities
Develop and assist with programs that strengthen relationships between police and members of the community and among community members, increase human and social capital in the community and linkages with private industry.

Performance indicators
Programs and resources allocated to strengthening relationships between police and the community and among community members, including traditional community relations programs, school programs and resources spent to meet with the public in a positive alliance. Innovative programs to develop a sense of community, organizational measures of decentralization, community storefront operations and officer contacts with citizens for positive relations and feedback on performance are aspects of developing strong relationships with members of the community.

Source: Alpert and Moore, 1993, p. 134.

bolic nature of police agencies' goals and objectives has complicated the measurement of police agency performance. Moreover, the public safety impact made by other municipal agencies has also been difficult to separate from the impact made by the police alone.

Police performance measurement has typically focused on tasks performed and on traits; until recently there was little focus on the behaviors of the police themselves. Current police performance measurement has sought to increase the behavioral content of such assessments.

Most recently, the advent of problem- and community-oriented policing has led to a slow but steady shift in philosophies and methods used in measuring what the police do and how effective police agencies are. Solving problems, influencing the social and physical context of community life, and activating the community to defend and preserve itself and to enhance its quality of life are now seen as ways of increasing police effectiveness. Opportunities for restructuring police productivity and performance measurement systems to make them more consistent with the emerging philosophies and practices of problem solving and community policing will require a rethinking of the missions, goals, and objectives of the police, as well as the design of measures that better capture the efforts and effects of law enforcement and public safety activities.

QUESTIONS FOR DISCUSSION

1. Define police productivity. How do the concepts of efficiency and effectiveness relate to the idea of productivity?
2. Why is it so difficult for the police to specify measures of police agency effectiveness? What are the implications of this specification for measuring police productivity?
3. What are the traditional and evolving measures of police productivity and performance, and what are their strengths and limitations? What are the bases for police job analysis, and how do they relate to performance appraisal?
4. How, and in what ways, have the philosophies and practices of community- and problem-oriented policing affected ideas about police performance and productivity?
5. What is good police work? How might police agencies measure good police work as part of a performance appraisal and performance measurement system?

NOTES

1. The "crime clock" was introduced by the FBI as a means of describing national crime statistics. The crime clock divided the total number of reported crimes in any category by 24 hours. The result would be statements to the effect that a robbery occurs every 12 minutes; an auto theft, each 8 minutes; an assault, every 75 minutes. This approach has many obvious failures, the most serious of which is its suggestion that crime occurs with equal frequency everywhere. Some have argued that the crime-clock approach was a police-generated scare tactic to increase police budgets (see Clark, 1970).

2. This list is adapted from Hatry (1975:87).

3. The abstract mission statements and mottos of the police are not the only examples of this phenomenon. Consider the difficulty of basing productivity measurement on such emotion-inspiring missions mottos as a local board of education's commitment to *Teaching Today for Tomorrow's Challenges* or the U.S. Marines' promise—*Semper Fideles*—to be always faithful.

4. For a review of this literature, see Mastrofski and Wadman (1991).

5. For a review of job-analytic techniques, see Schneider and Greene (1982).

6. Perhaps the most notable of these cases, involving the issue of the job-relatedness of screening for employment, is *Griggs v. Duke Power Company* (1972), in which the U.S. Supreme Court held:

> Congress has not commanded that the less qualified be preferred over the better qualified simply because of minority origins. Far from disparaging job qualifications as such, Congress has made such qualifications the controlling factor so that race, religion, nationality, and sex become irrelevant. *What Congress has commanded is that any test used must measure the person in the job and not the person in the abstract.* (emphasis added)

7. The Index, or Part I, crimes include murder/nonnegligent manslaughter, forcible rape and sodomy, aggravated assault, robbery, burglary, vehicle larceny, other forms of larceny, and arson.

8. This is due to the fact that police departments typically produce clearance rates annually, meaning that they are concerned about the relationships of arrests to crimes for any given year. Since court cases, particularly those of any magnitude, can take a long time to resolve, there is no way to adjust police clearance rate calculations to account for arrests not resulting in a criminal conviction. While some might argue that convictions are not a police responsibility, the use of arrests as an indication that a crime has been "solved" is therefore tenuous.

9. In the course of conducting research on police arrest statistics, colleagues of one of the authors encountered a police department that reported an annual crime clearance rate of more than 99 percent. Investigation of this extraordinary batting average determined that it had been derived by classifying traffic and parking offenses (all of which had been cleared with the issuance of tickets) in with other, more traditional, *criminal* offenses.

10. For a review of many of the dominant studies of police workload, see Cordner (1979).

11. For discussions of this more generalized approach to assessing police and community relations, as well as the pitfalls in such assessments, see Alpert and Moore (1993), Bayley (1993), and Bennett (1993).

12. This is not a suggestion that police officials should become official bleeding hearts. As long ago as 1936, O. W. Wilson's mentor, police pioneer August Vollmer, demonstrated that police chiefs could deplore and demand change in the social conditions that create crime without making themselves vulnerable to charges that they were surrendering to it. Vollmer's subject, "the juvenile transient movement," was memorialized by Woodie Guthrie and other songwriters of the period. More popularly known as "hoboing" or "riding the rails," this movement consisted of young men who jumped freight trains from place to place in search of work:

> This movement, which is in almost startling contrast to the splendid government-supervised youth hostels in Europe, is a matter of grave concern in the United States. According to rough estimates, 1,500,000 youths are wandering

about this country. They pass from one state to another, at first oftentimes honestly seeking work and with full desire and intent to lead an upright life. They meet other young men in circumstances similar to their own, and soon, especially when they are unable to find employment, they become discouraged and hopeless because of their economic position, and finally resort to any means of supplying their wants. Once having succeeded in wrongdoing and in escaping unpunished, they continue their criminal activities until apprehended or killed.

Meanwhile, however, the society that has permitted the development of a state of affairs that is directly contributory to antisocial living cheerfully lays the resulting serious problems, along with traffic, vices, strikes, riots—anything and everything—upon the broad doorstep of the police. The spirit in which society makes this gesture is by no means one of cooperation; it is a spirit of carping criticism that is to be reckoned among the handicaps imposed upon the police. (Vollmer, 1936:5)

Vollmer's fiery but humane and socially alert criticism shows little evidence of compromise with crime, the conditions that he believed cause it, or the public apathy that he believed responsible for those conditions.

SOURCES

ALPERT, GEOFFREY, and ROGER DUNHAM. *Political Multi-Ethnic Neighborhoods* (New York: Greenwood Press, 1988).

———, and MARK H. MOORE. "Measuring Police Performance in the New Paradigm of Policing," pp. 109–140 in U.S. Department of Justice, Bureau of Justice Statistics, *Performance Measures for the Criminal Justice System* (Washington, D.C.: U.S. Government Printing Office, 1993).

American Bar Association Project on Standards for Criminal Justice. *Standards Relating to the Urban Police Function* (New York: American Bar Association, 1973).

BAYLEY, DAVID H. "Back From Wonderland, or Toward the Rational Use of Police Resources," pp. 1–34 in Anthony N. Doob (ed.), *Thinking about Police Resources* (Toronto: University of Toronto, Centre for Criminology, 1993).

———, and EGON BITTNER. "Learning the Skills of Policing," *Law and Contemporary Problems*, 47:35–59 (1984).

BENNETT, TREVOR. "Community Policing in Britain," pp. 127–144 in Dieter Dolling and Thomas Feltes (eds.), *Community Policing—Comparative Aspects of Community Oriented Police Work* (Holzkirchen/Obb., Germany: Felix-Verlag, 1993).

BITTNER, EGON. *Aspects of Police Work* (Boston: Northeastern University Press, 1990).

———. "Legality and Workmanship: Introduction to Control in the Police Organization," pp. 1–11 in Maurice Punch (ed.), *Control in the Police Organization* (Cambridge, Mass.: M.I.T. Press, 1983).

BLACK, DONALD I. "Production of Crime Rates," *American Sociological Review*, 35:735–739 (1970).

———. "The Mobilization of Law," *Journal of Legal Studies*, 2:125 (1973).

BROWN, MICHAEL K. *Working the Street* (New York: Russell Sage Foundation, 1981).

CLARK, RAMSEY. *Crime in America* (New York: Simon & Schuster, 1970).

CORDNER, GARY W. "Fear of Crime and the Police: An Evaluation of a Fear-Reduction Strategy," *Journal of Police Science and Administration*, 14:222–223 (1986).

———. "Police Patrol Work Load Studies: A Review and Critique," *Police Studies*, 2:50–60 (1979).

CORDNER, GARY W. *The Baltimore County Citizen Oriented Police Enforcement (COPE) Project, Final Report* (New York: Florence V. Burden Foundation, 1985).

ECK, JOHN E. *Solving Crime: The Investigation of Burglary and Robbery* (Washington, D.C.: Police Executive Research Forum, 1982).

———. *Using Research: A Primer for Law Enforcement Managers* (Washington, D.C.: Police Executive Research Forum, 1984).

EDELMAN, MURRAY. *The Symbolic Uses of Politics* (Urbana: University of Illinois Press, 1964).

———. *Political Language: Words That Succeed and Policies That Fail* (New York: Academic Press, 1977).

ERICKSON, RICHARD V. *Making Crime: A Study of Detective Work* (Toronto: Butterworths, 1981).

FYFE, JAMES J. "Good Policing," pp. 269–290 in Brian Forst (ed.), *The Socioeconomics of Crime and Justice* (Armonk, N.Y.: Sharpe, 1993).

———. "The Split-Second Syndrome and Other Determinants of Police Violence," pp. 207–225 in Anne T. Campbell and John J. Gibbs (eds.), *Violent Transactions* (Oxford: Basil Blackwell, 1986).

GOLDSTEIN, HERMAN. "Improving Policing: A Problem Oriented Approach," *Crime and Delinquency,* 25:236 (April 1979).

———. *Policing a Free Society* (Cambridge, Mass.: Ballinger, 1977).

———. *Problem-Oriented Policing* (New York: McGraw-Hill, 1990).

GREENE, JACK R., GEOFFREY ALPERT, and PAUL STYLES. "Values and Culture in Two American Police Departments: Lessons from King Arthur," *Journal of Contemporary Criminal Justice,* 8:183–207 (1992).

———, GARY W. CORDNER, and TIM S. BYNUM. "Planning and the Play of Power: Resource Acquisition and Use among Criminal Justice Agencies," *Journal of Criminal Justice,* 14:529–544 (1986).

———, and CARL B. KLOCKARS. "What Police Do," pp. 273–285 in Carl B. Klockars and Stephen D. Mastrofski (eds.), *Thinking about Police,* 2d ed. (New York: McGraw-Hill, 1991).

———, and EDWARD D. MCLAUGHLIN. "Facilities for Communities through Police Work: Drug Problem Solving and Neighborhood Involvement in Philadelphia," pp. 141–161 in Robert C. Davis, Arthur J. Lurigio, and Dennis Rosenbaum (eds.), *Drugs and the Community* (Springfield, Ill.: Thomas, 1993).

Griggs v. Duke Power Company, 401 U.S. 424 (1972).

HATRY, HARRY P. "Wrestling with Police Crime Control Productivity Measurement," pp. 86–128 in Joan L. Wolfle and John F. Heaphy (eds.), *Readings on Police Productivity* (Washington, D.C.: Police Foundation, 1975).

KELLING, GEORGE L. "Measuring What Matters: A New Way about Thinking about Crime and Public Order," *City Journal,* 21–34 (Spring 1992).

KLOCKARS, CARL B. *The Idea of Police* (Beverly Hills, Calif.: Sage, 1985).

KUPER, GEORGE H. "Productivity: A National Concern," pp. 1–10 in Joan L. Wolfle and John F. Heaphy (eds.), *Readings on Police Productivity* (Washington, D.C.: Police Foundation, 1975).

MANNING, PETER K. *Police Work: The Social Organization of Policing* (Cambridge, Mass.: M.I.T. Press, 1977).

MASTROFSKI, STEPHEN D., and ROBERT D. WADMAN. "Personnel and Agency Performance Measurement," pp. 363–397 in William A. Geller (ed.), *Local Government Police Management,* 3d ed. (Washington, D.C.: International City Management Association, 1991).

MURPHY, PATRICK V. "Police Accountability," pp. 35–46 in Joan L. Wolfle and John F. Heaphy (eds.), *Readings on Police Productivity* (Washington, D.C.: Police Foundation, 1975).

National Advisory Commission on Civil Disorders. *Report of the National Advisory Commission on Civil Disorders* (New York: Dutton, 1968).

National Advisory Commission on Criminal Justice Standards and Goals. *Police* (Washington, D.C.: U.S. Government Printing Office, 1976).

O'BRIAN, ROBERT M. *Crime and Victimization Data* (Beverly Hills, Calif.: Sage, 1985).

OSBORNE, DAVID, and TED GAEBLER. *Reinventing Government* (New York: Plume, 1993).

PATE, ANTONY, WESLEY SKOGAN, MARY ANN WYCOFF, and LAWRENCE W. SHERMAN. *Reducing the Signs of Crime: The Newark Experience* (Washington, D.C.: Police Foundation, 1985).

PATE, ANTONY M., MARY ANN WYCOFF, WESLEY G. SKOGAN, and LAWRENCE W. SHERMAN. *Reducing Fear of Crime in Houston and Newark: A Summary Report* (Washington, D.C.: Police Foundation, 1986).

PETERSON, GEORGE E. "Urban Policy and the Cyclic Behavior of Cities," in George E. Peterson and Carol W. Lewis (eds.), *Reagan and the Cities* (Washington, D.C.: Urban Institute, 1986).

Police Foundation. *The Newark Foot Patrol Experiment* (Washington, D.C.: Police Foundation, 1981).

President's Commission on Law Enforcement and Administration of Justice. *Task Force Report: The Police* (Washington, D.C.: U.S. Government Printing Office, 1967a).

————. *The Challenge of Crime in a Free Society* (Washington, D.C.: U.S. Government Printing Office, 1967b).

REISS, ALBERT J., JR., *The Police and the Public* (New Haven, Conn.: Yale University Press, 1971).

REUSS-IANNI, ELIZABETH. *Two Cultures of Policing: Street Cops and Management Cops* (New Brunswick, N.J.: Transaction Books, 1983).

ROSENBAUM, DENNIS (ed.). *Community Crime Prevention: Does It Work?* (Newbury Park, Calif.: Sage, 1986).

SCHNEIDER, VICKI W., and JACK R. GREENE. *A Handbook for Human Resource Planning in Criminal Justice Agencies*, vol. III: *Human Resource Planning Guide: Part 2* (East Lansing, Mich.: Michigan State University, School of Criminal Justice, 1982).

SHERMAN, LAWRENCE W. "Policing Communities: What Works?" pp. 343–386 in Albert J. Reiss, Jr., and Michael Tonry (eds.), *Communities and Crime* (Chicago: University of Chicago Press, 1986).

SKOGAN, WESLEY G. *Disorder and Decline: Crime and the Spiral of Decay in American Neighborhoods* (New York: Free Press, 1990).

SKOLNICK, JEROME H. *Justice without Trial: Law Enforcement in a Democratic Society* (New York: Wiley, 1966).

————, and DAVID H. BAYLEY. *The New Blue Line* (New York: Free Press, 1986).

SPELMAN, WILLIAM A. *Beyond Bean Counting: New Approaches to Managing Crime Data* (Washington, D.C.: Police Executive Research Forum, 1988).

U.S. Department of Justice, Bureau of Justice Statistics. *Crime and the Nation's Households, 1991* (Washington, D.C.: U.S. Government Printing Office, 1992).

U.S. Department of Justice, Community Relations Service. *Principles of Good Policing: Avoiding Violence between Police and Citizens* (Washington, D.C.: U.S. Government Printing Office, 1987).

VOLLMER, AUGUST. *The Police and Modern Society* (Montclair, N.J.: Patterson Smith, 1972 reprint of original 1936 manuscript).

WHITAKER, GORDON P. *Basic Issues in Police Performance* (Washington, D.C.: U.S. Government Printing Office, 1982).

WILSON, JAMES Q. "The Problems of Defining Agency Success," in *Performance Measures for the Criminal Justice System* (Washington, D.C.: U.S. Department of Justice, 1993).

————, and GEORGE L. KELLING. "Broken Windows": The Police and Neighborhood Safety," *Atlantic Monthly* (March 1982), pp. 29–38.

WYCOFF, MARY ANN, WESLEY SKOGAN, ANTONY PATE, and LAWRENCE W. SHERMAN. *Police as Community Organizers: Executive Summary* (Washington, D.C.: Police Foundation, 1985).

APPENDIX 11-1
VICTIMIZATION SURVEY,
TAMPA POLICE DEPARTMENT
Public Housing Community Survey
City Police Department
Month, [year]

"Hello, my name is _____. I'm with the city police department and we're working on a study of neighborhood problems and crime here in your neighborhood. Our goal is to improve the quality of life in this area. Are you the head of the household? (OR May I speak with the head of the household?)

"We're interested in your opinions about what can be done to help improve living conditions here. We sent you a letter that described the study and mentioned how important your participation is to the study. Did you receive that letter?"

If no, give respondent a copy of the letter and time to read.

"Participation in the study is completely voluntary. All of your answers will be kept secret. Our study will in no way identify you or your household. Your address was selected at random to give us feedback about your neighborhood."

If possible, interview the head of the household. If not available, interview another adult living at the address. If inconvenient, schedule an appointment and record the date for follow-up.

Address _____
Date of first visit _____
Time of first visit _____
Date of appointment _____
Time of appointment _____

Record the following from visual information if interview proceeds. Clarify verbally if necessary.

Head of household? $\Box^0$ No
                    $\Box^1$ Yes
Sex of respondent? $\Box^0$ Male
                    $\Box^1$ Female
Race of respondent? $\Box^0$ Black
                    $\Box^1$ White
                    $\Box^2$ Hispanic
                    $\Box^3$ Other

Section III. Exposure to Crime

"These next few questions will be about things that have happened to you or members of this household in the last year in your community. We're not interested in crimes that were committed outside your neighborhood. Now I'd like you to think back to June of last year, about a year ago."

18. "Since June of last year, has anyone damaged or defaced the building where you live in this community, for example, by writing on the walls, breaking windows, setting fires or anything like that?"

☐⁰   No
☐¹   Yes—"How many times did this happen?" _____
☐²   Don't know
☐³   Refused to answer
    Missing

19. "Since June of last year, has anyone broken into or somehow illegally gotten into your home?"

   ☐⁰   No
   ☐¹   Yes—"How many times did this happen?" _____
   ☐²   Don't know
   ☐³   Refused to answer

20. "Since June of last year, has anyone stolen anything from you or someone in your household in your neighborhood? Something like a bicycle, clothing, tools, money, a purse or wallet?"

   ☐⁰   No
   ☐¹   Yes—"How many times did this happen?" _____
   ☐²   Don't know
   ☐³   Refused to answer

21. "Since June of last year in your neighborhood, has anyone taken money or other belongings from you or from other members of your household by force? For example, did someone use a gun or knife, or in any other way force one of you to give them something that did not belong to them?"

   ☐⁰   No
   ☐¹   Yes—"How many times did this happen?" _____
   ☐²   Don't know
   ☐³   Refused to answer

22. "Since June of last year, has anyone used violence against you or members of your household in an argument or quarrel, or in any other way attacked or assaulted one of you in your neighborhood?"

   ☐⁰   No
   ☐¹   Yes—"How many times did this happen?" _____
   ☐²   Don't know
   ☐³   Refused to answer

23. "Since June of last year in your neighborhood, has anyone tried to sell you or members of your family drugs?"

   ☐⁰   No
   ☐¹   Yes—"How many times did this happen?" _____
   ☐²   Don't know
   ☐³   Refused to answer
       Missing

24. "Since June of last year in your neighborhood, has anyone tried to get you or members of your family to help them sell drugs?"

   ☐⁰   No
   ☐¹   Yes—"How many times did this happen?" _____
   ☐²   Don't know
   ☐³   Refused to answer
       Missing

If respondent was not a victim of any crime, skip to question 28.

25. "We've talked about several crimes. Let me ask you a few questions about the most recent of these incidents. Which of these crimes happened most recently?"

(What)	(When)

- □⁰ Don't know
- □¹ Refused to answer

26. "Were the police informed or did they find out about this crime in any way?"

- □⁰ No, the police were not informed
- □¹ Yes, the police were informed (*skip to question 28*)
- □² Don't know
- □³ Refused to answer

27. "What was the reason this incident was not reported to the police? Was it because you felt there was no need to call, didn't think the police could do anything, didn't think the police would do anything, or was there some other reason?"

- □⁰ No need to call the police (Property recovered, unimportant matter, private or personal matter)
- □¹ Police couldn't do anything (No proof, no way to identify offender, difficult to recover property, unwilling to press charges)
- □² Police wouldn't do anything (Police wouldn't want to be bothered, or would think unimportant; police would be ineffective, inefficient or insensitive)
- □³ Fear of retaliation from offender
- □⁴ Any other reason _____
- □⁵ Don't know
- □⁶ Refused to answer

28. "Suppose your apartment were broken into while you weren't at home. If your neighbors saw the burglar break in, what do you think they would do?" (*Do not read list; mark all that apply.*)

- □⁰ They would call the police
- □¹ They would call someone else (*record who*) _____
- □² They would try to stop the crime themselves
- □³ They would watch the crime and investigate
- □⁴ They wouldn't know what to do
- □⁵ They would ignore it
- □⁶ Other (*record answer*) _____
- □⁷ Don't know
- □⁸ Refused to answer
    Missing

29. "Suppose you were robbed or assaulted somewhere on the street in your neighborhood. If your neighbors saw the attack, what do you think they would do?"

- □⁰ They would call the police
- □¹ They would call someone else (*record who*) _____
- □² They would try to stop the crime themselves
- □³ They would watch the crime and investigate
- □⁴ They wouldn't know what to do
- □⁵ They would ignore it
- □⁶ Other (*record answer*) _____
- □⁷ Don't know

$\square^8$ Refused to answer

405

CHAPTER *11*
Productivity and
Performance
Measurement

30. "In the last year have you done any of the following to avoid trouble or protect yourself against crime in this neighborhood? Have you . . . ?" (*Read the list and check all that apply.*)

    $\square^0$ Avoided taking the bus
    $\square^1$ Stayed in your home in the evening and night
    $\square^2$ Arranged to have someone go with you in the neighborhood
    $\square^3$ Had a neighbor pick up your mail while you were away
    $\square^4$ Had a neighbor watch your home while you were away
    $\square^5$ Engraved identification on your valuables
    $\square^6$ Bought additional insurance
    $\square^7$ Secured your home by adding locks, nailing windows shut or putting timers on lights
    $\square^8$ Kept a dog
    $\square^9$ Kept a gun or weapon in your home
    $\square^{10}$ Taken a course in self defense
    $\square^{11}$ Joined a neighborhood Crime Watch
    $\square^{12}$ Done something else to avoid crime or protect yourself against crime in your neighborhood (*ask what?*) _____

    _____

31. "Is there anywhere in your neighborhood that you avoid because of crime problems or other trouble?"

    $\square^0$ No
    $\square^1$ Yes—*Ask Where?*
    $\square^2$ Don't know
    $\square^3$ Refused to answer

If respondent answers "no," skip to Question 34.

32. "Do you avoid this area during the day?"

    $\square^0$ No
    $\square^1$ Yes
    $\square^2$ Don't know
    $\square^3$ Refused to answer

33. "What about at night?"

    $\square^0$ No
    $\square^1$ Yes
    $\square^2$ Don't know
    $\square^3$ Refused to answer

"In every neighborhood, there are some people who cause trouble for the other residents. They may have loud parties, leave trash around the area, bother people as they walk down the street, or even commit crimes such as selling drugs. I'd like to ask you a few questions about the people who make trouble in this neighborhood. We don't need to know their names but we would like to know a little about them."

34. "In your estimate, do most of the people who cause trouble in your neighborhood live in these apartments, or do most of them live elsewhere?"

    $\square^0$ Most live in this neighborhood

□¹   Most live somewhere else (*Go to Question 36.*)
□²   There are no troublemakers (*Go to Question 39.*)
□³   Don't know where they live (*Go to Question 39.*)
□⁴   Refused to answer (*Go to Question 39.*)

35. "Is there any particular part of this neighborhood where these troublemakers live?"

□⁰   No, they live all over.
□¹   Yes—*Ask where?* _____
□²   Don't know where they live
□³   Refused to answer

36. "Is there any other particular place—say one particular apartment complex or housing development where these troublemakers come from?"

□⁰   No, they live all over.
□¹   Yes—*Ask where?* _____
□²   Don't know where they live
□³   Refused to answer

37. "We're interested in knowing how old these troublemakers are. Are they mostly . . . (*Read list 0–3*)?"

□⁰   Under 14 years of age,
□¹   between 14 and 17 years old,
□²   between 18 and 24 years old,
□³   or older than 25?
□⁴   Don't know
□⁵   Refused to answer

38. "Is there a regular place in this neighborhood where these people tend to 'hang out'?"

□⁰   No, there's no regular place
□¹   Yes—*Ask where?* _____
□²   Don't know
□³   Refused to answer

39. "How visible do you feel that drug dealing and other crimes are in this neighborhood?"

□⁰   Very visible
□¹   Somewhat visible
□²   Hidden from the view of most people
□³   Don't know
□⁴   Refused to answer
       Missing

40. "Do you know of anyone in this neighborhood who has been bullied into having their apartment used for selling drugs?"

□⁰   No
□¹   Yes (*Ask to describe situation*)

_____

_____

□³   Don't know
□⁴   Refused to answer
       Missing

41. "Are you usually at home during the daytime hours?"

  - □⁰ No
  - □¹ Yes
  - □² Don't know
  - □³ Refused to answer

42. "Are you usually at home during the evening hours (6 P.M. to later)?"

  - □⁰ No
  - □¹ Yes
  - □² Don't know
  - □³ Refused to answer

43. "Do you have a telephone?"

  - □⁰ No
  - □¹ Yes
  - □² Refused to answer

Source: Victimization Survey. Tampa Police Department. Used by permission.

12

Discipline

KEY WORDS AND PHRASES

Training and socialization
Informal culture
Street cops
Management cops
Reward system
Transfers

Morale
Malfeasance
Misfeasance
Nonfeasance
Rulebook expansion
Grapevine

Discipline is a state in which an organization's members behave in ways that best serve its goals and purposes. If police discipline is to be more than adherence to empty bureaucratic motives and personal agendas, therefore, it is first necessary to carefully define organizational goals and to assure that they are in accord with the public interest. The movement to *value-driven policing* described in Chapter 7 is precisely such an effort, as are *management by objectives, problem-oriented policing,* and similar attempts to see that police personnel pull together to achieve desirable and clearly articulated purposes.

DISCIPLINE AND PUNISHMENT

Although we tend to think of discipline in punitive terms, there is a very important distinction between the words "discipline" and "punishment." Punishment is an extreme *disciplinary* action, a *negative* form of achieving discipline that should be employed only when other, more *positive* measures have failed to keep employees' conduct within acceptable bounds. Again, keep in mind this definition:

Discipline is a state in which an organization's members behave in ways that best serve its goals and purposes.

Clearly, all police organizations do more than punish in their attempts to achieve this state. As should be equally clear, discipline is not the exclusive responsibility of inspections and internal affairs units, review boards, and other department units established specifically to detect, investigate, and adjudicate violations of laws, policies, and rules (these are discussed extensively in Chapter 14). Instead, discipline is a responsibility that permeates a police department, that is shared by everyone in it, and that results from several nonpunitive processes that often are not included in lists of disciplinary activities. These include:

Recruitment and selection

Training and socialization

Supervision and policy formulation

Reward and incentive systems

Punishment fits at the end of this list and should come into play when none of these more positive disciplinary functions has produced the desired results.

POSITIVE DISCIPLINE

As Chapter 9 has demonstrated, there are many arguments about what the entry requirements for new police officers and civilian personnel should be. No matter where one stands on these issues, however, one point is clear: Since it is extremely difficult to instill in new employees an organization's commitments to excellence, integrity, and service during a short entry-level training period, police agencies must ensure that the people they hire share these values *before* they are added to the official payroll. Careful examination of candidates' backgrounds and character should be the keystone of police recruitment efforts.

Training and Socialization as Discipline

The evidence is by now clear that the operative definitions of "good policing" that most affect police performance and discipline come, either directly or by default, straight from the top of the police agency. When a department's top management plays a leadership role and inculcates in the agency a strong sense of commitment to clear values—*good or bad*—its efforts will be reflected directly in the performance and discipline of line officers. When a department's mission is ambiguous and/or when its administration is weak, out of touch, or invisible, officers will do as they please, with disastrous results for discipline. Indeed, the existence of what Reuss-Ianni (1983) calls two competing cultures of "management cops" and "street cops" is a direct result of the remoteness of management from those involved in the direct delivery of police services.[1]

At no point is the influence of top management more important in shaping discipline than at the very beginning of an officer's career. The chief executive should play an important symbolic role at this point, officiating at ceremonies and serving as a very visible sign of line officers' connection and accountability to the top of their agency.

In addition, by ensuring that training is realistic and that it adequately addresses the problem areas of policing—problems such as brutality, corruption, insensitivity, and malingering—the chief executive should play a substantive role in new officers' lives. Perhaps the most frequent complaint about entry-level police training is that it does not adequately reflect or prepare officers for the realities of police work on the streets.[2] Among those realities, unfortunately, are the temptations toward wrongdoing and the possibility that new officers will be exposed to it on the part of their colleagues. If, like parents reluctant to discuss the facts of life with their children, top police administrators do not make certain that new officers are prepared to deal with these issues—or if administrators adhere to the discredited theory that "discussing details of corruption might teach some recruits tricks they don't know" (Knapp et al., 1972:239)—trouble is certain. The fact is that, to some extent, brutality, corruption, insensitivity, and malingering have occurred in every large U.S. police agency and in many small ones as well. Further, even if they have not yet occurred, these breaches of discipline are a danger in police agencies of all sizes. To pretend otherwise and to trust that officers will have the common sense to do the right thing when confronted with them is too great a danger for administrators to tolerate.

All large police agencies should use their own experiences and disciplinary files as a basis for developing case-based training that illustrates both routine and extremely serious disciplinary problems, the consequences of engaging in wrongful conduct, and the appropriate responses to other officers' participation in such conduct. It is very easy to overlook the need for such training, but examples drawn from two of our largest police departments show precisely how important it is.

The early 1970s Knapp Commission investigation in New York demonstrated rather clearly that the city's police department did not adequately prepare officers to deal with corruption. The commission noted in its report that, rather than treating the need to avoid corrupt acts as a theme that ran through all substantive police training, the department had compartmentalized it into a single session that, according to the testimony of two young officers who had been caught accepting bribes, was "unrealistic, even comical." The commission stated that:

> Corruption used to be one of several matters treated by the chaplain in the course of his six hours of Academy lectures. Copies of the Policemen's Code of Ethics were also distributed. During regular instruction on the Penal Law the bribery statutes were covered, but corruption was traditionally regarded as a matter of individual conscience and not in any large sense as an environmental or departmental problem. Moreover, the realities of the extent of corruption and the specific corruption hazards to be faced by new patrolmen were avoided on the ostensible theory that they should not be taught how to go wrong. (Knapp et al., 1972:239)

More recently, the Christopher Commission's report of the Los Angeles Police Department, issued in the wake of the Rodney King incident, suggested

The best police departments recognize that positive discipline begins with training and socialization that encourage voluntary compliance with agency rules, and that minimize the need for negative discipline.
Bob Daemmrich/Image Works.

that LAPD training not only did not teach officers how to avoid misconduct but actually encouraged an overly aggressive style of dealing with citizens, particularly minorities. Noting that probationers' performance is most greatly affected by the lessons taught by their field training officers (FTOs), the commission wrote:

> The high levels of fear and anxiety exhibited by FTOs color the training provided to probationers. The probationers' world quickly is divided by their FTOs into "we/they" categories. One FTO stated that he routinely draws his gun whenever he approaches "suspicious" people, even though LAPD policy states that a gun should not be drawn unless the officer anticipates an imminent need to use deadly force. This officer further stated that he also encourages his probationers to draw their guns if they feel "uneasy" about citizens encountered in the field. Other FTOs noted that they routinely search or handcuff citizens, even absent reasonable suspicion of criminal activity or danger, in order to increase their own "comfort" level. These FTOs stated that they encourage their probationers to follow the same rule of "search or handcuff first, talk later."
>
> The "we/they" mentality is exacerbated by the failure to integrate cultural awareness or sensitivity training into field training. Few of the FTOs devote any attention to teaching probationers how to interact effectively and respectfully with minorities. Instead, probationers are often exposed to the derogatory comments, slurs and jokes that many officers have attempted to characterize as "locker-room" banter or good-natured fun. The FTO interviews

provide evidence that this problem is particularly acute with reference to gay men and lesbians. (Christopher et al., 1991:131)

In both these instances, as well as in others, blue-ribbon committees found that training deficiencies lay at the heart of disciplinary problems that led to major scandals (see also DiUlio et al., 1991; Kolts et al., 1992; Miami, 1984; St. Clair et al., 1992). These committees and other authorities also have offered several suggestions to strengthen training in ways that best serve departmental discipline and good order. Although training has been described in greater detail in Chapter 9, the training-related observations most germane to the maintenance of departmental discipline and prevention of misconduct include the following:

- All training must have clearly articulated behavioral objectives. *Every* lesson, lecture, reading assignment, and exercise should be designed to affect the trainees' conduct in specific ways.
- Training must go beyond prescribing specific skills. It must also explain the reasoning behind procedures and must reinforce the agency's values.
- Training must deal realistically with the temptations toward misconduct and the appropriate course of action when misconduct is observed among subordinates, supervisors, or colleagues.
- Training must sensitize officers to the significance of gender, racial, ethnic, cultural, and sexual preference differences among the public and their colleagues.
- Training cannot end at the recruit academy. It must be a continuing part of the development and career of all employees, and it should be designed specifically to aid each employee in fulfilling the duties of his or her individual assignment.
- Mistakes and unanticipated events should be used as learning devices. Every critical incident (e.g., police shooting, use of force, vehicle pursuit, injury to officer, disciplinary, criminal, or civil action against an employee) should be carefully reviewed with an eye to identifying and addressing its training implications (see Box 12-1).

Reward Systems as Discipline

It is hard to conceive of many institutions that have stronger informal cultures than policing. Several ties bind police officers together in this culture. Because they work strange hours, officers tend to become isolated from much of the public, from old friends, and even from their families. Much of their work and many of its frustrations and rewards are hard to explain to outsiders, and consist of experiences most easily shared with colleagues. By nature, police work is dangerous and unpredictable, characteristics that—especially in the busiest departments and most hazardous assignments—encourage great mutual loyalty among officers. In most police agencies, supervisors and administrators are people who have worked their way up from the lowest organizational rung. Consequently, they typically have great experience and identification with the work of all the people they supervise. To a much greater extent than is true of executives in organizations in which upward mobility is limited, top police administrators usually have a shared history and many relationships

BOX 12-1. Training Responses to Disciplinary Problems

The New York City Police Department's training responses to the Knapp Commission's revelations of corruption are a good example of training designed to address identified disciplinary problems. According to the Knapp Commission:

The new recruit program includes twenty hours of discussions and lectures that range through all known forms of police crime and corruption. These twenty hours are spread over the total days of recruit training. The old theory that discussing details of corruption might teach some recruits tricks they didn't know has been abandoned in favor of a more realistic approach. Extensive use is made of workshop and group discussion techniques. Role-playing is used to increase the impact and believability of the conditions to which the new recruit will soon be exposed. . . .

Academy training of superior officers. Sergeants: The Academy's training for officers being promoted to the rank of sergeant does not spare their feelings, and it is no longer presumed that they are "clean" simply because they are being promoted. They are taught that they must make arrests for corrupt acts which other persons (including themselves) may have committed with impunity even a short time ago.

The pre-promotional training for patrolmen who are about to make sergeant has been extended from six weeks a year ago and as few as three weeks some years back to a present total of seven weeks. The training course is entitled "Basic Management Orientation" and is meant to develop management and leadership skills as well as imparting supervisory techniques. The course now also contains thirty-four-and-a-half hours of anti-corruption training. It includes field work, actual duty with the Inspections Division, training in all areas of anti-corruption activities and many hours of guidance sessions in small groups aimed at discussing and resolving on a mutual basis problems and problem situations that have and will confront these men as they progress through their careers.

Lieutenants and Captains: Pre-promotional courses for lieutenants and captains are entitled "Middle Management I" and "Middle Management II." They carry forward the theory that the Department needs effective management in order to do an effective job. The courses last two and three weeks, respectively, and each contains eight hours of anti-corruption activity.

Field training. The most extensive anti-corruption training problem...is in the rank and file of the Department already on the job. The men on the beat, in the cars, and in the special squads have either participated in or been exposed to corruption for their entire careers. The Academy is trying to reach these men with a variety of field programs aimed at duplicating the "facts of life attitude" taken with recruits.

In keeping with the efforts at decentralization and command responsibility, the Academy supervises a program of workshops, lectures, and special classes at various command levels designed to penetrate to the places where anti-corruption strength is most sorely needed.

One of the Department's more encouraging innovations in anti-corruption training is a series of Ethical Awareness Workshops, run by a sergeant and a patrolman. In eight to ten three-hour sessions, using imaginative techniques like role-playing in a no-holds-barred atmosphere, the workshop leaders encourage the participants to explore what corruption really is and how it affects them, to confront their own attitudes toward corrupt acts, and to reach some conclusions about just what they feel is morally permissible and what is not. Surprisingly, almost all the officers who have been through the workshop have come to the conclusion that even accepting a free cup of coffee is compromising and even insulting.

While it remains to be seen how long these new attitudes prevail after the officers have left the workshop and returned to the pressures of the station house and the street, these workshops appear to be a most promising tool in the hardest phase of the anti-corruption fight, namely changing the attitude of the rank and file.

Group leaders from every command in the Department are now being trained in these techniques, and will return to their commands to head their own workshops, eventually reaching a substantial percentage of the Department.

In addition to special efforts being made at the Academy to professionalize the anti-corruption training of recruits in the Department, the Academy feels that in the long run future the Executive Development Program and the Management Techniques Program now being fully developed will be the strongest elements in the anti-corruption fight. From these programs will come the administrative and command staffs whose training and development hopefully will inculcate a professional attitude incompatible with dishonesty. (Knapp et al., 1972:239–242)

Unfortunately, recent revelations of recurrent but less widespread corruption in the New York City Police Department suggest that such programs are likely to assume a low priority over time, as the problem for which they were established is seen to have diminished (Mollen et al., 1993, 1994). The message, of course, is that the integrity of a police organization's members is not ensured by programs that are instituted after scandal and that gradually fade away as memories of the agency's embarrassment also recede.

with the people they command; it is probable that most American police chiefs have held every rank in their organizations.

For those who participate in it, the strong internal culture of police departments is one of the most enjoyable parts of a police career. It also can be a real asset in the administrator's attempts to strengthen esprit de corps, discipline, and a sense of shared values and mission. Conversely, however, it can also be a negative force, a group that sees itself as an embattled minority at war with an unappreciative public and led by an unsympathetic and isolated cadre of upper-level careerists (see, e.g., Daley, 1978; Rothmiller and Goldman, 1992). When this happens, the department is likely to devolve into two separate cultures of *street cops* and *management cops*, complete with different and conflicting values and reward systems (see Reuss-Ianni, 1983).

Some degree of differentiation between line and management is as desirable in police departments as in any other type of organization. Because of the great strength of the forces that create it, however, the informal culture of line police officers is so powerful and consuming that it can easily override an administrator's attempts to devise a working environment based on official values, policies, and rules. When there is a great split between the line and management, the street officers' *reward system*—the manner in which an organization or culture defines conduct as outstanding or undesirable and treats it accordingly—also may conflict with the official reward system. As a case in point, a department's administration should reward officers for exercising restraint in the use of force and for demonstrating a willingness to stop other officers from using force needlessly. Where a department's informal street culture defines the department's rule makers as unrealistic, however, officers are likely to earn prestige for being quick with their fists and are sure to be labeled as obstructionists or informers for interfering with such conduct by other officers.

The best way to make certain that police departments' informal and formal reward systems are not in conflict is to prevent line officers from becoming so alienated that they see themselves as being at war with the public and with their administrators. To accomplish this, a department's administrators must demonstrate every day that they live by the agency's values and standards, and they must hold themselves to the same codes of conduct that the department demands of officers on the line. Line officers are quick to recognize the hypocrisy of paper commitments to stamping out misconduct that are not followed by the brass themselves.

Commendations. Even when supervisors and administrators have little power to grant formal rewards to outstanding employees, they should not hesitate to compliment personnel on their good work, as publicly as possible. The desire for recognition is a key factor that motivates many employees, and administrators should use it to increase the effectiveness of the department. Commendation and praise are often more effective as tools of leadership than criticism and disciplinary measures.

Commendation may be given in a number of ways. Leaders should use every opportunity to call the attention of others to outstanding accomplishment. This may be done by personal praise in conferences or in the presence of

Supervising and command officers should watch for commendable acts and report them to the chief, and the chief also should be alert to discover officers who deserve praise. Care should be taken to avoid giving one officer undue praise to the exclusion of others having equal claim to credit. Successful supervisors give full credit to the officers of their unit and do not seek commendation for themselves.

The effectiveness of the commendation is sometimes reduced by ritualization, formality, and excessive use. If commendations become perfunctory and commonplace, their value is lost. Praise is most valuable when it is meaningful, not necessarily when it is formal. In small and medium-sized departments, the chief can make mental notes of individual accomplishments and mention them casually when meeting officers here and there. When this extends to work that has not otherwise been publicized, it is an even greater morale builder because the feeling grows within the department that the chief knows what takes place and gives credit where credit is due.

On this point, it is critical for police administrators to recognize that outstanding behavior not involving confrontations with violent offenders is no less worthy of commendation than blazing gun duels and spectacular arrests. In many agencies, the highest and most prestigious official rewards and commendations are reserved for those who have engaged in the most sensational "cops and robbers" activity. At the same time, those who may put their lives on the line in other circumstances—or even make major contributions in ways that do not involve physical peril—receive only an informal pat on the back or no official recognition at all.

Certainly, police officers who solve big cases and demonstrate great heroism in bringing violent offenders to justice deserve our highest acclaim. But the officer who saves lives at fires, auto wrecks, and the like—or who is part of a team responsible for a program that has made a major contribution to reducing crime, restoring police-community relations, or convicting offenders—is also deserving of high official recognition. If the police are to encourage this type of performance, which is so critical to the success of the entire police enterprise, they must also use their commendation systems to reward it.

Promotions and Desirable Assignments. Perhaps the most important rewards that a police department can bestow are promotions and assignments to desirable duty. Unless these are granted on the basis of objective, merit-based criteria, they not only become meaningless as incentives to performance but also damage officers' respect for administrators, supervisors, specialists, and the system that put them in place. Although it may be true that outstanding performance in a nonsupervisory position may not predict how well one will perform as a supervisor, special care should be taken to ensure that those promoted to supervisory ranks have not been substandard performers in their old positions. Often, this is overlooked. In some, mostly small, American police departments, there are supervisors who hold their positions only because they have more seniority than anybody else. In many large agencies, supervisors are promoted solely on the basis of their performance on written tests, assessment centers, or other *one-shot* tests. Neither system, however, takes into account the individual's actual performance and day-to-day adherence to agency policies and rules, both of which are plainly visible to those with whom the individual works. When failure to take such factors into account results in the promotion or assignment to desirable duty of people whose records are marred by such indicators of substandard performance as poor personnel evaluations, histories of complaints, civil suits, and disciplinary actions, departmental discipline is irreparably damaged. In short, nobody in policing should receive a promotion or plum assignment until his or her entire record has been taken into account.

Empowerment of Sergeants. One valuable way of building a record of employees' performance and of enhancing formal reward systems is to empower first-line supervisors. One of the reasons for the great strength of informal reward systems in many agencies is that the first-line supervisor has no significant power to formally reward good performance or to take disciplinary action in response to misconduct. In his study of the Chicago Police Department, for example, sociologist Larry Tifft (1975) found that patrol supervisors had little effect on officers' behavior because supervisors were essentially powerless to reward the outstanding or to correct the substandard. Sergeants' efforts in detective units, by contrast, were an extremely powerful incentive to good performance because, Tifft suggested, such supervisors had the carrot and the stick that were denied patrol sergeants. With a stroke of the pen or a recommendation to their supervisors, detective sergeants could assign detectives to the best cases—or ensure their return to uniformed duty. Their detectives knew this and performed accordingly. Patrol sergeants had no such authority. They could do little to reward their officers because they had no input into promotion and transfer decisions, and they could do nothing to punish patrol officers, who were already performing their department's most onerous and least prestigious job.

Ironically, such a situation often goes hand in hand with criticism of patrol sergeants as weak links in command structures, who identify more closely

Unless sergeants have authority to meaningfully reward and punish officers' conduct, their great potential influence on a police agency's discipline is lost.
George Godoy.

with those they supervise than with the management teams of which they purportedly are a part. But when, alone among members of the management team, sergeants have no formal authority to reward or discipline, it is the management structure rather than individual sergeants that damages department discipline and good order. If reward systems—both positive and negative—are to have any value at all, they must give first-line supervisors, who are best positioned to evaluate officers, the authority to grant significant rewards and to exact significant punishments.

Transfers.   It is long-term wisdom in the literature of administration and management that transfers should not be employed as a form of disciplinary action. This generally is true—shifting a problem to another unit does not correct the problem but merely passes it on—but it is a principle that must be qualified.

As Tifft's work indicates, people who hold the same rank in medium- and large-sized police agencies may perform very different duties, some of which are more sought after than others. People who hold the entry-level police officer title, for example, can be found in traffic, patrol, vice, and investigative work, as well as in rescue squads, SWAT units, scuba teams, laboratories, computer centers, dignitary protection details, police training classrooms, helicopters, boats, and canine units. Because so many officers seek assignments to these specialized units—and are qualified for such assignments—these assignments are *plums*, granted to applicants not only on the basis of objective qualifications but also on the basis of general performance and adherence to departmental values and policies.

When people who hold such positions commit serious violations of the rules, it is difficult to justify keeping them among the ranks of their department's elite. Such positions should be considered privileges that, as one penalty for egregious conduct, may be lost.

PUNISHMENT

As suggested earlier, punishment fits at the end of the list of disciplinary techniques. When it is necessary to employ punishment, administrators should not hesitate to do so—but they should also avoid the temptation to solve problems simply by chopping heads. At the same time, no administration can engage in or tolerate favoritism or arbitrariness in deciding which employees to reward or punish, or wink at some violations in order to preserve *morale* or to achieve some political purpose. A particular challenge on this score is the need to avoid adjudicating officers' actions not on the basis of their objective merits but rather on the basis of the character of the people they have affected. Like Rodney King, many victims of police abuse have checkered backgrounds and have done something outrageous to provoke officers to excesses. But in responding to the police conduct, administrators must take care to avoid finding justification for outrageous police action on the grounds that, like a rape victim dressed in provocative clothing, its victim somehow brought it upon himself or herself. Where both police abuse and rape are concerned, such arguments are usually spurious and do not address the issue of what the accused did and whether it was reasonable.

In dealing with violations of the rules, police officials should recognize that there is no such thing as *absolute* discipline. In police organizations, which rely heavily on the efforts of line officers who frequently work alone and out of sight of supervisors, some "goofing off" is inevitable. So, too, is some degree of dissent on the part of those who may doubt the legitimacy of organizational goals or the prescribed means of achieving them. In neither case should the administrative response be an immediate resort to punishment. Instead, as they do in formulating law enforcement policies, police administrators should set some priorities in deciding who and what activities are deserving of official punitive action. Failure to set such priorities and to interpret the rules in their spirit, rather than to the letter, creates a real danger that personnel will define the rules as obstacles and will see those who enforce them as enemies rather than as leaders. Every police agency has its stories of officers who were punished for bending the rules in creative ways or for committing minor violations during the course of extraordinary accomplishment. When these "locker-room legends" occur with enough frequency, the natural inclination of line officers to see their departments as consisting of two opposing camps—themselves and the "clerks and jerks" in management (see, e.g., Manning, 1977; Reuss-Ianni, 1983)—may become severe enough to cause major problems of control and trust.[3]

A related consideration in deciding whether and how harshly to punish rule violations is suggested by a traditional legal conceptualization. Three broad categories of illegal behavior by officials also have great import within the confines of police administrative rules, procedures, and policies:

> *Malfeasance* 1. Wrongdoing 2. Doing an illegal act (especially by a public official).
> *Misfeasance* The improper doing of an otherwise proper or lawful act.
> *Nonfeasance* The failure to perform a required duty (especially by a public official). (Oran, 1983:259, 272, 288)

Often, but not always, this characterization helps to define the differences among intentional wrongdoing, good-faith mistakes, and indifference or laziness. Those whose acts are *malfeasant*—abusive or corrupt officers, those who cheat their colleagues or the time clock, or those who disappear during their working hours—generally intend to do wrong. The *nonfeasant*—officers who don't take citizens' reports or complaints, who look the other way when their colleagues do wrong, who fail to enforce the law when they should; supervisors who tolerate wrongdoing by those they oversee; and the like—also generally act with intent. As its prefix suggests, *misfeasance* usually is a mistake rather than the result of conscious venality. It involves officers who are insensitive to racial or cultural differences, who force confrontations with emotionally disturbed people, and who fail in critical situations because they don't know the rules. As such, their actions often reflect inadequacies in department supervision and training rather than their own improprieties.

These three descriptors suggest one reason not to resort immediately to punishment in all cases of rules violations: such violations may indicate a problem with the rules themselves—or with how well officers have been trained to adhere to them—rather than a conscious inclination toward counter-productive behavior by the personnel involved.

In addition, every organization suffers from a tendency toward *rulebook expansion*—responding to situations that have ended unhappily simply by creating new rules prohibiting whatever conduct was involved. On occasion, these rules are merely a transparent means of shifting blame from the top of an organization to its lowest level. When this occurs, two results follow. First, workers become alienated from management and come to question every management decision, no matter how innocuous or necessary. Second, workers' decisions and ability to solve problems may be unrealistically limited, with the result that goal-oriented personnel are forced to choose between following an unworkable rule and running the risk of punishment in order to get the job done (see Box 12.2).

Whenever a rule is violated, therefore, administrators should evaluate not only the wrongful conduct but also the rule itself, as well as the extent to which following it in the circumstances might have furthered or impeded the attainment of legitimate police goals. A rule violation involves a conflict between what an employee has done and what the agency states should have been done. On most occasions, such conflicts occur because the employee was wrong. On some of these occasions, however, the employee was wrong only because he or she was not adequately prepared to do right. In still other cases, conflicts occur because the rule was wrong or because, in the specific circumstances involved, it did not offer a way of achieving a legitimate goal.

Severity of Punishment

In deciding whether and how severely to punish, administrators should focus heavily on the *good of the service* as well as on the welfare of the individual. One purpose of punishment is to inform the individual involved that his or her conduct was intolerable, but it is easy to forget a second important purpose of punishment: to reinforce the rules by informing everybody else in the organization of the distinction between acceptable and unacceptable behavior and of the costs of engaging in unacceptable behavior. The manuals of some police departments are replete with stringent rules and guidelines for behavior, but when these go unenforced or when administrators punish violations leniently, it takes little time for the *grapevine* to spread the word that the rules do not mean what they say.

In general, punishment should be progressive, increasing with the gravity of violations and the frequency with which they are repeated. Although Bittel and Newstrom wrote on supervision generally, their characterization of such a progression is as applicable to policing as to any other field:

> Warning and oral reprimand
> First written reprimand
> Second written reprimand
> Suspension
> Discharge (Bittel and Newstrom, 1990:367)

Management Tone

The overall *management tone* of a police organization is probably the major subject of police organizational grapevines. As Boxes 12-2 and 12-3 suggest, either an arbitrarily punitive tone or an overly permissive tone can have dramatic effects on the agency's operations. Equally important, this *tone*—the message sent by the leadership's demonstrations of its reactions to outstanding performance, as well as to conscious wrongdoing and simple mistakes by those inside and to criticism from those outside—has a great effect on the extent to which officers and others on the line regard the agency's managers and supervisors as legitimate leaders and sources of authority.

Thus, in deciding how to achieve discipline in specific cases, administrators in the tightly knit social groups that are police agencies must keep in mind that their actions—to reward, to retrain, to punish—will have effects that go far beyond the individual employees involved. When a police organization's management tone and disciplinary system are seen as arbitrary, the morale and performance of line officers—who come to see the department as *not on the level*—suffer, and consequently the public suffers as well.

Line officers are particularly alert to the following signals of inappropriate management tone and arbitrary punishment:

Unworkable rules that are routinely violated without disciplinary action as long as public embarrassment or negative consequences are avoided. If, as the disabled-vehicle example in Box 12-2 suggests, some rules exist only to place blame for embarrassing situations at the lowest organizational levels and are otherwise ignored, they should be abolished, and new ways should be sought to achieve the same purpose. The purpose of an organization's rules, after all, is to help employees to do their jobs, to accomplish the organization's purposes. When a rule fails to achieve this purpose—as when following it would actually hinder employees from completing their work—it should be stricken from the books.

There is a simple test to determine whether a rule furthers organizational goals or is merely a mechanism to pin the blame for embarrassing situations on the lowest levels. If it is possible for protesting or disgruntled employees to succeed in a *rulebook slowdown*—to grind the work of the organization to a halt by adhering stringently to the organization's own rules—the rulebook should be overhauled, and all the rules that make a slowdown possible should be altered or discarded. When following rules blocks an organization's progress, the rules serve no legitimate purpose. Instead, they function only as a means of pointing the finger of blame downward in the organization's hierarchy. On a day-to-day basis, the existence and routine violation of such rules diminishes the degree to which employees legitimize *all* rules; on the rare public occasions when such rules are enforced, employees become cynical and get the message that "it's not cheating unless you get caught." No police agency can afford such a situation.

Rules that are periodically ignored for political purposes. In virtually every jurisdiction, there periodically arise demands for police to "crack down" on

BOX 12-2. Punishing the Blameless

For many years, a large police department's manual included a rule that forbade officers from using patrol vehicles to push disabled vehicles out of traffic lanes. The widely held wisdom was that this rule had originated as a headquarters response to a complaint that an officer had broken a motorist's taillight while pushing her disabled car off a highway, where it was creating a major traffic jam.

Creating this rule may have been an easy way out for administrators, but honoring it was not easy for well-intended officers. Especially on this jurisdiction's many elevated highways, where there are no roadside shoulders or means of quick emergency access from the opposite direction, officers who responded to aid disabled motorists faced a dilemma. After fighting their way through the stop-and-go traffic stacked up behind a disabled vehicle, they could break the rule by simply pushing the vehicle off the highway, where its occupants would be out of danger and where it would no longer obstruct traffic. In doing this, however, they would be participants in a charade:

- If they pushed the vehicle off the roadway without damaging it, no questions would be asked, and the rule would go unenforced.
- If the towing contractor who held the franchise for that section of the highway happened by and complained that officers were undercutting his or her livelihood, the officers would be disciplined unless they denied what they had done.
- If the officers damaged the vehicle and the motorist complained about it, there would be no deniability, and they would be disciplined for violating the rule.

Or, they could do what the rule required:

- Notify their radio dispatcher of the vehicle's location.

- Ask the dispatcher to contact and request the aid of an authorized towing contractor.
- Calm the vehicle's occupants.
- Direct frustrated motorists around the vehicle while the tow wended its way through a growing traffic jam to the disabled vehicle—hoping that the tow was not diverted by other vehicles that might overheat in the delay.
- Stand by as the tow operator explained his or her financial requirements to the vehicle's driver, obtained the motorist's signature on a contract, hooked the vehicle, towed it off the roadway, and deposited it in a safe location.

This situation had several effects, all of them bad:

- It made martyrs of some few officers, who were punished for causing minor damage for doing what most officers viewed as the right thing or for telling the truth about what they had done.
- It made liars of other officers, who did the right thing and denied it in order to avoid punishment.
- It made officers less willing to assist motorists in trouble.
- It created a degree of cynicism among officers, who came to believe that their administrators didn't care if officers broke the rules unless they were caught at it.
- Finally, some few officers actually followed the rule, and this led to prolonged traffic jams, pollution, overheated vehicles, and complaints about officers who, instead of moving disabled vehicles off roadways as quickly as possible, had merely directed traffic around them.

After all the administrators who had been involved in creating this rule had left the department, it was finally revoked.

specific crime problems or to apprehend particularly heinous offenders. Politicians and police administrators frequently respond to these demands by flooding areas with police officers and by demanding that they produce *results*—arrests and other evidence of enforcement action. When such pressures to clean up neighborhoods and take dangerous individuals off the streets also encour-

BOX 12-3. Absolving the Blameworthy

One large police department prohibits officers from discharging their firearms at moving vehicles unless the vehicle occupants are "using deadly force other than the vehicle" against officers or other innocent persons. This provision apparently bans shooting at fleeing vehicles or at motorists driving in officers' direction. This latter section, common in police deadly force policies, is based largely on the theory that officers may more readily protect themselves from oncoming vehicles by moving out of the paths of these vehicles rather than by remaining stationary and firing at them.

Yet more than a third of this agency's firearms discharges involved shootings that apparently violated this policy. In only 1 of more than 60 cases over a five-year period, however, did the officer involved become the subject of disciplinary action. He had responded with several other officers to a large brawl at a tavern. While he was inside the tavern, an intoxicated woman jumped into his patrol wagon and drove off. A few moments later, she returned and, at high speed, buzzed the crowd that had gathered outside the tavern. As she did so, the officer fired a shot into his wagon's tire. The wagon sped off and was subsequently found a few blocks away with a tire flattened by the officer's shot.

Except for this case, the department's review board absolved every officer who had fired at a vehicle. When younger officers were involved, the justification for finding that no violation of the rules had occurred typically read:

It is true that Rule _____ prohibits shooting at vehicles unless the occupants of the vehicle are using deadly force other than the vehicle against the officer involved. This was a fast breaking situation, however, and the shooting was caused by Officer Jones's inexperience and highly aroused emotional state rather than by any intentional wrongdoing on his part. Thus, while his firearms discharge would have been intolerable on the part of a more seasoned, veteran officer, we find that Jones's discharge was a justifiable exception to Rule _____.

When older officers fired shots, the same review board typically wrote:

It is true that Rule _____ prohibits shooting at vehicles unless the occupants of the vehicle are using deadly force other than the vehicle against the officer involved. This was a fast breaking situation, however, and the vehicle involved was headed directly at Officer Smith. A younger, more lithe, officer might have been able to jump out of the vehicle's way and to refrain from shooting. Officer Smith, however, is 41 years old and made a mature judgment that he could not safely engage in such demanding gymnastics. Thus, while his shooting was a violation of Rule _____ that we would punish if it had involved a younger officer, we find that, in these circumstances, it was a justifiable exception to Rule _____.

The effects of this agency's routine toleration of violations of its deadly force policy were also all bad:

- Officers learned through the grapevine that this rule would not be enforced, and violations became routine. Again, one-third of the department's shootings involved unpunished violations of its own rule against shooting at vehicles.
- Some officers apparently adopted the unsafe tactic of walking directly in front of stopped vehicles, knowing that any attempt to flee on the part of the motorists involved would justify shooting.
- Several officers were seriously injured because instead of jumping out of the paths of oncoming vehicles, they stood their ground and fired.
- A number of the people shot in such circumstances were nonviolent offenders (unlicensed, underage, or intoxicated drivers; joyriders).
- The department's attorneys were forced to agree to extremely generous pretrial settlements in lawsuits emanating from such shootings because the department's record of not enforcing its own rule had proven indefensible in court.

This practice ended when the administrators who followed it were embarrassed into changing it.

age officers to disregard "technicalities" like citizens' constitutional rights and dignity, or when administrators wink at such violations, a dangerous Pandora's box is opened. No matter how noble the cause or how critical the emergency, neither politicians nor police administrators have any authority to suspend the Bill of Rights. Further, once they have done so, administrators can have no reasonable expectation that officers will behave lawfully once temporary emergencies—or political exigencies—have passed, or that they will regard as legitimate any directive to do so. In short, once a mayor or police chief directs the police to solve a crisis by any means necessary, he or she cannot again expect officers to follow the rules once the crisis has passed or to regard as anything but hypocrisy any attempts to see that they do so.

Rules that are enforced at the organization's lowest levels but that obviously do not apply to those at the top. Virtually all police departments prohibit officers from drinking on duty (with exceptions for undercover agents or some other investigators) and ban the consumption of alcoholic beverages in department facilities. It is not unusual, however, to find that such rules are violated at the highest levels, as, for example, when the chief's staff has its Christmas party or when high-ranking officials retire or are promoted. Such arbitrariness—one code for Reuss-Ianni's "management cops," another for the "street cops"—is readily apparent and drives a wedge of cynicism into the organization.

Other practices also strengthen this wedge: Are line officers punished for accepting free cups of coffee while the chief and high-ranking commanders attend fancy free lunches with business leaders in the interests of community relations? Are patrol officers punished for attending to personal business during working hours while the chief and commanders use their staffs to run errands and act as gofers? Certainly, such practices may encourage officers to advance to high ranks, but they do so for all the wrong reasons and cause severe damage.

Imposition of strict liability for violations and failure to consider the circumstances in which they occur. In law, convictions for offenses of strict liability, such as traffic violations, require no showing of intent or recklessness. All that must be demonstrated by the prosecutor in such cases is that the acts *happened;* the motorist who runs a red light is guilty, regardless of whether he or she intended to do so. Many police departments treat violations of their rules as offenses of strict liability and fail to take into account important factors that may mitigate or excuse officers' violations or, in rare circumstances, aggravate the degree of officers' culpability.

Police experience is replete with bizarre examples of such arbitrariness:

A police officer responds to a report of female calls for help atop the roof of a tenement. Hurrying to the scene, he leaves his patrol car unlocked. He saves the woman, apprehends the rapist, but receives an official reprimand from a captain at the scene for leaving his car unlocked in violation of department rules.

An off-duty police officer in the same department is in a local tavern when armed men burst in and rob the bartender. Finished with the bartender, the robbers demand the customers' money and valuables as well. When the robbers start toward him, the officer identifies himself and pulls his gun. A struggle ensues, and he is struck in the head by a gunshot that later is discovered to have caused only minor injury. While he is unconscious, the robbers take his wallet, gun, and badge. The commander who investigates this incident concludes that the officer acted with courage but should suffer the agency's prescribed five-day suspension for loss of his gun and badge.

During a loud and drunken argument, an off-duty officer gives his wife his service revolver and dares her to shoot him. She does, wounding him. His department punishes him with its prescribed five-day suspension for failing to safeguard his weapon.

Another contextual factor that should be considered in deciding whether and how severely to discipline is the career history of the employees involved. One of the purposes of discipline is *specific deterrence:* preventing the violator from committing his or her offense again. In many agencies, however, police officials treat repeated violations by employees as though they happened in a vacuum. In such cases, they simply continue to impose the same minor punishments—or no punishments at all—even though, with each repeated offense, it becomes clearer that the agency's actions are having no effect. Conversely, using the logic of strict liability, such agencies sometimes punish first-time violators whose records are otherwise exemplary, even though nonpunitive disciplinary action (e.g., counseling or retraining) would almost certainly achieve the deterrent effect sought.

This failure to take officers' histories into account has several effects, all bad. First, it instills in officers who are inclined to violate the rules a belief that they have a license to do so. As a consequence, as recent studies of the police departments in Boston, Los Angeles, and New York City indicate, some wind up causing major damage to citizens, their agencies, and themselves (Christopher et al., 1991; Mollen et al., 1993, 1994; St. Clair et al., 1992). Second, it embitters employees whose careers are marked by only a single deviation that has been punished no less harshly than the repeated offenses of the worst of their colleagues. Third, and somewhat less obviously, it discredits the agency's code of conduct in the eyes of other officers. They know that just as the courts take the records of accused persons into account in deciding what to do with them, police administrators should attempt to achieve discipline by considering officers' violations in a larger context.

Imbalance between treatment of administrative rule violations and handling of abuses of citizens. A longtime criticism of the police holds that administrators have tended to minimize the import of officers' violations of citizens' civil rights and safety while they have reacted most harshly to violations of internal regulations and protocols (President's Commission, 1967:197). On occasion, the police have given ammunition to those who make such criticisms. Consider the following cases that were resolved by one department on the same day. In the first:

Officer Jones, on station duty, emitted a "Tarzan-style" yell at about 0230 hours. Lt. Smith, the platoon commander, directed him not to do this again. At about 0515 hours, Officer Jones emitted another "Tarzan-style" yell. After a hearing, the board found Officer Jones guilty and recommended a seven-day unpaid suspension from duty.

In the second:

> After a hearing, the board found that Officer Adams had placed the barrel of his loaded service revolver into the mouth of a handcuffed prisoner in the interrogation room of his station. Since there was no justification for this, the board found Adams guilty of the charges against him. A seven-day unpaid suspension from duty was recommended.

No matter what underlying circumstances are not described in these summaries, exacting the identical penalty for such two widely divergent offenses is extremely hard to justify. It also gives officers a confusing and counterproductive message about the department's priorities: to wit, that offending a supervisor by horsing around during the wee hours in a quiet station merits the same punishment as serious—and probably criminal—treatment of people in police custody. Further, it is hard to counter the argument that an agency that treats these two offenses as equally serious is not in need of the insights a civilian complaint review process would provide.

SUMMARY

What should be clear is that discipline is primarily the result of leadership and that leadership is not the exercise of authority through the issuance of commands and the threat of punishment for noncompliance. Some police chiefs assume that the strength and frequency with which commands are barked and the exclusive use by the executive of the power of decision are evidence of strong leadership and are likely to produce disciplined organizations. They are wrong and, in the long run, create only dissent, division, and paranoia among the ranks.

The good executive makes fewer, rather than more, decisions; the strong leader directs and coordinates more by inspiration and enthusiasm than by the authority of command or by the threat of negative punishment. The good executive does everything possible to see that everybody in the agency has a positive spirit and a desire to attain organizational goals, and he or she shares the responsibility for stamping out misconduct. The good executive knows that the organization's discipline and good order are more dependent on the ability of its management team to persuade subordinates to get the job done with maximum harmony and effectiveness than on a willingness to punish.

At the same time, the good executive is not hesitant to punish wrongful conduct when necessary and knows that there is a need for departmental entities charged exclusively with the duty to maintain discipline and good order. Chapter 13 turns to a discussion of these entities.

QUESTIONS FOR DISCUSSION

1. Many critics have observed that police administrators are more likely to attribute wrongdoing to individual "rogue cops" than to look at systemic or organizational

causes of misconduct. Does this observation hold in the police agency that employs you or that serves the community in which you live? Is this tendency unique to the police?

2. An officer was dismissed by his department after he was videotaped beating a suspect. In news interviews and articles, he argued that he had only done what the agency had encouraged him to do and that he had been "betrayed" by his chief, who was anxious to avoid embarrassment to the department or himself. Privately, other officers suggested that this claim was valid. How would you expect the elected officials to whom the chief reports to respond to this claim? Should it be investigated? What if it is found to be grounded in fact?

3. Consider the disabled-vehicle example in Box 12-2. How else would you address the problem of disabled autos so that the officers are not put in untenable positions?

4. A union representative has complained to the press that supervisors are demoralizing patrol officers by disciplining them for such minor violations as wearing scuffed leathers or worn heels. A civil rights advocate has responded that supervisors use such technicalities to avoid giving abusive officers the punishment they truly deserve. What do you, as the chief, do?

5. Can you devise a schedule of punishments for specific violations of police rules? How much room should it leave for the assessment of such factors as officers' intentions and career histories?

NOTES

1. See, for example, the St. Clair Committee report on the Boston Police Department. Impaneled by the city's mayor to investigate the department's management, the committee reported that the department's leadership had:

   . . . failed to develop and articulate a shared vision or strategic plan to guide the Department's operation. Instead, the Department has adopted a purely reactive posture, and drifts from crisis to crisis. The Committee concurs with the numerous officers calling for the creation of a "plan of action" that would articulate values, establish measurable goals, and develop a strategy to achieve those goals. The absence of any strategic plan has resulted in divisive "turf wars" between different segments of the Department and a lack of cohesive policies; we found a profound lack of teamwork, communication and coordination between the Department's various Bureaus, Areas, and Units. In fact, the Department actually operates as many separate and nearly autonomous police departments, each with its own priorities and informal rules, rather than as a unified organization with shared goals and objectives. (St. Clair et al., 1992:ii)

2. Compare, for example, these statements from the Christopher Commission's report on the Los Angeles Police Department and the St. Clair Committee's report on the Boston Police Department:

   Experienced [Los Angeles] patrol officers expressed concern that some Academy instructors are not sufficiently familiar with field work as it exists today. That belief might be at least partially responsible for the much-reported statement to probationary officers: "Forget everything you learned at the Academy." (Christopher et al., 1991:125)

   According to [Boston] Academy staffers, field training officers often advise probationers to forget everything they have learned at the Academy. (St. Clair et al., 1992)

3. Indeed, there is even a school of thought that believes that it is desirable for managers to consciously and visibly tolerate minor delinquencies by personnel. In this view, supervisors build a reserve of goodwill among their personnel by letting them get away with petty offenses and, subsequently, are able to call on them to go beyond the call of duty in times of crisis. Most veteran managers in and out of policing know of successful applications of this somewhat Machiavellian style, but it is one that depends heavily on individual values and the strength of personalities and that draws only vague lines between the permissible and the impermissible and between judicious restraint and managerial arbitrariness. It is best avoided.

SOURCES

BITTEL, LESTER R., and JOHN W. NEWSTROM. *What Every Supervisor Should Know,* 6th ed. (New York: McGraw-Hill, 1990).

BOUZA, ANTHONY V. *The Police Mystique* (New York: Plenum, 1990).

BROWN, LEE P. *Policing New York City in the 1990s* (New York: New York City Police Department, 1991).

CHAPMAN, DENNIS. *Sociology and the Stereotype of the Criminal* (London: Tavistock, 1968).

CHRISTOPHER, WARREN, et al. *Report of the Independent Commission on the Los Angeles Police Department* (1991).

DALEY, ROBERT. *Prince of the City: The True Story of a Cop Who Knew Too Much* (Boston: Houghton Mifflin, 1978).

DiULIO, ALBERT, et al. *Report of the Mayor's Citizen Commission on Police-Community Relations* (City of Milwaukee, 1991).

FYFE, JAMES J. *Police Personnel Practices,* Baseline Data Reports, vol. 18, no. 6 (Washington, D.C.: International City Management Association, 1986).

International Association of Chiefs of Police. *Building Integrity and Reducing Drug Corruption in Police Departments* (Arlington, Va., 1989).

KNAPP, WHITMAN, et al. *Report of the New York City Commission to Investigate Allegations of Police Corruption and the City's Anti-Corruption Procedures* (New York: Bar Press, 1972).

KOLTS, JAMES G., et al. *Report of the Special Counsel on the Los Angeles County Sheriff's Department* (Los Angeles, 1992).

MANNING, PETER K. *Police Work: The Social Organization of Policing* (Cambridge, Mass.: M.I.T. Press, 1977).

Miami, City of. "Report of the Mayor's Blue-Ribbon Commission on Police Brutality" (mimeo) (Miami, Fla., 1984).

MOLLEN, MILTON, HAROLD BAER, JR., HERBERT EVANS, RODERICK C. LANKLER, and HAROLD TYLER. *Interim Report and Principal Recommendations of the Commission to Investigate Allegations of Police Corruption and the Anti-Corruption Procedures of the New York City Police Department* (New York: Dec. 27, 1993).

———, ———, ———, ———, and ———. *Report of the Commission to Investigate Allegations of Police Corruption and the Anti-Corruption Procedures of the New York City Police Department* (New York: July 7, 1994).

O'CONNOR, GEORGE W. *Survey of Selection Methods* (monograph) (Washington, D.C.: International Association of Chiefs of Police, 1962).

ORAN, DANIEL. *Oran's Dictionary of the Law* (St. Paul, Minn.: West Publishing, 1983).

President's Commission on Law Enforcement and Administration of Justice. *Task Force Report: The Police* (Washington, D.C.: U.S. Government Printing Office, 1967).

REUSS-IANNI, ELIZABETH. *Two Cultures of Policing: Street Cops and Management Cops* (New Brunswick, N.J.: Transaction Books, 1983).

ROTHMILLER, MIKE, and IVAN G. GOLDMAN. *L.A. Secret Police* (New York: Pocket Books, 1992).

ST. CLAIR, JAMES D., et al. *Report of the Boston Police Department Management Review Committee* (City of Boston, 1992).

SKOLNICK, JEROME. *Justice without Trial* (New York: Wiley, 1966).

TERRITO, LEONARD, CHARLES R. SWANSON, JR., and NEIL C. CHAMELIN. *The Police Personnel Selection Process* (Indianapolis: Bobbs-Merrill, 1977).

TIFFT, LARRY. "Control Systems, Social Bases of Power and Power Exercise in Police Organizations," *Journal of Police Science and Administration* 3:155–182 (1975).

VOLLMER, AUGUST. *The Police and Modern Society* (Montclair, N.J.: Patterson Smith, 1972 reprint of original 1936 manuscript).

WERTHMAN, CARL, and IRVING PILIAVIN. "Gang Members and the Police," pp. 56–98 in David J. Bordua (ed.), *The Police: Six Sociological Essays* (New York: Wiley, 1967).

WILSON, JAMES Q. *Varieties of Police Behavior* (Cambridge, Mass.: Harvard University Press, 1968).

13

Quality Assurance and Inspections

KEY WORDS AND PHRASES

Control
Inspectional services bureau
Rule of control
Vulnerability analysis
Customer satisfaction
Task accomplishment
Line inspections

Staff inspections
Control points
Effectiveness
Efficiency
Matériel
Follow-up
Community conditions

Control, according to management pioneer Luther Gulick, is "seeing that everything is carried out in accordance with the plan which has been adopted, the organization which has been set up, and the orders which have been given . . . control is in a sense the consequence of command in action" (Gulick, 1937:73). More recently, management experts have adopted the phrase "quality control" to speak of the same function.

Automobile manufacturers and other makers of material goods expend a great deal of effort on what is today called quality assurance. Although automobiles are extremely complex machines, their makers' attempts to see that they are built to high standards of quality are, in many ways, much simpler than the quality control tasks of the police and other institutions that turn out products one cannot physically see or touch. A careful check at the end of the assembly line or a few hours behind the wheel of a new car often allows a judgment about its quality, but the quality of policing is not so readily evaluated by either officials or the public. A community, for example, may be a good place to live or a bad place to live for reasons that have nothing to do with the police. Despite the most egregious police mistakes, some crimes may be solved quickly, while others may go forever unsolved no matter how hard and how well police work on them.

Because it is so hard to evaluate the output of policing, police administrators have historically been careful to organize their departments in ways that, it is believed, best lend themselves to discipline and high-quality performance. Once this is accomplished, it follows that police administrators also need to ensure that their departments' members conform to these organizational prescriptions and to examine the way things get done. As we have suggested earlier, this emphasis on *inspection* of structure and operations—rather than on direct measurement of output—can be overdone (see, e.g., Goldstein, 1979), but it does have an undeniably important place in police organizations.

THE CHIEF'S ROLE

The extent to which police chief administrators should participate directly in inspection and quality assurance cannot be precisely defined, because it is influenced by the organization and size of the department as well as by the department's history and demonstration of the need for such activity. In practice, then, chiefs' participation is influenced by their interests, the amount of time they must have available for direct services, their estimate of the priority of control over other activities, their confidence in the ability of their subordinates, and their own ability to delegate authority. But while chiefs may delegate the tasks of inspection and quality assurance to others, they cannot escape ultimate responsibility for seeing that these jobs are successfully accomplished. Neither can they escape the responsibility of continuously demonstrating and articulating their total commitment to quality and integrity.

Part of this commitment requires that the chief hold top and middle management strictly accountable through the use of powerful sanctions. This is essential if the police administrator is to deal successfully with police misconduct and avoid the high risk or personal blame for its existence. Yet—while the chief is rightly held accountable for any wrongdoing in the agency—the environment, protection, and mentality associated with civil service often insulate from accountability those immediately beneath the chief. Since the police chief cannot ensure the quality and integrity of the department alone, he or she must find ways to make subordinates in management actively participate and, despite civil service restraints, to hold them strictly accountable for doing everything possible to control misconduct. One of the most valuable tools for accomplishing this is an inspectional services bureau.

ORGANIZATION FOR INSPECTION AND QUALITY CONTROL

In most modern police departments, an inspectional services bureau or its equivalent is the major unit charged specifically with quality and integrity assurance. Such units may be responsible for inspection of persons, property, and procedures; investigations of personnel; and (with less regularity) intelligence and/or vice control operations.[1] Although the first two functions are seemingly similar, in actual practice the role of the inspector is very different from that of the internal investigator. Both functions are nevertheless logically grouped under one commander in a major department, even though it may be necessary to have personnel with different aptitudes assigned to the two functions. Certainly, in large departments, the same people should not perform both tasks.

The head of the department must remain informed about matters that vitally affect police operations. Some of what he or she must know is reflected in police records, but the chief must have firsthand information in order to operate successfully. In all but the smallest departments, the chief needs assistance in order to have this information available at all times. In the largest departments these inspectional duties may be so continuous and of such broad scope that a separate bureau may be required. Thus, Figure 13-1 on p. 441, should be interpreted not as a precise guide to organization but as a guideline that illustrates the functions that should be performed by the bureau charged with specific responsibility for inspection and control.

In medium-sized departments, the formal inspections function performed by the Inspections Division in Figure 13-1 may be assigned to one or more staff officers who can be given the working title of "inspector."[2] If there are several inspectors, their duties should be divided according to the functions inspected rather than geographically or by time of day. Platoons in both territorial and functional units should be inspected by the heads of their districts and divisions, and the inspector likewise should deal with the work of the district or of the functional unit as a whole. Inspectors are more likely to do so when they have a 24-hour responsibility for inspecting operations.

In larger departments, it may be necessary to staff the inspections function with high-ranking officials. Inspectors are theoretically staff officers acting on behalf of the chief of police, but when they are outranked by the people whose units they inspect, problems may arise. Persons assigned to inspections duty should have adequate rank to carry out their purpose. For example, if the common rank for platoon commander of the patrol division is lieutenant, and if it is obvious that inspectors will be required to be in contact with platoon lieutenants in each district, the officer assigned to inspectional duties should be a captain or higher.

INSPECTION AS AN IMPLEMENT OF QUALITY ASSURANCE

Accountability of Command

As suggested above, managers may delegate the authority to actually perform the tasks of their units, but they cannot rid themselves of any of their responsibility for accomplishing these tasks. Managers may tell subordinates that they are responsible for the successful conclusions of assignments, but managers remain ultimately accountable for finally accomplishing them.

Rule of Control. *Authority* is delegated by some form of command and should always be accompanied by *accountability*, the establishment of some form of control. This process requires evaluation of the manner in which the authority has been exercised and leads to the *rule of control: The person who gives an order must ascertain that it has been properly executed.*

It is far easier to give a command than to hold a subordinate accountable by seeing that the command has been properly carried out. The process of inspection is the one key to this determination. Inspection—critical review or examination involving careful scrutiny and analysis—may, in some cases, be accomplished by simple observation; in other instances, it may involve inquiry or the analysis of records and statistics.

Purpose of Inspection. There are four major purposes of inspection:

1. To learn whether a task is being performed as planned and in accordance with regulations and procedures
2. To learn whether the anticipated results are being realized
3. To determine whether resources of the department are being used to best advantage
4. To identify problems and needs, the first step in planning

Although inspection may uncover unsatisfactory conditions that should be changed, such discoveries by themselves may not suggest the precise direction of the change. For example, noncompliance with regulations and procedures, unsatisfactory results and conditions, and failure to use department resources to best advantage may be the result of simple misconduct. But, as suggested in Chapter 10, such problems may also reflect a need for additional or modified organization, regulations, procedures, equipment, personnel, training, direction, or leadership. Thus, when deficiencies are discovered in the course of inspections, they should be carefully analyzed by both the planning division and the operating units concerned.

Scope of Inspection

Since police departments must control all their operations and facilities, they must frequently inspect everything within their domains. Inspection procedures should be outlined in the same manner as procedures for all other police operations.

Every inspectional observation must be accompanied by a judgment as to whether a predetermined standard is being met. The standard in some cases might be simply compliance with the law or a police regulation rather than a performance standard. It follows, therefore, that inspection of procedures and operations will not be fully effective unless such standards exist. It is impossible to hold anyone accountable to an unstated level or standard of performance, and inspections unit staff can render a most useful service by assisting other units in developing performance and operational standards.

Such standards should be based on a careful analysis of points in the agency and on procedures that may be especially inviting or vulnerable to poor, or even criminal, performance or that otherwise might cause great public damage or bring discredit on the agency. It has become painfully clear, for example, that virtually any police operation involving drugs presents great temptations and opportunities for illicit profits. Consequently, inspections of all operations and facilities related to drug enforcement must be based on standards that have been formulated with special care. This form of *vulnerability analysis* may also be used to identify other high-risk police operations—preparations for disasters and disorders, interventions in domestic violence, vehicle and fleet management, management of jails and lockups, and purchasing are just a few of those that come to mind among many others—and to design clear standards and related inspection procedures.

One way to do this may be to enroll in the accreditation program of the Commission on Accreditation for Law Enforcement Agencies, Inc. (CALEA, 1994) and/or one of the state accreditation agencies or, at least, to conduct a self-assessment to determine whether the agency is substantially in conformance with accreditation standards. Although CALEA's standards serve more to identify areas where policy should be formulated than to prescribe specific policies or *how-to's* for line officers, they are comprehensive enough that responding in a meaningful way to each CALEA standard and commentary will help the agency meet its goals and avoid liability. As we use the term "meaningful," of course, it has more than just a paper connotation: a meaningful response to a standard of CALEA or any other professional body requires three steps:

1. *Research* designed to identify all the issues involved in a policy area. This should involve surveys of other agencies and consultation with line and staff personnel as well as with agency attorneys and other affected parties outside the department.
2. *Formulation of policies* or rules that take into account both the experiences of other agencies and the particular needs of the community and agency involved.
3. *Training* to ensure that resulting policies or rules are understood by everybody involved.
4. *Continuing evaluation* to determine whether policies or rules are workable and to determine whether affected personnel are abiding by them. Where appropriate, this should result in *correction* of defective policies, rules, or related procedures in order to bring them into line with the realities of the task involved. Similarly, when evaluation demonstrates that policies or rules are not achieving their purposes because individuals or groups are ignoring or otherwise resisting them, disciplinary action should follow.

Although there are obviously interrelationships among inspections of *persons, things, procedures,* and *results,* these four categories are useful for discussion purposes.

Persons. Determination of the health and physical appearance of personnel calls for an examination of individuals. Compliance with regulations on grooming, diet, and appearance may be ascertained by casual visual inspection, but matters of physical or psychological health and general fitness may require more thorough medical and laboratory examinations.

Similarly, morale and attitude toward work, both important factors in successful police operations, may be appraised only in part by observing the individual officer. A more accurate appraisal may require examination of the things the person uses and of his or her thoughts, attitudes, actions, reactions, and accomplishments. This is the purpose of personnel performance evaluations. In addition, many police agencies recently have adopted the practice of questioning citizens about the quality of police services they have received from officers (see Box 13-1). Under such programs, police reports are reviewed, and crime and accident victims and other individuals who have received police services are contacted by supervisors or inspections personnel for their comments on officers' courtesy and the degree of assistance rendered.

An emerging concern among police administrators involves the need to ensure that personnel are drug-free. The easiest way to deal with this problem, of course, is to insist that all employees submit to drug testing at unannounced times. Such a system, however, overlooks fundamental issues of privacy and dignity, as well as the constitutional provisions that guarantee them, and turns the inspections unit into an adversarial body. Two related sets of questions involve the accuracy of the tests and the effects of drugs on employees' ability to perform their jobs. First, doubts about accuracy have made it questionable that courts will sustain dismissals or other disciplinary actions based *solely* on positive test results. Second, the courts seem to indicate that the potential effects of drugs on police work are not sufficiently catastrophic to warrant routine random testing of all employees.[3]

Consequently, the prevailing view is that police drug testing is permissible in the following circumstances:

1. To screen applicants for jobs
2. Where members are involved in particularly sensitive work, such as that of vice, narcotics, internal affairs, and bomb squads and that of Special Weapons and Tactics (SWAT) units
3. As part of routine prepromotion or pretransfer physical examinations
4. Where erratic behavior or poor performance gives specific and articulable reason to suspect drug abuse
5. After members have been involved in controversial or unusual events, such as shootings, use of force, or vehicle accidents

Things. The physical inspection of things indicates whether equipment and facilities need repair or replacement and may also disclose the extent of compliance with regulations. This inspection cannot be allowed to become casual or superficial. Every item and aspect of the police building, offices, cell spaces, and corridors; all police vehicles and the police garage; the laboratory and its equipment; department and privately owned weapons; uniforms and uniform equipment; records, files, and other office equipment; officers' notebooks; radio and communications equipment; supplies of every kind; physical evidence; prisoners' property—all must be regularly inspected to determine whether they are in good condition and suitably cared for as required by regulations governing their maintenance and use.

Because it is a highly attractive target to corrupt personnel and other criminals, evidence is a particular concern in such inspections. An inspection system should supplement a solid property management system (which tracks the custody and whereabouts of all evidence from start to finish of case processing) and should focus carefully on safeguarding drugs, money, firearms, and other contraband or dangerous devices. The absence of such a system is an

BOX 13-1. Evaluating Customer Satisfaction

Perhaps one of the earliest and most extensive evaluations of citizens' satisfaction with the quality of police services rendered was undertaken in Troy, New York, during 1978. Scholar Dorothy Guyot, who worked with then-Police Commissioner George O'Connor in conducting this study, reports:

[C]onsumer satisfaction surveys are the most appropriate technique [for evaluating patrol officers' performance]. . . . Performance measures for police need to take account of the diversity of the problems and the outcomes. Since incidents are not recorded on videotape, such specific knowledge must come from those on the scene; the officers themselves, the citizens involved, and, if present, supervisors or alert bystanders.

Citizens who have requested police service can report the degree to which the officers listened to their problems and helped them toward solutions. Consider, for example, two residential burglaries investigated by Troy officers in the spring of 1978. Departmental records show they were basically alike and similar to the majority of burglary investigations that occur across the nation. In each case the householder discovered the break-in on returning home; patrol officers responded promptly and completed incident reports; no sergeant came, and no detective followed up; no property was recovered, and no one was caught. Despite the superficial similarity, however, comparison of what the householders told a survey interviewer reveals vast discrepancies in the quality of work performed.

A twenty-five-year-old woman used bitter words to describe the investigation of her ransacked apartment:

The officer walked in and looked around. He was very nonchalant. He asked me what was missing, filled out the report, and asked me if I lived alone. He came to the conclusion that it was my ex-husband who did it and told me to contact him. He said he would give the report to the detective. His whole attitude was as if he was just there from nine to five, as if he thought, "Why did I have to come for this?" He got annoyed when I asked why he suspected my ex-husband. I thought he would be a little more concerned. He could have taken fingerprints or something because a metal box was broken into. He told me the way the doors were secured that I might as well leave them open. I felt very degraded. I felt like I was the criminal.

In contrast to the woman's anger over [this officer's] callousness, an old man expressed gratitude to the officers who came after his vacation money was stolen from his home while he was visiting his wife in the hospital.

The officers made an investigation to find the point of entry, which I couldn't find. They made another call to headquarters for . . . someone to come down who took pictures and picked up fingerprints from various items. They waited till he came and just talked. They went out of their way to help me by giving me good pointers in things I could do. For example, I have eight switches that go on at night. They told me to set them for different times and they would check on my house when I'm on vacation. The patrol car in the neighborhood would make sure nothing was unusual when they went by. They told me I could leave my guns at the police station when I went on vacation. They were very courteous and knew their job.

These divergent assessments underscore the importance of citizens' perspectives in answering a major performance question . . . "To what extent do police officers use discretion to help people solve their problems?" For Commissioner O'Connor the most important work that a patrol officer can do is to respond to citizens' calls in an effective and caring manner. . . . [Through survey research to determine whether patrol officers have done so] citizens' views on the handling of their problems may be communicated to the department, so that patterns of excellence may be encouraged and patterns of shoddy service may be identified and corrected.

In Troy both a service survey of 349 citizens who had called the police and a cross-section of 950 residents were conducted during the spring of 1978, with financial support from the Law Enforcement Assistance Administration (LEAA). . . . The service survey dwelt on the citizens' perceptions of how an officer responded to their calls for service; the residential survey examined citizens' reactions to being stopped by the police, witnessing praiseworthy and blameworthy police actions, and directly cooperating with police in crime prevention, as well as their views of crime problems, recent experience with burglary, sense of personal safety, and priorities for the police department. . . .

The most general question asked in the service survey was this: "On the whole, how would you rate the service the police officer(s) gave you?" Overall, 62 percent rated the Troy service as very good, 25 percent as good, 6 percent as fair, 3 percent as poor, and 3 percent as very poor; 1 percent declined to say. Satisfaction with police handling of suspicious incidents was highest,

BOX 13-1. Evaluating Customer Satisfaction *(continued)*

close to 100 percent, for these are occasions when an officer's mere appearance scares off troublemakers. People were least satisfied, only 76 percent, with the handling of conflicts among acquaintances, incidents with long histories and little likelihood of conclusion. . . .

The service survey asked people what they particularly liked about the responding officers' actions. Courtesy was the most frequent answer, mentioned by 68 percent and listed first by 38 percent. We may speculate that courtesy is most important because citizens who call the police are doubly vulnerable; they are beset by the current crisis, yet faced with a powerful individual who could belittle them with impunity. The next most frequent response was that the officer was concerned. Typical answers here included "Reassuring"; "Sympathetic"; "Calmed me down"; "Seemed to know how I felt"; "Realized the situation embarrassed me"; "Suggested we could have lost a lot more." Overall, 65 percent of the citizens questioned gave their first praise to supportive actions such as courtesy, concern, and friendliness. Only 21 percent first praised task accomplishment. Another 8 percent expressed praises in a manner too vague to classify, and 6 percent liked nothing. . . .

The majority of citizens praised officers' courtesy in all types of incidents. Officers' concern was particularly appreciated by people who suffered personal harm or theft. Where citizens feared a repetition, they appreciated officers' suggestions for preventive action. Citizens who were agitated admired the officers' calm. We see that for task accomplishment, getting results was praised most often in the simple situation of a parking problem. Citizens emphasized efficiency only for handling traffic problems. Quick arrival was particularly praised only for violent attacks. . . . In sum, courtesy and concern were far more often praised than were all aspects of task accomplishment, a major finding of the survey. . . .

The finding that citizens place less importance on the accomplishment of tasks than on emotional support has far-reaching consequences. Generally, police task accomplishment is low because there are no easy solutions to the problems that prompt people to call the police; a purse snatcher's shove breaks an old woman's hip; a neighbor's child continually and deliberately smashes windows; neighbors disagree over the proper volume

for music. Officers are often weighed down with intimate knowledge of how much goes wrong in people's lives. Setting out on a burglary call, they know they are probably headed for failure to make an arrest and failure to recover the stolen property. Leaving a burglary scene, they often feel frustrated and discouraged that they "can't do anything." The survey found that in the seventy-five cases of burglary and theft, officers recovered the property of only three people, yet 90 percent of the victims considered their service good or very good. Helping people to feel better and motivating them to take precautions to prevent a recurrence have traditionally received little recognition as goals for patrol officers. Indeed, officers tend to discount supportive actions by labeling anything that helps a person to feel better as "a P.R. job." However, this survey shows that by listening sympathetically, officers have already done something important. In the 349 responses to the survey, no one ever said or implied that officers were insincere or manipulative.

Human nature is at work here. If we look beyond the technology of 911 emergency numbers, computer-aided dispatching, and speedy radio patrol cars, we see that someone who is seeking help is visited by a person whose job is to give help. That the seeker appreciates courtesy and concern from the giver is only natural.

As should be clear by now, the most appropriate performance measures are based on an assessment of what a situation requires and judgment of how well officers address the requirement of the specific situation. Police officers, patrol sergeants, and other experts can assess an officer's skill in both task accomplishment and psychological support. Citizens responding to surveys can make nontechnical judgments of how helpful and supportive an officer is. Yet despite the power of survey research to obtain citizen perspectives, police management has barely begun to use this tool for evaluating feedback on performance. The crying need for judgmental evaluation techniques was hidden until a few years ago by the denial that officers exercise discretion and by the reliance upon objective statistics on response time.

Source: Guyot, 1991:52–57. Reprinted with permission of Temple University Press.

invitation to disaster; during the early 1970s, for example, large amounts of heroin and cocaine were stolen from the New York City Police Department's custody and, no doubt, sold on the streets (Burnham, 1972). More recently, the Washington, D.C., Metropolitan Police Department's shoddy evidence and property system was exploited by corrupt employees who apparently stole

The large amounts of cash taken in drug
seizures is an important reason for a secure
property management system.
AP/WideWorld.

nearly 3,000 guns (Carlson, 1993). Furthermore, such police contributions to
the traffic in drugs and illegal weapons are not limited to the big cities; the national media frequently carry accounts of smaller-scale loss of evidence from
police departments throughout the country. In short, a sound, impenetrable,
regularly inspected property management system is a must if police are to be
confident that, once seized, contraband and other property will not find their
way back to the wrong hands.

Another set of things recently shown by history to be in need of regular inspection is the electronic record of officers' voice communications on car and
portable radios and their digital communications in mobile data transmissions.
The Christopher Commission report on the Los Angeles Police Department
disclosed patterns of racist, sexist, and otherwise dehumanizing commentary
in digital transmissions, which, as the commission observed, stood "in sharp
contrast to the LAPD's official policy against 'racially or ethnically oriented' remarks" (Christopher et al., 1991:73). If a department is to ensure that its officers' words and actions reflect the agency's values, it must systematically inspect these electronic records, perhaps on a random basis.

Procedures and Actions.   Conformity with procedures designed for use during the tour of duty—such as inspection of hazards, questioning of suspicious
persons, handling of violators, investigation of crimes or accidents, interrogation of suspects and witnesses, and search and transportation of prisoners—
may be determined more accurately by observation of acts than by an analysis
of the results or by a study of reports covering the particular incident. Obviously, not every action can be observed, and some—such as the stopping of
suspicious characters and the arrest of violators—are virtually impossible to

predict and observe. Still, it is important that inspections be made often to determine whether department procedures are being followed.

Results.   An examination of results indicates the success of an operation; it also indicates whether each task was performed in the manner outlined and whether the resources of the department were used to best advantage. In addition, it may reveal needs not previously recognized. The inspection of results includes the analysis of statistics, the examination of reports of incidents, interviews with police clients, and surveys of public opinions and reactions to specific events. In research and analysis, inspection goes hand in hand with planning.

Line and Staff Inspection

Police agencies conduct two types of inspections:

1. *Line* inspections, conducted by those in direct control of the persons and things being inspected, to see that tasks are satisfactorily performed.
2. *Staff* inspections, conducted by those who lack direct control but who have the responsibility to determine how well workers—including line inspectors—do their jobs.

Those who conduct line inspections should use their own authority over the work being performed to see that deficiencies are corrected. Similarly, the findings of staff inspections should be reported to the line supervisors and administrators who are best positioned to correct problems.

Line Inspection.   Line inspection is basically the supervisor's continuous inspection of the work performed under him or her. The complexity of line inspections varies directly according to the length of the chain of command and the number of employees under a manager's supervision. In a small department, for example, a chief might directly order a patrol officer to enforce a regulation and would ascertain by personal inspection that the order was being carried out. In a large department, such an order from the chief would travel through several command levels—an assistant chief, a captain, a lieutenant, and a sergeant, for example—before it reached the patrol officer. This delegation down the chain of command and the communication of results back up the chain, necessary if each level is to be held accountable, is not always easy and does not always occur without static (see Box 13-2).

The chief's main interest should be results; he or she should be most concerned with knowing that the order has been executed, rather than knowing all the nuances of the way it was communicated down the line. To furnish the chief with this information, each official in the chain of command must have some way of applying the rule of control—of ensuring that commands were carried out at the line level. The sergeant's day-to-day supervisory responsibilities enable him or her to obtain this information by frequent and regular inspection. The lieutenant, also responsible for the accomplishment of the task,

BOX 13-2. A Communication and Control Problem

Elizabeth Reuss-Ianni quotes an anonymous memo posted on many walls in New York City Police Department facilities:

THE POLICE COMMISSIONER ISSUED THE FOLLOWING DIRECTIVE TO THE CHIEF OF [DEPARTMENT]:

> "Tomorrow evening at approximately 2000 hours, Haley's Comet will be visible in this area, an event which occurs only once every 75 years. Have the men assemble in front of the station house in uniform and I will explain this rare phenomenon to them. In case of rain we will not be able to see anything, so assemble the men in the sitting room and I will show the films on it."

THE CHIEF OF OPERATIONS DIRECTED THE AREA COMMANDER:

> "By order of the Police Commissioner: Tomorrow at 2000 hours Haley's Comet will appear above the station house. If it rains, fall the men out in uniform and then march to the sitting room where the rare phenomenon will take place, something which occurs only once every 75 years."

THE AREA COMMANDER ORDERED THE PRECINCT COMMANDING OFFICER:

> "By order of the Police Commissioner in uniform at 2000 hours tomorrow evening the phenomenal Haley's Comet will appear in the sitting room. In case of rain in front of the station house, the Police Commissioner will give another order, something which occurs only once every 75 years."

THE PRECINCT COMMANDING OFFICER ISSUED THE FOLLOWING ORDER TO THE ADMINISTRATIVE LIEUTENANT:

> "Tomorrow at 2000 hours, the Police Commissioner will appear in front of the station house with Halley's Comet, something which happens every 75 years. If it rains, the Police Commissioner will order the Comet into the sitting room."

THE ADMINISTRATIVE LIEUTENANT MADE THE FOLLOWING ANNOUNCEMENT AT ROLL CALL:

> "When it rains tomorrow at 2000 hours, the phenomenal 75 year old Chief Halley, accompanied by the Police Commissioner will drive his Comet through the station house in uniform."

AN HOUR LATER ONE OF THE COPS ASKED THE SERGEANT FOR CLARIFICATION OF THE LIEUTENANT'S ANNOUNCEMENT AT ROLL CALL AND THE SERGEANT SAID:

> "Chief Halley, the new Area Commander, is going to test a new [patrol car] here tomorrow, if it doesn't rain."

A SHORT TIME LATER, A [CIVILIAN POLICE ADMINISTRATIVE AIDE] ASKED THE COP IF HE KNEW WHAT WAS GOING TO HAPPEN TOMORROW, THE COP SAID:

> "Forget it, you civilians can't get anything straight anyway."

Source: Reuss-Ianni, 1983. Reprinted by permission of Transaction Publishers. *Two Cultures of Policing: Street Cops and Management Cops.* Copyright © 1983 by Transaction Publishers. All rights reserved.

delegates the necessary authority to the sergeant but can hold the sergeant accountable only by ascertaining that the task has been performed. The lieutenant could personally supervise its performance, but limited time and other responsibilities make this impractical. It is for this reason that lieutenants have sergeants.

Lieutenants, therefore, must discover by some other means whether a task has been accomplished. They should watch for reports that may indicate a lack of attention, and they should make sample inspections to determine whether the regulation is being enforced. This inspection is essential if sergeants are to be held accountable for exercising the authority available to them. Captains

The sergeant is a key link in line inspections. Here, a sergeant visits an officer assigned to a truck weigh station.
Roberta Hershenson/Photo Researcher.

have access to the same inspectional procedures to determine whether lieutenants are holding their sergeants accountable.

Line inspection—or quality assurance—of this type is essential at each level of authority to ascertain that the job has been done. At each successively higher level, the amount of inspection by sampling is decreased, and thus the justification for staff assistance is increased.

Staff Inspection. Staff inspection itself may be divided into two categories. The first relates to, or may be part of, *functional supervision* and is most commonly encountered when the line commander lacks the necessary technical skill for (and sometimes, unfortunately, interest in) inspecting technical work carried out by employees. For example, the crime laboratory may inspect the work and equipment of evidence technicians assigned to a field operations bureau. Lack of time may also result in staff inspection for this purpose: when patrol sergeants are overloaded with work, vehicle maintenance units may temporarily assume that their duties are to inspect patrol cars, and records officers may assume that their responsibilities are to review case reports.

The second category of staff inspection involves the *general requirement that inspections be conducted on behalf of the chief by a formal staff inspection unit* to enhance control over the total supervision of the department and its personnel and to make certain that line supervisors are doing their jobs well. This is the norm for staff inspections and is the subject of the rest of this chapter.

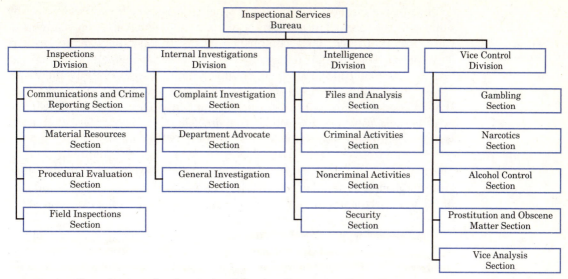

FIGURE 13-1. Organization of an Inspectional Services Bureau in a Large Department

Inspections by the Staff Unit

The functional assignment of duties, as shown in Figure 13-1, encompasses all phases of inspectional needs discussed earlier. The inspections undertaken by the inspections division should enhance the work of the internal investigations division, the intelligence division, and the vice control division (regardless of whether all three are part of an inspectional services bureau) but should not duplicate their inspections. An inspector who discovers discrepancies in property management procedures, for example, may at the same time be uncovering a breach of integrity by some member of the department. This is not the primary aim of the inspector, however, who should be interested primarily in discovering and pinpointing specific areas where irregularities or weaknesses occur and in keeping supervisory officers informed about them so that they may be corrected.

Inspections of communications and crime reporting, material resources, and procedures (the first three boxes under "Inspections Division" in Figure 13-1) should be conducted continuously, on an unscheduled, spot-check basis. Field inspections teams—who usually inspect headquarters operations, as well—should surprise nobody. Instead, they should make scheduled, simultaneous inspections of both field and headquarters operations. They may spend several days inspecting a district station, for example, and should examine in minute detail every phase of building maintenance, care of equipment, and records of every kind. They should also check on methods of handling calls for service.

A Straightforward Process. Inspection conducted by line supervisors is usually informal, without a sharp distinction between the casual observation involved in supervision and the somewhat more orderly observation characteris-

441

tic of formal inspection. Regardless of whether it is done by supervisors or by staff inspectors, formal inspection should be conducted in an open, straightforward manner. Inspections accomplished by stealth (such as searching lockers in the absence of tenants) are certain to have undesirable effects on morale and to lead officers to conceal all their activities from officials. Certainly, there may be reason to justify this kind of activity, but it should not be the work of the staff inspections unit. A related rule for staff inspectors is that they should *never allow employees to believe that they are doing anything but inspecting.* The staff inspection function is not an undercover or covert operation.

The Inspector's Relationships.   The inspector's relationship with the chief, best established by regularly scheduled conferences, should be open and candid. The inspector should not, out of a desire to shield the chief from bad news, fail to provide information for the chief.

The inspector must establish a relationship with operating personnel that will facilitate frank and direct interaction, using persuasion, suggestions, and personal requests rather than commands to correct irregularities without the assistance of high authority. To establish this relationship, the officer chosen for inspectional duties should be one whose maturity, experience, morality, integrity, judgment, character, and personality command the respect and admiration of all other members of the agency. A desirable relationship is further promoted by an attitude of friendliness reflected in the officer's demeanor, voice, and facial expression and evidenced by a willingness to be helpful.

To avoid friction, the inspector must be circumspect in relations with both commanding officers and subordinates. The inspector's findings and any resultant suggestions or requests to subordinates should be reported to commanders promptly and with further recommendations. Care must be used in making suggestions and requests, especially to subordinates, to avoid creating the impression that they are commands. A good relationship between operations personnel and those engaged in staff inspections is vital to the success of this kind of supervision. The relationship is a delicate one, and desirable results are achieved only when it is worked out to the satisfaction of all concerned.

Overly rigid interpretations of the principle of unity of command should not prohibit officers who make staff inspections from calling problems to the attention of the officers involved or at fault. In all but the largest departments, such an interpretation would necessitate reporting nearly all matters to the chief and, consequently, would defeat one of the important purposes of staff inspections. The evils of unnecessarily delaying corrective action and the desirability of lessening the routine duties of commanding officers justify cutting across the lines of direct authority when this may be done without jeopardizing harmonious relationships. For example, the report-review officer cuts across the lines of authority by reporting matters directly to the immediate superior of the officer involved. The lines can be successfully navigated only by friendly discussion—not by command. The level at which this can be done without friction is influenced by the personalities involved, their willingness to give and take, and the esprit of the organization.

Operating personnel should be instructed in the true purpose of staff inspection—they should understand that it is a service rather than a device for catching them in a dereliction of duty. When all members of the force understand the purpose and character of staff inspection, it can be used to the fullest extent to relieve commanding officers of heavy burdens and to promote a constructive and harmonious relationship between personnel of various units.

Appraisal of Intangibles. The inspector should spend most of the time inspecting operations and conditions concerning which there is no other way to receive reliable information. It is in the inspection of these latter, less tangible things that the inspector will render the greatest service to the chief.

Personal observation enables the inspector to ascertain the extent to which department procedures are being followed as intended or on paper only, to appraise officers' morale and their attention to duty, to evaluate public reactions to the police and their programs, and to determine conditions on the streets, in headquarters, and in station houses at all hours of the day or night. Rather than being restricted to what can be seen, the inspector should discuss duties and the way they are being performed with subordinate and superior officers alike.

Common Sense and Concentration on Important Matters. The inspection process can suffer needlessly when it is directed toward meaningless or perfunctory activities. Even when inspections are carried out with the best of intentions, they can be subject to misinterpretation and downright exaggeration if caution is not exercised regarding the importance of the subject matter. When inspections of overloaded and overworked line units conclude with criticisms of temporary equipment or administrative deficiencies that have little or no effect on the direct delivery of services, for example, resentment is bound to occur, and the credibility of inspections units—as well as the cooperation they receive—diminishes. The rule to be followed is that an inspector should consider things in the context of what is immediately important and what can wait.

Timeliness of Inspection. Inspection should occur as close as possible in time to any event that has precipitated it. Inspection carried out long after an incident or act takes place is much like shutting the barn door after the horse has gotten away; witnesses disappear or grow uncooperative, memories fade, and reconstructing an event becomes near impossible. Corrective action is also more meaningful when the time elapsed after a violation is short.

Control Points. Since it is often impossible to inspect an entire process, inspectors should generally focus their efforts on existing *control points*, or places in the process at which supervisory review is already routine. These control points, generally in effect because they provide line supervisors with the most logical opportunities for review, usually occur when actions have been documented—such as when a dispatcher records complaint information in a database or on a case-control form—or when responsibility shifts from one person to another. For example, the review of reports by a sergeant and the matching of reports with information received initially by the complaint officer or dispatcher are logical control points.

The dangers of relying on either a single control point or a very small number of such points as a means of inspecting a long and complicated process should be obvious. Either unintentionally or because line personnel come to know what inspectors look for and consequently "give them what they want" without regard to the overall soundness of a process, such *slice-in-time* investigations may not accurately measure the whole process. As a result, whether they are inspecting evidence handling, crime reporting, temporary lockup operations, or any other operation, staff inspectors should look at as many control points as possible and should vary the points examined from inspection to inspection.

The Cost of Inspections.   While inspections are generally directed at measuring and enhancing *effectiveness* (the degree to which organizational goals are attained), the *efficiency* of inspections (the extent to which their benefits outweigh their costs) should also be monitored carefully. Thus, unless a deficiency is likely to be repeated or reflects a problem of employee dishonesty, it makes little sense to spend $150 for an inspections unit to identify and describe a deficiency that itself accounts for only a $100 loss of tax funds.

It is, of course, impossible to predict such returns on cost in advance. Further, concern for finances must be balanced by the need to account for other less immediately apparent costs. Bad press, tensions between police and the community, and the threat of civil litigation may not immediately draw on an agency's checkbook, but, over time, they will add significantly to operating costs. Hence, in calculating financial return on investment, one must weigh not only immediate dollar costs but also the likely longer-term outcomes of failing to spend money to avoid potential problems.

As a general rule, therefore, inspections should focus on large expenses and on likely future expenses rather than on small expenditures and milk that is not likely to be spilled again. For example, absent the potential for major long-term damage to core department goals or relationships, inspections to ascertain that employees are making economical use of a product or service—such as the proper grade of paper—are justifiable if the inspection process costs less than the likely savings in expenditures for paper.

Frequency of Inspection.   The interval between inspections can be very important to the process. Key activities, such as reviewing crime-report classifications and spot-checking follow-up investigation reports, should take place on a weekly basis. Other activities, such as the inspection of facilities, can take place quarterly or semiannually. Of course, the degree of the problem has a strong bearing on the frequency of inspection. If an activity or process is being done well, the need for frequent inspection is less critical.

Staff Inspection of Line Inspection Reports.   Inspectors should promote the inspectional process throughout the organization, and their activities should stimulate, rather than retard, inspections by other members of the force.

Daily inspections of some aspects of the condition of personnel and matériel should be made by line supervisors and managers. For example, at the beginning of each tour of duty, sergeants should inspect the jail and the department-owned vehicles. Weekly or monthly formal inspections by line officers should also be carried out and should be documented by means of checklists that form a record of inspectional activity. These records can then be made available to staff inspectors as well as line commanders.

To lessen their own workload and to ensure more complete inspections, staff inspectors should rely heavily on documentation of these periodic inspections by line personnel. Suitably designed reports—when correctly and accurately prepared, promptly submitted, and used according to wisely conceived procedures—disclose much essential information and diminish the need for additional inspectors. Also, through the use of suitable reports that can be occasionally spot-checked, the inspector has more free time for making personal inspections.

A major advantage of the review of line inspection reports is that they force line supervisors and officers to make periodic inspections that, in the pressure of day-to-day work, might otherwise be neglected and to commit to writing statements of whether conditions are satisfactory or unsatisfactory. For example, patrol officers who are required to submit periodic reports on the vice conditions on their beats usually make greater efforts to learn whether such conditions exist. One of their principal tasks is to know the conditions on their beats, and failure to know—especially under community policing models—is as much a dereliction of duty as is the failure to take action in the face of such knowledge. When officers state that vice exists on their beats, they are bound to take some action against it or to report it to the vice division. If such officers periodically report that vice is present on their beats at certain times and locations and that the condition has been reported to the vice division, staff inspectors must ascertain why the vice division has permitted the condition to persist.

One reason for inspectors to perform personal inspections is to be assured of the accuracy of the reports of operating personnel. Inaccuracies arise from carelessness and indifference in inspection or in the preparation of the report or from a deliberate misrepresentation of facts. Additional instructions for the person making the inspection and preparing the report and for his or her supervising officer should eradicate the former; disciplinary action—up to removal from the department—may be necessary in the case of deliberate misrepresentation. Either of these actions, of course, would be initiated by order of the chief.

Follow-up.   A key element for the success of a formal inspection system is the certainty of actions taken to remedy deficiencies. If the inspection process continually discloses inadequacies that remain uncorrected, the system loses all effectiveness.

On a similar note, operating personnel often call attention to matters that they wish inspectors to report to a higher authority. Although reporting back to operating personnel is not within the scope of inspectors' duties, chiefs should make certain that the results of corrective action are made known to the inspectors—not only so that they can, if necessary, inform operating personnel of action to be taken but also to satisfy the inspectors themselves. In large departments, several months may go by before an inspection schedule brings the team into the same areas for repeat inspections. Inspectors' work quality is improved when they realize that constructive action is taken with respect to their views.

Box 13-3 states the purpose and nature of inspection and may be useful as the basis for a general order establishing an inspections program.

SUMMARY

Many action-oriented police personnel think of inspection as a dull subject, the work of bureaucrats more interested in neatness and in order than in ensuring the quality of line police services. Unfortunately, this negative view often is based on the manner in which some departments conduct the inspections function. When inspections are the work of isolated headquarters types who think of themselves as line units' adversaries, they are a counterproductive wedge in what should be a unified attempt to make sure that the public gets the police services it pays for. When done properly, by personnel who have an understanding of the primacy of police line operations and the problems of those on the line, staff inspections are one of the most important ways in which headquarters can assist line units. Similarly, when line inspections are conducted by supervisors and managers close to line personnel and their problems, they are immensely valuable.

To be useful, inspections should begin with the development of a clear set of performance standards. These should be crafted with special care in areas in which the public and the department can be most severely hurt by poor performance or misconduct. Most important, those who conduct inspections should never lose sight of the fact that their ultimate goal is the improvement of line police services.

QUESTIONS FOR DISCUSSION

1. Devise and discuss performance standards that might be used for the following purposes by staff inspectors in the department that employs you or that serves the community in which you reside:
   a. Preservation and storage of narcotics evidence
   b. Maintenance and distribution of portable radios
   c. Recording of officers' court-related overtime.
2. Some suggest that staff inspection is a task that requires great skill and that may create adversarial relationships between inspectors and the inspected. Consequently, they argue, staff inspection should be a permanent assignment. Others suggest that rotation between staff inspection and other assignments keeps inspections fresh and informed and strengthens the supportive aspect of inspectors' relations with other personnel. Evaluate and discuss these varying views.
3. In some departments, the line between inspections and internal affairs work is blurred. There, personnel perform both inspections and investigations of alleged misconduct by officers and other personnel. Do the advantages of such a practice outweigh its disadvantages?
4. A police chief has recently implemented a system of customer satisfaction surveys similar to that suggested and advocated by Dorothy Guyot in Box 13-1. In response, the leader of his department's union has claimed that the department is "looking over officers' shoulders" and that the new program is a "morale killer that proves the chief is more interested in having officers hold hands with citizens than in doing the real police work of finding and arresting criminals." What would lead to

BOX 13-3. Purpose and Nature of Inspection

PURPOSE

The purpose of an inspections program is to promote effectiveness and economy by the inspection of:

- Persons
- Things
- Procedures
- Results

In order to disclose:

- Conditions
- Situations
- Actions

That adversely influence the success of police operations because of weaknesses and failures in:

- Personnel
- Matériel
- Procedures

Which indicate a need for modified or additional:

- Organization
- Regulation
- Procedures
- Equipment
- Headquarters facilities
- Personnel
- Training
- Direction
- Leadership

NATURE

Inspection is accomplished by interviews with:

- Members of the department
- Persons involved in police incidents
- The general public

And analysis of:

- Inspection reports
- Police records
- Police statistics
- Police procedures

And observation of the condition of:

- Police quarters
- The jail
- Public places
- Equipment
- Personnel

In order to ascertain whether:

- Department morale is unsatisfactory
- Morale-destroying influences are at work
- The attitude, actions, reactions, and accomplishments of members of the department are satisfactory

- Training, direction, and supervision are satisfactory
- Rules governing personal care, hygiene, and fitness are being followed
- The integrity of all members is above reproach
- The moral standards of members of the department are satisfactory
- Regulations concerning the maintenance and use of equipment and property are being followed
- Equipment and property require repair or replacement
- Equipment and property are damaged or impaired because of improper use or inadequate maintenance
- Equipment and space are adequate
- Department procedures are suitable
- Department procedures are being followed
- Operations are being carried out as planned
- Department resources are being used to best advantage
- Department units are operating satisfactorily
- Any part of the police job is being neglected
- Community conditions affecting efforts to combat crime and disorder are satisfactory
- Public reaction to department policies, methods, and officials is satisfactory
- Department members are dealing satisfactorily with people and incidents

DUTIES OF THE POLICE INSPECTOR

As an agent of the chief of police, the police inspector should:

- Conduct open inspections of personnel, matériel, procedures, and results of police operations
- Inform the chief of:
  - Action that he or she has taken
  - Action desired by the chief
- Promote and stimulate supervision on the part of operating personnel by
  - Devising well-conceived inspection reports for their use that will require a positive statement that a condition is satisfactory or unsatisfactory
  - Instructing supervisory personnel in:
  - The use of inspection reports

BOX 13-3. **Purpose and Nature of Inspection** *(continued)*

- The nature of line and staff inspections
- Spot-checking inspection reports
- Inspect and correct reported unsatisfactory conditions
- Maintain satisfactory relationships with subordinate and commanding officers
- Focus attention on the appraisal of such intangibles as public relations, conditions in the community affecting police operations, and the morale of personnel

such a charge? What can be done to respond to it? What might have been done to anticipate and prevent it?

5. Inspections personnel in a major department recently told an investigative commission that they were reluctant to report deficiencies to the head of their agency because he had a reputation for "killing the messenger," or finding them at fault for not discovering misconduct or other problems earlier than they had. What *should* the agency head do when his or her inspectors find major operational problems in the course of their inspections?

NOTES

1. Intelligence and vice control are discussed in Chapter 17.
2. Another common title for this position is "integrity officer."
3. *O'Connor v. Ortega*, 480 U.S. 709 (1988); *Lovvorn v. City of Chattanooga*, 846 F. 2d 1539 (1988).

SOURCES

BURNHAM, DAVID. "$10-Million Heroin Stolen from a Police Office Vault," *New York Times* 1, 30 (Dec. 15, 1972).

CARLSON, TUCKER. "D.C. Blues: The Rap Sheet on the Washington Police," *Policy Review*, 63:26–33 (1993).

CHRISTOPHER, WARREN, et al. *Report of the Independent Commission on the Los Angeles Police Department* (July 1991).

Commission on Accreditation for Law Enforcement Agencies, Inc. *Standards for Law Enforcement Agencies* (Fairfax, Va., 1994).

GOLDSTEIN, HERMAN. "Improving Policing: A Problem Oriented Approach," *Crime and Delinquency*, 25:236 (April 1979).

GULICK, LUTHER. *Papers on the Science of Administration* (New York: Institute of Public Administration, 1937).

GUYOT, DOROTHY. *Policing as Though People Matter* (Philadelphia: Temple University Press, 1991).

Lovvorn v. City of Chattanooga, 846 F. 2d. 1539 (1988).

O'Connor v. Ortega, 480 U.S. 709 (1988).

REUSS-IANNI, ELIZABETH. *Two Cultures of Policing: Street Cops and Management Cops* (New Brunswick, N.J.: Transaction Books, 1983).

14

Police Misconduct and Integrity Control

KEY WORDS AND PHRASES

Nonprofit abuses
Brutality
Unnecessary force
Corruption
External corruption
Internal corruption
Gratuities

Victimless crime
Rotten apples
Rotten pockets
Pads
Scores
Integrity tests
Disciplinary action

To a greater degree than is true of most other organizations, control in police agencies requires checks on the behavior of individual employees. Police business requires officers to exercise authority over others and to engage in a variety of activities that require confidentiality and trust. Consequently, the most fundamental requirement for a police agency's aspirations to deliver high-quality service is the integrity of its own personnel. Police employees simply cannot be permitted to abuse either the citizenry or the powers of their office or to profit in improper ways from their work. For this reason, each police agency's system of inspection and control must have the capacity to deter, detect, and punish wrongdoing. Because inspections personnel should not directly participate in internal investigations of specific misconduct—especially those that may be covert—this task is usually the specific charge of internal affairs units or officers.

Despite the existence of inspections and internal affairs units, their functions—inspecting and controlling; and preventing, detecting, and punishing wrongdoing—cannot be exclusively delegated to any one supervisor or unit. Instead, like all other disciplinary and quality control functions, they permeate

449

the entire organization. At each level of authority, supervisors must plan and direct the work of others. From the chief down through each successive level to the officer on the street, therefore, they must also inspect and control the activities of subordinates to see that their work is done properly.

POLICE MISCONDUCT

Police misconduct is a very tough subject that is rarely dealt with candidly and thoroughly. While many, in and out of policing, may wish that police misconduct would simply go away, it has, like other types of sin, persisted in one form or another as long as police have been in business. Thus, it is clear that wishing will not make police misconduct disappear and that constant vigilance and persistent efforts to dig it out are central to the administrator's job. These efforts have not always occurred. Consequently, many of those outside policing are distrustful of officers and place little credence in the ability of police to police themselves.

Public Responses to Perceived Police Wrongdoing

Civilian Review. The perception that police did not deal forthrightly with wrongdoing in their ranks gave rise during the turmoil of the 1960s to calls for complaints against officers to be reviewed by panels composed of persons other than police officers (Ruchelman, 1974). Where such civilian complaint review boards have operated, they have often generated strong resistance. As a consequence, they often—and apparently deliberately—have been so badly understaffed and underfunded that they have not lived up to their adherents' expectations (Terrill, 1991).

Judicial Review and External Audits. Demands for civilian review have been renewed over the last several years, however, and have received a far more favorable reception (Walker and Bumphus, 1991). In addition to this increasingly widespread form of external oversight, police have been subjected to greater judicial scrutiny since 1978, when the U.S. Supreme Court expanded official liability for unconstitutional behavior by public employees.[1] Finally, elected officials have shown great willingness to subject police and their operations to critical study by blue-ribbon commissions and other external auditors (see Christopher et al., 1991; Kolts et al., 1992; Miami, 1984; Milwaukee, 1991; Mollen et al., 1993, 1994; St. Clair et al., 1992).[2]

Reasons for Increased Scrutiny

There are many reasons for this increased scrutiny of the police. The ineffectiveness of such other remedies as the exclusionary rule and criminal penalties to curb police abuse has encouraged the courts to expose the *deep pockets* of public treasuries to plaintiffs who have suffered police abuse. Two products of the civil rights movement—the political empowerment of urban minorities and the changing composition of police departments—have played a great part in increased receptivity to civilian review and independent external management studies. Spectacular incidents, such as the beatings of Rodney King in Los Angeles and Malice Green in Detroit, have sensitized much of the public to the need for police accountability.

Police Reluctance to Act.   Underlying all this has been a view that the police have been reluctant to make fair and vigorous efforts to root out and investigate wrongdoing in the ranks. There is considerable merit to this perception: in all too many places, a "blue curtain of silence" is routinely drawn over police transgressions. Indeed, without such a code of silence among police officers and their administrators, widespread corruption or abuse of citizens simply could not exist in police agencies.

This misdirected police solidarity is often attributable to a feeling by officers and administrators that they are a vilified minority that must band together for self-protection. Some misguided administrators believe that vigorously and objectively investigating suspected—or even *undeniable*—wrongdoing may demoralize their personnel. Often associated with this logic is a wrongheaded belief by administrators that acknowledging the existence of police misconduct is tantamount to admitting the failure of their own administrative efforts. Indeed, even from the most cynical perspective, police chiefs who learn of corruption are better advised to expose it themselves than to wait for someone else to do it instead.

Whatever their reasons, police who are unwilling to apply to police wrongdoing the same vigor that they apply to other criminality only strengthen the arguments for increased direct external oversight of the police. Further, no amount of external oversight excuses the police from doing everything possible to root out police misconduct.

TYPES OF POLICE MISCONDUCT

A prerequisite to any efforts to combat police misconduct is an understanding of the varieties of wrongdoing to which policing is vulnerable. Some improprieties—employee theft of supplies, padding of overtime, sexual harassment of subordinates or peers, and the like—are not unique to the police but are dangers in all organizations. Thus, like chief executives in any other line of work, police administrators have an obligation to fight these types of wrongdoing. But because police have such great authority over the lives and liberties of citizens, particularly heinous types of misconduct have appeared in U.S. police agencies and present a major challenge to all officials.

Police misconduct may be classified in several ways, but one of the most fundamental distinctions is between *profit-motivated corruption* and that which involves *nonprofit abuses of citizens* ranging from brutality through verbal abuse to simple discourtesy. The connection between these two types of activities is unclear, but it is noteworthy that some police agencies in which officers have been found guilty of abuses of the most serious types—brutality, fabricating evidence in criminal cases—have not been marked by any significant corruption. In many cases, brutality appears to be a form of overzealousness in anti-crime and order maintenance efforts on the part of officers who would never participate in money corruption. The reverse is not always true, however, and it appears that corrupt officers may also engage in brutality, either in the course of their profit-making efforts or because the rules generally have little meaning for them.

In other words, departments that have experienced scandals related to brutality often are free of profit-motivated corruption, but agencies with histories of corruption are sometimes also marred by brutality. This is so for two reasons. First, supervisors and administrators who are "on the take" have a very difficult time making certain that the field officers most likely to engage in brutality do not do so, or they are simply disinterested in preventing this form of misconduct (Goldstein, 1977:190). In addition, readiness to engage in brutality may be a signal that officers are also willing to take part in profit-motivated misconduct. The interim report of a commission that recently investigated allegations of police corruption in New York City suggested the following:

> A number of officers have told us that they were "broken in" to the world of corruption by committing acts of brutality; it was their first step toward other forms of corruption. A willingness to abuse people in custody or others who challenge police authority can be a way to prove that an officer is a tough cop who can be trusted and accepted by fellow officers. Brutality, like other kinds of misconduct, thus sometimes serves as a rite of initiation into aspects of police culture that foster corruption. (Mollen et al., 1993:9)

Nonprofit Abuses of Citizens

Brutality or Unnecessary Force? An important distinction between brutality and unnecessary force should be drawn.

Brutality is the conscious and intentional use of more force than officers need to defend themselves or others, to make arrests, or to accomplish any other legitimate police purpose. Brutality is purposeful abuse rendered by officers who employ it to punish rather than to defend themselves or to complete arrests, and it is usually committed by officers who make great efforts to keep their wrongdoing secret. Indeed, since brutal officers must lie about what they have done, the public is usually made aware of incidents of brutality despite, rather than because of, the reports of the officers involved.

Unnecessary force may cause as much damage as brutality, but it involves no ruthlessness on the part of the officers involved. Instead, it occurs when—through lack of training or expertise or because of recklessness, negligence, overconfidence, or haste—officers needlessly put themselves into dangerous situations in which they must subsequently use force to escape injury or death. While brutality involves needless *intentional* harm to others, unnecessary force usually occurs because *well-meaning* officers rush in where wiser and better-trained officers fear to tread.[3]

Emotionally Disturbed Persons. An illustrative example has been repeated in jurisdiction after jurisdiction in recent years. Over the last three decades, the national movement to deinstitutionalize mentally and emotionally disturbed people (EDPs) has reduced the populations of American mental asylums and

Broad police authority to use force sometimes makes it difficult to determine when police have crossed the line between necessary and unnecessary force.
AP/Wide World.

hospitals by more than 500,000 (Murphy, 1986). Certainly, neither police officers nor other nonmedical personnel can be expected to identify the specific disorders suffered by people whose behavior is dangerous or bizarre, but a walk through almost any big city's downtown area will confirm that many EDPs have joined the ranks of the homeless and have become a new sort of problem for the police. Formerly institutionalized, EDPs rarely came into contact with the police in years past; at present, however, the police are the officials called to deal with them when they act out.

In response to this problem, training has been developed for police encounters with EDPs and generally encourages a patient, nonthreatening approach in which officers keep their distance and demonstrate that they seek to help (Murphy, 1986). Unfortunately, not all police have been adequately trained to deal with EDPs in this manner. As a result, they sometimes apply to their encounters with EDPs the same techniques of deterrence through intimidation and threats of force that they have been trained to employ in their confrontations with more rational offenders. These techniques, however, often result in disaster when EDPs are involved. Pointing a gun at a knife-wielding robber, using a command voice to direct him or her to drop a knife and surrender, and advising the offender that there is no other viable option but surrender, for example, are likely to result in compliance and a bloodless arrest. But when police challenge knife-wielding EDPs in the same way—or worse, close in on them in attempts to disarm them—they are likely to precipitate attacks on themselves that can be halted only by resorting to deadly force. In short, trying to intimidate an EDP into submission is no less likely to result in explosion than is lighting the fuse on a stick of dynamite.

Shootings following hasty police attempts to intimidate EDPs are unnecessary because they are precipitated by inappropriate and needlessly volatile police action.[4] Often, they generate great criticism of the police, as well as civil liability. But, except when officers have ignored training that they have already received, the appropriate administrative response to such shootings is not to punish the officers involved. Instead, administrators should make certain that such officers—and all their colleagues on the line—are adequately trained to deal with EDPs.

This is not always easy. It is tempting to place the blame for situations that have gone wrong at the level of execution, rather than to acknowledge policy or training deficiencies—especially when doing so may expose a jurisdiction to liability for inadequate policy and training. Taking this easy way out, however, is counterproductive and damaging to the public, to officers, and to departmental discipline. In short, unnecessary force is usually a training problem rather than a reason for punishment.

Dealing with Brutality and Other Intentional Abuses

In cases of conscious abuses of citizens, it is appropriate to place blame at the level of execution. In addition, such instances should raise other questions. Brutality, for example, may be an individual aberration, but it may also demonstrate administrative weaknesses that should be addressed so that similar incidents may be prevented. Among the questions that should be considered after disclosures of brutality are the following:

1. Is the department unwittingly encouraging excesses by overemphasizing aggressiveness and such quantitative measures of crime-fighting effectiveness as arrests?
2. Does political rhetoric about wars on crime encourage officers to engage in brutality and other circumventions of citizens' rights?
3. Does training fail to prepare officers for situations in which their ability to control their tempers is put to severe tests?
4. Do policy and training adequately prepare officers to subdue resistance with the minimal degree of force?
5. Was the brutality a response to a misunderstanding caused by the officer's inability to deal sensitively with a member of a particular ethnic or cultural group? If so, to what extent can such inability be addressed by training?
6. Are official pronouncements and training related to the use of force and citizens' rights neutralized by middle managers or supervisors or by a street culture among officers that encourages toughness and aggressive behavior?
7. Are expectations by the public, the department, or other officials of what officers should accomplish in the way of ridding the streets of crime and undesirables so unrealistic that they frustrate officers and cause brutality?
8. Do brutal officers' histories include indications of instability or a propensity toward such conduct? If so, does the record also suggest supervisory

indifference to such indications of instability, prior questionable conduct, or other signs of a pattern of abusive behavior?

The Need to Consider the Whole Record. Brutality is not the only kind of intentional abuse in which officers have engaged. A recent scandal that has marred the excellent reputation of the New York State Police involves a group of investigators who fabricated latent fingerprints and other physical evidence in criminal cases ("Police Investigation," 1993:B5). Planting evidence—drugs, illegal weapons—on "dirty" suspects and giving perjured testimony designed to conceal violations of the laws of search and seizure or constitutional interrogation requirements have long been alleged and occasionally have been documented (Knapp et al., 1972:104). Allegations of wrongful arrests, illegal searches, harassment, and discourtesy also are made with some regularity against the police. When any of these abuses occur or are alleged, administrators should investigate them thoroughly and should consider any alleged misconduct in the context of an officer's entire career history.

This last is an extremely important consideration. In the great majority of circumstances, misconduct allegations by citizens cannot be sustained. Often, the only witnesses to controversial incidents are the officers and citizens most directly involved. In such cases, the citizen typically charges some wrongdoing that is denied by the officer. Then, in the absence of objective recording, physical evidence, or uninvolved witnesses, the complaint is ruled "not sustained."

Certainly, it would be inappropriate to punish any officer for an allegation that cannot be proved. At the same time, however, most large departments include a small number of officers who accumulate far larger numbers of unsustainable complaints—and who use force far more—than do their colleagues. The Christopher Commission's investigation of the 8,450-officer Los Angeles Police Department, for example, reported that:

> Of approximately 1,800 officers against whom an allegation of excessive force or improper tactics was made from 1976 to 1990, more than 1,400 had only one or two allegations. But 183 officers had four or more allegations, 44 had six or more, 16 had eight or more, and one had 16 such allegations.

> Of nearly 6,000 officers identified as involved in use of force reports from January 1987 to March 1991, more than 4,000 had fewer than five reports each. But 63 officers had 20 or more reports each. The top 5% of the officers (ranked by number of reports) accounted for 20% of all reports. (Christopher et al., 1991:IX–X)

The St. Clair Committee found a similar pattern in Boston. The committee sampled complaints filed against officers during 1989 and 1990 and reported that 74 percent had been subjects of prior complaints (St. Clair et al., 1992:110). Taken alone, this statistic means little, but the committee also reported:

> . . . it appears that a small number of officers are involved in excessive amounts of alleged misconduct. Of the 134 officers with prior complaints in our sample 13 (10%) had more than ten previous complaints. This small group of officers have generated an incredible total of *246* prior complaints (233 previous, 13 current). When we look at all of the prior complaints against our

sample of officers, we find that this 10% of officers are responsible for 45% of all previous complaints.

From the case records provided by the Department, we determined that very few of these complaints were sustained. Of the 246 complaints, only approximately 26 were sustained and 13 were still pending. (St. Clair et al., 1992:112)

Bargaining Away Authority to Consider the Past.   Many police departments have entered into agreements with bargaining units that prohibit or limit consideration of unsubstantiated allegations in dispositions of complaints or decisions about officers' careers. Such agreements are a mistake, and, where they exist, administrators should make every effort to rescind them. Where such agreements do not exist, administrators should take full advantage of their authority to have complete information before them when resolving complaints or use-of-force investigations.

To the argument that consideration of such information somehow contravenes officers' rights, the St. Clair report has an excellent retort:

> When asked about these officers with 10, 15, or 20 prior complaints, we were told by Department supervisors that prior complaints "can't be held against the officer unless they are sustained." The Department treats unsustained prior complaints similar to not guilty or dismissed criminal complaints, i.e., not relevant in deciding on the case in question. In most organizations, past behavior, whether alleged or confirmed, is used to assist the organization in identifying problem employees. . . . At the very least, officers who receive repeated citizen complaints of misconduct should be carefully monitored and more likely should receive counseling.
> . . . No police department and no community should tolerate a situation where officers with long histories of alleged misconduct, including some with histories of alleged physical abuse of citizens, remain on the street largely unidentified and unsupervised. (St. Clair et al., 1992:113–114)

The St. Clair Committee's recommendation makes good administrative sense and represents the only viable courtroom defense against questions about officers whose complaint jackets are much longer than those of the great majority of their colleagues. Most jurors who hear civil suits involving officers whose histories include long records of complaints, sustained or otherwise, believe that it is irresponsible for supervisors or administrators to overlook such histories. Given the opportunity, such jurors almost always punish jurisdictions that have ignored officers' pasts in this way.

Profit-Motivated Police Corruption

Herman Goldstein (1975:16) has observed that "one of the most amazing things about police graft is the endless variety of schemes that come to light." He provides a list of common activities that, although not exhaustive, includes many historic areas of bribery, extortion, and other unauthorized types of police entrepreneurship:

a. Failing to arrest and prosecute those the officer knows have violated the law.

b. Agreeing to drop an investigation prematurely by not pursuing leads which would produce evidence supporting a criminal charge.

c. Agreeing not to inspect locations or premises where violations are known to occur and where an officer's presence might curtail the illegal activity.

d. Refraining from making arrests in licensed premises where an arrest would result in license review that could lead to revocation.

e. Reducing the seriousness of a charge against an offender.

f. Agreeing to alter testimony at trial or to provide less than the full amount of evidence available.

g. Providing more police protection or presence than is required by standard operating procedures.

h. Influencing departmental recommendations regarding the granting of licenses.

i. Arranging access to confidential departmental records or agreeing to alter such records.

j. Referring individuals caught in a new and stressful situation to persons who can help them and who stand to profit from the referral.

k. Appropriating for personal use items of value acquired on the job. (Goldstein, 1975:18–19)

External and Internal Corruption.   All the types of corruption listed above are *external*, in the sense that they involve some interaction—bribery, theft, extortion—between corrupt police and people outside policing. In addition, hard lessons of experience have demonstrated that policing has also suffered from *internal* corruption. According to the Knapp Commission's investigation of New York corruption, the wide variety of assignments that may be performed by officers who hold the same rank and the range of opportunities they offer corrupt police accounted in part for a pattern of misconduct in which officers purchased desirable or lucrative assignments (Knapp et al., 1972:17).[5] More recent scandals in Massachusetts have involved the theft of promotional examinations by officers in several departments.

Gratuities.   Perhaps the most common form of police corruption is the small, usually unsolicited *gratuity*. Many administrators regard such gratuities as free or half-price meals, discount prices from local merchants, and Christmas gifts as the first step on a slippery slope to major corruption and, hence, try vigorously to eliminate them. Other administrators tolerate them, often writing them off as a traditional form of police-community relations. Whether either of these positions is absolutely correct is difficult to judge. When officers expect gratuities, they may find ways to punish restaurateurs and others who do not offer them. At the same time, their ability to deal objectively with those who have fed them *gratis* or furnished their homes at cost may also be compromised.

Corruption Trends.   In the years since Goldstein compiled his list, some corruption problems have become worse:

- As noted earlier, after the Washington, DC metropolitan police department discovered that a gun used in a criminal shooting was last located in its own evidence room, it conducted an audit and found that about 3,000 firearms had disappeared. Apparently, someone in the agency had joined the area's lucrative trade in high-capacity weapons.

- The profitable drug market has corrupted police and law enforcement personnel formerly thought untouchable. Among other more widely recognized problems, drugs have been removed from evidence packages, replaced with such substances as sugar and quinine, and sold back to drug dealers.
- Vice enforcement officers have seized gambling records and sold photocopies or duplicate computer disks back to arrestees so that they could check players' claims that they had bet on winning numbers, horses, or teams.
- The rapid expansion of computer intelligence and information files has made it easy for those so inclined to sell their access to these highly sensitive and confidential records.

Obviously, there can be no excuses for these types of conduct, and police are duty-bound to do everything possible to eliminate them. In dealing with them, and with any other categories of behavior that may be lumped under the heading of profit-motivated corruption, it is useful to know something about their causes and about the lessons of history.

Police Corruption Does Not Happen in a Vacuum. Some police jurisdictions have historically been free of significant corruption for a single reason: The nature of the communities they serve presents virtually no opportunities for officers to engage in it successfully. In places where nobody needs to buy police protection from arrest, or to ensure official inattention to wrongdoing, or to compromise the police in any other way, there are few chances for even personnel of the worst character to engage in corruption. Similarly, where communities are highly organized and quick to mobilize against criminal activity, corruption does not exist because the light of public scrutiny is sure to expose it.

Conversely, when communities—or periods in history—have been marked by widespread and profitable criminality, especially that involving the *victimless crimes*—public order offenses, including the vices, drugs, and violations of administrative ordinances—and by public apathy about such criminality, police corruption has been rampant. No period better exemplifies this than the era of Prohibition, when the manufacture or transportation for sale or the actual sale of alcoholic beverages was illegal. Unlike robbers, burglars, or other predatory criminals whose success depends on their ability to hide their operations from the police, the bootleggers and others involved in the illegal alcohol trade could not hide from the police. Instead, if they were to be successful, they had to be visible to their clientele—one cannot buy a drink unless one knows where to get it—and, hence, to the police. In order to operate, therefore, they had to reach an accommodation with the police, a task they usually accomplished by bribery. In the Chicago of Al Capone, Frank Nitti, and company, this pattern of corruption was so widespread that in 1931 the blue-ribbon commission impaneled to investigate the police drew a startling conclusion concerning the 6,700-member Chicago Police Department:

It is quite within the range of possibility that the shortest road to police reha- bilitation would involve mustering out the entire police personnel, and substi- tution of a new force, under new leadership, and guided by new statutory arrangements. Such a program would separate from the service a small minor- ity of police who have contributed their best efforts toward the upbuilding of the Police Department. That their efforts have failed is no reflection upon them as individuals. It will therefore be argued that the plan is too radical in that it does not recognize these personal factors. To that argument the answer must be given that separation of the sheep from the goats would in all likelihood prove an impossible task. It would necessarily involve conflicts among those committed to the work of reconstruction and thereby impair the prospects for success at the very outset. The swift, sure way of building anew should not concern itself with such factors but should concentrate upon a fresh start, unimpaired by even a trace of the old tradition. (Citizens' Police Committee, 1969:8–9)

It would be hard to argue that the police department had come to this sorry state because it employed only *rotten apples* whose major interest in po- lice work was graft. Instead, it is likely that many of even the most high- minded officers were absorbed into the liquor-related corruption because it was so commonplace that normal definitions of right and wrong had been turned on their heads. Officials at every level were involved in this corruption; the most upstanding figures drank at speakeasies; raids on and arrests at ille- gal distilleries and speakeasies seemed to please nobody; and gangsters like Capone were folk heroes. In such circumstances, not to engage in corruption— and to refrain from taking one's fair share of what everybody else is doing—is the conduct that marks one as an oddball who is not to be trusted. In short, the *system* itself had more to do with corruption than did a few rotten apples.

Nearly a half-century later, Officer Frank Serpico found much the same set of circumstances concerning illegal gambling in New York City. Virtually invis- ible in middle- and upper-class neighborhoods, illegal lottery betting—*num- bers*—is big business in urban ghettos and in some working-class neighbor- hoods. Unlike drug dealers, gambling operators have often been perceived as major benevolent figures in such areas, and their services are in great demand. During Serpico's time, as now, the Knapp Commission suggested, there was "no public pressure to crack down" on such offenders (Knapp et al., 1972:72; see also Maas, 1973). When gamblers are arrested, their records—and the bets and hopes of many poor people who engage in no other activities having to do with crime or the underworld—are taken as evidence. Obviously, police who make such arrests win no popularity contests among the urban poor, who often wonder why the police are not instead doing something about *real crime*. When brought to court to answer for their offenses, gamblers have historically received slaps on the wrist both from judges who legitimately accord a higher priority to filling cells with violent offenders and from judges who have them- selves been corrupted. According to Jonathan Rubinstein, for example:

- Only 17 of more than 9,000 persons arrested for gambling in New York City during 1970 received jail sentences;
- 2,096 persons were arrested for felonious gambling in New York State during 1969; 281 were indicted; 15 were convicted, and one went to jail;

- 517 of 4,720 persons arrested for gambling in Philadelphia during 1970 were convicted; five received jail sentences;
- 11,158 people were arrested for gambling in Chicago in 1963; 8,480 of these cases were dismissed; 2,678 were prosecuted; 1,118 were convicted; and 17 people received jail sentences. (Rubinstein, 1973:379)[6]

In this situation, it is not so surprising that police officers may come to see gambling as a harmless activity, invisible to all who do not take part in it, and to regard the gamblers' bribes as "clean" money, as opposed to the more "dirty" money that might be available from drug dealers, violent criminals, or others whose activities cause more obvious harm. Indeed, it is also not surprising that Serpico—who, alone in his squad of 16 vice enforcement officers, did not accept the envelope that came to him every month from his division's gamblers—was regarded as the deviant in his workgroup. Indeed, in the weird charade of Serpico's time—police accepting money for refraining from enforcing laws nobody seemed to care about—anybody who resisted the pressure to take part was a deviant.

The purpose of these two accounts is neither to apologize for corruption nor to single out either Chicago or New York for criticism. Since the Prohibition era, many other cities—including Albany, Atlanta, Baltimore, Boston, Cleveland, Denver, Detroit, Kansas City (Missouri), Louisville, Miami, New Orleans, Newark, Philadelphia, San Francisco, and Seattle—have suffered scandals related to widespread, profit-motivated police corruption (see, e.g., Fogelson, 1977).

Instead, the purpose is to point out that explanations attributing corruption to a few rotten apples in an otherwise unspoiled barrel are generally not valid when corruption is widespread. More logically, wrongdoing so endemic that officers like Serpico become labeled as deviants for *not* participating in it generally indicates that something is seriously wrong with the barrel itself. As Lawrence W. Sherman (1974:7–9) has pointed out, police corruption may be classified into three types that vary in terms of pervasiveness, organization, and the source of bribes or other illegal income:

> *Rotten apples and rotten pockets* are individual officers or small groups of officers who engage in corruption on their own. Recent scandals in New York involving teams of officers engaged in theft and sale of drugs (Kelly, 1992; McAlary, 1989) provide good examples of this type of corruption, as did the experiences presented in the book and movie, "Prince of the City" (Daley, 1978).

> *Pervasive unorganized corruption* occurs when most of a department's members are corrupt, but engage in wrongdoing independent of each other.

> *Pervasive organized corruption* is the worst of all, because it involves massive corruption schemes, such as existed during prohibition-era Chicago (Citizens' Police Committee, 1969) or among New York vice and gambling enforcement officers during the era of Frank Serpico (Knapp et al., 1972; Maas, 1973; Shecter, 1973).

Before police administrators succumb to the instinct to claim that publicly disclosed corruption is the province of a few outlaw or rogue cops, therefore, they should attempt to determine how widespread and widely known it is. If the answers they find demonstrate that corruption is neither isolated nor immediately exposed by others who learn of it, they should suspect that characteristics of the community and the police and the relationships between them—rather than simply the criminality of a few rogue cops—may contribute to it.[7]

Among the questions that may be asked to determine whether corruption is a problem of rotten apples or an indication of deeper systemic problems are the following:

1. *How many officers are involved in the corrupt activity?* Obviously, the greater the number or percentage of officers involved in the activity, the less likely it is to be an aberration by one or a few officers.

2. *How high up the chain of command does the corruption extend?*

3. *How many nonparticipating officers, members of the community, or other officials knew about the corrupt activity?*

4. *Did any nonparticipating person who knew about this activity report it? If so, how long did it take, and under what circumstances did this occur?* There is an important difference between voluntary disclosure of misconduct and disclosure by someone who uses his or her information as a means of getting a good deal in a case in which he or she is already accused. The former usually is a *choice* made by a person who is distressed by misconduct and is an affirmation of the integrity of a system. The latter is an attempt to bargain by one who has few choices and does nothing to affirm the integrity of the police, the community, or the relationship between them.

   An important issue that should be examined under this heading is the state of incentives and disincentives to reporting corruption or other misconduct. Nobody, in the old movie terms, likes a rat. No matter how egregious the conduct reported, *whistle-blowers* are sure to earn the enmity and suspicion of many people both in and out of the organization.

   Stigmatization of this type is a powerful disincentive to coming forward with information about wrongful conduct, especially when it may implicate colleagues and friends (see, e.g., Daley, 1978). This is a powerful disincentive that should be counterbalanced by rewards and reinforcement for the courage to expose wrongdoing. Police officers are routinely rewarded and promoted for important arrests and contributions to their agencies' effectiveness and productivity; their efforts and successes in exposing corruption should certainly be included among these reasons for recognition.

5. *Have previous attempts to report the misconduct gone unheeded? If so, why?* There is perhaps no better indication of a widespread lack of integrity than reluctance to accept or act on information that police officers may be involved in corrupt activities.

6. *Is the corruption associated with an activity that very visibly provides illegal goods or services for a large clientele?* Because of their high visibility, few enterprises that provide ready access to such illegal products as gambling, illegal liquor, or prostitution can long remain in business without compromising officials at some level. The greater the number of officials who have some jurisdiction over illegal activities (police patrol officers, detectives,

vice officers, prosecutors, judges), the more likely it is that illegal businesses that continually operate at the same location have corrupted an entire system or some crucial point in it.

7. *Is the corruption associated with the enforcement of laws or administrative ordinances (e.g., prohibitions on the hours during which liquor or other merchandise may be sold; construction or building codes) that are routinely ignored and that have no support in the community?* This is not a suggestion that laws that create administrative headaches should be ignored. Instead, it should be read as a reminder that some laws, once strongly supported and vigorously enforced, have lost their meaning over time. As was true of New York's gambling laws during the Knapp/Serpico period, attempts to enforce such laws often result in corruption.

8. *Is the corruption associated with a law enforcement activity about which the agency has not formulated a clear policy?* What the courts have called "unfettered discretion" on the part of criminal justice officials has been associated with a variety of abuses. When police officers are free to enforce or not enforce laws without having to account for their decisions, they have an important tool of extortion, especially where crimes involving no victim are concerned. It is very difficult for a corrupt officer to accept or extort a bribe from a robber because the robbery victim is sure to complain about the officer's inaction. But when police officers are free to arrest or not arrest gamblers, drug dealers, pimps, prostitutes, or others whose activities do not directly hurt unwilling specific individuals, corrupt officers are given a persuasive carrot and stick.

One way to eliminate this carrot and stick is to clearly articulate the circumstances in which police may or may not arrest, especially where victimless offenses are concerned. In New York City following the Knapp Commission scandals, for example, Police Commissioner Patrick V. Murphy abolished the carrot and stick by prohibiting officers from making arrests in cases of gambling and possession of small amounts of drugs except in response to documented complaints by citizens. Murphy did so, he later wrote with Gerald Caplan, because of his realization that "in the wrong hands, the discretion to decide whom to arrest becomes a hunting license for personal gain; the corrupt officer employs lawful authority to threaten arrest unless a bribe is forthcoming" (Murphy and Caplan, 1991:252).

Despite fears that Murphy's action would lead to more widespread criminality or would be the first step in a trend of weakened enforcement, few people in the city noticed the difference, and corruption related to gambling offenses was virtually eliminated.[8]

9. *Is the corruption consistent with some partisan end?* Because American police have historically been so directly accountable to local politicians, much of the most widespread police corruption has been encouraged or even directed by elected officials and political power brokers. Hence, when corruption appears to feed right into the goals of such officials—awarding licenses to big contributors, overlooking political figures' violations, accepting bribes in return for allowing parking or other violations outside political figures' restaurants or hotels, misreporting incidents involving

A trusting relationship like this does not last long where police corruption exists.
AP/Wide World.

political figures—police administrators should be attuned to the probability that something more than isolated wrongdoing by individual officers is afoot.

In other words, police departments are close reflections of the communities and general morality in which they function. Because some corruption is indeed attributable to outlaw police officers, there may occasionally be found police rotten apples in jurisdictions noted for high levels of public and official integrity. But in jurisdictions marked by obsolete laws, great public demand for illegal goods and services, and low levels of integrity in governance and public life generally, the corollary may also be true; the honest cop may be as rare in such places as is the rotten apple in otherwise excellent communities and agencies. As hard as it may be for police administrators to examine critically the systems and communities of which they are themselves such an important part, fighting corruption most effectively demands that they must do so when they become aware that it exists in the ranks.

If such examinations suggest that powerful community institutions either support or are apathetic about corruption and the activities that give rise to it, the administrator's task is a difficult one. He or she must make sure that the press, the public, and other officials are informed about the costs of corruption to the quality of life and reputation of a community.

Few major legitimate employers, for example, knowingly operate in or move to communities in which corruption is tolerated. Newspapers and television stations should be made to understand that a willingness to look the other way where corruption is concerned keeps potential advertisers and prosperous subscribers out of town and, consequently, has a great effect on advertising rates as well.

The public should also know that external police corruption involves two parties who (except when deals are made to convince one to turn on and testify against others) should be treated equally harshly by the police and the criminal justice system. Corrupt cops have long had to worry that accepting a bribe from the wrong gambler or traffic violator might put them in jail, but those who offer or give such bribes rarely have been treated as the felons their acts make them. This is perhaps understandable; the police officer who takes a bribe betrays a public trust and deserves harsh punishment. At the same time, officers often betray this trust only at the inducement of members of the public. It takes only a few well-publicized arrests and prosecutions of those who corrupt the police to send out a clear message that bribery is not an activity that can be conducted with impunity. To this end, the police must mobilize the prosecutor to assist in detecting and proceeding with vigor against corrupters of the police.

The fact that corruption rarely happens in a vacuum should also serve as a warning against complacency to chiefs in jurisdictions in which corruption is not a problem. Such chiefs and their departments should carefully monitor changes in their communities, as well as in society generally, in an attempt to predict and assess their impacts on the quality and integrity of their personnel and their work. Probably nowhere are these needs better illustrated than in the many formerly quiet southern jurisdictions that suddenly became corrupted by the big money associated with drug trafficking. The big money offered by drug traffickers who needed police protection while they unloaded their boats or planes at isolated airstrips and marinas corrupted several unprepared law enforcement agencies in the early 1980s.

Salary Has Little to Do with Corruption.   Except where police officers are grossly underpaid, there is little evidence that corruption may be eliminated or even significantly reduced by increasing the "clean dollars" in officers' paychecks. Indeed, even in departments that pay poverty-level salaries, corruption may be indirect, having more to do with the poor quality of applicants attracted to such low-paying jobs than with officers' perceived need to supplement their incomes with bribes and gratuities. Similarly, the absence of corruption in many comparatively well-paid police departments is often more closely associated with the fact that most of the communities they serve—prosperous suburbs, for example—are relatively free of the kinds of activities that generate corruption than with salary levels per se. In places where these activities have reached the level of scandal—as in New York immediately before the Knapp/Serpico investigations—corruption has existed even though police have been given very large salary increases. In other words, high salaries probably are associated with the absence of corruption only to the extent that they are found in places where gambling, drug trafficking, prostitution, illegal liquor sales, and the like, are rare or nonexistent.

Certainly, police should be amply compensated for their work, and, surely, by any objective measure they are underpaid in virtually all American police agencies. But despite what employee groups might argue, the message of this experience is that pay raises are not an easy way to avoid or reduce corruption.

Some Types of Corruption Are More Difficult to Control than Others.   The Knapp Commission discussed two types of police bribery and theft:

The "pad" refers to regular weekly, biweekly, or monthly payments, usually picked up by a police bagman and divided among fellow officers. Those who make such payments as well as policemen who receive them are referred to as being "on the pad."

A "score" is a one-time payment that an officer might solicit from, for example, a motorist or a narcotics violator. The term is also used as a verb, as in "I scored him for $1,500." (Knapp et al., 1972:66)

Most of the corruption experienced firsthand by Frank Serpico involved the *pad*, the gamblers' regular monthly payoff to vice officers.[9] Although pads were highly organized and disciplined, by any objective standard, they also should have been easy to eliminate. Every month during the existence of a pad or a note, some corrupt officer must pick up money directly from a briber or at a drop arranged by prior understanding. Since the regularity and predictability of this arrangement should facilitate detection and apprehension, it is likely that pads can exist for any sustained period only if law enforcement officials are less than enthusiastic about putting them out of business.

Scores, by contrast, are much more difficult to predict and control. Perhaps the definitive illustrations of the problems of controlling scores involve drug trafficking. How, for example, can a police administrator prevent a police officer—or a pair of police officers—from taking a suitcase full of a million or so dollars in small bills offered by a cocaine smuggler who has been discovered carrying a large quantity of drugs during a late-night car or boat stop on a lonely road or several miles from shore? This and other such situations are unpredictable encounters between strangers who hope never to see each other again.

These are also extremely tempting situations for even the best-intended personnel. Young officers who viewed involvement in corruption as not even the remotest possibility—but who have young families, big bills, and long-term obligations—may suddenly find themselves faced with a very tough test of their morality: Do I arrest this person and get a pat on the back from my superiors, or do I take the million dollars, let the offender go, and ensure my family's future and kids' educations?

Other scores involve less dramatic situations and lesser amounts of money. American police have been arrested for stealing money and goods at the scenes of burglaries and robberies, from drunks and arrestees, and from the bodies and homes of people who have died suddenly. Narcotics officers have withheld drugs and money from evidence they have seized. William Phillips, a corrupt police officer who worked as an undercover agent for the Knapp Commission after he was caught in an extortion attempt, told his biographer of a career full of scores that even included accepting a bribe in return for not arresting an assault suspect—and then selling the assailant's name and address to the assailant's hospitalized victim so that he could exact his own revenge (Shecter, 1973).

Scores differ from pads in another important way. Places that have never been the turfs of organized criminals and their regularized activities are the least likely settings for pads, but opportunities for extremely lucrative scores may strike anywhere. A drug "mule" driving a load of cocaine and a suitcase full of cash from Los Angeles to Seattle—or from Brownsville, Texas, to Chicago, or from Miami to Boston—for example, passes through police jurisdictions of all sizes and characteristics.

Clearly, therefore, dealing with opportunistic corruption requires more than the traditional, *reactive* investigative technique of waiting for complaints and then investigating. Absent the testimony of participants, unexpected scores are impossible to re-create. Among the more successful techniques for deterring and discovering scores are some adopted from practice where more traditional criminality is involved.

IAU field associates.   Following the Knapp/Serpico scandals, the New York Police Department established a *field associate* program, in which line officers were recruited to secretly report to the internal affairs unit (IAU) on any misconduct they observed while at work. The program received substantial publicity and reportedly included at least one field associate in each department unit. While the program's success in detecting corrupt activities is impossible to measure because of the agency's concerns about exposing associates who had provided information that precipitated investigations, several points can be made:

1. The program almost certainly had great effects on officers' willingness to engage in wrongdoing with, or in the presence of, colleagues. When officers could not be certain whether or which of their colleagues were field associates who reported regularly to internal investigators on their observations, their ability to trust that they would not be *given up* dissipated, and whatever wrongdoing they may have been involved in was driven underground.
2. The program almost certainly had negative effects on officers' morale and camaraderie; it is hard to be relaxed with peers when one or more may be members of the agency's own secret police. As Patrick Murphy, in whose administration the program was created, suggested, there is reason for concluding that this is an objectionable tactic that should be undertaken only when police wrongdoing is a substantial problem (Murphy, 1977:80).
3. Participants in such a program should not be encouraged to serve as *snitches* whose information on minor delinquencies will be used as the basis for disciplinary action. There is probably no faster way for an administrator to sow divisiveness in a police agency than to cause officers to distrust each other out of fear that their every misstep may be recorded and reported.
4. Such a program is, in a sense, an admission of failure. Why would a field associate program be necessary if a department had succeeded in inculcating in all its personnel a sense of responsibility for reporting whatever wrongdoing they witnessed? If a department's efforts to ensure integrity were truly successful, all officers would perform the role assigned to field associates.
5. The recent investigation of apparently renewed corruption in the NYPD was critical of the department's failure to continue using such undercover operations (Mollen et al., 1993:14).
6. From a truly Machiavellian perspective, it is probably more important that officers in a corrupt department *believe* that an announcement of a field associate program is true than that the program actually exist.

Integrity tests. Police integrity tests are *stings* designed to determine whether officers take advantage of opportunities to engage in corruption presented to them by undercover operatives. In New York City, these have included "wallet tests" in which uniformed officers were handed wallets filled with cash and owner's identification by "pedestrians" who claimed to have found them on the street but whose schedules made it impossible (e.g., by virtue of having to catch a train or an air flight) to turn them in at police facilities. After handing the wallets to these officers, the undercover pedestrians would dash off. The test, of course, was to determine whether the officers would then properly process the wallet and its cash contents as lost property. Other stings have tested whether officers would surrender all the contraband, cash, and valuables seized from "arrestees" and whether they could be induced to accept bribes from "wrongdoers."

Like all other undercover operations, stings may raise questions of entrapment. As long as they do not induce crime on the part of people not otherwise disposed to crime, however, they avoid this problem. They also can be executed arbitrarily and in ways that police employees—like anyone else subjected to such tests for no apparent reason—might find objectionable. When they involve targets selected on the basis of some reasonable criteria (e.g., an articulable reason to suspect that an individual or a group may be involved in wrongful conduct) that make them invulnerable to attack as fishing expeditions, however, integrity tests should be considered a valuable deterrent and detection device. In addition, when used to test the integrity of the complaint reporting system rather than to detect wrongdoing, they also are a good means of assessing the general level of integrity within the agency.

"Turning" those involved in corruption. A standard technique among criminal investigators is the practice of "using little ones to get big ones," of compromising minor violators and "turning" them for use in continuing investigations of more serious offenders. Until the Knapp/Serpico scandal and the sensational testimony and evidence provided by corrupt officers who were turned in this manner, however, this tactic was virtually unknown in investigations of suspected criminality by police. Instead, corrupt officers have generally been treated as pariahs by their agencies and, apparently on the belief that they would not violate the police *code of silence*, have not been asked to participate in further investigations as a way of minimizing their own problems. This is a mistake because, as experience suggests, officers caught in corruption frequently make zealous and effective operatives and witnesses.[10] Despite the administrators' distaste for dealing with corrupt officers, therefore, "turning" is a technique that may be useful in discovering unsuspected corruption and in arranging stings (see Shecter, 1973).

THE INTERNAL AFFAIRS UNIT

As discussed in this chapter and in Chapter 12, discipline is a responsibility that runs throughout police agencies. When minor violations of department rules, regulations, or policies occur or are suspected, sergeants generally handle them on an informal basis. When violations or allegations are more serious—or even criminal—they traditionally have been investigated by high-ranking personnel. As departments have grown, this task has become more routine and has become the province of specialists.

In large departments, these specialists should be located in an internal affairs unit (IAU) established to exercise staff supervision over all internal investigations and to conduct the actual investigations in selected cases. The IAU should have the responsibility for recording, registering, supervising, and controlling the investigation of complaints against officers and for ferreting out evidence of corruption within the force, but its responsibility should not include the actual dispensation of punishment or other disciplinary actions. The operation of this unit protects the reputation of the department by establishing, through complete and objective investigation, than any allegation of misconduct made against a police officer, regardless of the source, is either sustained by evidence or not so sustained; that, although the alleged act did occur, the officer was exonerated; or that the act did not occur and the case was unfounded.

In addition, the IAU should bear some responsibility for identifying and responding to apparent *patterns* of misconduct. As indicated earlier, these patterns may involve repeated complaints that cannot be individually sustained. But they also include other signals not readily visible to the IAU, such as:

- Vehicle accidents
- Frequent use of sick leave
- Frequent injuries, on-duty or off-duty
- Frequent tardiness or unexplained absence
- Changes in mood, performance, or relationships with colleagues and supervisors

These actions and characteristics may indicate that officers are suffering from personal or professional stresses that can explode in ways harmful to themselves, others, and the department. They usually are far more apparent to supervisors and colleagues than to headquarters units such as the IAU, but the IAU (and the personnel unit) should encourage those closest to such officers to call them to official attention.

In departments of fewer than 1,000 or so officers, the internal investigations function can be carried out without the need for subdivision of the unit. In larger agencies, however, it is necessary to group the activities of the unit in some logical way, such as shown in Figure 13-1. Another logical arrangement divides the IAU into three sections:

Complaint investigations section. The responsibilities of this section include staff supervision of the investigations carried out by line commanders and the investigation of the most serious complaints made against department personnel.

Administrative section. The purpose of this section is to receive, file, and process all complaints against department employees and to serve as a liaison with the trial board and complaint review board.

General investigations section. This section should be given the responsibility of conducting confidential investigations affecting department personnel, with work to be initiated at the direction of the chief of police. Since personnel are required to work covertly at times, security should be observed in the operations of such a section and in reporting the results of its activities. If stings and other proactive work are to be conducted, this section bears the logical responsibility for it.

IAU Responsibilities

Ferreting Out Violations.   The department may learn or suspect that officers or civilian employees are accepting gratuities for special favors; ignoring violations by favored persons; soliciting or accepting bribes; giving confidential information to lawyers, bond brokers, or others; stealing or extorting money from prisoners; rolling drunks; working in league with vice operators or drug dealers; and so on. The IAU must use various undercover techniques, including stings, to ferret out violations of this nature and to produce evidence that tests allegations against officers or other personnel. When such evidence is found, the chief or commanding officer of the accused should proceed as with any other complaint against the force, and where the seriousness of the offense warrants it, an arrest should be made and charges preferred.

Registration.   A register should be kept in a constantly occupied post in the division. All commanders, supervisors, and others who receive complaints or hear of suspected violations of laws, ordinances, or department regulations or policies should be required to report them by telephone within an hour and to obtain a register number from the IAU. All telephone calls into and out of the register line should be recorded, and the register should contain spaces for the registration number, name, rank, badge number, and duty assignments of the alleged violator; the date and hour of the first entry and receipt of the first written report; the date the case was considered by the department disciplinary board and/or the civilian complaint review board; and the date of the final action by the chief. There should be no index to the book, and access to it should be limited to the chief and the highest-ranking personnel in the IAU.

In larger agencies, especially, this register and all information related to both alleged and suspected police misconduct, as well as the use of force, should be automated. When such information is lodged in a computer database, as Box 14-1 suggests, questions concerning factors that may be related to both specific incidents and general trends can be quickly and regularly investigated. Obviously, security measures limiting access to such data only to specifically authorized personnel should be designed in consultation with computer specialists.

Supervisors and commanders must be allowed to exercise some discretion in deciding whether to register complaints that are observed by them and that are disposed of by oral reprimands. *They should exercise no discretion in deciding whether to register complaints reported to them by citizens.* In cases of internal complaints, versus those filed by citizens, it should be within the rights of unit commanders to give written reprimands and to exact predetermined minor penalties (e.g., up to two or five days' suspension without pay or denial of pay) without having to reprocess such decisions through the department's disciplinary machinery. Unlike oral reprimands, such actions should be reported to the IAU for review to ensure that they are justified and for recordation in the

BOX 14-1. The LASD's Personnel Performance Index

A recent blue-ribbon commission's investigation of the Los Angeles County Sheriff's Department (LASD) commented on the absence of a computerized system to track officers' conduct in that agency. Although the commission's primary focus was the use of excessive force, its observations are relevant to policing and to discussions of police misconduct generally:

To a large extent, [the absence of such a computerized system] is a result of a previous policy of self-imposed ignorance. Driven by fears that data on use of force and citizen complaints would be used against it in civil litigation, the LASD followed legal advice from County Counsel to avoid creating "paper trails" when it could. When it could not, the information was scattered throughout the LASD and kept haphazardly.

. . . The lack of concrete and specific information cripples management in several ways. First, it disables the LASD, its training bureaus and its task forces from adequately reviewing and evaluating weakness in current training and policy. Changes thus cannot be made in a timely fashion. . . .

Second, the lack of useful information prevents the Department from identifying individual problem officers, or cliques of problem officers, until after the damage has been done, possibly subjecting the County to millions of dollars in civil exposure. . . .

Third, failure to track force consistently and in a useful format disables managers from identifying officers with a propensity to use unnecessary force. . . .

Fourth, the absence of a uniform, Department-wide force tracking system gives rise to an inference that the LASD puts a low priority on identifying and rooting out those who use excessive force. . . .

Fifth, failure to document and track all uses of force disables the LASD from countering and putting to rest allegations by citizens' groups that either outright misconduct or questionable force is widespread within the LASD. An IAB officer's observation that, "[s]ure, we've got some bad guys out there doing all kinds of stupid stuff," is no substitute for hard data. (Kolts et al., 1992:169–170)

The LASD's response to this rather harsh criticism was to propose and begin the design of a computerized Personnel Performance Index (PPI). According to the commission's first subsequent staff report:

The LASD claims that the PPI is by far the most sophisticated computer tracking system of its kind. We agree. The LASD hopes to market the system to other law enforcement agencies and, accordingly, is protecting its intellectual property rights to the PPI's design and software.

The PPI records and tracks information pertaining to six separate areas: (1) uses of force; (2) officer involved hit and non-hit shootings; (3) citizen complaints or commendations; (4) formal administrative investigations of possible officer misconduct; (5) civil claims against the LASD filed with the County; and (6) lawsuits filed against the LASD. Each of these applications is linked, enabling managers to determine, for example, whether a use of force now the subject of litigation had ever resulted in any disciplinary action against the involved officers. The PPI also contains a powerful application permitting a manager to program the PPI to his or her own requirements for an early warning of potential problems. The PPI also contains a sophisticated program sharply delimiting the access to files on the basis of rank and case sensitivity.

The PPI has the following features, among others:

- Uses of force are documented according to the weapons used, the injury caused, and the location of the injury. This ensures that each use of force is given its proper weight by managers and executives.
- Managers are able, for the first time, to conduct sophisticated factual queries for purposes of training and managing risk. For example, the Training Bureau can, for the first time, test the effectiveness of a Department-approved weapon (such as the baton) by generating statistics on how frequently the weapon is used and in what circumstances, as well as the sorts of injuries (including those to LASD officers) associated with its use.
- Entries regarding force incidents, shootings, and citizen complaints will document which supervisors were on duty when the alleged incident occurred.
- Each application allows for the electronic "attachment" of notes and incident-related documents, including computer-imaged photographs, sketches, and handwritten materials.
- The PPI provides easy access to pertinent information regarding lawsuits, such as: (1) the parties to the lawsuit and their respective counsel; (2) the causes of action and damages sought; (3) a synopsis of the allegations giving rise to the lawsuit; (4) important dates in the litigation; and (5) the ultimate fate of the lawsuit, such as trial verdict or settlement amount.

BOX 14-1. **The LASD's Personnel Performance Index**
(continued)

- The PPI contains a powerful application which enables a limited number of managers to set electronic "triggers" for automatic reports on uses of force, citizen complaints, lawsuits, and the like. The triggers prompt the captain to intervene, in a nonpunitive fashion, and assess whether one of his or her officers is at risk. (Bobb et al., 1993:25–27)

As one might expect, considerable technical difficulty has been encountered in the development of this sophisticated system, but it is directed at highly laudable goals that, in this computer age, should be achievable.

Sources: Bobb et al., October 1993; Kolts et al., July 1992.

officer's personnel file. If an action is found to be unjustified, it should be rescinded by the chief, and the officer should be compensated for any loss that may have been sustained. Commanders who exercise this disciplinary authority arbitrarily should, of course, be corrected.

Many agencies permit no appeal of oral or written reprimands that remain at lower levels in the department (e.g., not in the officer's department or central personnel office file). But when disciplinary action consists of a formal written reprimand that can affect promotion or pay raises, or when loss of pay is involved, the right of appeal should be permitted.

Investigations. The IAU should serve as a clearinghouse for deciding whether to conduct investigations itself or to assign them to the districts or divisions in which they originated or in which suspected officers are assigned. This should not be a totally discretionary process, however, and the IAU should be required to employ some criteria in deciding how to apportion cases. Generally, cases that are very serious, involve suspected criminal activity, or affect supervisory or command levels should be retained for investigation by the IAU. All cases brought to the IAU's attention by district or division commanders should require at least preliminary investigations, complete with findings and recommendations, by those commanders.

Similarly, to ensure that accountability extends as far as possible along the managerial line, watch commanders or desk officers who receive complaints should be required to submit written reports to the IAU before going off duty. The best evidence from the officers involved is a verbatim transcript of an interview conducted as close in time to the event as possible. If this is proscribed by ill-advised labor contracts, legislation, or other arrangements, reports should be obtained from accused officers.

The first recommendation for actions should come from the lowest command level so that, in cases in which officers have been found guilty as charged, they and their colleagues will not feel that summary sentences have been given. The recommendation should pass up the channels to the chief, with each level reviewing and commenting on previous recommendations. The various suggestions may then be assessed and reevaluated by the internal investigations unit before the case is finally presented to the chief. Regardless of how a civilian complaint review may be involved in the process, the final decisions as to disposition should lie with the chief, who is both the operating manager and the chief executive officer of the department.

When a charge against an officer is not sustained by the investigation, he or she should be notified in writing of the final disposition, and the case should be closed. Regardless of whether charges are sustained, the allegation and disposition should be retained in the officer's personnel file, while the record of the investigation should remain with the IAU.

Staffing IAUs

Those charged with interrogating or interviewing personnel during internal investigations should outrank their interviewees, but most personnel investigations involve officers of lower rank. Hence, unless a department has substantial problems involving unethical activity and dishonesty among high-ranking officers, it usually is sufficient to staff internal affairs units with investigators of the sergeant and lieutenant ranks. Whatever their rank, obviously, internal affairs investigators must have strength of character, loyalty, and absolute integrity (see Box 14-2).

In small agencies, responsibility for internal affairs may necessarily lie with the chief or his or her immediate assistant, but there are varying schools of thought concerning the best way to identify those to be assigned to large departments' internal affairs units. In some large agencies, work in an IAU is seen as a *calling* and is conducted exclusively by officers who apply for such assignments or who agree to requests to engage in it early in their careers. One danger with this assignment pattern is that the IAU may come to be regarded by line personnel as an adversary, staffed by self-righteous and naive volunteers who seek to embarrass and harass field officers and staff.[11]

In some places, this attitude has been a rationalization on the part of line personnel whose wrongful activities give them plenty of reason to fear and loathe internal affairs personnel. But in departments in which misconduct is not endemic, internal affairs personnel may lend strength to this view by engaging in an overly rigid and punitive application of department rules. When they do, the likely result is an unnecessary and counterproductive divisiveness in which field personnel view themselves and internal affairs personnel as *us and them*. In such cases, field personnel define their quality control responsibilities not in terms of cooperating and working toward common goals with internal affairs but as protecting themselves and their units against the "headhunters" from the IAU.

One way to overcome this, it has been suggested, is to draft internal affairs personnel from the ranks of upwardly mobile members of the agency. Under this logic, all officers at an advanced rank—typically lieutenant, but perhaps also sergeant or even captain—would be required as a step in their career tracks to perform satisfactorily in an internal affairs assignment. Three desirable outcomes of such a schema are predicted. First, internal affairs would be destigmatized and humanized, less isolated from the field, and no longer vulnerable to the criticism—however unfair or unjustified—that it is a lair of overzealous volunteers who, in the view of detractors, lack the stomach for *real* police work. Second, in addition to this change in the perceived objectivity of

BOX 14-2. The Mollen Commission

About every twenty years since the 1890s, the New York City Police Department has suffered a corruption scandal. The 1994 report of the Mollen Commission, the blue-ribbon group that investigated the most recent such scandal, found that the extent and nature of corruption had changed since the 1970s revelations begun by Frank Serpico. "Unlike the situation a generation ago," the Mollen Commission noted, "this Commission can confidently report that the vast majority of New York City police officers are honest and hard-working, and serve this city with skill and dedication each day."

The corruption the Mollen Commission did find, however, was far more serious and more threatening than what had been uncovered twenty years earlier. Then, most corruption involved the licensing by bribe of illegal gambling and other "victimless crimes." In the 1990s, the Mollen Commission reported, corrupt officers were involved in drug dealing and thefts, robberies, and brutal enforcement of their presumed authority to operate beyond the law.

The commission commended the incumbent police administration's commitment to eliminating corruption, and it acknowledged that—in a very large police jurisdiction full of temptations—it was impossible to guarantee that no officers will become involved in corruption. But, the commission suggested, in the years since Police Commissioner Patrick V. Murphy had demonstrated during the 1970s that it was possible to change a police organizational culture in ways that eliminated tolerance for corruption, the department had grown fearful of renewed scandal and had directed its efforts at suppressing bad publicity rather than at suppressing bad policing.

In comments that are worth repeating, the commission indicated that the department had grown more interested in looking good than in doing good:

For at least the past decade, the system designed to protect the Department from corruption minimized the likelihood of uncovering it. In a Department with a budget of over one billion dollars, the basic equipment and resources needed to investigate corruption successfully were routinely denied to corruption investigators; internal investigations were prematurely closed and frag-

mented and targeted petty misconduct more than serious corruption; intelligence-gathering was minimal; integrity training was antiquated and often non-existent; Internal Affairs undercover officers were often placed in precincts where corruption was least prevalent; reliable information from field associates was ignored; supervisors and commanders were not held accountable for corruption in their commands; and corruption investigators often lacked experience and almost half had never taken the Department's "mandatory" basic investigative training course. Most Internal Affairs investigators and supervisors embraced a work ethic more dedicated to closing corruption cases than to investigating them. Most volunteered for Internal Affairs to get on a quick promotion track rather than to get corrupt cops off the job. Indeed, a survey of Internal Affairs investigators we conducted through an Internal Affairs "insider" revealed that over 50 percent of Internal Affairs investigators' time was spent on non-investigatory matters. And no one said a word about this state of affairs until this Commission commenced its investigations.

This was no accident. Weak corruption controls reduced the chances of uncovering serious corruption and protected police commanders' careers. Since no entity outside the Department was responsible for reviewing the Department's success in policing itself, years of self-protection continued unabated until this Commission commenced its independent inquiries.

This abandonment of effective anti-corruption efforts did more than avoid public exposure of corruption, it fueled it. It sent a message throughout the Department that integrity was not a high priority and that Department bosses did not really want to know about corruption. In short, it gave everyone in the Department an excuse for doing what was easiest: shutting their eyes to corruption around them.

And that is precisely what happened. The principle of command accountability, which holds commanders responsible for fighting corruption, completely collapsed. Supervisors and commanding officers were largely complacent about maintaining integrity. Few were concerned with corruption on their watch—unless it exploded into an embarrassing corruption scandal. One officer in a high-crime precinct related how his commanding officer went so far as to announce at roll call that he knew his officers were committing acts of corruption, and gave them this bit of advice: if you get caught, keep your mouth shut. Obviously, any officer who hears that message will conclude that his bosses are content to let corruption continue—despite the Department's rhetoric to the contrary. . . . The Department also failed—or refused—to recognize that police corruption is a multi-dimensional problem that cannot be overcome by

BOX 14-2. The Mollen Commission *(continued)*

focusing on the corrupt cop and inadequate investigations. In so doing, the Department failed to insure that corruption controls operated on a variety of fronts and in the daily operations of the Department, including: recruitment, screening, integrity training, supervision, deterrence, accountability and police culture. Because of that failure, the Department abandoned some of its best tools for conquering corruption: the honest cop and the community.

Source: Mollen et al., 1994:3–5.

the IAU, it might, in fact, become more objective because of the regular entry into it of new blood. As Herman Goldstein has suggested, the absence of personnel turnover:

> may intensify the difficulty in maintaining the unit's integrity. And it can be argued that officers assigned to investigating corruption over a long period of time, like those permanently assigned to vice investigations, eventually cease to be fair and objective investigators. (Goldstein, 1977:211)

Third, over the long term, such an assignment plan would fill the agency's top ranks with personnel who had an understanding of and sympathy for the work of internal affairs and who would therefore share its goals (Murphy, 1977:81).

This is not an easy issue, however, and Goldstein has also offered an observation that seems to argue against personnel turnover in IAUs. As he notes:

> The greatest weakness of special investigative units is one seldom acknowledged by police. It is absolutely unrealistic to expect officers on special assignment, however honest and dedicated, to investigate zealously the activities of fellow officers who may one day be their partners or superiors. (Goldstein, 1977:212)

However accurate, this observation is most relevant when those assigned to the IAU hold the entry- or first-level supervisory ranks. Future considerations may be a great issue when IAU officers, detectives, and even sergeants who can anticipate reassignment to field duty investigate—and perhaps testify against—field personnel. The future is less threatening, however, when the lieutenants and captains most likely to be the agency's future top executives conduct such investigations.[12]

Obviously, the question of who is assigned to internal affairs is secondary to the issue of whether there exists in the agency a real commitment to integrity and to objectivity in investigations. Once this primary question has been resolved, considerable thought should be given to personnel assignment. It is probably not a good idea to rely exclusively on either an *all-volunteer* or an *all-draftee* IAU; instead, an IAU should be staffed by using a combination of both methods, which should provide both continuity and the continuing staff turnover necessary to avoid isolation and loss of objectivity.[13]

Division of responsibilities among internal investigators can be made on the basis of whether the activity to be performed is overt or covert in nature. In large departments, this issue may be decided automatically with the assignment of IAU personnel to one of the unit's subsections. In addition, in very large departments, it is often possible and desirable to assign officers to specialized duty, such as the investigation of brutality cases and bad-debt cases.

DISCIPLINARY ACTION

When either internal investigations or civilian review results in a finding that a serious policy or rules violation has occurred, the chief should appoint a department disciplinary board composed of members of the department, none having a rank below that of the officer charged, to review the facts of the case, to make further investigation when necessary, and to submit a recommendation for action. While department regulations may establish the relative ranks of board members, it is best that they be selected by the chief on the basis of their competence and fairness. Before disciplinary action is imposed, an officer should have the right to a hearing before the department disciplinary board, if he or she so desires.

The use of a disciplinary board in this manner relieves the chief of some of the onus of disciplinary action, and it diminishes the likelihood of caprice and haste. On the other hand, since it makes only a recommendation to the chief, neither a disciplinary board nor a civilian complaint review board deprives the chief of disciplinary power. For example, the police departments in both New York and Los Angeles employ *department advocates*[14] who are charged with pretrial investigation of disciplinary cases and their prosecution before department tribunals.[15] In both agencies, the tribunals make their recommendations to the department's chief executive officer. The LAPD chief's final decisions are reviewed by the department's civilian Board of Police Commissioners, while the NYPD's CEO, the police commissioner, makes the agency's final disciplinary decisions.

The chief should have unrestricted disciplinary power subject only to the general direction and approval of the jurisdiction's chief executive officer. This power should be guarded zealously and used so judiciously that it will not be jeopardized.

Appeal of Disciplinary Action of the Chief

A central personnel agency, operating independently of the administrative head of the jurisdiction, or an independent appeal board may be authorized to hold a hearing on appeal by an employee who has been demoted, suspended, dismissed, or otherwise severely disciplined. Such an appeal board should not be authorized to increase the chief's disciplinary action but should be restricted to affirming or reducing the penalty imposed by the chief. The final level of appeal described by law should rest with the highest executive in the government. Such a process provides a suitable safeguard against capricious disciplinary action by the chief.

Recent court decisions imposing liability on government entities that have failed to adequately supervise aberrant employees raise two issues that should be addressed by police chief executives and government attorneys. First, some states require local governments to convene disciplinary tribunals in cases in which employees, particularly police officers and firefighters, have been accused by citizens of serious wrongdoing. At these tribunals, government attorneys act on behalf of complainants, serving as prosecutors of accused employees. Almost invariably, however, they take this advocacy role knowing that they will subsequently have to defend both accused employees and their employers in civil litigation stemming from the same charges brought by the same complainants. This situation is rife with conflicts of interest and greatly reduces the credibility of findings that employees are not guilty of the wrongdoing of which they have been accused.

The second issue is state usurpation of the disciplinary process in local police departments. Some states' civil service commissions, perhaps most notably New Jersey's, are empowered to hear local police officers' appeals of disciplinary action brought against them by their employers. In many cases, the result is the reinstatement of officers who, very justifiably, have been cashiered by their chiefs. This has damaging effects on discipline and replaces chiefs' best judgments with those of officials who are beyond accountability for such officers' subsequent misconduct. Where either of these conditions exists, chiefs should lobby against it.

Departmental Dispositions of Disciplinary Proceedings

Regardless of whether disciplinary proceedings are heard by individual judicial officers, police boards, or civilian review boards, several due process guarantees should apply:

1. The nature of the charge must be made known in advance to the accused.
2. The accused must be given reasonable notice of the time and place of the hearing.
3. The accused must be given the opportunity to call witnesses, to cross-examine opposing witnesses, and to testify in his or her own behalf.
4. The accused is entitled to have the hearing before those who are to decide the issue.

Although an administrative hearing is quasi-judicial in character and thus need not be strictly formal, it should be conducted in a dignified manner, free of distraction and interruption. The rules for the hearing should be reviewed carefully so that the accused is fully aware of the items listed above and the rules themselves. The procedure should include provision for opening statements for both the accused and the department advocate, as well as provision for cross-examination, questioning by board members, and other ground rules.

Their experience in criminal courts leads some police sometimes to confuse violations of regulations and the proceedings that follow with violations of law and the criminal trials to which they lead. Such confusion leads some police officers who receive adverse decisions based on evidence that does not prove guilt beyond a reasonable doubt to erroneously believe—or, at least, to claim—that their rights have been abridged.

Administrative proceedings and criminal trials are not the same, of course, and the high guilt-beyond-a-reasonable-doubt standard required in criminal trials should not be applied in internal administrative actions. Administrative proceedings are fact-finding exercises in which conclusions are based on a preponderance of the evidence and in which procedures are somewhat less formal and adversarial than in criminal trials.

If a hearing is held before a board, it should have a presiding officer who is knowledgeable about the procedure and familiar with parliamentary rules. Both the presiding officer and the department advocate (who should not be a member of the board) should be able to confer with the police legal adviser.

The board should end its deliberation by making its decision, accompanied by a statement summarizing the essentials of the hearing and findings. Each charge (if there are several) should receive a separate finding. If the decision sustains a charge, one of the following dispositions can be recommended:

- Oral reprimand
- Written reprimand
- Loss of time or of annual leave in lieu of suspension
- Suspension
- Fine, to be deducted from salary or pension payments
- Removal from service

If appropriate, any of these penalties can be supplemented with a recommendation or requirement that the officer undergo psychological or substance abuse counseling or treatment.

Summary Disciplinary Action

The disciplinary system should provide for a simple way to dispose of minor infractions which require some sort of formal action but which are not serious enough for a trial-board appearance. For example, a repeated violation of uniform regulations might require a supervisor to recommend summary action, which should be approved by a second-line supervisor. Summary action should not exceed more than two or three days' loss of leave or pay. The accused officer should have the right to appeal any action to the disciplinary board. Review of summary action should be a responsibility of the internal investigations unit.

Emergency Action

First-line supervisors should have the authority to suspend subordinates until the next business day for certain violations, such as insubordination or drinking on duty, which preclude the officer's remaining on the job until disciplinary action is taken. Sergeants should also be authorized to send officers home (without pay, if necessary) to secure missing equipment such as a handgun or a flashlight. In larger departments, this authority can rest with platoon or shift commanders.

SUMMARY

There is probably nothing than can bring down a police and government administration more quickly and more dramatically than a scandal involving intentional police misconduct. Even when they have not caused riots, police misconduct and official ineptitude in dealing with it create distrust and erode the relationship between the police and the community. Thus—especially because they are themselves charged with enforcing laws and maintaining order—the police have no more critical administrative responsibility than the duty to keep their own house clean. Indeed, all three branches of government, as well as the public and the bar, have made it plain that they will work hard to substitute their own forms of control for what they see as inadequate police efforts at integrity control.

In carrying out this responsibility, however, the police should not become locked into the trap of substituting gloss for substance, of paying more attention to the ritual of inspection and the appearance of doing good than to whether their efforts are actually accomplishing good. The best way to do this is to mount an aggressive integrity control program that involves both line personnel and those who work in internal affairs.

QUESTIONS FOR DISCUSSION

1. The reluctance of police to bring their colleagues' misconduct to official attention or to give full and accurate accounts when asked about it has been called a "code of silence" comparable to that said to exist in organized crime. Does such a "blue curtain" exist in the agency in which you work or that serves your community? If so, what accounts for it? Is it unique to the police and organized crime? To what extent does it also exist among other groups? What can be done to rechannel it?

2. Discuss the benefits and possible uses of the PPI system described in Box 14-1. What disadvantages does such a system have?

3. Distinguish between *unnecessary force* and *brutality*, using examples. What can be done to reduce them both?

4. The illicit narcotics trade has created situations in which young, low-paid officers and investigators have been offered enormous amounts of cash to refrain from arresting offenders or seizing their drugs. What can be done to minimize the chances that such officers will succumb to these temptations?

5. Why should internal affairs investigators not be permitted to impose punitive disciplinary action for the violations they uncover during their work?

NOTES

1. *Monell v. Department of Social Services*, 436 U.S. 658 (1978).
2. Civilian review and civil liability are discussed in more detail in Chapter 15.
3. See Fyfe (1986) for a more thorough discussion of this issue.

4. This is not to suggest that adequate training will *eliminate* shootings of EDPs or other controversial violence between police and citizens. In some circumstances, EDPs and other people the police encounter in adversarial circumstances leave even the best-trained and most competent officers no choice but to resort to the use of force. In all cases, the test should be whether officers have done everything reasonably possible to avoid or minimize the use of force.

5. Similar patterns were found in New York during the 1890s (New York State, 1895) and in Prohibition-era Chicago. In both cases, corruption related to the purchase of promotions and assignments was more clearly external in the sense that it was heavily influenced by organized crime interests concerned with maintaining control over police operations. In 1931, Chief Justice John P. McGoorty told a Cook County (Chicago) grand jury that:

> It is a matter of common knowledge that for many years there has been a fixed scale of prices for advancement in the police department, according to the rank and salary of the office sought. A determined and persistent effort by you should disclose that promotions have been paid for and bestowed by vice lords upon those thus promoted, like feudal barons conferring titles and emoluments upon their trusted vassals. Sums paid have been determined by the amount of profits derived from criminal operations in certain districts. Such evidence will tend to show why organized crime has flourished in Chicago. (Citizens' Police Committee, 1969:46)

6. The Knapp Commission, created in response to Serpico's allegations, cited three studies of court dispositions of gambling arrests in New York:

> A State Commission of Investigation study of eighty-eight gambling arrests made during one year at a Bronx social club revealed that forty-seven of the arrests—slightly over one half—resulted in conviction, and of these, one resulted in a jail sentence—and then only because the convicted gambler chose to go to jail for five days rather than pay a $50 fine. In the remaining forty-six convictions, the offenders were either given conditional discharges or ordered to pay fines ranging from $25 to $250.
>
> A similar study by the Police Sciences Center, Inc., came up with comparable figures. This study analyzed 356 numbers bank arrests made in Bedford-Stuyvesant over the past ten years. Such arrests can be assumed to have greater impact on the gambling power structure, because an arrest in a policy bank involves a greater number of slips and larger money volume, yet the courts did not show significantly greater punishments for such offenses. Of the 356 arrests, 198 resulted in dismissals, sixty-three in acquittals, and ninety-five in convictions. Of the ninety-five convictions, twelve resulted in suspended sentences, seventy-seven in a fine/time option, and six in jail sentences. Of the six jail sentences, one was for one year and the other five averaged seventeen days.
>
> Our study of 108 gambling arrests made by the plainclothes squad in one division over a five-month period showed that, of fifty convictions, not one resulted in a jail sentence; two resulted in conditional discharge; forty-seven in fines of under $300; and one in a $500 fine (five were pending). (Knapp et al., 1972:72)

7. This principle applies to brutality as well. The beating of Rodney King, for example, has been described by some police administrators merely as the aberrational act of four officers out of control. If this were so, however, it might be asked: Why was the

beating not stopped or brought to official attention by the more than 20 other officers who witnessed it?

8. Over the succeeding 20 years, the New York City Police Department's anticorruption mechanisms eroded, with the consequence that apparently more pernicious but less widespread narcotics corruption reappeared (Mollen et al., 1993).

9. According to Rubinstein (1973:397), the same arrangement was known as the *note* in Philadelphia.

10. In fact, the technique of "turning" corrupt officers seems to have been lost and refound over the last 100 years rather than to have been an innovation of the Knapp Commission. Nearly a century ago, the Lexow Commission investigation of police corruption (New York State, 1895) found a New York officer named Max Schmittberger with his hand in the till. Schmittberger was "turned," served as the commission's star witness, and went on to a long and successful career fighting corruption as a high-ranking New York police official (see Steffens, 1904).

11. Patrick V. Murphy and Gerald Caplan (1991:261) suggest another issue and an approach to dealing with it: "[Some] contend that corrupt officers may volunteer for the IAU to pursue corrupt ends or simply to undermine investigations. Thus, if a voluntary approach is adopted, the department should verify the volunteers' integrity through extensive background checks."

12. This should not be read as a suggestion that IAU lieutenant investigators and staff can work with impunity because high-ranking personnel do not become subjects of internal affairs investigations. Instead, the suspected or known involvement of high-ranking personnel in matters that fall within the IAU's jurisdiction should be brought to the attention of the department's highest levels.

13. As the Knapp Commission pointed out in recommending that the New York Police Department establish an IAU in which officers would spend their entire careers, the Internal Revenue Service has long, and apparently successfully, operated its Inspections Office in such a fashion (Knapp et al., 1972:17). Whether, despite its position on the organization chart, such a unit can truly be considered *internal*, however, is another issue.

14. The LAPD advocate is a sworn officer, while the NYPD advocate's position is reserved for an attorney and has been held by both civilian employees and high-ranking sworn personnel.

15. LAPD disciplinary hearings are heard by a board of rights consisting of sworn officers. NYPD hearings are heard by a civilian deputy commissioner for trials.

SOURCES

BOBB, MERRICK J., et al. *First Semiannual Report of the Special Counsel on the Los Angeles County Sheriff's Department* (Los Angeles, October 1993).

CHRISTOPHER, WARREN, et al. *Report of the Independent Commission on the Los Angeles Police Department* (July 1991).

Citizens' Police Committee. *Chicago Police Problems* (Montclair, N.J.: Patterson Smith reprint of 1931 original, 1969).

DALEY, ROBERT. *Prince of the City: The True Story of a Cop Who Knew Too Much* (Boston: Houghton Mifflin, 1978).

FOGELSON, ROBERT M. *Big-City Police* (Cambridge, Mass.: Harvard University Press, 1977).

FYFE, JAMES J. "The Split-Second Syndrome and Other Determinants of Police Violence," pp. 207–225 in Anne T. Campbell and John J. Gibbs (eds.), *Violent Transactions* (Oxford, Eng.: Basil Blackwell, 1986).

GOLDSTEIN, HERMAN. *Policing a Free Society* (Cambridge, Mass.: Ballinger, 1977).

————. *Police Corruption: A Perspective on Its Nature and Control* (Washington, D.C.: Police Foundation, 1975).

KELLY, RAYMOND W. "An Investigation into the Police Department's Conduct of the Dowd Case and an Assessment of the Police Department's Internal Investigation Capabilities" (New York City Police Department internal report, November 1992).

KNAPP, WHITMAN, JOSEPH MONSERRAT, JOHN E. SPRIZZO, FRANKLIN A. THOMAS, and CYRUS R. VANCE. *Report of the New York City Commission to Investigate Allegations of Police Corruption and the City's Anti-Corruption Procedures* (New York: Bar Press, 1972).

KOLTS, JAMES G., et al. *Report of the Special Counsel on the Los Angeles County Sheriff's Department* (Los Angeles, July 1992).

MAAS, PETER. *Serpico* (New York: Viking, 1973).

MCALARY, MIKE. *Buddy Boys* (New York: Charter Books, 1989).

Miami, City of. *Report of the Mayor's Blue-Ribbon Commission on Police Brutality* (Miami, 1984).

Milwaukee Mayor's Citizen Commission on Police-Community Relations. *Report to Mayor John O. Norquist and the Board of Police and Fire Commissioners* (Milwaukee, Oct. 15, 1991).

MOLLEN, MILTON, HAROLD BAER, JR., HERBERT EVANS, RODERICK C. LANKLER, and HAROLD TYLER. *Interim Report and Principal Recommendations of the Commission to Investigate Allegations of Police Corruption and the Anti-Corruption Procedures of the New York City Police Department* (New York, Dec. 27, 1993).

————, ————, ————, ————, and ————. *Report of the Commission to Investigate Allegations of Police Corruption and the Anti-Corruption Procedures of the New York City Police Department* (New York: July 7, 1994).

Monell v. Department of Social Services, 436 U.S. 658 (1978).

MURPHY, GERARD R. *Special Care: Improving the Police Response to the Mentally Disabled* (Washington, D.C.: Police Executive Research Forum, 1986).

MURPHY, PATRICK V. "Corruptive Influences," pp. 65–86 in Bernard L. Garmire (ed.), *Local Government Police Management*, 1st ed. (Washington, D.C.: International City Management Association, 1977).

————, and GERALD CAPLAN. "Fostering Integrity," pp. 240–271 in William A. Geller (ed.), *Local Government Police Management*, 3d ed. (Washington, D.C.: International City Management Association, 1991).

New York State Senate Committee Appointed to Investigate the Police Department of the City of New York. *Report and Proceedings* (Albany, 1895).

"Police Investigation Supervisor Admits Faking Fingerprints," *New York Times* (July 30, 1993:B5).

RUBINSTEIN, JONATHAN. *City Police* (New York: Farrar, Straus and Giroux, 1973).

RUCHELMAN, LEONARD. *Police Politics: A Comparative Study of Three Cities* (Cambridge, Mass.: Ballinger, 1974).

SHECTER, LEONARD, with WILLIAM PHILLIPS. *On the Pad* (New York: Berkeley Medallion Books, 1973).

SHERMAN, LAWRENCE W. *Police Corruption: A Sociological Perspective* (Garden City, N.Y.: Anchor Books, 1974).

ST. CLAIR, JAMES D., et al. *Report of the Boston Police Department Management Review Committee* (City of Boston, Jan. 14, 1992).

STEFFENS, LINCOLN. *The Shame of the Cities* (New York: McClure Phillips, 1904).

TERRILL, RICHARD J. "Civilian Oversight of the Police Complaints Process in the United States: Concerns, Developments, and More Concerns," in Andrew J. Goldsmith (ed.), *Complaints against the Police* (Oxford, Eng.: Clarendon, 1991).

WALKER, SAMUEL, and VIC W. BUMPHUS. *Civilian Review of the Police: A National Survey of the 50 Largest Cities, 1991*, University of Nebraska at Omaha Criminal Justice Police Research Group (monograph 91-3, 1991).

15

Police Standards and Accountability

KEY WORDS AND PHRASES

Accountability
Responsiveness
Rules
Policies
Brutality
Unnecessary force
Escalating force
Domestic violence
Emotionally disturbed persons

Special operations
Off-duty employment
Citizens' complaints
Sustained
Not sustained
Unfounded
Accreditation
Positional asphyxia

Accountability is the requirement that one demonstrate that one's conduct has been consistent with a predetermined standard of performance. Because police can have such powerful effects on the lives, liberties, rights, safety, and dignity of the public, it is especially critical that police be held closely accountable for their policies and actions.

In a democracy, police accountability does not stop at the top of the police department's organization chart. Certainly, everyone in a police agency must answer to its chief executive, and the heads of police departments must have sufficient authority to ensure the discipline and good order of their organizations. But police must also report to the elected executives who appoint them and, when asked, must also explain and defend their policies and actions to judicial and legislative officials, as well as to the press and to members of the public. As a general rule, police should be willing to provide these people and institutions with any and all information that does not endanger lives and/or investigations.

Few people enjoy being the subjects of close oversight by *outsiders* to their organizations, but perhaps because demand for police external accountability has been so strong, police resistance to it has been particularly strenuous. In the busy routine of day-to-day police operations, when the chief usually has the last word on everything, it is easy to believe that a police agency is a self-contained entity that should be free from oversight because its leaders and members know their work better than anybody from outside the ranks. When this philosophy prevails, police come to see those who champion close accountability as inexpert meddlers and Monday-morning quarterbacks. The highly politicized history of policing in the United States certainly offers some justification for this view, but such a perception generally is inconsistent with the everyday experience of the police. The reality of this experience is that, like the rest of government, the police are a part of the political system. As Chapter 3 suggested, the police are appointed by politicians; the police enforce laws enacted by politicians; the police bring those they arrest to prosecutors and judges who either are elected politicians themselves or are appointed by politicians. Police budgets, labor agreements, and job specifications are all created or approved by politicians. To argue that the police are—or *should be*—exempted from the political processes that affect the rest of government, therefore, is to defy what goes on every day in every U.S. police department and law enforcement agency. Worse, such an argument violates a fundamental precept of democracy: Like the military structure on which police organizational structure is based, police *must* be held accountable to the public through an elected civilian commander in chief. Where this reality is not recognized and where such a relationship does not exist, democracy ends and a police state begins.

THE POLICE AND POLITICAL ACCOUNTABILITY

It is not easy to maintain an appropriate system of police accountability to political officials and, thence, to the public. In virtually every large U.S. police jurisdiction, as well as in many small ones, police have at one time or another been improperly influenced by partisan politics or, simply, by crooks who have used political office as a means for accumulating personal wealth. Rather than serving as a justification for exempting police from accountability to officials, however, such experience should encourage attempts to distinguish between proper and improper political influences on police, as well as between appropriate and inappropriate mechanisms of accountability.

One way to begin such distinctions is to recall the discussion in Chapter 11 of *commonweal goals,* which are:

> . . . goals that affect everyone in the society, whether they use the services of those agencies directly or not. Such commonweal, or public goods, goals mandate that public agencies preserve the constitution and democracy, educate the public, improve the public health and preserve the public tranquility.

In the most general sense, political influences and accountability mechanisms that serve such commonweal goals are proper and appropriate; those that retard police progress toward such goals—damaging the public interest so that a small, usually partisan, group may benefit—are improper and inappropriate. This would be a simple distinction to make if it were not for the fact that small, partisan, and highly objectionable groups enjoy the same constitutional protections as the rest of the population. In the view of many people, for example, the public's interest in order and tranquility would best be served if unpopular groups like neo-Nazis, radical homosexuals, and vociferous pro-life demonstrators were denied the right to assemble and demonstrate. Police who responded to demands to break up demonstrations by such groups in the interest of tranquility, however, would be hard put to account for their actions. Recall the working definition that started this chapter: Accountability is the requirement that one demonstrate that one's conduct has been consistent with a predetermined standard of performance.

Accountability to Law

Every one of the 50 states has an extensive set of statutes and case law that tell the police what they can do and how they can do it. Underlying them all, however, is the U.S. Constitution, the fundamental American law and the yardstick for measuring the reasonableness of every official American action.

The Constitution's first 10 amendments, the Bill of Rights, are the provisions most significant to the police. As they are applied to the states by the Fourteenth Amendment, the most relevant of these declare:

> *Amendment I* Congress shall make no law respecting an establishment of religion, or prohibiting the free exercise thereof; or abridging the freedom of speech, or of the press; or the right of the people peaceably to assemble, and to petition the government for a redress of grievances.

> *Amendment IV* The right of the people to be secure in their person, houses, papers, and effects, against unreasonable searches and seizures, shall not be violated, and no warrants shall issue, but upon probable cause, supported by oath or affirmation, and particularly describing the place to be searched, and the persons or things to be seized.

> *Amendment V* No person shall be held to answer for a capital, or otherwise infamous crime, unless on a presentment or indictment of a Grand Jury, except in cases arising in the land or naval forces, or in the militia, when in actual service in time of war or public danger; nor shall any person be subject for the same offense to be twice put in jeopardy of life and limb; nor shall be compelled in any criminal case to be a witness against himself, nor be deprived of life, liberty, or property, without due process of law, nor shall private property be taken for public use, without just compensation.

> *Amendment VI* In all criminal prosecutions, the accused shall enjoy the right to speedy and public trial, by an impartial jury of the State and district wherein the crime shall have been committed, which district shall have been previously ascertained by law, and to be informed of the nature and cause of the accusation; to be confronted with the witnesses against him; to have compulsory process for obtaining witnesses in his favor, and to have the assistance of counsel for his defense.

Judging by its lead-off spot in the Bill of Rights, it is safe to assume that the Founding Fathers meant the First Amendment to be the primary standard for

Police responsibility to uphold the Constitution sometimes puts them in places they'd rather not be. These officers are keeping counter-demonstrators safely away from Ku Klux Klan marchers.
Bob Daemmrich/Stock, Boston.

measuring how well government protects citizens. Thus, if police are to honor the constitutional mandates upon them, they must vigorously safeguard the rights to free expression and assembly and to freedom of religion, even when these are exercised by groups and individuals whose extreme views are repugnant to police and most others.

The First Amendment also is the primary standard demanding police accountability to the media. Certainly, in these days of "bang-bang" police reporting, sensationalistic journalism, and immense pressure for scoops, dealing with the media may not always be pleasant. But if we are to continue the democratic tradition of an informed public that consents to be policed because it trusts the police, openness with the media is a requirement.

Remedies

The rights of free assembly, expression, and religion, as well as other guarantees defined by these amendments, were unique when they were written and remain a model for the rest of the world to emulate. As careful readers of contracts and warranties will have noted, however, these amendments say nothing about how to prevent violations or how to deal with those who commit them. In the years since the Bill of Rights was written, legislators and jurists have fashioned *remedies* that give it real teeth.

In 1871, primarily to protect newly freed slaves in the South from depredations by the likes of the Ku Klux Klan, the Congress passed a Civil Rights Act that created criminal and civil penalties for violations of guarantees in the Bill of Rights. In its most relevant part—42 U.S. Code Section 1983—this law states:

> Every person, who under color of any statute, ordinance, regulation, custom, or usage, of any State or territory, any citizen of the United States or other persons within the jurisdiction thereof to be deprived of any right, privileges, or immunities secured by the Constitution and laws shall be liable to the party injured in an action at law, suit in equity, or other proper proceeding for redress.

As interpreted in the years since the Supreme Court's landmark 1978 decision in *Monell v. New York City Department of Social Services* (see Chapter 2), this law imposes civil liability on everyone implicated in line-of-duty constitutional violations by police. For example, if it is shown in court that an arrest involving excessive force (a violation of the Fourth Amendment guarantee against unreasonable seizure) was part of a pattern of conduct that has been tolerated or encouraged by a police agency and its supervisors and chief, they—as well as the department and the officers—may all be ordered to pay judgments.[1]

Violations of Fourth and Fifth Amendment guarantees against unreasonable searches and interrogations also are subject to the *exclusionary rule,* which bars the use in criminal trials of unconstitutionally obtained evidence. Although it has lately been fashionable to attack the rule as liberals' unthinking handcuffs on the police, there is no evidence that it has affected public safety or police crime-fighting effectiveness in any measurable way (see Chapter 2). Also frequently overlooked in highly charged debates about the rule is its origin. It was put in place in 1914 by a very conservative U.S. Supreme Court which, frustrated by the failure of other remedies (e.g., civil suits and criminal prosecutions against law enforcement officials), created the rule to deter official intrusions into citizens' privacy (*Weeks v. United States,* 1914).[2]

ACCOUNTABILITY AND RESPONSIVENESS

The preceding discussion illustrates an important point. Especially in this era of community-oriented policing and great concern about crime, police are extremely conscious of the need to be responsive to the communities they serve. But police responsiveness to community demands should never outweigh police accountability for behaving in accord with the Constitution and other laws.

This is no mere academic exercise or semantic game. History includes many incidents and periods in which police have found it more expedient to be responsive than to be accountable. Police who brutalized demonstrators during the civil rights era, for example, certainly were responsive to the most powerful and influential individuals and interests in their communities; but they ignored their accountability to the Constitution and fundamental democratic principles. Today, it might be argued that these police simply responded to what was then "the tenor of the times." But, then or now, it would be impossible to explain how their actions accorded with the more enduring principles written into the First Amendment.

Police must keep this history in mind as they decide how to respond to community demands for action. It may be expedient and responsive to violate suspects' rights or to otherwise bend the law in dealing with such contemporary police problems as drugs or demonstrations for causes that many people regard as offensive, but such conduct ignores the requirement that police remain accountable to the law.

There is a simple way to balance responsiveness and accountability. Accountability dictates that police be able to explain the reasons for their programs, policies, and actions, as well as to describe their conformance to constitutional and professional standards. If it is not possible to write a full and comprehensive explanation of a police program or action without shading the truth or otherwise forcing the facts to fit the law, the accountability requirement is not met.

POLICE PROFESSIONAL STANDARDS

By definition, accountability to standards of performance must begin by establishing and articulating the standards. The Constitution and the law are such standards, but they are not the only standards by which the police must abide. Over the years, there has developed within policing a set of standards that, in a general sense, articulate the way police work should be done. These are found in the principles taught in training programs such as the FBI National Academy, the Southern Police Institute, and state and local training academies; in such sources as the International Association of Chiefs of Police *Training Keys* and *Model Policies*; and in the standards promulgated by the Commission on Accreditation for Law Enforcement Agencies and similar state-level accrediting groups. Increasingly, these standards also are found in formal police department policies designed to assist personnel in making critical operations decisions.

Resistance to Police Policy Making

For many years, police administrators resisted the increased accountability that came with creating policies to serve as standards for officers' conduct. In general, this resistance—which continues in some quarters—has had been based on three faulty arguments:

1. That the criminal law was an effective and sufficient control on the behavior of officers charged with enforcing it
2. That such policies were unworkable, because every police situation is different
3. That, by delineating restrictive policies, the police would create narrow new standards by which their conduct would be judged in court, and would therefore increase their exposure to civil liability

However apparently appealing these arguments may seem, they have been made moot by experience and by the decisions of courts charged with reviewing police behavior. Where they persist, they should be abandoned because they lead to a system of seat-of-the-pants policing, complete with all the mistakes and negative consequences that follow when important decisions are based on hunches rather than careful analysis.

Criminal Law: An Inadequate Control on Police Conduct.   The notion that, as law enforcement officers, police should be subject *only* to the criminal law is an old one; like some other old notions, though, it is simply wrongheaded. All professionals, including the police, certainly must abide by the law, but as in other professions the laws related to critical police behavior are far too broad to serve as meaningful guideposts to acceptable behavior. The criminal law was designed to draw the line between conduct which is serious enough to warrant prosecution and formal legal penalties and that which is not.

Where police use of force is concerned, the criminal law serves only to distinguish between criminal assault and other force, including much that may not be criminal but that should be regarded as unacceptable and unprofessional. This reality is neither revolutionary nor unique to the police, and the same principle applies to all occupations. Not all medical malpractice amounts to criminal assault; not all unethical conduct by lawyers or stockbrokers is criminal; not all sexual harassment by professors or supervisors is criminal. In all these cases, the law is simply too broad to provide parameters for professional discretion.

Policing is full of examples of unacceptable, but noncriminal, conduct. Most police departments prohibit officers from attempting to run fleeing motorists off the road, but criminal laws are usually silent on this point. No law prevents police from crashing into rooms in which armed criminals are holding innocent hostages, but generally accepted police practices based on the ideal of avoiding bloodshed do. Police professional standards typically forbid police firing warning shots and shooting at or from moving vehicles, but criminal laws do not.

The position that the criminal law, rather than internal police policies, should be the standard by which police conduct is judged is one frequently heard in two circumstances. First, police labor leaders often make this claim to protest police administrative actions against officers for incidents that have resulted in either prosecutorial declinations to proceed or acquittals after trial. This complaint—usually characterized by the phrase "double jeopardy"—is without basis because prosecutors' decisions not to bring charges and juries' acquittals in criminal cases have little to do with internal organizational discipline.

Second, police administrators sometimes make this claim after controversial police shootings, particularly in very small jurisdictions in which these events are so rare that neither the public nor the media know what to expect after such events happen. "Yes, we do have an internal deadly force policy," we have heard several police executives say in such situations, "but since one of our officers did the shooting and is the subject of this investigation, it would be a conflict of interest for me to conduct the investigation or determine how to deal with the officer. Instead, I have determined that we will rely on the findings of the prosecutor" (or the state police, or the county sheriff).

This may play well with a public and media who are unfamiliar with the procedures that should follow a police shooting, and the chiefs who have said it may even believe it. It does not play so well in civil suits that emanate from police shootings, because its weaknesses are easily demonstrated to juries, who invariably come to see it for what it truly is: buck-passing. At its core, the superficially noble and evenhanded position reflected in the statement above substitutes the broad provisions of the criminal law for more stringent police professional standards. It is simply another way of saying: "We have a policy for police shootings, but I'm washing my hands of this one and leaving it to the prosecutor. As long as the prosecutor does not obtain an indictment of the officer (or the state police or sheriff do not arrest the officer), we're all home free." Jurors in civil suits invariably ask: Why even have a policy on use of deadly force (or any other sensitive police problem), if it is not put to use or enforced when officers use deadly force?

The Every-Situation-Is-Different Argument. There are two problems with the argument that differences in police situations make it impossible to develop meaningful guidelines for police field decisions. First, *every* situation in *every* field of human endeavor is different from every other, but in most fields—especially the professions—meaningful standards of performance do exist. No two battles, heart attacks, cancer cases, football game situations, courtroom trials, fires, or cars that will not start are exactly alike, but the people who deal with these problems have professional standards to guide them. This being so, there is little justification for the position that meaningful guidelines cannot also be developed for such critical, but relatively frequent, police situations as responses to reports of crimes in progress, stops of suspicious persons, encounters with emotionally disturbed persons, or vehicle pursuits.

The second problem with this argument is that it confuses the difference between rules and policies. Contrary to the old saw, *rules* allow for no exception and are most useful in prescribing the manner in which routine activities are to be performed. Rules can ensure that paperwork is processed, that lost property is correctly described and safeguarded, and that complaints are investigated thoroughly. Rules focus on *process*, on the performance of tasks in which mistakes will generally not prove fatal or irreversible.

Policies, by contrast, are *goal*-oriented general statements of intent, designed to assist professionals through problems in which the stakes are very high. Consequently, policies are more flexible than rules, and they are interpreted with an eye to whether, in the particular circumstances involved, professionals have behaved reasonably and in a manner likely to achieve the desired outcome. As a general policy, doctors begin treatment with the least intrusive alternative; but every emergency room doctor can describe a particular case in which specific information indicated that the desired outcome—saving a life—would not be accomplished unless he or she went immediately to the most drastic alternative. Similarly, as a matter of general policy, police officers should not shoot at moving vehicles. But it is not difficult to imagine unusual circumstances in which shooting at a moving vehicle is the only way to fulfill the fundamental police obligation to protect life.

The point is that there is a major difference between rules and policies. Rules are to be applied to the *letter*, strictly as they have been written, with no room for alternative interpretations. Policies should be applied *flexibly*, with an eye to whether their spirit has been honored in ways most likely to achieve the goals they were designed to accomplish. This is not an easy task, and unwillingness to tackle it accounts for some of the historic police reluctance to write and enforce policies. Such unwillingness is a sign of weak leadership.

Policies as Paper Trails. The argument that policies create paper trails—or *traps*—by which civil courts can hold police officers and chiefs to account is probably the worst reason to avoid writing and enforcing policies. It is, in essence, an argument that nobody can be held to account for doing wrong if the difference between right and wrong is not described in policy.[3] If policy is to be meaningful, it should define this difference and should serve as a guidepost to both officers and jurors in the same way that medical standards serve as guideposts to doctors and to the juries who hear medical malpractice cases. Indeed, jurors recognize this, and they are harsh on police administrators and departments that fail to provide officers with policy definitions of right and wrong that may be applied in street-level emergencies. As Chapter 2 indicated, the U.S. Supreme Court has done the same thing formally, in *Monell v. New York City Department of Social Services* (1978), a decision that has led to a long line of cases in which police have been held liable precisely because they have failed to promulgate policy that gave officers meaningful guidance in the field.

Monell and other cases have made it plain that, where police have not been willing to define clear professional standards, the courts are ready to do so.[4] Even the most activist courts, however, do this with a reluctance born of their often-expressed knowledge that they are substituting their judgments for those of better-qualified police professionals who refuse to do what they should.

Policy Making

Formulation of police operational policies should include these steps:

1. Establish policies that guide the most critical decisions made by its personnel.
2. Make certain that personnel are trained in what these policies mean and how to apply them.
3. Hold personnel accountable for abiding by policy.
4. Continually review policies to ensure that they are responsive to community needs and that they hold personnel properly accountable as new problems are identified (see Appendix 15-1).

Establishing and Enforcing Policies. Policing is full of surprises. The most hazardous and sensitive situations confronted by police personnel occur suddenly, and at unpredictable times; however, it is predictable that, over a period of time, at least some personnel *will* encounter virtually every imaginable type of emergency. No police chief can predict, for example, when an estranged father may go berserk and hold his children hostage in a misguided, pathetic, and very dangerous attempt to regain their mother's affection. Unfortunately, it is absolutely certain that, over the next few years, police officers all over the country, in jurisdictions of all sizes, will find that their routines have been interrupted by precisely such situations. If these personnel have not been prepared to deal with these situations by a carefully formulated policy and related training (see Chapter 9), they are likely to help turn potential tragedies into the real thing. Thus, both *policy and training should prepare police both to do what all officers do every day and to do what some officers might have to do some day.*

On a more routine basis, police encounter a variety of dangerous and sensitive situations—responses to crimes in progress, vehicle stops, field interrogations of suspicious persons, domestic disputes, encounters with arrestees who resist—for which policy guidance is eminently useful. Again, in considering the establishment of such guidance, it is critical to bear in mind that whatever directives result should be goal-oriented statements of intent, rather than hard-and-fast rules. *The purpose of policy is to give general direction for how missions may best be accomplished, rather than to lock personnel into inflexible procedures.* The most important police mission is the protection of life, and in the formulation and enforcement of police policy, no other police mission should receive a higher priority than this one.

Further, it must be recognized that the most critical policies are designed for the most critical emergency situations and should be useful in them. This has become a major issue in recent years, as some law enforcement agencies have been criticized for abandoning operational policies in the midst of emergencies for which they were presumably designed. The justification offered for such abandonment (which usually has been accompanied by hasty adoption of ill-conceived approaches that resulted in disaster) typically is the argument that the situations involved were somehow *unusual* and that the relevant policies somehow did not fit—a variant of the *every-situation-is-different* argument described above. This argument is almost always spurious. It makes little sense to formulate a policy on barricade situations, for example, and then to say that it does not apply in a specific barricade situation because this particular event is unusual and different from precisely what was anticipated by policy makers. By definition, all barricade situations are unusual and not precisely as anticipated. But unless the people who have formulated policies for dealing with such encounters are totally removed from reality, it usually makes sense to follow their guideposts as closely as possible, adjusting them as necessary. To totally abandon them for a new and untried path in the midst of a crisis is unwise; the major reason that some roads are less traveled is that there is usually no way to know where they will lead.

To establish operational policy, police agencies should attempt to identify sensitive situations in which it is likely that officers and other personnel may at some point have to intervene and make critical decisions (some examples are discussed later in this chapter). This can be accomplished in several ways:

- Regular review of internal reports of unusual events (shootings, pursuits, in-custody deaths, uses of force, assaults on officers, complaints against officers, etc.) with an eye to identifying patterns of conduct and/or undesirable outcomes that might be addressed by policy and related training.
- Regular review of the police professional literature for information on operational problems emerging in other places, and consideration of their relevance.
- Regular contact with peers in other agencies, through professional organizations, training programs, informal networking, and the like. In many areas, regional police chiefs' groups (at metropolitan-area councils of government, for example) have found it valuable to set aside time for partici-

pants to introduce and discuss emerging operational problems, or concerns about potential problems, and what to do about them.

Then, by surveying other agencies and the major professional organizations for advice and examples of existing policies, as well as by involving line and staff personnel in the process, policies can be thoughtfully crafted. An outstanding example of this process is summarized in Appendix 15-1.

Training. No matter how carefully worded, no policy speaks for itself. Unless personnel are carefully trained to interpret and apply policy—especially when new policies are complex and/or mark dramatic changes from prior practice—attempts to advance the state of the art turn instead into sources of confusion.

The bane of the police instructor's existence may be the "What if . . . ?" question, as in:

- *What if* A happens? What should we do then?
- *What if* A happens, and B is also present?
- *What if* B happens, and we only *think* that A has also happened?

Such questions reflect a desire to have a pat answer for every possible police situation. However desirable this state might be, it is impossible to achieve. Thus, the appropriate answer to such questions usually is the one suggested above: The department will enforce its policies flexibly, with an eye to whether the spirit of department policies has been served in ways most likely to achieve the goals they were designed to accomplish.

The ambiguity of this answer illustrates the need for careful training in policies. What must be conveyed in a course related to policy is far more difficult than the mere recitation of facts in courses related to rules and routine procedures. If trainees in a policy course do not leave it understanding (1) what the agency expects to accomplish with the policy, (2) how trainees should attempt to set priorities among the issues involved in the policy, (3) how trainees will be required to demonstrate that their attempts to apply the policy are reasonable and in accord with the agency's goals, and (4) how their compliance with the policy in question will be judged, the policy has not been adequately explained—or may even be inadequate itself.

This is a different sort of training than has been provided by many agencies. It is *analytic* rather than merely *prescriptive*, and attempts to convey the logic—the *why*—of police work rather than simply a black-letter description of *how* it should be done. In policing, as in all of life, compliance with expectations increases when people understand both how and why to do something.

Policy Review. Like life's challenges, the problems confronting policing change continuously. Old police problems—drug abuse, for example—rarely disappear but, instead, constantly assume new shapes and forms. New social problems requiring police attention—AIDS, terrorism, political protest—arise regularly, and new information constantly becomes available to the police.

For all these reasons, it is critical that police agencies continually review existing policies to ensure that they anticipate and are responsive to community needs. At the same time, police must constantly look ahead to spot emerging problems that may require new or modified policies. Box 15-1 traces the growth of new information concerning one of the most critical police policy is-

Operational policies and related training should be specific to guide officers' decisions
in critical situations without unreasonably limiting their discretion.
James Fyfe.

sues, as well as its effects on the standards of the Commission on Accreditation
for Law Enforcement Agencies.

One major barrier to policy change is legal and financial—and uncon-
scionable. On occasion, embarrassment or tragedy strikes police agencies. In
attempting to determine why, administrators sometimes discover that—
through omission rather than willfulness—they have failed to provide adequate policy guidance to line personnel. Almost invariably, the response of
well-intended administrators is to correct their oversight and prevent future
problems by establishing appropriate policies and related training. Sometimes,
however, they are advised by their attorneys or other officials to avoid needed
changes in policy and training on grounds that these changes will serve as tacit
admissions that they have been doing things wrong, and that changes will lead
to liability in the case that has spawned the controversy.

An example: A large police agency encourages its officers to be "on-duty
24 hours a day" and to use "good judgment" in enforcing all the laws all the
time. Unfortunately, not all of this department's officers understand what the
agency means by "good judgment." As a result, off-duty officers have become
involved in brawls and shootings stemming from their attempts to intervene in
tavern fights and discourtesy on the roadways, and to resolve their own personal disputes by using laws against disorderly conduct, menacing, and terror-
istic threats to arrest their adversaries. This has led to considerable bloodshed
and ill will, and a spate of lawsuits. Recognizing the relationship between the
absence of a policy clearly defining "good judgment" and delineating the limits of off-duty officers' authority, the top administrators of this agency have at-

BOX 15-1. The Commission on Accreditation's Vehicle Pursuit Standard and Commentary

As standards that apply throughout the country, CALEA's standards on vehicle pursuit are understandably somewhat abstract. Still, their evolution since 1983 illustrates a trend toward more refinement and specific direction. The requirement under CALEA's 1983 standard is that:

41.2.8 A written directive governs pursuit of motor vehicles, to include:

- evaluating the circumstances
- initiating officer's responsibilities
- secondary unit's responsibilities
- dispatcher's responsibilities
- supervisor's responsibilities
- forcible stopping
- when to terminate pursuit
- inter- and intrajurisdictional pursuits

Commentary: The agency must balance the necessity for pursuit or apprehension against the probability and severity of damage or injury that may result. When air units are available, they should be used to direct the movement of the initial pursuing units and any other ground units that may be involved [mandatory for all agencies].

By 1994, the Supreme Court had ruled that the reasonableness of roadblocks as a means of apprehending fleeing subjects should be judged by trial courts within the framework of the Fourth Amendment's guarantees against unreasonable seizure. In addition, a series of lower-court cases involving pursuits had occurred (see Alpert and Fridell, 1992), and growing police sensitivity to the problem generally led CALEA to alter this standard (renumbered because of a top-to-bottom overhaul of the accreditation manual), to add another, and to cross-reference them to each other and to the deadly force standard:

41.2.2 A written directive governs pursuit of motor vehicles, to include:

a. Evaluating the circumstances;
b. initiating officer's responsibilities;
c. designating secondary unit's responsibilities;
d. assigning dispatcher's responsibilities;
e. describing supervisor's responsibilities;
f. using forcible stopping/roadblocks (refer to 61.3.4)
g. specifying when to terminate pursuit
h. engaging in inter- and intrajurisdictional pursuits involving personnel from the agency and/or other jurisdictions; and
i. detailing a procedure for a critique of the pursuit as soon as possible.

Commentary: The agency should have clear-cut policy and procedures for pursuits. The policy should be cross-referenced with the agency's deadly force policy (see 1.3.2). All sworn personnel should be provided with this written directive. Agencies may wish to consider frequent discussion and review of these policies/procedures during roll-call and/or in-service training sessions [mandatory for all agencies].

61.3.4 A written directive describes circumstances warranting the use of roadblocks and specific procedures for implementation.

Commentary: The extreme dangers inherent in the use of roadblocks mandate guidelines for their use. The directive should specify the types of roadblocks authorized for use, e.g., moving, fixed, or circle system, and the circumstances justifying their use, e.g., to stop a fleeing felon or conduct traffic checks. The procedures should specify who has authority to implement and/or cancel a roadblock, the person in charge at the scene, and staffing arrangements. Whenever possible, planning should take place prior to the implementation of the roadblock. Officers should be trained in roadblock techniques and properly equipped to set them up. Standards 1.3.2 [deadly force] and 41.2.2 are cross-referenced to this standard [mandatory for all agencies].

Sources: Commission on Accreditation for Law Enforcement Agencies, 1983, 1994.

tempted to implement a more adequate set of guidelines. Their efforts have been opposed by their government's attorneys, who apparently have convinced the department's head that creating such a policy will demonstrate to juries that the department has itself recognized the inadequacy of policies currently under attack in court. When these cases are over, the attorneys argue, you can change the policy without costing the city more money. The trouble with this logic, of course, is apparent: Without changes in policy, the cases will never be over, because officers will continue to operate under a policy that everybody recognizes is wrongheaded.

The point is that protecting the treasury of a city or county may be the primary obligation of its attorney, but the primary responsibility of its police chief is to protect its citizens. Whenever it is apparent that a policy is wrongheaded or inadequate, it should be changed immediately and without regard to the immediate costs in money or embarrassment. To do otherwise is to knowingly perpetuate bad practice.

CRITICAL POLICY ISSUES

Several critical policy areas are described elsewhere in this book (see Chapter 6 regarding deadly force policy and Chapter 16 regarding vehicle pursuits), but other critical issues remain. These include:

- Use of force and restraint of violent subjects
- Domestic violence
- Encounters with mentally and emotionally disturbed persons
- Special operations: hostage, barricade, and high-risk drug operations
- Prisoner transportation and lockup and detention facilities
- Off-duty conduct, weapons carrying, and employment
- Review of controversial police conduct that generates citizens' complaints, such as use of deadly force and vehicle pursuits

Use of Force

Egon Bittner (1970) has written that the core of the police role is the capacity to use force. In a democracy, this authority is subject to great limits, and one way to measure the success of police operations is the extent to which the police are able to do their work without having to resort to the use of force. This view—in effect, that police should become expert at getting the job done and avoiding the use of force at the same time—finds its best and most sophisticated expression in the elaborate protocols developed to resolve hostage situations.

To begin to apply similar sophistication to more routine police encounters, it is essential to understand the distinction between police brutality and unnecessary force. *Brutality,* or extralegal police violence, is "the willful and wrongful use of force by officers who knowingly exceed the bounds of their office." *Unnecessary force* is the result of carelessness or ineptitude and "occurs when well-meaning officers prove incapable of dealing with the situations they encounter without needless or too hasty resort to force" (Fyfe, 1986:207). Because brutal police officers try to keep their activities a secret, it is difficult to know how often such behavior occurs. Experience suggests, however, that brutality is rarely lethal and that it typically involves beatings at curbsides or in the back rooms of police stations. Unnecessary force, by contrast, typically occurs in public and may range from simple unnecessary restraint to police shootings that might easily have been avoided by the use of appropriate tactics.

Every law enforcement agency has policies forbidding brutality, but it is more difficult to control unnecessary force. In attempting to do so, it is vital to recognize the importance of encouraging officers to approach potentially violent circumstances cautiously and in ways that do not unnecessarily create or contribute to the need to use force (see Appendix 15-2). When officers attempt to break up street disputes alone rather than waiting the short time necessary for help to arrive, for example, they increase the chances both that they will be hurt and that they will hurt someone else. Thus, policy should make it plain that officers will be held accountable for structuring their encounters with potential adversaries in ways that minimize the likelihood that someone will be hurt. Methods of doing this include:

- Calling and waiting for help whenever it is reasonably possible to do so without endangering life or property
- Delaying encounters such as field interrogations and traffic stops until their subjects are in places (away from intersections; on lighted streets) in which the opportunity for flight or forcible resistance is minimized
- Avoiding statements or actions likely to produce violence or forcible resistance

Policy should also require officers to employ the minimal degree of force necessary to accomplish their missions. While laws related to police use of force are necessarily vague—including only such broad descriptors as "reasonable and necessary"—police policy must be quite specific, prescribing in as much detail as possible the degree of force appropriate for various situations and holding officers accountable for using no greater degree of force than necessary. Many police departments by now have adopted scales of *escalating force* that, with some semantic variation and in decreasing order of severity, resemble the following:

- *Deadly force.* Force capable of or likely to cause death or serious physical injury. Deadly force usually involves firearms[5] and should be employed in order to protect officers or others from imminent death or serious physical injury or, in some jurisdictions, to apprehend violent felons whose conduct indicates that they will pose a great danger to the community if not immediately apprehended.
- *Impact devices and techniques.* Nightsticks, martial arts techniques involving fists and feet, and other impact techniques. To be used when lesser means fail or are inadequate to protect officers or other innocent persons against physical assault.
- *Pain compliance.* Gaining compliance with officers' directions through infliction of temporary pain that causes no lasting damage. Includes such techniques as wristlocks, hammerlocks, and fingerlocks and typically is used to move resisting sit-in demonstrators or disorderly persons.
- *Firm grips.* Grips on the arm, shoulder, or other body part that are intended to direct subjects' movements without inflicting pain. Typically used to separate disputants, to guide drunk driving suspects during field sobriety tests, and to restrain persons already in police custody.
- *Voice commands.* Verbal commands to do specific things: "Come out!" "Police! Don't Move!" "Raise your hands!" "Leave this street now!" are exam-

ples. When used in combination with drawn guns, voice commands constitute threats to use deadly force, actions that are merited only in life-threatening situations.

- *Persuasion.* Requests to do specific things. "You were speeding, sir. May I see your license, registration, and proof of insurance?" When these persuasive attempts fail, officers escalate to voice commands: "I asked you nicely, sir. Now I am telling you that I want to see your license, registration, and proof of insurance."
- *Mere presence.* Police wear uniforms because their mere high-visibility presence has an effect on peoples' behavior. Often, just by showing up, for example, police can cause motorists to slow down, disorderly kids to leave their corner hangouts, and panhandlers and other street people to disperse.

Policy should create an understanding that officers are to begin their encounters with potential adversaries as low as possible on this scale. In addition to the general legal and moral requirement that officers employ no more force than necessary, there is a practical reason for this principle. Beginning an encounter high up on the scale makes it very difficult to deescalate to lower levels. An officer who begins an intervention in a domestic dispute by barking commands rather than by attempting to persuade is very unlikely to be able to reduce the tension of the situation but, instead, is quite likely to provoke an escalation by its participants.

Domestic Violence

Police often describe themselves as "law enforcement" officers, but they have not always regarded *domestic violence* as an activity that called for enforcing laws. Instead, for generations, police treated both criminal domestic violence and simple noncriminal domestic arguments in the same way: by attempting to avoid doing anything that might cause or accelerate the disintegration of families.[6] Since it was reasoned that the spectacle of a father being taken in handcuffs from his own home was likely to precipitate family dissolution, arrest was generally to be avoided even when serious crimes had been committed. The downside of this logic, we have since learned, was that it gave domestic abusers a license to continue their brutal and demeaning ways, perpetuated family dysfunction, and made it more likely that children would also grow up to become abusers (see, e.g., Buzawa and Buzawa, 1990; Hirschel et al., 1992; International Association of Chiefs of Police, 1976; Loving, 1980; Martin, 1976).

The conventional wisdom is that police have always treated domestic violence in this way (see, e.g., Calvert, 1974). This is not so: Sherman's analysis (1992:45–48) shows that U.S. policies and attitudes toward wife beating have not been unvaryingly tolerant. Centuries ago, the Puritan colonists' strong moral condemnation of domestic violence found its way into law. Ironically, this view fell out of favor during the Enlightenment era, when the prevailing view held that only public conduct should be criminalized, while activities that occurred in the home—such as wife beating—were private matters, not appropriate for official intervention. The legalistic approach was revived when modern enforcement-oriented police departments were created in the mid-nineteenth century. Later in that century, anti-domestic violence legislation and provisions for legal assistance for its victims grew, in reflection of elite reformers' concerns that immigrants conform to American standards of conduct. Like most of the causes of the Progressive reformers, wife beating faded as a policy issue during the 1920s, when the most recent period of official tolerance of wife beating began. Then, in the 1970s, the current trend toward stringent enforcement of assault laws in domestic violence cases began.

This trend toward equitable police treatment of violence in the home demands that police do everything possible to ensure that its victims have access to law. Although this has not been welcomed by all police officials, it should be. It treats domestic violence as what it is—*crime*—and thereby requires officers to serve only as law enforcers, relieving them of the onerous and rarely successful burden of attempting to serve as midnight social workers in the homes of highly emotional abusers and victims. The International Association of Chiefs of Police Model Policy on Domestic Violence is an excellent basis for a policy statement tailored to the needs of individual communities and agencies (see Box 15-2).

Mentally and Emotionally Disturbed Persons

Since the 1950s, the population of U.S. mental institutions has shrunk by nearly 500,000 (Murphy, 1986:23). This trend is attributable largely to the movement to deinstitutionalize disturbed persons whose conditions cannot clearly be demonstrated to be dangerous to themselves or others, and it has had enormous consequences for the police. As a walk on many downtown American streets will demonstrate, people who would likely have been confined to mental institutions a generation ago are now out and about.

On these streets, these *emotionally disturbed persons* (EDPs) sometimes act out in ways that draw police attention. On occasion, because officers have been given inadequate policy and training guidance for dealing with such situations, a terrible scenario is played out:

Day 1

2:00.00 P.M.: An obviously disturbed person becomes loud and alarming on a downtown street.

2:01.00 P.M.: A citizen calls the police.

2:02.30 P.M.: Officers arrive and try to restore order by talking to the man.

2:02.45 P.M.: As they approach the man, he becomes hysterical and defensive, backing away and pulling out a small penknife or handtool.

2:02.48 P.M.: The officers draw their guns and shout commands for him to drop the weapon.

2:02.58 P.M.: He continues backing away, waving the weapon ineffectually and telling the police to leave him alone.

2:03.05 P.M.: Other citizens call the police, and the sound of sirens is heard as additional officers respond to assist their colleagues. The noise and arrival of additional officers obviously increase the man's panic.

2:03.15 P.M.: The man backs against a wall, and several officers, with guns drawn, form a semicircle around him, shouting warnings for him to drop his weapon.

2:03.20 P.M.: Trapped and by now hysterical with fear, he bolts for freedom. No matter what direction he chooses, he heads toward an officer. Fearing that he is attacking, several officers simultaneously shoot him down. *Fifty seconds have elapsed* since the police arrived on the scene.

3:00.00 P.M.: The police chief tells a hastily called press conference that the man has been hit by 10 of the 14 shots fired, and that he has expired. The chief says also that the shooting appears justifiable, because officers' lives were in danger when they fired.

BOX 15-2. The International Association of Chiefs of Police Model Policy on Domestic Violence

The International Association of Chiefs of Police National Law Enforcement Policy Center was established in 1987 in cooperation with the U.S. Justice Department's Bureau of Justice Assistance. Since then, it has published a quarterly *Policy Review* and has generated model policies and extensive explanatory papers dealing with several critical police problems, including the following on domestic violence.

I. PURPOSE

The nature and seriousness of crimes committed between family or household members are not mitigated because of the relationships or living arrangements of those involved. It is the intent of this policy to prescribe courses of action which police officers should take in response to domestic violence that will enforce the law while also serving to intervene and prevent future incidents of violence.

II. POLICY

It is the policy of this agency to:

- Reduce the incidence and severity of domestic violence.
- Protect victims of domestic violence and provide them with support through a combination of law enforcement and community services.
- Promote officer safety by ensuring that officers are fully prepared to respond to and effectively deal with domestic violence calls for service.

III. DEFINITIONS

A. "Family/household member" includes persons who:
  1. Are legally married to one another;
  2. Were formerly married to one another;
  3. Are related by blood;
  4. Are related by marriage;
  5. Have a child in common;
  6. Are living together, who have lived together, or who have a dating relationship; or
  7. Are specified as such by state law.
B. "Domestic violence" occurs where a family or household member commits or attempts to commit the following types of offenses against another:
  1. Bodily injury or fear of imminent bodily injury;
  2. Sexual assault;
  3. Interference with freedom of movement;
  4. A property crime directed at the victim;
  5. Violation of a court order; or
  6. Criminal trespass.

IV. DISPATCHER'S PROCEDURES

The dispatcher who receives a domestic violence call can provide the responding officers with vital information that could save the victim's and the officer's life. The dispatcher will give a domestic violence call the same priority as any other life-threatening call and will, whenever possible, dispatch at least two officers to every incident.

A. In addition to information normally gathered, an effort should be made to determine and relay the following to responding officers:
  1. Whether the suspect is present and, if not, the suspect's description and possible whereabouts;
  2. Whether weapons are involved;
  3. Whether the offender is under the influence of drugs or alcohol;
  4. Whether there are children present;
  5. Whether the victim has a current protective or restraining order; or
  6. Complaint history at that location.
B. Dispatchers shall *not* cancel police response to a domestic violence complaint based solely on a follow-up call from the residence requesting such cancellation. However, the dispatcher shall advise the officers of the complainant's request.

V. RESPONDING OFFICER PROCEDURES

A. On-Scene Investigation
  When responding to a family violence call, the officers shall:
  1. Restore order by gaining control of the situation.
  2. Take control of all weapons used or threatened to be used in the crime.
  3. Assess the need for medical attention and call for medical assistance if indicated.
  4. Interview all parties.
  5. After each party has been interviewed, responding officers should confer to determine if an arrest should be made or whether other actions should be taken.
  6. Collect and record evidence and, where appropriate, take color photographs of injuries and property damage.
  7. Complete appropriate crime or incident reports necessary to fully document the officer's response, whether or not a crime was committed or an arrest made.

6:00.00 P.M.: The story headlines on the evening news, beginning a media blitz that questions why six large officers had to fire 14 shots to subdue a mentally ill man who had been armed with only a small screwdriver.

Day 2
The press reports that the dead man had been a successful civil engineer who had suffered an apparent nervous breakdown. The coroner reports that six of the shots that hit the man struck him in the back.

Day 3
The police union president defends the officers, saying that they had no choice but to shoot. He is attacked as inhumane by advocates for the mentally disturbed, and as unprofessional and counterproductive by the media.

Day 18
The man's heartbroken family files a civil rights suit.

Day 75
After a study of other agencies' policies for dealing with mentally and emotionally disturbed persons, the police department changes its policies and training.

Day 1,047
After expending enormous amounts of money, the city settles the civil rights suit and agrees to change its policies and training. Their attorneys, colleagues, and supervisors try unsuccessfully to convince the officers that they had done nothing wrong. Instead, these supporters argue, the officers had done the best they could and the settlement reflects only the city's acknowledgment that training and policy were deficient. In the years to come, it becomes clear that the officers and their performance have been grievously affected by the whole experience.

The best way to avoid this sad drama begins with understanding that the tried-and-true police techniques of bringing more rational offenders under control are not likely to work where EDPs are concerned. When officers deal with suspects in robberies and burglaries, their adversaries are persons who understand that police are entitled to use force to bring them before justice and that resistance is only likely to make their lot worse. EDPs, by definition, are irrational and not capable of understanding the consequences of their actions. Typically, they have no grasp of why the police have appeared and hold no interest in complying with demands to submit to police authority. On occasion, EDPs are even likely to regard police threats and commands—"Drop the knife!"—as challenges to physical action. As in the example above, responding to such challenges almost invariably kills EDPs rather than the police. But if the police are to conform to their primary responsibility for protecting life, officers must be sophisticated enough to avoid issuing such challenges unknowingly or otherwise unnecessarily. Instead, they should avoid threatening behavior and must take as much time as necessary to take dangerous EDPs into custody without precipitating needless bloodshed.

Perhaps the best single source of information for dealing with EDPs is Gerard R. Murphy's *Special Care: Improving the Police Response to the Mentally Disabled* (1986). This publication includes many suggestions for policy, as well as model policies, and should be on all law enforcement executives' bookshelves. Its most important directions are presented in Box 15-3 and suggest general principles that should be followed during line officers' encounters with EDPs.

Special Operations

The principles of defusing potential violence and delaying confrontation useful in handling EDPs have perhaps been applied with greatest success in the development of protocols for hostage and barricaded-person situations, two of the most critical police special operations. Following the confused and tragic police responses to hostage taking during the 1971 Attica (New York) prison riot and the 1972 Munich Olympics, the New York City Police Department developed strategies and implemented training for resolving both of these crisis types. Since then, police throughout the country have enjoyed enormous success in resolving these situations nonviolently (see, e.g., Bolz and Hershey, 1979). Indeed, evidence suggests that violence at such incidents usually occurs because police have strayed from the principles of containment and control described in Box 15-4. This often occurs because, apparently acting without adequate direction and/or feeling some compulsion to put a quick end to these situations, police have forcibly entered barricaded premises or scenes of hostage taking, forcing confrontations that have come to fatal endings. The temptation to engage in such heroics should be resisted at all costs. *Success in a hostage or barricade situation is a bloodless resolution, and police should strive for that outcome regardless of how long it takes.* In extreme circumstances, accomplishing this goal may consume a considerable amount of time and resources, but even in the most understaffed police jurisdictions, there is no justification for putting innocent lives at risk in order to end a diversion that has taken officers away from routine duties. Where a small agency does not itself have the personnel to staff a protracted hostage or barricaded incident, it should assure, through cooperative agreements with state police and adjoining jurisdictions, that it will have the ability to do so with its neighbors' help.

It should also do so where other emergencies requiring special operations expertise are concerned. Among the types of incidents cited by the Commission on Accreditation for Law Enforcement Agencies as requiring special planning, policy, and training are natural and man-made disasters, civil disturbances, emergencies at correctional or other institutions, bomb threats and bomb emergencies, and dignitary and VIP protection (Commission on Accreditation, 1994: chap. 46).

As the war on drugs has intensified, a more recent problem requiring formulation of policy and training has been large-scale drug raids and operation of interagency drug enforcement teams. The ground rules for such endeavors often are governed by statute and case law. Officers must know thoroughly the requirements for obtaining and executing search and arrest warrants and should be closely supervised to prevent mistaken intrusions into the lives and homes of innocent people or other overzealousness. In addition, all participating agencies should have a clear understanding of these operations' chains of command, operational protocols, provisions for accountability, and the extent to which their personnel may be committed to operations and duties that may either conflict with individual agencies' philosophies and policies or incur liability on agencies. The IACP Model Policy presented in Box 15-5 is a good basis from which to tailor an interagency agreement and operating policies.

Prisoner Transportation and Detention and Lockup Facilities

The most challenging prisoner transportation and detention issues are addressed in Appendix 15-1, but other issues remain. On many occasions, police officers and agencies have been justifiably held liable for causing or contribut-

The International Association of Chiefs of Police Model Policy on Hostage/Barricaded Subject Incidents

I. PURPOSE

It is the purpose of this policy to provide general guidelines for handling hostage/barricaded subject situations.

II. POLICY

In hostage/barricaded subject situations it shall be the policy of this law enforcement agency to consider the lives of the hostages, civilians and officers involved to be of the utmost importance; whenever possible, to enhance the prospects of peacefully resolving the incident through communication with the suspect; whenever possible, to develop and maintain the ability to use alternative approaches to resolve the incident should communications fail; and in hostage situations, to make every reasonable effort to effect the safe release of the hostages.

III. DEFINITIONS

A. Barricaded Subject: Any individual who is reasonably believed to be a threat to commit serious bodily injury or death to hostages, officers or others in the community and who is in a stronghold position.

B. Hostage: Any person held by another against his will by force or threat of force, expressed or implied.

IV. PROCEDURES

A. Patrol Officers

Patrol officers confronting hostage/barricaded subject incidents shall not initiate tactical actions other than those necessary to protect the lives and safety of themselves or others consistent with this department's use of force policy. Officers shall then

1. notify a supervisory officer of the incident and circumstances;
2. contain and isolate the incident scene, establishing an inner containment perimeter to provide a reasonable degree of safety while maintaining contact with the incident scene and—as time and resources permit—establish an outer containment perimeter to control pedestrian and vehicular traffic into the area; and
3. whenever possible, evacuate occupants of affected residences and businesses to a point beyond the perimeter.

B. Officer in Command (OIC)

The ranking officer at the scene shall be in command until specifically relieved by a superior.

The OIC shall

1. inform the watch commander about the nature and circumstances surrounding the incident;
2. delegate the tactical mission to the OIC of the tactical response team;
3. ensure development of a communications/negotiations process and an emergency response team reaction;
4. ensure establishment of an inner and outer perimeter, command post, tactical operations center, negotiations center and a staging area for officers and others arriving for assignment;
5. assign a press center and an officer for press liaison;
6. ensure that responsibility for traffic and crowd control is established, and that routes for emergency vehicles have been designated;
7. make provisions for recording personnel assignments and developing a chronological record of events at the command center and tactical operations center;
8. ensure that necessary equipment from the fire department is made available at the staging area together with any other units or equipment such as canine teams, aviation or marine units; and
9. ensure that emergency medical services are available at the site.

C. Tactical Response Team Commander

The commander of the tactical response team shall

1. assist the OIC in assessing the situation and formulate and provide the OIC with recommended tactical alternatives should communications with the subject fail to resolve the incident;
2. determine equipment needs and assign personnel to control and contain the inner perimeter;
3. designate marksmen and entry teams as necessary;
4. ensure that personnel manning the inner perimeter maintain firearms discipline and are provided with periodic relief by appropriate tactical response team members;
5. prepare appropriate logistical plans to include diagrams of the location in question;
6. ensure the establishment of a tactical operations center if necessary; and
7. maintain contact with and keep the command

post informed of all developments and operations.

D. Hostage Communications Team

The individual in charge of communicating with the subject shall . . . .

1. provide any requested assistance to the OIC;
2. provide trained primary and secondary negotiators and, as available and necessary, a negotiations investigator;
3. obtain all pertinent information about the hostage taker, the hostages, hostage site and other barricaded subjects;
4. designate a location to interview witnesses, released hostages and others; and
5. debrief hostages following the incident.

E. Psychological Services

Psychological services shall serve as a resource to the hostage communications team and will

1. monitor communications between the negotiators and subjects and provide negotiators with assessments of effectiveness, recommended strategies and other relevant information;
2. assist in interviewing witnesses and debriefing hostages; and
3. provide professional assistance to hostages, witnesses and others as may be necessary.

ing to injuries to prisoners they have transported or detained in a plainly unsafe manner that should have been prohibited by policy. Among the policy implications of the injuries and deaths that led to these judgments and settlements are the following:

- Prisoners should be thoroughly searched before being transported.
- Whenever possible, prisoners should be transported in vehicles specially designed for that purpose.
- Policy and training should dictate the seating position of officers and prisoners traveling in patrol cars or vehicles not especially designed for prisoner transportation.
- Victims and witnesses should not be transported in the same vehicles as prisoners.
- Except in unusual conditions (e.g., injured, handicapped, pregnant, extremely obese prisoners), officers should rear-cuff prisoners with their palms facing outward and should double-lock cuffs.
- Prisoners should be seated erect and securely belted into transporting vehicles.
- Transporting officers must be required to keep prisoners under constant observation.
- Sick or injured prisoners should be transported directly to medical facilities.
- Whenever possible, prisoners should be transported by officers of the same sex. When staffing limits make this impossible, special care should be taken to document departure and arrival times and vehicle mileage.
- Except in emergencies (e.g., getting prisoners away from volatile street scenes), juvenile prisoners should not be transported with adult prisoners, and male prisoners should not be transported with female prisoners.

I. PURPOSE

The purpose of this policy is to promote a cooperative effort among law enforcement agencies in order to reduce the amount of regional illicit drug-related activity.

II. POLICY

It is the policy of this law enforcement agency to maximize the effectiveness of its drug enforcement efforts through active participation in the Cooperative Drug Enforcement Unit. This cooperative approach to addressing the region's illicit drug-related problems may result in the following benefits:

1. Establish regional priorities so that a comprehensive, ordered plan of action is developed;
2. Provide local law enforcement agencies with the ability to combine and coordinate their individual resources to more effectively address the regional drug problem;
3. Provide the ability to conduct cross-jurisdictional investigations that would normally have to be terminated when going beyond jurisdictional lines;
4. Establish a regional networking of information and intelligence on drug-related activity; and
5. Provide smaller agencies with an opportunity to participate in narcotics operations and further provide "on-the-job training" to participating officers who may not receive this exposure and expertise in their own agency.

III. PROCEDURES

A. Formal Agreement Establishing the Cooperative Drug Enforcement Unit
   1. The Cooperative Drug Enforcement Unit shall be established by express written agreement.
   2. The authorized chief executive officer of each member jurisdiction shall sign and execute the agreement and secure the approval of their governing bodies where required by law.
   3. Termination of participation in the Cooperative Drug Enforcement Unit agreement shall take effect as provided for under the terms of that agreement.

B. Responsibilities of the Supervisory Board
   1. The chief law enforcement executive from each participating jurisdiction shall serve on a Supervisory Board that shall be responsible for the operation and activities of the Cooperative Drug Enforcement Unit.
   2. The Supervisory Board shall meet on a regular basis for the purpose of overseeing the operations and activities of the Cooperative Drug Enforcement Unit.
   3. Each member of the Supervisory Board shall have an equal vote in the conduct of its business.
   4. A commanding officer for the Cooperative Drug Enforcement Unit shall be appointed by, and work under the direction and guidance of, the Supervisory Board and shall serve at its pleasure. The commanding officer shall be an officer from one of the participating law enforcement agencies.
   5. The commanding officer shall prepare and submit a monthly and yearly report of unit activities to the Supervisory Board.
   6. The Supervisory Board shall annually submit a written report to the chief executive officer or chief elected official of the participating jurisdictions. That report shall contain all information necessary to inform the participating jurisdictions of the activities and accomplishments of the Cooperative Drug Enforcement Unit, providing that all precautions have been taken by the Supervisory Board to maintain security and protect confidential information or sources.
   7. All disputes between participating jurisdictions arising from the operations and activities of the Cooperative Drug Enforcement Unit shall be settled by the Supervisory Board.

C. Personnel Assignment and Authority
   1. Each participating jurisdiction may have one or more law enforcement officers of their agency assigned by the chief law enforcement executive to temporary full-time duty with the Cooperative Drug Enforcement Unit.
   2. The number of law enforcement officers assigned to the Cooperative Drug Enforcement Unit from each participating agency shall be determined by the Supervisory Board with the determination based on:
      a. The size of the jurisdiction and its law enforcement agency;
      b. The level of unit activity within the jurisdiction; and
      c. The amount of resources available beyond current enforcement obligations.
   3. Any law enforcement officer so assigned shall work under the immediate supervision and

direction of the commanding officer and shall adhere to the rules and regulations of the Cooperative Drug Enforcement Unit.

4. For the purposes of indemnification of Cooperative Drug Enforcement Unit personnel and their participating jurisdictions against losses, damages, or liabilities arising out of the activities of the unit, the personnel assigned by any jurisdiction shall be deemed to be continuing under the employment of that jurisdiction and its law enforcement agency.

5. Any sworn officer, while assigned to the Cooperative Drug Enforcement Unit, working under the direction of the commanding officer of the unit, and adhering to the operational procedures of the unit, shall have the same powers, duties, privileges, and immunities as are conferred upon him as a law enforcement officer in his own jurisdiction and in any jurisdiction participating in the Cooperative Drug Enforcement Unit.

D. Financial Support
1. Each participating jurisdiction shall be responsible for the full payment of the personnel temporarily assigned to the Cooperative Drug Enforcement Unit.

2. The operations of the Cooperative Drug En-

forcement Unit shall be financed by assessments to the participating jurisdictions and shall be based upon a per capita share of necessary operating expenses utilizing the most recent and valid census data.

E. Coordination of Asset Forfeitures
1. In asset forfeiture cases, a formal agreement as to the division of functions, responsibilities, and the share of assets shall be reached before the conclusion of the operation.

2. All applications for assets in federal asset forfeiture proceedings shall be submitted within 30 days of the seizure for forfeiture. The application shall contain the following information:
   a. Identification of the property against which the claim is made;
   b. Details concerning the requesting agencies' participation, documenting the resources and manpower expended;
   c. Statement on the intended use of the property; and
   d. Designation of the proper governmental authority to which disbursements or transfers should be made, and a statement from the appropriate legal officer indicating that the transfer is not prohibited under applicable federal, state, or local statutes.

- Lockup personnel should be required to document prisoners' physical conditions and to obtain medical help for any who are obviously sick or injured or who complain of sickness or injury.
- All property in prisoners' possession must be inventoried and documented by lockup personnel.
- Strip searches may be conducted only in private and secure facilities by same-sex officers and only in situations involving violent offenders and/or articulable reason to suspect that such searches may find weapons, evidence, or contraband.
- Body cavity searches may be conducted only under authority of a judicially issued search warrant, in private, and by either a physician or medically trained personnel under the direct supervision of a physician.
- Whenever possible, prisoners should be held in separate cells.
- Prisoners in cells should be kept under constant observation (e.g., by closed-circuit television), and lockup personnel must be required to certify in writing to prisoners' well-being every quarter hour (see, e.g., Commis-

sion on Accreditation, 1994: chaps. 71, 72; International Association of Chiefs of Police, 1992: Model Policy 24).

507

CHAPTER *15*
Police Standards
and Accountability

Off-Duty Conduct, Weapons Carrying, and Employment

During a normal workweek, officers are on-duty for 40 hours and off-duty for 128 hours. What they do in these off-duty hours has an enormous effect on the discipline, good order, and reputation of their agencies and, when circumstances arise that may call for police action, on the safety of citizens and officers, as well. Thus, as suggested in Chapter 9, it is imperative that police agencies promulgate policies and provide training that define both their expectations of off-duty officers and methods by which officers will be held accountable for abiding by these expectations.

The 24-Hour-a-Day Officer.   The first step in this process should be a careful reexamination of the tradition that officers are on-duty and required to take appropriate police action 24 hours a day. There is a considerable difference between what may be appropriate when one is on-duty, in uniform, and detached from an emergency situation and what may be appropriate when one is off-duty, in civilian clothes, and, probably, caught in the physical—*and emotional*—center of a police situation. When an *on*-duty police officer encounters armed robbers, it is usually because the officer is told about them by the radio dispatcher. When this happens, the officer is well rested, removed from the scene, readily identifiable, and in radio contact with other officers and so can plan a tactically sound approach. When an *off*-duty officer encounters an armed robber, it is usually in a restaurant or store and the stranger next to the officer suddenly pulls out a gun and demands that the staff and customers stand and deliver. Alone except for terrified citizens—and caught up in this without warning (and without being able to determine whether the robber is alone or has hidden accomplices in the store)—such a dilemma is likely to become a tragic nightmare if the officer has not been given careful guidance about what to do next. If the officer is armed and acts in a way that might be appropriate for an on-duty uniformed officer (e.g., seeking cover, pulling one's gun, announcing oneself), the officer is virtually bound to precipitate a gun duel in the middle of a crowd and to make a bad situation much worse (see, e.g., Fyfe, 1975, 1980, 1988; Geller and Scott, 1992:161–167, 266–267). Clearly, therefore, officers are best advised to act in some other way. But unless they have previously been given some policy and training guidance, they are likely to choose an inappropriate course of action.[7] Their actions must also be guided by a reward and disciplinary system that, formally or otherwise, does not penalize restraint in the face of overwhelming odds.[8]

If officers find themselves in such circumstances while unarmed, the police reaction to their actions should be based on the following IACP Model Policy statement:

> An officer who elects not to carry a handgun while off duty shall not be subjected to disciplinary action if an occasion should arise in which he could have taken police action if he were armed. Exception: Off-duty officers while oper-

ating a department vehicle shall be armed with an approved weapon. (Matulia, 1985:76)

Off-Duty Employment. It would be ideal if police officers' compensation
were sufficient to make moot any questions concerning off-duty employment.
In many U.S. jurisdictions, however, police salaries are so low that officers simply cannot get along without the income generated by *moonlighting,* or finding
secondary employment. Further, even where officers' compensation is comparatively large, they generally have won or been accorded the right to supplement their income with second jobs or businesses.

The fact that moonlighting is a widespread practice among U.S. law enforcement officials does not lead to the conclusion that officers should be free of
restrictions related to such work. The relevant standards put forth by the Commission on Accreditation for Law Enforcement Agencies (CALEA) require that:

22.3.3. A written directive governs the types of off-duty employment in
which agency personnel may engage.

22.3.4. If the agency permits sworn personnel to engage in extra-duty employment, a written directive addresses the following:
   a. the requirement that sworn personnel must receive agency permis-
      sion to engage in extra-duty employment;
   b. policies that address the behavior and activities of officers during off-
      duty employment;
   c. approval, review, and revocation processes pertaining to officers' off-
      duty employment;
   d. designation of a point of coordination or administration within the
      agency to oversee adherence to the aforementioned policies,
      processes, and other matters deemed appropriate by the agency; and
   e. documentation of the significant aspects of each officer's extra-duty
      employment (Commission on Accreditation, 1994: Standard 22–32)

There is a plethora of compelling specific questions that should be resolved in such regulations. Obviously, no officer should be permitted to work
so many hours for a secondary employer that she or he becomes exhausted or
is otherwise unable or unavailable to perform effectively. Consequently, a cap
must be placed on the number of off-duty hours officers can work. In addition,
officers should not be permitted to work in positions that embarrass their departments or that exploit their police positions in inappropriate ways. Several
years ago, the police department in a relatively conservative large city was
mortified when it came to light that many of its officers and supervisors served
as a sort of private army of bodyguards, chauffeurs, and "gofers" for an inter-
nationally renowned pornographer. In other cases, officers have established or
been employed by landscaping, home improvement, or burglar alarm businesses to which they have referred citizens contacted during their normal police working days. Regulations must prohibit police officers from acting as
shills in such fashions.

Less obvious, but equally critical, are questions concerning whether and
under what conditions officers should be allowed to engage in private security
work while off-duty. An assumption that seems operative in many circles is

that, by virtue of their training for public policing positions, officers require no additional training for private security positions. This is a faulty assumption that is no more valid than the reverse proposition that training as a private security officer qualifies one for public police work.

Police officers wear uniforms and badges and carry weapons in order to protect and serve the public impartially. Private security officers carry guns in furtherance of the private parties or businesses that employ them and to which they are expected to be partial. Changing back and forth between the two mind-sets required for success in these positions is not something that can be accomplished without special training. Hence, where police officers are permitted to wear their uniforms, guns, and badges to protect private interests, those interests must be required to train officers for their jobs.

Other differences between public policing and private security also merit special training. When on-duty officers take action in the line of duty, they usually are dispatched to scenes of suspicious conduct and/or have access to immediate assistance by use of their radios. Especially in heavily policed big cities, this means that they rarely are alone in suspicious circumstances for more than the most brief periods. This reduces the urgency of confrontations with suspicious people because, rather than feeling compelled to confront them immediately and alone, officers often can surreptitiously stand by and observe while they wait for and coordinate reinforcements before they come face-to-face with suspects. It also reduces urgency in another way: When suspects leave places where they are being observed by on-duty officers who do not feel that they can safely confront suspicious people alone, officers can use their radios to transmit descriptions and directions of travel, so that colleagues may assist in apprehensions at other places. Consequently, except where officers must intervene immediately to protect life (e.g., when an officer observes a robbery, rape, assault, or other violent crime in progress), on-duty officers rarely have to confront criminal suspects alone. This is not so where private officers are concerned.[9]

But the line between police officer as public servant and police officer moonlighting as private security guard often is difficult to draw, especially when officers are permitted to work as security guards—or *uniformed bouncers*—in bars and nightclubs. For example:

- When officer security guards stop and question customers or other persons they regard as suspicious (or underage), are they acting in the public interest or the interests of their private employers? Who assumes any liability that may result?
- Do police officers working in bars or nightclubs have an obligation to cite their employers when they witness them serving alcohol to persons who are intoxicated? This is an act that is against the law in most U.S. jurisdictions, but it occurs regularly in bars and nightclubs.
- Must such officer-bouncers prohibit obviously intoxicated bar patrons from driving?
- Do officer-bouncers have an obligation to arrest disorderly customers or bar fighters? If such an obligation exists, how is it reconciled with officers' knowledge that, in many jurisdictions, the mere fact of an arrest in a

liquor establishment causes licensing authorities to carefully review the qualifications of bar owners—the officers' secondary employers—to hold liquor licenses?

- When officer-bouncers intervene in barroom disputes, are they acting as public police officers or as private employees?
- When such officer-bouncers make arrests or take other action, are their police employers or their private employers—or both—liable for any misconduct that may occur?
- If such arrests result in repeated court appearances, do taxpayers or private employers foot the bill for the officers' time in court and away from their normal duties?
- To what extent may public liability be increased because, in response to employers' wishes that they handle problems informally, officer-bouncers may refrain from official action? If an officer does not arrest a man who blackens his girlfriend's eye in a bar fight, for example, is the officer's public employer liable for failing to protect the woman from any further violence?
- To what extent is police officers' responsibility to act impartially compromised by private employers' expectations that they will overlook violations of law or otherwise grant special favors even when they are on-duty?

Even when off-duty employment programs are well administered, the conflicts of interest that arise in private security work, especially in bars and nightclubs, are inevitable, difficult, and potentially dangerous to departments' reputations and to municipal treasuries. When such programs are poorly administered, they may totally compromise an agency's integrity and command structure. In several jurisdictions, low-ranking officers have used their personal connections with private employers to control their supervisors' and commanders' access to lucrative off-duty employment opportunities. This is devastating to agency discipline and integrity because, for example, it is impossible for a lieutenant to command an officer effectively when the officer can determine with a phone call whether the lieutenant will enjoy a profitable off-duty job.

In short, while loose restrictions on off-duty employment are a tempting and apparently low-cost perk for cash-strapped agencies to offer officers, they present many problems that are not readily obvious. Off-duty employment should be carefully and closely regulated to see that it does not interfere with the agency's ability and responsibility to achieve the commonweal goals discussed earlier.

Review of Controversial Police Conduct

Three types of police conduct seem to create great amounts of controversy and are therefore worthy of consideration in this discussion. They are conduct that generates complaints from citizens, use of deadly force, and vehicle pursuits.

Procedures for Citizens' Complaints. As suggested above, no police controversy has been more polarizing than the debate about whether allegations of police misconduct should be reviewed by citizen advisory or review boards (see, e.g., Fyfe, 1985; Perez, 1978, 1994; Ruchelman, 1974; Skolnick and Fyfe,

1993). No matter what the view of parties to this debate, however, there is consensus that citizen review boards should serve in an advisory capacity only and that the disciplinary authority of the police chief executive should not be compromised. As the day-to-day operating head of his agency, the chief must be the person with whom the buck stops. Many debates about the establishment of citizen review boards focus on fears that the chief's authority will be usurped by the new panel. These debates might be avoided if it is made clear by advocates of review that they intend boards only to serve in an advisory capacity rather than to replace them as ultimate disciplinary authorities.

Increasingly, however, citizen review panels have been created to review misconduct complaints and advise police chiefs on the results of their reviews. According to Walker and Wright (1994:1), the number of citizen review procedures in the nation's 100 largest cities increased from 1 in 1970, to 20 in 1985, to 38 in 1990, and to 66 in 1994. Thus, there presently exists some form of citizen review in two-thirds of the largest American police jurisdictions.

There are no doubt many reasons for this dramatic increase which, typically, has occurred despite the strong objections of most police officials and, often, their mayors. African Americans and Hispanics, who have frequently championed such boards, have grown more politically powerful and have insisted on creating them. In addition, the police in many places—like government generally—have given citizens and elected officials reason to believe that the ability of the departments to police themselves has not been nearly as great as claimed (see, e.g., Christopher et al., 1991; DiUlio, 1994; Kolts et al., 1992; Mollen et al., 1994; St. Clair et al., 1992). In the face of sensational exposures of inept internal investigations of corruption and brutality, it has been hard to argue that external review of police conduct is superfluous.

Internal review as a conflict of interest. In addition, there has been a recognition by many police officials that there is a conflict of interest in any system that leaves exclusively to the chief the responsibility for investigating and resolving citizens' complaints against his or her personnel. Police historically have claimed, with reference to law and medicine, that the best assessors of the reasonableness of professional conduct are peers. This analogy to the historic professions is flawed, however, because the professionals who typically review allegations of police misconduct are not impartial peers who have no stake in the outcomes of their deliberations. Instead, those who currently review allegations against officers are their *bosses,* who, whether they consciously acknowledge it or not, have a great stake in demonstrating that their personnel are well-trained, well-supervised professionals who do things by the book. A real professional peer review system includes a number of professionals assembled by a licensing body (e.g., the bar or medical associations) from among people who do the same sort of work as the accused but who do it in different places and for different employers.

The purported "professional peer review systems" that characterize policing, by contrast, are comparable to the chief surgeons' panels that review and dispose of complaints against the doctors who work under them. Chief surgeons and hospital administrators know that findings of malpractice by the doctors they have employed, trained, and supervised may create liability for them and the hospitals to which they have devoted their careers. No layperson would place much credence in the findings of such a system or in a legal malpractice system run by the senior partners of the law firms in which accused attorneys work. Indeed, even the demonstrably more objective American Medical Association and American Bar Association peer review procedures that currently supplement hospitals' and law firms' reviews are viewed as highly suspect. Certainly, therefore, the police—who are trained and socialized to be skeptical—should understand why many citizens do not take seriously review procedures in which police investigate police and, as is usually the case in swearing contests between citizens and officers, in which chiefs report tersely that the investigation did not sustain allegations of wrongdoing. As their agencies' heads, police chief executives must ultimately determine and announce whether officers involved in controversial circumstances have acted appropriately, but it is simply wrong to suggest that they do so as officers' peers.

Citizen participation as an ideal. Recognition of a second, closely related factor has also strengthened the move to citizen review. Civilian participation in review is an *inclusionary* strategy that addresses fundamental democratic principles. In this sense, it is much like the jury system. While we take juries for granted, the jury system is hard to justify purely as a rational fact-finding process. Far more easily and efficiently than juries, two intelligent people, perhaps with some sophisticated computer software, could make decisions about guilt, innocence, or liability and contributory negligence in ways that could be justified on paper.

If we were to switch to such a system on grounds of pure rationality and efficiency, however, the *quality* of justice would undoubtedly suffer. Abolition of juries would cause the system to lose credibility and would create speculation that we are on the way back to an easily manipulated Star Chamber system. The justice system would lose the ability to take into account jurors' assessments of witnesses' credibility, a factor not easily put to paper or put in a computer-readable form. Other important considerations better interpreted by the broad and representative perspectives of six or twelve jurors would also fall by the wayside if we abandoned the jury system for a purely rational process. Pure rationality does not easily interpret the law in its spirit, rather than by the letter, or allow for consideration of mitigating or aggravating factors. In short, the jury system is an acknowledgment that reasonable application of the law is an art as much as it is a science and that inclusion and openness are as important to its success as the purely intellectual merits of its decisions.

For many of the same reasons, citizen review enhances the credibility of investigations and adjudications of alleged police misconduct. Research conducted by Douglas Perez in Oakland and Berkeley, California (1978, 1994), provides evidence of the credibility of citizen review systems relative to that of internal review systems. He reports that the internal system of processing complaints employed by Oakland at the time of his study was thorough and fair.[10] Berkeley, Oakland's neighbor city, also boasted a thorough and fair complaint adjudication system, but it included a citizen police review commission (PRC), which advised the chief on its findings, and it also built in more procedural safeguards for accused officers than did Oakland's internal system. Indeed, in comparison with the stringent Oakland system, one experienced police official

TABLE 15-1. Citizen Complainant Satisfaction with Investigation in Berkeley and Oakland

	Berkeley PRC*	Berkeley IAD†	Oakland
Percentage of complainants who believed that investigation was:			
(1) Impartial	64.9%	29.4%	9.5%
(2) Thorough	85.7%	47.0%	23.1%
(3) Fair	73.3%	35.3%	11.5%
Percentage of complainants who were satisfied with outcome:			
(4) Complainants whose allegations were found justified	60.0% (*n* = 5)	66.7% (*n* = 6)	60.0% (*n* = 5)
(5) Complainants whose allegations were not found justified	66.7% (*n* = 6)	0.0% (*n* = 1)	0.0% (*n* = 15)

*Period when complaints against Berkeley officers were reviewed by the Police Review Commission.
†Period when complaints against Berkeley officers were handled entirely by the department's Internal Affairs Division.
Source: Derived from data collected by Douglas Perez, "Police Accountability: A Question of Balance," Ph.D. dissertation, University of California, Berkeley (1978), as presented in Wayne A. Kerstetter, "Who Disciplines the Police? Who Should?" pp. 162, 168–169 in William A. Geller (ed.), *Police Leadership in America: Crisis and Opportunity* (New York: Praeger, 1985).

noted, "the Berkeley civilian review system [analyzed by Perez] may enhance procedural fairness for the [accused] at the cost of some loss in substantive fairness for citizens" (Kerstetter, 1985:163).

One might expect, therefore, that the Oakland system would be viewed by citizens and complainants as far more credible than the Berkeley system. This is not so. Perez's findings showed that the Berkeley PRC was granted substantially more credibility by complainants than either the Oakland system or the previous Berkeley internal system. In Berkeley, as Table 15-1 illustrates (line 1), two of every three complainants (64.9 percent) viewed the investigations of their complaints as "impartial," but fewer than one in ten Oakland complainants (9.5 percent) held the same view. Line 2 shows that seven out of eight Berkeley PRC complainants (85.7 percent) viewed investigations as thorough; less than one in four Oakland complainants (23.1 percent) felt the same way. Line 3 discloses that nearly three of four Berkeley PRC complainants felt that they had been fairly treated (73.3 percent); only one in eight Oakland complainants (11.5 percent) gave such responses. Favorable views of the old Berkeley IAD (Internal Affairs Division) procedures generally fell midway between these two extremes.

Further, complainants' favorable views of the Berkeley proceedings held regardless of the outcome of complaint investigations. This is not true of the other systems Perez studied. Line 4 of Table 15-1 demonstrates that about three in five of those whose complaints were substantiated were satisfied with what happened. Perez managed to contact six complainants whose allegations were dismissed by the Berkeley PRC. Line 5 shows that four of these six (66.7 percent) were satisfied that they had received a fair hearing and that the PRC had acted appropriately *despite* the dismissals of their allegations. Line 5 also shows, however, that none of the 15 Oakland complainants whose cases were dismissed felt that they had been treated fairly.

These numbers are small and must be interpreted with care, but they suggest the importance of the *process* of investigating and reviewing citizens' complaints. Apparently, formalization and citizen participation in investigating and reviewing is a better way than internal police proceedings to enhance relations between police and those who are dissatisfied enough with police to complain against officers. This conclusion is consistent with the findings of legal scholars who have studied court proceedings. There, it has been reported that, regardless of outcome, victims generally view the courts more favorably when they are allowed to air their grievances in formalized and inclusive legal proceedings than when, for example, overworked prosecutors or fast-buck lawyers pressure them into quick plea bargains or pretrial settlements that do not give them a chance to state their cases in public settings (see, e.g., Lind and Tyler, 1988; McCoy, 1993).

Thus, the experience in Berkeley suggests that citizen review is a good thing for all concerned. The Berkeley system has enhanced the department's credibility among the community and complainants; the chief has retained ultimate disciplinary power; and the civil libertarians who helped create the system built into it due process guarantees that have benefited accused officers. Even those who have differences of principle with the idea of citizen review should not view this as a cause of the great divisiveness with which it has historically been associated.

Funding citizen review.   Critics of citizen review frequently suggest that the success in Berkeley is an aberration and that the history of citizen review is littered with failure. The successes in Berkeley and in Dade County (Florida), where an independent review panel oversees investigations of complaints against all county employees, however, suggest that the major difference between success and failure involves one of commitment and resources. In both places, officials have strongly supported the boards, politically and with capital sufficient to allow the hiring of staff adequate to do the job. In places where boards have failed, this has generally not been true.[11]

The mechanics of processing citizen complaints.   Regardless of whether review of complaints is internal or external, several philosophical issues and matters of fact should be reflected in agency policies related to handling allegations against officers.

First, because police officers typically work alone and out of the sight of their commanding officers, their supervisors and commanders are at a real disadvantage in attempting to gather firsthand information about their performance and about the continuing merits and appropriateness of department policies and procedures.

Second, complaints are a valuable form of management information, rather than just documents to be viewed exclusively in negative, punitive terms. Complaints serve as a check on officers and other personnel, but they also are an important means of identifying obsolete policies and sources of misunderstanding between the agency and its clientele.

Third, most people who complain about the police do so only reluctantly and with great anxiety concerning the consequences of doing so. Many police officials believe that citizens file complaints against officers frivolously. On occasion, in some places more than in others, this belief certainly is accurate. But for most people—especially those who have inarguably been mistreated—filing a complaint against a police officer is a real act of courage. Out-of-towners who do so may fear they will be greeted with derision—or even threats or illegal arrests—when they enter police stations to lodge complaints. It is very rare indeed that these fears have anything to do with objective reality, but they are very real to the people who harbor them. Out-of-town complainants are, after all, strangers in foreign lands who at least believe they have been treated badly by the only local officers they have met. Residents who have been mistreated must go on living in the jurisdictions policed by the officers about whom they wish to complain. Consequently, they may also be reluctant to make enemies in this way.

This third point is important because it places on police agencies a responsibility to make it as easy as possible for citizens who believe they have been aggrieved to lodge complaints. It is not easy to file complaints against officials who exercise such broad authority as the police,[12] and many people are discouraged from doing so by provisions that require them to come to police facilities to complain—or even by requirements that they identify themselves before a complaint is investigated thoroughly. Often, especially in really serious cases, the reluctance of complainants has nothing to do with the merits of the complaint or with the question of whether misconduct did occur.

Fourth, administrators too often view discontinuance of a complaint as an opportunity to take the easy way out of a nasty allegation by closing the case without determining the facts. This is a mistake; a citizen's desire to withdraw a complaint that has already been lodged usually does not indicate that the complaint was without merit or that the misconduct did not occur. Some complainants run out of courage after initially filing their complaints, or they make deals with police and prosecutors in which criminal charges against themselves are dropped in return for their waiving of charges against police. Neither of these developments speaks to questions of whether accused officers actually did wrong or whether policy and training are in need of revision. Instead, administrators are dutybound to make both determinations regardless of whether, for whatever personal reasons, citizens no longer wish to cooperate with police.

Fifth, there is enormous pressure on field supervisors, who frequently are the first to hear about citizens' complaints, to "support the troops" by dissuading complainants from proceeding or by treating citizens' complaints informally. Ironically, therefore, when supervisors are given the discretion to reject a complaint because, for example, it does not appear meritorious, their job is more stressful than the jobs of those in agencies in which all complaints must be accepted and referred to internal investigators regardless of their apparent merits.

More important, however, permitting supervisors to determine whether to accept complaints damages organizational discipline in two significant ways:

- This practice creates an enormous loophole for supervisors who are tempted to succumb to pressures to "back up the troops" by short-circuiting complaints out of the system. Administrators' access to the information on which decisions to accept or reject complaints are made is controlled by the supervisors involved, who have considerable leeway in deciding what to include in or omit from their reports. Hence, supervisors who bend the rules can easily make it impossible for administrators to reconstruct precisely what they knew when they decided that a complaint had no merits (see Box 15-6). In such situations, there is no meaningful way to hold supervisors accountable for properly dealing with citizens' complaints.
- This practice may allow supervisors to reject complaints on grounds that officers acted in accord with policies that may themselves be in need of revision. When this occurs, chief administrators are denied information about the extent to which existing policies and practices are offensive to the public.

Sixth, the great majority of citizens' complaints are "swearing contests" in which there is no dispositive physical or other objective evidence. Most complaints allege minor verbal or physical abuse which officers deny and which, therefore, cannot be resolved one way or the other.

There are several specific policy implications of these issues and facts:

- Agencies must do everything possible to avoid "chilling" complaints in any way. They must make it as easy as possible to file complaints and should treat anonymous, telephoned, and third-party complaints in exactly the same way as signed first-party complaints. It is hard to defend doing otherwise, because police do investigate anonymous, telephoned, and third-party complaints of crime as thoroughly as possible. Police executives who are seriously interested in determining the merits of complaints are obliged to make accommodations for citizens' fears just as they accommodate people who, for a variety of reasons, only reluctantly claim that they have been victims of crime.
- Agencies should make it mandatory that field supervisors and others accept and treat formally *all* citizen complaints, regardless of whether they spell out only minor violations or no violations at all. As indicated above, this relieves supervisors of the unstated, but very real, expectation among officers that their supervisors will do everything possible to resolve complaints as informally as possible, or even to avoid accepting them altogether. It also facilitates examination of departmental policies and demonstrates the agency's openness and willingness to investigate allegations

BOX 15-6. An Attempt to Complain about the Police

According to hospital and court records, Rodney King's March 3, 1991, encounter with the police left him with 20 stitches, a broken cheekbone, a broken right ankle, 11 skull fractures, permanent brain damage, broken teeth, kidney damage, and emotional and physical trauma. Consider the implications of two attempts to spur an investigation into the circumstances in which these injuries occurred:

Paul King

Paul King was awakened by Rodney King's passenger, Bryant Allen, on Sunday, March 3, at approximately 4:00 A.M., and told that his brother Rodney had been beaten and arrested by the police. Allen also said someone might have videotaped the incident. On Monday morning, Paul King went to the Foothill Station to complain about the treatment of his brother.

The officer at the front desk told Paul King he would have to wait. After waiting and then growing impatient, Paul King returned to the front desk as a sergeant came out from the back of the station. Paul King said he wanted to make a complaint about his brother; the sergeant took Paul King back to a detective's interview room.

According to Paul King, the sergeant went in and out of the interview room several times during the 40 minutes Paul King was there, spending approximately half of that time out of the room. The sergeant states that he left the room once for about 30 minutes to find the arrest report and to attempt to locate a use of force report, which is required after any LAPD officer uses force more severe than a "firm grip." Paul King specifically asked about the procedures for making a complaint and advised the sergeant that a videotape of the incident existed.

According to Paul King, the sergeant began by asking whether he had ever been in trouble. Paul King responded that he was there to talk about Rodney King, not himself. The sergeant recalls discussing the public perception of and reaction to police officers in general in an effort to make Paul King feel more comfortable.

The sergeant told Paul King that he would check the logs and said something to the effect that an investigation was going on. In response to Paul King's inquiry as to what was being investigated, the sergeant told him that Rodney King was in "big trouble," that he had been caught in a high-speed chase going 100 m.p.h. or so and that, according to the reported ground for the arrest, Rodney King had put someone's life in danger, possibly a police officer.

The sergeant told Paul King that he should try to find the video, and that the video could be of help. The sergeant did not at any time fill out a personnel complaint form. According to Paul King, when he left Foothill Station "I knew I hadn't made a complaint."

The sergeant told the Commission staff he followed usual procedures when conducting the Paul King interview. The sergeant explained that when an individual makes a general complaint of police misconduct without specific details, he conducts a preliminary investigation. If that investigation reveals facts that, if true, would warrant discipline, a personnel complaint is prepared. If no complaint is prepared, the information he gathers is written down and passed along to his superior officers. Based on the general information he received from Paul King, the sergeant reported in his daily log that no further action was necessary, pending completion and evaluation of the use of force report or receipt of additional evidence such as the videotape.

George Holliday

George Holliday [who videotaped the beating] reported that he called the Foothill Station on Monday, March 4, intending to offer his videotape to the police. Holliday informed the desk officer who answered the call that he had witnessed an incident involving a motorist who had been beaten by LAPD officers. Holliday said he inquired as to the condition of the motorist and was told that "we (the LAPD) do not release information like that."

According to Holliday, the desk officer made no attempt to learn any details of the event Holliday witnessed. No personnel complaint was generated as a result of his call. Holliday said he did not inform the Foothill officer that he had videotaped the beating.

Confronted with what he viewed as disinterest on the part of the LAPD, Holliday made arrangements with Los Angeles television station KTLA to broadcast the videotape on Monday evening. The following day the tape received national exposure on the Cable News Network, and thereafter was reported widely in the media.

Source: Christopher et al. (July 1991:9–11).

against its officers, which, in turn, diminishes calls for civilian review based on allegations that administrators wrongly quash complaints.

- Agencies should not distinguish between complaints in which complainants wish to proceed and those in which they do not. In both cases, the key question is whether wrongful police conduct occurred, rather than what the complainant may wish to do about it. It is up to police administrators, rather than complainants, to correct bad police behavior or policies.
- Agencies must carefully monitor officers who appear to accumulate a large number of complaints that cannot be sustained (e.g., "The officer hit me unnecessarily" . . . "I used necessary force"; "He called me a $@*$!!" . . . "Never happened.") In every agency, some few officers seem to fall into this category (see, e.g., Christopher et al., 1991; DiUlio, 1992; Kolts et al., 1992; Mollen et al., 1994; St. Clair et al., 1992), and although it would be inappropriate to discipline them for allegations that cannot individually be sustained, where there is smoke, there is often fire. Like most citizens, juries just do not accept the idea of innocence when plaintiffs in suits against the police demonstrate in court that defendant officers have long records of unsustained complaints that were ignored because a department could not decisively prove that allegations made by different citizens at different times and places were true.

There are two costs of treating all complaints formally and documenting and investigating them as far as they can be taken. First, some small number of people will make frivolous complaints. These costs are minimal, however, because most baseless complaints can be identified with little effort. Second, some officers will openly resent formal treatment of complaints, but most will be quietly happy that the department investigates carefully all allegations and is doing what it can to keep control of its disciplinary system in-house. Further, these costs pale when compared with the problem of trying to explain to a jury or a roomful of reporters why nothing has been done to determine why an accused officer has previously been the subject of far more citizen complaints than any of his colleagues.

Dispositions of citizen complaint investigations.   Regardless of whether complaints are reviewed internally or by citizen panels, investigations of citizen complaints and other allegations generally cannot end in simple guilty/not guilty determinations. Such dispositions are appropriate in adversarial criminal prosecutions, where decisions makers have to answer only one question—Did the prosecutor prove guilt beyond a reasonable doubt?—but they are insufficient to cover the range of conclusions possible during police administrative fact-finding investigations. Instead, some variation of the following set of potential findings (which are not mutually exclusive and which may apply in whole or in part when multiple charges are involved) probably is most useful:

- *Sustained.* The acts or omissions alleged did occur and did violate department policy or regulations.

- *Not sustained.* Evidence is insufficient to allow a determination of whether the acts or omissions alleged did occur. This finding, in other words, indicates that there is no way to know what happened.
- *Unfounded.* Investigation has affirmatively determined that the acts or omissions alleged did not occur. This finding differs from *not sustained* because it indicates that reviewers have found out what occurred, and that it was proper.
- *Exonerated.* Investigation has disclosed that the acts or omissions alleged did occur but that they were proper and in accord with agency policy and regulations. As suggested above, when such a conclusion is reached, reviewers should carefully reexamine the policies in question to determine whether they should be changed.
- *Referred for prosecution.* Investigation has developed reason to believe that accused personnel have committed criminal acts, and the department's internal review process will be held in abeyance until the disposition of criminal charges by the prosecutor. In such cases, especially when serious crimes are suspected, suspension pending the outcome of prosecutorial action may lead to summary dismissal upon conviction in the criminal courts.

Review of Vehicle Pursuits and Deadly Force. Few police actions are more spectacular or generate more public attention than vehicle pursuits and use of deadly force. Although police chief executives are ultimately responsible for determining whether police actions in both types of situations were proper and in conformance with agency policy, their decisions should be informed by information, conclusions, and recommendations furnished by people at several organizational levels.

If the principle of accountability is to be honored, pursuits and police shootings must be investigated by the supervisors and commanders of the officers involved, who should be required to explain in writing their findings about the propriety of police actions involved. These reports and any other information necessary to reach a final determination should be provided to boards of review, perhaps best composed of field and personnel administrators, trainers, community relations personnel, officers of the same rank and similar (but not identical) assignment, legal staff, and any legally authorized or required civilian participation.

Before such boards convene as a group, members should review case folders alone and independently and should commit to writing their findings, recommendations, and the reasons therefor. This process ensures that the case folder eventually received by the chief executive includes independent perspectives that, to the greatest extent possible, are unaffected by the dynamics of a meeting that may be dominated by one charismatic and/or high-ranking individual who manages to press his or her views on the whole panel.

When boards meet, depending on local provisions, they may take testimony, examine witnesses, or simply discuss their interpretations of the facts and circumstances. However this is accomplished, the board's findings, recommendations, and reasoning should be committed to writing, and, like appellate judges, each participant should be required to indicate and explain in writing either agreement or disagreement with the end result.

As is true of adjudication of complaints and allegations of wrongdoing, investigation and review of pursuits or deadly force (or other uses of force) should not simply end in "Okay"/"Not okay" findings. Instead, the following (a composite of the disposition alternatives of several large agencies) can serve as a model:

- *Justified.* The pursuit or use of deadly force was appropriate, necessary, and in accord with law and department policy and practice.
- *Administrative disapproval.* The pursuit or use of deadly force was in accord with law and department policy and practice, but the actions of the officer(s) indicate a need for retraining in tactics, law, and/or policy. This finding is perhaps most frequent in cases (such as those involving EDPs, as discussed above) in which officers' poor tactical choices put them in danger from which they can extricate themselves only by shooting.[13]
- *Violation.* The pursuit or use of deadly force was in violation of department policy and practice.
- *Referred for prosecution.* There is reason to believe that the pursuit or use of deadly force involved criminal acts by the officer(s) involved, and the department's internal review process will be held in abeyance until the disposition of criminal charges by the prosecution.

In addition to the above, board recommendations may include the following:

- *Counseling.* The actions of the officer(s) may indicate a need for psychological or psychiatric treatment and/or substance abuse counseling.
- *Mandatory transfer.* The officer(s) should be transferred to a less sensitive assignment or, if he or she holds a sought-after assignment, to a less desirable assignment.
- *Voluntary transfer.* The officer(s) has acted properly but should be given the opportunity to transfer to less sensitive or less dangerous work.

Accreditation

As suggested throughout this chapter, the process of professional accountability must begin with the formulation of professional standards, or policies. In Chapter 6, we saw that this movement really did not get under way in policing until the 1960s, when scholars and blue-ribbon commissions began to study the police. One of the major attempts to define professional police standards since that time is found in the accreditation process, first applied to policing by the Commission on Accreditation for Law Enforcement Agencies.

CALEA has its roots in the late 1970s, when a variety of nonpolice groups proposed formal standards to govern police conduct (see, e.g., American Bar Association, 1973; National Advisory Commission, 1973). Subsequently, with a seed grant from the U.S. Department of Justice, four major law enforcement professional groups (the International Association of Chiefs of Police, the National Organization of Black Law Enforcement Executives, the National Sheriffs' Association, and the Police Executive Research Forum) collaborated in developing a standards manual and a process for reviewing and accrediting agencies that apply for CALEA accreditation.

The more than 900 standards that appeared in CALEA's original accreditation manual were largely administrative. With the exception of requiring that accredited agencies authorize officers to employ deadly force only in defense of life (CALEA, 1983: Standards 1.3.2, 1.3.3), the standards generally identified areas in which policies and training should exist, but they did not prescribe precisely what the policies should say. Since that time, the number of standards has been pared down to under 500, and in many cases their content has been edited and refined. Still, they generally remain guides to areas in which policy should be formulated, rather than models for direct adoption. The standard and commentary concerning police vehicle pursuit presented in Box 15-1, for example, are an encouragement to take certain important factors into account, rather than a precise guide.

At present, CALEA has accredited more than 300 law enforcement agencies (for five-year periods, renewable on reassessment and demonstration of continued compliance with CALEA requirements). Several hundred additional agencies currently are undergoing the several-year process of self-assessment and preparation for evaluation by CALEA's peer assessors, most of whom are administrators and managers from accredited agencies. CALEA has spawned several state-level accreditation programs which, like New York's, have generally adopted a pared-down version of CALEA's standards and processes for proof of compliance and assessment.

Successful participation in the accreditation process includes several benefits. First, it produces knowledge and certification that an agency's administration is addressing the policy and training areas deemed essential by the country's four major police professional organizations. Again, it does this not by telling departments specifically how to address these areas but, instead, by encouraging them to apply prevailing standards to their own needs. It is hard to see how this cannot result in improvements in delivery of police services, in enhancement of an agency's status and image in the community, and in greater pride among personnel.

Second, the intense self-assessment that is part of the process of bringing an agency into accord with accreditation standards helps to identify its strengths and weaknesses—to exploit the former and to correct the latter. Third, because it effectively compels agencies to bring their administrative practices into compliance with the state of the police art, accreditation probably reduces agencies' exposure to liability; at least, insurers in several states have concluded that this is so and have offered reduced rates to departments that have successfully completed the process.[14]

Even if an agency declines to participate in formal accreditation, however, it is well advised to acquire CALEA's *Standards Manual* and other documents and to hold its policies, practices, and facilities to the degree of sophistication prescribed by them.

SUMMARY

At its core, this chapter is an argument for continuing development and refinement of a fairly specific standard of care for police operations. Some administrators are reluctant to undertake or continue this task, but there is an excellent reason to do so: If the police do not, legislators, judges, and jurors, who know far less about policing, will do it for them, often at great expense and after great pain.[15] As the reluctance of courts and legislators to intervene in what they regard as police administrative prerogatives suggests, defining appropriate police conduct is properly the business of the police, rather than of representatives of the other two branches of government. Professional police make sure that they make it their business and, consequently, rarely find that judges or legislators feel it necessary to tell them what to do.

This chapter argues also that police agencies must be willing and able to explain to the public and the media their standards of conduct and the reasons for them. Accountability demands that one must be able to explain why one took a particular action. In this era of public skepticism about government, no official can get away with the claim that only professionals can understand or are fit to judge why other professionals did something. This is a ploy that may have worked before Vietnam, Attica, Watergate, and Rodney King, but it is no longer accepted by the public.

Especially since *Monell*, police should be aware that, where any controversial police action or practice is concerned, they are eventually likely to have to tell it to the judge. It is better to avoid this by carefully formulating policies and explaining why they exist before trouble arises. In doing so, they will deliver better service and make their officers' jobs easier by more clearly defining what is expected of them.

QUESTIONS FOR DISCUSSION

1. You have been called to a staff meeting by the chief of your department. A local television station has surreptitiously videotaped several incidents in which undercover reporters attempted to report fictitious misconduct to supervisors at several police stations. Last night, the first in a series of reports on their investigation was broadcast. It showed that, in almost all cases, the officials with whom the reporters spoke were cold, impolite, accusatory, or even threatening. In only one of the ten incidents broadcast did the alleged victim actually succeed in filing a complaint. In the others, complainants were improperly referred to the chief's office, sent on their way with advice to "think over what they were doing," or told that their complaints would be "taken care of informally."

   The chief has thrown the floor open for a discussion of the series and what to do about it. Where do you stand?

2. Read Appendix 15-1. Then discuss the principles used by the San Diego Police Department in addressing the problem of in-custody death and explain how you would apply them to the problem of delineating the circumstances in which police canines may be used to search for and assist in apprehension of suspects.

3. Starting from scratch, design an off-duty employment policy directive for the department in which you are employed or that serves the jurisdiction in which you reside.

4. What information should be released to the public concerning the investigation of police shooting by police officers during and after investigations of these events?

5. How should the following case and related policy be handled?

A man has been arrested for disorderly conduct and resisting arrest after being stopped by Officer Walters for a traffic violation. The man claims that Walters cursed him, dragged him from his car, arrested him for no reason, and punched him in the face after he was handcuffed. Walters denies all this and says that he used only necessary force to defend himself when the man jumped out of his car and attacked Walters for no reason. Walters says that the man's nose must been broken when they both fell to the ground during this struggle. There are no other witnesses.

Walters works in a tough neighborhood, and this is the seventh time in his three-year career that he has been the subject of an unnecessary force or abuse complaint; not all complaints were sustained. No other officer in the district has had to answer more than three complaints during this period, and the majority have never been the subject of a complaint.

NOTES

1. See Kappeler (1993) for a nontechnical and easy-to-read primer on police liability.
2. As originally operationalized by the Supreme Court in *Weeks,* the exclusionary rule applied only to federal enforcement. In 1961, by which time courts in about half the states had adopted the rule, the Supreme Court decided *Mapp v. Ohio,* which made the rule mandatory in all U.S. criminal prosecutions—federal, state, and local.
3. This argument gained considerable strength with *Peterson v. City of Long Beach,* a 1979 California case in which it was ruled that police policy could be used by jurors in assessing the reasonableness of police actions.
4. See, for example, *Brower v. County of Inyo* (1989), concerning roadblocks during vehicle pursuits; *Los Angeles v. Lyons* (1983), concerning neckholds; *Tennessee v. Garner* (1985), concerning shootings of unarmed nonviolent fleeing felons; *Thomas v. Williams* (1962), concerning conditions and security in police lockups; *Thurman v. Torrington* (1985), concerning arrest policies in domestic violence cases; and *Zuchel v. Spinharney* (1993), concerning failure to adequately train officers to deal with emotionally disturbed persons.
5. Neckholds such as the bar arm and carotid control holds also are capable of causing death or serious physical injury, just as—depending on the circumstances in which they are used—batons and police dogs are.
6. Certainly, as many critics have suggested, casual police treatment of domestic violence has also involved sexist attitudes and issues.
7. Police experience suggests that she is best advised to continue to play the shocked—nonpolice—citizen the robber has apparently taken her to be, unless some forceful action is made absolutely necessary because the robber has begun to hurt or kill people. There are no guarantees, but the great majority of armed robberies—*including those in which off-duty officers have surrendered to people who have pointed guns in their faces*—do not result in injury to victims or bystanders. When officers pull their guns in such circumstances, however, innocent people—including the officers—are very likely to be hurt or killed (see Fyfe, 1975, 1980; Geller and Karales, 1981). Thus, the primacy of the police obligation to protect life dictates that this officer delay forceful action unless there is no alternative or until it can be done without unreasonably endangering everybody in the vicinity.

8. Joseph Wambaugh's novel *The Onion Field* (1973) is an excellent account of the terrible effects of a police department's less-than-official condemnation of the actions of such an officer.

9. In some jurisdictions, officers who moonlight are permitted to carry and use department portable radios. This practice, of course, raises another sensitive question about whether the taxpayers should be required to subsidize the security of private employers in this way.

10. Fyfe also had the opportunity to review the Oakland internal complaint procedure while working as a consultant to the city, and he verifies Perez's assessment.

11. In Philadelphia, for example, the unpaid Police Advisory Commission created by the city council in 1993 over the objections of the mayor, the district attorney, and the police commissioner has been greatly limited in its effect by an annual budget allotment ($275,000) that approximates the cost of staffing a single police beat on a 24/7 basis. This has enabled the unpaid commissioners to hire a director, two investigators, and a secretary to provide oversight for this 6,600-officer department. Thus, it appears likely that in Philadelphia, as in other places, those who have failed to prevent the creation of a citizen review mechanism will attempt to kill it off over the long run by funding it inadequately and by subsequently pointing to its lackluster performance as an indication that it should be abolished in favor of a return to the old ways (see, e.g., Ruchelman, 1974).

12. An analogy is appropriate here. Over the years, we have known a great number of police officials and officers who have been reluctant to take any enforcement action against federal officials (especially those who work for the Internal Revenue Service) out of fear that they will be subjects of such future retaliation as repeated and unnecessary income tax audits. It really doesn't matter whether such fears are justified. What matters is that they exist and that they affect conduct.

13. As discussed earlier in this chapter, some departments have begun to develop formal standards that prescribe tactics for particular situations and to punish officers for violating them (see Appendix 15-2).

14. See Gerald Williams's (1989) evaluation of the benefits of accreditation for more detailed discussion.

15. Among notable cases in which courts have defined the police standard of care are *Miranda v. Arizona* (1966), concerning interrogations; *Los Angeles v. Lyons* (1983), a case that reached the U.S. Supreme Court after the California Supreme Court rewrote police policy concerning neck restraints; *Brower v. County of Inyo* (1989), concerning roadblocks; *Tennessee v. Garner* (1985), concerning deadly force; *Thurman v. Torrington* (1985), concerning domestic violence policies and practices; *Zuchel v. Spinharney* (1993), concerning standards and training for police encounters with EDPs; and *Chew v. Gates* (1994), concerning deployment of canines.

SOURCES

ALPERT, GEOFFREY P., and LORIE A. FRIDELL. *Police Vehicles and Firearms: Instruments of Deadly Force* (Prospect Heights, Ill.: Waveland, 1992).

American Bar Association Project on Standards for Criminal Justice. *Standards Relating to the Urban Police Function* (New York: American Bar Association, 1973).

BITTNER, EGON. *The Functions of the Police in Modern Society* (Rockville, Md.: National Institute of Mental Health, 1970).

BOLZ, FRANK and EDWARD HERSHEY. *Hostage Cop* (New York: Rawson, Wade, 1979).

Brower v. County of Inyo, 489 U.S. 593 (1989).

BUZAWA, EVA, and CARL BUZAWA. *Domestic Violence: The Criminal Justice Response* (Newbury Park, Calif.: Sage, 1990).

CALVERT, ROBERT. "Criminal and Civil Liability in Husband and Wife Assaults," pp. 88–91 in Suzanne R. Steinmetz and Murray A. Straus (eds.), *Violence in the Family* (New York: Dodd, Mead, 1974).

Chew v. Gates, 55 Cr.L. 1342 (9th Cir. 1994).

CHRISTOPHER, WARREN, et al. *Report of the Independent Commission on the Los Angeles Police Department* (July 1991).

Commission on Accreditation for Law Enforcement Agencies. *Standards for Law Enforcement Agencies* (Fairfax, Va.: Commission on Accreditation for Law Enforcement Agencies, Inc., 1983).

———. *Standards for Law Enforcement Agencies* (Fairfax, Va.: Commission on Accreditation for Law Enforcement Agencies, Inc., 1994).

DIULIO, ALBERT, et al. *Report of the Mayor's Citizen Commission on Police-Community Relations* (City of Milwaukee, Wisc.: 1991).

FYFE, JAMES J. "Always Prepared: Police Off-Duty Guns," *Annals of the American Academy of Political and Social Science,* 452:72–81 (November 1980).

———. "Avoiding Reflexive Response," New York City Police Academy In-Service Training Program, 1975.

———. "Police Use of Deadly Force: Research and Reform," *Justice Quarterly,* 5:65–205 (1988).

———. "Reviewing Citizens' Complaints against Police," pp. 76–87 in James J. Fyfe (ed.), *Police Management Today: Issues and Case Studies* (Washington, D.C.: International City Management Association, 1985).

———. "The Split-Second Syndrome and Other Determinants of Police Violence," pp. 207–225 in Anne T. Campbell and John J. Gibbs (eds.), *Violent Transactions* (Oxford: Basil Blackwell, 1986).

GELLER, WILLIAM, and KEVIN KARALES. *Split-Second Decisions: Shootings of and by Chicago Police* (Chicago: Chicago Law Enforcement Study Group, 1981).

———, and MICHAEL S. SCOTT. *Deadly Force: What We Know* (Washington, D.C.: Police Executive Research Forum, 1992).

HIRSCHEL, J. DAVID, IRA W. HUTCHISON, CHARLES W. DEAN, and ANN-MARIE MILLS. "Review Essay on the Law Enforcement Response to Spouse Abuse: Past, Present, and Future," *Justice Quarterly,* 9:247–284 (1992).

KAPPELER, VICTOR E. *Critical Issues in Police Liability* (Prospect Heights, Ill.: Waveland, 1993).

KERSTETTER, WAYNE A. "Who Disciplines the Police? Who Should?" pp. 149–182 in William A. Geller (ed.), *Police Leadership in America: Crisis and Opportunity* (New York: Praeger, 1985).

KOLTS, JAMES G., et al. *Report of the Special Counsel on the Los Angeles County Sheriff's Department* (Los Angeles, Calif., 1992).

LIND, ALLAN, and TOM R. TYLER. *The Social Psychology of Procedural Justice* (New York: Plenum, 1988).

Los Angeles v. Lyons, 461 U.S. 95 (1983).

LOVING, NANCY. *Responding to Spouse Abuse and Wife Beating* (Washington, D.C.: Police Executive Research Forum, 1980).

Mapp v. Ohio, 367 U.S. 643, 81 S. Ct. 1684, 6 L.Ed.2d 1081(1961).

MARTIN, D. *Battered Wives* (San Francisco: Glide, 1976).

MATULIA, KENNETH R. *A Balance of Forces,* 2d ed. (Gaithersburg, Md.: International Association of Chiefs of Police, 1985).

McCOY, CANDACE S. *Politics and Plea Bargaining: Victims' Rights in California* (Philadelphia: University of Pennsylvania Press, 1993).

Miranda v. Arizona, 384 U.S. 436 (1966).

MOLLEN, MILTON, HAROLD BAER, JR., HERBERT EVANS, RODERICK C. LANKLER, and HAROLD TYLER. *Anatomy of Failure: A Path for Success. The Report of the Commission to Investigate Allegations of Police Corruption and the Anti-Corruption Procedures of the New York City Police Department* (New York, July 7, 1994).

Monell v. New York City Department of Social Services, 436 U.S. 658 (1978).

MURPHY, GERARD R. *Special Care: Improving the Police Response to the Mentally Disabled* (Washington, D.C.: Police Executive Research Forum, 1986).

National Advisory Commission on Criminal Justice Standards and Goals. *Police* (Washington, D.C.: U.S. Government Printing Office, 1973).

PEREZ, DOUGLAS. *Common Sense about Police Review* (Philadelphia: Temple University Press, 1994).

———. "Police Accountability: A Question of Balance," Ph.D. dissertation, University of California, Berkeley (1978).

Peterson v. City of Long Beach, 24 Cal. 3rd 238, 595 P. 2d 447 (1979).

RUCHELMAN, LEONARD. *Police Politics: A Comparative Study of Three Cities* (Cambridge, Mass.: Ballinger, 1974).

ST. CLAIR, JAMES D., ADOLO CATALA, WILLIAM COUGHLIN, DANIEL DENNIS, JOHN P. DRISCOLL, JR., JANE E. LEUNG, PATER MADDEN, NORMAN ROSENBLATT, and BARBARA SALISBURY. *Report of the Boston Police Department Management Review Committee* (City of Boston, Jan. 14, 1992).

SHERMAN, LAWRENCE W. *Policing Domestic Violence* (New York: Free Press, 1992).

SKOLNICK, JEROME H., and JAMES J. FYFE. *Above the Law: Police and the Excessive Use of Force* (New York: Free Press, 1993).

Tennessee v. Garner, 471 U.S. 1 (1985).

Thomas v. Williams, 124 S.E.2d 409 (Ga. App. 1962).

Thurman v. City of Torrington, 595 F. Supp. 1521 (D. Conn. 1984).

WALKER, SAMUEL, and BETSY WRIGHT. *Citizen Review of the Police, 1994: A National Survey* (Washington, D.C.: Police Executive Research Forum, 1994).

WAMBAUGH, JOSEPH. *The Onion Field* (New York: Delacorte, 1973).

Weeks v. United States, 232 U.S. 383 (1914).

WILLIAMS, GERALD L. *Making the Grade: The Benefits of Law Enforcement Accreditation* (Washington, D.C.: Police Executive Research Forum, 1989).

Zuchel v. Spinharney, 997 F.2d 730 (10th Cir. 1993).

APPENDIX 15-1
THE SAN DIEGO POLICE DEPARTMENT'S IN-CUSTODY DEATH TASK FORCE

The manner in which the San Diego Police Department dealt with a critical problem is a sterling example of policy development and commitment to the primary police responsibility of protecting life. The products of this work also can serve as a model for development of police policy related to restraint of violent subjects.

In 1992, the San Diego Police Department became alarmed by a series of seven deaths in slightly more than two years. All befell men, six of whom were under the influence of drugs, who had been acting bizarrely and violently and who had been taken into custody by officers after furious struggles.

Then-Chief Robert Burgreen directed the establishment of a task force that was headed by Assistant Chief Cal Krosch and "comprised of 27 members, including police officers and supervisors, a representative of the Citizens' Advisory Board on Police-

Community Relations, the County Medical Examiner, the director of the department's Psychological Services Unit, representatives from the Paramedic, Fire, and County Medical Services units, and a number of medical experts." The task force divided itself into four groups to study and report on *medical issues, training and tactics, legal and policy issues,* and *research.*

The task force surveyed the relevant medical literature and found that other cities had experienced similar deaths that had generally been attributed to the application of "law enforcement–style neckholds" during restraint of hyperactive subjects. The groups also then surveyed 223 law enforcement agencies across the country, inquiring whether they had experienced in-custody deaths, which were defined as:

> Any unintentional death that occurs while a subject is in police custody. Such deaths usually take place after the subject has demonstrated bizarre and/or violent behavior, and has been restrained. The deaths appear similar to sudden deaths in infants.

One hundred forty-two agencies provided enough information to be usable to the task force. Of these, 39 percent reported that they had experienced a total of 326 such deaths over the previous 23 years. Many of these deaths, however, were suicides and justifiable homicides that did not meet the criteria of sudden death after restraint described above. When the task force pared down these figures, it verified 94 restraint-related in-custody deaths across the United States in the preceding 10 years. The task force also was surprised to encounter a great deal of confusion in the rulings regarding "manner of death" assigned to in-custody death cases, a finding it attributed to the "still-evolving nature of the knowledge about these types of death."

Perhaps the most important finding and recommendation of the task force began with the discovery of a number of medical articles on *positional asphyxia.* The task force wrote:

> Most of the work on positional asphyxia has been done by Dr. Donald R. Reay, Chief Medical Examiner for King County, Seattle, Washington. Dr. Reay is widely recognized as a leading expert in the area of police custody deaths, and has been studying the issue for well over a decade. According to Dr. Reay, . . . positional asphyxia "occurs when the position of the body interferes with respiration, resulting in asphyxia." He goes on to report that, whenever positional asphyxia occurs, there are "contributing factors" which account for the "inability of the victim" to move him or herself from the ultimately fatal position. Among these factors are intoxication; illness; injury; or physical disability; and restraint or entrapment. The heretofore common law enforcement practice of transporting particularly violent suspects in a maximally restrained (i.e. "hogtied") and prone position in the back of a police car [see the discussion in Chapter 9 of this volume] provides an obvious example of a circumstance in which a subject would likely be unable to move him or herself into another position to relieve a breathing difficulty, if, in fact, the subject realized a problem was occurring. Although the San Diego Police Department banned the use of the "hogtie" procedure in October, 1991 following [an in-custody] death, the hazards inherent in the practice of transporting a suspect in a prone position were not then known to the department. After becoming aware of Dr. Reay's work, Task Force director Chief Krosch recommended an immediate ban on the procedure. That recommendation was approved by Chief Burgreen, and an Order announcing the ban was issued on March 9, 1992.

Members of the task force met with Dr. Reay, who advised them that detailed "freeze-frame" reviews of entire encounters between police and victims of in-custody deaths would assist investigators in isolating specific causes of death. This recommendation was adopted by the San Diego Police Department.

The task force also found medical evidence, again in research by Dr. Reay and a colleague, that neckholds were most likely to result in deaths for some categories of persons:

1. Men over the age of 40 and older people with cardiac conduction abnormalities
2. Persons with a history of seizure disorder
3. Mentally disturbed persons, particularly manic-depressive psychotics in the manic phase
4. Persons using alcohol and street drugs, including PCP, mescaline, LSD, amphetamines, and cocaine
5. Persons taking prescription drugs, specifically drugs with side effects that predispose the user to cardiac arrhythmias

The task force contacted Dr. Charles V. Wetli, Deputy Chief Medical Examiner of Metro-Dade County, Florida, who had written extensively on *cocaine psychosis* and sudden death. Dr. Wetli told the group that individuals in cocaine psychosis typically were violent, confused, irrational, and paranoid and suffered from highly elevated temperatures. These seem "to be the key to identifying those incidents in which sudden death is most likely to occur. He noted that persons with normal or only slightly elevated body temperatures are 'expected to survive.'"

Given this information, Deputy Chief Krosch:

recommended that department policy be revised to require that any person suspected of being under the influence of any drug who has had the carotid restraint applied to him/her be transported to a hospital for medical evaluation. That recommendation was approved by Chief Burgreen, and an Order announcing the new procedure was issued on June 15, 1992.

The task force also surveyed its officers for information on methods they used to restrain violent offenders. In addition, it found evidence to support the following recommendations, all of which were adopted as policy:

1. The carotid hold should be retained, not as a "control" device, but as a restraining device.

   * Full pressure should be maintained for no more than 30 seconds, after which officers should relax their grips while waiting for help or using another restraint method.
   * The carotid restraint should ordinarily not be used more than twice on the same individual in the same incident.
   * The carotid restraint should ordinarily be used as a "two-officer" technique, with one officer monitoring the hold to see that it is applied correctly and to monitor its effects.

2. It may sometimes be necessary to use the weight of several officers to hold down a violent subject, but they should move and place the individual on his or her side or in a sitting position as quickly as possible.
3. "High-risk" subjects should be transported by two officers, one of whom is responsible for monitoring the condition of the subjects. Doubt regarding a subject's condition will be resolved by transporting him or her immediately to a hospital or by summoning paramedics, whichever is likely to result in the quickest access to advanced life support.

4. Any subject exhibiting symptoms of cocaine psychosis or a drug-induced syndrome will be taken to a medical facility for evaluation before booking.

5. Maximally restrained subjects who are unconscious or less than "functionally conscious" are to be transported to a hospital by advanced life support personnel. Maximally restrained subjects who do not fall into these categories but who cannot be transported in a police car will be transported to a hospital by a basic life support ambulance. Whenever ambulances transport maximally restrained individuals, officers will ride in the ambulance with them.

6. All officers will receive updated training on the use of force.

7. No new training in tactics or use of force will be put in place without advising the Internal Affairs Division and obtaining the express permission of the Assistant Chief of Human Resources.

8. The department has installed a significant number of special restraining seats in their patrol cars and at the entrance to the police lockup facility.

9. Arrest reports and misdemeanor citations now require detailed information about the use of force and injuries.

Importantly, as the task force was advised early on, some cocaine psychoses and other drug-induced syndromes are so severe that they will prove fatal no matter what officers do. In the years since the task force submitted its work, two such in-custody deaths have occurred in San Diego—but there have been no deaths resulting from hog-tying, positional asphyxia, or neckholds.

Sources: Lieutenant Vickey Binkerd, San Diego Police Department, personal communication, Mar. 7, 1995; Assistant Chief (ret.) Cal Krosch, San Diego Police Department, personal communication, Mar. 13, 1995; Donald T. Reay, Corinne L. Fligner, Allan D. Stilwell, and Judy Arnold, "Positional Asphyxia during Law Enforcement Transport," *American Journal of Forensic Medicine and Pathology*, 13:90–97 (1992); Donald T. Reay, John D. Howard, Corinne L. Fligner, and Richard J. Ward, "Effects of Positional Restraint on Oxygen Saturation and Heart Rate Following Exercise," *American Journal of Forensic Medicine and Pathology*, 9:16–18 (1988); and San Diego Police Department, *Final Report of the Custody Death Task Force* (unpublished, June 1992).

APPENDIX 15-2
THE DALLAS POLICE DEPARTMENT'S DIRECTIVE AND TRAINING FOR RESPONSES TO REPORTED BURGLARIES

Police tactics, use of force, and officer safety are inextricably woven together. The use of appropriate and well-reasoned tactics in approaches to potentially violent situations helps officers to structure their confrontations with likely adversaries and reduces the chances they will hurt others or be hurt themselves. Recognizing this, many police departments have begun to describe in great detail their recommendations for responses to commonly encountered, but potentially very dangerous, field situations.

As the following excerpts illustrate, the Dallas Police Department is one of those that has attempted through policy and related training to take much of the guesswork out of officers' responses to several such situations.

PROCEDURE 1809

Burglary-in-Progress, Burglar Alarm, Open Building

A. When the call is received, indicate that you are enroute . . . on your [computer] or by voice transmission.

B. Proceed Code 1, normal driving, obeying all traffic laws. Use the safest and most direct route to the call.

1. Two one-officer elements may respond to two-officer calls.
2. In order to enhance officer safety, when responding to a two-officer call, two one-officer elements should meet at a location other than at the scene. The officers could then respond to the location of the call together.

C. Raise the Call sheet on the [computer] screen.
   1. If additional details are needed, contact the dispatcher.
   2. Consider contacting the complainant by cellular phone.

D. *Considerations enroute to the call. Plan, think ahead! Use enroute time to size up the situation and formulate a plan based on known factors.*
   1. What is the configuration of the building: one story, two or more stories?
   2. Where are doors and windows located?
   3. Are there adjacent structures as in shopping centers?
   4. Is there outside lighting?
   5. What is vehicle or pedestrian traffic flow?
   6. Due to the above considerations, it may be possible to make a decision to call or not to call for support elements prior to being Code 6. If not, make decision after arriving at offense location.
      a. K-9
      b. Helicopter
      c. Additional patrol officers
   7. What, based on your knowledge of the building, might be the point of entry?
      a. This can alter your approach. You would not approach entry area with noise or lights to alert suspect to your presence.
   8. What, based on your knowledge of the building, might the suspect be attempting to take?
   9. Where, based on your knowledge of the building, might a suspect hide?
   10. Determine the safest direction of vehicle approach to the building.

E. [Advise the dispatcher of your arrival] when in the block of the call, prior to actual arrival. When you arrive, your concentration should be on the scene.
   1. Arrive quietly. At night turn off headlights as you approach the building. Do not alert suspects to your presence.
      a. As you make your approach, be alert for goodeyes (lookouts).

F. Do a drive-around search, as allowed by the configuration of the building.
   1. Fences and multi-level terrain will prevent a full drive around.
   2. Do not illuminate the vehicle interior.
   3. Turn down volume on the radio.
   4. Consider using spotlight on doors, windows, possible points of entry.
   5. Focus your attention on the scene.

G. If no entry is found on drive around or if drive around can't be completed, place your vehicle in a tactical position off-set from the corner of the building and begin foot search procedure.

H. If entry is found, call for additional cover elements. The driver of the vehicle should move to a position of cover that will allow him to observe both the point of entry and possible alternative escape routes. The passenger officer should move to a position of cover at the diagonally opposite corner of the building to contain possible suspects.
   1. Cover can be solid walls, or different levels of terrain.
   2. The police vehicle can be used for cover when placed in a tactical position, off-set from the corner of the building.

I. If entry is not found on the drive around, prepare for a foot search of the perimeter of the building. A foot search is conducted by no less than two officers. They will walk the perimeter of the building, looking for a point of entry. Utilizing this method, officers are often able to find a point of entry that may have been missed using the drive-around search. Be sure to use the considerations listed below when doing a foot search.

1. Cover can be solid walls, or different levels of terrain. Even darkness and shadows can be used in selecting a dismount site.
2. Consideration should be given to being able to return quickly and safely to vehicle if the need arises.
   a. Remove your keys. Do not give the suspect an escape vehicle.
   b. Determine if you will lock the car doors or leave a door unlocked for radio access.
3. Make a decision on what equipment will be needed for foot search.
   a. Flashlight, PR-24, shotgun, walkie-talkie.
4. *Do not separate. Officers will search together but tactically separate, not side by side.*
5. Officers should use a leap-frog or cover move system while searching the perimeter. Using available cover, one officer searches an area and signals when it's secured, the second officer goes past the first officer into a new area and searches and secures it. The officers will search back and forth as the search progresses.
   a. You should be able to see your partner at all times. This will allow you to warn one another of danger and prevent the possibility of shooting each other.
6. On reaching corners of buildings, use wide angle techniques and quick peek prior to going around the corner.
   a. *Wide Angles* (Slicing the pie) Any time you need to move around a corner or other cover and feel a threat may be imminent on the other side. As you near the corner, carefully move out from the wall 3 feet or so, assuming space permits. Face the corner with your body straight, your feet and legs together. Your sidearm should be out in a two-hand hold, but keep your elbows close together, pulled back and tucked in toward the center of your body. This steadies your sidearm in a third-eye position while keeping your body as narrow as possible. It also tends to reduce the tendency to "lead" with your sidearm, exposing it around the corner prematurely. By shuffling your feet to the side a little bit at a time, tightly following one with the other, you can move in little slices toward the corner, gradually increasing your field of view around it. If someone is hiding there, chances are that you will be able to pick up his protruding feet.
   b. You may have to fight an impulse to hug up close against the wall because it is hard material. What you're fighting, really, is a false sense of protection. By swinging out in this slow fashion, you can gain an advantage of angle that will better serve your safety.
   c. *Quick Peek* With speed, move your head past the corner to see if the area is clear and bring your head back to cover. Do not use a head level peek that will be anticipated. A low peek is safer, and less likely to be seen. The peek will allow you to prepare for an imminent confrontation to withdraw to a position of cover if a suspect is seen. If a second peek is required, do it at a different level.

J. If entry is found, call for additional elements to cover the building. The officers will move to a position of cover at diagonally opposite corners of the building to contain suspects and observe the point of entry.
   1. The building will not be entered until it is contained, with all sides, entrances and exits covered. If possible, have the owner of the building give a layout of the premises prior to entry.
   2. If there is an indication that the suspect is still inside, determine if canine can be used.
      a. Needed for large buildings and warehouses. If K-9 is to be called, ensure that entrance and building are not contaminated until use of K-9 is complete.

3. If circumstances do not allow for use of K-9, you may search the building.
    a. Exterior of building will remain covered. Consider calling for helicopter to check the roof of the building.
    b. One officer, [who] should be a supervisor, will be in charge and will direct search based on physical layout of the building.
    c. Make sure all officers understand their assignment and where other officers will be.
    d. Ensure that entry officers have communications with those on the outside.
    e. Entry will not be made through small openings or windows unless there is sufficient visual access to the inside of the building to provide cover for entering officers.
    f. Entry will never be made by less than two (2) officers.
    g. Use quick peek and wide angle techniques, one officer moving, being covered from a cleared area, clearing one area at a time.
    h. Locate lights and illuminate the area to be searched as search progresses. Do not "backlight" yourself. You can be seen. Your shadow will precede you as you move.
    i. Anticipate ambush points.
    j. Use your imagination in finding hiding places; look up, check trash containers, air conditioning vents, etc.
        (1) Suspects have been found in places you would not normally think they could or would be able to hide.
K. If a suspect is found, consider the following steps.
    1. From a position of cover, identify yourself as a police officer and give loud clear verbal commands.
        a. Let the suspect know what you want done. If you want to see their palms, or raise their hands, or lie down in a prone position—*Tell them.*
        b. If the suspect is found to have a weapon and refuses to lay it down, or verbal commands fail to bring the suspect into an open handcuffing position, consider a tactical retreat, and handle the situation as a barricaded person.
    2. According to space, light and cover in the area, decide the best method to take custody of the suspect.
        a. With hands raised, have suspect walk backwards to you.
        b. The decision may be made to approach the suspect.
            (1) One officer covers the suspect while the second officer approaches from an angle. *Do not cross in front of cover officer.*
            (2) Handcuff suspect. Have an officer come from outside the building to remove the suspect.
    3. Continue search until entire building is cleared.
        a. It is possible that additional suspects will be found. . . .
M. When responding to a burglar alarm call, follow the above written procedures. If the officer determines that there is no offense and the alarm is false consider:
    1. Clearing the call. . . .
    2. Issuing a False Alarm Notification.
    3. If an audible alarm must be turned off, and the owner is needed, notify the dispatcher.
    4. Is the owner in violation of any City of Dallas Alarm Ordinances? (See Procedure 900.)
N. When responding to an Open Building/Door Call, follow the above written procedures. If the officer determines that there is no offense, consider:
    1. Have an owner respond to secure the building, notify the dispatcher for assistance.

Problem Two (2) Evaluation—Search of Store Room/Office Area
Score (1) or (0) for each problem question. If a question is not applicable, write N/A. Total the (1) and then divide the total into the number of questions with either a (1) or (0). Example: Total (1)s = 25. Total questions with either a (1) or (0) = 28. 25 divided by 28 = 89. The Recruit Officer's score for the Problem is 89.

1. Did the officers after entering the building, make use of tactical cover and concealment?
   Score: _____
2. Did an officer properly utilize the shotgun?
   Score: _____
3. Did the officers carry flashlights in non gun hand?
   Score: _____
4. Did officers have batons?
   Score: _____
5. Did officers utilize light control by lighting poor illuminated areas, but not back-lighting each other?
   Score: _____
6. Did officers work as a Team by communicating and keeping each other informed?
   Score: _____
7. Did officers keep each other in view?
   Score: _____
8. Did the officers keep their weapons pointed in the direction of possible assailant and not at each other?
   Score: _____
9. Did the officers utilize the quick-peek method?
   Score: _____
10. Did the officers locate the 1st suspect?
    Score: _____
11. Did the officers locate the 2nd suspect?
    Score: _____
12. Did the officers locate the 3rd suspect?
    Score: _____
13. Did the officer who moved in to control the suspect properly holster his side-arm?
    Score: _____
14. Did the officer with the shotgun switch to his sidearm when his partner moved in to handcuff and search?
    Score: _____
15. Did the officer handcuff the suspect before searching?
    Score: _____
16. Did the officer properly and effectively search the suspect?
    Score: _____
17. Did the officer remove his aim or holster his weapon while partner searched the suspect?
    Score: _____
18. Did the officer keep his gun side away from the suspect?
    Score: _____
19. Did the officer turn the suspect over to cover? (The Staff Member was the assumed cover officer.)
    Score: _____

20. Did the officers complete the Store Room/Office area search?
   Score: _____

Total points: _____

Total applicable questions: _____

Recruit's score: _____ *= Total applicable questions divided by total score*

Evaluation comments section: (Use this section to describe strengths and weaknesses of individual Recruits)

Part THREE

Operations

16

Uniformed Services: Patrol, Traffic, and Special Operations

KEY WORDS AND PHRASES

Uniformed services
Patrol
Random preventive patrol
Community-oriented patrol
Personnel allocation
Personnel distribution
Patrol beat
Workload assessment
Continuous assignment

Territorial accountability
Rotation of shifts
Broken windows theory
Traffic enforcement
Delaware v. Prouse
Selective enforcement
Accident investigation
Traffic safety education
Special operations

Police *uniformed services* are the operational activities of police officers engaged in the direct delivery of police services to citizens. In O. W. Wilson's terms, these officers are the "backbone of policing," the department's most important representatives, the front line that all other units and specialists exist to help. The two major activities of police uniformed services are patrol and traffic enforcement, but, especially in large departments, uniformed officers also may be assigned to specialized operational units created to respond to specific workload needs and objectives.

Every year, police departments allocate billions of dollars to maintain and operate uniformed services. In 1990, police protection in the United States cost local governments $31.8 billion (Lindgren, 1992), and it is a fair guess that most of this money went directly to patrol and other uniformed services. As a general rule, at least half the officers in large urban departments are assigned to patrol duty, while smaller departments may consist only of patrol officers. Thus, the monies spent on patrol and other uniformed services are a substantial investment of public revenue that police administrators are duty-bound to put to efficient and effective use. To this end, as Chapter 6 pointed out, police executives have been involved in nearly a generation of critical self-examination, testing, and experimentation with different operational strategies. This chapter will discuss the controversy surrounding these strategies, as well as the administration and organization of the patrol, traffic, and special operations functions.

PATROL

Although the word "patrol" suggests little more than a perfunctory inspectional activity, it is the most important police function, the activity for which policing was created. Police patrol embraces many more activities than just the physical act of patrolling a designated area. Patrol officers are responsible for the performance of all primary police tasks. They interact with citizens on a daily basis in a variety of situations in which they may:

- Prevent crime
- Conduct investigations
- Engage in problem-solving activities
- Maintain order, or restore it where it has been breached
- Aid persons in need of assistance
- Engage in conflict resolution
- Control traffic
- Enforce laws
- Write tickets
- Issue warnings
- Make arrests
- Write reports
- Use physical, or even deadly, force

These activities account for the majority of contacts between police and citizens, and to a great extent the public's view of the police is formulated by its impression of the patrol officer. Indeed, because patrol officers are the most visible street-level representatives of officialdom, their behavior and willingness to serve has enormous impact on how citizens perceive *all* government operations. These factors and the diverse nature of patrol activities have led many scholars to conclude that patrol officers are among the most important decision makers in both police departments and local governments generally (see, e.g., Goldstein, 1977; Muir, 1977).

In virtually every department, patrol is the largest independent police organizational subdivision and the only operational unit the police administrator cannot afford to disband (Alpert and Dunham, 1992:68). It functions as the nucleus of a police department, and all other units should be organized to support it. The patrol division is organized to be a department's *first responder*, bringing police services to those who need them as quickly as possible. Consequently, in places in which citizens are not expected to take matters into their own hands, patrol services must be available as first responders on a 24-hour, 7-day-a-week basis. In jurisdictions so small that they cannot staff such an arrangement, round-the-clock service typically is accomplished through contracts or mutual-aid agreements with state or county police or with neighboring departments. Often, this is supplemented by "on-call" systems, in which designated officers remain available to respond to calls for service during their off-duty hours. A simple call-forwarding system that transfers calls from police facilities to the homes of on-call officers usually is sufficient to facilitate such operations.

The Patrol Function

The uniformed patrol officer in most police agencies is a generalist responsible for (1) crime prevention, (2) law enforcement, (3) criminal apprehension, (4) order maintenance, (5) traffic enforcement, and (6) provision of public services. This last task—really another way to say that *police must do everything no other service exists to do, and they must do it promptly*—is a major problem for both police administrators and patrol officers. For those at the top of police agencies and the government leaders to whom they report, it creates the problem of deciding where to set the border between what is legitimate police work and what is not. Should patrol officers check the security of residents' homes while they are on vacation? Get cats out of trees? Open the cars and homes of people who have locked themselves out? Walk local merchants to night depositories? In some jurisdictions, these tasks are performed by patrol officers or other uniformed specialists; but in others, they are not.

For many patrol officers, such tasks are a sour part of the job, something they did not sign on for, a distraction from *real* police work, for which they often are given little or no training and, usually, no credit at all for a job well done. These tasks add to the ambiguity and uncertainty of the patrol officers' job and should be carefully explained to new officers, defined as part of the core of police work, and included in police evaluation and reward systems.

Whatever their tasks include, patrol officers perform them by responding in a timely manner to citizens' requests for service, conducting investigations of the facts and circumstances involved with these requests, and deciding on the best approach to resolve the situation at hand. They are, in Herman Goldstein's terms, "diagnosticians" and "problem solvers" (Goldstein, 1979). When not responding to calls for service, they are expected to maintain a visible presence and a sharp eye on their respective patrol areas. When patrol officers observe suspicious circumstances, dangerous conditions, or threats to order, they are expected to do whatever is reasonable and constitutional to maintain the security and safety of the communities they police.

The Traditional View of Patrol

In the days of Robert Peel and for most of this century, police administrators believed that the most effective and efficient means of achieving crime prevention and control was visible random preventive patrolling by uniformed police officers. This logic holds that officers should engage in unpredictable patrolling—*random preventive patrol*—so that offenders could never be certain of where they were or where they might turn up. When crime did occur, it was believed that rapid response to the scene of the crime would enable arrests, prevent harm to citizens, and assist in the recovery of stolen property.

O. W. Wilson, the dominant voice in police administration for many years, was a great champion of random preventive patrol. Like Peel and Wilson's mentor, August Vollmer, Wilson and his junior colleague Roy McLaren (1977:319) believed that the most important thing for police to know about crime was that it was a result of *desire* and *opportunity*. Certainly, all these police pioneers recognized that crime was attributable to many social, psychological, and economic factors. But, they reasoned, the police had no control over these factors. Instead, they postulated that police crime-fighting efforts should begin by recognizing that crime resulted from the desire to commit a criminal act and the belief that there existed an opportunity to do so successfully, and that the absence of either of these factors made crime impossible. Since the police could not affect potential criminals' desire, Wilson and McLaren argued, they should try to eliminate opportunity, and the best way to do this was by frequent and conspicuous patrolling at every hour and in all sections of the community. In this manner, they reasoned, the patrol service would create an impression of police *omnipresence* and thus invulnerability. In their view, then, the basic function of patrol was the elimination of the opportunity (or of the belief that the opportunity exists) for successful criminal conduct. This is a simple formula. The more that highly visible random patrol can convince potential offenders that they have little chance to get away with crime, the less likely crime is to occur.

Under the Wilson formula, random preventive patrol requires the assignment of a majority of a department's police officers to patrol units that roam their jurisdiction's streets at all times. However, beginning in the 1960s, the creation of 911 emergency telephone systems made it easier for the public to obtain immediate responses by patrol units and increased the workload demand of patrol officers to such an extent that this *incident-driven* style replaced random preventive patrol as the dominant operational strategy (Sparrow, Moore, and Kennedy, 1990). Radio dispatchers, rather than patrol supervisors and commanders, soon took charge of patrol operations, and responding to calls for service evolved into the most time-consuming patrol task (Kessler, 1993).

Unfortunately, instead of preventing crime, random motorized patrol, rapid response, and 911 emergency systems helped to create a very reactive patrol function that—as the Kansas City Preventive Patrol Experiment (Kelling et al., 1974) showed—did little to prevent crime. Instead, in this mode, which remains the norm in many places, patrol units responded after incidents had taken place, and patrol officers did little beyond conducting preliminary investigations for the purpose of filing reports. In addition, this mode of operation reduced the citizen's responsibility for crime prevention to that of an activator of police service, and the police came to be assumed capable of doing the impossible: bearing total responsibility for community safety and security. Citizens came to believe that when something happened or when they were suffering difficulties, all they needed to do was to call the police, the people responsible for responding to and correcting all of one's problems.

This development fostered a form of police professionalism grounded in the technical skills and values associated with putting criminals in jail, rather than in living up to Peel's ideal of preventing crime (Moore, 1992). When the patrol research of the 1970s (discussed in Chapter 6) failed to find support for the belief that increased patrol intensity affected crime rates or for the presumed value of rapid response, there began to emerge a different conception of the patrol function, the focus of the next section.

Evolving Views of Patrol

Community-oriented policing is a challenge to conventional wisdom about the effectiveness of patrol methods; it is an attempt to offer an alternative to random preventive patrol. As described earlier in this book, it envisions a police mission that involves crime prevention and control through community engagement and problem solving. It is designed to expand and direct patrol officers' attention from individual incidents alone to include the problems and conditions that underlie and create such events (Goldstein, 1990; Moore, 1992:99). Operationally, it does not rely on random visible patrol and a standard set of operating procedures as its principal tactics. Instead, by encouraging a variety of directed patrol tactics designed to match the security and safety needs of specific neighborhoods with the resources and capabilities of the department and the local community, it seeks to turn patrol into a proactive function. These operational strategies reflect the following common set of characteristics:

- Decentralization of patrol units by geographical assignment (foot beats, substations, community-policing zones)
- Selection of certain number of sworn personnel as community police officers to patrol and manage the beats, zones, and/or substations
- Selection of a line supervisor, usually a sergeant or lieutenant, to oversee the community officers
- Directed and structured patrol activities designed to develop a closer interpersonal relationship between citizens and community patrol officers
- Citizen-police joint efforts in problem identification, analysis, and resolution
- Problem response strategies developed at the operational level
- Enhancement of communication between the department, community, and other agencies within and outside city government

Community-oriented patrol involves tactics that are designed to enhance both the quality and the quantity of police contacts with citizens as well as to identify community problems that contribute to the lessening of a neighborhood's security and safety. Decentralization of patrol units into neighborhood foot beats and substations operated by community police officers lessens the anonymity of the patrol car, puts officers in direct contact with the community, and enhances their opportunity to obtain information regarding neighborhood problems and possible solutions. Departments experimenting with this mode of operation free community officers from the 911 response system or assign them to nonemergency service calls emanating from their neighborhood beats. Working more directly with citizens, community patrol officers are expected to find ways—in addition to the traditional response of reporting, citing, or arresting—that will enhance the lives of the most vulnerable citizens: juveniles, the elderly, minorities, and the poor (Skolnick and Bayley, 1988; Trojanowicz and Bucqueroux, 1990).

The specific activities community patrol officers engage in to accomplish their mission include:

- Operating neighborhood substations

- Meeting with community groups
- Analyzing and solving neighborhood problems
- Working with citizens on crime prevention programs
- Conducting door-to-door surveys of residents
- Talking with students in school
- Meeting with local merchants
- Making security checks of businesses
- Dealing with disorderly people (Mastrofski, 1992:24)

This new operational direction involves a major redefinition of not only patrol operations but also the mission, functions, and administrative and personnel practices of policing. Not surprisingly, therefore, it has both vigorous advocates and very skeptical detractors. Some, like Trojanowicz and Bucqueroux (1990), claim that it will emerge as the dominant patrol operational philosophy and strategy of modern policing, while others question its utility and ability to achieve its objectives (Clark, 1994; Greene and Mastrofski, 1988). Specifically, there is a serious question about its capability to achieve its objectives in low-income, heterogeneous, deteriorating, high-turnover, drug-ravaged, disorderly neighborhoods (Skogan, 1990). In such places, it is argued, the very absence of *community* in the traditional sense—a large number of people who share commitment to the common cause of preserving, or restoring, the quality of life in their neighborhoods—dooms this style of policing. Community policing cannot succeed where there is no "community."

To this, adherents generally respond that the job of community police officers is to take the lead in bringing the disparate groups in a neighborhood to a sense of community. To do this, they must become leaders and major pillars of the *potential* for community that is thought to exist in every area. This, obviously, is no easy task. Instead, it is a job that requires skills not traditional to policing and, assertedly, not readily learned by veteran officers who have long worked under the different values of incident-driven patrol work. This is certainly a valid argument, and to address it several police departments have designated junior personnel as their community police officers, while leaving senior officers in their patrol cars where they respond to the 911 calls that continue to pour into police headquarters. This transition has not always gone smoothly, however, and it is certain to create some degree of polarization between veteran officers, who see themselves as *real* police officers, and junior community police officers, who, as one New York City officer told one of us, are viewed by their senior colleagues as "social workers and community activists rather than as cops."

Regardless of the extent to which its potential for success is limited by neighborhood characteristics or division within police ranks, the community policing movement does represent a serious commitment to make uniformed services more responsive to local needs. It has enhanced debate and revitalized operational experimentation. It encourages an organizational philosophy dedicated to providing quality service and has renewed commitment on the part of line officers involved in community programs, while at the same time enhancing their job satisfaction. In these senses alone, it is a positive accomplishment for any police executive, and it should not be quickly abandoned merely be-

cause it suffers some teething problems. It is, after all, such a major overhaul of
police philosophy and operations that it would be naive to anticipate that it
could be put in place without implementation problems.

Patrol Administration

Patrol efficiency and effectiveness can be attained only with adequate staffing
and deployment of patrol resources. Selection of patrolling methods and tactics—whether random preventive patrol, community-oriented patrol, or a
combination of both—is up to the chief and command staff. Identification of
the primary responsibilities of the patrol component and its methods should
be established through departmental plans, policies, and directives. In departments using such community-oriented strategies as special patrol teams,
neighborhood beats, or storefront substations, the functions of these units and
their officers should also be included in policy statements. Where such programs are new enough that substantial evaluation and adjustment may be anticipated, these statements should take the form of *temporary operating procedures.* The benefit of committing missions and functions to paper is that it
connects operational strategy to the department's mission and to the chief's vision, while it also provides patrol officers with direction in performing their
daily activities.

In addition, chief administrators, aided by their ranking patrol commanders—and with considerable input from officers on the line—should establish
an annual auditing process that assesses the patrol division's workload and
performance. This is necessary for the identification, review, and reinforcement
or restatement of patrol unit objectives. This annual process should reflect and
reinforce the department's broad operational philosophy and values as well as
its specific performance goals. The benefit of this process is that it provides the
chief executive and any other interested parties in or out of the agency with an
ongoing evaluation on which to assess how effectively and efficiently the patrol function has performed during a specific period.

Allocation and Distribution of Patrol Resources

At the very core of the chief's responsibilities is the allocation and distribution
of personnel resources. *Personnel allocation* is the determination of the overall
number of department personnel to be assigned to a function (e.g., patrol, investigations, traffic). *Personnel distribution* is the assignment of a given number
of personnel according to functional, spatial, and temporal workload demands
(Commission on Accreditation, 1994: Section 16.1). Assigning more officers to
the patrol shift that has the greatest demand for police services is an example
of personnel distribution.

The primary objective of these administrative tasks is the provision of
basic police services to a community on a 24-hour basis every day of the week.
As noted above, however, in departments that are unable to support such 24/7
patrol service because of limited personnel resources, mutual-aid agreements

for emergency response coverage are usually arranged with either a nearby police department, the county sheriff, or the state police agency.

Establishing Patrol Beats and Working Hours

The allocation of personnel to the patrol function should be based on a formula reflective of geography, organizational operations, and service demand. Division of a jurisdiction or police district into the lowest police geographic subdivision—variously called a *beat*, *post*, or *sector*—should take into account four major considerations: terrain, geographical size, population, and workload.

Terrain. *Natural boundaries, such as rivers and main thoroughfares, should be used to divide beats whenever possible.* This typically keeps response time to a minimum and, experience suggests, facilitates officers' understanding of the communities and terrain in which they work.

Size. In addition to designing beats so that major geographical barriers do not have to be traversed in order to respond promptly to calls for service, beats should not be so large that officers cannot quickly travel from one end to the other.

Population. The social character of the beat should be as uniform as possible. Obviously, police have little control over who frequents, or lives, or does business in particular neighborhoods. But, especially in larger jurisdictions, traditional neighborhoods composed of people who share similar backgrounds, interests, and socioeconomic status have developed, often existing side by side with neighborhoods that are quite different. In one geographically small police precinct where one of us worked as a patrol officer, for example, there existed a busy commercial and civic area; an upper and upper-middle-class residential neighborhood that included a large gay population; a poor tenement community populated mostly by Caribbean Hispanics and Native Americans; another neighborhood consisting largely of the families of Spanish American and Irish American longshoremen and construction workers; a largely African American housing project; several middle-class apartment complexes; a district of Middle Eastern businesses, churches, and homes; and a growing neighborhood of recent Byelorussian immigrants that had grown up around a newly established church. In such a polyglot environment, as in less diverse areas, officers' understanding of the cultures and folkways of the community they police, as well as their knowledge of individuals within it, usually is facilitated when, as far as possible, beats conform to such informal boundaries. This practice also serves to improve police-community relations, as community members come to the realization that the officers who serve them have developed quite a knowledge of (and, it is hoped, an interest in) their neighborhood. Often, these neighborhoods grow up within the natural boundaries described previously, so that this issue is not as complicated as it might appear.

Workload. Insofar as possible, the workloads among beats should be equal. Personnel distribution on patrol beats (and patrol shifts) should be based on proportionate need, established by a *workload assessment.* This assessment is a detailed study of the content and distribution of the patrol unit's workload in order to identify the category, number, complexity, location, and service time of the demand for police services. A workload assessment should include evaluation of:

1. Number of incidents handled by patrol personnel during a specific time period
2. Average time required to handle an incident at the patrol level (or measurement of a sampling of cases)
3. Calculation of the percentage of time, on average, that should be available to the patrol officer for handling incidents during a specific period (such as an eight-hour shift)
4. Time lost through vacation, off days, holidays, and other leave, compared to the total time required for each patrol assignment (Commission on Accreditation, 1989: Standard 16.1.3)

Obviously, many other factors can also be included in a formula to distribute patrol personnel over time and space, including, for example, the amount and nature of vehicle and pedestrian traffic; the existence of such large public gathering places as sport arenas, theaters, and parks; temporary or longstanding tensions within neighborhoods; and the presence of such illegal and disorderly street conditions as drug dealing, prostitution, and panhandling. Rather than simply dividing personnel equally into three different shifts and across neighborhoods, the most salient of these factors can be identified by individual departments and should be included in distribution calculations. Because of limited personnel and the absence of many such considerations, of course, many smaller police departments simply split patrol resources into equal, round-the-clock coverage.

In recent years, a number of police departments have computerized their management information systems. Most of the computer software developed for this purpose can be used on microcomputers, which enhances their accessibility to small and medium-sized departments. These programs are designed to assist in the allocation and distribution of patrol resources as well as to help design the number and size of patrol beats. No matter what system is used, the department should establish a service-demand evaluation process so that it can adjust for changes that may occur.

Assignment/Availability Factor

The department should regularly calculate the assignment/availability factor for patrol personnel. This is the ratio between the total person-days available during a given time period and the number of patrol assignments that must be covered during the same period. Obviously, this is greatly affected by person-days lost through days off, leave, holidays, training, court appearances, and the like. As Box 16-1 illustrates, it is a safe estimate that, over the course of a

Some simple math helps to illustrate the demands of providing round-the-clock patrol services:

1. As we know, there are 52 weeks in a year.
2. Each 7-day week includes 168 hours, so that, over the course of a year, continuously staffing a single officer patrol car on a 24/7 basis requires 8,736 person-hours per year.
3. Police officers typically work only 40 hours a week, so that their work schedules include 2,080 hours per year.
4. Thus, to staff a patrol car on a 24/7 basis over a year, it is necessary to *begin* calculating personnel requirements by assuming that more than four officers (8,736/2,080 hours = 4.2 officers), each working different hours, will be required to field the car 168 hours (40 hours per officer = 4.2 officers).
5. Fortunately for them, police officers do not spend 2,080 hours a year in their patrol cars. From this total, deductions for vacations, holi-

days, training, court appearance time, and sick and line-of-duty injury time must be made. Thus, the time an officer may have available for patrol service over a year is more likely to look like this:

```
2,080  hours per 52 week at 40 hours per week
  160  hours for 4 weeks vacation
  104  hours for 13 holidays
   40  hours for in-service training
  160  hours for 20 days in court
   64  hours for an average of 8 days sick
          and injured leave
 -528  hours
1,552  hours per year available for patrol per
          officer
```

6. Now, calculate again:

$$\frac{8{,}736 \text{ hours per year}}{1{,}552 \text{ hours per officer per year}} = 5.95 \text{ officers}$$

year, approximately six officers are required to staff a single patrol beat or patrol car around the clock.

Scheduling

Scheduling involves the assignment of officers by shift hours and frequency of beat and shift rotation. The distribution of officers and other 24/7 personnel may be based on seniority, officer choice, department choice, or, as is common, some combination of all three factors. But in all cases it is important that an impartial scheduling policy be established and followed consistently and that it provide the best possible service to the public. This should be based on a careful analysis of workload and potential hazards and should not merely result in assignment of equal numbers of personnel across the days of the week and the hours of day.

Despite the best efforts to introduce predictability into policing, it remains a vocation that must respond to unpredictable emergencies. Hence, the work schedules that result from careful analysis must always be flexible enough to allow for public crises, community policing needs, personnel hardships, or the need to accommodate school attendance by officers or other personnel involved in 24/7 services (e.g., radio dispatchers and other communications personnel). Further, it should be kept in mind that the job of a police officer does not always end at the conclusion of an eight-hour tour of duty. Officers are

A patrol sergeant describes his department's patrol beats to new officers.
Spencer Grant/Photo Researchers.

often required to work overtime because of personnel shortages, involvement
in ongoing cases, and attendance at court or training sessions.

Continuous assignment of patrol officers to specific neighborhood beats has
occasionally been avoided on the theory that too much familiarity with a
neighborhood is likely to cause officers to lose their objectivity in dealing with
citizens and even to become corrupted. Such a policy is totally incompatible
with community policing. Officers cannot identify with communities from
which administrators consciously isolate them. Even before the current movement to this philosophy of policing, however, it was generally believed that a
better quality of patrol service results from continuing assignments to the same
geographical areas.

There is good reason for this belief, even though officers who know their
beats well may be exposed to opportunities to engage in corruption more often
than officers who are strangers to those they serve. But in addition to sending a
troubling message to both police and the public that officers are not trusted,
isolating officers from the community by rotating their assignments places
great limits on their ability to serve. This type of isolation should be avoided in
favor of an adequate system of positive incentives for officers who adhere to
ethical and legal standards and strong discipline for those who ignore or violate these standards. Indeed, using a system of rotating assignments as an anti-
corruption measure is a poor substitute for an adequate system of inspections
and integrity control, as described in Chapters 13 and 14.

The justifications for steady assignments are many. Both local cultures and
police hazards—and, occasionally, the best means for dealing with them—vary

from place to place. Frequent beat changes prevent officers from becoming well acquainted with the streets and buildings, people, hazards, and problems in their area. Invariably, the consequence is that police officers come into citizens' lives only in times of crisis, when the officers suffer the additional burden of appearing as strangers, rather than as well-known and trusted members of the community.

Further, officers who rotate assignments have a difficult time developing a sense of *territorial accountability,* the feeling of responsibility or ownership for the conditions that exist in a patrol beat or zone. Officers whose mind-set includes a sense of territorial accountability pride themselves on the level of service they render to the residents in their areas and strive to keep their beat areas safe and secure. Officers who fail to develop this value, however, have a tendency to render superficial responses to calls for service and the needs of the citizens they serve.

Fixed beat assignments also permit management to hold officers accountable for conditions in their assigned areas. In addition, officers who know an area and its people probably are less likely to have to resort to force to control situations than are officers who are foreign to the area and suddenly find themselves injected into situations involving unfamiliar people (Goldstein, 1990:160).

Rotation of shifts at some regular interval is common in many police departments. Among cities of over 300,000 population, periodic rotation of shifts remains a frequently encountered method of assigning shift hours. In some places, shifts rotate monthly, biweekly, weekly, or—as among many Boston officers—even *daily.*

Such a system results in equal treatment of all officers, but it is a terrible equality that should be avoided in favor of more regular assignments or, at least, infrequent rotation. Although the police bookshelf includes little research on the social, psychological, and physiological effects of rotating shifts, a considerable body of literature involving other occupations provides great justification for avoiding frequent shift rotation. Aschoff (1965) found that the body's natural, or "circadian," rhythms do not adjust quickly to new working hours and that something akin to terminal jet lag—fatigue, poor work performance, and unbalanced emotions—is the likely result of frequent shift changes.

Other research has shown that frequent shift changes disrupt family and social life and cause sleep disorders (Weitzman et al., 1968) and are associated with increased use of sick leave and diminished productivity (Taylor, 1967). When one puts these findings alongside the studies of DeLaMare and Walker (1965), who found that 24/7 employees were far more concerned with whether their shifts were relatively permanent than with the particular hours to which they were assigned, it is difficult to justify frequent shift changes on grounds that they are equitable to everybody. Further, police incidents and citizens' service demands vary according to the hour of the day or night. Consequently, knowledge of conditions on one shift may be only tangentially useful to service on another shift.

Although shift rotation varies with departments, usually the first shift, midnight to 8 A.M. (*midnight* or the *graveyard shift*) is considered the least desirable assignment, and the second shift, 8 A.M. to 4 P.M. (*daylight*) the most desirable and most compatible with a traditional social and family life. The third shift, 4 P.M. to midnight (*evenings*) usually has the most demanding workload, requiring well-trained, experienced, skilled patrol officers. However, if a department's workload assessment discloses that this is not the case, officers should be assigned to the shift on which they are needed. Many departments assign their senior, more experienced, and sometimes less physically active officers to the day shift as a reward for long service. However, competent senior officers should be used as field training officers, acting supervisors, and peer leaders on high-service-demand shifts where high-liability or high-vulnerability situations are most likely to occur. Their knowledge of the police service and their years of experience will prove most useful on these shifts. It is not an uncommon practice to initially assign recruits to a shift where the less frequent service demand permits time for coaching and the development of competency in handling patrol duties. In doing so, however, it is critical that new officers not be isolated, to learn by themselves through a process of trial and error and, no doubt, to pick up bad habits that will endure throughout their police careers. It is critical that all shifts be carefully supervised and that some measures be taken to ensure that no shift—especially the low-visibility graveyard shift—comes to see itself as a group apart from the rest of the agency.

Permanent shifts make it easy to assign varying numbers of officers to each shift, in proportion to the workload. Rotation of shifts, on the other hand, may force a chief to adopt the same number of beats on each shift simply because of scheduling difficulties. Community-oriented patrol programs usually have permanent beat assignments. Shift rotation should be the responsibility of the community patrol unit supervisor. The supervisor should base this decision on the needs of the officer's beat and the demands of the specific problems the officer is addressing. For example, foot assignment in commercial areas may need an officer only during normal business hours. However, officers assigned to particular neighborhoods may require greater flexibility and need to rotate between day and evening shifts in order to accomplish specific tasks or, more generally, to become acquainted with their communities. Rarely will foot-beat officers be assigned to the midnight shift.

Some departments use fixed shifts that operate on a forced seniority basis, but with the same effect as described above. New officers are assigned to the midnight to 8 A.M. shift on the basis of order of appointment, and they have no choice in subsequent movements to the evening shift or (eventually) to the day shift. In other systems, there is more freedom of choice; officers are allowed to pick shifts, based on the order of seniority.

PATROL METHODS

Responsibility for the performance of police tasks within areas is placed on individual patrol officers. The accomplishment of these duties requires not only competency in police procedures but also knowledge of the citizens and conditions in the assigned area. Automobiles, motorcycles, scooters, and, increasingly, bicycles are the most frequently used patrol vehicles. Choices of whether and when to use each of these should be based on an appraisal both of the primary purpose of the patrol or specific task to be accomplished and of the area involved. The following factors influence the choice of patrol methods:

- Population density
- Concentrations of special populations, e.g., schoolchildren, the elderly
- Distribution and character of police hazards
- Frequency and nature of the police service demand
- Geographical size and topographical characteristics of the beat
- Social and physical disorder that exists in the neighborhood
- Volume of pedestrian and vehicular traffic
- Adequacy of area regulation by signs, signals, and markings
- Adequacy of illumination
- Surface and condition of streets and sidewalks
- Weather conditions during the various seasons
- Character of business establishments and residences

As can be seen, the factors that should be considered by administrators when selecting specific patrol methods vary with the geographical, demographic, and criminogenic conditions of a community. Conditions that justify a certain method of patrol vary with such factors as the presence and number of intersections and crosswalks with heavy vehicular and pedestrian traffic and areas containing establishments in which a large number of incidents calling for police service may originate. The conditions also may vary between day and night. In business districts, for example, burglary prevention tactics useful at night are not needed when establishments reopen for business the following day.

The demands for patrol services are not evenly distributed in a community. Serious levels of felony crime are more often found clustered in neighborhoods characterized by high unemployment, poor housing conditions, overcrowding, and transience. People living in these areas usually generate the majority of the calls for police service (Reiss, 1971).

In an experiment conducted by the Crime Control Institute and the Minneapolis Police Department to locate chronic repeat call locations, it was found that 3 percent of the estimated 115,000 addresses and intersections in Minneapolis generated 50 percent of the 321,174 calls to the police between December 15, 1985, and December 15, 1986 (Sherman, 1989; Sherman, Gartin, and Buerger, 1989). This information was used to identify 110 *hot spots* that were subjected to a one-year directed patrol experiment during 1988 and 1989. An initial analysis of this project found that directed patrol—patrol designed with attention to these hot spots and the times at which they were most active—had a modest effect on robbery in the hot spots (Sherman, 1992). This finding suggests that the traditional patrol tactic of assigning increased levels of police officers to proactively patrol troubled areas for repeated brief periods may bring about a reduction of crime in these areas. It also supports the general thesis that a highly visible police presence in clearly defined areas can affect both crime and citizens' sense of safety and order.

Motor Patrol

Under ordinary conditions, the automobile has advantages over all other general patrol methods. Its speed in response to emergency service calls and its ability to cover large geographical areas have established motorized patrol as the principal police operational tactic. An automobile can be operated under almost all weather and road conditions, and it provides protection against inclement weather to its occupants. It easily carries other officers, prisoners, extra clothing, a radio, a computer, additional weapons, riot control gear, a fire extinguisher, a first-aid kit, and other equipment that makes the patrol car a mobile police office. The advantages of the automobile in enforcement of moving traffic regulations are so great that, in all but the most crowded city and highway conditions, there is little reason to use two-wheeled motorcycles for this purpose.

The automobile, however, is not without major disadvantages. It isolates patrol officers from the citizens they serve and often leads to a reactive, rather than a proactive, style of dealing with crime and other police business. Officers traveling in vehicles even at slow speeds are less likely to observe conditions that would alert them to the necessity of stopping and conducting investigations. Their primary focus is on the safe operation of their patrol vehicle and on the observation of traffic conditions. The sporadic service demand on different shifts subjects motor officers to alternating bouts of inactivity and intense periods of work overload. During quiet periods officers frequently fail to use their uncommitted time proactively or productively. Crime control–oriented motor officers tend to perceive of community service as "social work" and prefer to engage in "real" police work such as "hot pursuit," investigation, and arrest (Payne and Trojanowicz, 1985). Motor officers are usually *single-incident-oriented*, overlooking patterns of conduct in favor of getting to the scenes of individual calls, getting information, resolving the conflict the best they can, leaving, and returning to service for the next assignment. Goldstein observes that this:

> erodes the strength and self-image of the police. The agency commonly viewed by the outside world as so powerful, and frequently criticized as having too much autonomy, is often viewed by its own personnel as extraordinarily weak, as not having a direction of its own, as buffeted about and responding, in a feeble fashion, to the demands of every Tom, Dick, and Harry. Operating almost exclusively in a reactive mode results in the police resigning themselves to providing a limited type of service; to responding repeatedly and inadequately to the same calls, often from the same persons or addresses. Officers become frustrated and cynical, and the public is left unsatisfied. (Goldstein, 1990:20)

These conditions, in addition to experiments in Flint, Michigan, and Newark, New Jersey, during the 1970s and 1980s, have led many police administrators to return to foot patrol as an operational tactic in addition to patrol by automobile.

Foot Patrol

The Newark Foot Patrol Experiment (Police Foundation, 1981) and the Flint Neighborhood Foot Patrol Program (Trojanowicz, 1982) found that foot patrol enhanced citizen satisfaction with the police. In addition, foot patrol reduced fear of crime and contributed to residents' and merchants' belief that their neighborhoods were safer.

The value of foot patrol was also pointed out in Wilson and Kelling's semi-nal *Atlantic Monthly* article "Broken Windows" (1982). In this piece, Wilson and Kelling identified fear as a contributing factor to the spread of both crime and neighborhood decay. Their *broken windows theory* suggests that when neighborhood incivilities and disorder go unchecked, residents' fear of victimization increases, and their sense of responsibility for what happens in their community lessens. This lack of concern invites more disorder and criminal activity, which, in turn, increases citizens' fear even further. Those who can afford to move out of the neighborhood do so, abandoning it to additional criminal invasion—and adding to the overall sense of hopelessness. All this hastens the eventual decline and destruction of the community (see Skogan, 1990).

Wilson and Kelling argue that police can stem the tide of community destruction by maintaining order through the control of disorder and other quality-of-life offenses. They posit that foot patrol is the appropriate operational tactic to accomplish this task because, in their concentration on service calls, motor patrol officers ignore these types of offense. In part because of Wilson and Kelling's thinking, police departments began to change their patrol strategies to include foot patrol in order to halt the cycle of fear, crime, and community decline (Moore, 1992).

As it is used today, foot patrol is different from the traditional method of past years. Community-oriented foot patrol makes officers accessible to all types of neighborhoods, not just downtown business districts. Officers now are expected to lend more than just their physical presence to their beats and can no longer just pass time without working as they await assignments from sergeants or requests from citizens. Instead, they are expected to patrol the same area day after day and to assume continuing responsibility for their beats.

They must proactively profile their beats. *Beat profiling* is a systematic means by which community patrol officers capture and record critical information about their areas (Bieck, Spelman, and Sweeney, 1991:92). Officers are expected to use this information to analyze workload demands, problems on the beat, and community resources. Once these analyses are completed, the officers are expected to use their ingenuity to devise strategies that enhance beat safety and crime prevention. Besides their normal law enforcement duties, community foot patrol officers are expected to be planners, problem solvers, community organizers, and information links between the residents on their beat and their departments and other governmental and social service agencies. They are assessed on how well they accomplish their problem identification activities, resolve beat conditions, and create safe areas.

The ongoing administrative evaluation of foot patrol programs will prove whether they are worthy of continuation. As with any program, administrators must base their resource allocation and operational strategies on facts, rather than on unsubstantiated beliefs. In his study of Flint's foot patrol experiment, Trojanowicz (1982:17–19) suggested a specific set of objectives that can be used by administrators to evaluate their foot patrol programs. These include:

- Decrease of the actual or perceived criminal activity
- Increased citizen perception of personal safety
- Delivery of police services consistent with community needs

- Creation of community awareness of crime problems and methods of increasing the ability of the department to deal with actual or potential criminal activity
- Development of citizen volunteer groups and supporting action
- Elimination of citizen apathy about crime reporting
- Increased protection for women, children, and the aged

Foot patrol will never replace motor patrol as the principal operational strategy of patrol, but it should be part of an integrated patrol plan designed to meet specific community conditions. If, on evaluation, the program is found not to meet its objectives, then it should be reorganized or eliminated.

One-Officer versus Two-Officer Patrols

O. W. Wilson was a strong advocate of one-officer patrol vehicles. He argued that they were a more efficient use of personnel resources. However, the argument whether to field a one-officer or a two-officer patrol vehicle operation is moot for the majority of police departments in the United States because personnel resources dictate that they function with one-person patrol units (Police Executive Research Forum, 1982).

Still, in larger urban police departments, the conflict between perceived patrol officer vulnerability and operational cost efficiency remains a dominant issue. Unfortunately, there are disorderly and crime-ridden sections of U.S. cities that rank-and-file police officers view as extremely dangerous places to work. Police fraternal groups and unions support the use of two-person patrol vehicles in these areas and have imposed their wishes in contractual agreements. In addition, the volume of potentially violent police business requiring two-officer responses often is so great that administrators simply deploy police officers in two-person patrol units. In New York City, 98 percent of auto patrol division is conducted in two-person units. The comparable figure in Cleveland is 93 percent, and all Chicago police officers ride in pairs on the evening shift (Police Executive Research Forum, 1982:611–615).

A comprehensive evaluation of the one-officer, two-officer issue was conducted by the Police Foundation in San Diego during the 1970s. This evaluation found that one-person patrol unit officers were less often assaulted and also were less frequently involved than the two-officer vehicles in resisting-arrest charges. The one-officer vehicles also produced more arrests and field crime reports, generated fewer citizen complaints, and were less expensive to operate. However, there was little difference between the productivity of one- and two-officer units in handling calls for service or in officer-initiated investigative or enforcement actions. The study concluded that the one-person units were about equal to, or at times safer than, two-officer units and that they were more efficient (Boydstun, Sherry, and Moelter, 1977).

Although such findings may appear counterintuitive, there are several apparent reasons for them. Our experience working with and observing both solo officers and those in pairs suggests that paired officers may be somewhat more daring and less cautious than officers who work alone. Paired officers also are likely to be distracted by conversations with one another and, because they often come to depend on each other, may be more reluctant to call for help when they need it. Regularly paired officers develop close relationships and regular working styles, while officers who work alone usually must be flexible enough to match their efforts to whoever happens to show up to assist them.

On the objective merits, these findings and this experience logically support administrators who favor the use of one-officer vehicles. At the same time, this research has done little to change officers' perceptions of their vulnerability. Therefore, this issue will continue to confront administrators, who often must make a choice between costly labor unrest and operating efficiency.

Bicycle Patrol

Bicycles were used frequently for patrol before the beginning of this century, and their use has been rediscovered. Approximately 20 percent of municipal police departments employing 100 or more sworn officers now use bicycle patrols (Reaves, 1992), and it is likely that the number is higher still among such agencies as housing and campus police and those that serve other large off-street jurisdictions, such as parks and beach boardwalks.

Officers on bicycles are able to go where patrol cars find traveling difficult and to cover more area than foot patrol officers. Bicycle patrol officers have only slightly less opportunity for observation and contact with people than officers on foot, and the bicycle's silent operation makes it especially useful at night. In Seattle, for example, bicycle patrols have proved effective in controlling the activities of street-level drug dealers. At another level, in Louisville, they were used to control huge crowds of people attending city events associated with the Kentucky Derby.

The cost of the bicycle and the special equipment required for this type of patrol is expensive. This has caused some departments to seek private contributions (usually from merchants' groups, local philanthropic foundations, and corporate donors) to finance their bicycle operations. Also, bicycle officers require special training and must be physically fit at all times. Lastly, weather conditions limit the use of the bicycle as a patrol tactic.

Motorcycle Patrol

For a major part of this century, the motorcycle—usually a big Harley ridden by a dashing leather-clad officer—was the vehicle of choice for traffic control and police escort duty. The maneuverability of the motorcycle in congested traffic and its great acceleration have long made it a favorite among some highway patrols and traffic units. Over time, however, the disadvantages of motorcycles have become plain. Motorcycles cannot be used in inclement weather, are dangerous in subfreezing temperatures, and, at least in the case of the large Harleys, long ago lost their advantages of speed and acceleration to the powerful cars now available to police. Motorcycles also have contributed to disabling injuries and death among the officers who have ridden them. The cost of lost time to injuries, the cost of disability retirements, and the permanent loss of veteran officers are unnecessary and excessive liabilities that far outweigh the motorcycle's benefit to a department. Beyond some ceremonial and escort duties and limited traffic enforcement, therefore, it is difficult to justify the use of motorcycles in policing.

Scooters and Three-Wheeled Vehicles

Many police departments have adopted motor scooters and three-wheeled vehicles for use in traffic enforcement and specialized patrol operations on college campuses and in urban parks. Scooters and three-wheeled vehicles also are flexible and easily maneuvered in congested urban traffic areas, thus making them especially suited for parking enforcement. However, operating them beyond their capacity can result in unnecessary injury to the operator. Consequently, it is best to regard them as a means of increasing the mobility of officers who would otherwise work on foot, rather than as a substitute for motorcycles or cars.

Special-Purpose Vehicles and All-Terrain Vehicles (ATVs)

Severe climatic conditions and terrain in remote mountainous or woodland areas have resulted in the use of snowmobiles and ATVs by law enforcement departments in the United States and Canada. These modes of transportation are used as necessary in normal patrol operations and in emergency situations.

Other Specialized Patrol Methods

State police and suburban and rural sheriff departments are more likely than municipal and county police departments to make use of helicopters and airplanes (Reaves, 1992). Fixed-wing aircraft with short take-off and landing characteristics are more economical than helicopters, have lower maintenance costs, and can do most of what helicopters can do in the way of slow-speed flight, surveillance, vehicle pursuits, and illumination of crime scenes. They have two major disadvantages, however, that have severely limited their use in policing. First, they cannot land anywhere other than at airports or airstrips, and, second, they cannot be used for airlifting victims in rescue situations.

The recreational use of boats has increased dramatically on our nation's waterways. This increase, however, is not without serious problems. There have been increases in boating accidents and fatalities due to the inexperience of and use of alcohol by operators, as well as thefts of boats and their equipment. Many departments in jurisdictions that include recreational and commercial waterways maintain either permanent or seasonal boat patrols.

Called-for Services and Differential Response

The two principal activities of the patrol officer are handling called-for services and engaging in routine preventive patrol activities. *Called-for services* is a term used by police to describe the activity generated by crime complaints and requests for service, other police work that cannot be categorized as preventive patrol activity, or administrative activity, such as time spent refueling the po-

A

B
It's harder to adjust to some new patrol vehicles than to others.
A *St. Petersburg, Florida Police Department.*   B *Barbara Rios/Photo Researchers.*

lice vehicle or time out of service (e.g., meals and coffee breaks). A called-for service usually results in the completion of a report and ordinarily becomes part of the measurable workload of the patrol officer.

Called-for services relate to incidents reported by police officers as well as to complaints of crime and requests for service by citizens. They include:

- Disposing of violations in every field of police control by warning, citation, or arrest
- Investigating and disposing of miscellaneous complaints
- Investigating accidents
- Doing a preliminary investigation of crimes
- Recovering stolen property
- Searching for, interviewing, and investigating suspects and witnesses
- Doing follow-up investigations of crimes and incidents

Obviously, called-for services vary in nature and number by day and by time. Consequently, some control must be exercised over them, or else during peak periods life-or-death emergencies will go unattended because officers are unavailable to respond to them. By now, most police agencies have developed some sort of *differential response* program, usually coordinated with computer-assisted dispatch (CAD), that assigns varying priorities to calls depending on their urgency and that delays response to noncritical calls until peak periods have passed.

Thus, for example, almost all urban police departments experience a large. number of reported *past burglary* calls between 5 P.M. and 8 P.M., as working people return to their apartments and discover they have been victimized. In such cases, immediate police response and rapid *response time*—the time elapsed between the receipt of a citizen's request for help and the arrival of officers at the scene—accomplish little. This is so because traditional definitions of response time do not take into account the time elapsed between the *occurrence* of a crime and the receipt by police of a telephone report. Instead, the traditional definition of response time operates on the assumption that crimes are promptly discovered and that victims call police immediately after they have been victimized. But the crimes involved in our apartment burglary example typically occur long before they are discovered so that their perpetrators no longer present threats to victims' lives or property and there is little hope of apprehension regardless of how promptly police respond (see, e.g., Gay et al., 1977). Further, as suggested above, immediate response is likely to divert officers from assignments in which their presence is important.

Thus, if the police continue to provide (or, at least, to promise) immediate response to such calls, officers are compelled to work in a reactive mode that is counterproductive to other efforts to prevent crime or to provide police presence at potential problem scenes. In addition, because of the heavy workload at peak hours, calls become backlogged, so that even the promise of immediate response becomes an illusion. Stated most simply, without careful management, 911 becomes a bottomless pit, and the radio dispatcher, rather than the patrol commander or supervisor, runs the department. His or her priorities, which usually emphasize reducing the radio call backlog, become those under which the department operates.

The catch in the development of differential response programs involves another traditional assumption about police work. Even given objective evidence that immediate response to all calls is not necessary to protect life and property and to effect arrests, many police believe that good community relations and retention of departmental credibility require that police appear promptly whenever their presence is requested by citizens. This widely shared belief has remained a major impediment to implementation of differential response programs.

This belief is a significant obstacle to the adoption of differential response because it is so reasonable. It is clear that the police cannot effectively accomplish their varied and challenging missions unless they enjoy broad public support and credibility. But, contrary to what one might expect, several studies have found that citizens are willing to accept delayed responses for certain calls *provided they are informed of an estimated arrival time and that the police arrive within the designated time* (see Farmer, 1981; McEwen, Connors, and Cohen, 1986; Scott, 1981). Thus, the historic assumption that police must respond immediately to all calls if they are to enjoy public support has generally not been supported by the research. Where it interferes with police ability to respond immediately to all life-or-death calls, it should be abandoned for a differential response program and related public education.

Preventive Patrol Activity

Preventive patrol activity includes patrol by vehicle or foot as well as "hazard-oriented" patrol intended to curb specific crimes or to curtail disorderly or criminal activity at specified hot spots. It also includes inspections directed at lessening the threat of identifiable security or safety hazards. These services include routine examination of the doors and windows of business premises and of vacation homes likely to be burglarized, as well as inspection of public garages, where stolen automobiles may be stored or temporarily parked. In addition, preventive patrol activity involves inspection and supervision of places under license; of questionable establishments such as taverns, bars, massage parlors, and cocktail lounges; and of parks, bowling alleys, poolrooms, skating rinks, dance halls, and other recreational places. Preventive patrol should also take officers off the street and into such locations as shopping malls, landmark commercial buildings, parks, and other places where they eventually are likely to run into crises. As Jonathan Rubinstein has suggested, however, patrol officers typically learn their beats very well—as long as they do not have to leave their cars to do so:

> The patrolman's territorial knowledge of his sector is dictated largely by what he needs to know for the effective use of his car. Alleyways too narrow to drive through are rarely patrolled. Since he is not worried about wearing out the car, he is willing to drive any place that will not crack an axle or scrape a door. When he finds he cannot get his car into a place, he loses interest. Very few men make any effort to examine systematically the many passageways and alleys that can be navigated only on foot. If a patrolman is in pursuit on foot, he does not hesitate to go into these places, but he rarely takes the time to examine them for breaks in the fences, branches, concealed passageways, or

dead ends. He even acknowledges the tactical superiority of teenagers, whose skill in exploiting local topography frequently allows them to escape capture. Even his frustration and momentary anger do not encourage him to examine these partially hidden places with the meticulous care he gives to areas where his car can go. (Rubenstein, 1973:139)

To the extent that this early 1970s observation of Philadelphia police holds true there and in other jurisdictions today, administrators and supervisors are duty-bound to encourage officers to get out of their cars and learn what lies beyond the curblines of their beats.

Preventive patrol is directed primarily at diminishing community hazards that are not readily isolated and identified. Officers lessen opportunity for misconduct by observing and supervising persons and things during routine movements from one point to another on their beats, especially when they give particular attention to specific locations that are vulnerable crime targets or to areas in which incidents calling for police service most frequently occur. Beat profiling—visits with residents and owners of commercial establishments on the beat to discuss beat conditions, their safety concerns, and potential problems—is an essential part of preventive patrol tactics. Field interrogations of persons whose appearance and actions arouse the suspicion of alert patrol officers are important tasks in preventive patrol. In accomplishing this purpose, of course, officers must be attuned to constitutional rights and law, and they must not intervene in people's freedom of movement on arbitrary or subjective grounds.

Handling of Noncriminal Incidents and Services. A substantial part of patrol officers' time is devoted to noncriminal incidents and services. Officers must handle incidents involving such things as traffic accidents, runaway or missing persons, family crises, lost property, and lockouts; must render aid to persons who are handicapped or incapacitated by injury; and must respond to fire calls. Administrators should be on the alert for the tendency of officers to think of this activity as something other than "real" police work.

Identification of Hazards. Any situation that may induce an incident calling for some police action is a police hazard. Police hazards may result in crimes, minor violations, traffic accidents and congestion, lost persons and property, incivility, disorder, and other incidents that destroy the quality of life in a community. Hazards may vary according to the house of the day, the day of the week, and the season. They may be of high or low frequency and of high or low value. Some create a desire, and others present an opportunity to misbehave. Some hazards are temporary, and some are permanent. Some may be corrected or minimized by target-hardening tactics, regulation, or public education, and some may be affected only by the actions of a police officer.

Importance of Knowing Beat. Prevention, in the broadest sense, is the process of eliminating hazards or diminishing their effects. A patrol officer's beat is composed of persons and things that may constitute hazards in some cases. In other instances, these same people and things may be useful as resources that aid in the disposition of the resultant incidents. Knowledge of hazards and facilities, therefore, is essential to the successful performance of patrol duty.

Patrol officers should develop information sources that may be of help to them. They should develop personal contacts with residents, businesspeople, and proprietors or employees of businesses frequented by persons of questionable character. They should also know sources of readily obtainable emergency equipment—such as wreckers, diving equipment, armored cars, and boats—as well as city and private agencies that may assist in the resolution of beat problems.

Services to Merchants and Residents.   Police officers should establish speaking acquaintanceships with the businesspeople and residents on their beats. In community policing operations, beat officers are expected to profile their beats as a means of identifying and establishing communication with these people. This relationship creates information sources for the officer, facilitates communication of police information to the public, enables citizens to become personally acquainted with members of the department, and helps to establish a partnership between community members and the police. Consequently, when crises arise, the officers who respond to them do so as trusted and knowledgeable members of the community rather than as strangers in blue or brown suits.

Crime Prevention Activities.   Officers should pass on to the merchants on their beats information about bad-check passers, credit-card and cash-card swindlers, shoplifters, frauds, and other criminal operations that they have learned about from active investigations or from crime analysis bulletins or other department releases. Patrol officers should give merchants descriptions of suspects and their methods of operation and should request them to notify the department if suspects appear. Crime-prevention officers or the community policing officers should inform the personnel of retail establishments, either in a group or individually, about security methods.

Banks and Hazardous Business Places.   Banks, check cashing establishments, liquor stores, all-night convenience stores, franchise stores, and restaurants are potential robbery targets. Patrol officers should pay particular attention to these when they are on patrol and should check their security procedures from time to time. A relationship should be established between the department and all private security personnel guarding these premises. This relationship can help to maintain secure facilities and to resolve problems in the event of a crime or other emergencies.

Security Inspections.   Patrol officers should conduct security inspections of the commercial establishments on their beats. A security survey form is appropriate for this task. Officers can check off unsatisfactory conditions and list recommendations to proprietors or other management personnel. This form will serve as a record to be checked to see if the recommendations were followed on subsequent inspections. In addition, the proprietary information on this record will assist the department in notifying the owner or agent responsible for the premise when emergencies arise.

Assistance from Merchants.   The merchants on a beat are often willing to assist the officers in the resolution of beat problems. A safe and secure neighborhood is in their best interest as well as in the department's. Beat officers should strive to develop a positive relationship with merchants by asking their assistance and advice. In addition, officers should be willing to listen to the merchants' complaints and to try to resolve them in the best way possible. These individuals are taxpayers who are the lifeblood of many local communities. When they abandon a neighborhood and their stores are boarded up, the spiral of decay and crime takes over, and police problems increase (Skogan, 1990; Wilson and Kelling, 1982).

Inspection of Vacant Homes.   To minimize the threat of burglary, some departments keep a special watch on homes from which residents are temporarily absent. To get off the ground, this service requires advertising so that people will notify the department of their anticipated absence. Beat officers then inspect the premises on each tour of duty and see that the neighbors keep the front porch clear of the accumulation of newspapers, advertisements, and other deliveries that clue potential housebreakers that nobody is at home. A log of these checks and of the conditions noted should be maintained by the department. Occupants should be instructed at the time of their requests to notify the department immediately on their return.

Meeting Residents.   All beat officers should be instructed to become acquainted with everyone on their beats. In community policing operations this is a basic responsibility of all community officers. Motorized patrol officers, however, are apt to ignore this requirement, especially in single-incident-driven, high-service-demand areas. Several departments have established procedures to ensure contact by the beat officers with residents. In one method, the department uses a list of new residents in the community, furnished by the chamber of commerce or some similar source, to make a welcoming contact and provide the new resident with information about the department and its services. In Boston, beat officers assigned to a team policing operation in the late 1970s and early 1980s arranged to hold neighborhood meetings with residents, usually over coffee and cake, in a local school. To draw attendance, they delivered an invitation to every mailbox on their beat, and they succeeded in meeting virtually everybody, demonstrating their interest in and ties with the community and building strong support for their efforts to help residents address the community's police problems.

   Another method is to require beat officers to make residential visits in their assigned areas during uncommitted service time, on tours when the service demand is low and residents are home. Early evenings and Saturday mornings and afternoons typically are good times to accomplish this. Like the Boston public meeting program, this procedure can be activated and directed by the patrol supervisor. The assigned officer should be instructed to fill out a resident profile report of the person(s) contacted and the information obtained. This report should become part of the neighborhood profile record kept by the department.

Lastly, as community policing is introduced, officers should be assigned to conduct a residential survey of their beats. The officers are expected to visit each residence, identify who lives there, and obtain the residents' feelings about their personal safety and neighborhood problems. This activity is designed to do more than just obtain intelligence, and it should not be treated as a method of spying or otherwise intruding on citizens' privacy. Instead, community-oriented beat officers should be expected to use these visits to break down any barriers between the residents and themselves, to form partnerships with the residents in which both take ownership for the security and safety of the beat.

Residential contacts by community police officers are a directed and structured process. In addition to beat surveys, in some departments officers are expected to maintain a *beat conditions log* and a *persons interviewed log.* They are also expected to provide their supervisors with self-generated work plans by which officers identify the manner in which they intend to resolve beat problems. Their progress in resolving beat conditions and problems serves as the foundation of their performance evaluation.

Supervisors in charge of community-oriented units should meet daily with their officers. These meetings should be used to exchange information, review beat logs, evaluate beat conditions, and develop operational strategies. Supervisors should visit the officers' beats, observe conditions, and talk to citizens about police contact and services in their neighborhoods. Although it has been suggested that community policing supervisors practice a more participatory style of supervision, these visits are necessary for the supervisor to maintain oversight of the officers' activities and to evaluate the impact of problem-solving strategies.

TRAFFIC OPERATIONS AND TRAFFIC ENFORCEMENT

The use of motor vehicles on public roadways is carefully controlled by motor vehicle codes and traffic ordinances. Police officers are responsible for enforcing these regulations, and it is among the most important of their tasks. *The loss of life and money from automobile accidents each year is greater than all other losses the police are charged with preventing.* More people are injured or killed each year in traffic accidents than by the combined total of all other crimes and incidents.

Patrol officers are in the unique position of being the first to observe and become aware of conditions that affect traffic safety. As a result, traffic enforcement has evolved into an important police function. The duties associated with traffic control include (1) monitoring and directing the flow of traffic, (2) investigating accidents, (3) enforcing laws and regulations, and (4) assisting in planning, design, and maintenance of transportation systems (Bufe and Thompson, 1991:159).

Investigation of traffic accidents, especially those involving serious injury and death, requires specialized skills and training and is very time-consuming. Information gathered by the police during enforcement and accident investigation activities assists public works, state highway, and engineering departments in creating and maintaining traffic management systems. However, because traffic control involves the conflicting responsibilities of ensuring motor vehicle operator safety and enforcing regulations through the application of such sanctions as citation and arrest, many patrol officers do not like traffic control work because it subjects them to a great amount of citizen hostility and animosity. If transportation systems are to work with any degree of safety, however, the police must shoulder a heavy responsibility to prevent traffic accidents and congestion. Traffic regulations are an important tool in achieving this purpose; they set the boundaries of acceptable motor vehicle usage, and they should be enforced at a level sufficient to deter drivers from committing offenses.

Traffic Control Administration

Unlike the operational functions of patrol and criminal investigation, the administration of traffic operations is characterized by the existence of a vast external supporting network made up of public and private organizations associated with the nation's highway transportation system. The network has had a distinct influence on police traffic operations, ranging from the impact of legislation that created the National Highway Traffic Safety Administration to local government highway safety programs. Over the years, there has been increasing standardization of state traffic laws, primarily because of the influence of the Uniform Vehicle Code and Model Traffic Ordinance published by the National Committee on Uniform Traffic Laws and Ordinances. The code itself, first published in 1926, is refined and updated periodically.

The highway transportation system has some similarities to the criminal justice system, with national, state, and local sections each engaged in planning and engineering, while state and local governments also are concerned with traffic law enforcement. The state, influenced to some extent by the national government and its role in funding and overseeing the national highway system and interstate roadways, is heavily involved in the promulgation of traffic laws. Local governments create traffic ordinances—usually with titles such as *Municipal Traffic Ordinances* or *County Traffic and Parking Regulations*—to address specific conditions within their jurisdictional control. Although most of the traffic prosecution and court function is local, the state is involved in hearing appeals and prosecuting and trying felony traffic cases.

Police traffic operations are closely tied to the traffic-related responsibilities of other local government departments. These include the following:

- Transportation planning, often carried out by a city planning section. This activity is concerned with projections of traffic flow by various kinds of vehicles, such as buses, private vehicles, and commercial trucks, and the anticipation of problems and solutions. Often such a section is concerned with the layout or approval of streets being planned for new subdivisions.
- Analysis and design related to improvement, traffic flow, and prevention of accidents. In many cities this function is found in the city engineering department or in a department of public works. Activities can range from the planning of new streets, bridges, and interchanges to the planning and installation of signs, signals, and street marking.

- City or township organizational components responsible for the planning of on- and off-street public parking facilities and other revenue-related activities related to motor vehicles.

All these functions require the cooperation of the police department in supplying opinions (useful in long-range planning), data for analysis (e.g., accident investigations), or enforcement action.

Successful traffic administration also depends on the ability of the department's management team to develop a cooperative working relationship with prosecutors and courts. As in most situations that depend on cooperation, problems can be resolved through the development of an open, communicative relationship. This can be accomplished either by direct contact by the chief of police or through the creation of court liaison officers. These officers should develop close relations with prosecutors and judges and must have the authority to resolve problems.

The influence of the chief of police and his or her management team is essential in the direction of traffic operations because of the wide discretion police officers exercise in enforcing traffic regulations (see Fyfe, 1988; Gardiner, 1968; Lundman, 1979). All traffic functions, activities, and programs should be described in department directives. The modern approach to reducing traffic accidents is prevention (Bufe and Thompson, 1991). This approach demands not only a focus on traffic laws and ordinances but proper attention to the qualifications and training of traffic officers. Training in traffic laws and regulations, as well as enforcement guidelines, should be provided regularly to all operational personnel.

Over the years, various observers have questioned whether police should be engaged in traffic enforcement. It has been suggested that, instead of being handled by the police, traffic enforcement should be handled by a separate department within local government. The hypothesis supporting this position claims that the unpopularity of traffic law enforcement among normal, law-abiding citizens has created an unfavorable image of the police in their minds, and has resulted in a lack of cooperation for other police activities. However, it would be highly inefficient if police officers patrolling in conspicuously marked vehicles did not engage in traffic law enforcement in situations where violations occurred in their presence. In addition, traffic enforcement by uniformed officers is desirable because many criminal activities are detected through this form of enforcement (Pilant, 1993:39). In all, traffic enforcement is a major police task that is perfectly consistent with the primary police responsibility to protect life. It should be regarded in these terms rather than, as has sometimes been the case, as a cash cow or a source of operational revenues. The purpose of traffic enforcement is to protect the public, not to generate cash.

The Traffic Unit

No matter what their size, police departments usually have traffic units. The factors that influence the staffing of these units and their duties include the geographical size of the service, its population and volume of traffic, the demand for services by citizens, and the availability of personnel to be assigned to this function. The rank and position of the traffic unit's commanding officer is a good indicator of a department's commitment to traffic management. The staffing limitations on smaller departments often lead to the assignment of a single officer to this function, usually to investigate accidents or to conduct traffic education programs. The operational objectives of the traffic unit should include traffic law enforcement and analysis, accident investigation, traffic direction and control, public education, and parking control.

Enforcement Tactics

Random enforcement of traffic laws has recently been curtailed greatly by the courts. Previously, it was conducted largely by stopping vehicles that had not been involved in any offenses and whose occupants gave police no reason to suspect they had violated any laws. Now, however, it generally includes stopping only vehicles occupied by suspicious persons or driven by people whom officers have observed violating traffic regulations. This change is attributable to judicial redefinitions of police authority over vehicles and their drivers and occupants. For generations, police were trained that citizens' use of the highways was a *privilege* conditioned upon their willingness to be stopped, detained, and questioned by the police at any time, and to produce their drivers' licenses and proof of vehicle ownership and insurance whenever officers demanded them. In 1979, however, the U.S. Supreme Court ruled that citizens could not be required to waive their rights against unreasonable search and seizure merely because they had stepped off sidewalks and into vehicles. Commenting on an arrest that occurred when evidence of a crime was discovered by an officer who had arbitrarily decided to stop and question a motorist who had given the officer no reason to believe that he was involved in any wrongdoing, the Court wrote:

> The Fourth and Fourteenth Amendments are implicated in this case because stopping an automobile and detaining its occupants constitute a "seizure" within the meaning of those Amendments, even though the purpose of the stop is limited and the resulting detention quite brief. (*Delaware v. Prouse* 440 U.S. 648 at 653 [1979]).

In effect, therefore, the Court ruled in *Delaware v. Prouse* that officers would no longer be free to stop vehicles just because they felt like doing so. Two years later, the Court clarified this by ruling that the same reasonable suspicion standard governing stops of suspicious pedestrians or loiterers (*Terry v. Ohio*, 392 U.S. 1 [1968]) applied to motorists:

> Officers [who stop and detain a motorist] must have a particularized and objective basis for suspecting the particular person stopped of criminal activity. First, the assessment must be based upon all of the circumstances. The analysis proceeds with various objective observations, information from police reports, if such are available, and consideration of the modes or patterns of operation and certain kinds of lawbreakers. . . . The second element contained in the idea that an assessment of the whole picture must yield a particularized suspicion

is the concept that the process just described must raise a suspicion that the particular individual being stopped is engaged in wrongdoing. (*U.S. v. Cortez* 449 U.S. 411 at 417–418 [1981]).

In other words, the Court has forbidden the longtime police practice of stopping vehicles at will and demanding that their drivers identify themselves and document their authority to be behind the wheel. In *Prouse*, the Court also drew a distinction between a *rolling stop* (pulling up behind a moving motorist and signaling him or her to stop with emergency lights and sirens) and a *roadblock* (in which motorists who have been singled out for stopping are not suddenly alarmed by flashing lights in their mirrors and pulled to the sides of lonely roadways). The former, the *Prouse* Court suggested, is a procedure that is extremely alarming to the motorists involved. Hence, it should be carefully restricted by allowing officers to make such stops only when they observe specific traffic violations or, as in *Terry* stops, when they have *articulable* reasons to suspect that motorists may be involved in criminal behavior or other lawbreaking.

Roadblocks, however, have received greater approval by the courts. As long as roadblocks are operated on the basis of neutral and articulable principles that limit the opportunity for officers to be arbitrary or discriminatory, the courts have generally not objected to roadblocks. Thus, for example, if a police department's analyses demonstrated that a significant number of drunk-driving-related accidents occurred on a major roadway late on weekend evenings, it would be free to establish a roadblock at that time to briefly stop every car—or every fifth car, or every tenth car—for the purposes of conducting brief checks on drivers' sobriety and/or drivers' licenses. Without probable cause, of course, officers at such roadblocks have no authority to search the cars they have stopped.

Where the data suggest that roadblocks may be a valuable deterrent to traffic violations and/or an effective way of apprehending violators, they should be part of an agency's program of *selective enforcement*, or planned activities against the kinds of violations that cause accidents. Whether it involves roadblocks or heavy concentrations of moving patrol vehicles, selective enforcement is carried out at the same time and in the same locations as targeted violations and accidents.

Selective enforcement is not easy, however. It requires an ongoing analysis of traffic data in order to link specific offenses or road conditions with traffic accidents at given times and places. To ensure that selective enforcement programs are maximally effective, police management information systems should be programmed to track accident locations and times, and the driver behavior and traffic violations that caused them. Computer analysis can produce the necessary data by which to determine selective enforcement plans. Traffic officers can then be assigned to these locations and times to strictly enforce the regulations governing the accident-causing incidents.

The National Highway Traffic Safety Administration has established the Selective Traffic Enforcement Program (STEP) to provide demonstration grants to assist police departments in carrying out selective enforcement efforts. STEP grants may be obtained through individual state coordinating agencies. To date, some of these projects have proved effective in reducing accidents and enforcement costs.

Speed Enforcement

The most common citations for moving traffic violations are issued for speeding, which is a frequent and easy-to-prove offense. Law enforcement agencies use a variety of instruments and techniques to control violators, ranging from the use of marked vehicles to electronic speed identification devices, VASCAR, and selective enforcement.

Speed enforcement can involve officers in pursuit situations, and the traditional police practice of chasing fleeing vehicles has become the subject of increased attention both within and outside police organizations. The issues surrounding this controversy are explored later in this chapter.

Recently, concerns have been expressed about the possibility that microwave emissions of radar units used in speed enforcement have a carcinogenic effect (Violanti, 1992). Presently, there is no conclusive evidence that the low-level microwave radiation emitted from police radar devices is either dangerous or safe (Hannigan and Crescenti, 1993). Until current, and extensive, scientific research is completed, traffic radar is likely to continue to be an important speed control device. In the meantime, the National Highway Traffic Safety Administration has recommended minimum standards for radar units, as well as a 40-hour training course for unit operators, and has proposed that unit antennae be aimed only at distant target vehicles and away from the occupants of police cars.

Driving under the Influence

Since the 1980s, most police departments have placed a high priority on apprehending and arresting people who are driving under the influence of alcohol or controlled substances. This enforcement effort has come in response to enhanced public awareness of the dangers of drunk driving and the political pressure brought to this issue by such groups as Mothers Against Drunk Driving (MADD) and Students Against Drunk Driving (SADD). It is by now virtually certain that intoxicated individuals are the greatest cause of traffic accidents and fatalities and that drunk drivers are many times more likely than sober operators to become involved in traffic accidents, particularly serious ones. It is also by now clear that former blood alcohol levels establishing a legal presumption of intoxication (typically 0.15 percent blood alcohol) were far too high and that serious impairment of motor skills begins at much lower levels. Consequently, many states have lowered the levels of the legally permissible percentage of alcohol in the blood and have passed harsher mandatory sentences for convicted drunk drivers.

The enforcement of drunk driving laws is not always easy. Officers must be trained in methods of field sobriety testing and the use of breath analysis testing devices, as well as in safety procedures demanded in these incidents. In addition, conviction of intoxicated drivers often depends on officers' observations of arrestees' driving conduct and general behavior during stops and arrest processing. Despite enforcement difficulties, however, this is one enforcement area in which police enjoy the unanimous support of the public and the courts.

Accident Investigation

Accident investigation is the application of standard police investigation methods to the traffic field. The traffic regulations in most states require police officers to respond to the scenes of traffic accidents only if serious injury has occurred or property damage exceeds a specific amount. Still, police can expect that they will be summoned to accidents no matter how minor the damage. It is often the motorists' perception that a police officer is needed to determine and document who caused accidents, and these calls should be handled with courtesy and dispatch.

Department regulations should direct officers to respond to accident scenes when there is a report (or other indication) of any of the following:

* Death or injury likely to cause death
* Hit and run
* Impairment of an operator due to alcohol or drugs
* Damage to public vehicles or property
* Disturbances between principals
* Major traffic congestion resulting from the accident
* Vehicle damage requiring towing

The general purpose of accident investigations, which should be a requirement in the first four categories above, is to obtain information that will contribute to the overall safety of the driving public. This objective is accomplished by locating and interviewing witnesses; taking measurements and photographs of the locations and positions of vehicles and debris knocked from them by impact (and if appropriate, of the victims); taking photographs of the roadway or fixed objects nearby; collecting and preserving physical evidence; noting and recording information on weather, roadway, and traffic conditions; and facilitating the exchange of information between drivers.

There are four rather distinct types of accident investigations:

1. The most comprehensive and thorough investigations involve cases that have had unusual causes or especially tragic consequences such as multiple deaths, apparent intentional behavior, or public transport vehicles (buses, trains). They are generally carried out by teams of police accident investigation specialists, department legal advisors, traffic engineers, and psychologists.

   These investigations include all the activities described above, plus intensive examination of such factors as drivers' past accident histories and previous traffic convictions; psychological profiles derived from interviews with family and employers; review of influences such as problems or stress which may have contributed to the accident; and examination of physical actions immediately before, during, and after accidents.

2. More commonly, the investigation is conducted by only a trained police accident specialist. This is appropriate for cases involving injury likely to cause death, felony hit-and-run cases, felony drunk driving, and other serious, but unfortunately more routine, traffic offenses and tragedies.

3. In cases involving only property damage and/or minor injury, patrol or traffic officers most frequently conduct investigations. These are abbreviated versions of category 2, in which investigation proceeds to the point at which responsibility for the accident can be determined.

4. Last is accident reporting. This requires patrol or traffic officers to record information on accident report forms or to give drivers copies of forms they must complete and submit. This kind of report can be considered an investigation in the sense that the officer inquires into the circumstances to the extent that will permit its classification into this category.

The information obtained during the accident investigation is used to:

1. Identify hazards related to the engineering of streets, or to problems with signs, markings, or traffic laws that may cause accidents, so that hazards may be corrected.

2. Identify the types of violations that cause accidents, so that the most appropriate educational and enforcement efforts can be designed.

3. Provide evidence for the conviction of violators.

4. Furnish all parties, insurers, and licensing authorities all relevant information related to parties' liability and insurance.

This last purpose has been the subject of some debate. Some police administrators and some of the literature relating to accident investigations suggest that the police should not be concerned with civil fault or liability and that officers should restrict their activities to gathering evidence on violations of traffic regulations and criminal laws. This logic holds that the police investigative responsibility is solely to determine what happened, to enforce apparent violations of law, and to leave entirely to other authorities questions about who or what caused the accident. Attempting to distinguish so finely between responsibilities, however, is much like trying to split hairs. Identifying, citing or arresting, and assisting in the eventual prosecutions and convictions of offending drivers are integral components and consequences of finding out what happened in accidents involving drinking drivers, manslaughter, hit-and-run cases, deliberate violations, or reckless driving. Further, even if it could be neatly drawn, the distinction between finding out what happened and determining who or what caused it to happen in accident cases draws an arbitrary line between the police accident investigation role and their task in investigating other incidents in which lawbreaking may be a factor. In both accident investigations and criminal investigations, the police role should be to determine what happened and who did it, and to assist in seeing that culpable parties are brought to justice.

Most accident report forms used by police officers have provisions for listing violations committed by each driver, and many law enforcement administrators direct their officers to issue citations to one or more of the drivers for any violations they have committed. This position is taken because it is expected that the police should decide, if they can, whether and which driver actions contributed to the accident. Even in states where this practice is not forbidden by law, however, many administrators feel that issuance of a citation for a violation not witnessed by the officer is inappropriate.

Traffic Records

A traffic records system should be maintained by all police departments and, at minimum, should contain traffic accident report and investigation data, traffic enforcement data, traffic hazard reports, traffic volume and distribution data, and traffic safety education reports. These records enable the administrator to evaluate the accomplishments and effectiveness of traffic operations and also provide administrative control over day-to-day activities.

Traffic records provide administrators with the information necessary for planning, evaluating, and directing traffic operations. The preparation of useful data requires (1) gathering facts related to accidents, arrests, or engineering; (2) turning these facts into useful summary statistical form; and (3) analyzing the statistical data for planning purposes.

Accident location records and computer-generated incident maps assist in identifying dangerous locations, conditions that contribute to traffic accidents, repeat violators, and the impact of enforcement activities. Analysis of traffic summary data should enable administrators to discover whether their programs are achieving desired objectives or whether modifications are necessary. For example, a primary use of traffic records involves the comparative analysis of enforcement and accident data. As suggested above, since the major objective of traffic operations is the reduction of accidents, enforcement should be linked to the frequency and severity of accidents.

Traffic Safety Education

Traffic law enforcement is a deterrent and educational opportunity that reminds motorists to obey the rules of traffic safety. Because so many accidents are caused by inadvertent violations on the part of people of goodwill, it is critical that they be cited. For such persons, citations are, in effect, notices that they had better pay closer attention to what they do behind the wheels of their potentially lethal vehicles. At the same time, "apologetic people who didn't mean to do it and who promise to make sure that it will never happen again" often feel that they are not deserving of tickets and citing them often creates an undesirable attitude and ill will toward the police, no matter how undeserved. Certainly, these nasty sentiments often are rationalizations for the offenders' own wrongdoing, but they can be reduced if citations are supplemented by formal programs for dissemination of traffic safety information.

Police traffic safety education programs are attempts to win public understanding of traffic problems and to gain support for programs, policies, and methods used in their solution. They are also directed at stimulating safe practices among individual drivers, pedestrians, and schoolchildren. These programs often consist of classroom lectures by traffic safety officers, either to students before they obtain their driving licenses or to such select groups of drivers as senior citizens and persistent violators to re-educate and train them. Many departments have created traffic safety officer positions or units who function primarily to develop and conduct these programs. Programs of this type include explanation of traffic regulations, instruction in safe driving practices, bicycle safety training, and training of school safety patrols. The effectiveness of these programs is difficult to assess because their outcome—safe driving—is affected by such factors as program delivery quality, receptivity of students, and instructors' ability. In general, however, programs aimed at young people are more likely to be effective than those involving older drivers who already suffer from bad habits.

Police Pursuits

Vehicle pursuits are among the most difficult and dangerous police situations. Pursuits involve attempts by law enforcement officers to apprehend motorists who knowingly flee from officers. Long a staple of "cop movies" and television shows and long regarded as a necessary means of deterring flight and apprehending serious violators, pursuits recently have come under careful and critical scrutiny from many quarters.

In a series of cases, for example, the courts have awarded great damages to persons hurt or the families of persons killed in police pursuits—often without regard to whether they were themselves the initiating offenders—and seem to demand that police carefully weigh the dangers of continuing to pursue against the costs of slowing down and increasing the possibility that offenders will escape (see Alpert, 1988; and Alpert and Fridell, 1992, for a concise summary of cases and research).

This breakpoint in this cost–benefit equation is not always an easy one to strike, particularly in the heat of the moment when, surprised by drivers' refusals to stop, police officers typically are in highly aroused emotional states. Consequently, clear policy, supervision, and training should guide officers' decisions in such cases and should put flesh on the bones of such ambiguous phrases as "reasonable and prudent."

In formulating a pursuit policy, some information on past pursuits is necessary. But there are severe limitations on the information that is available because many pursuits go unreported. In addition, some of the research engages in the apples-and-oranges exercise of lumping together under one heading very short attempts to flee by offenders who quickly come to their senses and stop and very long high-speed chases by offenders who care little for life. Obviously, the probability and severity of accidents generated by these widely varying pursuits also varies greatly.

While it is consequently difficult to generalize from the research, it is justifiable to draw some broad conclusions that have implications for policy and practice:

1. Each year, in almost every police department, pursuit situations occur.
2. Estimates put the number of U.S. police pursuits as high as 50,000 annually and the number of injuries they cause at approximately 20,000 (Charles, Falcone, and Wells, 1992).

3. Although one cannot predict with accuracy precisely when particular officers will find themselves in potential pursuit situations, it is extremely predictable that such situations will arise during virtually every uniformed officer's career.

4. Most pursuits are initiated for traffic violations rather than serious criminal offenses. For example:

   - One study (Physicians for Automotive Safety, 1968; cited in Fennessy et al., 1970) reported that this was the case in about 80 percent of pursuits.
   - The California Highway Patrol (1983) found that 63 percent of pursuits were initiated for traffic violations and that another 26 percent involved suspected drunk drivers.
   - The Solicitor General of Canada (1985) reported that 14 percent of pursuits in that country involved auto theft (9 percent) or other serious crime (5 percent) and that the remainder started with simple traffic offenses (57 percent), dangerous or impaired driving (27 percent), or suspended licenses (2 percent).
   - The state of Minnesota reported that 82 percent of its chases involved traffic violations (76 percent) or suspected drunk driving (6 percent) (Alpert and Fridell, 1992:108).
   - Even in the relatively high-crime Miami area, Alpert and Dunham (1988) reported that 56 percent of pursuits began with traffic offenses (54 percent) or reckless or impaired driving (2 percent).

5. Great numbers of these pursuits result in accidents:

   - 29 percent, according to the California Highway Patrol (1983)
   - 23 percent in Canada (Solicitor General, 1985)
   - 38 percent in the Miami area (Alpert and Dunham, 1988)
   - 44 percent in Minnesota (Alpert and Fridell, 1992:108)

6. A good number of these pursuits result in injury:

   - 11 percent, according to the California Highway Patrol (1983)
   - 20 percent in Canada (Solicitor General, 1985)
   - 17 percent in the Miami area (Alpert and Dunham, 1988)
   - 24 percent in Minnesota (Alpert and Fridell, 1992:108)

7. Somewhat less than one in a hundred pursuits kills *at least* one person:

   - 1 percent, according to the California Highway Patrol (1983)
   - 0.5 percent in Canada (Solicitor General, 1985)
   - 0.7 percent in the Miami area (Alpert and Dunham, 1988)
   - 0.2 percent in Minnesota (Alpert and Fridell, 1992:108)

8. The percentages of pursuits that result in injury or death do not accurately reflect the numbers of people killed. Often, several pedestrians or motorists are killed or severely injured in single spectacular accidents.

9. There are no accurate statistics on what pursuit victims were doing when they were injured or killed. Very often, the victims of pursuits are totally innocent motorists or pedestrians who happen into the paths of fleeing drivers or pursuing officers.

10. Passengers in pursued vehicles often are unknowing persons who suddenly, and unwillingly, find themselves in the middle of extremely perilous situations over which they have no control. They are in effect, along for a ride they usually cannot stop.

It is small wonder, therefore, that pursuit has become a major police policy issue, as well as a major source of criticism and liability for police. In order to properly address this issue police administrators must:

1. Develop a pursuit policy that clearly emphasizes the value of life over the need to apprehend even the most serious offenders
2. Maintain close supervision and evaluation of pursuits
3. Provide officers with both legal instruction and driver training for pursuit situations

Pursuit policy should be restrictive in nature. It should limit the degree of individual discretion and risk by the officer by defining what the department's priorities and limitations are regarding apprehension and safety. The policy should be clearly written, easily understood, and strictly enforced. Like the example in Appendix 16-1, it should include provisions that address:

- The need to carefully evaluate the circumstances
- A statement of the initiating officer's responsibilities
- A statement of secondary units' responsibilities
- A statement of dispatchers' responsibilities
- A statement of supervisors' responsibilities
- Clearly stated general prohibitions against forcible stopping, caravaning, ramming, "boxing," or attempting to overtake pursued vehicles and against shooting at or from moving vehicles
- A clearly stated rule that roadblocks may be employed only in circumstances authorizing use of deadly force, and then only in circumstances that do not endanger the public or officers and that do not totally block the roadway
- A clear statement of when pursuits should be terminated
- A clear statement of responsibilities related to interjurisdictional pursuits (see, e.g., Commission on Accreditation, 1994: Standard 41.2.2)

The department's pursuit policy should also be evaluated annually by the department's command staff and legal advisor to ensure its utility and adherence to current legal decisions. This policy should be disseminated to all members of the department.

Administrators and supervisors must be held accountable for actively maintaining and enforcing the established pursuit policy. Accountability must be accompanied with empowerment. Supervisors must be directed by policy to take disciplinary action when violations of the policy occur. The monitoring of pursuits and reporting on each incident should be required of all supervisors. This will provide a means to effectively deal with and prevent problems as well as demonstrate a commitment to the policy on the part of the department's management.

Training should define the limits of officer discretion as defined in both policy and case law. In essence, decisions about what to do should be made in advance so that, under stressful pursuit situations, officers are not forced to reinvent the wheel but may instead revert almost instinctively to what they have already been taught. In addition, all officers should be made to attend and qualify in a certified tactical training course. Officers who fail to meet certification as tactical drivers should not be permitted to engage in pursuit driving.

These suggestions accompanied with a strong commitment on the part of the department's management team should ensure that appropriate safety standards will be applied in these incidents. However, all officers involved in emergency incidents should always operate their motor vehicles with the strictest regard for the safety of others as well as themselves.

SPECIAL OPERATIONS

Today, police departments are required to confront a complex array of special situations. Many tactical situations and events arise that require flexibility in deployment of personnel, as well as an expertise and skill level beyond that possessed by the ordinary patrol officer. These situations may involve policing of hot spots, sporting events, visiting dignitaries, hostage and barricade situations, demonstrations, bomb threats and bomb disposal, civil disturbances, tactical drug enforcement measures, and parades. In many major metropolitan areas, these events are almost daily occurrences. As a result, many police departments have employed special operational methods and units to meet the demands of these occurrences.

Specialized operational methods involve relieving patrol personnel of the responsibility of handling routine calls for service in order to concentrate on a specific problem or event. These methods are usually directed at the deterrence of suppressible crimes and the on-site apprehension of offenders (Schack, Schell, and Gay, 1977). They include directed patrol tactics, such as saturation patrol and suspect-oriented techniques, as well as stakeouts and the surveillance of places and offenders. Specialized units may be created to address specific problems and situations that occur at ongoing or irregular intervals if the department's personnel resources are sufficient to support them. They provide many benefits to a department such as assignment of responsibilities, development of expertise, creativity and innovation in the handling of complex problems, and career development opportunities.

Before establishing such units, however, administrators should keep in mind the principle that *specializations should be created only when it is clear that specialists can perform the task at hand substantially better than can generalists.* This is so because specialization is not without disadvantages. Increasing the number of boxes on a department's organization chart adds to the difficulty of administrative coordination, communication, and control, and it sometimes creates conflict, as when units compete for resources and recognition.

The importance of this last consideration often is not fully grasped by administrators. When *Tac* units and the like are created, they usually seek to recruit the very best patrol officers. Not only does this drain patrol of highly qualified personnel, but it also creates divisions within the agency, increasing the schisms between the patrol officers (who come to see themselves as "grunts" and "warm bodies") and the "elites," whom patrol officers must call for assistance with problems they cannot handle. This further diminishes the prestige of patrol—which, again, is the most visible, critical, and important component of any police agency—and gives the most competent patrol officers yet another reason to seek to leave their work for specialized, and more obviously appreciated and prestigious, jobs.

Where such a caste system can be avoided, it should be; where the workload demands the establishment of special operations units, every effort must be made to ensure that the patrol officers' role and status are diminished no more than necessary. One way to do this is to involve patrol officers as much as possible in the operations of special units and in the credit that comes to the department through joint patrol–special operations efforts. In New York City, for example, divisions between the special operations unit (the Emergency Service Division) and hostage negotiators on the one side and patrol officers on the other have been minimized by assigning patrol personnel to highly visible roles in hostage and barricade situations and by designating the primary patrol officer on each such scene as the arresting officer who gets the credit and recognition for the sensational arrests that often result.

The Metro-Dade Police Department's Special Response Team (SRT) is more substantially integrated with its patrol operation. SRT officers are full-time patrol officers who work across the county, as do all other patrol officers, and who leave their patrol assignments only when they are mobilized for specific situations. By all observable measures, this program has been a success. Obviously, however, it requires considerable effort to ensure that a sufficient balance of SRT patrol and patrol officers are on duty at any time. In return, however, the department enjoys the benefits of a closely integrated crisis intervention service and the knowledge that it has not created a new bureaucratic empire that, as often occurs, might eventually become more concerned with its own survival and narrow goals than with the overall mission of the agency.

Special Operations Administration

As these two examples suggest, the use of special operational methods and units varies among law enforcement departments. In general, however, larger departments tend to be more specialized, creating specialized operations units and employing special patrol tactics on the basis of careful planning and consideration by the chief and the command staff. This planning should entail identifying problems or events that require special attention, studying and forecasting potential issues related to these, and identifying operational strategies or tactics for dealing with them. The process of creating special operational units should involve:

1. Identification of the unit's primary objective and its place in the organizational structure
2. Identification of staffing requirements
3. Selection of unit managers and members based on identified knowledge, skills, and abilities demanded by the operational objectives
4. Development of unit personnel through specialized training

5. Deployment of the unit
6. Evaluation of the unit's performance and the continued need for it

Units created by this process are usually classified under a tactical or special operations section. Grouped under such an organizational subdivision may be any or all of the following functions:

- Special weapons and tactics (SWAT) teams
- Hostage negotiations
- Special-purpose vehicle operation
- Decoy operation
- Undercover surveillance and stakeout
- Bomb threats and bomb disposal
- Coverage of special events
- VIP protection
- Coverage of disasters
- Coverage of civil disorders and emergencies

The chief of police and the command staff should create a policy statement that governs the direction of the special operations before, during, and after their utilization. This policy directive should include:

- Position or person authorized to activate special operations
- Procedures governing the use of special operations personnel in specific situations
- Guidelines for the use of special operations officers to supplement other operations
- Reporting and evaluation procedures to be used upon termination of special operations

Selection of Special Operations Personnel

Since special operations personnel are deployed in dangerous and emergency situations, these units require staffing by qualified and specially trained personnel. The selection process should include:

- Selection standards that match the candidates' knowledge, skills, and ability with that of the unit's operational requirements
- A psychological evaluation
- Physical fitness testing for those officers who will be assigned to specialized field units
- Situational testing to assess the officer's problem-solving and response skills
- Mandatory drug screening before appointment

Once selected, officers should be required to maintain an appropriate level of physical fitness and should be subjected to annual psychological and drug review. The results of these annual tests should remain in the officers' personnel file. The nature of special operations work requires that both the officers and the department take necessary precautionary measures to overcome the effects of the stress that is a natural part of these assignments.

SUMMARY

577

CHAPTER 16
Uniformed Services:
Patrol, Traffic, and
Special Operations

This chapter has examined the work of the uniformed services in patrol, traffic, and special operations, all of which are at the heart of the police operation. Patrol work is a demanding and complex police function that requires staffing by the department's best people, and every effort must be made to ensure that those who perform it are not treated as ugly ducklings among personnel involved in more specialized work. Patrol officers are a department's eyes and ears, society's first responders to a dazzling array of minor problems and potential social upheavals of major dimensions. When patrol officers do not perform their jobs well, citizens routinely are offended and hurt. In more extreme circumstances, police departments and entire municipal administrations have been turned out of office, and streets have exploded into riot after police officers—almost always police *patrol* officers—have acted inappropriately. This is a terrible responsibility, and patrol officers should be put on notice through their training and by their prestige in and out of the department that they perform their department's most crucial service.

The selection of patrol methods should bring together the chief's vision, the department's mission, and the needs of the community. Many administrators are attempting to experiment with a variety of methods to accomplish this objective. However, good basic police work has always required that patrol officers actively become involved in and assume responsibility for the areas they police. Technology may have changed the way police patrol their beats, but in the final analysis police officers will respond to what they think management feels is important. It is therefore critical that the chief administrator and the command staff actively manage and continually evaluate the patrol function. In this manner this most important of all police functions will be carried out in an effective and efficient manner.

The traffic and special operations functions are important specialized activities that should support the patrol function. Traffic officers enhance public safety by enforcing the traffic laws, investigating traffic accidents, and educating the public in safe driving methods. Special operations allow a department to provide a level of response and expertise in special tactical situations that would be difficult for conventional patrol units to provide. However, the selection, training, and management for personnel of both of these functions must be carefully handled. Specialization adds to the difficulty of administrative coordination, communication, and control, and it sometimes can lead to interunit conflict. All special operational units should be subject to periodic review by the command staff to ensure that they are accomplishing their original purpose and that they are integrated properly into the department's overall mission and goals.

QUESTIONS FOR DISCUSSION

1. In the late 1960s, a police agency in a mid-sized eastern city suffered a terrible multi-fatality accident during a high-speed pursuit of a young traffic violator. Stricken by grief and anger, the department's chief then hastily enacted the following pursuit

policy, quoted in its entirety: "High-speed pursuits of traffic violators are stupid, ridiculous, and dangerous. Officers will not engage in them." Critics of this policy argued that motorists would routinely flee from officers who were "handcuffed" in this manner. But the policy has been in place for more than a quarter century, and none of the predicted disastrous effects of this policy have occurred. Indeed, the only pursuit that has since occurred in the city involved another agency whose officers chased a traffic violator into town, where he crashed, killing himself and a passenger and causing four other serious injuries—and outraging both the local police and the city's residents. How would you explain the results of this policy?

2. A major police department recently canceled its year-old policy of assigning patrol officers to steady shifts. It did so for two reasons. First, as the police commissioner reported, communication among officers who worked different shifts was minimal, so that community problems rarely were addressed in a significant way. Second, he claimed, officers working one shift never got to know the people and conditions encountered by officers on other shifts. The police union has fought this change, arguing that it would renew the great disruption of alternating shifts just as officers were becoming accustomed to regular schedules and normal private lives. The union has also challenged the commissioner, asserting that his justifications are ruses designed to conceal his true motive: reducing arrest and court-related overtime for officers who work midnights and who spend many mornings in court with persons they have arrested. If you were a mediator in this dispute, what would you do to resolve it?

3. Many police chiefs and officials believe that even though some research shows that delayed responses to some noncritical calls for services make good sense, especially reports of past crimes, it has no relevance to their jurisdictions because their citizens have always expected police to show up immediately. Are their arguments valid?

4. What can be done to improve the status, prestige, and morale of police patrol officers relative to personnel in other specialized units?

5. A veteran police officer claims that one-officer patrol units are purely an economic measure, and that officials who abandon two-officer cars for solo units will eventually "have the blood of dead officers on their hands." How would you respond to this statement?

SOURCES

ALPERT, GEOFFREY P. "Questioning Police Pursuits in Urban Areas," *Journal of Police Science and Administration,* 15:298–306 (1988).

———, and ROGER G. DUNHAM (eds.). *Policing Urban America,* 2d ed. (Prospect Heights, Ill.: Waveland, 1992).

———, and ———. "Research on Police Pursuits: Applications for Law Enforcement," *American Journal of Police,* 7:123–131 (1988).

———, and LORIE A. FRIDELL. *Police Vehicles and Firearms: Instruments of Deadly Force* (Prospect Heights, Ill.: Waveland, 1992).

ASCHOFF, J. "Circadian Rhythms in Man," *Science,* 148:1427–1432 (1965).

BIECK, WILLIAM H., WILLIAM SPELMAN, and THOMAS J. SWEENEY. "The Patrol Function," pp. 59–95 in William A. Geller (ed.), *Local Government Police Management,* 3d ed. (Washington, D.C.: International City Management Association, 1991).

BOYDSTUN, JOHN E., M. E. SHERRY, and N. P. MOELTER. *Patrol Staffing in San Diego: One- or Two-Officer Units* (Washington, D.C.: The Police Foundation, 1977).

BUFE, NOEL C., and LARRY N. THOMPSON. "Traffic Services," pp. 159–184 in William Geller (ed.), *Local Government Police Management,* 3d ed. (Washington, D.C.: International City Management Association, 1991).

California Highway Patrol. *Pursuit Study* (Sacramento: State of California, 1983).

CHARLES, MICHAEL T., DAVID N. FALCONE, and EDWARD WELLS. "Police Pursuit in Pursuit of Policy," *The Pursuit Issue, Legal and Literature Review, and an Empirical Study* (Washington, D.C. AAA Foundation for Traffic Safety, 1992).

CLARK, JACOB R. "Does Community Policing Add Up?" *Law Enforcement News,* xx:1–8 (Apr. 15, 1994).

Commission on Accreditation for Law Enforcement Agencies, Inc. *Standards for Law Enforcement Agencies,* 2d ed. (Fairfax, Va.: CALEA, 1989).

———. *Standards for Law Enforcement Agencies,* 3d ed. (Fairfax, Va: CALEA, 1994).

Delaware v. Prouse 440 U.S. 648 (1979).

FARMER, MICHAEL T. (ed.). *Differential Police Response Strategies* (Washington, D.C.: Police Executive Research Forum, 1981).

FYFE, JAMES J. *The Metro-Dade Police/Citizen Violence Reduction Project: Final Report* (Washington, D.C.: Police Foundation, 1988).

GARDINER, JOHN A. "Police Enforcement of Traffic Laws: A Comparative Analysis," in James Q. Wilson (ed.), *City Policy and Public Policy* (New York: Wiley, 1968).

GAY, WILLIAM. *Patrol Emphasis Evaluation: Cleveland Heights, Ohio* (Philadelphia: University City Science Center, 1977).

GOLDSTEIN, HERMAN. *Policing a Free Society* (Cambridge, Mass.: Ballinger, 1977).

———. "Improving Policing: A Problem Oriented Approach," *Crime and Delinquency,* 25:236–258 (April 1979).

———. *Problem-Oriented Policing* (New York: McGraw-Hill, 1990).

GREENE, JACK R., and STEPHEN D. MASTROFSKI (eds.). *Community Policing: Rhetoric or Reality?* (New York: Praeger, 1988).

HANNIGAN, MAURICE J., and PAUL E. CRESCENTI. "The Effects of Police Radar Exposure: Another Perspective," *Police Chief,* LX(7): 53–55 (July 1993).

KELLING, GEORGE L., TONY PATE, DUANE DIECKMAN, and CHARLES E. BROWN. *The Kansas City Preventive Patrol Experiment: A Technical Report* (Washington, D.C.: Police Foundation, 1974).

———, and JAMES K. STEWART. "The Evolution of Contemporary Policing," pp. 3–21 in William Geller (ed.), *Local Government Police Management,* 3d ed. (Washington, D.C.: International City Management Association, 1991).

KESSLER, DAVID A. "Integrating Calls for Service with Community and Problem Oriented Policing: A Case Study," *Crime and Delinquency,* 39:485–508 (October 1993).

LINDGREN, S. *Justice Expenditure and Employment, 1990* (Washington, D.C.: Bureau of Justice Statistics, 1992).

LUNDMAN, RICHARD J. "Organizational Norms and Police Discretion: An Observational Study of Police Work with Traffic Violators," *Criminology,* 17:159–171 (August 1979).

MASTROFSKI, STEPHEN D. "What Does Community Policing Mean for Daily Police Work?" *National Institute of Justice Journal* (August 1992): 22–27.

McEWEN, THOMAS J., EDWARD F. CONNORS, and MARCIA J. COHEN. *Evaluation of the Differential Police Response Field Test* (Alexandria, Va.: Research Management Associates, 1984).

MOORE, MARK H. "Problem Solving and Community Policing," pp. 99–158 in Michael Tonry and Norval Morris (eds.), *Modern Policing* (Chicago: University of Chicago Press, 1992).

MUIR, WILLIAM K. *Police: Streetcorner Politicians* (Chicago: University of Chicago Press, 1977).

New York State Law Enforcement Accreditation Program. *Standards Manual* (Albany, N.Y.: Division of Criminal Justice Services, 1989).

PAYNE, DAVID M., and ROBERT C. TROJANOWICZ. *Performance Profiles of Foot versus Motor Officers* (East Lansing, Mich.: National Neighborhood Foot Patrol Center, Michigan State University, 1985).

PILANT, LOUIS. "Speed-Measuring Devices," *Police Chief,* LX(11):33–39 (November 1993).

Police Executive Research Forum and Police Foundation. *Survey of Police Operational and Administrative Practices—1981* (Washington, D.C.: Police Executive Research Forum, 1982).

Police Foundation. *The Newark Foot Patrol Experiment* (Washington, D.C.: Police Foundation, 1981).

REAVES, BRIAN A. *Law Enforcement Management and Administrative Statistics, 1990: Data for Individual State and Local Agencies with 100 or More Officers* (Washington, D.C.: Bureau of Justice Statistics, 1992).

REISS, ALBERT J. JR. *The Police and the Public* (New Haven, Conn.: Yale University Press, 1971).

RUBINSTEIN, JONATHAN. *City Police* (New York: Farrar, Straus and Giroux, 1973).

SCOTT, ERIC J. *Calls for Service: Citizen Demand and Initial Police Response* (Washington, D.C.: U.S. Government Printing Office, 1981).

SCHACK, STEPHEN, THEODORE H. SCHELL, and WILLIAM G. GAY. *Improving Patrol Productivity, vol. II: Specialized Patrol* (Washington, D.C.: National Institute of Law Enforcement and Criminal Justice, 1977).

SHERMAN, LAWRENCE W. "Repeat Calls for Service: Policing the 'Hot Spots,'" pp. 150–165 in Dennis Kenney (ed.), *Police and Policing: Contemporary Issues* (New York, Praeger, 1989).

———. "Attacking Crime: Police and Crime Control," pp. 159–230 in Michael Tonry and Norval Morris (eds.), *Modern Policing* (Chicago: University of Chicago Press, 1992).

———, PATRICK GARTIN, and MICHAEL E. BUERGER. "Hot Spots of Predatory Crime: Routine Activities and the Criminology of Place," *Criminology,* 27(1):27–55 (1989).

SKOGAN, WESLEY G. *Disorder and Decline: Crime and the Spiral of Decay in American Neighborhoods* (New York: Free Press, 1990).

SKOLNICK, JEROME, and DAVID H. BAYLEY. "Theme and Variation in Community Policing," pp. 1–38 in Michael Tonry and Norval Morris (eds.), *Crime and Justice: A Review of Research* (Chicago: University of Chicago Press, 1988).

Solicitor General of Canada. *Special Report from the Solicitor General's Special Committee on Police Pursuits* (Ontario: Solicitor General's Office, 1985).

SPARROW, MALCOLM K., MARK H. MOORE, and DAVID H. KENNEDY. *Beyond 911: A New Era for Policing* (New York: Basic Books, 1990).

TAYLOR, P. J. "Shift and Day Work: A Comparison of Sickness, Absence, Lateness, and Other Absence Behavior at an Oil Refinery from 1962–1965," *British Journal of Industrial Medicine,* 24:93–102 (1967).

Terry v. Ohio 392 U.S. 1 (1968).

TROJANOWICZ, ROBERT. *An Evaluation of the Neighborhood Foot Patrol Program in Flint, Michigan* (East Lansing, Mich.: National Center for Community Policing, Michigan State University, 1982).

———, and BONNIE BUCQUEROUX. *Community Policing: A Contemporary Perspective* (Cincinnati: Anderson, 1990).

U.S. v. Cortez 449 U.S. 411 (1981).

VIOLANTI, JOHN M. "Police Radar: A Cancer Risk?" *FBI Law Enforcement Bulletin* (October 1992):14–16.

WEITZMAN, ED, et al. "Reversal of Sleep Waking Cycle: Effect on Sleepstage Pattern and Certain Neuroendocrine Rhythms," *Transcripts of the American Neurological Association,* 93:153–157 (1968).

WILSON, JAMES Q., and GEORGE L. KELLING. "Broken Windows," *Atlantic Monthly* (March 1982):29–38.

WILSON, O. W., and ROY C. MCLAREN. *Police Administration,* 4th ed. (New York: McGraw-Hill, 1977).

APPENDIX 16-1
NEW JERSEY'S VEHICLE PURSUIT POLICY

In 1993, The Attorney General of New Jersey disseminated the following model policy to all police and law enforcement agencies in his state. It serves as a good basis for construction of a pursuit policy in any law enforcement agency:

NEW JERSEY POLICE VEHICULAR PURSUIT POLICY
PURPOSE OF POLICY

The primary purpose of this policy is to secure a balance between the protection of the lives and safety of the public and police officers, and law enforcement's duty to enforce the law and apprehend violators. Since there are numerous situations which arise in law enforcement that are unique, it is impossible for this policy or any standard operating procedure to anticipate all possible circumstances. Therefore, this policy is intended to guide a police officer's discretion in matters of vehicular pursuit.

This policy has been formulated to provide minimum statewide requirements to direct law enforcement activities in this very critical area of police practice. However, police department size, population density and other characteristics vary among communities in this state. Therefore, county and local law enforcement agencies are expected to develop individual standard operating procedures which account for departmental variations, yet are consistent with this policy.

Deciding whether to pursue a motor vehicle is among the most critical decisions made by law enforcement officers. It is a decision which must be made quickly and under difficult, often unpredictable circumstances. In recognition of the potential risk to public safety created by vehicular pursuits, no officer or supervisor shall be criticized or disciplined for a decision not to engage in a vehicular pursuit or to terminate an ongoing vehicular pursuit based on the risk involved, even in circumstances where this policy would permit the commencement or continuation of the pursuit. Likewise, police officers who conduct pursuits consistent with this policy will be strongly supported by the law enforcement community in any subsequent review of such actions.

DEFINITIONS

A. *Boxing In:* The surrounding of a violator's moving vehicle with moving pursuit vehicles which are then slowed to a stop along with the violator's vehicle.

B. *Divided Highway:* A road which includes a physical barrier between traffic traveling in opposite directions.

C. *Heading Off:* An attempt to terminate a pursuit by pulling ahead of, behind or toward a violator's moving vehicle to force it to the side of the road or to otherwise come to a stop.

D. *Law Enforcement Officer:* Any person sworn to uphold the law who is certified by the Police Training Commission or whose training has included Pursuit/Emergency Driving and who is currently employed by a public safety agency.

E. *Paralleling:*
  1. *Street Paralleling:* Driving a police vehicle on a street parallel to a street on which a pursuit is occurring.
  2. *Vehicle Paralleling:* A deliberate offensive tactic by one or more patrol vehicles to drive alongside the pursued vehicle while it is in motion.

F. *Pursuit Driving:* Pursuit driving is an active attempt by a law enforcement officer operating a motor vehicle and utilizing emergency warning lights and an audible device to apprehend one or more occupants of another moving vehicle when the officer reasonably believes that the driver of the fleeing vehicle is aware of the officer's attempt to stop the vehicle and is resisting apprehension by increasing vehicle speed, ignoring the officer or otherwise attempting to elude the officer.

G. *Pursuit Vehicles:*

1. *Primary Unit:* The police vehicle that initiates a pursuit or any unit that assumes control of the pursuit as the lead vehicle (the first police vehicle immediately behind the fleeing suspect).

2. *Secondary Unit:* Any police vehicle which becomes involved as a backup to the primary unit and follows the primary unit at a safe distance.

H. *Roadblock:* A restriction or obstruction used or intended for the purpose of preventing free passage of motor vehicles on a roadway in order to effect the apprehension of a violator.

1. *Avenue of Escape:* A gap in a roadblock which requires the violator to decrease the vehicle's speed to permit the violator to bypass the roadblock.

2. *Blocking Vehicle:* A motor vehicle, often a law enforcement vehicle, which is placed perpendicular to a roadway or angled in such a way as to create a roadblock.

I. *Supervisor:* A police officer who, by virtue or rank or assignment, is responsible for the direction or supervision of the activities of other police officers.

J. *Vehicle Contact Action:* Any action undertaken by the pursuing officer intended to result in contact between the moving police vehicle and the pursued vehicle.

K. *Violator:* Any person who a police officer reasonably believes: (1) has committed an offense enumerated in Appendix A of this policy or (2) poses an immediate threat to the safety of the public or other police officers.

I. DECIDING WHETHER TO PURSUE

A police officer has the authority, at all times, to attempt the stop of any person suspected of having committed any criminal offense or traffic violation. It is clear that while it is the officer who initiates the stop, it is the violator who initiates the pursuit. The officer's decision to pursue should always be undertaken with an awareness of the degree of risk to which the law enforcement officer exposes himself and others. The officer must weigh the need for immediate apprehension against the risk created by the pursuit.

A. Authorization to Pursue

1. A police officer may only pursue

a. When the officer reasonably believes that the violator has committed an offense of the first or second degree, or an offense enumerated in Appendix A of this policy, or

b. When a police officer reasonably believes that the violator poses an immediate threat to the safety of the public or other police officers.

2. Pursuit for motor vehicle offenses is not authorized under the above criteria unless the violator's vehicle is being operated so as to pose an immediate threat to the safety of another person.

B. In the event that one of the authorization requirements is satisfied, a pursuit should not be automatically undertaken. An officer must still consider the following factors:

1. Likelihood of successful apprehension.

2. Whether the identity of the violator is known to the point where later apprehension is possible.

3. Degree of risk created by pursuit

a. Volume, type, speed and direction of vehicular traffic.

   b. Nature of the area: residential, commercial, school zone, open highway, etc.
   c. Population density and volume of pedestrian traffic
   d. Environmental factors such as weather and darkness
   e. Road conditions: construction, poor repair, extreme curves, ice, etc.
 4. Police Officer characteristics
   a. Driving skills
   b. Familiarity with roads
   c. Condition of police vehicle
C. Terminating the pursuit
 1. The pursuing officer shall terminate the pursuit
   a. If instructed to do so by a supervisor, or
   b. If the officer believes that the danger to the pursuing officers or the public outweighs the necessity for immediate apprehension of the violator, or
   c. If the violator's identity is established to the point where later apprehension may be accomplished and where there is no immediate threat to the safety of the public or police officers, or
   d. If the pursued vehicle's location is no longer known or the distance between the pursuing vehicles and the violator's vehicle becomes so great that further pursuit is futile, or
   e. If there is a person injured during the pursuit and there are no police or medical personnel able to render assistance, or
   f. If there is clear and unreasonable danger to the police officer or the public. A clear and unreasonable danger exists when the pursuit requires that the vehicle be driven at excessive speeds or in any other manner which exceeds the performance capabilities of the pursuing vehicles or police officers involved in a pursuit, or
   g. If advised of any unanticipated condition, event or circumstance which substantially increases the risk to public safety in the pursuit.

II. ROLE OF THE PURSUING OFFICER

A. The decision to initiate and/or continue a pursuit requires weighing the need to immediately apprehend the violator against the degree of risk to which the officer and others are exposed as a result of the pursuit.
B. Upon the commencement of a pursuit, the pursuing officer will immediately activate emergency lights, audible device and headlights.
C. Once the pursuit has been initiated, the primary unit must notify communications and a superior officer providing as much of the following information as is known:
 1. Reason for the pursuit.
 2. Direction of travel, designation and location of roadway.
 3. Identification of the violator's vehicle: year, make, model, color, vehicle registration number and other identifying characteristics.
 4. Number of occupants.
 5. The speed of the pursued vehicle.
 6. Other information that may be helpful in terminating the pursuit or resolving the incident.

III. VEHICULAR PURSUIT RESTRICTIONS

A. No pursuits will be conducted
 1. In a direction opposite to the flow of traffic on a divided highway.
 2. In a police vehicle in which an individual who is not a law enforcement officer is either the driver or passenger.
B. No more that two police vehicles (primary unit and secondary unit) shall become actively involved in a pursuit unless otherwise specifically directed by a supervisor.

C. A motorcycle officer may initiate a pursuit, but will relinquish primary unit status immediately upon the participation of a marked police vehicle.

D. An unmarked police vehicle will not participate in a vehicular pursuit unless it is equipped with an emergency light and an audible device. The unmarked car shall relinquish primary unit status immediately upon the participation of a marked vehicle.

E. To diminish the likelihood of a pursuit, a police officer intending to stop a vehicle for any violation of the law shall, when possible and without creating a threat to public safety, close the distance between the two vehicles prior to activating emergency lights and an audible device.

F. Throughout the course of a vehicular pursuit, pursuing officers shall not attempt to overtake or pass the violator's moving vehicle.

G. Upon approaching an intersection controlled by traffic signals or signs, or any other location at which there is a substantially increased likelihood of collision, the operator of any pursuit vehicle shall, prior to entering the intersection, reduce the vehicle's speed and control the vehicle so as to avoid collision with another vehicle or a pedestrian. The officer shall observe that the way is clear before cautiously proceeding through the intersection.

H. Officers involved in a pursuit will not engage in vehicle paralleling.

I. There shall be no street paralleling along the route unless the pursuit passes through a patrol's assigned area. A patrol that is parallel-street-pursuing shall not join or interfere with a pursuit, and shall stop all pursuit-related activity at the boundary of its assigned area.

J. Boxing in or heading off a violator's moving vehicle is permitted only under extraordinary circumstances. These tactics substantially increase the risk inherent in the pursuit and shall only be employed:

  1. At low speeds, and
  2. With the approval of a supervisor, or
  3. In response to an imminent threat to the safety of the public or a police officer.

K. Roadblocks must only be employed as a last resort in circumstances where deadly force would otherwise be justified.

  1. The use of a roadblock must be authorized by a supervisor.
  2. At no time will a roadblock be established until all pursuing police vehicles are made aware of the roadblock and its location and have acknowledged this awareness.
  3. Once a roadblock has been established and a vehicle or barricade has been positioned in the roadway, there shall be:
    a. adequate distance to see the roadblock
    b. an avenue of escape
    c. no one in the blocking vehicle(s).

L. Officers involved in a pursuit shall not fire any weapon from or at a moving vehicle nor engage in any vehicle contact action except as a last resort to prevent imminent death or serious injury to the officer or another person where deadly force would otherwise be justified.

IV. ROLE OF THE SUPERVISOR

Upon being notified or becoming aware of the pursuit, the supervisor shall decide as quickly as possible whether or not the pursuit should continue.

A. The supervisor shall permit a pursuit to continue only if

  1. There is a reasonable belief that the violator has committed an offense of the first or second degree, or an offense enumerated in Appendix A of this policy, or
  2. There is a reasonable belief that violator poses an immediate threat to safety of the public or other police officers.

B. The supervisor shall order a pursuit terminated at any time if he or she concludes that the danger to the pursuing officers or the public outweighs the necessity for immediate apprehension of the violator.

C. The supervisor shall order the pursuit terminated if the suspect's identity is established to the point where later apprehension may be accomplished and where there is no immediate threat to public safety.
D. In recognition of the overall population density and volume of vehicular traffic in this State, and the increased risk attendant to prolonged vehicular pursuits, a supervisor shall order the termination of any pursuit of protracted duration unless the supervisor determines that further pursuit is justified to respond to an immediate threat to public safety.
E. The supervisor shall ensure, for the duration of the pursuit, that this policy and agency procedures are followed by all officers.

V. ROLE OF POLICE COMMUNICATIONS

A. The communications operator shall:
  1. Immediately notify a police supervisor of a pursuit in progress if a supervisor has not already been otherwise notified;
  2. Keep the supervisor apprised of the duration and progress of the pursuit.
B. When possible, a police supervisor shall determine whether there is a need to assume control over and coordinate pursuit related communications.
C. All law enforcement agencies shall establish procedures to ensure that radio channels remain open for pursuit related transmissions and that all necessary information is made available to officers involved in the pursuit.

VI. REINSTATING PURSUITS

A. Reinstatement of any previously terminated pursuit shall be undertaken consistent with the authorization criteria for originally initiating a pursuit.

VII. INTERJURISDICTIONAL PURSUITS

A. The original pursuing jurisdiction shall provide timely notification of a pursuit in progress to any other jurisdiction into which the pursuit enters.
  1. Notifying another jurisdiction that a pursuit is in progress is not a request to join the pursuit. The pursuing agency shall advise if assistance is necessary. Whenever the pursuing officers are unfamiliar with the roadways and terrain of the jurisdiction into which the pursuit has entered, the pursuing agency shall, when possible, seek the assistance of, and be prepared to relinquish the pursuit to, the other agency.

VIII. PURSUIT REPORTING

A. All law enforcement officers who operate law enforcement vehicles in vehicular pursuit situations shall be required to file a pursuit incident report. Pursuit incident reports are to be filed in a manner established by agency operating procedures and should contain, at a minimum, the following information:
  1. Location, date and time of pursuit initiation.
  2. Location, date and time of pursuit termination.
  3. Highest speed achieved, weather conditions, road surface and description of pursuit area.
  4. Reasons for initiating and terminating the pursuit.
  5. Consequences of the pursuit, such as accidents, injuries or fatalities.
  6. Whether or not the violator was apprehended.
  7. The offenses with which the violator was charged.
B. All law enforcement agencies shall prepare an annual agency Vehicular Pursuit

Summary Report for submission to the county prosecutor. The annual report shall be submitted on the Police Vehicular Summary Report Form and shall contain the following information:

1. Total number of pursuits
2. Number of pursuits resulting in accident, injury, death and arrest.
3. The number and type of vehicles involved in accidents (police, violator, third party).
4. A description of individuals injured or killed (police, violator, third party).
5. The number of violators involved and arrested in pursuit incidents, including passengers.

IX. VEHICULAR PURSUIT REVIEW

A. All law enforcement agencies shall establish procedures for the formal review of all pursuit incident reports.
B. Pursuit incidents should be reviewed for compliance with applicable policy and department operating procedures.
C. Pursuit incidents should also be reviewed to identify the need for remedial training of individual officers or specific areas of emphasis in agency-wide training regarding pursuit situations and the application of pursuit policies and procedures.
D. Periodic review of pursuit incidents and summary pursuit information should be conducted in order to identify any additions, deletions or modifications warranted in departmental pursuit procedures.

X. TRAINING

A. All officers shall attend in-service vehicular pursuit training twice annually. This in-service training shall be held simultaneously with use of force training which is provided in the firearms requalification process.
B. Vehicular pursuit training shall consist of knowledge of applicable statutes, familiarization with statewide police pursuit policy and departmental procedures, and decision making skills.
C. An annual report shall be filed with the county prosecutor or, in the case of certain state law enforcement agencies, with the Director of the Division of Criminal Justice. The report will confirm in-service pursuit training of all police officers in conjunction with semi-annual firearm requalification and the use of force training.

INDIVIDUAL AGENCY POLICIES

Law enforcement agencies may adopt more restrictive policies as to pursuit procedures or more extensive training and reporting requirements. In the event an agency chooses to do so, the agency policies and procedures will prevail with respect to applicability to that agency's personnel.

Dated: *January 29, 1993*

APPENDIX A

OFFENSES IN ADDITION TO THOSE OF THE FIRST AND SECOND DEGREE FOR WHICH VEHICULAR PURSUIT MAY BE AUTHORIZED UNDER SUBSECTION IA(1)(a)

Death by Auto 2C:11-5	Burglary 2C:18-2
Aggravated Assault 2C: 12-1b	Automobile Theft 2C:20-2
Criminal Restraint 2C:13-2	Theft by Extortion 2C:20-5
Aggravated Criminal Sexual	Escape 2C:29-5
Contact 2C:14-3a	Manufacturing, Distributing or
Arson 2C:17-1b	Dispensing of CDS 2C:35-5b

Source: New Jersey Division of Criminal Justice, Trenton, N.J. Used by permission.

17

Crime Prevention and Criminal Investigation

KEY WORDS AND PHRASES

Opportunity reduction programs
Informal social control programs
Crime analysis
Target hardening
Operation Identification
Preliminary investigation
Uniformed crime investigator
Criminal investigation division
Probable cause
Physical evidence

Case management
Solvability factors
Interviewing
Interrogation
Neighborhood contacts
Informants
Evidence Technicians
DNA testing
VICAP
Psychological profiling

The traditional view of the police crime control role can be stated very simply: The police should prevent crime, and they should investigate and solve all the crimes they have failed to prevent. However neat this mission statement, it is somewhat misleading in its suggestion that the existence of crime and of unsolved cases is a failure of policing. Police failures may allow some crimes to occur and may allow some criminals to escape justice, but such cases are the exception. In general, most crime has roots in social, economic, and psychological factors that can be affected by the police only indirectly, if at all.

Recognition that most crime is more closely associated with failures at the societal and community levels than with any inadequacies of the police is not new. Sixty years ago, August Vollmer, father of modern American policing and mentor of O. W. Wilson, wrote:

> Although there are still policemen who believe there is more crime prevention
> in the end of their nightsticks than in all efforts to find the causes of crime and

devise methods of treatment, long experience with delinquents and criminals has demonstrated to others that attempts to discourage adult offenders from their antisocial deeds is only surface treatment of disorders that go much deeper. Studies of juvenile delinquents bear out this theory; for when unadjusted boys and girls in school can be traced step by step in their development into habitual professional criminals, the corrective value of punishment for the adult misfits appears futile and absurd. Such habit and behavior patterns are not easily changed; certainly there is evidence that the punitive and reformative methods now employed have not effected great improvement. Information now available indicates that the causes of crime are many, and that probably only concerted, coordinated action by all social agencies will reduce criminality. The police, with their opportunities for firsthand information, and their primary responsibility for protection of society against crime and criminals, must take the lead in community programs for crime prevention. (Vollmer, 1936:3)

Vollmer's commentary is worthy of close attention for two reasons. First, unlike similar observations by more recent scholars and social critics, it was made by the foremost *police* practitioner of his era, rather than by someone whose conclusions, however accurate, were based almost exclusively on studies of what others had done. When Vollmer wrote, he was informed not only by the best scholarship of the time but also by his own work on the front lines of American policing. Thus, he was exempt from the criticism that he viewed the world from an ivory tower, and the fact that he reached conclusions so close to those of scholars and alleged bleeding hearts—and so different from what one might expect from a hardened police veteran—should cause us to pay close heed to them.

Second, and more important, like similar conclusions and observations of the scholars and critics who followed him (e.g., Fogelson, 1977; National Advisory Commission on Civil Disorders, 1968; President's Commission on Law Enforcement and Administration of Justice, 1967; Silberman, 1978; Skogan, 1990), Vollmer's commentary is enduringly accurate. Vollmer's experience and studies taught him that no matter how smartly deployed and individually capable police officers may be, it is unrealistic to expect them to have effects that would be in any way comparable to improvements in such correlates of crime as weak or nonexistent family structure; the absence of positive role models for young people; the absence of strong, supportive community networks; poverty; racism; ineffective educational systems; nonexistent recreational resources and chances to take part in legitimate leisure resources; and lack of opportunity. To understand the power of these forces relative to that of the police and the criminal justice establishment, all one must do is look carefully at our most crime-free environments. Almost invariably—and like most nearly crime-free Western industrial democratic nations—these areas are tightly knit, prosperous communities where the problems described above are minimal or nonexistent and where the work of the police and criminal justice officials is a stress-free pleasure.

Over the long term, therefore, the answer to the U.S. crime problem is not to be found in hiring more officers and training them better, or in building more and better prisons. Instead, it lies in attempting to change conditions in our most crime-ridden environments so that they more closely resemble those in places in which crime, violence, and fear do not shape and diminish everyday life. This is a massive undertaking, and if it is ever to be accomplished, it is likely to take generations. It is, however, an undertaking in which—by virtue of their front-row view of crime, violence, and the conditions that cause them—police can serve as *activists,* promoting and stimulating the kinds of changes necessary to have meaningful effects on crime. In addition, until the ideal state of a crime-free society is achieved, the police must continue to do everything possible to prevent and investigate crime; but they must do so in the knowledge that they hold no magic bullet that will solve the *crime problem.*

CRIME PREVENTION

The core of Sir Robert Peel's mission for the police is the prevention of crime and disorder. In Peel's view, the best measure of whether this task is being accomplished is an absence of police business. Operationalizing this view has been problematic. As suggested above, the presence or absence of police business—whether related to crime, disorder, or any other matter—may have little or nothing to do with the effectiveness of the police. Second, it is easier—and perhaps more fun—to measure how often and well police take action in response to crime and disorder than it is to assess the effects of their prevention efforts. Counting crimes solved is no problem, but there is no precise way to determine how many crimes police may have prevented. Newspaper headlines, movies, and television shows praise and glamorize the detectives who solve crimes, but they rarely pay heed to the crime prevention specialists whose quiet efforts may have far greater effects on the quality of life in a community or throughout the society. Consequently, in the consciousness of the public—and of many police officials—crime prevention has always taken second place to criminal investigation.

Recent serious rethinking of the police role and the limits on police ability to prevent and detect crime, however, has led to many new realizations about crime prevention. The team policing experiments of the 1970s, along with the Los Angeles Police Department's basic car plan and the more recent adoption of community and problem-oriented policing models are attempts to move closer to Vollmer's notion of a police service that is at the vanguard of mobilizing communities to address the conditions that cause crime and that allow it to go unpunished.

Commentators have suggested that crime prevention programs may be classified into two broad types based on the theories that underlie them. *Opportunity reduction programs* are designed to make it more difficult, or even impossible, to commit crimes. *Informal social control programs* are designed to strengthen the forces and institutions—family, schools, communities, and the others discussed above—that may influence potential offenders' behavior into more positive directions (see, e.g., Rosenbaum, Hernandez, and Daughtry, 1991:98–100). These theories provide a useful way to think of crime prevention. One of the major reasons that these theories are useful is that they reject the former conventional police wisdom, which held that although it was possible for police to reduce the opportunity to commit crime, they could not affect the desire to commit crime. This logic has been displaced, as police have conducted successful programs that have reduced both the opportunity and the desire to engage in crime.

Opportunity Reduction Programs

The fundamental opportunity reduction program, of course, is *preventive patrol:* a highly visible, uniformed police presence that is designed in large measure to present an image of police omnipresence and to make potential offenders think twice about attempting to commit a crime. As suggested earlier in this volume (see especially Chapters 6 and 16), much has been learned about the presumed value of preventive patrol in the years since the establishment of the London Metropolitan Police. More specifically, the Kansas City Preventive Patrol Experiment (Kelling et al., 1974) suggested that it is not sufficient to merely assign uniformed officers to random patrol and that more sophisticated means of deploying personnel may be necessary. In addition, more recent experience has suggested that, through proactive problem-solving and community mobilization techniques, patrol officers may be able to ameliorate some of the social and community conditions that make crime attractive to young people (Eck and Spelman, 1987; Goldstein, 1990; Trojanowicz and Bucqueroux, 1990). In this sense, preventive patrol officers who make it a point to get to know the people on their beats, who serve as role models for young people, and who work with other institutions to identify and solve problems are engaged in strengthening informal social controls, as well as in carrying out opportunity reduction programs.

Crime Analysis. One of the prerequisites of a sound preventive patrol program is *crime analysis,* or *field operations analysis* (see Chapters 6 and 7). Such programs are most effective when they are based on information gained through officers' close ties to the communities they patrol, as well as on such seemingly objective data as reported crimes. Residents and businesspersons often know much more about what ails a community than is reflected in the accounts of those who choose to report their victimizations to the police. The existence of a newly established drug trafficking location, for example, is not likely to be reflected in official reports until those who operate or frequent it have hurt someone in the community. It is far better for officers to have their antennae out for information about such places than to wait for innocent victims to report that they have been mugged by drug addicts or to be caught in the middle of drive-by shootings involving drug dealers.

Several principles are useful in ensuring that crime analysis is informed by community input. First, the agency's community relations apparatus should be used extensively, and its personnel should never lose sight of the fact that their task—in effect, making friends for the department—is a way of improving a community's quality of life and of preventing crime, rather than an end in itself. In some agencies, because of mistakes and questionable motives on one or both sides, community relations offices have turned into isolated enclaves, at odds with the rest of their agencies. Community relations personnel who share their departments' goals and who know that their efforts are supported by the top administration are an invaluable asset in building liaisons with any jurisdiction's most troubled people, as well as with its best informed and most influential.

Second, the flow of information about crime and suggestions for methods of preventing it often are facilitated by the establishment of formal police-community councils that bring citizens and police together on a regular basis. Where such bodies do not exist, they should be established. In doing so, it should be kept in mind that actively involving any citizen complaint review board or other such body in this process pays several benefits. It involves these groups in work that officers see as more positive than simply determining whether police have acted wrongly in specific cases, and may reduce police resistance to their role in reviewing complaints. In addition, it expands the role of such bodies beyond that of simple after-the-fact criticism of policies. Instead, it involves them in policy formulation, a task that is likely both to avert complaints and to increase the board's appreciation for the difficulty of designing policies or programs (involving crime prevention or anything else) that are likely to satisfy everybody.

Third, *the most important component of any police-community relations effort is the officer on the street.* This is a fact that sometimes has been forgotten or ignored by police administrators. Especially after the civil disorders of the 1960s, many police agencies established very elaborate and sophisticated community relations and crime prevention programs but ignored the reality that the first and most influential contact between citizens and their agencies almost invariably was the patrol officer. As a consequence of police failure to involve such officers in crime prevention planning and programs, citizens often were not advised that headquarters had available crime prevention specialists who could suggest ways to make their homes or businesses less vulnerable to crime. More typically, because they had been excluded, patrol officers simply did not take crime prevention or community relations seriously or, even, became antagonistic to it. Many inner-city police chiefs are familiar with the complaint that, when asked for advice on preventing crime, officers have told citizens to move out of town to safer places. If community relations programs in support of crime prevention are to be effective, those who perform preventive patrol must be a part of such programs.

Fourth, bringing patrol officers into the fold on these programs probably requires a rethinking of agency reward systems so that they honor demonstrable excellence in crime prevention. Officers do not take seriously official messages that prioritize crime prevention when they see that it carries no rewards, and that a department's system of official recognition focuses exclusively on arrests, shootings, and other spectacular actions that take place after crimes have occurred (see Box 17-1).

Providing Information That Helps Citizens Avoid Victimization.

A public that has a clear understanding of the extent and nature of crime in its community and on ways to avoid it is less likely than an uninformed citizenry to suffer victimization. By definition, an informed public also does not suffer from the misconception—common in many comparatively quiet neighborhoods—that their communities are far more dangerous and crime-ridden than is true.

BOX 17-1. CALEA Crime Prevention and Community Relations Standards

45.1.1 The agency's crime prevention function provides for the following:

a. targeting programs by crime types and geographic area on the basis of analysis of local crime data;
b. targeting programs to address community perceptions or misperceptions of crime; and
c. evaluating the effectiveness of crime prevention programs.

45.1.2 The agency assists in organizing crime prevention groups in residential and business areas targeted for such activity in standard 45.1.1 and maintains liaison with these and other interested community groups.

45.1.3 If granted the opportunity by the jurisdiction's governing authority, the agency provides crime prevention input into development and/or revision of zoning policies, building codes, fire codes, and residential/commercial building permits.

45.2.1 The community relations function provides the following at a minimum:

a. establishing liaison with formal community organizations and other community groups;
b. informing all personnel that they are responsible for achieving the agency's community relations objectives;
c. developing community relations policies for the agency;
d. publicizing agency objectives, problems, and successes;
e. conveying information transmitted from citizens' organizations to the agency;
f. improving agency practices bearing on police-community relations;

g. identifying training needs through interviews with citizen representatives, consultations with those involved in internal investigations, and conference with supervisors;
h. establishing community groups where they are needed.

45.2.2 At least quarterly, the person or persons responsible for the community relations function prepares and submits to the chief executive officer a report that includes, at a minimum, the following elements:

a. a description of current concerns voiced by the community;
b. a description of potential problems that have a bearing on law enforcement activities within the community;
c. a statement of recommended actions that addresses previously identified concerns and problems.

45.2.3 A survey of citizen attitudes and opinions is conducted at a minimum of every two years with respect to:

a. overall agency performance;
b. overall competence of agency employees;
c. officers' attitudes and behavior toward citizens;
d. concern over safety and security within the agency's service area as a whole;
e. recommendations and suggestions for improvement.

Source: Commission on Accreditation for Law Enforcement Agencies, 1994.

This latter point is critical, and it mandates that police counter the false impression of constant warfare and violence on the streets which often is transmitted by television news and sensational tabloid newspapers. Citizens—especially seniors who have seen influxes of people from unfamiliar cultures change their communities' demographics—may link these news stories with

the strangers they see on the streets and may wrongly come to believe that
they are in great personal danger whenever they venture from home.

Police should not attempt to convince citizens that streets are not dangerous when they may be, but the enormous costs of unrealistic fears of crime
mandate that police counter such misimpressions. When people are too fright-
ened to use their streets, their neighborhoods deteriorate, businesses close,
and the quality of their lives suffer. Wesley Skogan describes this cycle in
greater detail:

> Fear . . . can work in conjunction with other factors to stimulate more rapid
> neighborhood decline. Together, the spread of fear and other local problems
> provide a form of positive feedback that can further increase levels of crime.
> These feedback processes include (1) physical and psychological withdrawal
> from community life; (2) a weakening of the informal social control processes
> that inhibit crime and disorder; (3) a decline in the organizational life and mo-
> bilization capacity of the neighborhood; (4) deteriorating business conditions;
> (5) the importation and domestic production of delinquency and deviance;
> and (6) further dramatic changes in the composition of the population. At the
> end lies a stage characterized by demographic collapse. (Skogan, 1986:210)

Broken windows theory

Sensitized to the need to avoid this cycle, police should be capable of providing citizens with information regarding security and crime prevention techniques. These include such simple expedients as advising citizens to make certain that they avoid being on streets alone late at night, plan their walking
routes to include well-lighted areas, park their cars in well-lighted areas, lock
their doors and remove their ignition keys from their cars, do not leave packages or valuables exposed in their parked cars, and refrain from cashing pension, welfare, or unemployment checks on the days when they traditionally arrive in the mail.

More specific information can be provided to groups who are vulnerable
to certain types of crime. Elderly citizens, for example, frequently are targeted
by those whose income is derived from confidence games and sales frauds.
Homeowners should be alerted to such home improvement scams as "paving"
driveways with used motor oil rather than asphalt. Gays, women, and the
lonely also are prone to specific types of victimization and, wherever possible,
should be advised on how to avoid it.

Target Hardening. *Target hardening* involves a variety of techniques and
strategies designed to reduce the vulnerability of potential targets of crime,
whether they be things, places, or people. As CALEA Standard 45.1.3 (Box
17-1) suggests, a very important component of such an effort is the law. The
prevention efforts of fire departments have long been supported by elaborate
building codes that prescribe in great detail the steps that builders and building operators must take to avoid fires and the victimizations that might otherwise be associated with them. For generations, however, developers have put
up shopping malls and *gallerias,* hotels, motels, apartment complexes, bus terminals, indoor parking lots, and even roadways with nary a thought nor a restriction related to crime prevention.

This has changed. In recent years, many jurisdictions have come to see that
there is such a thing as *criminogenic architecture* that, always by oversight,

Bud Lee for McGraw-Hill.

makes it easy for offenders to complete and escape from their crimes. In some cases, some of the crime risks related to engineering and architecture are unavoidable. New York City's labyrinthine subway system has no doubt fostered crime by making it possible for offenders to run down into crowded subway stations and quickly disappear in any of several directions.[1] In Los Angeles, the elaborate freeway system has had a similar effect above the ground. In other cases, experience has taught that some types of architecture produce crime that can be reduced by alternative, albeit more expensive, designs. The high-rise public housing projects built in so many U.S. cities a few decades ago may have made efficient use of small parcels of land. In many cases, unfortunately, they also provided the anonymity, impersonality, and escape routes that made them centers of much crime and violence (see, e.g., Newman, 1972). Smaller, low-rise developments, we have since learned, preserve a sense of community, are easier to police, and enjoy far lower crime rates.

Police should seek out opportunities to participate in the development of building codes and debates about land use to offer their views on what is likely to advance or retard the cause of crime prevention. They should do their best to see that standards comparable to those involving fire prevention are developed for construction, alarms, and the like, and to offer regular inspection and suggestions for preventing crime in existing locations. They should also see that the public and its decision makers understand that it is in everybody's interest to take into account how easy or how difficult it will be to police any proposed public works project or private development. A place that is easy to police is usually a very safe place.

A target-hardening program in which U.S. police have participated successfully is *Operation Identification*. This involves a system of marking valuable items with the owner's social security number or other unique identifier and maintaining documentation of such markings in police files for ready identification in the event of theft and recovery. At first glance, this seems to be exclusively a crime *detection* device, but it also is a deterrent. Thieves and fences know they cannot be convicted for possessing stolen property that cannot be positively identified. They know also that most people make such positive identification impossible because they do not record the serial numbers of their television sets, VCRs, cameras, and other valuables. Without such marking, as an illustration, it is impossible for a victim to positively tell the court that *this* particular television set is the one that was stolen, rather than merely one of the thousands just like it. A marked item changes the thief's rationale because it gives notice that someone has taken the time to document ownership of property and that, if caught with the property, the thief and the person who buys it can be convicted for possessing stolen property.

Building Liaisons with Other Groups and Institutions. Throughout the United States, public service and special-interest groups have long been deeply involved in crime prevention. Traditionally, these have included organizations such as chambers of commerce and other merchants' groups, homeowners' associations, chapters of the American Association of Retired Persons, and service clubs such as the Lions and the Rotary Club. More recently, groups that serve as advocates for victims of domestic abuse, as well as organizations such as Mothers Against Drunk Driving (MADD) and Students Against Drunk Driving (SADD), have been established and have become eager to work with police on programs designed to minimize specific offenses. Every police agency should know who these groups are and should engage in mutual assistance programs with them.[2]

Imaginative police administrators have also enlisted local corporations in significant crime prevention efforts. After a series of violent crimes on the bicycle and jogging paths of Brooklyn's Prospect Park, for example, the New York City Police Department conceived of a means of creating instant access to police emergency telephones. The department asked for persons who frequently use the park to volunteer to wear distinctively colored jackets or T-shirts on their jogs, hikes, and bicycle tours and to carry cellular phones programmed for quick access to the 911 emergency number. After hundreds of people volunteered to serve as the community's eyes and ears in this way, the department's representatives solicited NYNEX, the local telephone carrier, to provide the phones that would be required for the programs to succeed. NYNEX did so, the program was operationalized and was widely advertised in the vicinity of the park, and crime dropped precipitously (Julian, 1995).

Like this unusual program, citizen patrols can be a valuable adjunct to police crime prevention efforts, but they present many problems. Often, they are formed in reaction to spectacular crimes or debilitating neighborhood conditions, and they have about them some aspects of vigilantism and maintenance of a particular racial or social status quo. Consequently, police should assess these groups carefully before doing anything that appears to approve of them. In addition, police should work out ground rules with them. It is important that they understand that they are not police officers or substitutes for police officers and that they must not interfere with police officers. They should also understand that they are most valuable when they call the police to situations worthy of investigation and that they should refrain from attempting to investigate suspicious matters themselves.

Informal Social Control Programs

The police history of involvement in programs designed, in effect, to reduce the desire to commit crime may be traced to the establishment of Police Athletic Leagues and the introduction of women in policing to serve as counselors for troubled youngsters. At present, police participate in or run Police Explorer programs through the Boy Scouts; youth centers, including the oft-maligned "midnight basketball" and safe haven programs that, usually with federal support, provide people of all ages with safe places to spend their time constructively.

CRIMINAL INVESTIGATION

Criminal investigation is a primary police function. It is the process through which police discover, preserve, gather, and evaluate evidence in order to identify, apprehend, and prosecute criminal offenders. A primary objective of the criminal investigation process is to reconstruct events at crime scenes through complete and impartial inquiry. The responsibility for the investigation of crimes and other serious incidents belongs to the department's operational level.

Since the early nineteenth century, the public's understanding of the criminal investigation process has been influenced by the exploits of mystery novel detectives.[3] As a result, the investigator's role has become enshrined with a mystique that has made it the most celebrated position in modern policing and a cultural institution of gigantic proportions (Klockars, 1985:63). The public's fascination with the detective as portrayed in the media—a clever, individualistic, imaginative, and streetwise cop who outwits criminals—has inspired a belief that criminal investigators are always able to discover evidence and successfully apprehend the offender. The reality of criminal investigation is far from the media image.

Much of what detectives do involves routine, elementary, boring chores associated with an endless amount of paperwork (Goldstein, 1977). Not all crimes can be solved, and those that are solved do not necessarily result in prosecution and conviction of the offender. However, for the police administrator, a more critical factor is the research finding that:

> the single most important determinant of whether or not a case will be solved is the information the victim supplies to the immediately responding officer. If information that uniquely identifies the perpetrator is not present at the time the crime is reported, the perpetrator, by and large, will not be subsequently identified. Of those cases that are ultimately cleared but in which the perpetrator is not identifiable at the time of the initial report, almost all are cleared as a result of routine police procedures. (Greenwood and Petersilia, 1975:vii)

As a result, the preliminary investigation conducted by the first officer to respond to the crime scene is an extremely important operational task. It is the foundation on which the success of the entire criminal investigation process rests. Therefore, it is important that a department's entire criminal investigation process and the procedures for routing case information between patrol and the investigation division be viewed by the administrator as an important area of administrative control that must be managed appropriately if these efforts are to be successful. Information is the lifeblood of criminal investigation.

In order to ensure the accountability and responsibility of a department's criminal investigative function, written procedures should be established by administrators to set guidelines for:

- Preliminary investigation by patrol officers
- Case evaluation by patrol supervisors
- Assignment of cases to the investigation division
- Case management procedures for the investigation division
- Case clearance procedures for the investigation division

Criminal activity and administrative discretion determine the degree of specialization needed by a department to accomplish the criminal investigation function. In most medium-sized and large police departments in the United States, criminal investigation is the joint responsibility of the patrol division and the criminal investigation division. In many small police departments, however, responsibility for the total investigation process is assigned to the patrol division. As the need arises, cases that require investigation beyond the preliminary stage in these departments are assigned to experienced, trained patrol officers under the control of the patrol commander.

Because of their first-responder role, patrol officers have the responsibility for conducting the preliminary investigation as well as for conducting the initial search for and gathering of case evidence (informational and physical). The investigative division is responsible for all follow-up investigations and the preparation of cases for prosecution. Promptness and speed are essential in criminal investigation because the opportunity for apprehension often decreases with the passage of time. Because of its 24-hour service and complete personnel coverage, the patrol division is able to meet this need and also is available for the immediate continuation of the investigation in the event that important leads are revealed. This use of patrol makes 24-hour service by the criminal investigation division unnecessary, except in departments that experience an exceptionally high demand for criminal investigative services. Departments with fewer than 200 members usually provide detective service on the daylight shift only and thus avoid the withdrawal of additional officers from patrol on other shifts.

Preliminary Investigation by the Patrol Force

The *initial,* or *preliminary,* investigation begins with an incident that is brought to police attention. This investigative stage should continue uninterrupted up to the point at which postponement of further inquiry would not jeopardize the chances of successful completion. The primary investigative responsibility of the first patrol officer is to respond to the scene of an incident and to establish in fact that a crime has been committed. Upon arrival at the scene, it is important that the officer make a quick visual survey of the area and persons present and that he or she also act to:

- Provide assistance to the injured as needed
- Locate and identify the complainant (victim) and all witnesses
- Interview the complainant and witnesses
- Observe all conditions (weather, etc.), lighting, events, and remarks
- Establish the time and place the crime occurred
- Maintain the security of the crime scene
- Locate and protect evidence
- Arrange for the collection of evidence
- Interrogate the suspect
- Effect the arrest of the perpetrator if present
- Determine solvability factors
- Report the incident fully and accurately
- Yield the responsibility to the follow-up investigator

These duties are the same for all preliminary investigations, but it should be remembered that crimes seldom are identical to others. This negates the possibility that the same sequence of investigative steps is applied in each case. It is important that the officer in charge of the investigation be flexible and respond to the case demands as they arise, while keeping in mind the objective of the preliminary investigation.

After establishing that a crime has been committed, the first officer's most important responsibility is to protect the scene from everyone not directly involved in the investigation. This includes other officers, the media, and curiosity seekers as well as family members and friends of victims. The presence of large numbers of officers at a crime scene is usually a waste of resources. Patrol officers and supervisors alike have a responsibility to stay away from the scene if it is determined that the suspect is gone and that no further assistance at that location is required. The identity of all persons who enter the crime scene should be carefully recorded in a case log along with the time of entry, purpose, and time of leaving.

Preliminary investigations of such priority cases as homicides and rapes are often conducted under the close supervision of the shift commander, the patrol supervisor, or a detective. The patrol supervisor should respond to the scenes of all serious crimes. In many departments, these supervisors have had extensive investigative experience and are as well qualified as detectives to investigate crimes. Any part of the preliminary investigation left incomplete by one shift should be continued by the next, until all the obvious clues have been analyzed. The supervisor in charge of the investigation has the responsibility to determine at what point in the investigation a case will be referred to the investigation division.

Crimes—such as frauds, bad-check cases, and vice activities—that elicit no immediate protest from victims and/or that are not reported to the police until after some time has elapsed usually do not require immediate action and consequently do not ordinarily justify preliminary investigation by patrol officers. Instead, these cases should be referred directly to the specialized investigators who will follow them through to conclusion.

Follow-up Responsibility for Patrol Officers. Patrol officers should take an active interest in investigating all crimes committed in their assigned areas. In many jurisdictions, however, follow-up investigation by patrol officers is impractical because of heavy demand for the patrol division's services. Clearances of these crimes by arrest and the recovery of stolen property are not ordinarily the responsibility of patrol officers because they do not have the necessary time and freedom of movement to conduct a protracted investigation. In addition, patrol officers often lack the specialized investigative training and experience required in many cases. These factors have led to the establishment of a separate investigative division in those departments that have a demanding investigative caseload and sufficient personnel to permit specialization.

In small departments, it is necessary to assign follow-up investigations to patrol officers, because they are the only personnel available or because the investigative staff is extremely limited. Where this is true, investigators should be assigned primarily to the most serious cases such as homicides, assaults likely to cause death, rape, and other index crimes.

These conditions have led some police administrators to create *uniformed crime investigator* programs in their departments (Berry, 1984). These programs select a specific number of competent and committed patrol officers to serve as uniform crime investigators and then train them to provide investigative coverage for each shift. These officers are responsible for handling felony investigations from beginning to end, including consultations with prosecuting attorneys and preparation of cases for court. In the Oceanside, California, Police Department, the major functions performed by uniformed crime investigators include (1) managing the crime scene, (2) photographing the crime scene, (3) developing latent prints, (4) conducting interviews and interrogations, (5) obtaining search and arrest warrants, (6) collecting, preserving, and cataloging physical evidence, (7) sketching crime scenes, (8) collecting body fluids, (9) making impressions, (10) making composites using the "Identi-Kit" process, (11) conducting neutron activation tests, (12) attending autopsies, and (13) maintaining field activity records (Berry, 1984:3).

Uniformed crime investigator programs provide trained criminal investigators without draining scarce patrol resources. The concept is a cost-effective use of personnel resources and enriches the role responsibilities of the officers selected for this assignment.

Patrol officers' involvement in criminal investigation also is stimulated by giving patrol officers credit for their accomplishments. Detectives and patrol supervisors should try to make sure that the chief recognizes praiseworthy accomplishments of individual officers by public commendation (e.g., in the department bulletin or newsletter, in departmental orders), where all members of the department can read that their efforts are appreciated. Patrol officers' service records also should reflect arrests for serious offenses and the recovery of property. Finally, media representatives should be influenced to give credit to the patrol division, whenever possible citing the names of the patrol officers who make arrests. Administrative responsibilities and problems associated with the criminal investigation process are lessened when investigators and patrol officers work well together. In addition, case clearances and stolen property recoveries—*the* measures of success in criminal investigation—cannot help but increase as cooperation between patrol and detective units grows.

Investigation by the Criminal Investigation Division. Preliminary investigations by patrol officers often result in arrest at the crime scene or very soon after the crime was committed. When this happens, detectives' responsibilities are reduced to the recovery of stolen property, postarrest preparation of the case for presentation in court, and investigation of other crimes, either reported or unreported, which the offender may have committed.

In most cases, however, members of the detective division responsible for conducting follow-up investigations should conduct a thorough review of all current case information relating to the commission of the crime. This review should include:

- Interviewing the initial investigating officer, the victim, and witnesses
- Examining all evidence seized
- Reviewing results from laboratory examinations
- Inspecting the crime scene
- Seeking and collecting additional evidence (physical and informational)
- Conducting searches
- Conducting interrogations
- Conducting identification lineups
- Identifying and arresting the offender(s)
- Determining the offenders' involvement in other unsolved crimes
- Maintaining liaison with the prosecutor's or state attorney's office
- Preparing cases for prosecution
- Preparing and maintaining case reports and files

Investigators' ability, training, experience, knowledge, and possession of information from past investigations qualify them to continue investigations until criminals have been apprehended or further effort seems futile. Investigators may utilize the facilities of the patrol division in routine additional searches for witnesses, physical evidence, and suspects and thus save their own time and energy for more difficult phases of the investigation. Detectives may reinterview a victim and principal witnesses in the hope that closer and more skillful questioning will uncover additional information or information acquired since the preliminary investigation. However, routine reinterviews that cover little more than the area of the preliminary investigation are decidedly undesirable.

In addition to the duties listed above, and no matter what type of crime they are attempting to solve, investigators must keep in mind the following factors necessary for a successful case prosecution: probable cause, identification, physical evidence, statements, and witness tracking data.

Probable Cause. *Probable cause* is sufficient evidence to lead a reasonable person to believe that a crime has taken place and that a particular individual or group of individuals is responsible for it. Investigators must collect sufficient case information to clearly establish the existence of probable cause in order for an arrest to take place. They should keep in mind that, while probable cause is the constitutional standard for arrest, a conviction requires proof beyond a reasonable doubt—and that prosecutors are unlikely to be interested in proceeding with cases in which this standard of evidence is plainly absent. Therefore, it is important that the investigator uncover sufficient evidence to support each element of the crime under investigation, as well as the identification of the person responsible for the crime.

Identification. In cases where an arrest has occurred, information on how the suspect was identified is extremely important to a successful prosecution. For example, was the arrest made on the basis of the complainant's description? Were the witnesses or complainant present at the time of arrest, or did they make an identification after a lineup was conducted? Did any distinctive personal features or clothing lead to the arrest of the defendant?

Physical Evidence. In the event that evidence has been secured, all factors relating to the method of identification, location, possession, condition, and seizure of the evidence must be recorded and maintained in the case file. An important rule in the collection of physical evidence at the crime scene is to never alter the position of, pick up, or even touch any object before it has been photographed and minutely described in official notes.

Statements. Whatever statements are taken from complainants, witnesses, and/or perpetrators should be recorded verbatim, either on tape or in the form of signed statements. In addition, when, where, and under what conditions the statement was given should be recorded as part of the investigative record. Sometimes suspects make conflicting statements to different officers; since these are invaluable to prosecutors, officers should compare notes on all statements obtained so that prosecutors have the best possible picture of the evidence. In addition, the record of each statement by suspects should indicate whether the statement was given before or after the *Miranda* advisements of the rights to silence and counsel, and whether the warnings were given at the beginning of any renewed sessions with suspects.

Witness Tracking Data. The cooperation of the complainant and witnesses is essential to the prosecutors' case. Since trials often are conducted months after arrest, prosecutors may have considerable difficulty locating important witnesses. Therefore, it is excellent practice for follow-up investigators to obtain as much identifying information as possible from complainants and witnesses. In addition to the information that investigators normally obtain (name, address, phone number), they should learn parties' work addresses and tele-

Despite its glamorous reputation, criminal investigation often involves tedious work.
Bud Lee for McGraw-Hill.

phone numbers, names of immediate work supervisors, social security numbers, and any other items that would assist in searching for such persons.

Case Management

After a preliminary investigation has been conducted, the final determination to close a case or to refer it for further investigation should rest with the patrol supervisor or shift commander. Thus, supervisors should be held specifically responsible for screening preliminary investigation information. This arrangement will fix accountability and will control decisions about the allocation of investigative resources. A primary objective is to provide enough early information to determine whether additional investigative resources should be devoted to the case. The supervisor should base this decision on case screening procedures established by a department directive. This directive should specify how such screening is to be conducted, by whom, and what criteria (e.g., solvability factors or agency experience) should be used (Commission on Accreditation Agencies, 1994: Standard 42.2.3).

An important criterion in case screening is the existence of *solvability factors,* elements of case information that have in the past proved to be important in determining the likelihood of solving a case (Greenberg et al., 1975). Especially in crimes that do not involve face-to-face contact between offenders and victims, research has found that the characteristics of the case, rather than the quality of the follow-up effort, generally determine overall investigative success or failure (Eck, 1979:3). Consequently, a number of police departments have developed case screening procedures based on a predetermined set of case solvability factors (Cawley et al., 1977; Urlacher and Duffy, 1990). These procedures are probably most often used by burglary investigators, and they include factors such as the following:

1. Were there witnesses to the crime?
2. Can a suspect be named?
3. Can a suspect be located?
4. Can a suspect be described?
5. Can a suspect be identified?
6. Was the suspect previously seen?
7. Can the suspect's vehicle be identified?
8. Is the property taken traceable?
9. Is a significant modus operandi present?
10. Is significant physical evidence present?
11. Was there opportunity for anyone but the suspect to commit the crime?
12. Is there some other significant reason to believe that the crime may be solved with a reasonable amount of investigative effort?
13. Is there an administrative or supervisory priority for investigating this case? Supervisory priority is governed by:
    a. Department policy
    b. Seriousness of the crime
    c. Totality of case circumstances
    d. Investigators' caseload

Except for more serious crimes, cases in which solvability factors are lacking should be eliminated from further investigation at this point. In all such instances, victims should be informed of this decision and the basis for it. However, they should be advised that if additional information should arise or a connection is made with similar cases, the investigation will be reopened and they will be contacted by the department. A case that is to be assigned to the investigation division for follow-up investigation should be taken over by an investigator within 24 to 48 hours of the crime (Eck and Williams, 1991).

Organizing and Staffing the Investigation Division

Adherence to organizational principles is as important in the structuring of the investigative function as it is in any other area of the department. In large police departments, the investigative division is a primary operational subdivision, similar to patrol and reporting directly to the commander of the operations division. In many of these departments, the organization of the investigation division is extremely specialized, with separate squads or details for each of the various crime categories and activities, such as homicide, burglary, and robbery. In most departments, however, the detective function is organized according to the kind of offenses to be investigated. There is a tendency toward grouping by functional specialty—e.g., by creating a *crimes against persons section* and a *crimes against property section*. However, since a substantial percentage of crime is related to drugs and/or youths, functional specialization may also be needed in jurisdictions in which these problems drive most of the investigative caseload; thus, a separate *juvenile section* may also be appropriate.

If further specialization is required within the crimes against persons section, units may be established for homicide, assault and sex offenses, and robbery offenses. In the crimes against property section, similar subdivisions should be established, if necessary, for burglary, theft, and auto-theft units. Pawnshop work should be carried out by personnel assigned to this section.

A *general assignment section* should conduct investigations of check cases, frauds, bomb and arson cases, and other non-index felony crimes, including crime categories not mentioned for the other sections as well as fugitive or warrant-service assignments from outside the agency.

The investigative division should ordinarily have an administrative unit, which should be responsible for review of all investigative reports to ensure compliance with Uniform Crime Report system requirements. This unit should also offer report processing and stenographic help (for all reports in small divisions and in major cases in larger investigative divisions) and general administrative support for the division, such as arrangements for travel and other administrative duties.

The classes of crimes that are assigned to individual detectives (or to groups of detectives who make up a section of the division in a large department) are determined by the proportional incidence of the various crimes, by offense seriousness, by the average length of time required in investigating them, and by investigators' ability. The small number of crimes in some classes may make it necessary to assign more than one class to a detective. When this is the case, the classes of crimes assigned to one detective should be similar or related in some manner.

For example, crimes such as passing bad checks, shoplifting, and short-changing are related because they are frequently committed against retail merchants. A detective assigned to these crimes enjoys some of the advantages of specialization because his or her field of attention is narrowed in terms of area and prospective victims. The merchants also become better acquainted with the investigator than they would if these three classes of crimes were divided among three detectives, who, in addition, were given other assignments.

Some classes of crimes may be grouped for assignment purposes because they are related, in the sense that one may grow out of another. For example, robberies, aggravated assaults, rapes, and sexual offenses sometimes result in homicide. Frauds, bad-check passing of all kinds, and counterfeiting are other examples of crimes that are similar in character.

In some jurisdictions, the number of crimes in one class may be more than can be adequately investigated by one detective. Because burglars who break into dwellings usually do not break into stores, or vice versa, burglaries may be advantageously divided into residential and nonresidential offenses. While individual house burglars may direct their attention almost exclusively to apartment houses, one-story dwellings, or duplexes—and individual store burglars may specialize in supermarkets, clothing stores, or warehouses—there generally is not a sufficient degree of persistency in such specialization to warrant further division by the police department. In the very largest departments, however, an advantageous further division may be made by analyzing the patterns of burglars who direct their operations against one type of property. For example, the separation of hotel crime from residential burglaries and of warehouse burglaries from other commercial burglaries may be desirable when the number in either category justifies the full time of one detective.

Staffing

In most medium-sized and large police departments, approximately 10 to 20 percent of sworn personnel are assigned to the investigation division (Heaphy, 1978; Eck and Williams, 1991). In individual departments, the number of detectives or investigators actually assigned to the division should largely be a matter of adjustment to workload, and some standards should be adopted to facilitate this kind of decision. Many experienced detective supervisors believe that the number of new cases (*routine* or *average* felony cases, such as burglaries or armed robberies without such complications as the injury of a victim) should not exceed a given amount per day, and that the number of active cases kept in pending status should be restricted. Finally, a specific period of time should be established as an automatic limitation on caseload—beyond which permission should be required for continuing with the assignment. Each of these determinants should be established in operational procedures by the division's commander. The number of detectives can be determined by the application of this kind of information.

Selection of Investigators

Routine patrol service, with its manifold problems and opportunities for experience in preliminary investigations, provides invaluable training for future detectives. In the past, some departments have promoted individuals to the position of detective based on one exemplary act, an outstanding arrest record, or the ability to fit in with the personalities of the officers in the investigative unit. This is an inappropriate practice. Sound management dictates that selection be based on criteria that carefully match the person with the performance needs of the investigative position to be filled.

The selection of personnel should be based on an assessment process that measures the potential candidate against criteria derived from a task analysis of each investigative position, the potential candidate's past performance evaluations, and supervisory recommendations. This candidate should possess the potential to develop the skills, knowledge, and abilities required to perform the duties of the investigative assignment as well as the minimum standard of formal education and police experience.

Investigators should possess a number of qualifications that include, but are not limited to, an interest in criminal investigation; knowledge of criminal law and rules of evidence; good analytical, problem-solving, communication, and interpersonal skills; initiative, imagination, ingenuity, and judgment; thoroughness in work habits; and an interest in people. DeLadurantey and Sullivan (1980:17) claim that the most desirable qualities in an investigator are thoroughness and tenacity. Since so much investigative work involves the chore of painstakingly checking and rechecking case information and a willingness to continue searching for leads, they probably are right.

The qualities needed in investigators are not exactly the same as those needed in supervisory officers. Some sergeants and lieutenants of superior ability would make mediocre detectives; similarly, some of the best investigators would not prove satisfactory as supervisory officers. For this reason it seems wise to select detectives from the patrol force but to refrain from rewarding them for their new responsibilities with a promotion to the rank of sergeant, since this practice automatically places them in an important supervisory position.

Detectives should be appointed to their positions, serving at the pleasure of the chief, not frozen into their positions by civil service. In no other operational division may the accomplishments and abilities of individual officers be so accurately appraised as in the detective service; within assignment types (e.g., burglary, homicide), clearances by arrest and percentages of property recoveries reflect rather closely the ability and effort of investigators. Administrators should consider this in evaluating patrol officers for potential service as investigators and in transferring detectives who have not demonstrated the skills necessary to remain in their position.

Managing the Investigation Division

The commanding officer of the investigation division should establish a case management system for all follow-up investigations. The object of this system is to enhance supervisory direction and control of the investigative process. This system should include the following steps:

1. All cases assigned to the division for follow-up investigation should be logged by time, date, type of crime, and investigator assigned.
2. Investigators should submit an initial investigation follow-up report within three working days of receipt of a case.
3. The investigation supervisor together with the investigator should review each case within seven working days after receipt of the initial follow-up report. The review should determine if the case should be closed or continued.
   a. If it is to be closed, a follow-up report must indicate that the complainant was interviewed, informed of the decision, and told the reason for closing the case. The closure report should also include a statement that the case was reviewed and that the supervisor authorized closing.
   b. If the investigation is to be continued, a case file should be established. The file should contain all case documentation as well as a case index sheet. All case follow-up reports should be numbered consecutively on the case sheet.
4. The investigative supervisor should review all active cases by the twenty-first working day following assignment.
5. Active investigations should not be closed, nor should they be permitted to extend beyond thirty working days without supervisory review.
6. The investigative supervisor should maintain an individual case assignment log for each investigator.

Successful administrative control of detective operations depends on the maintenance of records by the division administrative unit, secretary, or clerk. The following are needed as a minimum:

1. Attendance record, showing hours worked for each detective.
2. A performance record for each investigator listing all cases assigned to this individual, as well as case results (closures, arrests, property recovered).
3. A record of the court disposition of cases. Each case filed should be registered according to class of crime, listing:
   a. The date filed
   b. The number and names of defendants
   c. The court and docket number
   d. The date disposed of
   e. The disposition:
      (1) Whether the defendant pleaded guilty to the charge or to a lesser one
      (2) Whether the defendant was tried
      (3) Whether the defendant was found guilty or not guilty or whether there was no verdict
4. Monthly work summaries for each investigator, showing the number of days worked, number of cases assigned, and number cleared by arrest.

Individual case files for investigators are necessary even if a computerized case management system exists. The case file for each open case usually includes copies of reports, original crime scene notes, checklists, rough notes written by the investigator, statements of suspects and witnesses, and supervisors' instructions. The file may be kept in the detective's immediate work area during active investigation. When the case becomes inactive, however, only the investigator's original field notes and the original copies of statements should be retained by the criminal investigation division because of the need to protect these documents for court purposes. Central records should also receive supplemental or follow-up reports, together with copies of statements, diagrams, photographs, case summaries, and other material.

The criminal investigation division should not operate a separate case records and indexing system, nor should it administer the identification records function. Such arrangements almost invariably result in divisiveness and turf battles within the department.

Supervision

The nature of criminal investigation duties necessitates close and continuous supervision of detectives. This should include sound case management procedures, continuous review of the daily work of each investigator, and appraisal of his or her accomplishments in terms of clearances, recoveries, arrests, and convictions. Supervision will usually be adequate when the supervisor knows the extent of each detective's workload as well as the daily whereabouts and activities of each subordinate on duty.

In the criminal investigations division, the supervisor's span of control is influenced by so many variables that it is impossible to categorically establish a maximum number of subordinates who may be satisfactorily supervised. Experienced and capable detectives typically have developed great expertise in their work, especially when they perform highly specialized tasks, and they require little advice or consultation in handling their cases. As a rule, they refer only important matters to their supervising officers for decisions or information. Each detective should be instructed to confer with his or her immediate supervisor on important matters without unreasonable delay. Consequently, it seems desirable that the number of detectives reporting to a supervisor should not exceed ten. When two or more are assigned to the same class of crime investigation, there is some justification for designating one as the head to direct the investigations of all, thus creating a section within the division.

Qualifications of Supervisors

Most departments overstress the value of the seasoned investigator as a detective supervisor. Many administrators also believe that an effective supervisor in another division, such as traffic or patrol, would be completely unsuccessful in supervising investigators or detectives. While it is true that a first-line supervisor in a detective division must have a certain amount of appreciation for, and understanding of, investigative techniques, it should be emphasized that a supervisor in a detective or investigation division should be a good supervisor and handler of personnel first and an investigator second.

Planning Detective Operations

Two principles are useful in planning detective operations: (1) Relatively stable changes in crime frequency should lead to permanent changes in assignments and, perhaps, in organization; and (2) temporary fluctuations that result in unequal workloads should lead only to temporary changes in regular assignments, rather than to major organizational change.

The head of the detective division, who is responsible for such assignments, also participates in the development of procedures used not only by the detective division but also by the patrol division in the preliminary investigation of crimes. Procedures that involve patrol, records, and other divisions must, of course, be developed in cooperation with the commanding officers of these units.

Plans of operation must also be developed by the detective supervisor to meet intermittent and unusual needs created by criminal activity. In departments having a task force, the relationship of the detective division and the task force must be worked out by the detective and patrol division commanders, in conjunction with the task force supervisor. Operational plans designed to uncover information concerning crimes or to effect the discovery and seizure of suspects, wanted persons, personal property used for criminal purpose, stolen property, and evidence necessarily include tasks to be performed by the members of other divisions, principally the patrol division. Consequently, these plans must be prepared in cooperation with the other unit commanders concerned. Such plans will include special assignment of personnel to an area canvass or to certain places or businesses for stakeouts and surveillance.

Police administrators must be aware of some of the key concepts in operations conducted by the criminal investigation division. The department's directive system should specify the circumstances under which detectives should be summoned to crime scenes to carry out immediate investigations, detectives' working arrangements and hours of assignment, detectives' routine patrol duties, nighttime and on-call basis duties, and responsibilities regarding juveniles.

Immediate Investigation by Detectives. While on duty, all detectives available to investigate major crimes should be notified of reports of any serious crimes likely to be assigned to them. This is necessary so that they can respond to the scene of the crime and participate in the investigation to the extent warranted by the seriousness of the crime and by their own availability. When a patrol officer conducts the preliminary investigation, it is usually not necessary for the detective to be right there. Written guidelines should stipulate the level of seriousness that warrants active participation by a detective during the initial investigation. For example, homicides deserve the prompt attention of detective investigators. Frequently, so do such serious crimes as rape and aggravated assault, especially when the victims are in danger of dying. And robberies and burglaries resulting in heavy property loss occasionally may justify similar prompt detective investigation. But it is infrequently required for other classes of crimes.

Hours of Detective Duty. The need for 24-hour detective service typically exists only in larger cities (in excess of 500,000 population) but may be influenced by the extent and quality of the patrol division's preliminary investigations. In most departments, detective division quarters are usually open, and detectives are regularly on duty, from 8 A.M. until 5 P.M. Most cases may ordinarily be investigated with the least inconvenience to the victim, witnesses, and suspects during business office hours. Also, agencies and business houses whose records may contain information useful in crime investigations, as well as the courts and the prosecutor's office, are usually not open except during business hours.

The prevalence of two-wage-earner families, however, has resulted in an increase in the number of homes that are unoccupied during daytime hours during the business week. This is a special problem for detectives in some suburban departments, where homes are relatively isolated from each other and where all adult members of a family may be working in the central city during the day. For these departments, some detective operations are best scheduled during hours such as 12 noon to 8 P.M. Detectives may occasionally find it necessary to work at other hours in the investigation of some cases, and each should be permitted to vary his or her hours of work, with supervisory approval, to suit the immediate needs of the cases under investigation.

Detectives assigned to shifts after 5 P.M. usually cannot be given specialized assignments but must investigate all crimes committed during their tour of duty. Consequently, their work typically consists largely of preliminary investigation for the detective who is regularly assigned to that class of crime on the day shift. Since every on-duty police officer should be supervised, the absence of detective supervising officers necessitates administrative supervision of detectives after 5 P.M. by the commanding officer of the patrol division, as previously described, or by patrol supervisors.

There is greater need for detectives on duty during the early evening hours than in the period after midnight or 1 A.M. Indeed, even between 5 P.M. and midnight, the need for detectives usually is far less than one might anticipate. In cities of less than 150,000 population, these hours typically are marked by few crimes that require the immediate attention of detectives. The head of the detective division and individual detectives in departments that do not provide detective service after 5 P.M. should confer with the patrol division commander and platoon commanders regarding types of crimes that deserve immediate detective attention. (See Box 17-2.)

The Assignment of Detectives.   As a general rule, all cases should be investigated by detectives specializing in the particular type of crime involved. This does not mean, however, that there should be no deviation from the plan of assignment. Specialization of assignment fixes responsibility, simplifies training, permits a selection of personnel for assignment on a basis of special interest and ability, and provides a more accurate measure of the accomplishment of the individual detective. Frequent repetition of tasks increases skill and narrows the field of attention, thus permitting the detective to make informational contacts more effectively and to keep informed about a particular class of criminals and their operations. For example, detectives assigned to nonresidential burglaries are able to concentrate their attention on this class of crime and to learn about the type of persons who commit such burglaries, where they spend their time, and where they dispose of their stolen property.

Investigation of Juvenile Crimes.   For the following reasons, detectives should usually investigate to conclusion all crimes in the classes assigned to them, even though juveniles may be involved in some cases as victims or offenders:

1. The assignment of crimes for investigation on the basis of the offender's age is unsound because the age can rarely be established before arrest. Instead, it is usually determined when the offense is investigated.
2. To assume the offender's age before his or her identity is known usually results in controversy and friction, and the detective may initiate the reclassification of an offense as juvenile in order to avoid work or the embarrassment of a low percentage of clearances.
3. Divided responsibility is undesirable. The assignment of all crimes of a class to one division for investigation and clearance is feasible and avoids the splitting of responsibility.
4. The investigation division has as its primary purpose the investigation and clearance by arrest of the most serious crimes, and its members are usually best qualified by training and experience to investigate them. The juvenile division is not designed for this purpose.
5. The accomplishments of the investigation division and of its individual members are measured in terms of the clearance by arrest of assigned classes of crimes. Consequently, detectives should have authority to conduct investigations to conclusion. When responsibility for the investigation of a class of crime is divided between the investigative and juvenile

BOX 17-2. CALEA Criminal Investigation Standards

42.1 ADMINISTRATION

42.1.1 If the criminal investigation function does not provide 24-hour coverage, an on-call schedule of investigators is maintained.

42.1.2 The agency uses a case-screening system and specifies the criteria for continuing and/or suspending an investigative effort.

42.1.3 A written directive establishes a system of case file management for the criminal investigation function, to include:

a. a case status control system;
b. administrative designators for each case;
c. types of record to be maintained;
d. accessibility to the files; and
e. procedures for purging files.

42.1.4 A written directive specifies accountability for conducting preliminary and follow-up criminal investigations.

42.1.5 A written directive requires the following:

a. specification of criteria designating certain offenders as habitual/serious offenders;
b. identification of all cases in which a designated/serious offender is a party; and
c. notification to the prosecuting agency of such cases.

42.2 OPERATIONS

42.2.1 A written directive establishes procedures to be used in criminal investigation, to include:

a. information development;
b. interviews and interrogations;
c. collection, preservation, and use of physical evidence
d. execution of background investigations, and
e. surveillance.

42.2.2 A written directive establishes steps to be followed in conducting preliminary investigations, to include:

a. observing all conditions, events, and remarks;
b. locating and identifying witnesses;
c. maintaining and producing the crime scene and arranging for the collection of evidence; and

d. interviewing the complainant, witnesses, and suspects.

42.2.3 A written directive establishes steps to be followed in conducting follow-up investigations, to include at a minimum:

a. reviewing and analyzing all previous reports prepared in the preliminary phase, departmental records, and results from laboratory examinations;
b. conducting additional interviews and interrogations;
c. seeking additional information (from uniformed officers, informants);
d. planning, organizing, conducting searches, and collecting physical evidence;
e. identifying and apprehending suspects;
f. determining involvement of suspects in other crimes;
g. checking suspects' criminal histories;
h. preparing cases for court presentation; and
i. making a "second contact" with principals involved in a case requiring follow-up investigations or which has been closed.

42.2.4 The agency provides checklists to aid in criminal investigations.

42.2.5 Sworn positions in the criminal investigation function are the same as those used in the patrol function for:

a. rank titles;
b. salary schedules.

42.2.6 The agency has a system that provides for periodic attendance of criminal investigators at roll-call meetings conducted for patrol officers.

42.2.7 If investigative task forces are used, a written directive governs their activities, to include:

a. identifying the purpose;
b. defining authority, responsibilities, and written agreements;
c. establishing accountability; and
d. evaluating results and their continued necessity.

42.2.8 If technical aids for the detection of deception are used, a written directive governs their use

BOX 17-2. CALEA Criminal Investigation Standards *(continued)*

in criminal investigations. Examiners must be graduates of institutions providing training for this purpose.

42.2.9 A written directive specifies policies and procedures to be followed when using informants, to include:

a. inclusion of informants in a master file;
b. content of the informant file, to include biographical and background information, criminal history record, if any, and code name or number of each informant;
c. maintenance of an informant file;

d. security of informant file and related codes;
e. other methods to protect the identity of informants;
f. criteria for paying informants, if applicable;
g. precautions to be taken with informants, generally;
h. special precautions to be taken with juvenile informants
i. procedures for the use of informants by patrol officers.

Source: Commission on Accreditation for Law Enforcement Agencies, 1994.

---

divisions, the clearance rate no longer reflects the effectiveness of one division or of one detective.

A distinction must be made, however, between the investigation of crimes committed by juveniles and the disposition of individual juvenile offenders. The latter should be the exclusive responsibility of the juvenile division. Care must be observed to ensure that the handling of juveniles complies with legal guidelines. All interrogations of juvenile suspects should be conducted in the juvenile division area designated for this purpose and/or in the presence of a member of the juvenile division's staff.

Investigative Methods and Techniques

Investigative issues and matters that should be of greatest concern to police chief administrators include interviewing and interrogation, neighborhood contacts, second contact with complainants, use of available sources of information, school contacts, and use of information.

Interviewing and Interrogation. The fundamental skill required of the detective—the sine qua non of the investigating officer—is the technique of interviewing and interrogation. Authorities generally make a distinction between the two, preferring to say that *interviewing* is the method used to obtain information from victims and witnesses, while *interrogation* (implying the solicitation of information that is not voluntarily given under most circumstances) is reserved for suspects and prisoners.

Interrogation of suspects after their arrest is an important investigative task. Interrogation serves not only to obtain specific facts about the crime the person is believed to have committed but also to discover information about past crimes, as well as the criminal activity of others. Especially if they are supporting a drug habit, many offenders engage in numerous illegal activities. In many instances, information about past crimes and active criminals can be obtained by skillful interrogation.

Police executives must be certain, however, that citizens' rights are not abridged and that criminal cases are not lost through improper police handling of persons who would otherwise be convicted. Improper handling related to interrogations generally occurs in the following areas, all of which are regulated by constitutional law and by judicial interpretation:

- Coercion or involuntary confessions or admissions
- Delay in appearance before a magistrate
- Failure to properly inform suspects of their rights
- Failure to provide or allow access to counsel
- Pretrial publicity tending to prejudice a fair trial

Chief executives must make certain that each of these areas is covered by written policy and procedure so that there is no mistake about the intent to comply with constitutional requirements. At the stage where suspicion focuses on a suspect, the suspect must be advised of his or her right to remain silent, to have counsel, and to be informed that what is said may be used in a court of law.

Neighborhood Contacts. *Neighborhood contacts,* or the canvass of neighbors, merchants, and others in the vicinity of a crime are basic tools in any investigative system. It is estimated that the systematic use of neighborhood canvassing within a short time after the commission of a crime (such as the following morning) results in positive information of investigative value in 20 percent of cases. The neighborhood-contact procedure also has preventive value and leads to better relations between police and the community. Police administrators should require neighborhood canvasses as a routine part of criminal investigation, and when such canvasses have not been conducted, administrators should demand specific explanations of why not.

Second Contact with Complainants. Another useful concept is the second contact with complainants and victims. The police administrator should make certain that investigators recontact the complainant or victim in any criminal case that does not result in arrest or a closed case. Before action on the case can be suspended, the investigator should be required to indicate that he or she contacted the complainant a second time about one week or so after the initial call.

The second contact is valuable for supplying leads that are not available in any other way. Complainants and victims are usually very much interested in the circumstances of a crime or incident involving them; they may often learn additional details themselves because of this interest, or they may have remembered information that is helpful to the solution to the case. Since complainants are sometimes reluctant to take the initiative by calling the department, the second contact is of vital importance, and a substantial percentage of cases can be closed through this technique.

Use of Available Sources of Information. The ability to make use of whatever information may be available is one of the hallmarks of successful investigators. Sometimes investigators have no other information than part of a name or a fragment of some other identifying data, but through diligent search of various sources of information, they often develop this partial information into a complete case.

Police administrators should make sure that investigators are supplied with listings of sources of information which are available in their area. The following public and governmental sources should be listed in written directives concerning criminal investigations:

- Departments of motor vehicles
- City directories, particularly street-address directories (increasingly rare in recent years)
- Probation and parole offices
- Public welfare and social service agencies
- Offices of prosecutors in the local and neighboring jurisdictions
- Office of the state attorney general
- Repositories of court records in criminal, juvenile, civil, and probate proceedings
- County or municipal assessors' and recorders' offices
- Boards of elections
- Coroners' offices
- Boards of education and schools
- Bureaus of vital statistics
- Licensing bureaus
- U.S. Postal Service
- U.S. Immigration and Naturalization Service
- U.S. Coast Guard
- U.S. Drug Enforcement Administration
- U.S. Internal Revenue Service and the Alcohol, Tobacco, and Firearms Division
- Federal Bureau of Investigation
- Social Security Administration

The number of private organizations and businesses capable of providing information are as numerous as the investigator will permit them to be. Almost any business transaction or credit investigation can become a valuable resource. The following sources have frequently been used by investigators:

- Telephone directories (Each vehicle in the department should carry a telephone book and, if available, the telephone company's street-address directory.)
- Telephone company records and transactions
- Utility companies
- Bonding companies
- Commercial credit agencies
- Insurance companies
- National Auto Theft Bureau

- National Board of Fire Underwriters
- Churches and parish houses
- Banks and local businesses
- Transportation agencies
- Laundry and dry-cleaning establishments
- Union hiring halls
- Proprietary private security departments

School Contacts. Frequent police contacts with school officials have proved particularly effective in detecting juvenile offenders. Young people who are no longer in school are likely suspects for offenses, such as drug sales and usage, auto theft, theft of auto accessories, and residential burglaries.

Use of Informants. Administrators must facilitate the use of *informants* by giving investigators sufficient funds to pay them and by expediting the confidential relationships that must exist between informants and investigators. A special investigation fund should be a part of the police budget in any department that has a formalized investigative function. Use of such funds should be accepted as a normal operating practice, and, with proper control, administrators may assure themselves of reasonably secure operations. The system should require the investigator to complete a voucher for each payment, listing the date, amount, and code name or number of the informant. Voucher forms and cash should be kept under strict control, accessible only to an investigator or supervisor and the chief. To preserve the confidential nature of information provided by informants, each investigator should be required to keep the coding information in a separate location which is secure and accessible.

Investigative Procedures

This volume is not a technical police investigative handbook, so that giving specific advice for investigations of various kinds of offenses is beyond its scope. Instead, we focus on fundamental concepts useful to administrators and students of police management.

For convenience, the investigative procedures described in this text are grouped into the three offense categories described earlier in this chapter: crimes against persons, crimes against property, and general assignment.

Police executives must make certain that each of these areas gets sufficient attention in the in-service training program and that standard operating procedures or instructional materials cover at least these broad categories. Finally, administrators should make sure that these areas are carefully examined in formal inspections of their departments' investigative apparatus.

Crimes against Persons. Crimes against persons—homicide, assault, robbery, rape, and other sex crimes—usually involve some form of communication as well as face-to-face visual and/or physical contact between victims and offenders; these factors generally are not present in crimes against property. In addition to the collection of physical evidence, therefore, investigations of crimes against persons should include careful interviews of victims and witnesses, who may provide the only possible means of linking offenders to their crimes. Instructions to investigators should emphasize the value of systematic and patient interviewing to elicit a proper description. Investigators should be supplied with extensive physical description checklists and other aids, such as the use of police sketches, Identi-Kit, and computerized graphic software programs for the construction of composite photos of suspects.

A second important aid in investigation of crimes against persons is a set of photo files containing identification photos arranged by type of offender or crime classification. In addition, books containing photos of persons previously arrested for particular types of crimes also are useful because they can be taken by detectives to victims and witnesses in crimes currently under investigation. However, investigators should be instructed in the legal requirements regulating photo identification. When a suspect is arrested as a result of photo identification, a lineup must be held so that the identification can be verified in person. This is critical in order to lessen the chance of mistaken identification. Suspect files contain pictures taken at the time of the last arrest and include only part of subjects' descriptions. Therefore, they are not current and can contribute to a case of mistaken identification.

The lineup is an indispensable part of investigations of crimes against persons. When properly carried out, a lineup that results in identification of a suspect is often the key evidence in a successful prosecution. Consequently, the U.S. Supreme Court ruled in *United States v. Wade* (1971), postindictment lineups are also a *critical stage* at which suspects are entitled to be represented by legal counsel. The seriousness of the lineup places a great responsibility on administrators to ensure that lineups are conducted fairly. More specifically, administrators should be certain that the facilities for conducting lineups are adequate, that there is no possibility of witness-suspect contact, that the light level at the scene of the crime is approximated in the lineup, and that security for the identity of witnesses is maintained. Participants in the lineup must be selected carefully so as not to make the suspect the most obvious choice.

Investigators must make sure that any person who makes a lineup identification is absolutely certain the suspect selected is the perpetrator of the crime. A doubt on the part of the witness will negate the validity of the identification.

At times, police can lose sight of the economy involved in certain investigative procedures. For example, some departments spend countless hours pursuing leads that may or may not be productive—as in investigating a series of armed robberies of liquor stores—and yet not realize that the same level of manpower, if stationed in or near these same stores, would prevent such crimes during the course of the stakeout, with a very good likelihood of making arrests in the process.

A significant aspect of investigations of crimes against persons is that of alerting the public, particularly potential victims, when a crime pattern is known. On occasion, police investigators have had reliable advance information that offenders were planning very specific crimes against persons and, without warning the planned victims or taking any preventive action, have conducted surveillance to catch the miscreants in the act. This is a practice that makes for spectacular headlines, but it puts innocent lives at great risk and is difficult to justify on moral, legal, or professional grounds. It should be avoided.

More typically, investigators possess information about a series of crimes, rather than a particular offense planned for a specific location. In such circumstances—a series of gas station or convenience store holdups, for example—patrol officers and investigators should visit service station or store personnel to alert them to descriptions of suspects and their vehicles and to give them instruction about safety precautions, the level of cash to be kept in registers, the dangers of resisting armed robbers, and the importance of promptly notifying the police. At times (even though there is a risk of generating crime-related hysteria), it is a good idea to publicize a notorious crime pattern through the press and broadcast media. The way police handle information of this sort has a great deal to do with the amount of hysteria generated. If information is presented in a calm and reassuring manner, the public can accept such alerts almost as if they were an everyday occurrence.

Crimes against Property.   As discussed earlier, this category of offense includes such crimes as burglary, auto theft, and arson. Burglars look to steal property of value that they can convert into cash as quickly as possible. Arson can be the product of vengeance, the desire to reap the benefits of insurance fraud, or the desire to conceal another crime. In burglary cases, investigators should try to obtain descriptions of the stolen property that are as complete as possible. The records system of the department (as well as regional and state identification systems) should make it possible to establish identification of stolen property and to retrieve it if it is imprinted with a serial or social security number, if the property is valuable, or if there are distinctive markings on the property. A records search may prove productive, particularly if there is adequate description of the property.

Most solutions of crimes against property hinge on the ability to recognize physical evidence and on the adequate search of crime scenes. Departmental procedures should require searching the crime scene in some formal way for most categories of offenses.

A routine search of the crime scene helps cultivate an appreciation for the value of physical evidence. Just the fact that such searches are carried out is sometimes a stimulus to greater learning by officers, evidence technicians, and investigators. Training is obviously important in this area. If common sense does not indicate to an investigator that two distinct ignition sites at a fire suggest arson, for example, then training is needed and will serve the police purpose.

In investigations of crimes against property, it is essential to become familiar with potential outlets for stolen property, such as pawnshops, junkyards, secondhand stores, and antique shops. Administrators should make certain that investigators spend sufficient time with the proprietors of these businesses, either through constant attention if the owners or employees are uncooperative or through the cultivation of their cooperation if they are responsible citizens.

Auto theft deserves special recognition as a crime against property because it is a crime that involves a high percentage of youthful offenders. The crime can generally be divided into two categories—*theft for the purpose of stripping a vehicle* for its engine or other valuable parts and *joyriding*, theft for simple temporary transportation. Regardless of the motive, auto theft accounts for a staggering loss to the economy. In terms of life, accidents related to stolen-car joyrides take far more lives—not only of guilty drivers but also of innocent victims who may be in or outside the stolen vehicle—than murders committed during armed robberies.

Investigative procedures relating to auto theft should stress close scrutiny of possible suspects and should call for public education to encourage people to take such simple security measures as not leaving their keys in their cars and not leaving the cars unlocked. Potential locations for vehicle stripping—typically, garages of known offenders and remote or rural areas—should also be surveilled regularly and closely.

The General Assignment Grouping. Offenses such as bad-check cases, credit card frauds, the acquisition of money or property by false pretenses, and embezzlement typically involve more sophistication than traditional property crime offenses like burglary and simple theft. Consequently, they require different and, in many ways, more complex investigative techniques.

Crimes involving abuse of credit cards have reached epidemic proportions. These offenses are usually solved when offenders take too many chances, such as using cards to purchase identifiable or traceable merchandise, or persist in credit card spending over a long period of time, thus allowing evidence to accumulate. Since the majority of the credit card issuers have a stake in their security, the police have received help in the recovery of property by investigators working directly for these corporations.

Evidence Collection and Crime Scene Search

Searching crime scenes for physical and psychological evidence calls for the services of specialists—typically called *evidence technicians*—supplied with essential equipment and assigned or available on a 7/24 basis. The crime laboratory's usefulness is dependent on the receipt of physical evidence in an unchanged condition. Crime scene searches must therefore be conducted before crime scenes have been altered or contaminated, and physical evidence must be recorded, preserved, and transported to the laboratory. Such searches should include:

- Sketching and photographing crime scenes
- Searching for, developing, photographing, and lifting latent fingerprints
- Searching for articles or impressions left by criminals
- Making casts of impressions of tires, tools, and feet or other body parts
- Searching for and preserving lethal instruments, such as knives, bludgeons, firearms, bullets and cartridge cases, poisons, and suspect food
- Searching for any other articles that may have been left at scenes by offenders

The evidence technician's primary mission is to gather physical material at crime scenes, in order to assist in determining what has taken place and to identify or associate perpetrators with victims and/or crime scenes. Evidence technicians should be given intensive training in evidence collection and preservation, but these techniques should not be thought of as replacements for criminal investigators or detectives. Because of their training and skill, evidence technicians save time and ensure that an increased proportion of crimes is cleared by arrest.

The Beat Officer and the Evidence Technician. During preliminary investigations, beat officers are concerned primarily with locating and identifying or interviewing people, whereas evidence technicians are concerned primarily with locating and identifying things. In crime or accident investigations, beat officers and technicians should work as a team, with beat officers in charge and evidence technicians furnishing all pertinent information discovered in the course of the search.

In preliminary investigations of some crime and accident scenes, beat officers need no assistance. In others, there arises a need for extra investigators or for officers to assist in traffic or crowd control. Assistance should be provided by the officers dispatched to the scene, or a call should be made to headquarters for additional officers. The evidence technician, in most cases, will need no assistance except in making measurements and, infrequently, in performing other tasks. The beat officer can assist in these. Conditions will seldom require the assignment of other officers or of a second evidence technician.

When two or more evidence technicians are assigned to the same tour of duty, the area of the city should be divided into sectors having approximately equal numbers of crimes and accidents. When the number of patrol sergeants is equal to the number of evidence technicians, one technician should be assigned to each. In this case, the patrol beats in the sector assigned to each sergeant should be the area covered by the sergeant's evidence technician.

Supervision of Evidence Technicians. The need for continuous supervision of evidence technicians and the desirability of the close integration of their work with preliminary investigations by patrol officers make it most advantageous to assign these specialists to the patrol division. Also, this way they are available during slack periods for general patrol in areas needing special attention and for special assignments. Regular staff inspection of the accomplishments, procedures, and equipment of the evidence technicians should be conducted. In addition, the detective and traffic divisions should provide staff inspection of procedures and reports relating to crime and accident investigations.

Technical Investigative Services

In recent years, a variety of technological advances have had enormous influence on police investigative procedures. While administrators need not—and, practically speaking, cannot—become experts in these technologies, they should be aware of the capacities and limitations of these techniques. Three that are particularly noteworthy have been developed and/or applied to criminal investigations by the Federal Bureau of Investigation, which continues to coordinate and manage them. They include DNA testing; VICAP, the FBI's Violent Criminal Apprehension Program; and psychological profiling.

DNA Testing. DNA technology was not originally developed for police purposes, but it has provided one of the most significant scientific advancements for modern criminal investigation. DNA testing of crime scene evidence obtained in cases involving violent physical contact and sexual offenses conclusively connects criminal suspects to their crime. It provides police and prosecutors with a powerful forensic weapon to identify the criminal and clear the innocent who may have mistakenly been identified. In recent years, for example, DNA testing has cleared several prison inmates who had been serving time for rapes they did not commit (see, e.g., "DNA Testing," 1993). This new technology permits forensic analysts to identify individuals based on the genetic patterns found in a drop of blood, a drop of semen, or a single hair (Hicks, 1988). It provides more conclusive proof than serology tests on body fluids.

DNA—deoxyribonucleic acid—is a naturally occurring organic substance and is the principal component of chromosomes located in the nucleus of living cells. It supplies the hereditary code that determines a living creature's unique characteristics. This code contains an arrangement of four basic materials, termed "nucleotides," which are identified by the letters *A, G, C,* and *T* (for adenine, guanine, cytosine, and thymine, respectively). These nucleotides are linked in chainlike sequences, and their order can vary to provide an almost infinite number of possible arrangements. Our genetic code contains 3 billion combinations of nucleotides shared in common by all human beings (Hicks, 1988; Osterburg and Ward, 1992). The unique genetic patterns found in each person's DNA can be as distinctive as fingerprints.

The FBI laboratory, located at the Forensic Science Research and Training Center at the FBI Academy in Quantico, Virginia, has become the principal provider of DNA testing to law enforcement. This valuable service, as well as all FBI laboratory forensic testing and examiners' testimony, is provided free to any duly constituted law enforcement agency. Approximately 2,000 DNA cases are submitted each year to the laboratory's DNA unit, two-thirds of which involve the crime of rape, with the remainder consisting of murders and other violent crimes. About 75 percent of these cases result in a conclusive determination that the biological evidence collected from the crime scene can be associated with the subject in question or, conversely, that the subject can be excluded from consideration. Evidence of this quality can be used to rebut alibis, to corroborate eyewitness identification, and to aid in criminal prosecution by inducing the defendant to plead guilty.

The FBI is presently working with state and local crime laboratories to establish a national DNA index. This will eventually become a valuable investigative tool that will permit crime laboratories to make a comparison of DNA crime scene evidence with DNA stored in a national data bank of known sex offenders and other violent criminals.

VICAP: The Violent Criminal Apprehension Program. VICAP is part of the FBI's National Center for the Analysis of Violent Crime, a national law enforcement resource for the identification of criminals who perpetrate crimes of violence, especially serial murders. Established in 1985, VICAP is also quartered at the FBI's Quantico Training Academy. The effectiveness of this program depends on the cooperation of local and state police departments who submit case reports to the program on the 15-page VICAP crime report form. Crime report forms should be submitted to VICAP for a number of circumstances. When a case is solved and the offender is known and arrested, a crime report form should be submitted to the program so that a search of the VICAP files can be conducted in order to link the known offender with unsolved cases. When a link is made, the departments involved are informed so that they can exchange information and coordinate their efforts. In this manner, it is hoped that all the offenses committed by violent offenders may be identified so that offenders might be held to account for all their wrongdoing.

Crime report forms should be submitted to the VICAP program whenever cases meet the following criteria:

- *Homicides.* Whether solved or unsolved, cases of homicide or attempted homicide should be submitted when they involve abduction; and/or appear to be random, motiveless, or sexually oriented; and/or suspected or known to be part of a series of offenses.
- *Missing persons.* Missing-person cases should be submitted when the circumstances indicate a strong possibility of foul play and victims remain missing.
- *Unidentified dead bodies.* Cases involving unidentified dead bodies should be submitted when it is known or suspected that death resulted from criminal homicide.

Thus far, VICAP's effectiveness has been encouraging. Not long ago, for example, the Hillsborough County (Florida) Sheriff's Department used this program to link a truck driver, convicted of three murders near Tampa, with ten murders in other states. This department asked VICAP to provide information about young white females who had been strangled and dumped in remote areas in the 26 states that the driver's records disclosed he had visited. This provided a possible suspect to the investigators working independently on these cases in each of the states (Bulkeley, 1993).

Psychological Profiling. In crimes of personal violence, such as rape and sex-related homicide, it is important that investigators attempt to understand offenders' psychological motives. Clues to motives may be found in behavioral evidence left at the crime scene. The possible manifestations of offender behavior at a crime scene include modus operandi and personation, or signature.

Modus operandi, the methods of operation used by individual offenders to commit their crimes, is a learned behavior that usually changes as the offender gains experience. The *signature* is conduct that is a unique, integral part of the offender's behavior and that extends beyond behavior which is needed to commit the offense. One such pattern reported by the FBI involves sexual sadist rapists who intentionally manipulate and inflict suffering to their victims in the same manner during each sexual assault (Hazelwood, Dietz, and Warren, 1992). Unlike a modus operandi, a signature appears to be a constant, enduring characteristic of each offender that never changes (Douglas and Munn, 1992). Searching for and identifying a signature, therefore, may help in developing a psychological profile of the offender, which, in turn, may serve to narrow and limit the investigation.

Psychological profiles are developed from an assessment of a crime scene and may help to identify offenders' motives. Profilers attempt to recognize and interpret visible items of evidence at crime scenes; obviously, their attempts are limited when little evidence exists. Profiles, therefore, are not inclusive and do not contain the same information from one case to another. Profiles may include the perpetrator's race, sex, age range, marital status, general employment, reaction to questioning by police, and degree of sexual maturity. Profiles may also speculate on the possibility that the individual will strike again, that he or she has committed a similar offense in the past, and that he or she may have a police record.

The research in offender profiles was conducted by the FBI's Behavioral Sciences Unit, which is a part of the National Center for the Analysis of Violent Crime. State and local police departments interested in using this service and others offered at the national center should contact their local FBI field office.

SUMMARY

The subjects of this chapter—crime prevention and criminal investigation—are two of the principal roles for which the police as we know them were created. Certainly, one role—investigation—is more glamorous than the other, but it would be hard to say that either is more important than the other. Indeed, recent great increases in citizen self-help groups and the enhancements in the technology of personal and community security suggest that we are only beginning to appreciate how important a task crime prevention is.

Police agencies should invest heavily in the technologies of both crime prevention and criminal investigation. In doing so, however, they should keep in mind a major lesson of police history: Technology may help police deal with the crime problem, but it will never solve the crime problem. At base, crime has much to do with problems of the community, the economy, and the psyche. Technology can only get at the fringes of these issues and can generally serve only to reduce the *opportunity* to commit crime. If the police are to be maximally effective in preventing crime, they must also attempt to reduce the *desire* to commit crime. They can do this only by working with other institutions and concerned individuals to strengthen the informal social controls—families, communities, schools, and the like—that have failed where crime flourishes and that flourish in crime-free areas. As August Vollmer observed, the role of police in society is to lead in this effort. This task frequently is criticized as social work, as work that is unfit for police. But this view is obsolete and short sighted. As crimefighters, the police should take every opportunity to make our streets and neighborhoods safer.

The technology of investigation has changed in recent years, with the development of such advances as DNA testing and computerized identification and fingerprint files. Still, these are only supplements to, rather than substitutes for, the traditional skills of detectives: the ability to develop information during interaction with criminal suspects, witnesses, victims, informants, and community members. Good investigators—and the administrators to whom they report—understand this, and make sure that both their interpersonal and technological skills are at high levels.

QUESTIONS FOR DISCUSSION

1. What is the major crime problem in the community in which you work or reside? What would you do to reduce offenders' opportunity to engage in it? What informal social controls might be strengthened to reduce the desire of potential offenders to commit this offense? How should—or can—the police help to strengthen these forces?

2. How would you advise the chief administrator of the police department in which you work or that serves the community in which you reside to go about setting up a rape prevention crime team?

3. It has been argued that traditional measures of investigators' performance—arrest and clearance rates, amounts of property recovered—encourage investigators to violate citizens' rights in order to remain in their bosses' good graces. What steps should be taken to assure that this does not occur?

4. Computer technology has created a whole new set of offenses and criminals. Local police generally are poorly prepared to deal with these acts and offenders. What would you recommend to improve their ability to prevent and detect offenses such as computer fraud and other abuses of electronic networks?

5. Police detectives enjoy enormous prestige in their agencies and their communities. How would you go about attempting to spread some of their glory and good publicity to crime prevention specialists and their work?

NOTES

1. The builders of the newer METRO subway system in Washington, D.C., went to what many regard as the other extreme. Nighttime and restroom muggings in the D.C. system are impossible because the system closes at night and has no restrooms. In addition, for the system's first 10 or more years of operation, it generally provided access only to the Washington region's "nice" neighborhoods and had no stations in the areas that account for Washington's high crime rates.

2. The National Crime Prevention Council's *Taking the Offensive to Prevent Crime: How Seven Cities Did It* (1994) is a good primer on this aspect of crime prevention and on building crime prevention programs generally.

3. In police departments, the terms "investigator" and "detective" are used to refer to persons who conduct follow-up investigations or who initiate undercover investigations; they have the same meaning as in this chapter.

SOURCES

BERRY, GENE N. "The Uniformed Crime Investigator: A Unique Strategy to Protect and Serve," *FBI Law Enforcement Bulletin,* (March 1984):1–6.

BULKELEY, WILLIAM M. "Police Turn to Databases to Link Crimes," *Wall Street Journal,* (Mar. 1993):16.

Commission on Accreditation for Law Enforcement Agencies. *Standards for Law Enforcement Agencies*. Standards for Law Enforcement Agencies (Fairfax, Va.: Commission on Accreditation for Law Enforcement Agencies, Inc., 1994).

DeLadurantey, Joseph C., and Daniel Sullivan. *Criminal Investigation Standards* (New York: Harper & Row, 1980).

Cawley, Donald F., H. Jerome Miron, William J. Araujo, Robert Wasserman, Timothy A. Mannello, and Yale Huffman. *Managing Criminal Investigations* (Washington, D.C.: University Research Corporation, 1977).

"DNA Testing Frees Man Jailed in Rape," *New York Times* (Apr. 25, 1993):29.

Douglas, John E., and Corenne Munn. "Violent Crime Scene Analysis: Modus Operandi, Signature, and Staging." *FBI Law Enforcement Bulletin,* 61(2):1–16 (1992).

Eck, John E. *Managing Case Assignments: The Burglary Investigation Decision Model Replication* (Washington, D.C.: Police Executive Research Forum, 1979).

———, and William Spelman. *Problem Solving: Problem Oriented Policing in Newport News* (Washington, D.C.: Police Executive Research Forum, 1987).

———, and Gerald L. Williams. "Criminal Investigations," pp. 131–158 in William A. Geller (ed.), *Local Government Police Management,* 3d ed. (Washington, D.C.: International City Management Association, 1991).

Fogelson, Robert M. *Big-City Police* (Cambridge, Mass.: Harvard University Press, 1977).

Goldstein, Herman. *Policing a Free Society* (Cambridge, Mass.: Ballinger, 1977).

———. *Problem-Oriented Policing* (New York: McGraw-Hill, 1990).

Greenberg, Bernard, Carol V. Elliot, Lois P. Kraft, and Steven Proctor. *Felony Investigation Decision Model: An Analysis of Investigative Elements of Information* (Menlo Park, Calif.: Stanford Research Institute, 1975).

Greenwood, Peter W., and Joan Petersilia. *The Criminal Investigation Process,* vol. 1: *Summary and Policy Implications* (Santa Monica, Calif.: Rand Corporation, 1975).

Hazelwood, Robert R., Park E. Dietz, and Janet Warren. "The Criminal Sexual Sadist," *FBI Law Enforcement Bulletin,* 61(2):12–20 (1992).

Heaphy, John F. (ed.). *Police Practices: The General Administrative Survey* (Washington, D.C.: Police Foundation, 1978).

Hicks, John W. "DNA Profiling: A Tool for Law Enforcement," *FBI Law Enforcement Bulletin,* 57(8):1–5 (1988).

Julian, Michael. Former New York City Police Department Chief of Personnel, personal communication (June 30, 1995).

Kelling, George L., Tony Pate, Duane Dieckman, and Charles E. Brown. *The Kansas City Preventive Patrol Experiment: Summary Report* (Washington, D.C.: Police Foundation, 1974).

Klockars, Carl B. *The Idea of Police* (Beverly Hills, Calif.: Sage, 1985).

Osterburg, James W., and Richard Ward. *Criminal Investigation: A Method for Reconstructing the Past* (Cincinnati, Oh.: Anderson, 1992).

National Advisory Commission on Civil Disorders. *Report of the National Advisory Commission on Civil Disorders* (New York: Dutton, 1968).

National Crime Prevention Council. *Taking the Offensive to Prevent Crime: How Seven Cities Did It* (Washington, D.C.: National Crime Prevention Council, 1994).

Newman, Oscar. *Defensible Space: Crime Prevention through Environmental Design* (New York: Macmillan, 1972).

President's Commission on Law Enforcement and Administration of Justice. *The Challenge of Crime in a Free Society* (Washington, D.C.: U.S. Government Printing Office, 1967).

Rosenbaum, Dennis P., Eusevio "Ike" Hernandez, and Sylvester Daughtry, Jr. "Crime Prevention, Fear Reduction, and the Community," pp. 96–130 in William A. Geller (ed.), *Local Government Police Management,* 3d ed. (Washington, D.C.: International City Management Association, 1991).

SILBERMAN, CHARLES E. *Criminal Violence, Criminal Justice* (New York: Vintage Books, 1978).

————. "Fear of Crime and Neighborhood Change," pp. 203–229 in Albert J. Reiss, Jr., and Michael Tonry (eds.), *Communities and Crime,* vol. 8 of *Crime and Justice: A Review of Research* (Chicago: University of Chicago Press, 1986).

TROJANOWICZ, ROBERT, and BONNIE BUCQUEROUX. *Community Policing: A Contemporary Perspective* (Cincinnati, Oh.: Anderson, 1990).

United States v. Wade, 401 U.S. 745 (1971).

URLACHER, GORDON F., and ROBERT J. DUFFY. "The Preliminary Investigation Process," *FBI Law Enforcement Bulletin,* 59(3):1–6 (1990).

VOLLMER,, AUGUST. *The Police and Modern Society.* (Montclair, N.J.: Patterson Smith, 1972 reprint of original 1936 manuscript).

Index

National Organization of Black Law Enforcement Executives (NOBLE), 203, 521
National Sheriffs Association, 21, 521
Needs, 114–116
Neighborhood contacts, 613
Neighborhood context, 394–395
"New Police," 7, 8
New York City:
blackout of 1977, 229–230
Crown Heights civil disturbance of 1991, 230–232
New York City Police Department, 307, 321
central planning in, 222
Newark, New Jersey riot, 200–201
Newark Foot Patrol Experiment, 551
Newman, Oscar, 594
Newstrom, John W., 419
Niederhoffer, Arthur, 18
911 systems, 168–169, 595
effects on staffs of, 295–296
patrol and, 540, 541, 542, 557
problem-oriented policing and, 159
Noncriminal incidents and services, 559
Nonfeasance, 418
Nonprofit abuses of citizens, 452–456
brutality as, 452
dealing with, 454–456
considering the whole record, 455–456
limiting considerations of the past, 456
questions to ask, 454–455
emotionally disturbed persons and, 452–454
profit-motivated corruption and, 450–451
unnecessary force as, 452
Not sustained disposition of complaint, 519
"Notes on the Theory of Organization," 154
Numbers, 459
NYNEX, 595

Object/line item budgeting, 259–262
Objectives of state and local police, 37
O'Brian, Robert M., 382
Occupational mandates, 29–30
confusion about, 34–36
failure to distinguish the police from other occupations, 31–32
problems in setting priorities, 30–31
responsibilities, 30, 36–38
O'Connor, George W., 281, 294, 435
Off-duty conduct, 507–510
employment, 508–510
line between police officer and private citizen, 307
training for, 306–308
24-hour a-day officer, 507–508
weapons carrying, 507–508
Office of Personnel Management, U.S., 321
Officer-reported offenses, 384–385
Ohio State University leadership study, 97–98
Ombudsmen, 72
O'Meara, Stephen James, 12
Omnipresence, 14, 540
"On-call" systems, 538–539
One-officer versus two-officer patrols, 553–554
Onward Industry! (Mooney and Reiley), 153–154
Open organizational system, 144–146, 157
Open police department, 80
Open-system, 368
Operating expenses, 260
Operation Identification, 594–595
Operational plans, 236–239
Operational research, 183–184
-behavioral, 184
-technological, 184
Operations research, 220–221
Opportunism management, 99
Opportunities and threats, 167
Opportunity reduction programs, 589, 590–595

crime analysis and, 590–591
liaisons with groups and institutions, 595
preventive patrol and, 590
target hardening, 593–595
victimization-avoiding information, 591–593
Organic organizations, 156
Organization and management theories, 147–158
contingency management, 156–157
environmental uncertainty, 157–158
Fayol and, 151–153
general theory, 151–153
Gulick and, 154
mechanistic and organic, 156
Mooney, Reiley and, 153–154
overview of, 150–151
POSDCORB, 154
schools of thought influencing, 148
scientific management, 155–156
Taylor and, 155–156
traditional, 148–150
Weber and, 148–150
Organizational complexity and size, 146–147, 169–170
Organizational specialization, 137–138
Organizational technology, 168–169
Organizational theory, 148
Organizations, 136–137, 158–164
as brains, 159–160
as cultures, 160–161
"ideal," 149–150
as instruments of domination, 164
as machines, 158–159
as organisms, 159
as political systems, 161–162
as psychic prisons, 162–163
as social constructs, 158
as structures in flux and transformation, 163
systems for management of, 166–175
communications, 170–173